Free Money For Everybody

by
Matthew Lesko

with
Mary Ann Martello

Researchers
Cindy Owens, Jean Neuner, Bev Matson
Jessica Neuner, Chelsea Noble, Dixie St. John

Production
Beth Meserve

Marketing
Kim McCoy

Support
Mercedes Sundeen

Cover & Illustrations
Tom Ford

Clip art used in this publication © Dynamic Graphics, Inc.; Totem Graphics; One Mile Up; Tech Pool; Image Club Graphics, Inc.; and Corel Corp.

ISBN-13: 978-1-878346-81-0

Other books available from Matthew Lesko:

Free Money To Change Your Life

Free Money To Change Your Life
    6-hour instructional audio cassette/CD

Lesko's Info-Power III

Government Giveaways for Entrepreneurs IV

Free Legal Help

Free Health Care

Gobs and Gobs of Free Stuff

Free Stuff For Busy Moms

Free Stuff For Women's Health, Fitness and Nutrition

Free College Money And Training For Women

Free Money And Help For Women Entrepreneurs

Free Money to Change Your Life CD-ROM

Free Money For Your Retirement

How to Write and Get a Grant

Free Money To Pay Your Bills

For ordering information on any of Matthew Lesko's publications, call 1-800-UNCLE-SAM, or contact his web site at www.lesko.com.

TABLE OF CONTENTS

Table of Contents

FREE MONEY FOR ARTISTS, WRITERS, DANCERS, POETS, MUSICIANS, ACTORS, ETC 269

Table of Contents

Table of Contents

Table of Contents

Free Money For Everybody

Introduction

I should not be writing this book, the government should. I believe the IRS should include a book like this to every American when they send you your tax forms. That way every American would know how to get their tax money back, because even though I call this "free money," it really isn't free. This is money that you gave to the government to pay your taxes and now you can get it back.

Get 100% of the Cash Back You Give The IRS

IRS data show that each year about 131 million individuals file tax returns and pay an average of $7,633 to the IRS (1). The U.S. Office of Management and Budget and recent independent studies show that the government gives out over $1.5 Trillion a year to individuals through its free money programs (2). One and one half trillion dollars in government money programs, divided by 131 million taxpayers, means that the average taxpayer is getting $11,450 a year in cash back from the government in free money programs. Are you getting yours?

Taxes Paid By Individuals	# of Taxpayers	Avg. Tax Paid
$987 Billion	131 million	$7,534

Free Money To Individuals	# of Taxpayers	Avg. Free Money Given
$1.5 Trillion	131 million	$11,450

No wonder the government is in debt.

Only 12% OF Gov't Money Goes To Poor

You're probably not getting yours. And why not? Because the government does not advertise. An even greater reason you may not actively seek this money is because a lot of us live with misinformation. Most Americans think that government money programs are for everyone else but them, for instance only the poor, minority or friends of the president. The facts show otherwise. I bet you did not know that:

☐ Only 12% of Government Handouts Go To The Poor (3)
☐ Only 25% of Government Programs Have Income Requirements (4)
☐ Seniors Making Over $150,000 Receive 200% More In Government Benefits than Seniors Making Less Than $15,000 (5)
☐ People Making Over $100,000 Get More in Grant Money for College Than People Making Less Than $100,000 (6)

The rich and famous, including Donald Trump, H. Ross Perot, Dick Cheney and George W. Bush, all made millions as private citizens with the help of government money programs.

50 Million People Don't Know They're Eligible

It's understandable that most people don't know about all government money programs. I don't even know about every government money program available and I've been studying these programs for over 25 years. But what should surprise you, because it surprised the heck out of me, is that there are millions of Americans who are eligible to call the government today and get thousands of dollars from some of the government's basic programs. For example:

☐ 4 Million Seniors can receive up to $1,000 from Medicare but they don't apply because they are unaware of the program (7)

☐ 6 Million Families are missing out on free health insurance for their kids (8)

☐ 10 Million Families can get up to $4,000 a year for groceries but don't apply (9)

☐ 800,000 College Students can receive grants up to $4,050 but don't apply (10)

☐ Single Moms can receive some of the $673 million in collected unclaimed child support payments (11)

☐ 29 Million Seniors don't know they can get colonoscopies, bone mass measurement, prostate cancer and glaucoma tests paid for by Medicare (12)

Only 20% of Free Money Is Called "Grants"

Most people know that grant money refers to money that the government gives out and you don't have to pay it back. And that's true But what most people do not know is that most free money programs are not called "grants" by the government, they're called "direct payments." It is very easy for someone not to know all about government jargon. I've even seen government officials get thoroughly confused on this issue. Here's the data from Budget of United States Government 2005, Historical Tables, page 117 (2).

2005 Budget In Millions of Dollars

Direct Payments For Individuals	$1,198,333
Grants For Individuals	$275,904

Total Free Money For Individuals   **$1,474,237**

And this does not account for other free money programs the government has like the one they call "forgivable loans." This reminds me of when I used to ask my father to lend me $5.00. I usually never paid him back.

The Gov't Considers You Disadvantaged With $750,000 in the Bank

There are people who come up to me on the street and tell me they called the government about a program and the office said that they make too much money. Well, that may be true for that program. But the important thing to remember is that the government has thousands of programs covering all incomes and  backgrounds. Just because you are not eligible for one program, does not mean that there aren't dozens more around the corner that may have your name on it. Remember what I said earlier: only 12% of government money goes to the poor and only 25% have an income requirement.

I make a good deal of money and I was able to get government money and other grants to pay for almost half of the costs of sending our two sons to college. I've seen housing programs at the local level where they consider families disadvantaged if their incomes are under $80,000. There are even government programs for women entrepreneurs where they consider you disadvantaged if you have $750,000 in the bank. Wow, that is almost a millionaire. Even the programs that give people the basic necessities of life have income requirements for a family of 4 at $38,000 a year.

You Can't Make One Call And Get A Check in the Mail

Sure, there may be one in 100 of you reading this that will make a call to the government and get a check in the mail next Thursday that will solve your problems. But that is unlikely to happen to the other 99%. If you are one of those lucky one in a hundred, call me and I'll put you in my next infomercial. The people I put in my commercials are the people who say, "Hey, look. I made one phone call and got a check in the mail." The rest of us have to work at it.

Getting government money is like looking for a job. When you knock on one door and ask about a job, and they tell you that you are not qualified, you don't go home and wait for them to change their mind. No Way. You'd never find a job that way. If you really want a job, you go to the next company and ask about their qualifications, and then the next company, and then the next. This is the purpose of this book. It gives you not one, but a list of programs to keep contacting.

Free Money Keeps Growing
No Matter Who Is In The White House

We constantly hear about government budget cuts and that makes people believe that government money is going away or will soon be gone. It's all lies in my mind. Look at the facts below. Every year for the past 30 years the amount of free government money given out to individuals keeps growing. It keeps increasing no matter if it's the republicans or the democrats who are in charge.

So don't believe the headlines about budget cuts. What really happens is that some programs will not grow as fast as in the past, but will still grow. Others will continue to grow as normal and very few if any, will actually decrease. The total amount of available money will continue to increase. These scare headlines actually create greater opportunities for you to get the money. Most people will believe the headlines, causing fewer people to apply for the funds that will actually be available.

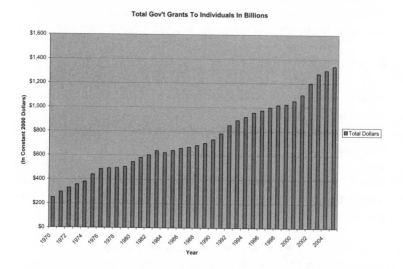

Total Gov't Grants To Individuals In Billions

Don't Worry: You Don't Need A Professional Grant Writer

So many people worry their heads off about what they are going to do when the get an application. They worry so much that they are buying professional grants writing services to the tune of hundreds or even thousands of dollars just so they don't have to worry when they get an application in hand. That's like buying a prom dress before you are invited to the prom.

Nine out of ten times you will not need help in filling out an application. Most free money programs to pay for your bills, education, health care, housing and even business require just a few pages of blanks to fill in. A major source for business money is only one page long to get $150,000. There are only 15 questions to answer to apply for a $4,000 grant to fix up your home. And artists can apply for grants by just filling in a form with 6 or 7 questions.

And if you decide you need help once you get an application you can get people to help you for free. Many offices offer this help at no charge. Also there are special government offices around the country that help business and entrepreneurs fill out forms. They are called Small Business Development Centers and are run by your state government. There are over 1,000 of these offices around the country. For a Center near you contact 1-800-8-ASK-SBA or {http://www.sba.gov/sbdc/sbdcnear.html}.

The only likely area where you might need professional help with an application is if you are a non-profit organizations. And if you are a non-profit or want to be a non-profit here are the 2 best places to get help. Don't hire anyone until you check out the services and help that they can offer you.

A. The Foundation Center of New York City maintains a database of all foundations that provide money to non-profit organizations or individuals. The information is available on the web at {http://fdncenter.org} or from their participating libraries by contacting 212-620-4230

B. The Guidestar Company in Williamsburg, VA also maintains a database of foundations and they can be reached at 757-229-4631 or at {www.guidestar.com}. Much of their database is accessible for free on the web.

You Can Do It Yourself If You Have 2,000 Hours

That is a conservative estimate of how long it took us to find and collect all the information for this book. And I feel that we are probably the country's leading expert in government money programs. So imagine how long it would take a non-expert to collect this information. Sure you can do it. There is no magic to what we do. It is mostly just a lot of hard work. But the average person does not have the time, the patience, or the expertise to take on such a task. Instead of doing it yourself, if you hired someone, even at $10 an hour, it would cost $25,000 to gather this information.

This book gives you the easiest way to take ONE BIG GIANT STEP towards getting free and cheap money for your anything. You won't have to spend the thousands of hours it takes in chasing down these little-known programs. And more importantly, you won't have to deal with the bureaucratic dance of wrong numbers, unanswered phones and voice mail in order to get the necessary applications.

We Still Don't Have It All

This book is not intended to be a complete collection of free money programs. The rain forest could not handle it if that were true. This book is intended to give every American an understanding of the major programs available and a number of minor ones that we found to be the most interesting.

It's impossible for any one publication, database or anything else really, to be able to collect everything in the universe on a given subject. I know I'm biased, but I certainly believe that we are the best people in the world for collecting information on government money programs. I also know that we cannot possibly get every single program that is available.

One problem is that programs come and go. Our world is changing every second. It is a big complex society we are living in, and people are making decisions throughout the day that make subtle or big changes which affect the contents of this book. Budgets keep changing. Priorities keep changing. People keep changing. Offices keep changing.

A bigger problem is that the world of free money is enormous. Preparing a book for a national audience makes us excellent at identifying national and state programs. But truthfully, it is sometimes beyond our capabilities to completely cover all local, county and nonprofit programs. First of all, if we did collect all of these programs in the country, you would not be able to pick up the book. There are thousands and thousands of local communities in the United States and each of them can have 5 to 50 programs. Fifty times 5,000 would be 250,000 programs. We would never finish researching.

Our goal is to arm you with knowledge. We want to show you the money, but you are going to have to do a little work yourself.

This Book Is Out Of Date

Sorry to disappoint you, but I have to warn you of the truth. In our modern society, it is virtually impossible to expect to include every program possible and have every item completely accurate. The problem is that the world is too big and it is always changing. Every day programs come and go. Every day people change their address, phone number and websites. It is just a fact that these things happen in our modern society.

But remember, if a listing in this book leads you to a non-working number or website, it does not necessarily mean that the program is gone. In all likelihood it is still there, but has changed since we completed our search. Here are some tricks you can try to locate the program:

♦ call the information operator and ask for the telephone number for the agency listed in the program description
♦ search the web for the agency name in any of the web search engines like {www.dogpile.com} or {www.google.com}
♦ contact the Federal Information Center at {http://www.pueblo.gsa.gov/}, or call 1-800-FED-INFO. This is a free service that will help you locate a federal government agency
♦ go to {www.govengine.com} on the web for a listing of most federal, state and local government agencies
♦ contact your federal, state or local elected official. They all have staff people who will help you find what you need at any level of government

It Doesn't Matter If It Sounds Like You Don't Qualify

You are going to find programs that excite you at first and then when you read further it may seem that you will not qualify. Or you will gather more information on a program in this book and you will run into some phrase, or sentence in the description that makes you feel you do not have a chance. You may encounter things like:

A. "all the money is given out by June 30th" and it is already September 1st
B. "the money is only for people who live in the country" and you live in the city
C. "the money goes to non-profit organizations" and you are not one

D. "you have to come up with 20% of the money for the project" and you don't have any"

E. "the money is only for people who live in Minnesota" and you live in New Jersey"

F. "the money is for people making less than $60,000/yr" and you make $70,000"

Don't look at phrases like these as impassable boulders that stand in your way of getting the money you need. In reality, they can simply be small pebbles in the road that you may not even feel at all. If you don't follow up, you will never know.

Here's what I've seen happen in each of these situations:

1. "all the money is given out by June 30th": The end of the accounting year for most government agencies is September 30th, but the agency can start giving out more money beginning October 1, and you can be the first in line. I think you can wait another 30 days for your money.

2. "the money is for people who live in the country:" That may be so. But it will still pay to get the details of the program to see if there is something in the description that was not obvious to others. A young man in Boston was trying to get money from a program that gave money for teenage entrepreneurs that lived in the country. He lived in Boston. When he got the materials it said that it was for people in the country, but the description also said that it was for people who wanted to start lawn mowing businesses. That is what he wanted to do and he convinced the office that he was qualified. Government officials do not know everything. Get the facts and find out for yourself.

3. "the money is for non-profits": for about $100 in fees you can become a non-profit. Just call up the IRS and your state

capital and ask for the office that registers non-profit organizations. Fill out the paperwork. Don't worry. You'll do it wrong. Send it in anyway. And they will send it back telling you how you messed up and then you will correct your mistakes. Another way to solve the problem is to find a local non-profit, like a community college, church, or community group. Tell them you would like  to use their name to apply for a bunch of money and that you will give them 15% if you get the money. They have nothing to lose and everything to gain.

4. "you have to come up with 20% of the cost of the project": There is always more than one way to come up with the extra money than having the cash in your pocket. Some programs allow you to provide services or equipment that you already have as part of your 20%. You may be able to use your sweat as your contribution. The fact that you will work for free in helping to get the house built or the refurbishing done is worth something. You can call yourself a general contractor or just a handy man who pounds in the nails. Or you may need equipment, like the use of a car, to get the project done. This can be your car. The one that you already have and it can count as a percentage of the project.

5. "the money is only for people in Minnesota": Contact them anyway. It's likely that if this is a unique program then the program administrators will be aware of similar programs around the country that do the same thing. People doing similar work around the country have a tendency to organize and share information on how they are doing. We are one of

the best organized countries in the world. If there are 10 people in the country doing the same thing they will start an association, a newsletter and have annual meetings.

6. "the money is for people making less than $60,000": We all know that rules are made to be broken and many bureaucrats who hand out money have the power and authority to break the rules. It is especially easier for them to bend a few rules if they like you or they like your project. Or they may be having trouble giving away all their money this year and you are one of the best ideas they have seen. Remember, bureaucrats are human too. They have feelings. Like all of us, unless they are having a bad day, their instinct is to help. Always give them a chance to see if they can help.

14 Steps To Getting The Money You Need

Step #1: Review The Book
It is important to go through the entire book. You don't have to read everything, but you have to at least review the title of every entry. Place a check mark on those entries that you feel MIGHT be of some interest to you. You can also place a post-it on the edge of the page or turn town the corner of the page so you can easily return to it.

Step #2: Assign A Grade To Likely Programs
Two grades can be enough. But it must be at least 2. Read each entry in detail and place either an "A" or "B" next to the entry. Using a "1" or "2" is also good. The higher grade should identify those entries that seem more likely and the lower grade should identify programs that are a little less likely but are "maybes."

Step #3: Follow Up Immediately
As you probably guessed from reading the step above, you should now go back and contact all your "A" list programs first.

Leave your "B" list programs for a later round. You want to tackle the most obvious first. You can start digging deeper later, but you may not have to. I know it sounds like an obvious choice, but some people get overwhelmed with so many places to go to. This prioritizes the process for you.

Step #4: Contact the Agency Directly
This is a must. Do not assume that you know everything about the program just by reading the description in the book. You have to get the details before you make the decision if this is a program for you. You can contact the agency in any of the following ways:

A. by telephone,
B. by email,
C. by website, or
D. in person

You may even want to do a combination. You can go to the website and review their programs and then call and ask for specifics. But remember; even if you get details about a specific program on the web be sure you contact the agency by phone or email to insure you have the complete information. Like printed material in books, a lot of material on the web can also be out of date or even misleading.

Step #5: Be Careful What You Ask For
Your initial contact with an agency should be friendly. Many people are intimidated to contact any government agency. Remember you don't have to know what you are talking about, because most of the bureaucrats don't know what they are talking about either. This is the government, remember. Your best approach is to try to be as inclusive as possible in your initial contact. Try not to say things that can get you a "no" answer right off the bat. For example, don't let the first words out of your mouth be:

"Hi, I want a grant to start a bakery. Will you give me one?"

This can get the door closed on you right away when in fact there may be lots of money sitting there waiting for you. The bureaucrat answering the phone may not be aware of any grant programs because he just started working there a few weeks ago and is really not aware of all the programs. Or he may not be aware of any money that says "bakery" on the label. Or if you  are looking for a townhouse he will look down his list for the word "townhouse" and tell you that there is no money available. Or the government may be offering other kinds of money that does not have the name "grant" attached to it but it means the same thing. They may be offering money in the form of "direct payments" or under a program called "loans," but in fact you never have to pay back the money if you live in the house for more than 3 years. That's just as good as a grant.

You can miss a lot by trying to be very specific. The problem is that most people in the government don't even now what is available. By being specific the official can find an easier way to tell you "no" and send you on your way. You'll be happy, because this is what you sort of expected anyway. And the official will be happy because they don't have to do any more work. So it is much better to start with something like:

"Hi. I'm trying to get a description of all the money programs that are available for housing or real estate."

You want the official to stretch her imagination and try to come up with a complete list for you. When you get a complete descriptive listing, review it in close detail and call the office back and tell them all the programs for which you would like to apply.

Step #6: Be Nice To Bureaucrats

When you are calling the government, getting a lot of voice mails or being put on hold, it's hard to remember how important that person is who finally answers the telephone. That's the person who can give you the money. So how well you treat them can determine your success or failure in getting what you need. If you start yelling when the person answers the phone because you've been sitting on hold for the past 10 minutes, you don't sound like you are going to be the highlight of any bureaucrat's day. That bureaucrat gets paid the same amount of money whether they help you for free for 2 weeks or if they hang up on you right after you say hello. What you have to do is try to get that person to want to spend time with you. You want them to enjoy talking with you. The more comfortable they are in talking with you, the more likely they are to share inside information that will increase your chances and make it easier for you to get the money. It is basic common sense that can easily be forgotten, like: a) Don't be nasty when they answer the phone because the first words out of your mouth can set the stage for the entire conversation. b) Don't act like you hate them except for the fact that they are sitting on the money (even though it may be true) because this will come through in your conversation and they will not want to help you. c) Send "thank you" notes when people are exceptionally nice because it is the best way to ensure that you are remembered the next time you call. I can go on and on, but simply put …. TREAT PEOPLE LIKE YOU WANT TO BE TREATED.

Step #7: Make It Personal

Think of it as being back in school when you would go and brown nose the teacher. The good brown nosers would meet with the teacher after class and not only talk about school, but also talk about their life. They would show the teacher pictures of their dog and talk about how much they like baseball; anything to get the teacher to relate to them not as a student but as a person. Once the teacher sees a student as a person, it's hard to flunk them no matter how bad they are. These bureaucrats have the power to pass or fail you on your money exam. So the more they get to know you as a person, the more likely they are to help you pass the test. So when you are talking to them, don't be afraid to talk about personal stuff along with the professional. They certainly have the power to help, because they are the ones who give out the money.

Step #8: Belly To Belly Is Best

If being good on the phone increases your odds of getting the cash, then face to face will do even more. This may not be practical or even possible all of the time, but it is certainly another way for a bureaucrat to put a face with an application and this will make it that much harder for her to just say "no".

Step #9: Don't Wait

I really mean don't wait until the last minute to apply. Especially with those offices that only give out money at certain times of the year. As deadline time approaches, the bureaucrats can become too busy to provide you with any individualized help. So the best strategy is to call early and to call often.

Step #10: Don't Leave Empty Handed

If after reviewing all of their programs you decide that they have nothing for you, you have one more important thing to do before you move on. Call up one of the program officers and tell them about your search. See if they are aware of any programs that may suit your needs, or if they know of other agencies that have ANY kind of financial assistance for your project.

These people are in the business and are likely to attend meetings and conventions with people from other agencies who also hand out money. They are on the front line of government programs and will likely know other people who do this work.

Step #11: Apply, Apply, Apply

Keep going through this process and keep applying to as many

programs as possible. Apply even if people tell you that you have a very small chance of getting the money. Apply even if they tell you that you "may" not be qualified. When you hear terms like "may"  or "small chance" this still means that you do have a chance, and that is all you need. Don't worry about filling out so many applications. Once you've done the first one the rest are pretty much the same. The whole process is a numbers game. Just like the lottery, you have to play to win.

Step #12: No Application Is A Problem

No matter how easy the application may appear you are likely to encounter some difficulty with at least one question. But this is not a real problem. There is plenty of help.

The best way to handle this is to call the office giving out the money and ask to speak to a "program officer" for the program to which you are applying. They are the people who are directly involved in handing out the money. Be blunt and tell them that you "have no idea what they are talking about in question #6 on the application." You are probably not the first person in the world who had trouble with that question. The office probably realizes it is confusing, but they didn't have money in the budget to reprint the forms.

If for some reason you are not getting help directly from the office giving out the money, you can always contact the office of your elected official. This is your Congressman or Senator at the federal level, your state elected official for state programs and your councilman or mayor at the local level. They all have people on their staff whose job it is to solve problems that taxpayers are having with the government.

Step #13: It's Important To Be A Nag
We all hate to be nags. But it is important because an application can get lost so easily in a mountain of paperwork.

- ☐ Call to make sure they sent out your application.
- ☐ Call to make sure they received your application.
- ☐ Call to make sure you know when you will be notified if you are accepted.
- ☐ Call a few days after the notification date if you have not heard anything yet.

It may be uncomfortable at times. But the squeaky wheel does get the grease.

Step #14: Success and Failure are Both Good
If you get the money, call. Make sure you thank them and ask all the stupid questions you think are necessary to know when, where, and how you are going to get your money. If your application is rejected, be sure you call anyway. This is the only way you may learn the truth about why you did not get the money. Ask how soon you can apply again. They may be accepting applications every month and too many people applied last month. You always have to keep learning how and why

organizations give out money and by being an applicant you are in a wonderful position to ask.

Where To Find More Programs

You can't stop if you don't find what you need in this book. As I mentioned earlier space precludes us from listing the thousands more that are available and publishing deadlines prevent us from having the latest. So, here is where you can turn to continue your work in getting what you need:

1) *Find More Federal Money Programs*
Look at a book called the *Catalog of Federal Domestic Assistance*. It contains all the federal government programs that give out money. This book is available at your local public library or the U.S. Government Printing Office {www.gpo.gov}. You can also search the contents of this book, by key word or government department, for free on the web at {www.cfda.gov}.

2) *Find More State Money Programs*
Every state government has dozens of money programs that help people pay their expenses. The problem is that there is never one central place to look. You have to go agency by agency, or department by department and search for what is available. Some good departments to start with are health, agriculture, commerce, and social services. You can find them by dialing 411 and asking for your state capitol operator or by going to the web at {www.govengine.com} and clicking on your state.

3) *Find More Local City and County Programs*
Start looking at every local city and county government for programs that might help. If you don't know where to go, you can call 411 and ask for the mayor's office or the office

of the county executive. Just tell them you are looking for programs that might provide financial assistance to residents. You can also go to {www.govengine.com} and under each state there will be a listing of all cities and counties. Click on those of interest and start searching for programs.

4) Find More Money From Non-Profit Organizations
There are two major sources for finding money from these groups:

☐ The Foundation Center of New York City maintains a database of all foundations that provide money to non-profit organizations or individuals. The information is available on the web at {http://fdncenter.org} or from their participating libraries by contacting 212-620-4230

☐ The Guidestar Company in Williamsburg, VA also maintains a database of foundations and they can be reached at 757-229-4631 or at {www.guidestar.com}. Much of their database is accessible for free on the web.

5) Find More Money From Local Non-Profit and Volunteer Organizations
There are a number of national volunteer organizations around the country that offer grants and other free services to solve problems for people in their community. The Lions Club awarded over $340 million in grants since they started, and the Kiwanis Clubs gives out over $100 million every year.

Catholic Charities USA
1731 King St., #200
Alexandria, VA 22314
703-549-1390

www.catholiccharitiesinfo.org
Over 14,000 local organizations offer a variety of services for many different community problems including child care, elderly services, emergency financial services, rental assistance, and more. To find an office near you go to their main web site and see "Need Assistance? Find A Local Agency?" and put in your state.

Salvation Army National Headquarters
615 Slaters Lane
P.O. Box 269
Alexandria, VA 22313
703-684-5500
www.salvationarmyusa.org/

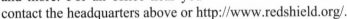

Families in need can receive a wide range of services, including utility assistance, transitional housing emergency food, clothing, and more. For an office near you contact the headquarters above or http://www.redshield.org/.

6) *Find A Local Non-Profit With Money And Services*

The United Way is a national organization that raises money for thousands of local non-profit organizations who offer money and services to people in their community. Your local United Way can identify non-profits in your area that may offer the resources or services you are looking for. Contact:

United Way of America
701 North Fairfax Street
Alexandria, VA 2314
703-836-7112
www.unitedway.org

To find a local chapter go to the website and enter your zip code under "Find A Local United Way."

When All Else Fails

Your elected representatives are in the business of seeing how they can help you locate money, services or anything else you need. They can also be handy if you have applied for government money and you can't seem to get a specific government agency to respond to you. Most elected officials have people on their staff whose job it is to do just that for voters. This is why politicians are always getting re-elected. If they do a favor for you, you will vote for them forever, no matter what they do.

☐ You have 1 congressman and 2 senators at the federal level. You can contact all 3.
☐ You have more than one elected official in your state capital.
☐ You also have an elected representative at your city and county level.

Contact them all. They are all getting a government salary to help you and they all have access to different resources. The worst that can happen is that more than one person solves your problem. If you need help finding them go to {www.congress.org }or your local library.

This Book Is More Than Just Money

I know that most people buying this book are looking for money and this is what this book is mostly about. But this book also serves as an introduction to all the other programs, services and information that our government has to offer. Money may be important in life but it may be even more important to know about the latest cure to your disease or the latest law that will make your insurance company pay a claim, or the best business investment that can make your portfolio double in size in one year.

The government spends billions of dollars a year studying almost anything you can think of, and they have nothing to sell because they give it all away for free. Government experts are there waiting to give it out if you know where to go and what to ask. You can literarily get better information than you can get from your doctor, lawyer or investment advisor, and you can get it free.

1) http://www.irs.gov/taxstats/article/0,,id=102886,00.html (the remainder of government spending comes from corporate, gift, employment, excise and estate taxes.
2) http://www.whitehouse.gov/omb/budget/fy2005/pdf/hist.pdf (see page 117)
3) Page 151 "Running On Empty", Peter G. Peterson, former Chairman of Federal Reserve Bank of New York, Farrar, Straus and Giroux, New York, 2004
4) Page 150 "Running On Empty", Peter G. Peterson, former Chairman of Federal Reserve Bank of New York, Farrar, Straus and Giroux, New York, 2004,
5) Page 151 "Running On Empty", Peter G. Peterson, former Chairman of Federal Reserve Bank of New York, Farrar, Straus and Giroux, New York, 2004
6) U.S. Office Of Education, National Center For Education Statistics, http://nces.ed.gov/pubs2003/2003060c
7) http://www.gao.gov/new.items/d04363.pdf
8) http://www.kff.org/medicaid/loader.cfm?url=/commonspot/security/getfile.cfm&PageID=28333
9) http://www.gao.gov/new.items/d04346.pdf
10) http://www.acenet.edu/resources/HigherEdFacts/issue-briefs/2004FAFSA.pdf
11) http://www.gao.gov/new.items/d04377.pdf
12) http://www.gao.gov/new.items/d03958.pdf

Life in a Question Mark Suit

Finding out where to get the money you want in life can be an easy task compared with trying to decide how one should actually live one's life. I'm not a philosopher, I'm a researcher. And although I've been researching government money programs for over 25 years, I'm sure I've spent more of my waking hours, and even my non-waking ones, thinking about how I should live my life. I also believe that the manner in which you live your life is an important part of how successful you are going to be at getting the money you need to do what you want to do in life.

I believe that, deep down, we are all scared and have no idea what we are doing. The problem is that no one seems to ever admit this. If more people would admit this, it would be a friendlier world to live in.

Question Mark Suits Changed My Life

I didn't get the courage to wear question mark suits until about 8 years ago in my early 50s. Now I wish I did it 30 years ago. My suits have nothing to do with some grand marketing strategy or in creating a brand. It was just a result of boredom. Life can be boring and mundane if you don't work at trying to make it exciting. If no one is going to throw a party for you, you have to throw one yourself.

Wearing these suits has changed my life. People smile at me when I walk into a room, even if they don't know me from the TV commercials. It gets me free upgrades on the airlines. I get better service at hotels, restaurants and bars. For the first time in my life pretty girls come up and talk to me. Where were they years ago when I had a lot more hormones?

It's not only what it does for me but what it does to other people. It makes people nicer. It lightens their day. I feel that I can walk into the toughest biker bar at 2 am and still feel secure. The suit just seems to melt people. As a result it makes me nicer, because everyone is kinder to me.

But I'm still the same guy who flunked English in college, got picked last on the basketball team, and couldn't get a date with any of the cheerleaders in high school.

The Most Important Thing in Life is Failure

We don't glorify failure enough in our country. It is the most important part of life. We glorify success but since our early days in school we are all taught how bad it is to fail, and as a result we avoid it like the plague when in fact we should embrace it as the most important part of life.

You are never going to learn anything unless you start failing. Only one in a million of us will ever wake up and become an instant success at something we want to do. Think about how a child learns to walk. They fall down 100 times before they make it across the room on two feet. It is the basic lesson in life. Falling down and failing is the only way we all learn to do anything. If you wanted to have a life that is protected from failure your mother would be pushing you around in a wheelchair today because you never learned to walk. We all know this about walking, but when we want to do anything else new in life we're told not to do it because we could fall down, get hurt or fail. Well of course that is going to happen. So if you want to live an exciting life, get out there and fail.

No One Cares If You Fail

I always dreamed of starting a business. But my biggest fear of starting a business was failure. I believed that everyone would point at me as I walked down the street and whisper behind my back that I was a failure. It would be like having a big red F on my forehead. But after my first two businesses failed, I realized that no one else really cared if I failed. Everyone is so involved in their own lives that they really don't have the time nor interest in the details of my life. Sure, for a few seconds, they may mention something behind my back at the next family reunion, but that will be about it.

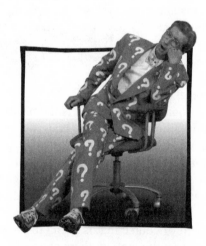

Failure Was The Best Thing That Ever Happened To Me

After my first 2 businesses failed and I saw that no one cared, it was the most liberating experience of my life, I felt that now I had nothing to lose. I didn't have much fun in my first two businesses and they failed anyway. So the third time I said to myself, "if the worst thing that can happen to me if I start another business is that I fail, then this time at least I'm going to have fun."

That's when things changed. I started a business that was in my soul and I started having fun. Now I was different than anyone else out there and it attracted people to me. I was not longer walking on egg shells every time I made a decision because I was so worried about making a wrong decision and failing. I was out there generating new ideas, solving new problems in the world, having fun, and people liked it.

Looking back I am very grateful that my first 2 businesses failed. If either of them had succeeded they would have been just a mediocre business because I wasn't having fun. The failures led me to a business where I have a good time and as a result I can do it better than anyone else, because I'm having fun.

Having an MBA Caused My First 2 Businesses To Fail

I really believe that it took me two failed businesses to unlearn all that I learned in MBA school. Back in the 70's business school taught me how to run General Motors and not run a little business out of my bedroom. It taught me how to spend a lot of money and waste a lot of time in starting a business. It taught me how to hire the high priced lawyers and accountants and to make sure I have the right tax structure. It taught me how to buy the "power" office space, the "power" drapes and the "power" business cards.

When my first two businesses failed, I looked around and began thinking, who won? The accountants, the lawyers, and the people I purchased the furniture and drapes from. They were the winners and I was out on the street. Then when I started my third business I forgot about everything I learned in MBA school and concentrated on just those things that were critical to the success of my business.

I decided that tax structure, drapes, or furniture were not critical to the success of my business. The only thing that my business could not live without was customers. If I didn't have customers, I was out of business. I could always survive with a less than perfect business card or organizational structure, but could not survive without customers.

For my third business I didn't even file paperwork with the government. I figured that the way the government works, it would take them 3 years to find me. And by that time I would either be out of business or I would be able to afford the $50 fine they would charge for not filing.

When starting a small business, the most important resource you have is your time. You can't be wasting it on things like meetings with lawyers, picking out drapes or other activities that are not critical to your success, You should be spending your time figuring out how to get customers, as that is the only thing that is critical to your success; the rest is detail.

Your Worst Enemies Are Your Loved Ones

Your loved ones can be your worst enemies in achieving the greatness you deserve in life. They believe that it's their job to project you from failure, so they will constantly keep telling you that you should not do something because you can fail. But by keeping you from failure they are keeping you from success because the only way anyone can achieve success is through failure. So ignore your loved ones and get out there and fail.

> # Loving Someone Is Helping Them Do Whatever THEY Want To Do— Not What You Want Them To Do

I grew up in an environment where I thought everyone loved each other. But they showed love by trying to control each other. "I want you do what I say because I love you." "You will be happy in life if you do what I say." I thought this was how everyone showed love, but it never felt good. It felt more like criticism. It made me feel that I could only get love if I did what other people told me to do.

Now, I have an entirely different definition of love. If I love you, I will never tell you what I think you should do in life. My job is to help YOU, find out what YOU want to do in life and then I have to do everything in my power to help you achieve it. And if you love me, I want the same.

What gives me the audacity to think I can ever tell anyone one else how to live their life. Someone's life is the most important possession they have, and only they, alone, have the right to decide what to do with it. And, anyway, I certainly don't have the answers in life for everyone else. The older I get the more I realize I've been guessing every day.

If You Want To Retire You Have The Wrong Job

Growing up in Pennsylvania during the 50s the ideal life was to work until you were in your 60s and then retire to Florida and play golf for the rest of your life. That seems dumb to me now. Sure I like playing golf but I'm pretty mediocre at it. I also feel I'm great at my job and I love doing it. So why would I want to leave something I'm good at and spend the rest of my life doing something I'm just mediocre at? My advice is to find something you love to do and you never have to worry about retirement.

Find Your Art And Solve Your Aging Problems

If you find something you love doing, you never have to retire. Retirement is an idea from the Industrial Age when most jobs were in factories or transportation and required a lot of muscle power. By the time you were 60 or 65 it was physically impossible to do most of those jobs anymore. But now we are out of the industrial age and into a service and information based economy. Muscle power is no longer the main requirement, it's brain power that's needed and those skills we can use forever.

Also, I think a lot of the problems of aging can be solved by finding work you really want to do. Contributing to society must be one of the main reasons why we are on earth. I can't imagine that if there is some big master plan for life, the top of the chart doesn't say, "Sit On The Beach Your Whole Life." Why are we here if we are not helping someone else? Sitting on your butt watching the weather channel and playing mediocre golf doesn't sound like a whole lot of contribution.

If you find work you love you will want to do it forever and most of the problems of aging will go way. You won't have to worry about how much money you have to retire because you'll keep on working forever. You won't be yelling at the TV news everyday about how the rest of the world is so stupid and you have everything figured out, because you will still be trying to put your ideas into action. And a lot of the aches and pains of old age will go away because you will have something bigger than yourself to worry about. You will be concentrating on getting up in the morning to go and do the things you love doing and feeling important because you are still needed and wanted in the world. We are not just here to fill up a doctor's waiting room.

What's Weird About You Is Your Best Part

Every organization that you come into contact with in life seems to want to stomp out what is best about you. If you have a knack for cracking jokes in a room full of people, you'll face as least 12 years of teachers who will try to beat it out of you. If you have a talent for seeing how to solve problems differently or if you like to wear different clothes, every boss you ever have will likely create a culture that will make you feel uncomfortable.

I remember when I was in school. I had ants in my pants. I couldn't sit still in class. I was always jumping around trying to make a fool out of myself and get a laugh. If I was a kid today they probably would have given me Ritalin. The teachers were always beating on me to sit down and be quiet. I was good at having ants in my pants. And it took until I was in my 40s to realize that I could make a whole lot of money jumping around TV shows selling books. For my first 10 years of acting like a fool jumping around on TV, my parents did not admit I was their kid. But it worked. It sold books and I loved doing it. I was good at it. And I make a boat load of money doing it. If someone said this was my good part and helped me develop the talent I was born with, I would not have wasted 40 years getting around to profiting from it.

So look into yourself, your kids or your loved ones, and try to discover the weird things about you and develop it to the fullest. Quit trying to be like everyone else. Other people are doing that better than you if it comes natural to them. What is weird about you, you will do better than  anyone else in the world because it will come natural to you. We are all attracted to different. So show the world what is different about you, and you will be loved for it. No one is going to love you for being the same as everyone else, and anyway you're not.

Living Inside Out

Walking around in question mark suits made me finally feel that I am living inside out. I am finally showing the world what I feel like inside of me. Our culture seems to want all of us to cover up what is inside of us. Why?

It Doesn't Take A Lot of Brains To Be A Boss. Look At All The Dumb People You've Worked For

It does not take a mental giant to run most things in this country. Look at all the idiots we've all worked for. It usually took me 6 months in a job to start feeling that I knew more than my boss. And by that time I was spending a lot of wasted energy talking behind their backs about how dumb they were.

That's when I figured out that instead of wasting energy talking behind the boss's back, it's better the BE THE BOSS and have other people waste their energy talking behind my back.

Increase Your Success With Your Heart

With all the idiots running things out there, you certainly can be running things too. The key ingredient to success is perseverance. You just have to hang in there long enough until you figure out how to do it. Eighty percent of us seem to have enough intelligence to run 80% of what is out there, if we really want to. That is why it's important to find out what you really want to do in life. Because if you really want to do something, you will work harder at it, and longer at it, until you figure it out.

Everything you do will have its ups and downs and there will be roadblocks for you to go over, under, around or through. If you are just doing something because your brother-in-law says you can make a lot of money at it, you will probably give up as soon as the first couple of bad days hit. You'll then be looking for another easy way to succeed. For 99% of us it's not going to be easy. So find something you really want to do and you won't mind doing what it takes to get there.

Easy Isn't Fun

Looking for the easy way is a trap to having no fun. If you were playing baseball as an adult with a bunch of 9 year-olds in a little league park, you would be able to hit the ball over the fence every time you were at bat. That would get old quickly and wouldn't be fun. The fun in life is trying to grow and stretch yourself as a human being as much as you possibly can. You can easily win a race if the rest of the field was on crutches and you had two good legs. That's why easy isn't fun. Trying to do the best you can against the best competition you can find and trying to grow the most out of your god given ability is what is really fun and satisfying too.

Be Your Own Hero

Is it because the media today tells us too much about our heroes? It's hard to find true heroes today, whether it's in sports figures, politicians, scientists, or whoever. The media always seems to like telling us something bad about our favorite person. I think the answer is to become your own hero. We all can be the kind of hero we dreamed about as a kid. The kind that goes out and carves a path into the unknown, slays the dragon, and then comes back to enlighten the village. We all are capable of doing this in our own way. There are still dragons around. They may not have fire coming out of their mouths, but they are real. Like providing a good meal at a good price. Or offering a day care service that provides real nurturing and real love. Or going back to school and becoming the best damn teacher the school system has ever seen. Or finally paying off all your bills and concentrating on what is really important in life.

None of these acts are easy. Real heroes don't do easy, or they wouldn't be heroes. Approach your struggle like you are the star of your own movie. Tell yourself you are going to solve your problem in a bold and courageous way. You are going to find unique answers to the problems that confront you. And most importantly, you are going to persevere, no matter what, to accomplish your goal. You've read books like this. You've seen 100 movies containing the same theme. So why don't you live your own movie. Be your own hero. You have nothing to lose except going back to doing what you already have been doing. On the other hand, you have a chance at becoming a star.

You Can Always Get Another Job You Hate

Many of us are sitting in jobs that we dislike and fear leaving to look for something else or to start your own business. Why does staying with something we hate stop us from trying something we may love for the rest of our lives? I always try to ask myself, "What is the worst that can happen if I leave?" And the answer I would come up with is that I can always find another job I hate, and you can too. There are plenty of them around.

Bad Is Beautiful

No one likes to ask for bad things to happen in their life. But many times the bad things create the best opportunities in life. Being fired from a job you didn't like is a blessing in disguise. You probably never would have left it by yourself because you didn't know exactly what you wanted to do. Being fired is probably the best thing your boss can ever do for you. Then you have no excuse but to go out and find something you really want to do in life.

The older I get the more I see that there is good in almost everything bad that happens. The Vietnam War and the military draft were going on when I graduated from college. I tried to get a deferment by going to graduate school. But my grades and test scores were so bad no school would have me. I joined the Navy to avoid being drafted into the Army and I'll tell you, I never had more responsibility again for the rest of my life. It turned out to be one of the best experiences of my life and I was trying to get out of it. As a 22 year-old kid out of college, the Navy gave me billion dollar ships to drive around the South China Seas. They gave me big guns to shoot, and made me a diplomatic currier traveling the world.

I have two failed marriages and I found divorce to be the most hurtful experience I have ever had. But without the experience of divorce I would have never thought through how much work a relationship really takes and what are the most important elements required for finding someone you can be compatible with in order to raise a family.

I already talked about having 2 failing businesses was the only way I could have found out what I really wanted to do in life.

And even recently, I relearned this important lesson again when a government consumer protection agency accused me of making false statements in my commercials. They did this even though they had no consumer complaints against me and they were not investigating me. It was just some kind of political thing because they saw me promoting government programs. It was still a kick in the gut. But when I decided to fight back on their false acquisitions I learned that I know more about government programs than even the government. And I am now stronger to fend off anyone else who has something bad to say about what I am doing. I can now be even bolder in my efforts to educate people about government programs, because my fight has reassured me of my knowledge and made me stronger in my convictions. I should now thank them for the wake up call.

> ## You Don't Have To Know Where To Go, Just Where Not To Be

So many people hang around doing a job, or even stay in a relationship, they dislike because they are waiting to identify the perfect job or person to jump to before they leave the imperfect one. The problem with this is that you may not live long enough for this strategy to work. The perfect job or person is unlikely to come and hit us in the head while we are in a place we know we should not be. You have a moral obligation to get away from what you know for sure is bad even if you have no idea where you are going to go.

You don't even have to be certain that your next step will be any better than the last one. But you still have a responsibility to leave what you positively know is not for you. That is the only way you can offer life a chance to present you with what you really should be doing. Being in the wrong place is like being in jail. Get out of there no matter what and give yourself a chance for perfect.

You Can Rest For Eternity When You Are Dead

It is puzzling to me why so many people think that the ultimate in life is to sit on the beach and rest. They must hate their jobs. Doing nothing may seem nice for awhile, but it gets pretty boring in short order if you have something in life that you feel is important to do. Once you find what you are dying to do, sitting on the beach seems like a waste of time. You can rest for eternity when you are dead. So why do it now, when there are so many fun things to do?

Don't get me wrong. I've been known to sit on my butt doing much of nothing. But things like resting, having a family, and living a full life are indeed important to me in that they also help my main mission in life and that is trying to contribute as much to someone else's life as I can before it's over.

Love Is A Muscle You Can Use For The Rest Of Your Life

The problem with aging is that the body does not work as well as it used to, and so we think we are missing out on pleasures of life that we once appreciated. But I think what really happens is that there are new pleasures that present themselves that we don't even realize exist. It seems to be a pattern throughout life.

We certainly didn't enjoy the same activities in high school as we did in kindergarten, so why should we think that we have to enjoy all of the same things in our 50s in the same way we enjoyed them in our 20s. By taking a pill to enjoy an experience the same way we did 30 years ago is missing out on exploring a deeper and more meaningful way to enjoy the experience. You don't want to act like a kindergarten kid when you are in high school.

I hope by now you know that I'm talking about love. Because I find it can be an experience that can grow deeper and more meaningful with age, especially when you don't have to react like a teenager anymore. It's a lovely experience that can be developed forever. I only wish I was able to take it more seriously when I was younger.

So don't give up on learning how to love. Unlike sports and a lot of life's other pleasures, it's one activity that can provide you with rewards forever.

Forget The Rules, Use The Tools

All the tools you need seem to be available for you to do anything you want in our society. Look at this book alone. It shows you where society is giving out over $1 trillion a year for people to solve their problems and to do fun stuff. We live in a bountiful society that has so much to offer those who are willing to put in the time to search for it. I think that not having the tools is not what stops people, it's trying to follow some stupid rules that have been put into their head for no reason at all.

It was like that for me. I used to believe that I couldn't write a book not just because I didn't go to a prestigious college, but more importantly because I flunked English in college and graduated, just barely, with a 3.0000001 average. Three point zero was passing. But I now have over 100 books to my name and two have been on the New York Times Best Seller lists. In

this country you can forget all the silly little rules people put in your head. The tools are out there for everyone to use. Is this a great country or what?

Plan For Failure Because Anyone Can Handle Success

Whether it's filling out a grant application for yourself or preparing a new marketing strategy for your business, we all love to think about what we are going to do once we get the grant, or once the millions of sales come in from the marketing plan. I used to do that too. But now I don't waste the time because I realize that success in anything is a nice problem to have and you should only worry about it once it happens. Reality

in life is that 9 out of 10 attempts at anything usually fail. I've written over 100 books but only about 10 or 15 have sold enough copies to be proud of. But before each book was published I would swear that each was going to be on the cover of Time Magazine. So if failure is likely to happen 90% of the time, I might as well gear my life around it and plan for failure, because if I'm wrong, that will be wonderful.

The way I plan for my books failing is to always have a few extra book ideas that I would like to do if I had the time. This way when a book fails I don't have to spend too much time wallowing in self pity over my failure because I will have another idea that I can get working on right away that I can now be positive will make it to Time Magazine.

45

Always Invest In YOUR Future or SOMEONE Else's Future

It seems to me that money is best spent by continually investing in yourself so that you have a better future. And if you're so old or rich that you don't need to worry about your future anymore, your money should be spent investing in someone else's future.

The money you spend on a cruise or even investing in the stock market can be put to better use in your life by investing in your education, your own business, or a place to live. If you can do both the cruise and the education that would be great. But most of us don't have that luxury.

Choosing the long-term gain will always better serve you and your family. Investing in the stock market or similar investment scheme can be a fool's game. Why invest in something you have very little knowledge of and very little control over. Plus you are giving your money to a stock broker who will be having all the fun with it while you have all the worry. The best investment is always in yourself. That is the one thing you have the most knowledge of and the most control over.

Get Comfortable With Discomfort

We seem to experience some of our best growth when we find ourselves in uncomfortable situations. That's when we have to dig down into ourselves for something new that we have not used before. That's what makes us grow. I find this to be true even more so as I get older. Age makes you believe you know more about what works and what doesn't work, because you've gone through so many uncomfortable situations already. There seems to be something in us that wants to avoid uncomfortable situations. And if we do that, we are going to stop growing. So as you grow older and figured out how not to be uncomfortable, reverse the process and throw yourself into situations that are uncomfortable so you can keep learning and growing.

The Only Thing Constant In Life Is Change

The only people in life who really like change are wet babies and busy cashiers. The rest of us go kicking and screaming if anyone introduces change into our life. But the world has turned into a force of constant change. Nothing seems to last long. Nothing seems to work twice. Can you name the top 10 TV shows from 2 years ago. It seems that everything but 60 Minutes is probably history. Computers are out of date as soon as they are introduced into the market. Everything is going out of date faster and faster.

At the turn of the century information arrived by letter on horseback. The process speeded up when we expected our letters in a few days. Now overnight is not even fast enough. We need it by email or instant messenger. The jobs that you thought were good to have a few years ago are no longer good. On September 11 a group of people armed with box cutters hurt a country with more missiles, bombs and tanks than anyone else in the world. The world keeps changing faster and faster every day. Don't fight it. Teach yourself how to live with it. Adapt to it and you will survive.

In my business I plan that everything I am making money with this year will not make money for us next year. I have to continually think of new products and new lines of income in order to survive. You either change yourself or someone else is going to change you.

Doing Something You Love Brings You More Love

When I had my first child I worried so much that my house and car would not be grand enough for my family or that I wouldn't have enough money to pay for my kids to go to college. I found myself beginning to make business decisions based solely on how much money the decision might bring me. I started to see myself not having as much fun in what I was doing because I was working more for the money and less for joy of what I was doing and in solving other people's problems. I was watching my mood change and I was becoming less and less happy.

Then the light bulb turned on over my head. I asked myself, as an adult, did I remember my own father for the house or car he had? The answer was no. I remembered my father for how he acted day by day. So I said to myself that my kids are only going to have a good experience with me as a father if I am happy with what I am doing in my work. That way I could come home every day and share my joy and happiness with the whole family. That was a better gift to give my children than a bigger house or a nicer car.

Giving Is Selfish

When I was young and my in-laws wanted to give us money or gifts to help us out I used to not accept them because I wanted to do things myself. I didn't want to be beholden to anyone. Then I realized that what I thought was a brave and independent act on my part was actually a very selfish act.

The nicest thing in the world is to be able to give to someone. We all know that. The problem is trying to find someone deserving enough that you want to give to. So if someone believes that you are a very deserving person and they want to give you something, but you refuse, then you are actually preventing that person from being able to experience one of the greatest feelings in the world. That's why I now believe that giving is a very selfish act and not an act of generosity. It's a very selfish act because it feels so great to give. And we should not deprive others of that wonderful feeling.

Less Money Makes You Stronger

When I was trying to start my first business I used to think things like, "If I only had $1 million I could be successful. I used to see studies at the time that said the main reason people went out of business was because of lack of capital. What I believe now is that that kind of thinking is stupid. It's like saying, "The reason the man died is because he stopped breathing." That may certainly be the reason the man died, because that's the reason all people die. But it's not the cause. The easiest thing for any entrepreneur to say when they go bankrupt is that they didn't have enough money. You are not going to hear them say things like, "Oh, I wasted a lot of money on stupid things."

Anyone can start and run a business if they have a lot of money. But if you have a lot of money you are going to be a lot less likely to have a strong business. The easiest thing for any entrepreneur to do is to throw money at a problem. If you need more sales and you have a lot of money, you will start throwing it at advertising. This is what all those dot com businesses did in the 90s when they were rolling in dough.

People were giving these upstarts millions of dollars to run businesses that had no customers. Because they had all this money they would buy the most expensive advertising in the world, like TV commercials during the Super Bowl. It would cost them $30 million for a commercial and it would generate only $1 million in sales. This was a stupid business decision. All the dot com businesses were doing things like this in the 1990s and that is why there are only a handful left.

If someone gave me a bunch of money to start my business, I would probably do the same thing. But because I didn't have the money, I had to figure out a way to get sales without any money. The first way I did this was by being a professional guest on talk shows. I quickly saw that TV producers would put me on their show because I acted goofy. I would get on their shows, act crazy telling people about my book, and give my 800 number so people could order. And it was all for free.

I remember sitting on Letterman and getting 7 minutes of air time for my segment as a guest and we would stop in the middle for a commercial from some company that had to pay something like $30,000 for only 1 minute of air time. I got 7 minutes for free because I figured out how to act like an idiot on TV.

This gave me a strong business. I found a way not to pay for advertising because I didn't have any money. There is always more than one way to accomplish an objective. Real entrepreneurs figure out how to do it without a lot of money.

You Can't Learn When You Blame Others

I wrote 12 books for the big publishers in New York City. Two of them became New York Times best sellers. One or two others did pretty well and the rest were failures. When I realized a book was failing, it was wonderful to have all those fat cat executives in New York to blame. I would blame the publishers' publicity department for not sending me to enough cities to do publicity. I would blame their marketing department for not spending enough on advertising. I would blame their production department for coming out with the book at the wrong time of

year. There were so many handy punching bags on which to work out my depression.

But this was bad because it took my energies away from trying to learn from all those failures and from trying to use the experience to improve the success of my next book.

Now that I publish my own books I learn from every single book that comes out. I have to learn. I have no one else to blame but me. I have to take apart the entire publication process and see if I can learn where I went wrong. I want to be here tomorrow and the only way to do that is to learn by the mistakes of today.

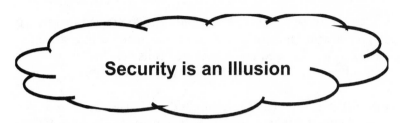

Security is an Illusion

I wonder why we as a species all run around trying to do everything possible to become secure. Have enough money, have a secure job, have a secure relationship, secure, secure, secure. When it really seems that the ultimate in life is insecurity. No matter what our bank account, job or relationships wind up to be we are all going to die anyway. So life seems like it is the ultimate insecurity.

Not Doing What You Were Told Is Still The Best Way To Have Fun

When I was a kid it seemed that the real fun things in life were doing those things that my parents told me not to do. Don't climb that tree, it may be dangerous. Don't hang around that Jimmy, he's a trouble maker. I never told my parents when I climbed that tree or played with Jimmy, but it was fun when I did it, and I never seemed any worse for it.

Business seems the same way. After 7 years of business school I feel that my first two businesses failed because I was trying to operate them like I was told to in business school. When I threw away the books and started doing things the experts said I should not be doing, I started having fun. I was told to slow down when I spoke on TV because no one could understand me, but that wasn't fun. When I started I was told I had to pretend I was a big company with fancy offices, when I was really a guy starting a business in his bedroom, making calls in his underwear. Pretending I was something I wasn't was no fun either.

Life never really changes from childhood. The real fun comes from doing the things you are told not to do, because that is where the adventure is.

I Made Good Money Selling Stuff I Get For Free

I'm really a plagiarist. I copy information available to anyone from the government and sell it for as much as I can get. My first New York Times Best Seller was practically all copied from a book anyone could get from the U.S. Government Printing Office called the Catalog of Federal Domestic Assistance. Nothing in the government is copyrighted. Anyone can take government documents and sell them for as much as they like.

In our information age most businesses are like me in that they are rearranging reality for other people and selling it. People in the news business go out and get the news for free and then sell it to people. Accountants put numbers to what is going on in reality and then sell it to people. Psychologists get paid to interpret the reality that may or may not be going on in your head. Getting information for free and selling it for as much as you can get is a growth industry.

You Can Always Find A Reason NOT To Do Something

Have a good idea. Ask a dozen experts, or friends, to help you evaluate it and the majority of them will always come up with a reason why you should NOT do it. It's never been done before. It will cost a lot of money. So and so did something like that and failed. Experts love telling you why things can fail because; it is a safer answer to give. If they talk you out of doing it, you can't prove them wrong by trying it to see if you would have succeeded.

Things get done in this world by people who do things no matter what anyone says. Anyone with half a brain can identify potential obstacles in any plan. But the hero does it anyway, and uses her will and determination to overcome any obstacles that may present.

Experts Tell You What Worked Yesterday

We all want to be able to go to some expert and have them tell us what is the right thing to do, what is the right job to take, what is the right business decision to make, etc. Most experts are wrong because it is impossible to predict the future.

The Best Decisions Are The Hardest Ones To Make

Life offers you few chances to make those difficult decisions that will turn out to be life changing character builders. And when these decisions present themselves, the forces around us will pressure us to make the easy, the safer, but the wrong choice.

I only started wearing question mark suits about 8 years ago. And in the beginning years Home Shopping Network came under new management. They wanted to change their image so they could try and attract a more upscale customer. This meant that they did not want me to wear my question mark suit on the air. It was a very difficult decision for me to make. On the one hand it took me 30 years of building up the courage to wear this suit and on the other hand Home Shopping had a right to say what the dress code was for their party. But more importantly Home Shopping was close to half of my business at the time. If I didn't take off the suit I would lose a bunch of easy money.

The advice I was getting from my staff was mostly variations of how I was silly to give up that much money if I left. But there was something inside of me that was urging me not to give up wearing the suit. I felt so proud of myself for finally finding the courage to wear it that I was very reluctant to give up the thrill. I felt that this suit was me. It was who I wanted to be. And I decided to bite the bullet and tell Home Shopping that I could not be on if I could not wear the suit. I was gone.

It was a very scary decision, especially when there were few, if any, around me who encouraged me to follow my heart. But it turned out to be one of the most important decisions in my life. Closing one door behind me opened up a bunch of other doors in front of me that I didn't even know were there. Within a few years my business got twice as big as it was when I was with Home Shopping and I couldn't have done it WITH THEM. But I certainly didn't know it at the time.

Following your heart and not your pocket book, your friends, or generally accepted theories, can give you the greatest joy that you can ever experience.

I Think We're Here To Help

Better minds than mine have wrestled with the eternal question of "Why Are We Here". But is seems to me that we must be here to help other people. We all want to be wanted. And that seems to come from using what ever we have inside of us to help other people.

It's easy to get caught up in making money, making muscles or making wrinkles disappear, but if you're not doing something that is also helping other people, making money, muscles or making wrinkles go away is going to get old real fast. What are you going to do when you have all the money, muscles or smooth skin you need. Probably you'll want more. They become just another addictive drug in our society, and they become insatiable. They are false gods.

That's why if you develop a product, a profession, a skill, or whatever, that you also feel is helping someone else, in addition to you making money, it can keep you satisfied and balanced after you get your money.

Making money is certainly not bad. I enjoy making money because it is a great way to keep score and see if what you are doing is helping  someone. If people are not going to pay you for it, maybe you should not be doing it.

I wish you as much joy and growth as possible so that I can travel in a world that is filled with many more people who are grateful to be doing what they want to be doing each day.

Matthew Lesko

START OR EXPAND A BUSINESS

The programs below are for those who are looking for money and help to start or expand a business or a non-profit organization. Although we have listed mostly grants, we have also included some low interest loans and special services that can be worth thousands.

Remember the programs below are nowhere near the amount of programs that are available in the United States. There are not enough trees in the rain forest for us to list every single program. Our hope is that if you do not find what you need, you will keep pursuing your mission through other sources. We do have another title that describes about 30,000 sources for business. It's called "Free Money For Entrepreneurs" and you can get more information on this title at 1-800-955-POWER or at {www.lesko.com}.

If you wish to do the research necessary yourself you can follow the outline below of the major sources of getting money and help to start or expand a business or non-profit organization.

1) Find Federal Money Programs for Business

Look at a book called the *Catalog of Federal Domestic Assistance*. This book is available at your local public library or the U.S. Government Printing Office {www.gpo.gov}. You can also search the contents of this book for free on the web at {www.cfda.gov}. In this chapter you will find items which have a five digit number associated with them (such as 10.471). These numbers refer to the *Catalog of Federal Domestic Assistance*.

2) *Find State Money Programs for Business*

Look for the state office of economic development located in your state capitol. You can find them by dialing 411 and asking for your state capitol operator or by going to the web at {www.govengine.com} and clicking on your state. Then start looking for web sites on business or economic development. Every state offers a wealth of help and information on starting a business. Some offer job training funds, export assistance, technology resources, tourism promotion, industrial revenue bonds, revolving loan funds, and more. Most have a State Business Resource Guide to assist you in your search.

3) *Find Local City and County Programs for Business*

Start looking at every local city and county government for programs that help businesses. They all have them. If you don't know where to go you can call 411 and ask for the mayor's office or the office of the county executive. Just tell them you want to start or expand a business and want to know about any and all programs. You can also go to {www.govengine.com} and under each state there will be a listing of all cities and counties. Click on those of interest and search for economic development or business programs. Remember, you can start a business in any state, city or county and not live there. The people who give out the money just want your business to be there and you can commute.

4) *Find Money From Non-Profit Organizations for Business*

There are 3 major sources for finding money from these groups:

A. The Association for Enterprise Opportunity in Arlington, VA maintains a database of non-profit organizations that provide financial assistance to entrepreneurs. Contact them at 703-841-7760 or {www.microenterpriseworks. org/nearyou/}

B. The Foundation Center of New York City maintains a database of all foundations that provide money to non-profit organizations or individuals. Their information is available on the web at {http://fdncenter.org} or from their participating libraries by contacting 212-620-4230 or 800-424-9836.

C. The Guidestar Company in Williamsburg, VA also maintains a database of foundations and they can be reached at 757-229-4631 or {www.guidestar.com}. Much of their database is accessible for free on the web.

D. The Aspen Institute's mission is to identify, develop, and disseminate microenterprise program information. To find resources near you contact The Aspen Institute, One Dupont Circle, NW, Suite 700, Washington, DC 20036; 202-736-1071; Fax: 202-467-0790; {http://fieldus.org}.

5) Find Help With Any Part Of Starting Or Expanding A Business
The government supports over 1,000 offices all over the country called Small Business Development Centers. They will sit down with you and help tackle any problem you may be having with your business like: finding money, filling out forms, taxes, marketing, technical problems, contracting, etc. All their services are free or for very little cost. These Centers do not have money for entrepreneurs, but will know of local money

sources available. For a Center near you contact 1-800-8-ASK-SBA or {http://www.sba.gov/sbdc/sbdcnear.html}.

6) *Fill out 1 to 3 pages for grants up to $50,000*

I keep trying to dispel the myth that all grant applications are big and complication. Some do have large applications, but they are normally for people going after money as a non-profit organization. But a majority of grant money for business, housing, education or personal expenses normally requires only a few pages of a form to fill out. Here are some real sample applications for business façade grants:

- 2-Pages Gets You a $32,500 Grant To Build A Business {www.ci.toledo.oh.us/images/EconDev/0428ccfacadeapp.pdf}
- 1-Page Application Gets A $7,500 Grant For New Landscaping For Your Business {www.chooserockledge.com/Facade%20%20and%20LandscapeGrant%20Program.pdf}
- 2-Pages Gets You a $50,000 Grant For Your Business {www.downtownbillings.com/dbp/docs/Download/AppsFY05/Facade05.pdf}
- 2-Pages Get You A $10,000 Grant To Fix Up Your Business {www.sumter-sc.com/client_resources/departments/downtown/2005%20facade%20grant%20program.pdf}

Don't stop here. Because next year the government is going to give money to over 1 million entrepreneurs and you can be one of them.

$1,500 a Month To Live On While You Start Your Own Business

There are a number of states, including New York and Iowa that will allow you to collect unemployment money while you try to get your business started. It used to be that you could only receive unemployment compensation if you were actively looking for a job. Now Uncle Sam considers entrepreneuring to be a

legitimate job. Contact your state unemployment labor office to see what your local rules are on entrepreneuring.

$10,000 to Take Entrepreneur Training Courses

Each state has established local job-training centers that provide money to job seekers to upgrade their skills and get better jobs. Many of these local centers allow residents to use this money to train to become an entrepreneur. Contact your state's One-Stop Labor Information Center headquarters located in your state capital and they can direct you to a local office. Check them out at {www.doleta.gov/usworkforce/onesto p/onestopmap.cfm}.

$100,000 to Become A Freelancer Working From Your Kitchen Table

My wife got over $100,000 of government money to do consulting right out of our home. My sister got over $350,000 from the government to frame pictures. They are both government freelancers. There are free offices around the country that will help any freelancer get government contracts. The government buys: legal services, web design, aerobic instructors, landscaping, cleaning, and even stand-up comics.

Contact the state Office of Economic Development located in your state capital or your local Procurement Assistance Office who can match the product or service you are selling with the appropriate agency, and then help you market your wares effectively. To find the office nearest you, contact Small and Disadvantaged Business Utilization Office, Cameron Station, Room 4B110, Defense Logistics Agency, Alexandria, VA 22304; 703-767-1661; {www.dla.mil}.

Free Help to Turn Your Hobby Into a Career

There are dozens of little businesses that you can start for free around any area of interest and get all the free help you need to get them started. A back packer can sell back-packing equipment on the internet or be a back packing tour operator. An avid golfer can sell golf-related equipment or supplies, be a golf tour organizer. An animal lover can sell unique pet supplies on the web or offer pet sitting services. And none of these businesses require money to start. If you need marketing, management, legal or any other kind of help, contact your state Office of Economic Development and ask for your local Small Business Development Center {www.gov ngine.com}.

$250,000 to Buy Out Your Boss

There are a number of federal and state programs for employees who want to purchase the company where they are working. Some programs offer money for any reason and some for specific reasons like: making your company employee owned or keeping your employer from moving out of state. Contact the state Office of Economic Development located in your state capital (www.govengine.com) for a starting place for locating these programs.

Free Accounting Services for Non-Profits and Small Business

There are a number of organizations around the country that provide free accounting services to help non-profits, small businesses, and even needy individuals get the accounting help they need. They can help with bookkeeping instruction, system analysis, preparation of 990 forms, preparation for audits and free publications. A minimal one-time cost may be required. To find free accounting help in your area, contact Accountants for the Public Interest, University of Baltimore, Thurnel Business Center, Room 519, 1420 North Charles Street, Baltimore, MD 21201; 410-837-6533; Fax: 410-837-6532. You can also contact your state association of Certified Public Accountants, as many may be able to direct you to a volunteer CPA who would be willing to help.

Get $75,000 in Trees and Bushes

If you are a landscaper/orchardist and had plants damaged or destroyed by natural disaster, you can be reimbursed up to $75,000 for the cost to replant eligible trees, bushes, and vines. Contact the Department of Agriculture, Farm Service Agency, 1400 Independence Ave., S.W., Washington, DC 20250-0506; 202-720-7809; {www.fsa.usda.gov/pas/publications/facts/html/tap04.htm}.

Get Paid $75,000 to Send Product Samples Overseas

Through the Quality Samples Program, let the government help you transport and market your products overseas, with funding up to $75,000. You can introduce new foreign buyers to your agricultural products with the help of the USDA. Contact the USDA-FAS Marketing Operations Staff, AG Box 1042, 1400 Independence Ave., Washington, DC 20250-1042; 202-720-4327; {www.as.usda.gov/mos/programs/qsp.html}.

Free Interns for Your Business from the Middle East

The Middle East Partnership Initiative provides young women from the Middle East unique opportunities to learn management and business skills while working in the U.S. business environment. To find out how your company can benefit from this program, contact U.S. Department of State, Harry S. Truman Building, NEA/PI, 2201 C Street, NW, Rm. 5253A, Washington, DC 20520; {www.state.gov/p/nea/rls/24795.htm}.

Free Air Transportation to Send Supplies Overseas

Through the Denton Program, you can ship approved cargo weighing 2,000 to 100,000 pounds to approved countries. Contact Information Center, U.S. Agency for International Development, Ronald Reagan Building, Washington, D.C. 20523-1000; {www.usaid.gov/our_work/cross-cutting_programs/private_voluntary_cooperation/denton.html}.

$25,000 to Start A Business In The Middle East

Though the Middle East Partnership Initiative's Small Grants Program, grass-roots Middle Eastern companies can get up to $25,000 in funding. Contact Middle East Partnership Initiative, U.S. Department of State,

Harry S. Truman Building, NEA/PI, 2201 C Street, NW Rm. 6258, Washington, DC 20520; 202-776-8570; {http://www.mepi.state.gov/}; {http://mepi.state.gov/28088.htm#mep isgrants}.

$7,000 to Work At Home With Your Kids

The United Planning Organization has created a project entitled Childcare Entrepreneurial Expansion Development Initiative that is designed to expand childcare services to provide 24 hour care and to create new businesses through training, certification, and start-up of consumer owned home based child care businesses. Contact the U. S. Department of Health and Human Services, Administration for Children and Families, Office of Community Services, Division of Community Discretionary Programs, 370 L'Enfant Promenade, S.W - 5th Floor West, Washington, D.C. 20447; 202-401-5307; {www.acf.hhs.gov/programs/ ocs/dcdp/joli/revised/sum2000.htm}.

$30 Million to Invest Overseas

The Overseas Private Investment Corporation (OPIC) provides financing for projects sponsored by private U.S. businesses in developing countries and emerging economies throughout the world. OPIC's goal is to provide financing for investments in developing countries in projects that contribute to the economic and social development of the host country while having a positive impact on the U.S. economy. To get more information, contact the Information Officer, Overseas Private Investment Corporation, 100 New York Ave., NW, Washington, DC 20527; 202-336-8799; {www.opic.gov/}.

$300,000 for a Small Town Business

The New Markets Venture Capital Program is a developmental venture capital program designed to promote economic development and the creation of wealth and job opportunities in low-income geographic areas. Recipients use funds to make equity capital investments in smaller enterprises located in low-income geographic areas. Recipients can also use funds to provide management and technical assistance to smaller enterprises in connection with such investments. Contact the New Markets Venture Capital Program, 409 3rd Street, NW, Suite 6300, Washington, DC 20416; 202-205-6510; {www.sba.gov/INV/}.

$800,000 to Start an Airline

The Essential Air Service (EAS) program guarantees that small communities served by air carriers before deregulation maintain a minimal level of scheduled air service. Currently commuter airlines are subsidized to serve approximately 100 rural communities. Any interested air carrier may submit a proposal to provide subsidized service. Contact the Office of Aviation Analysis, X-50, Department of Transportation, 400

Seventh Street, SW., Washington, DC 20590; 202-366-1053; {www.dot.gov/ost/index. html}.

$75,000 for Businesses Hurt By Imports

Through Trade Adjustment Assistance, the Economic Department Administration uses a national network of twelve Trade Adjustment Assistance Centers to help manufacturers and producers affected by increased imports prepare and implement strategies to guide their economic recovery. Contact your local regional EDA office or the U.S. Department of Commerce, Economic Development Administration, 14th Street and Constitution Ave., N.W., Washington, DC 20230; {http://www.eda.gov/}.

$10,000 to Start a Cleaning Business

Through the help of the Utah Microenterprise Loan Fund (UMLF), individuals have started up their own cleaning businesses, quilting companies, and even a group home for autistic children. The Micro-Loan is available to start-up and existing businesses, offering up to $10,000. This program is available in Salt Lake, Davis, Summit, Tooele, Utah, Box Elder, Morgan, Wasatch, and Weber counties in Utah only. Contact the Utah Microenterprise Loan Fund, 154 East Ford Avenue, Salt Lake City, UT 84115; 801-746-1180, Fax: 801-746-1181; {www.umlf.com}.

$10,000 to Start a Business in St. Croix

Find out how you can start a business in the exotic Virgin Islands, or one of 16 qualified States. Loans are made available through the USDA Rural Development Intermediary Relending

Program. The aim of business revolving loan funds is to finance business facilities and community development projects in rural areas. Loans from intermediaries to the recipients must be used to establish new businesses, expand existing businesses, create employment opportunities, save jobs or complete community development projects. Contact the USDA, Rural Business-Cooperative Service, 1400 Independence Avenue, SW, Room 5050 South Building, Washington DC 20250; 202-720-1400; {http://www.rurdev.usda.gov/rbs/busp/irp.htm}.

$3,000 to Help Your Business Grow

The Utah Microenterprise Loan Fund (UMLF) helps people who cannot qualify for traditional small business loans. The Next Small Step Micro-Loan is available to existing small businesses, and offers up to $3000 in funding to help businesses take the next small step forward in growth. This program is available in Salt Lake County only. Contact the Utah Microenterprise Loan Fund, 154 East Ford Avenue, Salt Lake City, UT 84115; 801-746-1180, Fax: 801-746-1181; {www.umlf.com}.

$10,000 to Start a Child Care Business

The Child Care Provider Micro-Loan is available to home or center-based child care providers. This loan can help individuals to start or grow their child care business with funding up to $10,000. This program is available in Salt Lake, Davis, Summit, Tooele, Utah, Box Elder, Morgan, Wasatch, and Weber counties only. Contact the Utah Microenterprise Loan Fund, 154 East Ford Avenue, Salt Lake City, UT

84115; 801-746-1180, Fax: 801-746-1181; {www.umlf.com}.

$20,000 to Open a Market

The Vocational Rehabilitation Micro-Loan of the Utah Microenterprise Loan Fund is available to individuals who have been injured on the job and have an open Workers Compensation claim. This loan can help individuals to start a new business as an avenue to return to the workforce. Funding up to $20,000 is available. This program serves the entire state of Utah only. Contact the Utah Microenterprise Loan Fund, 154 East Ford Avenue, Salt Lake City, UT 84115; 801-746-1180, Fax: 801-746-1181; {www.umlf.com}.

$25,000 to Open a Coffee Shop

The Salt Lake City Micro-Loan is available to start-up and existing businesses located inside Salt Lake City limits. Funding is available up to $25,000. Contact the Utah Microenterprise Loan Fund, 154 East Ford Avenue, Salt Lake City, UT 84115; 801-746-1180, Fax: 801-746-1181; {www.umlf.com}.

$10,000 to Start a Cookie Business

Count Me In offers women access to business loans, consultation, and education, making loans of $500-$10,000 available to women who are trying to obtain their first business loan. The organization provides access to networks that expand contacts, markets, skills, and confidence. Loans can be used for working capital, purchase of inventory or equipment, marketing materials for a sales event, or other uses. Contact Count Me In, 240 Central Park South, Suite 7H, New York, NY 10019; 212-245-1245; {www.count-me-in.org}.

Money to Start a Small Business in Dorchester, Massachusetts

The Dorchester Bay Economic Development Corporation small business loan program awarded ten small business loans totaling $132,300 in the past year. This is for the Dorchester Bay area only. Contact Dorchester Bay Economic Development Corporation, 594 Columbia Rd., Dorchester, MA 02125; 617-825-4200; {www.dbedc. com}.

$50,000 to Start a Support Hose Store

The GO TEXAN Partner Program is a dollar-for-dollar matching fund program open to small businesses that are members of GO TEXAN, Texas Department of Agriculture's comprehensive marketing campaign for Texas agricultural products. The program's funding assists with promotional and marketing costs. Contact the GO TEXAN Partner Program, Texas Department of Agriculture, P.O. Box 12847, Austin, TX 78711; 512-463-7731; {www. gotexan.org}.

$50,000 in Venture Capital for Small Business

The Growth Opportunities Fund (GO Fund) provides financing to small businesses that does not require immediate repayment. Through this funding, it is easier to attract investors, and the GO Fund does not take an ownership stake in the business. This program serves the Ithaca community only. Ccontact the Alternatives GO Fund, 301 W. State St. Ithaca, NY 14850; 607-273-3582; {e-mail: GoFund@alternatives.org}; {www. alternatives.org/GoFund.html}.

Money and Help to Start Food Businesses

The Food Ventures Project works to create opportunities for new specialty food jobs and businesses in Southeast Ohio only. The program offers market and trend information, access to loan and venture funds, small business and financial planning assistance, food production information and training, links to industry exports, and links to other specialty food businesses within a network of firms. To find out more, contact Appalachian Center for Economic Networks, Inc., Food Ventures, 94 North Columbus Road, Athens, OH 45701; 740-592-3854; {www.acenetworks.org/frames/frames about.htm}.

Over $10,000 for Entrepreneurs

This foundation works with partners to encourage entrepreneurship across America and improve the education of children and youth. The foundation

focuses its operations and grant making on two areas: entrepreneurship and education. Giving is limited to the U.S., with emphasis on the bi-state Kansas City area (KS/MO) for youth development. Contact Ewing Marion Kauffman Foundation, 4801 Rockhill Road, Kansas City, MO 64110-2046; 816-932-1000; Fax: 816-932-1100; {www.kauffman.org}; {info@kauffman.org}.

$10,000 for Business Ventures on Reservations

The Four Times Foundation awards fellowship grants up to $10,000 for individuals to pursue a business venture on one of five specific reservation sites: Blackfeet Nation and Northern Cheyenne Nation, Montana; Rosebud Lakota Nation, South Dakota; White Earth Ojibwa Nation, Minnesota; and Pueblo of Zuni, New Mexico. Contact Four Times Foundation, P.O. Box 309, 16 1/2 North Broadway, Red Lodge, MT 59068; 406-446-1870; Fax: 406-446-1013; {http://www.fourtimes.org/}; {e-mail: info@fourtimes.org}.

$90,000 for Entrepreneurs

Through the two-year fellowship program, the Foundation helps passionate social entrepreneurs develop new solutions to some of society's most difficult problems. These social entrepreneurs and their organizations work to close deeply-rooted social, economic and political inequities to ensure equal access and help all individuals reach their potential. Fellowships are awarded to individuals and are $30,000 a year for two years. Fellowships awarded to partnerships are $45,000 (total per project not per individual) for two years. Echoing Green pays the grants in four equal installments over two years. Contact Echoing Green Foundation, 60 East 42nd Street, Suite 520, New York, NY 10165; 212-689-1165; Fax: 212-689-9010; {www. echoinggreen.org}; {e-mail: info@ echoinggreen. org}.

$10,000 for Women to Start or Expand a Business

Balance Bar annually awards four grants of $10,000 to creative and dynamic entrepreneurial women who want to implement a new and creative business idea to improve their existing business or organization. Contact Balance Bar Company Contributions Program, 800 Westchester Avenue, Rye Brook, NY 10573; {http://www.balance.com/grants/default.asp}. Application address for Balance Grants: c/o Grants Program, Hunter PR, 5th Fl., 41 Madison Ave., New York, NY 10010.

$1,000 for Pharmacists

The Incentive Grants for Practitioner Innovation in Pharmaceutical Care awards up to twenty $1,000 grants each year to practitioners in all practice settings to develop innovative services and to share their experiences with other pharmacists. Applicants must be members of APHA, currently licensed and actively engaged in ambulatory pharmacy practice. Contact American Pharmaceutical Association Foundation (also known as The APHA Foundation), 2215 Constitution Ave., N.W., Washington, DC 20037-2985; 202-429-7565; Fax: 202-429-6300; {http://www.aphafound ation.org}; {e-mail: info@aphafound ation.org}

Funding for Harness Racers

The Horsemen's Welfare Trust provides grants to distressed horsemen in the harness racing industry or their

families on the basis of need for essential items such as medical care, food, clothing and basic necessities. Contact Horsemen's Welfare Trust, c/o Delaware SOA, 830 Walker Sq., Dover, DE 19904-2748.

Grants to Dairy Farmers Whose Milk is Contaminated Because of Pesticides

This program provides money to dairy farmers and manufacturers of dairy products who are forced to remove their products from commercial markets due to contamination. For more information on the program (10.053 Dairy Indemnity Program) contact the U.S. Department of Agriculture, Farm Service Agency, 1400 Independence Av., SW, Washington, DC 20250-0512; 202-720-7641; {www.fsa.usda.gov}.

Grants to Producers of Wheat, Corn, Grain Sorghum, Barley, Oats, Upland Cotton and Rice

This program provides financial assistance to farmers in order to ensure a steady supply of food, while maintaining the flexibility necessary to adjust to the condition of the economy while complying with farm conservation and wetland protection requirements. For more information on the program (10.055 Production Flexibility Payments for Contract Commodities) contact Philip W.

Stronce, U.S. Department of Agriculture, Farm Service Agency, Economic and Policy Analysis Staff, Stop 0508, 1400 Independence Ave., SW, Washington, DC 20250-0508; 202-720-2711; {www.fsa.usda.gov}.

Money to Implement Emergency Conservation Programs

This program enables farmers to perform emergency conservation measures to control wind erosion on farmlands, to rehabilitate farmlands damaged by wind erosion, floods, hurricanes or other natural disasters and to carry out emergency water conservation or water enhancing measures during periods of severe drought. For more information on the program (10.054 Emergency Conservation Program) contact the U.S. Department of Agriculture, Farm Service Agency, Stop 0513, 1400 Independence Ave., SW, Washington, DC 20250-0513; 202-720-6221; {www.fsa.usda.gov}.

Grants to Livestock Producers

This program provides grants to eligible livestock producers who suffered grazing losses due to drought, hot weather, disease, insect infestation, fire, hurricane, flood, earthquake, severe storm or other disasters occurring after January 1, 2000. Benefits are provided to producers who suffered 40% or greater grazing loss for three or more months. For more information on the program (10.066 Livestock Assistance Program) contact the U.S. Department of Agriculture, Farm Service Agency, Production, Emergencies and Compliance Division, Emergency Preparedness and Program Branch, Stop 0517, 1400 Independence Ave.,

SW, Washington, DC 20250-0517; 202-720-7641; {www.fsa.usda.gov}.

Loans to Purchase and Construct On-Farm Storage Facilities

The purpose of this program is to support the construction of on-farm grain storage facilities and to help farmers adapt to identify preserved storage and handling requirements for genetically enhanced production. For more information on the program (10.056 Farm Storage Facility Loans) contact the U.S. Department of Agriculture, Farm Service Agency, Director, Price Support Division, 1400 Independence Ave., SW, Washington, DC 20250; 202-720-7935; {www.fsa.usda.gov/dafp/psd/FSFL.html}.

Grants to Producers of Cattle, Sheep, Goats, Buffalo, and Catfish

This program provides financial compensation to livestock producers in counties that received primary disaster designation due to drought in 2001 and 2002. For more information on the program (10.077 Livestock Compensation Program) contact the U.S. Department of Agriculture, Farm Service Agency, Production Emergency and Compliance Division, Washington, DC 20250; 202-720-7641; {www.fsa.usda.gov}.

Grants to Bioenergy Producers

This program provides financial assistance to producers of Bioenergy. The money is to be used to increase purchases of eligible commodities for the purpose of expanding production of Bioenergy, such as ethanol and bio-diesel, and to support new production capacity for Bioenergy. For more information on the program (10.078

Bioenergy Program) contact the U.S. Department of Agriculture, Farm Service Agency, Kansas City Commodity Office, Contract Reconciliation Division, P.O. Box 419205, Stop 8758, Kansas City, MO 64141-6205; 816-926-6525; {www. fsa.usda.gov/daco/bio_daco.htm}.

Money to Farmers, Ranchers, and Aquaculture Businesses

Loan funds may be used to enlarge, improve, and buy family farms; provide necessary water and water facilities; provide basic soil treatment and land conservation measures; construct, repair, and improve essential buildings needed in the operation of a family farm; construct or repair farm dwellings; or provide facilities to produce fish under controlled conditions. For more information on the program (10.407 Farm Ownership Loans) contact the U.S. Department of Agriculture, Farm Service Agency, Director, Loan Making Division, Ag Box 0522, Washington, DC 20250; 202-720-1632; {www.fsa.usda.gov}.

Loans to Family Farms That Can't Get Credit

Operating loans obtained through the Interest Assistance Program can be used to finance livestock or farm equipment; to pay annual operating expenses or family living expenses; or to refinance debts under certain conditions. For more information on

the program (10.437 Interest Assistance Program) contact the U.S. Department of Agriculture, Farm Service Agency, Director, Loan Making Division, Ag Box 0522, Washington, DC 20250; 202-720-1632; {www.fsa.usda.gov}.

Grants to Market Food Related Products Overseas

The purpose of this program is to develop, maintain and expand long-term export markets for U.S. agricultural products. Funding from this program may be used for trade servicing, market research and technical assistance to actual or potential foreign purchasers of U.S. commodities. For more information on the program (10.600 Foreign Market Development Cooperation Program) contact the U.S. Department of Agriculture, Foreign Agricultural Service, Deputy Administrator, Commodity and Marketing Programs, 1400 Independence Ave., SW, Washington, DC 20250; 202-720-4761; {www.fas.usda.gov/mos/ programs/fmd.html}.

Grants to Sell Food Related Products Overseas

Program funds may be used for consumer advertising, point of sale demonstrations, public relations, trade servicing activities, participation in trade fairs and exhibits, market research and technical assistance. For more information on the program (10.601 Market Access Program) contact the Deputy Administrator, Commodity and Marketing Programs, Foreign Agricultural Service, U.S. Department of Agriculture, 1400 Independence Ave., SW, Washington, DC 20250; 202-720-4761; {www. fas.usda.gov/mos/programs/mapprog.h tml}.

Loans and Grants to Build Housing for Farm Laborers

Funds from this program can be used for construction, repair, or purchase of year-round or seasonal housing; land acquisition and the improvements necessary to build; and developing related support facilities such as central cooking and dining areas, small infirmaries, laundry facilities, day care centers, and other essential equipment and facilities or recreation areas. For more information on the program (10.405 Farm Labor Housing Loans and Grants) contact the Multi-Family Housing Processing Division, Department of Agriculture, 1400 Independence Ave., SW, Washington, DC 20250; 202-720-1604; {www.rurdev.usda.gov}.

Grants to Nonprofits to Lend Money to New Businesses

The grant funds may be used for learning networks or programs that provide educational or job training instruction; to establish revolving loan funds; or refinancing services and fees. Funds may also be used to develop, construct or purchase land, buildings, plants, equipment, access streets and roads, parking areas, utility extensions, or necessary water supply and waste disposal facilities. Television Demonstration Grants (TDG) may be used for television programming to provide information on agriculture and other topics of importance to farmers and rural residents. All uses must assist a small or emerging private business enterprise except for the TDG Program. For more information on the program (10.769 Rural Business Enterprise Grants) contact Director, Specialty Lenders Division, Rural Business-Cooperative Service, U.S. Department of Agriculture, Washington, DC 20250-3222; 202-720-1400; {www.rurdev.usda.gov}.

Grants and Loans to Telephone Companies That Then Provide Financing to Small Businesses

The goal of this program is to fund rural economic development and job creation projects through electric and telephone utility companies. For more information on the program (10.854 Rural Economic Development Loans and Grants) contact Director, Specialty Lenders Division, Rural Business-Cooperative Service, U.S. Department of Agriculture, Washington, DC 20250; 202-720-1400; {www.rurdev. usda.gov}.

Free Plants for Conservation Studies

This program's goal is to develop technology for land management and restoration with plant materials by promoting the use of new and improved plant materials for soil, water, and related resource conservation and environmental improvement programs. For more information on the program (10.905 Plant Materials for Conservation) contact Deputy Chief for Science and Technology, Natural Resources Conservation Service, U. S. Department of Agriculture, P.O. Box 2890, Washington, DC 20013; 202-720-4630; {www.nrcs.usda.gov}.

Grants to Communities That Provide Money and Help to Small Business Incubators

The EDA provides funding for special projects to support long-term economic development in areas experiencing substantial economic distress. Such projects could include water and sewer system improvements, industrial access roads, industrial and business parks, port facilities, railroad sidings, distance learning facilities, skill training facilities, business incubator facilities, eco-industrial facilities and telecommunications infrastructure improvements needed for business retention and expansion. For more information on the program (11.300 Grants for Public Works and Economic Development) contact David L. McIlwain, Director, Public Works Division, Economic Development Administration, Room H7326, Herbert C. Hoover Building, U.S. Department of Commerce, Washington, DC 20230; 202-482-5265; {www.doc.gov/eda}.

Grants to Fisherman Hurt by Oil and Gas Drilling on the Outer Continental Shelf

This program compensates U.S. Commercial fishermen for damage/loss of fishing gear and 50% of resulting economic loss due to oil and gas related activities in any area of the Outer Continental Shelf. For more information on the program (11.408 Fishermen's Contingency Fund) contact Michael Grable, Chief, Financial Services Division, National Marine Fisheries Service, 1315 East-West Highway, Silver Spring, MD 20910; 301-713-2396; Fax: 301-713-1306; {www. noaa.gov}.

Grants to Communities That Help Finance New or Old Businesses Due to Military Base Closings

The goal of this program is to assist state and local areas in the development and/or implementation of strategies designed to address structural economic adjustment problems resulting from sudden and severe economic dislocation such as plant closings, military base closures and defense contract cutbacks, and natural disasters, or from long term economic deterioration in the area's economy. For more information on the program (11.307 Economic Adjustment Assistance) contact David F. Witschi, Director, Economic Development Administration, Room H7327, Herbert C. Hoover Building, U.S. Department of Commerce, Washington, DC 20230; 202-482-2659; {www.doc.gov/eda}.

Grants to Develop New Technologies for Your Business

Working in partnership with industry, the Advanced Technology Program provides funding for development of new, high-risk technologies that offer the potential for significant, broad based economic benefits for the entire country. For more information on the program (11.612 Advanced Technology Program) contact Barbara Lambis, Advanced Technology Program, National Institute of Standards and Technology, 100 Bureau Drive, Stop 4700, Gaithersburg, MD 20899-4700; 301-975-4447; Fax: 301-869-1150; {Email: Barbara.lambis@nist.gov}; {www.atp. nist.gov/atp}. To receive application kits call ATP customer service staff at 800-ATP-FUND.

Grants to Organizations That Help Minorities Start Their Own Businesses

The Minority Business Development Agency provides funding for Minority Business Development Centers. For a nominal fee, these centers provide a wide range of services from initial consultations, to the identification and resolution of specific business problems. For more information on the program (11.800 Minority Business Development Centers) contact Barbara Curry, Business Development Specialist, Room 5071, Minority Business Development Agency, U.S. Department of Commerce, 14th and Constitution Ave., NW, Washington, DC 20230; 202-482-1940; {www. mbda.gov}.

Grants to Organizations That Help Native Americans Start Their Own Businesses

This program provides funding for eight Native American Business Development Centers that provide electronic and one-on-one business development service to Native Americans interested in entering, expanding, or improving their efforts in the marketplace. For more information on the program (11.801 Native American Program) contact Barbara Curry, Business Development Specialist, Room 5071, Minority Business Development Agency, U.S. Department of Commerce, 14th and Constitution Ave., NW, Washington, DC 20230; 202-482-1940; {www. mbda.gov}.

Grants to Help Minority Businesses Enter New Markets

This Program supports minority business development through indirect business assistance programs that identify and develop private markets and capital sources; expand business information and business services through trade associations; promote and support the utilization of Federal, State and local government resources; and assist minorities in entering new and growing markets. For more information on the program (11.803 Minority Business Opportunity Committee) contact the Office of Business Development, Minority Business Development Agency, Department of Commerce, 14th and Constitution Avenue, NW, Washington, DC 20230; 202-482-1940; {www.mbda.gov}.

Grants to Organizations That Will Help You Sell to the Department of Defense

The Procurement Technical Assistance Program assists business firms in obtaining and maintaining Federal, State, and local government contracts. Recipients of project funds are to provide marketing and technical assistance to businesses in selling their goods and services to the Department of Defense, other Federal agencies, and local and State governments. For more information on the program (12.002 Procurement Technical Assistance for Business Firms) contact the Defense Logistics Agency, Office of Small and Disadvantaged Business Utilization, 8725 John J. Kingman Road, Suite 2533, Fort Belvoir, VA 22060-6221; 703-767-1650; {www. dla.mil/db}.

Grants to Build or Improve an Airport

Using grants, advisory services, and counseling, this program's goal is to assist owners or operators of public airports in the development of a nationwide system of airports sufficient to meet needs of civil aeronautics. Grants can be made for integrated airport system planning in a specific area, airport master planning, construction, or rehabilitation of a public-use airport. For more information on the program (20.106 Airport Improvement Program) contact the Federal Aviation Administration, Office of Airport Planning and Programming, Airports Financial Assistance Division, APP-500, 800 Independence Avenue, SW, Washington, DC 20591; 202-267-3831; {www.faa.gov}.

Grants to Bus Companies

This program provides technical and financial assistance to rural transportation providers. Funding may be used for operating and administrative expenses, and for the acquisition, construction, and improvement of facilities and equipment. For more information on the program (20.509 Formula Grants for Other Than Urbanized Areas) contact the Federal Transit Administration, Office of Program Management, Office of Capital and Formula Assistance, 400 Seventh Street, SW, Washington, DC 20590; 202-366-2053; {www.fta.dot.gov}.

Grants to Become a Women-Owned Transportation Related Company

This program provides financial assistance to national, regional, and local initiatives that address public transportation. Projects may include employment training programs; outreach programs to increase minority and women's employment in public transportation activities; research on training and public transportation manpower needs; and training and assistance for minority businesses. For

more information on the program (20.511 Human Resources Program) contact Director, Office of Civil Rights, Federal Transit Administration, U.S. Department of Transportation, 400 Seventh Street, SW, Room 9102, Washington, DC 20590; 202-366-4018; {www.fta.dot.gov}.

Money for Airlines to Fly to Small Towns and Make a Profit

The purpose of this program is to assure that air transportation services are provided to eligible communities. Subsidy payments are made to air carriers providing air services to eligible locations in order to ensure the continuation of service. Subsidies are paid to cover the carrier's prospective operating loss plus an element of profit. For more information on the program (20.901 Payments for Essential Air Services) contact Director, Office of Aviation Analysis, X-50, U.S. Department of Transportation, 400 Seventh Street, SW, Washington, DC 20590; 202-366-1030; {www.ost.dot.gov}.

Grants to Women-Owned Businesses to Help Get Contracts from the Department of Transportation

This program is designed to help small businesses, socially and economically disadvantaged persons, and businesses owned and operated by women increase their participation in Department of Transportation programs and funded projects. For more information on the program (20.903 Support Mechanisms for Disadvantaged Businesses) contact the Office of Small and Disadvantaged Business Utilization, S-40, Office of the Secretary, 400 Seventh Street, SW, Washington, DC 20590; 800-532-1169; 202-366-1930; {www.dot.gov}.

Loans to Start a Credit Union
The Community Development Revolving Loan Program for Credit Unions provides funding to support low-income credit unions' efforts to provide a variety of financial and related services designed to meet the needs of their community. For more information on the program (44.002 Community Development Revolving Loan Program for Credit Unions) contact Mr. Anthony Lacreta, Community Development Revolving Loan Program for Credit Unions, National Credit Union Administration, 1775 Duke Street, Alexandria, VA 22314-3428; 703-518-6610; {www.ncua.gov}.

Help for Contractors and Others to Get Bonded to Obtain Contracts
Under this program, small contractors unable to obtain a bond are guaranteed surety bonds issued by commercial surety companies. Guarantees are for up to ninety percent of the losses incurred and are paid by participating sureties when conditions are met. For more information on the program (59.016 Bond Guarantees for Surety Companies) contact Associate Administrator, Robert J. Moffitt, Office of Surety Guarantees, Small Business Administration, 409 Third

Street, SW, Washington, DC 20416; 202-205-6540; {www.sba.gov}.

Grants to Local Organizations That Help Women Start Their Own Businesses
Private, non-profit organizations can receive funding through this program to provide training and counseling to small businesses owned and operated by women in an effort to eliminate discriminatory barriers women may encounter in obtaining credit and promoting their businesses. For more information on the program (59.043 Women's Business Ownership Assistance) contact Sally Murrell, Office of Women's Business Ownership, Small Business Administration, 409 Third Street, SW, Washington, DC 20416; 202-205-6673; {www.sba.gov/womenin business}.

Money to Local Organizations to Provide Micro-loans
The Micro Loan program provides very small loans to start up, newly established or growing small businesses. Its objective is to help business owners, especially women, low-income entrepreneurs, minorities, potential entrepreneurs, and those located in areas with a lack of credit due to economic conditions. These micro-loans can only be used for working capital, supplies, furniture, fixtures, inventory, equipment and/or machinery. The SBA makes grants to participating intermediary lenders to provide marketing, management and technical assistance to micro-loan recipients. For more information on this program (59.046 Micro-loan Demonstration Program) contact the Small Business Administration, Office

of Financial Assistance, Micro-Enterprise Development Branch, 409 Third Street, SW, Eighth Floor, Washington, DC 20416; 202-205-6490; {www. sba.gov}.

Grants to Local Organizations That Help Veterans Start Their Own Businesses

This program establishes Veteran Business Outreach Centers to provide long term training, counseling, and mentoring to small businesses and potential small businesses owned and operated by eligible U.S. Veterans. For more information on this program (59.044 Veteran's Entrepreneurial Training and Counseling) contact Reginald Teamer, Office of Veteran Affairs, Small Business Administration, 5th Floor, 409 Third Street, SW, Washington, DC 20416; 202-205-6773; {www.sba.gov}.

Help for Disabled Veterans to Start New Businesses

This Vocational Rehabilitation Program provides services and assistance to help disabled veterans get and keep a suitable job. The program also provides the needed services and assistance to help individuals achieve the necessary skills to maximize independence in daily living. Veterans who meet certain requirements may receive an initial supply of goods and commodities to start a small business. For more information on the program (64.116 Vocational Rehabilitation for Disabled Veterans) contact the Veterans Benefits Administration, Vocational Rehabilitation and Counseling Service (28), U.S. Department of Veteran Affairs, Washington, DC 20420; 202-273-7419; {www.va.gov}.

Help for Retired Military to Start a Business

This program provides vocational and counseling to recipients of VA pensions so they may get and keep a suitable job. Veterans who meet certain eligibility requirements may be provided with the goods or commodities to start a small business. For more information on the program (64.123 Vocational Training for Certain Veterans Receiving VA Pension) contact the Veterans Benefits Administration, Vocational Rehabilitation and Counseling Service (28), U.S. Department of Veterans Affairs, Washington, DC 20420; 202-273-7419; {www.va.gov}.

Money to Invest in Companies Overseas

The Overseas Private Investment Corporation provides financing for investments in developing countries for projects that contribute to the social and economic development of the host country and at the same time have a positive impact on the U.S. economy. OPIC disqualifies projects that may have a negative effect on the environment, U.S. employment, the host country's development, or would violate internationally recognized worker rights. For more information on the program (70.002 Foreign Investment Financing) contact Information Officer, Overseas Private

Investment Corporation, 1100 New York Ave., NW, Washington, DC 20527; 202-336-8799; Fax: 202-336-8700; {Email: info@opic.gov}; {www.opic.gov}.

Money to Privately Owned Community Drinking Water Utilities for Security Improvements

Large privately owned community drinking water utilities that serve 100,000 or more people are eligible to apply for this funding. The money may be used to conduct a vulnerability assessment, develop or revise an emergency response operating plan, enhance security plans, or a combination of these efforts. For more information on this program (66.477 Vulnerability Assessments and Related Security Improvements as Large Privately Owned Drinking Water Utilities) contact U.S. Environmental Protection Agency, Private Water Utility Security Grant Program, Room 2104A, EPA East Building, 1201 Constitution Avenue, NW , Washington, DC 20004; 800-426-4791; 202-564-3750; {www.epa.gov}.

Grants for Security Improvements at Drinking Water Utilities

Large publicly owned community drinking water utilities that serve at least 100,000 people are eligible to apply for this funding. Recipients of these grants may use the money to conduct a vulnerability assessment, develop or revise an emergency response operating plan, enhance security measures, or any combination of these efforts. For more information on the program (66.476 Vulnerability Assessments and Related Security Improvements at Large Drinking Water Utilities) contact the U.S.

Environmental Protection Agency, Public Water Utility Security Grant Program, 1201 Constitution Ave., NW, Washington, DC 20004; 800-426-4791; {www.epa.gov}.

Insurance Against Your Business in Another Country Being Hurt by Foreign Politics

To encourage private U.S. investment in developing countries, OPIC provides insurance to protect against the risks of inconvertibility, expropriation and political violence. Insurance is available for contractors and exporters against arbitrary drawings of letters of credit posted as bid, performance or advance payment guaranties; petroleum exploration, development and production; leasing operations; and debt financials, including securities. For more information on this program (70.003 Foreign Investment Insurance) contact the Information Officer, Overseas Private Investment Corporation, 1100 New York Avenue, NW, Washington, DC 20527; 202-336-8799; Fax: 202-336-8700; {Email: info@opic.gov}; {www.opic.gov}.

Free Patent Licenses to Develop and Market Energy Saving Inventions

The Department of Energy grants nonexclusive, revocable patent licenses to qualified applicants with plans to develop and/or market one of the more that 1,200 DOE owned U.S. Patents. For more information on the program (81.003 Granting of Patent Licenses) contact Robert J. Marchick, Office of the Assistant General Counsel for Patents, U.S. Department of Energy, Washington, DC 20585; 202-586-2802; {www. doe.gov}.

Money to Work on an Energy Related Invention

The U.S. Department of Energy's Inventions and Innovation program provides financial and technical support to inventors and businesses to develop energy saving concepts and technologies. Grant recipients are selected through a competitive process. For more information on this program (81.036 Invention and Innovations) contact Lisa Barnett, Office of Industrial Technologies (EE-23), U.S. Department of Energy, Weatherization and Intergovernmental Programs, 1000 Independence Avenue, SW, Washington, DC 20585; 202-586-2212; {www.eere.energy.gov/inventions}.

Help for Farmers to Control Plant and Animal Diseases

This program's objective is to protect U.S. agriculture from harmful plant and animal diseases and pests. It provides for inspections to detect and evaluate infestations and carries out regulatory actions to prevent the interstate spread of diseases and infestations. For more information on the program (97.003 Agricultural Inspections) contact the Department of Homeland Security, 245 Murray Drive, SW, Washington, DC 20528; 202-282-8000; {www. dhs.gov}.

Grants for Commercial Fisheries Failing Due to a Natural Disaster

This program provides assistance to fishing vessel owners, operators, and crew, and fish processors that are facing failure due to a fishery resource disaster. For more information on the program (11.477 Fisheries Disaster Relief) contact Alicia Jarboe, Financial Services Division (F/CS2), National Marine Fisheries Service, 1315 East-West Highway, Silver Spring, MD 20910; 301-713-2358; Fax: 301-713-1939; {Email: Alicia.jarboe@noaa.gov}; {www.fakr.noaa.gov/omi/grants/default.htm} for Alaska, or {http://caldera.sero.nmfs.gov/grants/programs/disaster.htm} for the Southeast.

Grants to Work on Solar Energy Products

The Department of Energy provides funding to conduct research and development efforts in the following energy technologies: distributed energy and electric reliability, solar, hydrogen, biomass, fuel cells and infrastructure, geothermal, wind and hydropower. Grants are also offered to develop and transfer these renewable energy technologies to the scientific and industrial communities, and state and local governments. For more information on the program (81.087 Renewable Energy Research and Development) contact the Office of Energy Efficiency and Renewable Energy (EERE), Mail Stop EE-1, Department of Energy, Washington,

DC 28585; 800-DOE-3732; 202-586-9220; {www.eere.energy.gov}.

Grants to Develop Uses of Fossil Fuels

The focus of the Fossil Energy Research and Development program is to promote the development and use of environmentally and economically advanced technologies for supply, conversion, delivery and utilization of fossil fuels. For more information on the program (81.089 Fossil Energy Research and Development) contact Mary J. Roland, Fossil Energy Program, Mail Stop FE-3, 19901 Germantown Road, Department of Energy, Germantown, MD 20874; 301-903-3514; {www.fe.doe.gov}.

Grants to Develop Energy Saving Products

This program offers grants to conduct research in the areas of buildings, industry and transportation. Grants are also offered to develop and transfer conservation technology to the non-federal sector. For more information on this program (81.086 Conservation Research and Development) contact the Office of Energy Efficiency and Renewable Energy (EERE), Mail Stop EE-1, Department of Energy, Washington, DC 28585; 800-DOE-3732; 202-586-9220; {www.eere.energy.gov}.

Grants to Telecommunications Companies to Provide Services to Schools

This program provides grants to telecommunications companies to provide facilities and equipment, educational and instructional programming, and necessary technical assistance to elementary and secondary schools. Priority is given to companies that provide services to schools in underserved areas, individuals excluded from careers in math and science due to discrimination or economic disadvantages, areas with scarce resources, and areas with limited access to courses in math, science, and foreign languages. For more information on this program (84.203 Star Schools) contact Joseph Wilkes, U.S. Department of Education, Office of Innovation and Improvement, Technology in Education Programs, 555 New Jersey Ave., NW, Washington, DC 20208-5645; 202-219-2186; {Email: joseph.wilkes@ed.gov}; {www.ed.gov/offices/OII}.

Money to Develop Health and Safety Programs for Construction Workers

The purpose of this program is to develop health and safety programs for construction workers in order to reduce occupational injuries and illnesses. Funds may be used for salaries of personnel employed specifically for the project, consultant fees, supplies and equipment necessary to conduct the project, essential travel expenses, and other project related expenses. For more information on this program (93.955 Health and Safety Programs for Construction Workers) Grant Management Contact: Mildred Garner, Grants Management Branch, Procurement and Grants Office, Centers for Disease Control and Prevention, 2920 Brandywine Road, Atlanta, GA 30341; 770-488-2745 or Program Management Contact: Office of Extramural Programs, National Institute for Occupational Safety and Health, Centers for Disease Control and Prevention, 1600 Clifton Road, Mail Stop E-74, Atlanta, GA 30333; 404-498-2530; {www.cdc.gov}.

Grants to Improve Emergency Medical Service in Rural Areas

This program makes grants for research and demonstration projects designed to improve the quality and availability of emergency medical services in rural areas. Funds may be used to develop and use new, innovative communications technologies; develop model curricula for training emergency medical services personnel; make training, certification, and continuing education more accessible; develop increased access to pre-hospital care and improve the availability of emergency transportation services; and evaluate the effectiveness of current emergency medical services and systems. For more information on the program (93.952 Improving EMS/Trauma Care in Rural Areas) contact Richard J. Smith III, Chief, Injury/EMS Branch, Maternal and Child Health Bureau, Health Resources and Services Administration, Public Health Service, Department of Health and Human Services, Parklawn Building, Room 18A-38, 5600 Fishers Lane, Rockville, MD 20857; 301-443-0324 or Grants Management Branch, Maternal and Child Health Bureau, Health Resources and Services Administration, Public Health Service, Department of Health and Human Services, Parklawn Building, Room 18-12, 5600 Fishers Lane, Rockville, MD 20857; 301-443-1440; {www.mchb.hrsa.gov}.

Pension Plan Termination Insurance for Small Businesses

This program encourages the continuation and maintenance of voluntary private pension plans, provides for timely and uninterrupted payment of pension benefits to participants and beneficiaries in plans covered by the PBGC, and maintains premiums at the lowest possible level. For more information on this program (86.001 Pension Plan Termination Insurance) contact the Pension Benefit Guaranty Corporation, 1200 K Street, NW, Washington, DC 20005-4026; 202-326-4000; {www.pbgc.gov}.

Crop Insurance for Owners or Operators of Farmlands

The Federal Crop Insurance Corporation (FCIC) is a government owned corporation created to provide comprehensive crop insurance nation wide. Catastrophic crop insurance protection (CAT) is fully subsidized except for administrative fees paid by the producer. This coverage compensates the producer for yield losses greater than 50% at a price equal to 55% of maximum price. For more information on the program (10.450 Crop Insurance) contact the Department of Agriculture, Administrator, Risk management Agency, Ag Box 0801, Washington, DC 20250; 202-690-2803; {www.fsa.usda.gov}.

Money for Livestock Owners Hurt by a Natural Disaster

This program provides emergency assistance to eligible livestock owners in an area, county or state where an official emergency has been declared due to insect infestation, disease, fire, drought, flood, hailstorm, hurricane, earthquake, hot weather, c old weather, ice, snow, freeze, winter kill, or other natural disaster. For more information on this program (10.452 Disaster Reserve Assistance) contact the Department of Agriculture, Farm Service Agency, Emergency and Noninsured Assistance Program Division, Mail Stop 0526, 1400 Independence Avenue, SW, Washington, DC 20250-0526; 202-720-3168; {www.fsa.usda.gov}.

Help for Farmers and Ranchers on Indian Lands

This program helps Indian farmers, ranchers and landowners manage and develop their land for farming and grazing. It also provides for noxious weed eradication by means of chemical, mechanical, cultural, and biological control methods. For more information on this program (15.034 Agriculture on Indian Lands) contact Mark Bradford, Office of Trust Responsibilities, Division of Water and Land Resources, Branch of Agriculture and Range, Bureau of Indian Affairs, 1849 C Street, NW, Mail Stop 4513 MIB, Washington, DC 20240; 202-208-3598; {www.doi. gov/bia/otrhome.htm} or {www.doi. gov/bureau-indian-affairs.html}.

Money to Indian Tribes for Economic Development

Funds from this program can be used to administer revolving loan and guaranty loan programs to promote economic development on tribal lands. Assistance is provided to American Indian owned businesses in obtaining financing from private sectors. For more information on the program (15.032 Indian Economic Development) contact Woodrow Sneed, Office of Economic

Development, Bureau of Indian Affairs, 1849 C Street, NW, Mail Stop 4640, Washington, DC 20240; 202-208-4796; {www.doi.gov/bia/ecodev/ index.htm} or {www. doi.gov/bureau-indian-affairs.html}.

Grants to Market Food Related Products to Emerging Markets Overseas

The Emerging Markets Program's goal is to promote, enhance, or expand the export of U.S. agricultural commodities in low to middle income counties that are likely to emerge as promising export markets in the near future. U.S. agricultural and agribusiness firms, especially those that need assistance in obtaining or maintaining access to overseas markets, may be eligible for cost-share assistance to implement an Emerging Markets Program. For more information on this program (10.603 Emerging Markets Program) contact the Director, Marketing Operations Staff, Foreign Agricultural Services, Department of Agriculture, Washington, DC 20250; 202-720-4327; {www.fas.usda.goc/mos/em-markets/em-markets.html}.

Help for Farmers and Ranchers to Conserve Natural Resources

This program provides technical, educational and financial assistance to eligible farmers and ranchers to address soil, water and other natural resource concerns on their lands through the implementation of structural, vegetative, and land management practices. Technical assistance is provided for conservation planning measures. Educational and financial assistance is provided for the implementation of structural, vegetative and land management practices. For more information on the program (10.912 Environmental Quality Incentives Program) contact the Deputy Chief for Natural Resource Conservation Programs, Natural Resources Conservation Service, U.S. Department of Agriculture, P.O. Box 289, Washington, DC 20013; 202-720-1845; Fax: 202-72-4265; {www.nrcs.usda.gov}.

Money for Great Plains Farmers and Ranchers to Conserve Soil and Water

In order to conserve and develop the Great Plains water and soil resources, technical and financial assistance is provided to farmers and ranchers to plan and implement conservation practices. Cost-share funds are available for many of the soil and water conservation measures necessary to protect and stabilize a farm or ranch against the effects of climate and erosion in the Great Plains area. Land must be located in one of the 556 designated counties in Colorado, Kansas, Montana, Nebraska, New Mexico, Oklahoma, South Dakota, Texas or Wyoming. For more information on the program (10.900 Great Plains Conservation) contact the Deputy Chief, National Resources Conservation Programs, Natural Resources Conservation Services, Department of Agriculture, P.O. Box 2890, Washington, DC 20013; 202-720-1873; {www.nrcs.usda.gov}.

Money for Businesses to Reduce High Energy Costs in Rural Communities

This program provides assistance to rural communities with extremely high energy costs. Funds must be used to acquire, construct, extend, upgrade, or otherwise improve the energy generation, transmission, or distribution facilities in these communities. For more information on this program (10.859 Assistance to High Energy Cost-Rural Communities) contact the Administrator, Rural Utilities Service, Department of Agriculture, Washington, DC 20250-1500; 202-720-9540; {www.rurdev.usda.gov}.

Grants to Agricultural Producers and Rural Small Businesses to Conserve Energy

The Rural Business-Cooperative Service provides direct loans, loan guarantees and grants to farmers, ranchers, and rural small businesses for measures to help reduce the cost and consumption of energy. Funds must be used to purchase renewable energy systems or energy efficiency improvements. For more information on this program (10.775 Renewable Energy Systems and Energy Efficiency Improvements Program) contact Rural Business-Cooperative Services, Department of Agriculture, 1400 Independence Avenue, SW, Washington, DC 20013; 202-720-1400; {www.rurdev.usda.gov/rbs}.

Money to Enhance Production and Marketing in the Sheep and Goat Industries

The National Sheep Industry Improvement Center provides financial assistance to the U.S. Sheep and Goat

Industries to strengthen and enhance the production and marketing of sheep, goats, and their products within the United States. For more information on this program (10.774 National Sheep Industry Improvement Center) contact the National Sheep Industry Improvement Center, U.S. Department of Agriculture, 1400 Independence Avenue, SW, Room 2117, Washington, DC 20250; 202-690-0632; Fax: 202-236-6576; {www.rurdev.usda.gov/coops/cssheep.htm}.

Grants for Rural Businesses and Communities

Grant funds from this program can be used to improve the economic development of rural areas by providing technical assistance for rural businesses, training for rural entrepreneurs and economic development officials, or planning for business and economic development. For more information on the program (10.773 Rural Business Opportunity Grants) contact the Rural Business-Cooperative Service, U.S. Department of Agriculture, Specialty Lenders Division, Mail Stop 3225, Room 6767, 1400 Independence Avenue, SW, Washington, DC 20250-1521; 202-720-1400; {www.rurdev.usda.gov}.

Grants to Improve and Extend Public Telecommunications Services in the U.S.

This program's purpose is to assist in the planning, acquisition, installation and modernization of public telecommunication facilities. Grants are given to extend public telecommunications service by the most efficient and economical means; including the use of broadcast and non-broadcast technologies; increasing public telecommunications services

and facilities owned and operated by women and minorities; and strengthening the capability of existing public television and radio stations to provide public telecommunications service to the public. For more information on this program (11.550 Public Telecommunications Facilities-Planning and Construction) contact William Cooperman, Director, Public Telecommunications Facilities Program, Office of Telecommunications and Information Application/NTIA, Room 4625, Department of Commerce, 1401 Constitution Avenue, NW, Washington, DC 20230; 202-482-5802; {www.ntia.doc.gov/ptfp}.

Money to Help Bus Operators Comply With "Transportation for Individuals with Disabilities" Requirements

This program provides funding to private operators of over-the-road buses to assist with the costs and training necessary to comply with the Department of Transportation's "Transportation for Individuals with Disabilities" rule. Capital projects eligible for funding include adding wheelchair lifts and other accessibility equipment to new vehicles, and purchasing lifts to retro-fit existing vehicles. Eligible training costs can be included. For more information on this program (20.518 Capital and Training Assistance Program for Over-the Road Bus Accessibility) contact Brenda Younger, Program Coordinator, Federal Transit Administration, Office of Program Management, Office of Resource Management and State Programs, 400 7th Street, SW, Washington, DC 20590; 202-366-2053; {www.fta.dot.gov}.

Help to Establish and Operate a Credit Union

NCUA staff will explain Federal Credit Union chartering requirements to any group interested in forming a credit union. They also help with the preparation of the charter application, assist newly chartered credit unions begin operation, and will assist credit unions and their members in consumer matters. For more information on the program (44.001 Credit Union Charter, Examination, Supervision, and Insurance) contact the Chairman, NCUA Board, National Credit Union Administration, 1775 Duke Street, Alexandria, VA 22314-3428; 703-518-6300; {www.ncua.gov}.

Institutional, Collections Management, Public Dimension and Governance Assessments for Museums, Nature Centers, Science and Technology Centers and Botanical Gardens

The Museum Assessment Program (MAP) is funded by the Institute of Museum and Library Services and administered by the American Association of Museums. It is designed to help museums assess their strengths and weaknesses and plan for the future. The program provides non-competitive grants of technical assistance for four types of assessments: Institutional, Collections

Management Public Dimension, and Governance. For more information on this program (45.302 Museum Assessment Program) contact Jeannette Thomas, Institute of Museum and Library Services, 1100 Pennsylvania Avenue, NW, Room 510, Washington, DC 20506; 202-606-8339 (Public Affairs) or 202-606-8458 (Jeanette Thomas); {Email: imlsinfo@imls.gov}; {www. imls.gov}.

Grants to Museums, Aquariums, Zoological Parks, and Planetariums for Conservation Programs

The Conservation Assessment Program (CAP) supports a two day site visit by conservation professional to perform the assessment and up to three days to write the report. The general conservation survey or assessment provides an overview of all the museum's collections, as well as its environmental conditions, policies and procedures relating to collections care. For more information on the program (45.304 Conservation Assessment Program) contact Noelle Giguere, Institute of Museum and Library Services, 1100 Pennsylvania Avenue, NW, Room 510, Washington, DC 20506; 202-606-8339 (Public Affairs) or 202-606-8550 (Noelle Giguere); {Email: imlsinfo@imls.gov}; {www. imls.gov}.

Grants to Museums, Botanical Gardens, Arboretums, and Nature Centers for Conservation Projects

The IMLS Conservation Project Support program awards matching grants to help museums identify conservation priorities and needs, and perform activities to ensure the safekeeping of their collections. The primary goal of each project must be conservation care and not collection management or maintenance. Conservation Project Support also funds exceptional projects with far reaching effects that benefit multiple institutions. For more information on this program (45.303 Conservation Project Support) contact Steven Shwartzman, Institute of Museum and Library Services, 1100 Pennsylvania Avenue, NW, Room 510, Washington, DC 20506; 202-606-8339 (Public Affairs) or 202-606-4641 (Steven Shwartzman); {Email: imlsinfo@imls.gov}; {www.imls.gov}.

Business Development Help for Small Businesses

This program provides assistance to prospective, as well as present, small business persons to improve the skills necessary to manage and operate a business. The assistance includes workshops for prospective small business owners; management counseling including assistance from the Service Corps of Retired Executives (SCORE) and other volunteer groups; management courses, conferences, and seminars; and educational materials to assist in the management of a small business. For more information on this program (59.005 Business Development Assistance to Small Business) contact the Associate Administrator for Business Initiatives, Small Business Administration, 409 3rd Street, SW, Washington, DC 20416; 800-8ASK-SBA; 202-205-6665; {www.sba.gov}.

Help in Obtaining Federal Contracts for Small Businesses

This program helps small business obtain a "fair" share of contracts and sub-contracts for Federal government supplies and services, and a "fair" share of property sold by the government. Assistance includes: the application of small business set-asides to increase the Federal procurement and disposal requirements awarded to small business; consultations to optimize procurement activities; review and analysis of small firms in order to certify competence as a prime contractor; review of large prime contractors' sub-contracting plans and programs to insure sub-contracting opportunities; consultation and advice for small firms regarding government procurement and property sales matters; assistance in specific contract administration problems; and determination of small business eligibility for SBA's procurement financial programs. For more information on this program (59.009 Procurement Assistance to Small Businesses) contact the Associate Administrator for Government Contracting, Small Business Administration, 409 3rd Street, SW, Washington, DC 20416; 800-8ASK-SBA; 202-205-6460; {www.sba.gov}.

New Markets Venture Capital for Small Business in Low-Income Geographic Areas

The goal of this program is to promote economic development and job opportunities in low-income geographic areas through developmental venture capital investments in smaller businesses located in such areas. The SBA designates New Markets Venture Capital companies which are eligible to receive guaranteed loans and project grants. The guaranteed loan funds are used to make equity capital investments in smaller businesses located in low-income geographic areas. For more information on the program (59.051 New Markets Venture Capital) contact the Director, New Markets Venture Capital Program, 409 3rd Street, NW, Suite 6300, Washington, DC 20416; 800-8ASK-SBA; 202-205-6510; Fax: 202-205-6013; {www.sba.gov/INV/venture.html}.

$500,000 for Small Businesses

The SBA's Small Business Loan Programs provide guaranteed loans to small businesses that are unable to obtain traditional financing, but have shown the ability to repay loans granted. Priority is given to low income business owners, businesses located in high unemployment areas, nonprofit sheltered workshops, small businesses owned or being established by handicapped individuals, and the support of small businesses in the manufacturing, design, marketing, installation or serving of specific energy measures. For more information on this program contact the Director, Policy Procedures Branch, Small Business Administration, 409 Third Street, SW, Washington, DC 20416: 202-205-6570: 800-UASK-SBA; {www.sba.gov}.

Help to Start or Expand a Micro-enterprise

The PRIME program was created to help the smallest of small businesses, those with fewer than six employees. Under the Program for Investment in Micro-entrepreneurs (PRIME), the SBA provides federal funds to community based organizations that in turn offer training and technical assistance to low-income and very low-income micro-entrepreneurs. For more information on the program

(59.050 Micro-Enterprise Development Grants) contact Judy Raskind, Office of Financial Assistance, Small Business Administration, 409 Third Street, SW, Washington, DC 20416; 800-UASK-SBA; 202-205-6497; {www.sba.gov/INV}.

Free Counseling and Mentoring Services for Potential and Existing Small Businesses

SCORE uses the management experience of retired and active business professionals to counsel and train potential and existing small business owners. SCORE members volunteer their counseling and mentoring services to the public free of charge, though small business training workshops are offered for a low fee. For more information on the (59.026 Service Corps of Retired Executives Association) program contact W. Kenneth Yancey, National SCORE Association Office, Small Business Administration, 409 Third Street, SW, Washington, DC 20025; 800-634-0245; 202-205-6762; {www.score.org} or {www.sba.gov}.

Business Development Help for Asian American, African American, Hispanic American, Native American and Asian Pacific American Businesses

This program offers business development assistance to business owners who are both socially and economically disadvantaged. The assistance provided includes: management and technical assistance, access to capital and other forms of financing, business training and counseling, and access to sole source and limited competition Federal Contract opportunities. For more information on the (59.006 8(a) Business Development) program contact the Associate Administrator for 8(a) Business Development, Small Business Administration, 409 Third Street, SW, Washington, DC 20416; 202-205-6421; 800-UASK-SBA; {www.sba.gov/8abd}.

Grants to Museums for Projects that Sustain Our Cultural Heritage and Support Life Long Learning in the Community

Museums for America Grants support projects and activities that strengthen museums as active resources and centers of community engagement. These grants may be used to fund ongoing museum activities; purchase equipment or services; research and scholarships; upgrading and integration of new technology; improve institutional infrastructure; or to plan new programs or activities. For more information on (45.301 Museums for America Grants) contact Christine Henry, Senior Program Officer, Office of Museum Services, Room 609, Institute of Museum and Library Services, 1100 Pennsylvania Avenue, NW, Washington, DC 20506; 202-606-8687; Fax: 202-606-0010; {Email: chenry@imls.gov}; {www.imls.gov/grants/museum/mus_mfa.htm}.

Grants to Non-Profit Museums for Innovations in Public Services and Meeting Community Needs

National Leadership Grants support innovation in providing public service and meeting community needs through the creative use of new technologies; model projects to be replicated though out the field; increased public access to museum collections; and collaborative projects to extend the impact of funding. Museum Online Grants address the technological needs and issues of museums. Museums in the Community Grants support museum and community partnerships that enhance the quality of community life. Professional Practice Grants support projects that improve the professional practices in the museum field. For more information on (45.312 National Leadership Grants for Museums) contact Dan Lukash, Senior Program Officer, Office of Museum Services, Room 609, Institute of Museum and Library Services, 1100 Pennsylvania Avenue, NW, Washington, DC 20506; 202-606-4644; Fax: 202-606-0010; {Email: dlukash@imls.gov}; {www.imls.gov/grants/museum/mus_n lgm.asp}.

Grants to Libraries that Serve Native Americans and Native Hawaiians

Grants from the Native Hawaiian Library Services Program can be used to support improvements in library services to Native Hawaiians. Funds may be used to establish or enhance electronic links between libraries; link libraries electronically with social, educational or information services; help libraries access information through electronic networks;

encourage libraries in different areas, and different types of libraries to establish consortia and share resources; pay costs for libraries to acquire or share computer systems and telecommunications technologies; and target library and information services to persons having difficulty using a library and to underserved urban and rural communities. For more information on the Native American and Native Hawaiian Library Services Program contact Alison Freese, Senior Program Specialist, Office of Library Services, Room 802, Institute of Museum and Library Services, 1100 Pennsylvania Avenue, NW, Washington, DC 20506; 202-606-5408; Fax: 202-606-1077; {Email: afreese@imls.gov}; {www. imls.gov/grants/library/lib_nhls.asp}.

Help for Manufacturers and Producers Hurt by Increased Imports

The EDA provides assistance to manufacturers and producers injured by increased imports. A network of 12 Trade Adjustment Assistance Centers (TAAC) help affected firms complete and submit an eligibility petition to the EDA. Once approved, the TAAC helps the firm to prepare an adjustment proposal that includes an objective analysis of the firm's weaknesses, strengths, and opportunities. After the EDA approves the adjustment plan, the firm can receive cost share assistance from the TAAC. For more information on the Trade Adjustment Assistance Program contact David A. Sampson, Economic Development Administration, Department of Commerce, 1401 Constitution Avenue, NW, Washington, DC 20230; 202-482-5081; {www.eda.gov/Investments Grants/Investments.xml}.

Help for Marine Suppliers and Owners and Operators of U.S. Shipbuilding and Repair Facilities to Improve Their Competitiveness in International Markets

The Maritime Administration (MARAD) established the National Maritime Resource and Education Center to assist marine suppliers, and the owner/operators of U.S. shipbuilding and repair facilities in improving their international competitiveness. For more information on the National Maritime Resource and Education Center contact Joseph Byrne, Director, Office of Shipbuilding and Marine Technology, Maritime Administration, U.S. Department of Transportation, 400 7th Street, SW, Washington, DC 20590; 202-366-1931; 800-99-MARAD; Fax: 202-366-7197; {www.marad.dot.gov/ NMREC/index.html}.

Help for Owners and Operators of U.S. Flag Ships to Construct, Reconstruct or Acquire New Vessels

The CCF Program was established to help owners and operators of U.S. Flag vessels accumulate the capital necessary to modernize and expand the U.S. Merchant Marine. The program promotes the construction, reconstruction or acquisition of vessels by deferring Federal Income Taxes on money or property placed into a Capital Construction Fund. For more information on the Capital Construction Fund contact the Office of Ship Financing, Maritime Administration, U.S. Department of Transportation, 400 7th Street, SW, Room 8122, Washington, DC 20950; 202-366-5744; 800-99-MARAD; {www. marad.dot.gov/TitleXI/ccf.html}.

Help for Exporters of U.S. Dairy Products

The Dairy Export Incentive Program helps exporters of U.S. dairy products meet world prices for certain dairy products and destinations. Through this program, the USDA pays cash bonuses to exporters, allowing them to sell certain U.S. dairy products at prices lower that their acquisition costs. The goal of this program is to develop export markets for dairy products where U.S. products are not competitive due to the presence of subsidized products from other countries. For more information on the Dairy Export Incentive Program contact the Operations Division, Export Credits, Foreign Agricultural Service, USDA, Mail Stop 1035; 1400 Independence Avenue, SW, Washington, DC 20250-1035; 202-720-3224 or 202-720-6211; Fax: 202-720-0938; {www.fas.usda.gov/excredits/deip.html}.

Cash Bonuses to Exporters of U.S. Agricultural Products

The main objectives of the program are to expand U.S. agricultural exports and to challenge unfair trade practices. The EEP helps products produced by U.S. farmers meet competition from subsidized products from other countries, and especially the European Union. To achieve these objectives, the USDA pays cash bonuses to exporters, allowing them to sell U.S. agricultural products in targeted countries at prices below their cost of acquiring them. For more information on the Export Enhancement Program contact the Operations Division, Export Credits, Foreign Agricultural Service, USDA, Mail Stop 1035; 1400 Independence Avenue, SW, Washington, DC 20250-1035; 202-720-3224 or 202-720-6211; Fax: 202-720-0938; {www.fas.usda.gov/excredits/eep.html}

Money for Farmers to Incorporate Conservation into their Farming Operations

Agricultural Management Assistance (AMA) provides cost share assistance to agricultural producers to voluntarily incorporate conservation efforts, such as water management, water quality and erosion control, into their farming operations. AMA provides the personnel and resources needed to conduct conservation planning, conservation practice surveys, layout design, installation and certification, quality assurance and assessment of the program. For more information on Agricultural Management Assistance contact David B. Mason, National AMA Program Manager, Natural Resources Conservation Service, USDA, 1400 Independence Avenue, SW, Room 5242-S, Washington, DC 20250; 202-720-1873; {Email: dave.mason@usda.gov}; {www.nrcs.usda.gov/programs/ama}.

Money for Farmers and Ranchers to Conserve Soil and Water

The SWCA program helps farmers and ranchers address threats to water, soil and other related natural resources, including grazing land, wetlands and wildlife habitat, by providing cost share and incentive payments. SWCA also helps landowners comply with Federal and state environmental laws, and make cost effective changes to nutrient management, irrigation, grazing management and cropping systems. For more information on the Soil and Water Conservation Assistance, SWCA program contact Walley Turner, National Program Manager, Natural Resources Conservation Service, USDA, 1400 Independence Avenue, SW, Washington, DC 20250; 202-720-1875; {Email: walley.turner@usda. gov}; {www.nrcs.usda.gov/programs/swca}.

Grants to Convert Military Airfields for Civilian Use
The Military Airport Program (MAP) provides financial assistance to civilian sponsors who are converting or have already converted a military airfield for civilian or joint military/civilian use. Eligible projects include utility work, building or rehabilitating surface parking lots, access roads, hangars, fuel farms, passenger terminal facilities, and projects to construct, improve or repair building facilities with up to 50,000 square feet of floor space. For more information on the Military Airport Program contact Oliver Murdock, Office of Airport Planning and Programming, Federal Aviation Administration, Military

Airport Branch (APP-420), 800 Independence Avenue, SW, Washington, DC 20591; 202-267-8244; {www.faa.gov/planning/MAP}.

Grants to Business Partnerships to Provide Technical Skills Training to American Workers
The goal of the H-1B Technical Skills Training Grant Program is to raise the technical skill levels of American workers. Grants are awarded to local Workforce Investment Boards and business partnerships. The grants are to be used for training workers in high technology, information technology and biotechnology skill areas, including software and communications services, telecommunications, systems installation and integration, computers and communication hardware, advanced manufacturing, health care technology, biomedical research and manufacturing, and innovation services. For more information on the H-1B Technical Skills Training Grant Program contact Mindy Feldbaum, Program Officer, U.S. Department of Labor, Employment and Training Administration, Room 4659, 200 Constitution Avenue, NW, Washington, DC 20210; 202-693-3382; Fax: 202-693-2982; {Email: Feldbaum.Mindy@dol.gov}; {www. doleta.gov/h-1b/h-1b_index.cfm}.

Loans and Technical Assistance for Small Businesses in New Market Areas
Community Express is a SBA loan program with the National Community Reinvestment Coalition (NCRC). It is offered in pre-designated geographic areas that primarily serve low and moderate incomes and New Market

small businesses. The program also includes hands-on technical and management assistance. Loan funds may be used for start-up, working capital, expansion, real estate acquisitions or equipment purchases. For more information on Community Express Loans contact the Office of Financial Assistance, Special Purpose Loan Programs, Small Business Administration, 409 Third Street, SW, Washington, DC 20416; 800-UASK-SBA; 202-205-6490; {www.sba.gov/f inancing/lendinvest/comexpress.html}.

Grants for Small Businesses to Research and Develop High-Tech Innovations

The Small Business Innovation Research Program encourages small businesses to conduct research and development on high-tech innovation. SBIR funds the start up and development stages of the technology, product or service and encourages its commercialization. Small businesses must be American owned and independently operated, for-profit, have less than 500 employees, and the principal researcher must be employed by the business to be eligible for this program. Awards are based on small business qualification, degree of innovation, technical merit, and future market potential. Small businesses that receive awards or grants then enter into a three phase program. The start-up phase is Phase I. Awards, up to $100,000, are given for six months to explore the technical merit or feasibility of an idea or technology. Phase II consists of up to $750,000 for as long as 2 years to expand Phase I results. Research and development is completed and the developer evaluates commercial potential. Phase III is where the innovation moves from the lab into the marketplace. There are no SBIR funds to support this phase. For more information on the Small Business Innovation Research Program contact Robert Connolly, SBIR/STTR Program, Office of Technology, U.S. Small Business Administration, 409 Third Street, SW, Mail Code: 6540, Washington, DC 20416; 202-205-6450; Fax: 202-205-6390; {Email: robert.connolly@sba.gov}, {www.sba.gov/sbir}.

Additional SBIR Program Contacts
Department of Agriculture
Charles Cleland PhD., Director, SBIR Program, Cooperative State Research, Education & Extension Service, U.S. Department of Agriculture, Stop 2243, Waterfront Centre, Suite 2312, 1400 Independence Avenue, SW, Washington, DC 20250-2243; 202-401-6852; Fax: 202-401-6070; {Email: CCLeland@reeusda.gov}; {www.reeusda.gov/sbir}.

Department of Commerce
Joseph Bishop, Ph.D., Director, Office of Research and Technology Applications, U.S. Department of Commerce/NOAA, 1335 East-West Highway, Room 106, Silver Spring, MD 20910; 301-713-3565; Fax: 301-713-4100; {Email: Joseph.Bishop@ NOAA.GOV}; {www.ofa.noaa.gov/~ amd/sbir/sbir.html}.

Department of Defense
Jeff Bond, Acting SBIR/STTR Program Coordinator, OSD/SADBU, U.S. Department of Defense, 1777 North Kent Street, Suite 9100, Arlington, VA 22209; 703-588-8616; Fax: 703-588-7561; {Email: Jeff.Bond@osd.mil}; {www.defenselink.mil}.

Department of Education
Joseph G. Teresa, Ph.D., U.S. Department of Education, Institute of Education Sciences, Room 620, 555 New Jersey Avenue, SW, Washington, DC 20208; 202-219-2046; Fax: 202-501-3005; {Email: Joe.teresa@ ed.gov}; {www.ed.gov/programs/sbir/ index.html}.

Department of Energy
Arlene M. DeBlanc, J.D., SBIR/STTR Program, Office of Science, U.S. Department of Energy, 100 Independence Avenue, SW, SC-32, Germantown Building, Washington, DC 20585-1290; 301-903-3199; Fax: 301-903-5488; {Email: Arlene. deblanc@science.doe.gov}; {www. science.doe.gov/sbir}.

Department of Health and Human Services
Debbie Ridgely, Director, OSBDU, Office of the Secretary, U.S. Department of Health and Human Services, 200 Independence Avenue, Room 360G, Washington, DC 20201; 202-690-7235; Fax: 202-260-4872; {Email: Debbie.ridgely@hhs.gov}; {www.hhs.gov/osdbu}.

Department of Transportation
Joseph D. Henebury, SBIR Program Director, U.S. Department of Transportation, Volpe Center, 55 Broadway, Kendall Square, Cambridge, MA 02142-1093; 617-494-2712; Fax: 617-494-2370; {Email: Henebury@volpe.dot.gov}; {www.volpe.dot.gov/sbir}.

Environmental Protection Agency
James Gallup, Ph.D., Office of Research and Development, U.S. Environmental Protection Agency, ORD/NCER (8722R), 1200 Pennsylvania Avenue, NW, Washington, DC 20460; 202-564-6823; Fax: 202-565-2447; {Email: Gallup.James@epa.gov}; {http://es.epa.gov/ncer/sbir}

NASA
Robert L. Norwood, Ph.D., Director, Commercial Development and Technology Transfer, National Aeronautics and Space Administration-HQ, 300 E Street, SW, Code XC, Washington, DC 20546-0001; 202-358-2320; Fax: 202-358-3878; {http://sbir.gsfc.nasa.gov/SBIR/ SBIR.html}.

National Science Foundation
Kesh S. Narayanan, Director, Industrial Innovation Programs, U.S. National Science Foundation, SBIR Program, 4201 Wilson Boulevard, Room 550, Arlington, VA 22230; 703-292-7076; Fax: 703-292-9057; {Email: knarayan@nsf.gov}; {www.eng.nsf.gov/sbirspecs}.

Grants for Small Business and Non-profit Research Partners to Research and Develop High-Tech Innovations

The Small Business Technology Transfer Program (STTR) is a competitive program that sets aside a certain percentage of federal research and development funds for awards to small business and non-profit research institution partnerships. To be eligible, small businesses must be American owned and independently operated, for profit, and have fewer than 500 employees. STTR awards are based on the qualifications of the small business/non-profit research institution, degree of innovation, and future market potential. Small businesses that receive awards or grants enter into a three phase program. Phase I is the start up phase. It consists of awards up to $100,000 for one year to fund the exploration of the technical, scientific and commercial feasibility of an idea or technology. Phase I consists of awards up to $500,000 for two years to expand on Phase I results. Research and development work is performed and commercial potential considered, Phase I must be completed in order to be considered for Phase II. During Phase III, the innovation moves from the laboratory into the marketplace. The small business must acquire funding from the private sector or other non-STTR federal agencies. For more information on the Small Business Technology Transfer Program contact Robert Connolly, SBIR/STTR Program, Office of Technology, U.S. Small Business Administration, 409 Third Street, SW, Mail Code: 6540, Washington, DC 20416; 202-205-6450; Fax: 202-205-6390; {Email: robert.connolly@ sba.gov}; {www.sba.gov/sbir}.

Additional STTR Program Contacts:
National Science Foundation
Kesh S. Narayanan, Director, STTR Program, National Science Foundation, 4201 Wilson Boulevard, Room 550, Arlington, VA 22230; 703-292-7076; Fax: 703-292-9057; {Email: knarayan@nsf.gov}; {www.nsf.gov}.

National Aeronautics and Space Administration
Robert L. Norwood, Ph.D., Director, STTR Program, National Aeronautics and Space Administration-HQ, 300 E Street, SW, Code-XC, Washington, DC 20546-0001; 202-358-232; Fax: 202-358-3878; {www.nasa.gov}.

Department of Health and Human Services
Debbie Ridgely, Director, STTR Program, OSBDU, Office of the Secretary, U.S. Department of Health

and Human Services, 200 Independence Avenue, Room 360G, Washington, DC 20201; 202-690-7235; Fax: 202-260-4872; {Email: Debbie.ridgely@hhs.gov}; {www.hhs.gov/osbdu}.

Department of Energy
Arlene M. DeBlanc, J.D., STTR Program, Office of Science, U.S. Department of Energy, 1000 Independence Avenue, SW, SC-32, Germantown Building, Washington, DC 20585-1290 ; 301-903-3199; Fax: 301-903-5488; {Email: Arlene. deblanc@science.doe.gov}; {www.science.doe.gov/sbir}.

Department of Defense
Jeff Bond, Acting STTR Program Coordinator, OSD/SADBU, U.S. Department of Defense, 1777 North Kent Street, Suite 9100 Arlington, VA 22209; 703-588-8616; Fax: 703-588-7561; {Email: jeff.bond@osd.mil}; {www.defenselink.mil}.

Venture Capital to Start a Water Related Business in an Emerging Market County
This fund supports equity investments in operating and special purpose companies involved in the treatment, bulk supply and distribution of water in emerging market countries. The Aqua International Partners Fund is a privately owned, privately managed investment fund supported by the Overseas Private Investment Corporation. For more information on the Aqua International Partners Fund contact John Sylvia, Chief Operating Officer, Texas Pacific Group, 345 California Street, Suite 3300, San Francisco, CA 94104; 415-743-1570; Fax: 415-743-1504; {Email: jlyvia@texpac.com}; {www.opic.gov/investmentfunds}.

Venture Capital to Start Infrastructure Projects in the Baltic Region

This fund provides equity investments in the Baltic, Russia, and NIS for large infrastructure projects including transportation, power, natural resource development and related industries. The AIG Brunswick Millennium Fund is a privately owned, privately managed investment fund supported by the Overseas Private Investment Corporation. For more information on the AIG Brunswick Millennium Fund contact Peter Yu, American International Group, 175 Water Street, 24th Floor, New York, NY 10038 ; 212-458-2156; Fax: 212-458-2153; {www.opic.gov/investmentfunds}.

Venture Capital to Start a Business in Russia

This program supports equity investments in Russia in natural resource related companies, telecommunications, light manufacturing, and consumer services and products. This fund may also invest in other OPIC covered NIS states. The Russia Partners Fund, A is a privately owned, privately managed investment fund supported by the Overseas Private Investment Corporation. For more information on the Russia Partners Fund, A contact Drew Guff, Managing Director, Siguler, Guff & Company, 630 Fifth Avenue, 16th Floor, New York, NY

10111; 212-332-5108; Fax: 212-332-5120; {www.opic.gov/investment funds}.

Venture Capital to Start a Business in the Ukraine, Russia and Other East European Countries

This fund provides equity investment in consumer products, financial and service industries, and diversified manufacturing in the following target areas: Latvia, Ukraine, Lithuania, Russia, Estonia, Kazakhstan, Moldova, Armenia, Bulgaria, Romania, Belarus, and Georgia. By supplementing the capital of privately owned, privately managed investment funds, OPIC can help profit oriented enterprises in emerging market areas gain access to venture capital, management guidance and financial expertise. For more information on the New Century Capital Partners LP Fund contact George Rohr, Chief Executive Officer, NCH Advisors, 712 Fifth Avenue, 46th Floor, New York, NY 10019-4018; 212-641-3229; Fax: 212-641-3201; {www.opic.gov/investment funds}.

Venture Capital to Start a Telecommunications Business in Southeast Asia

This program funds equity investment in consumer products, financial services and telecommunication in the emerging market areas of Bangladesh, India, Vietnam, Thailand, Indonesia, Korea, Sri Lanka, Laos and the Philippines. By supplementing the capital of privately owned, privately managed investment funds, OPIC can help profit oriented businesses in emerging market areas gain access to venture capital, management guidance, and financial expertise. For more information on the Asia Development

Partners LP Fund contact Daniel Mintz, Managing Director, Olympus Capital Holdings, Asia, 153 East 53rd Street, 43rd Floor, New York, NY 10022; 212-292-6531; Fax: 212-292-6570; {Email: dmintz@zbi.com}; {www.opic.gov/investmentfunds}.

Venture Capital to Start a Business in South America

This program supports equity investments in South America, with emphasis on Argentina, Brazil, Chile and Peru, for diversified manufacturing, service and financial services. By supplementing the capital of privately owned and managed investment funds, OPIC can help profit oriented enterprises in emerging market areas gain access to venture capital, management guidance and financial expertise. For more information on the South American Private Equity Growth Fund contact Varel D. Freeman, Vice President and Managing Director, Baring Latin American Partners, LLC, 230 Park Avenue, New York, NY 10169; 212-309-1795; Fax: 212-309-1794; {www.opic.gov/investmentfunds}.

Venture Capital to Start a Business in Southern Africa

This fund provides equity investment in South Africa and regional SADC countries for financial and service industries and diversified manufacturing. By supplementing the capital of privately owned and

managed investment funds, OPIC can help profit oriented businesses in emerging market areas gain access to venture capital, management guidance, and financial expertise. For more information on the New Africa Opportunity Fund contact Thomas C. Barry, Chief Executive Officer, Zephyr Management, LP, 320 Park Avenue, New York, NY 10022-6815; 212-508-9410; Fax: 212-508-9494; {Email: info@opic.gov}; {www.opic.gov/investmentfunds}.

Venture Capital to Start a Manufacturing or Computer Business in India

This fund supports equity investment in India for basic manufacturing, consumer goods, computer, banking and related industries. By supplementing the capital of privately owned and managed investment funds, OPIC can help profit oriented enterprises in emerging market areas gain access to venture capital, management guidance and financial expertise. For more information on the India Private Equity Fund contact Michele J. Buchignani, Managing Director, CIBC Oppenheimer & Company, Oppenheimer Tower, World Financial Center, New York, NY 10281; 212-667-8190; Fax: 212-667-4468; {Email: Michele.buchignani@us.cibc.com}; {www.opic.gov/investmentfunds}.

Venture Capital to Start a Business in Latin America

This program funds equity investments in Belize, Bolivia, Brazil, Columbia, Ecuador, Peru, Argentina, Venezuela, El Salvador, Costa Rica, Honduras, Guatemala, Uruguay, Panama, Paraguay, Nicaragua and Chile for diversified manufacturing, financial and service industries. By supplementing the capital of privately owned, privately managed investment funds, OPIC can help profit oriented businesses in emerging market areas gain access to venture capital, management guidance and financial expertise. For more information on the Newbridge Andean Partners LP Fund contact Bernard Aronson, ACON Investments, LLC, 1133 Connecticut Avenue, NW, Suite 700, Washington, DC 20036; 202-861-6060 ext. 103; 202-861-6061; {Email: infp@opic. gov}; {www.opic.gov/investment funds}.

Venture Capital to Start an Environment Related Business in an Emerging Market

This fund provides equity investments in all OPIC eligible countries for environment oriented sectors relating to the development, financing, operating or supplying of infrastructure relating to clean water and energy. By supplementing the capital of privately owned, privately managed investment funds, OPIC can help profit oriented enterprises in emerging market areas gain access to venture capital, management guidance and financial expertise. For more information on Global Environment Emerging Markets Fund I contact H. Jeff Leonard, President, GEF Management, 1225 Eye Street, NW, Suite 900, Washington, DC 20005; 202-789-4500; Fax: 202-789-4508; {Email: info@opic.gov}; {www.opic. gov/investmentfunds}.

Venture Capital to Start a Business in Southeast Europe

This program provides equity investments in Albania, Bosnia, Bulgaria, Croatia, Herzegovina, FYR

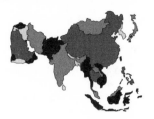

Macedonia, Montenegro, Romania, Slovenia, Turkey, and should they become eligible, Serbia and Kosovo. By supplementing the capital of privately owned, privately managed investment funds, OPIC can help profit oriented businesses in emerging market areas gain access to venture capital, management guidance and financial expertise. For more information on Soros Investment Capital Ltd contact David Matheson, Manager, Soros Private Funds Management, LLC, 888 Seventh Avenue, New York, NY 10106; 212-333-9727; Fax: 212-397-0139; {Email: info@opic.gov}; {www.opic.gov/ investmentfunds}.

Venture Capital to Start an Agriculture Business in the Baltic Region

This program provides equity investments in the NIS/Baltic region for agriculture, food firms, infrastructure projects, privatizations, and food storage and distribution facilities. By supplementing the capital of privately owned, privately managed investment funds, OPIC can help profit oriented enterprises in emerging market areas gain access to venture capital, management guidance and financial expertise. For more information on Agribusiness Partners International contact Robert Peyton, President, Agribusiness Management Company, c/o America First Companies, 11004 Farnam Street, Omaha, NE 68102; 402-930-3060;

Fax: 402-930-3007; {Email: bpeyton@am1st.com}; {www.opic. gov/investmentfunds}.

Venture Capital to Start an Environment Related Business in an Emerging Market

This fund provides equity investments in all OPIC eligible countries for environment oriented sectors relating to the development, financing, operating or supplying of infrastructure relating to clean water and energy. By supplementing the capital of privately owned, privately managed investment funds, OPIC can help profit oriented enterprises in emerging market areas gain access to venture capital, management guidance and financial expertise. For more information on the Global Environment Emerging Markets Fund II contact H. Jeff Leonard, President, GEF Management, 1225 Eye Street, NW, Suite 900, Washington, DC 20005; 202-789-4500; Fax: 202-789-4508; {Email: info@opic.gov}; {www.opic.gov/investmentfunds}.

Venture Capital to Start a Business in a Sub-Sahara Country

This fund supports equity investments in all sub-Saharan countries, except South Africa, with a focus on telecommunications, natural resources and manufacturing. By supplementing the capital of privately owned, privately managed investment funds, OPIC can help profit oriented businesses in emerging market areas gain access to venture capital, management guidance and financial expertise. For more information on the Modern Africa Growth and Investment Fund contact Steve Cashin, Managing Director, Modern Africa Fund

Managers, 1100 Connecticut Avenue, NW, Suite 500, Washington, DC 20036; 202-887-1772; Fax: 202-887-1788; {Email: info@opic.gov}; {www.opic.gov/investmenfunds}.

Venture Capital to Start a Business in Central Europe

This fund supports equity investments in basic manufacturing, distribution networks, consumer goods and related services networks. Eligible countries include Central Europe/Baltic Republics, Albania, Bulgaria, Croatia, the Czech Republic, Estonia, Hungary, Latvia, Lithuania, Poland, Romania, Slovakia and Slovenia. By supplementing the capital of privately owned, privately managed investment funds, OPIC can help profit oriented enterprises in emerging market areas gain access to venture capital, management guidance and financial expertise. For more information on the Bancroft Eastern Europe Fund contact Fred Martin, President, Bancroft UK, LTD, 7/11 Kensington, High Street, London W8 5NP; 44-20-736-8334; Fax: 44-20-738-3348; {Email: martin@bancroftgroup.com}; {www. opic.gov/investmentfunds}.

Venture Capital to Start a Telecommunications Business in Armenia, Georgia or Azerbaijan

This fund provides equity investments for telecommunications projects in Georgia, Armenia and Azerbaijan. By supplementing the capital of privately owned, privately managed investment funds, OPIC can help profit oriented enterprises in emerging markets gain access to venture capital, management guidance and financial expertise. For more information on the Caucasus Fund contact Irakli Rukhadze, CEO, Caucasus Advisors, Suite 901, 31 Milk

Street, Boston, MA 02109; 617-646-4512; Fax: 617-646-4512; {Email: info@opic.gov}; {www.opic.gov/investmentfunds}.

Venture Capital to Start a Business in Southeast Asia

This program supports equity investments in financial, construction, high tech, light manufacturing and telecom services in Indonesia, Singapore, Taiwan, Malaysia, Thailand and the Philippines. The Asia Pacific Growth Fund is a privately owned, privately managed investment fund supported by the Overseas Private Investment Corporation. It is designed to promote and facilitate U.S. investment in emerging markets by working with private capital to make direct equity and equity related investments. For more information on the Asia Pacific Growth Fund contact Ta-Lin Hsu, Chairman, Hambrecht & Quist Asia Pacific, 156 University Avenue, Palo Alto, CA 94104; 650-838-8098; Fax: 650-838-0801; {Email: info@opic.gov}; {www.opic.gov/investmentfunds}.

Venture Capital to Start a Business in West Bank/Gaza and Jordan

This program provides equity investments in West Bank/Gaza and Jordan for basic services and manufacturing companies. The West Bank/Gaza & Jordan Fund is a privately owned, privately managed investment fund supported by the Overseas Private Investment Corporation. It promotes and facilitates U.S. investment in emerging markets by working with private capital to make direct equity and equity related investments. For more information on the West Bank/Gaza & Jordan Fund contact Scott Stupay, International

Capital Advisors, 6862 Elm Street, Suite 720, McLean, VA 22101; 703-847-0870; Fax: 703-847-3068; {E-mail: info@opic.gov}; {www.opic.gov/investment funds}.

Venture Capital to Start a Business in Central and Eastern Europe

This program supports equity investments in Central and Eastern Europe for sustainable development industries. Eligible countries include Poland, Czech Republic, Slovakia, Romania, Bulgaria, Hungary and Slovenia. Investments are capped at 40% of commitments in any single country. By supplementing the capital of privately owned, privately managed investment funds, OPIC can help profit oriented enterprises in emerging market areas gain access to venture capital, management guidance and financial expertise. For more information on the Emerging Europe Fund contact Jamie Halper, Managing Director, TDA Capital Partners, Inc, 15 Valley Drive , Greenwich, CT 06831; 203-625-4525; Fax: 203-625-4525; {Email: jhalper@templeton.com}; {www.opic.gov/investment funds}.

Venture Capital for Starting a Business in India

This program supports equity investments in India for information technology, telecommunications and

consumer goods. Draper International India Fund is a privately owned, privately managed investment fund supported by the Overseas Private Investment Corporation. It promotes and facilitates U.S. investment in emerging markets by working with private capital to make direct equity and equity related investments. For more information on the Draper International India Fund contact Robin Richard Donohoe, Draper International, 50 California Street, Suite 2925, San Francisco, CA 94111; 415-616-4056; Fax: 415-616-4060; {Email: rarichards@draperintl. com}; {www.opic.gov/investment funds}.

Venture Capital for Starting a Business in Poland

This program provides equity investments in Poland for consumer goods, manufacturing, distribution networks, merchandising, and related service networks. The Poland Partners LP Fund is a privately owned, privately managed investment fund supported by the Overseas Private Investment Corporation. OPIC promotes and facilitates U.S. investment in emerging markets by working with private capital to make direct equity and equity related investments. For more information on this program (Poland Partners LP Fund) contact Landon Butler, President, Landon Butler & Company, 700 Thirteenth Street, NW, Suite 1150, Washington, DC 20005; 202-737-

7360; Fax: 202-737-7604; {Email: info@opic.gov}; {www.opic.gov/investmentfunds}.

Venture Capital for Starting a Business in Oman, Jordan and West Bank/Gaza

This program supports equity investments in Oman, Jordan and West Bank/Gaza for basic industries that create intra/inter-regional synergies. By supplementing the capital of privately owned and managed investment funds, OPIC can help profit oriented enterprises in emerging market areas gain access to venture capital, management guidance and financial expertise. For more information on this program (Inter-Arab Investment Fund) contact Dr. Fuad S. Abu Zayyad, Chairman, Inter-Arab Management, Inc, 2468 Embarcadero Way, Palo Alto, CA 94303; 650-917-0390; Fax: 650-856-9864; {Email: info@opic.gov}; {www.opic.gov/investmentfunds}.

Venture Capital to Start a Business in Israel

This program supports equity investment in Israel for technology, telecommunications, consumer retail and consumer products. The Israel Growth Fund is a privately owned, privately managed investment fund supported by the Overseas Private Investment Corporation. OPIC promotes and facilitates U.S. investment in emerging markets by working with private capital to make direct equity and equity related investments. For more information on this program (Israel Growth Fund) contact Allan Barkat, General Manager, Apax-Leumi Partners, Inc, Herzliya Business Park, 2 Maskit Street, 6th Floor, P.O. Box 2034, Herliza, Israel 46120; 972-3-696-5992;

Fax: 972-9-958-8366; {Email: allan@apax.co.il}; {www. opic.gov/investmentfunds}.

Venture Capital for Starting a Mining or Manufacturing Business in Sub-Sahara Africa

This program provides equity investments in Sub-Sahara Africa for mining, manufacturing and financial services. The Africa Growth Fund is a privately owned, privately managed investment fund supported by the Overseas Private Investment Corporation. OPIC promotes and facilitates U.S. investment in emerging markets by working with private capital to make direct equity and equity related investments. For more information on this program (Africa Growth Fund) contact Joe Jandreau, Managing Director, Equator Overseas Services, LTD, 45 Glastonbury Boulevard, Glastonbury, CT 06033; 860-633-9999; Fax: 860-633-6799; {Email: info@opic.gov}; {www.opic. gov/investmentfunds}.

Venture Capital to Start a Small Business Overseas

This program supports equity investments for basic manufacturing and service industries sponsored by qualifying U.S. small businesses in any OPIC eligible country. The Allied Small Business Fund is a privately owned, privately managed investment fund supported by the Overseas Private Investment Corporation. OPIC promotes and facilitates U.S. investment in emerging markets by working with private capital to make direct equity and equity related investments. For more information on this program (Allied Small Business Fund) contact Cabell Williams, Allied Capital Corporation, 1919

Pennsylvania Avenue, NW, Washington, DC 20006-3434; 202-973-6319; Fax: 202-659-2053; {Email: info@opic.gov}; {www.opic.gov/ investmentfunds}.

Fight Suppliers Who Won't Give You Credit

The Federal Trade Commission (FTC) enforces the laws that prohibit creditors and credit bureaus from discriminating against women because of their sex or marital status, and they can send you the free publication, *Equal Credit Opportunity*. This pamphlet explains your credit rights under the law, how to get help in establishing your own credit, and what to do if you feel your credit application has been unfairly denied. Contact the Federal Trade Commission (FTC), 600 Pennsylvania Ave., NW, Washington, DC 20580; 877-FTC-HELP; 202-326-2222; {www.ftc.gov/bcp/conline/ pubs/credit/ecoa.htm}.

28 States Offer Free Consulting To Women Only

Contact your state office of Economic Development located in your state capital. 28 states have set up special offices just for women entrepreneurs. Contact your State Office of Economic Development to see what your state has to offer. If they don't have a "Women Only" office, don't let that stop you. It just means you'll have to share the help available with the men in your state.

Grants, Loans and Loan Guarantees for Women-Owned Businesses

All federal money programs aimed at small business do not discriminate between women and non-women-owned businesses. However, at the state level there are a number of specific money programs that are set aside only for women-owned businesses. The programs vary from state to state and are changing all the time so it is best to check with your State Office of Economic Development in your state capital to insure you have the latest available information.

Federal Government Set-Asides for Women Entrepreneurs

Many Federal government contracting offices are trying to insure that a certain percentage of their contracts go to women entrepreneurs. Most even have special offices that will help women entrepreneurs sell to their agencies. For help in selling your product or service to the government, contact your State Economic Development Office in your state capital and obtain a copy of Equal Credit Opportunity. It is available from the Government Printing Office or free online. Contact Superintendent of Documents, Government Printing Office, Washington, DC 20402; 866-512-1800; Fax: 202-512-2168; {www.onlinewbc.gov/DOCS/procure/sellgov.doc}.

15% Set-Aside for Women Entrepreneurs

Not only is the Federal government active in insuring that women get a fair share of government contracts, but many state governments are becoming involved. Some states, like California for example, have passed laws that force their state agencies to give at least 15% of their contracts to women and minority-owned firms. Other states like Illinois, Iowa, Maine, Minnesota, Montana, New Jersey, Oregon, and Washington are among those who are active in insuring that women obtain a

fair share of state government contracts. Contact your State Office of Economic Development located in your state capital to see how your business can take advantage of set-asides in your state.

What To Do If You Suspect Your Bank Denied You Credit Because You Are a Woman or Divorced

The Federal Trade Commission (FTC) enforces the Equal Credit Opportunity Act, which prohibits any creditor from denying credit to a consumer on the basis of sex or marital status. If you think you've been discriminated against by a lender, contact the Federal Trade Commission. While the Federal Trade Commission won't act on individual complaints, a number of complaints against the same lender may force them to investigate. If you want your complaint investigated and action taken immediately, contact one of the following agencies, depending on the type of lending institution involved:

National Banks
Comptroller of the Currency, 1301 McKinney St., Suite 3710, Houston, TX 77010; 800-613-6743; {www.occ.treas.gov}.

Savings & Loans
Office of Thrift Supervision, U.S. Department of Treasury, 1700 G St., NW, Washington, DC 20552; 800-842-6929; {www.ots.treas.gov}.

FDIC State-Chartered Bank (not member of Federal Reserve System)
Federal Deposit Insurance Corporation, Consumer Affairs Division, Washington, DC 20429; 800-934-3342; {www.fdic.gov}.

Federally-Chartered Credit Union
National Credit Union Administration, Consumer Affairs Division, Washington, DC 20456; 800-827-3255; {www.ncua.gov}.

Small Loan/Finance Company, Public Utility, Credit Card or Government Lending Program
Consumer Response Center, Federal Trade Commission, Washington, DC 20580; 877-FTC-HELP; {www.ftc.gov}.

For all other complaints against creditors, contact: Department of Justice, Civil Rights Division, Washington, DC 20530. For more information contact Credit Practices Division, Federal Trade Commission, 600 Pennsylvania Ave., NW, Washington, DC 20580; 877-FTC-HELP; 202-326-2222; {www.ftc.gov/bcp/bcpcp.htm}.

Free Publications For Women Business Owners
If you're interested in finding out more about women in the workforce, including trends and future projections, you might find the following free publications informative:

Characteristics of Self-Employed Women
Developments in Women's Labor Force Participation
Employed Women About as Likely as Men to be Looking for Jobs
Marriage, Children and Women's Employment: What Do We Know
Married Women, Work and Values
Much Variation in Women's Employment Across Metropolitan Areas
'Second-Chance' Strategies for Women Who Drop Out of School
Twenty Facts on Women Workers
Women Business Owners
Women in High-Tech Jobs
Women in Jobs Recessions
Women in Jobs Recoveries
Women at the Millennium
Women's Share of Labor Force to Edge Higher by 2008
Differences in Women's and Men's Earnings by Age
Income and Spending Patterns for Working Women
Women in Managerial, Professional Occupations Earn More Than Others
Women's Earning's: An Overview
Job Absent Rate Higher for Women Than for Men
Women in the Construction Workplace: Providing Equitable Safety and Health Protection
Work Injuries and Illnesses Occurring to Women
These titles can also be accessed online at {www.dol.gov/dol/audience/aud-women.htm}. Contact the Women's Bureau, Office of the Secretary, U.S. Department of Labor, 200 Constitution Ave., NW, Room S-3311; Washington, DC 20210; 800-827-5355; 202-693-6731.

How to Get Start-Up Capital from Being Pregnant, Sexually Harassed, or From A Bad Shopping Experience
As a business owner, there are times you may come across unscrupulous wholesalers who try to sell you some

counterfeit products at cut-rate prices. Instead of risking your business by buying and reselling the bogus products, report the fraud to the U.S. Customs Service. If your complaint, which will be kept completely anonymous, leads to the seizure of counterfeit goods, you could receive a reward of up to $250,000, depending on the size of the case. Contact the U.S. Customs Service, Fraud Division, 1300 Pennsylvania Avenue, NW, Washington, DC 20229; 800-BE-ALERT; {www.customs.ustreas.gov}.

So you want to start your own business because you've just been fired because you were pregnant, or wouldn't sleep with your boss to get a promotion? Contact the Equal Employment Opportunity Commission (EEOC) and report how you think your former boss discriminated against you. The EEOC will investigate your complaint, and if they think there are grounds for prosecuting your former boss, they'll proceed with the case. If they prove the case, you could end up with enough money in back pay and other remedies to finance your own company. Contact the Equal Employment Opportunity Commission (EEOC), 1801 L St., NW, Washington, DC 20570; 202-663-4900; 800-669-4000; 800-669-3362 (publications); {www.eeoc.gov}.

Health Insurance for Divorcees Who Start Their Own Business

Under the new law, divorced and separated women and their children can continue to receive the same health insurance coverage they had before they were divorced or separated from their husbands at the group rate. The only difference is that they must pay the premium. This law applies to all private businesses that employ more than 20 people and to federal, state, and local government plans. For more information on this law, contact Women Work, 1625 K St. NW, #300, Washington, DC 20006; 202-467-6346; Fax: 202-467-5366; {www.womenwork.org}.

Seminars on How Women Can Sell to the Government

If you're not sure how to start doing business with the government, you might consider taking a seminar sponsored by the U.S. Small Business Administration on the procurement process. These seminars will give you a complete overview on what you'll need to know and do to get involved in bidding on and landing government business contracts. For information on when these seminars are scheduled in your area, contact the Office of Women's Business, U.S. Small Business Administration, 409 3rd St., SW, Washington, DC 20416; 202-205-6673; 800-8-ASK-SBA; {www.sba.gov/womeninbusiness/wnet.html}.

Creative Financing for Women Entrepreneurs

The Women's Business Ownership Office runs seminars on how women can use creative ways to locate financing if they've been turned down for loans by regular banks. For more information about these seminars, contact the Office of Women's Business Ownership, U.S. Small Business Administration, 409 3rd St., SW, Washington, DC 20416; 800-8-ASK-SBA; 202-205-6673; {www.sba.gov/womeninbusiness/wnet.html}.

Millions Set Aside For Welfare Moms To Start Their Own Businesses

The Job Opportunities for Low Income Individuals (JOLI) program can turn any good idea into a money making powerhouse, and it won't cost you a cent. Under the JOLI program, grants are awarded each year to nonprofit organizations that, in turn, work to create permanent jobs for people who are interested in running their own successful small businesses. As a collaborative partnership, the JOLI projects bring together community support services to lend a hand to those who want to climb that tough ladder of success.

For federal information on grants in your area, contact the federal JOLI office at the Department of Health and Human Services, Office of Community Services, 370 L'Enfant Promenade, SW, Fifth Floor, Washington, DC 20447; 202-401-9346, Fax: 202-401-4687; {www.acf.hhs.gov/programs/joli/welcome.htm}. They have a complete list.

Minority Business Development Centers

The Minority Business Development Agency funds Business Development Centers (MBDC), Native American Business Development Centers (NABDC), Business Resource Centers (BRC) and Minority Business Opportunity Committees (MBOC) nationwide to assist with the start-up, expansion, and acquisition of competitive minority owned firms offering quality goods and services. These centers provide business assistance for bonding, bidding, estimating, financing, procurement, international trade, franchising, acquisitions, mergers, and joint ventures to increase opportunities in domestic and international markets for minority entrepreneurs. The centers provide one-on-one counseling for accounting, administration, business planning, construction, and marketing information. They also identify minority owned firms for contract and subcontract opportunities with federal, state, and local government agencies, and the private sector. The centers identify both private and public sector sources of financing for minority owned firms and assist with the preparation of financial documents and plans for submission to lenders. Contact the national headquarters at Minority Business Development Agency, 14th and Constitution, Washington, DC 20230; 202-482-3917; 888-324-1551; {www.mbda.gov}; {Email: help@mbda.gov}.

Free Help and Money for the Disabled

The Federal Government has stepped in and funded programs across the country to help the disabled and handicapped reach their goals by providing them with all kinds of services to get them on their way. The help available ranges from free information services, self help groups, free legal aid, and independent living programs, to free money for education, job training, living expenses, transportation, equipment, and mobility aids. You can even get money to have your home retrofitted to make it more accessible to you, given your specific handicap. And if you're denied any of these programs or services, there are several free sources of legal help that can get you what you're legally entitled to. Your state Vocational Rehabilitation office will evaluate your skills, needs, and goals, and work with you to keep you a productive member of society.

The Office of Disability Employment Policy {www.dol.gov/ odep} knows that people with disabilities have a strong interest in working for themselves. The U.S. Department of Labor has developed a new office call Small Business Self-Employment Service that links to other entrepreneurship sites, provides information on a variety of technical assistance resources, as well as resources for writing business plans, financing, and other issues. Contact: Small Business and Self-Employment Service, Job Accommodation Network, P.O. Box 6080, Morgantown, WV 26506; 800-526-6234; Fax: 304-293-5407; {www.jan.wvu.edu/SBSES}.

You can also learn about programs and activities in your state for people with disabilities who want to work by checking out {www.ssa.gov/work}. Also don't forget to check out the federal government's website {www.disability.gov} that lists all the government programs relating to disabilities.

Banks Friendly To Those In Need

The government supports certain banks and credit unions who help people who have trouble getting loans elsewhere, so they can make their dreams come true. The U.S. Department of Treasury's Community Development Financial Institutions (CDFI) Fund is designed to award money to banks in support of their activities benefiting needy communities across the county. These banks provide a range of financial products and services including: mortgage financing for first-time-home-buyers, financing for needed community facilities, commercial loans and investments to start or expand small businesses and more. To learn what CDFI Fund institutions are near you contact Community Development Financial Institutions Fund, 601 13th St., NW, Suite 200, Washington, DC 20005; 202-622-8662; Fax: 202-622-7754; {www.cdfifund.gov}.

Money For Americans With Disabilities

The Abilities Fund is a nationwide developer targeted exclusively to advancing entrepreneurial opportunities for Americans with disabilities. They deliver a combination of training, technical assistance services, and advisory supports to individuals with disabilities and the organizations that support them. For more information contact The Abilities Fund, 332 S. Linn St., Suite 15, Iowa City, IA 52240; 866-720-38631 319-338-2521; Fax: 319-338-2528; {www.abiltiesfund.org}.

Entrepreneurial Loans and Assistance

The goal of the National Community Reinvestment Coalition's CommunityExpress program is to provide financing and technical assistance to entrepreneurs who have been underserved by financial institutions. The SBA guarantees business loans, community-based organizations provide the technical support, and lenders compensate these groups for the cost of support. Eligible small businesses must be located in low-income areas, or owned by women, minorities or veterans. Contact National Community Reinvestment Coalition, 733 15th St., Suite 540, Washington, DC 20005; 202-628-8866; Fax: 202-628-9800; {www.ncrc.org}.

Help For DC Area Businesses

The Foundation for International Community Assistance (FINCA) works hard to help metropolitan

Washington DC entrepreneurs achieve economic and personal success. FINCA offers self-employment loans to business founders through its unique Village Banking program. The program offers market-rate loans and savings products to those who could not otherwise obtain them. Services in the DC area include monthly training classes in entrepreneurship, marketing strategies, and more. Contact FINCA International Inc., 1101 14th St., NW, 11th Floor, Washington, DC 20005; 202-682-1510, {www.villagebanking.org}.

Loans For Low-Income Entrepreneurs

Very low-income individuals can start their own businesses with the assistance of a loan from the Grameen Foundation USA. This international organization dedicated to stopping poverty administers a microcredit program for poor Americans looking to start a small or home-based commercial business. Contact

Grameen Foundation USA, 1029 Vermont Ave., NW, Suite 400, Washington, DC 20005; 202-628-3560; Fax: 202-628-3880; {www.gfusa.org}.

Money For Environmentalists

Entrepreneurs with a focus on environmental and energy conservation have a source of business funding in the Strategic Environmental Project Pipeline (StEPP) foundation. They specialize in finding loans and grants for renewable energy, energy efficiency or pollution prevention projects to be undertaken by emerging businesses. The program is primarily designed for businesses that have past the start-up stage and are looking to expand. Contact The StEPP Foundation, P.O. Box 468, Golden, CO 80402; 303-277-0932; Fax: 303-384-3636; {www.steppfoundation. org}.

$8,000 For a Car, School, Business, or Home

Over 500 programs run by nonprofit organizations will give you up to $5 for every $1 you place into a savings account that is used to complete a life goal like education, housing, starting a business, or even transportation. They are called Individual Development Accounts, and they are designed for people with little money to save. To find a program near you contact IDA Network, Corporation for Enterprise Development, 777 N. Capitol St., NE, Suite 800, Washington, DC 20002; 202-408-9788; {www.idanetwork.org}.

$700 Grant To Start Your Business

Trickle Up provides grants of $700 (in two installments) to people wishing to start a business. Frequently these businesses are based in the home. They provide business training and seed capital to low income individuals who want to become entrepreneurs. Trickle Up works with 250 different coordinating agencies to provide the business training necessary to receive this grant. To see if there is a program near you contact Trickle Up, 104 W. 27th St., 12th Floor, New York, NY 10001; 212-255-9980; 866-246-9980; Fax: 212-255-9974; {www.trickleup. org}.

Money For Youth Entrepreneurs

Young entrepreneurs can learn skills that can be translated into successful business ventures, better job opportunities, and enhanced real-world skills. They can also meet other entrepreneurs and successful business people, have access to PYEP facilities, and may be eligible for $15,000 in loans to assists the launching of a business. For information on where programs are located contact Prudential Young Entrepreneur Program, 240 Dr. Martin Luther King Jr. Blvd., Newark, NJ 07102; 973-643-4063; {www.njit-edc.org/PYEP.htm}.

$35,000 Loan For Your Business

The U.S. Small Business Administration's Microloan Program was developed for those times when just a small loan can make the real difference between success and failure. Under this program, loans range for less than $100 to $35,000. The SBA has made these funds This program is currently available in 44 states. To learn which nonprofit organizations in your area offer this program contact U.S. Small Business Administration, 409 3rd St., SW, Suite 8300, Washington, DC 20416; 800-8-ASK-SBA; {www.sba.gov}.

$1.3 Million To Help Your Business

The Certified Development Company (504) Loan Program is a financing tool for economic development. The 504 Program provides growing businesses with long-term fixed-rate financing for major fixed assets such as land and buildings. Funds can be used for purchasing land, and improvements, including existing buildings, grading, street improvements, utilities, parking lots and landscaping, construction of new facilitates or purchasing long-term machinery and equipment. To learn more about these programs contact U.S. Small Business Administration, 409 rd St., SW, Suite 8300, Washington, DC 20416; 800-8-ASK-SBA; {www.sba.gov}.

Business Incubators Can Be The Answer

A business incubator can come in many different shapes and forms. Typically an incubator provides basic office space and services at a reduced rate or is an exceptional value for the services provided. Generally a variety of sized office spaces are available, with the flexibility for growth. Since incubators are places where companies are encouraged to grow, many offer mentoring, business planning, accounting, and tax services, and more. To see if a business incubator is located near you contact National Business Incubation Association, 20 E. Circle Dr., #37198, Athens, OH 45701; 740-593-4331; Fax: 740-593-1996; {www.nbia.org}.

Cities And Counties Have Help

Cities and counties often offer economic development programs as well to help businesses get off the ground. Some have tax abatements or tax credits, others offer low-interest loans. Some programs are designed to improve the exterior of your building to help improve the look of the town. Contact your local economic development office to see what programs they may offer. Some examples include the following, although these are for businesses in these communities only:

❑ $2,500 Grant From The City Of Wilmington, Delaware: Office of Economic Development, 800 French St., Third Floor, Wilmington, DE 19801; 302-576-2120; {www.ci.wilmington.de.us}.

❑ $3,000 Grant to make your building prettier from: Pinellas County Community Development, 14 South Fort Harrison Ave., Suite 3050, Clearwater, FL 34616; 717-464-8210; {www.pced.org}.

❑ A Matching Grant of $4 for Every $1 You Save To Start A Business from The City of Savannah: Economic Development Department, 2 E. Bay Street, Savannah, GA 31401; 912-651-3653; {www.ci.savannah.ga.us}.

❑ $5,000 Forgivable Loan For Every Job You Create In Union County Iowa: Union County Development Association, 208 W. Taylor, P.O. Box 471, Creston, IA 50801; 641-782-2003; {www.ucda.us}.

❑ $15,000 Grant To Train Your New Employees In Jeffersontown, KY: Jeffersontown Economic Development, 10416 Watterson Trail, Jeffersontown, KY 40299;

502-267-8333; {www.jeffersontownky.com}.

❑ $20,000 Grant To Start A Business In Carroll County Maryland: Carroll County Department of Economic Development, 225 N. Center Street, Suite 101, Westminster, MD 21157; 410-386-2070; {www.carrollbiz.org}.

❑ $7,000 Grant To Fix Up Your Storefront In Boston, MA: Massachusetts City Economic Development, 2201 Washington Street, Roxbury, MA 02119; 617-989-9100; {www.city ofboston.gov/dnd/OBD}.

❑ Tax Increment Financing: Low-interest loans for interior and exterior renovation of existing commercial or retail structures in an Urban Renewal District. Economic Development Grants are available for the creation of well paying jobs in the city. City of Kalispell, 284 Third Avenue East, Kalispell, MT 59901; 406-758-7740; Fax: 406-758-7742; {www.kalispell.com/community}.

❑ The White Mountain Investor Alliance provides equity capital for business startup, expansion or recruitment opportunities in Grafton County. The Grafton County Economic Development Council offers business assistance to develop and structure a financing package when quality jobs are retained or created. Grafton County Economic Development Council, 20 Highland Street, Suite 2-5, Plymouth, NH 03264; 603-536-1273; Fax: 603-536-1291; {www.graftoncountyedc.org}.

❑ Real Property Tax Exemption: New and expanding businesses in the Empire Zone are eligible for certain exemptions from real property taxes. A refund or credit of local sales taxes paid on building materials used in the construction, improving or rehabilitating industrial and some commercial property. Ogdensburg Growth Fund Development Corporation offers low-interest loans for acquisition, renovation equipment and working capital. A special program for construction assistance may allow for short-term borrowing at 0% when permanent financing has been arranged. Ogdensburg Economic Development, 330 Ford Street, City Hall, Room 10, Ogdensburg, NY 13669; 315-393-7150; {www.ogdensburg. org/econ.html}.

❑ Agri-Business Loan Fund: 6% loans for small businesses in Delaware County with 5 or fewer employees. It is expected that 1 new job will be created for each $5,000 of requested loan funds. Microenterprise Business Training Program: Free fourteen three hour classes for qualifying entrepreneurs to help in the business planning process. Main Street Revitalization Loan Program: Low-interest loans of up to $25,000 are available to new and existing main street businesses. Site Location: The Economic Development Office will help you find the perfect site for your new or expanding business. Delaware County Department of Economic Development, 97 Main Street, Delhi, NY 13753; 607-746-8595; Fax: 607-746-8836; {www.co.

delaware.ny.us/depts/ecodev/eco dev.htm}.

❑ Training Grants: Reimbursement of up to 50% of training costs for new employees with a maximum of $1,000 per person. Local Tax Incentives: 50% abatement on real property taxes for the first year, decreasing 5% each year for a nine year period. Niagara Mohawk Power Corporation: Incentives to reduce initial utility costs. Warren County Economic Development Corporation, 234 Glen Street, Glen Falls, NY 12801; 518-761-6007; Fax: 518-761-9053; {www.warren county.org}.

❑ Site Location: Corvallis-Benton County Economic Development Partnership maintains a current listing of industrial sites available to meet the needs of your business. Import/Export Assistance is available through the Willamette International Trade Center, the World Trade Center in Portland and the Oregon International Trade Division. Access to Finances: Access to "Angel" investment through the Corvallis Venture Forum. Corvallis-Benton County Economic Development Partnership, 1600 SW Western Boulevard, Corvallis, OR 97333; 541-757-1507; Fax: 541-757-2556; {www.corvallisedp.com}.

❑ Façade Improvement Program: Grants of up to 20% of total renovation and new construction costs with a $10,000 maximum for façade improvements within the Pleasantburg Drive Corridor Plan Overlay District. Upper Story House Loan: Low interest loans to create or rehabilitate residential units in the upper stories of buildings in the Central Business District or the West End Tax Increment District. Business License Tax Abatement: A graduated 3-year abatement of the City business license fee for new corporate offices, manufacturing, research and development and technology services on a city-wide basis. City of Greenville Economic Development, P.O. Box 2207, Greenville, SC 29602; 864-467-4401; {www.greenville.com/development/eco_dev.asp}.

☐ The Amarillo Economic Development Corporation maintains a current listing of available sites to meet the needs of your business. Amarillo offers business incentives in the form of cash grants and interest-free loans to companies creating new jobs in Amarillo. Businesses constructing new industrial facilities may be eligible for local tax abatement. Amarillo Economic Development Corporation, Bank One Center, Suite 1503, 600 South Tyler, Amarillo, TX 79101; 806-379-6411; Fax: 806-397-0112; {www.amarillo-tx.com}.

☐ The Albany/Dougherty Economic Development offers economic information for businesses in the area. The Albany area is designated an Enterprise Zone and businesses in the community are eligible for incentives which include: Facility Bonds: up to $3 million in tax free bonds. Working Opportunity Tax Credits: up to $2,100 per employee. Low Interest Loans: loans at 75% of Prime rate. Georgia Counties Economic Councils, Albany/Dougherty Economic Development Commission, 225 West Broad Street, Albany, GA 31701; 229-434-0044; 800-475-8700; Fax: 229-434-8716; {www.albanyga.com}.

☐ The St. Charles Economic Development Department strives to create a business-friendly environment so that existing businesses will choose to expand in St. Charles and new businesses will locate there. Small Business Classes and Counseling: A variety of classes and counseling is available. Corridor Improvement Grants Program: The Corridor Improvement Grant Program is designed to help property owners on highly visible corridors with landscape improvements. St. Charles Economic Development Department, 2 E. Main Street, St. Charles, IL 60174; 630-443-4093; {www.stcharles.org/departments/edd/index.asp}.

$$$ In Facade Improvement Grants

Listed below are a dozen programs that will give you a good idea of the kinds of programs that are out there. These are just examples of grants being offered around the country. To find a program that you are eligible to receive, contact your local economic development department.

1)   2-Pages Gets You $50,000 Grant For Your Business
The Façade, Sign & Awning Grants Program offers dollar-for-dollar matching grants for exterior improvements and renovations

including signs and awnings. Eligible applicants must be a commercial or non-profit business in the Downtown Billings area. For additional information, contact the Downtown Billings Association, Inc., 2906 3rd Avenue North, Billings, MT 59103; 406-294-5060; {www.downtown billings.com/dbp/FacadeSignAwningG rantPage.html}.

2) $1,000 Grant + 5 Gallons of Free Paint to Fix Up Your Business

The Faquay-Varina Revitalization Association offers the Façade Incentive Grant Program for businesses in the historic downtown area of Faquay-Varina. The grant offers as much as 30% of the total cost of the project up to $1,000. In addition, the grant recipient is given 5 gallons of free paint to update the exterior of their buildings. For additional information, contact the Faquay-Varina Revitalization Association, 121 N Main St, Suite A, Fuquay-Varina, NC 27526; 919-552-0848; {www.fuquay-varinadowntown.com/id9.html}.

3) 1-Page Application Gets A $7,500 Grant For New Landscaping For Your Business

The Façade and Landscape Treatment Grant Program offers matching grants of up to $7,500 for façade and on-site landscaping. All eligible applicant businesses located in the Rockledge Community Redevelopment Agency District may apply. If you are interested, contact the Rockledge Community Redevelopment Agency, 1600 Huntington Lane, Rockledge, FL 32955; 321-757-3197; {www. chooserockledge.com/incentives.htm}.

4) $20,000 Grant To Fix Up Your Real Estate Investment

The Washington Convention Center Authority Historic Preservation Grant Program was administered by the National Trust for Historic Preservation organization. They received 500 inquiries, 267 applications, $1,655,265 grants requested, 73 grants totaling $584,845 were awarded, 65 grants completely funded. Look for similar programs in your area. You may also contact National Trust Historic Preservation, 1785 Massachusetts Avenue, NW, Washington, DC 20036-2117; 202-588-6000; {www.nationaltrust.org/co mmunity_partners/applicationinfo.html}.

5) $27,000 In Business Grants Goes Unclaimed

The City of Oneida won a state grant two years ago for downtown facades. Several merchants applied but not all of the money had been used. {www.syracuse.com/news/poststandar d/index.ssf?/base/news-7/110337 2392315630.xml}.

6) Renters Can Get A $2,500 Grant To Paint Their Store

The City of Baltimore offers matching grants of up to $2,500 for commercial revitalization in designated areas of Baltimore. Contact the Facade Improvement Grant Program Commercial Revitalization, Baltimore Development Corp, 36 S Charles Street, Suite 1600, Baltimore, MD 21201; 410-545-0153; {www.ci. baltimore.md.us/news/press/030624b.h tml}.

7) $10,000 Grant To Fix Up A Movie Theater

The Roseville Development Façade Grant Program provides 2:1 matching grants to business and property owners in the redevelopment area to improve their building façade. The maximum grant is $10,000. If you don't live in Roseville. If you do live in Roseville, contact the City of Roseville Economic

& Community Services Department, 311 Vernon Street, Roseville, CA 95678; 916-774-5270; {www.roseville.ca.us/upload/files/FacadeGrant2.pdf}.

8) ***2-Page Application For a $32,500 Grant To Build A Business***

Toledo's Core City Façade Grant Program improves exteriors of existing buildings within the downtown Overlay District and the Warehouse District. Grants of one-third of the investment up to $75,000, with a maximum grant of $32,000 are available. Contact the Dept of Economic & Community Development, 640 Jackson Street, One Government Center, Suite 1710, Toledo, OH 43604; 419-245-1470; {www.ci.toledo.oh.us/index.cfm?Dept=Dept3Nav&Page=Page4176}.

9) ***$37,000 Grant and 15 Hours of Free Architectural and Design Services***

Medford offers a Façade Grant Program to business and property owners that want to rehabilitate their commercial building facades in the designated area of Medford. Grants are 50/50 cost-share up to $37,500 with an additional 15 hours of free architectural design consultation. Contact Medford Urban Renewal Agency, 45 South Holly Street, Medford, OR 97501; 541-774-2700; {www.downtownmedford.com/Projects.asp?ProjectID=100}.

10) ***Schmitt's Watch Repair Received $1,000 Grant To Fix Up His Store***

The Façade Grant Program helped Schmitt's clean, repair the building and install canvas on the side of the

building through the City of Washington. Eligible businesses must be located in the designated area of Washington. For information, contact the City of Washington, NC, P.O. Box 1988, Washington, NC 27889; 252-75-9354; {www.wdnweb.com/articles/2004/11/20/news/news01.txt}.

11) ***2-Page Application For A $10,000 Grant To Fix Up Your Business***

The Façade Grants Program helps businesses located in the designated area of the City of Sumter. Grants may be used on the exterior of the building that is visible to the public. To see the grant application, check {www.sumter-sc.com/client_resources/departments/downtown/2005%20facade%20grant%20program.pdf}. For additional information, contact the Facade Grant Program, City of Sumter, Downtown Development Manager, 21 N Main Street, Sumter, SC 29150; 803-436-2535; {www.sumter-sc.com/Departments/DowntownSumter_Yesterday_Facade.aspx}.

12) ***Hoglunds Western Wear Received $750 Grant (up to this amount) To Set Up Internet Access***

Great Falls offers businesses in the downtown area, an incentive to install broadband Internet connections. For additional information, contact Broadband Internet Connectivity Grant, Great Falls Business Improvement District, Downtown Great Falls, 419 Central Avenue, Great Falls, MT 59401; 406-453-6151; {www.downtowngreatfalls.com/ws/aboutus3.php?page_id=4111&PHPSESSID=2d6bd22a94f1cf0a1ae99af37ab6ee38}.

HEALTH CARE

There are few in America that really know how to take advantage of the current health care system. Some of the best health care services are free or cost very little and are even available to millionaires.

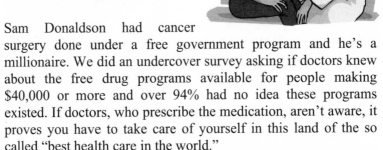

Sam Donaldson had cancer surgery done under a free government program and he's a millionaire. We did an undercover survey asking if doctors knew about the free drug programs available for people making $40,000 or more and over 94% had no idea these programs existed. If doctors, who prescribe the medication, aren't aware, it proves you have to take care of yourself in this land of the so called "best health care in the world."

There are thousands of free programs available for people of any income level. It's well documented that there are 6 million families eligible for free health care for their kids and don't apply. Four million seniors are eligible for an extra $1,000 to pay their health premiums, but don't apply. Over 29 million are eligible for free exams and don't take advantage of them. Here are some of the major programs you and your family can take advantage of immediately. If you are looking for thousands more like this, see our book, *Free Health Care* at {http://www.lesko.com/health/} or 1-800-955-POWER.

1) ***Get Health Information Better Than Your Doctor***
   Want to find out the latest information on your health condition? All you need to do is pick up the phone or go online to get the most up-to-date information from the government's team of health professionals. There is plenty

of free help available from government sponsored and non-profit organizations. Here is where you can go:

National Health Information Center
P.O. Box 1133
Washington, DC 20013
800-336-4797
www.health.gov/nhic

National Women's Health Information Center
U.S. Public Health Service
Office of Women's Health
1600 Clifton Rd., NE
Atlanta, GA 30333
800-944-WOMEN
www.4women.gov

National Institutes of Health,
Office of Communications
Building 1, Room 344
1 Center Dr., MCS 0188
Bethesda, MD 20892
301-496-4000
www.nih.gov

9000 Health Hotlines and Other Free Health Sources
http://healthhotlines.nlm.nih.gov/

2004 Toll-Free Numbers For Health Information
http://www.health.gov/NHIC/Pubs/tollfree.htm

2) *Self-Help Groups Teach You How To Beat The System*
They are certainly cheaper than a doctor visit, because they're free, and are probably a lot friendlier. In addition to offering advice on treatment options, they can be a great

source for learning the system and how to get the most from it. Here are some sources for finding a self-help group near you.

American Self-Help Clearinghouse
http://mentalhelp.net/selfhelp/

Self-Help Hotlines
http://mentalhelp.net/selfhelp/selfhelp.php?idx=44

Anxiety Disorders Self-Help Groups
Anxiety Disorders Association of America
www.adaa.org/Public/index.cfm

3) *Free Health Care When You Have No Insurance Coverage*
Healthcare centers around the country offer everything from mental health to dental services. Contact Health Resources and Services Administration, U.S. Department of Health and Human Services; 888-275-4772; {www.ask.hrsa.gov/Primary.cfm}. Another database, The Free Clinic Foundation of America, 1240 Third Street S.W, Roanoke, VA 24016; 540-344-8242; {www.freeclinic. net}.

4) *$2,000 Worth Of Free Prescription Drugs*
Make over $40,000 and get everything except Viagra. Drug companies do not want everybody to know this, but they will give certain people who cannot afford their medications their drugs free of charge. Your doctor needs to write a note to the drug companies stating that you cannot afford the prescriptions. Your doctor will also need to fill out a form, and then the company will ship the medications to your doctor's office. Contact Pharmaceutical Research and Manufacturers of America, 1100 15th St., NW, Washington, DC 20005; 800-PMA-INFO; {www.pharma.org}.

5) Non-Profits Will Pay For Health Expenses

There are thousands of non-profit organizations that provide help and even financial assistance to individuals and families who are suffering with most any illness or condition you can think of. You can get:

☐ $1,000 if you are suffering with pancreatic cancer to pay for transportation to treatment, medication or child care from Hirshberg Foundation, 800-813-4673, {www. pancreatic.org/html/financial. html}

☐ $3,000 for special expenses related to being a cancer patient from Cancer Care, 800-813-HOPE, {www. cancercare.org/FinancialNeeds/FinancialNeedsList.cfm? c=387}

☐ $750 for people who care for Alzheimer's patients from Alzheimer's Family Relief Programs; 800-437-AHAF; {http://198.63.60.19/afrp/guide.htm}

☐ $450 for an eye examination and eye glasses from Vision USA, 800-766-4466; {www.aoa.org/vision usa/}

☐ $1,000 to pay for rent, car repairs, handicap equipment or even horseback riding classes for families with seriously ill children, Kelly Anne Dolan Memorial Fund, 325-643-0763; {www. kadmf.org}

☐ $5,000 to purchase prosthetic limbs from The Barr Foundation, 561-394-6514; {www.oandp.com/resources/ organizations/barr/index2.htm}

You can look for relevant organizations by researching National Health Information Center, P.O. Box 1133, Washington, DC 20013, 800-336-4797, {www.health. gov/nhic}.

There is also a database of over 400 non-profit and government organizations that was set up to help families that have special needs when they are stuck with a health-related problem. It says it is for kids, but many of the organizations help anyone in need. Go to {www.bravekids.org} and take a look.

6) *$10,000 To Care For Grandma And Grandpa*

Does your mom need Meals on Wheels? Is she having trouble paying her bills? Need a new roof on the house? Grandma needs free legal help to divorce grandpa? Want to know what programs exist for seniors? All these questions and more can be found by contacting the Eldercare Hotline at 800-677-1116 or contact Administration on Aging, Washington, DC 20201; 202-619-0724; {www.eldercare.gov}.

7) *Emergency Rooms Have To Take You*

Emergency rooms are now required to provide an initial screening to assess a patient's condition, which is designed to stop the automatic transfer of people unable to pay. Emergency rooms must also treat emergency situations until they are stabilized, then they can refer you to other hospitals or clinics for further treatment. If you feel you have been denied service, contact Centers for Medicare and Medicaid Services, 7500 Security Blvd., Baltimore, MD 21244; 410-786-3000; {www.cms.hhs.gov}.

8) *Free Care By The Best Doctors In The World*

Bob Dole and Sam Donaldson knew where to go to get treatment - The National Institutes of Health (NIH). To see if your diagnosis is currently being studied, you can contact the Clinical Center, National Institutes of Health, Patient Recruitment, 6100 Executive Blvd., Suite 3C01, MSC 754, Bethesda, MD 20892; 301-496-2563; 800-411-1222; {www.cc.nih.gov}; National Institutes of Health, Office of Communications, Building 1, Room 344, 1 Center Dr., MCS 0188, Bethesda, MD 20892; 301-496-4000; {www.nih.gov};

or to search a database, contact CRISP, Office of Reports and Analysis, Office of Extramural Research, 6700 Rockledge Dr., Room 3210, Bethesda, MD 20892; 301-435-0656; {http:// crisp.cit.nih.gov}.

9) *$5,000 Worth Of Free Health Care For Kids*

Make up to $38,657 and get free health care for your kids. Almost every state now has a Children's Health Insurance Program (CHIPS), which extends medical coverage to many children who may not be covered. Contact your state Department of Health to see what version of the CHIPS program is offered in your area; or call a new government hotline to help locate free health care for kids at 877-KIDS-NOW (toll-free 877-543-7669); {www.insurekidsnow.gov}.

10) *Get An Extra $1,000 For Mom, Dad Or Grandparents*

Even if you're not a senior, check into this for your mom, dad or grandparents. Each year over 3 million eligible seniors and people with disabilities fail to apply for a program that will give them over $1,000 extra in their Social Security check. The program is called Qualified Medicare Beneficiaries Plan, or Specified Low-Income Medicare Beneficiaries Plan. Contact Social Security Office at 800-772-1213. You can also contact the Medicare Hotline and request the publication Guide to Health Insurance for People with Medicare; contact Medicare Hotline at 800-MEDICARE or online at {www.medicare.gov}.

11) *See If You Qualify For Your State Health Care Programs*

Every state has a number of health care programs that are paid for by the federal and state government funding. Most of the programs have income requirements, but the income can go up to $40,000 or more for a family. Every state has a number of programs to protect people in financial trouble.

There are programs to help pay for food, day care, and medical bills. {www.cbpp.org/1-14-04tanf.htm}.

12) *Free Help To Fight The Health Care System*

You can call government offices and advocacy groups that will help you fight the system. Before you call a lawyer, call these free offices first. Your state Insurance Commissioner will inform you of legal rights regarding insurance. Your state Medical Board will review your complaint and help resolve disputes. Your state HMO Board will also resolve disputes. Contact Patient Advocate Foundation, 700 Thimble Shoals Blvd., Suite 200, Newport News, VA 23606; 800-532-5274; {www.patientadvocate. org}.You can also use the Health Insurance Partnership program {www.healthassistancepartnership.org/site/Page Server?pagename=Program_Locator}.

13) *$2,000 To Pay Your Dental Bills*

There are close to 60 dental schools in the country that offer quality care at a fraction of the cost of private dentists. I used them for years. An $800 crown can cost you only $200. Sure you get a senior student, but you also get a professor who is better than most private practitioners. Contact {www. datreview.com/dentalschools.htm?source=overture}.

14) *Free Dental Care For Kids*

Many dentists will provide free dental care, according to an American Dental Association survey that states, "75% of its members provide charitable care." You can find free dental services offered in your state at {www.prnews wire.com/mnr/ada/10357}. Just click on your state. American Dental Association, 211 East Chicago Ave., Chicago, IL 60611-2678; 312-440-2500.

15) $20,000 Worth Of Free Alcohol And Drug Treatment

Georgia provides outpatient counseling services, short-term residential programs, and even school student assistance programs. A friend of mine received one- and two-week resident treatments for free in Maryland. So if you need help, keep looking for local free stuff or contact National Drug and Treatment Routing Service, Center for Substance Abuse Treatment, National Institute on Alcohol Abuse and Alcoholism (NIAAA), 600 Executive Blvd., Willco Bldg., Bethesda, MD 20892; 800-662-HELP; {www. niaaa.nih.gov}; or National Clearinghouse for Alcohol and Drug Information, 11426 Rockville Pike, Suite 200, Rockville, MD 20852; 800-729-6686; {www.health.org}.

16) Free Preventive Health Services For Seniors

A report for the U.S. Congress estimates that over 29 million seniors don't take advantage of free preventive health services like flu shots, tetanus shots, pap smear, mammography, vaginal cancer, colorectal cancer - colonoscopy, osteoporosis - bone mass measurement, prostate cancer test, and glaucoma test. They are all covered under the Medicare laws, but most doctors are not aware of this. Tell you senior friends to check it out at: {www.medicare.gov} or 800-633-4227.

Free Plastic Surgery For Children

Austin Smiles provides free reconstructive plastic surgery, mainly to repair cleft lip and palate, to the children around Austin, Texas. They do about 75 surgeries a year. Austin Plastic Surgery Foundation, P.O. Box 26694, Austin, TX 78755-0694; 512-451-9312; Fax: 512-451-9300; {www.austin.smiles.org}. To see if similar services are available anywhere near you contact Cleft Palate Foundation, 1504 East Franklin Street, Suite 102, Chapel Hill, NC 27514; 800-24-CLEFT; 919-933-9044; {www.cleftline.org}.

Discounts On Dental and Vision Care

If you live near a university that has a dental or optometry school, then you may be in luck. Many of these schools offer reduced fee services for dental care or vision screening. You will receive treatment from students, but they will be supervised by some of the best people in the field.

These schools also often conduct research studies, so if you qualify, you may be able to receive treatment for free. My eleven-year-old daughter gets glasses, contacts, plus free contact solution for three years, because she is part of a study on nearsightedness in children. Not a bad deal!

Contact American Dental Education Association, 1400 K Street, NW, Suite 1100, Washington, DC 20005: 202-289-7201; Fax: 202-289-7204; {www.adea.org}. Contact American Optometric Association, 243 N. Lindbergh Blvd., St. Louis, MO 63141; 314-991-4100; Fax: 314-991-4101; {www.aoa.org}.

Grants Up To $4,000 and Loans To Finance Adoptions
The National Adoption Foundation helps arrange loans and provides limited grants for parents to cover expenses before and after adoption. Contact: National Adoption Foundation, 100 Mill Plain Rd, Danbury, CT 06811; 203-791-3811; Fax: 203-791-3801; {www.nafadopt. org}.

The following organizations also provide free publications, referral services, advice on adoption and searching for birth relatives, financial help and tax credits available:
- **National Adoption Information Clearinghouse**, National Adoption Information Clearinghouse, Administration for Children and Families, 330 C Street, SW, Washington, DC 20447; 888-251-0075; 703-352-3488; Fax: 703-385-3206; {http://naic. acf.hhs.gov}.
- **National Adoption Center**, 1500 Walnut St, Suite 701, Philadelphia, PA, 19102; Answer

Line: 215-735-9988, 800-TO-ADOPT; {www. adopt.org}.
- **National Council For Adoption**, 225 N. Washington Street, Alexandria, VA 22314; 703-299-6633; Fax: 703-299-6004; {www.ncfa-usa.org}.

Camp WheezeAway Is Free For Kids With Asthma
Every year, about 100 kids with asthma, between 8 and 12 years of age, can go to summer camp for free in Jackson Gap, Alabama. Contact American Lung Association of Alabama, 3125 Independence Dr., Suite 325, Birmingham, AL 35209; 205-933-8821; Fax: 205-930-1717; {www.ala bamalung.org}.

For more information on other camps for children with asthma, Contact The American Lung Association, 61 Broadway, 6th Floor, New York, NY 10006; 212-315-8700; 800-LUNG-USA; {www.lungusa.org}.

Free Flu Shots
Who should get flu shots? The U.S. Center for Disease Control recommends it for specific groups of people. Almost anyone can get free or low cost flu shots from their county health office or other community sources. Some doctors, like Dr. Donald McGee in New Hampshire {www.drmcgee.com}, offer free shots in their office. Medicare Part B pays for flu shots. Contact your county office of public health listed in your telephone book or your state Department of Health. Contact

National Immunization Information Hotline at 800-232-4636; {www.cdc.gov/nip}.

Kids Get Free Expert Care At 22 Hospitals

Children suffering from orthopedic injuries, diseases of the bones, joint and muscles, or burns can get free treatment from one of the 22 Shriners Hospitals. The requirements for admission are that the child is under the age of 18, and there is a reasonable possibility the condition can be helped. Contact Shriners Hospitals, 2900 Rocky Point Dr., Tampa, FL 33607-1460; 813-281-0300; 800-237-5055; {www. shrinershq.org}.

Free Speech Therapy For Toddlers

You can have your child tested to see if any speech problems are developing and even get free speech therapy. The U.S. Individuals with Disabilities Education Act (IDEA) assures that children in need receive special education beginning on their third birthday, and in some states, it starts at age 2. The program is run through your local school district, so check with them, or your state Department of Education. Contact Office of Special Education and Rehabilitative Services, U.S. Department of Education, 400 Maryland Ave., SW, Washington, DC 20202; 202-245-7468; {www.ed.gov/about/offices/list/osers/index.html}.

$2,000 Worth Of Dental Care For Seniors and Disabled

The National Foundation of Dentistry for the Handicapped started the Donated Dental Services program to help disabled and elderly persons who are low-income by matching them with volunteer dentists. Volunteer dentists agree to treat one or two people each

year with dental problems, and dental laboratories also donate services. The Dental House Call project has been started where dentists will come to you. Contact National Foundation of Dentistry for the Handicapped, 1800 15th St., Suite 100, Denver, CO 80202; 303-534-5360, Fax: 303-534-5290; {www.nfdh.org}.

Grants For Vision Care

The Pearle Vision Foundation offers grants to nonprofit organizations for vision-care assistance. Vision-related services include, eye exam & eyeglass assistance programs, and programs that improve the quality of life for the visually impaired. Contact Pearle Vision Foundation, 2465 Joe Field Road, Dallas, TX 75229; 972-277-6191; {www.pearle vision.com}.

Sightless Get Free Seeing Eye Dogs, Training, Travel and Air Fare

Pilot Dogs gives its trained dogs to the blind at no charge. They also include four weeks of training and will pay for room and board, all equipment, and round trip transportation. Other groups provide similar services:

- *Pilot Dogs, Inc.*, 625 West Town Street, Columbus, OH 43215; 614-221-6367; Fax: 614-221-1577; {www.pilotdogs.org}.
- *Guide Dog Foundation for the Blind, Inc*, 371 East Jericho Tpke., Smithtown, NY 11787-2976; 800-548-4337; 631-930-9000; Fax: 631-361-5192; {www.guide dog.org}.

Free Help— For The First 3 Weeks After Childbirth

The Healthy Families America Project helps new mothers cope with the pressures of being a new parent by offering volunteer home visitors. They can show you how to deal with the physical, emotional and financial strains of a new baby. Contact Healthy Families America, 200 S. Michigan Ave., Suite 1700, Chicago, IL 60604; 312-663-3520; Fax: 312-939-8962; {www.healthyfamilies america.org}.

Free Wheelchairs

Easter Seals, the American Cancer Society and other helpful organizations provide free wheelchairs and other medical related equipment. Some programs require deposits that are refundable. Contact your local Easter Seals or American Cancer Society. You can also contact your state Department of Health.

- American Cancer Society, Inc., 1599 Clifton Road, NE, Atlanta, GA 30329-4251; 800-ACS-2345; {www.cancer.org}.

- Easter Seals, 230 West Monroe Street, Suite 1800, Chicago, IL 60606; 800-221-6827; 312-726-6200; Fax: 312-726-1494; TTY: 312-726-4255; {www.easterseals.com}.

Alcohol and Drug Abuse Counseling & Treatment

Georgia provides outpatient counseling services, short-term residential programs, and even student assistance programs. Florida provides substance abuse treatment programs through a partnership with not-for-profit community providers. Contact your state Department of Health to see what your state has to offer. Contact Center for Drug-Free Living in Orlando, Florida P.O. Box 538350, Orlando, FL 32853-8350; 407-245-0012; Fax: 407-245-0011; {www.cfdfl.com}.

- ◆ *National Drug and Treatment Routing Service*, Substance Abuse

and Mental Health Services Administration's (SAMHSA), National Institute on Alcohol Abuse and Alcoholism (NIAAA), 5635 Fishers Lane, MSC 9304, Bethesda, Maryland 20892-9304; 800-662-HELP; {www.niaaa.nih.gov/other/referr al.htm}.

- ◆ *The National Clearinghouse for Alcohol and Drug Information*, 11420 Rockville Pike, Suite 200, Rockville, MD 20852; 800-729-6686 24 hours a day; 800-487-4889 TDD; {www.health.org}.

Make Over $40,000 And Get Free Health Care For Your Kids

Over 10 million children are eligible for this program and are not enrolled. Most states have the Children's Health Insurance Program (CHIPS) which extends medical coverage to many children who may not be covered. A family of four living in Connecticut can make up to $43,240 and still qualify to get free health care for the kids. A family of four making $55,200 can join a health care program for their children and pay only $30 per month.

Benefits and eligibility vary from state to state, so check with your state. Call 1-877-KIDS-NOW for more information about the Children's Health Insurance Program or check out the Insure Kids Now website at {www.insurekidsnow.gov}.

Free Care Even If You Don't Qualify

You or your child may still be able to get free health care from local government programs even if you don't qualify. Many local health offices have the authority to stretch the rules if they see fit. These offices can direct you to local nonprofit organizations or groups that can give you the care you need at the price you can afford. Contact your county office of public health listed in your telephone book or your state Department of Health

Free Mammograms /Free Tests For Breast and Cervical Cancer

An estimated half a million will lose their lives from breast or cervical cancer in the next decade. Screening could prevent up to 20% of these deaths for women over 40. The government's Center for Disease Control maintains a state-by-state program to establish access to screening and follow-up services. To find the program contact for your state, go to {www.cdc.gov/cancer/nbccedp/ contacts.htm}. Each state runs their program a little differently.

Contact your county office of public health listed in your telephone book or your state Department of Health. Contact Division of Cancer Prevention and Control, National Center for Chronic Disease Prevention and Health Promotion, Center for Disease Control and Prevention, 4770 Buford Highway, NE, MS K-64, Atlanta, GA 30341, 770-488-4751; 888-842-6355; Fax: 770-488-4760; {www.cdc.gov/ cancer/nbccedp/}.

More Free Mammograms

Not all insurance companies pay for mammograms, and not every woman

is eligible for the government's program described earlier. The following organizations can help you identify free and low cost mammograms in your area.

1) The American Cancer Society: 800-ACS-2345; {www.cancer.org}.
2) YWCA's Encore Plus Program: 800-95-EPLUS
3) National Cancer Institute: 800-4-CANCER; {www.nci.nih.gov}
4) State Office of Breast and Cervical Cancer: contact your state Department of Health
5) October is National Breast Cancer Awareness Month: many mammogram facilities offer their services at special fees during this period. {www.nbcam.org/ index.cfm}.
6) Medicare: 800-MEDICARE.

Free Hospital Care

Don't have money for your gall bladder surgery? What about that hospital visit you had two months ago? You might not have to pay a cent. Call the Hill-Burton Hotline. Certain hospitals and other health care facilities provide free or low-cost medical care to patients who cannot afford to pay. You may qualify even if your income is up to double the Poverty Income Guidelines. That's $36,200 for a family of four! You can apply before or after you receive care, and even after the bill has been sent to a collection agency.

Call the Hotline to find out if you meet the eligibility requirements and to request a list of local hospitals who are participating. Contact Hill-Burton Hotline, Health Resources and Services Administration, U.S. Department of Health and Human Services, Parklawn Building, 5600

Fishers Lane, Rockville, MD 20857; 800-638-0742; 800-492-0359 (in MD); {www.hrsa.gov/osp/dfcr/about/aboutdiv.htm}.

Free Food At School For Your Kids

A 1998 Tufts University study states: "Children who participate in the U.S. Department of Agriculture's School Breakfast Program were shown to have significantly higher standardized achievement test scores than eligible non-participants. Children getting school breakfasts also had significantly reduced absence and tardiness rates."

Your child can get a free breakfast at participating schools at one income level ($23,920 for a family of four) and at a reduced fee at another level ($34,040 for a family of four). Families who pay full price still get a bargain. Lunch is also available under the U.S. Department of Agriculture's National School Lunch program at 98,800 schools serving 26 million children. The same general requirements apply to both programs.

Contact your local School Food Service Authority in your school system. If all this fails, contact your state Department of Education. Check out the Food and Nutrition Services web page at {www.fns.usda.gov/fns}.

Rich Kids Pay 2 Cents For Half-Pint of Milk

Milk at this price is available to students, no matter what the family income, at over 7,000 schools, 1,300 summer camps, and 562 non-residential child care institutions. The program is called the **Special Milk Program**. Ask your school if they participate, or contact your local School Food Service Authority in your

school system. If all this fails, contact your state Department of Education.

Low Cost Immunizations for Travelers

In order to prevent contracting diseases like yellow fever, cholera or Japanese encephalitis when traveling in other countries, the government's Center for Disease Control recommends certain vaccines. Some local Public Health offices offer these vaccines at a fraction of what you would pay at a doctor's office.

To find your local county office of health, look in your telephone book or contact your state Department of Health. Contact Center for Disease Control and Prevention, National Center for Infectious Diseases, Division of Global Migration and Quarantine, 1600 Clifton Road, MS E-03, Atlanta, GA 30333; 877-394-8747; 404-639-3534; {www.cdc.gov/travel/}.

How To Fight Your Doctor, Hospital, Or Insurance Company — Call The Marines

Well, not the actual Marines from the Department of Defense, dressed in fatigues and armed with high tech weapons. But you can call other government offices and advocacy groups that will do your fighting for you or give you the needed weapons to do your own fighting.

Before you call a lawyer, call these free offices first:
☐   State Insurance Commissioner: will help you learn your legal rights regarding insurance.

☐ State Medical Boards: will review your complaint and help resolve disputes.

☐ State HMO boards: will review your complaint and help resolve disputes.

☐ Center for Medicare Advocacy, Inc, P.O. Box 350, Willimantic, CT 06226; 800-262-4414 (toll free in Connecticut); 860-456-7790; 202-216-0028; {www.medicareadvocacy.org}. Free legal help for elderly and disabled who are unfairly denied Medicare coverage in the state of Connecticut. Legal help is also available to residents outside of Connecticut for a fee.

☐ American Self Help Clearinghouse, Mental Help Net, St. Clares Health Services, 25 Pocono Road, Denville, NJ 07834-2995; 973-625-3037; {www.mentalhelp.net/selfhelp}

☐ National Self-Help Clearinghouse, Graduate School and University Center of the City University of New York, 365 5th Ave., Suite 3300, New York, NY 10016; 212-817-1822; {www.selfhelpweb.org}

☐ Patient Advocate Foundation, 700 Thimble Shoals Boulevard, Suite 200, Newport News, VA 23606; 800-532-5274; Fax: 757-873-8999; {www.patientadvocate.org}

Fund Helps Foster Independence of Physically Disabled

Individuals with physical disabilities residing in Oregon may be eligible to receive financial assistance through the Blanche Fisher Foundation. The fund assists with the expense of hearing aids, eyeglasses, wheelchairs, ramps, tuition and skills training. Contact

Blanche Fisher Foundation, 1511 SW Sunset Blvd., Suite 1-B, Portland, OR 97239; 503-819-8205; Fax: 503-246-4941; {www.bff.org}.

Working People With Disabilities Can Get Cheap Health Insurance

A change to the Balanced Budget Act of 1997 passed by Congress allows states to offer Medicaid to individuals who are working and who have a disability. Contact your state Department of Health to identify your Medicaid office. You can also check out the website of the Bazelon Center for Mental Health Law at {www.bazelon.org}.

Grants and Fundraising Help For Transplant Patients

National foundations can assist patients, their families, and friends in raising significant amounts of money for the patient's transplant care when there is no public or private insurance that will cover all the costs. They also provide grants to help pay for medications, or money for transplant-related emergencies, and one-time assistance grants of $1,000.

☐ National Foundation for Transplants, 1102 Brookfield, Suite 200, Memphis, TN 38119; 800-489-3836, 901-684-1697, Fax: 901-684-1128; {www.transplants.org}.

☐ National Transplant Assistance Fund, 3475 West Chester Pike, Suite 230, Newtown Square, PA 19073; 800-642-8399; 610-353-9684; Fax: 610-353-1616; {www.transplantfund.org}.

☐ American Liver Foundation, 75 Maiden Lane, Suite 603, New York, NY 10038; 800-GO LIVER; 888-4HEP-USA; 212-

668-1000; Fax: 212-483-8179; {www.liverfoundation.org}.

Assistance to Children of Emergency Medical Technicians

Medical and dental assistance is available to children under the age of 18 through the Eagles Memorial Foundation, Inc. Educational Assistance not to exceed $6000/yr. or $30,000/4 yrs. is available through the Eagles Memorial Foundation. These benefits are offered to children of members of the Fraternal Order of Eagles and the Ladies Auxiliary who die from injuries or diseases incurred while in military service; while serving as a volunteer law enforcement officer, volunteer firefighter, or volunteer emergency medical service (EMS) officer; or in the commission of their daily employment.

Contact Eagles Memorial Foundation, Inc., 4710 14th St. W., Bradenton, FL 34207; 941-775-1976; Fax: 941-758-4042; {www.foe.com/memorial}.

Free Transportation To Medical Appointments

Mom has to get to a doctor's visit in the middle of the day and you can't take her. Or you have a disability that may cause you to miss an appointment if someone else doesn't drive. You may be able to get free transportation and escort services provided by either your local health office or local office on aging. Some communities even provide very low cost door-to-door services for seniors to go anywhere.

If you can't find your local area agency on aging or public health office in your telephone book, contact your state Department of Aging or Health. Contact the Eldercare Locator Hotline

at 1-800-677-1116; {www.eldercare. gov/Eldercare/Public/Home.asp}.

Cancer Patients Receive Help with Expenses

Limited financial assistance is available nationwide through Cancer Care, Inc. to cancer patients and their families for home care, child care and transportation expenses. Contact Cancer Care, Inc., 275 7th Ave., 22nd Floor, New York, NY 10001; 800-813-HOPE; 212-712-8080; Fax: 212-712-8495; {www. cancercare.org}.

Low Cost Home Health Care

Montgomery County in Maryland provides home health care free or on a sliding scale, depending on income, through the local public health office. You don't have to be a senior to qualify. Contact your county office of health listed in your telephone book or your state Department of Health. For similar services for seniors, contact your local area agency on aging or your state Department on Aging. If that fails, contact the Eldercare Locator hotline at 1-800-677-1116.

Free Insurance Counseling

Free one-on-one counseling is available to seniors and, in most areas, people with disabilities, to answer questions like:

- How much insurance is too much?
- If something sounds like fraud, where can I go for help?
- What's the best Medigap insurance plan?

The program is called **Health Insurance Counseling and Advocacy Program (HICAP)** and is sponsored by the Centers for Medicare & Medicaid Services. In most states, it is usually run by the state Department on Aging or the State Insurance Commissioner's office. If that fails, contact the Eldercare Locator hotline at 1-800-677-1116.

Free Health Insurance

Health insurance can be quite confusing, but you may qualify for help. Medicaid helps low income people pay for medical bills, doctor visits, and even prescription drugs. This program covers approximately 40 million individuals including children, the aged, blind and/or disabled, and those who are eligible for federally assisted income maintenance payments. Services include: inpatient hospital, outpatient, physician services, medical and surgical dental services, family planning, laboratory services and prenatal care. People that receive SSI benefits are automatically eligible for Medicaid benefits in most states. Income and resource guidelines must be met for an individual, couple, or family to qualify. Some services not covered by Medicare: medicine, nursing home care, eye exams, glasses, transportation for medical care, and other medical services, may be paid for under the Medicaid program. Each State establishes their own eligibility standards and administers their own program. For a list of each State's Medicaid toll-free phone number, go to {www.cms.hhs.gov/medicaid/statemap.asp}. To view the Federal poverty limits, go to {www.cms.hhs.gov/medicaid/eligibility/}.

For more information, or to find information on each State's Medicaid program, check out the Centers for Medicare and Medicaid Services (CMS) {www.cms.hhs.gov}. You can contact the lead agency at CMS, 7500 Security Boulevard, Baltimore, MD 21244-1850; 410-786-3000; 877-267-2323; TTY: 866-226-1819 or 410-786-0727.

$$$$$ Money To Buy A Van, A Talking Computer Or Rubber Door Knob Grips

People with disabilities now have a place to learn about how the latest in technology can improve their lives. It can be a specially equipped van, a talking computer, a special kitchen or eating aid or adaptive toys for children.

A project funded by the U.S. Department of Education, called Technical Assistance Project has established an office in each state that can provide: information services, epipment loan program, recycling program, funding and loan information.

Contact your state Office of Social Services or Vocational Rehabilitation. Contact Rehabilitation Engineering and Assistive Technology Society of North America, (RESNA), 1700 North Moore Street, Suite 1540, Arlington, VA 22209-1903; 703-524-6686; Fax: 703-524-6630; TTY: 703-524-6639; {www.resna.org}.

Free Take Out For Seniors

People 60 and over who are homebound because of illness, incapacity, or disability, or who are otherwise isolated can receive hot meals delivered to their home. The program is funded in every state by the Older Americans Act. Contact your local area agency on aging or your state Department on Aging. If that fails, contact the Eldercare Locator hotline at 1-800-677-1116; {www. eldercare.gov/eldercare/Public/Home.a sp}.

Free Hepatitis B Shots

Oswego County Health Department offers free shots for children 18 and younger. The same with Buena-Vista County in Iowa, but people 19 and over are charged $31.75 for the shot. However, you won't be turned away if you cannot pay. Contact the county office of health listed in your telephone book or your state Department of Health, or call CDC's Immunization Information Hotline at 800-232-2522.

Free Computers to People With Disabilities

Washington State chapter of Easter Seals has a free loan program, and the chapters in Missouri offer computer classes. Contact your local Easter Seals Society to see what they may offer in the way of computers and computer skills for people with disabilities. If you can't find your local office, contact: Easter Seals, 230 West Monroe Street, Suite 1800, Chicago, IL 60606; 800-221-6827; 312-726-6200; Fax: 312-726-1494; TTY: 312-726-4258; {www. easterseals.com}.

Free & Low Cost Dental Care

Many of the local health offices provide dental services to children and to income-eligible adults on a sliding fee scale. Contact your county office of health listed in your telephone book or your state Department of Health.

Many states have special free or discount services just for seniors. Contact your local Area Agency on Aging or your state Department on Aging. If that fails, contact the Eldercare Locator Hotline at 1-800-677-1116; {www.eldercare.gov/ eldercare/Public/Home.asp}.

Service Organizations Provide Free Care

Need help with child care, elderly services, substance abuse treatment? What about youth programs or disaster assistance? Many large service organizations have local offices that provide all this and more. Services vary depending upon the needs of the community, but before you fight your battles alone, contact these main offices to find out about local programs:

- *Catholic Charities USA*, 1731 King St., Alexandria, VA 23314; 703-549-1390; Fax: 703-549-1656; {www. catholiccharitiesusa.org}.
- *Salvation Army*, 615 Slaters Lane, P.O. Box 269, Alexandria, VA 22313; 703-684-5500; 800-SAL-ARMY; Fax: 703-684-3478; {www.salvation armyusa.org}.
- ◆ *United Way of America*, 701 N. Fairfax St., Alexandria, VA 22314; 800-411-UWAY; 703-836-7112; {www.unitedway.org}.

Money For New Hearing Aids

You can get information on hearing loss, lists of hearing professionals, and information on locating financial assistance for assistive hearing devices by calling The Better Hearing Institute, 515 King St., Suite 420, Alexandria, VA 22314, P.O. Box 1840, Washington, DC 20013; 800-EAR-

WELL; 703-684-3391; Fax: 703-684-6048; {www. betterhearing.org}.

Are You Eligible for Free Health Care?

Health insurance can be quite confusing. What exactly do you qualify for? Medicare is a health insurance program, generally for people age 65 or older who are receiving *Social Security* retirement benefits. You can also receive Medicare if you are under 65 and receive Social Security or Railroad Retirement Board disability benefits for 24 months, or if you are a kidney dialysis or kidney transplant patient.

Medicaid is a federal program administered by each state, so eligibility and benefits vary from state to state. The program is administered by a state welfare agency, and it provides health insurance to people with low income and limited assets.

To determine your eligibility, contact your state Office of Social Services by checking the website below. For Medicare eligibility, contact Medicare Hotline, Centers for Medicare & Medicaid Services, 7500 Security Blvd., Baltimore, MD 21244-1850; 800-MEDICARE; {www.medicare.gov}

Free Eye Care

If you or someone you love needs eye care, but cannot afford it, the following organizations can help:

- *Seniors EyeCare Program*, EyeCare America, 655 Beach

Street, San Francisco, CA 94142; 415-561-8500; 800-222-3937; Fax: 415-561-8567; {www.eye careamerica.org/eyecare}.

- *VISION USA*, American Optometric Association, 243 North Lindbergh Blvd., St. Louis, MO 63141; 314-991-4100; 800-766-4466; Fax: 314-991-4101; {www.aoanet.org}.

- *Lions Clubs International*, 300 West 22nd St., Oak Brook, IL 60523-8842; 630-571-5466; {www.lionsclubs.org}.

- *EyeCare America – Glaucoma EyeCare Program*, EyeCare America, 655 Beach Street, San Francisco, CA 94142; 415-561-8500; 800-391-EYES; Fax: 415-561-8567; {www.eyecare america.org/eyecare}.

Free Help For Cancer Families

Local chapters of the American Cancer Society sponsor a wide range of services for cancer patients and their families, including self-help groups, transportation programs, and lodging assistance for those who must travel far for treatment.

Contact American Cancer Society, 1599 Clifton Rd., NE, Atlanta, GA 30329-4251; 800-ACS-2345; {www. cancer.org}.

Financial Assistance for Ill Registered Nurses

Nurses House, Inc. offers short-term financial assistance to ill and indigent U.S. Registered Nurses to help meet basic living expenses. Costs of medical and educational expenses are not funded. Contact Nurses House, Inc., 2113 Western Ave., Suite 2, Guilderland, NY 12084-9559; 518-

456-7858; Fax: 518-452-3760; {www.
nurseshouse.org}.

Discounts On Bike Helmets

You can start with a free *Toolkit for
Helmet Promotion Programs* from
Bicycle Helmet Safety Institute, 4611
Seventh Street South, Arlington, VA
22204-1419; 703-486-0100; Fax 703-
486-0576; {www.helmets.org}. This
organization will also send you a free
copy of *A Consumer's Guide to
Bicycle Helmets.*

Eye Care Helpline

The Eye Care Helpline puts callers in
touch with local ophthalmologists who
have volunteered to provide medical
eye care at no out-of-pocket expense.
Individuals must be 65 or older and not
have had access to an ophthalmologist
within the past three years. The
emphasis of this program is to help
disadvantaged people. For more
information, contact Seniors EyeCare
Program, EyeCare America, 655
Beach Street, San Francisco, CA
94142; 415-561-8500; 800-222-3937;
Fax: 415-561-8567; {www.eyecare
america.org/ eyecare}.

Spinal Cord Injuries Help

The William Heiser Foundation for the
Cure of Spinal Cord Injuries, Inc.
provides general welfare assistance to
individuals with spinal cord injuries
residing in the Wantagh, New York
area. Contact: William Heiser
Foundation for the Cure of Spinal
Cord Injuries, 3434 Hawthorne Dr N,
Wantagh, NY 11793; 516-826-9747;
{www .theheiserfoundation.org}.

Money For Dental Bills

Dental care can be expensive, and
therefore cost-prohibitive to many
families. In Colorado, Denver's Kids
In Need Of Dentistry program (KIND)

offers free or discounted care. KIND,
2465 S. Downing, Suite 207, Denver,
CO 80210; 303-733-3710; 877-544-
KIND; {www.kindsmiles. org}.

Quantum Foundation in Florida has
developed an orthodontic program for
low-income residents which reduces
the price for braces in half;
{www.quantumfnd.org}. The Scioto
County Community Action
Organization in Ohio has a Center for
Dental Wellness for low-income
children and their families. Contact:
Center for Dental Wellness, 1112
Gallia Street, Portsmouth, OH 45662;
740-351-0880.

Contact your local dental society or
community action agency to see what
may be available in your area.

$$ To Pay Your Shrink Bills

Many people are suffering needlessly
because they think they cannot afford
to see a mental health professional. It
is estimated that over 38 million
people think that they cannot afford
the high cost of mental health care.
Before all hope is lost, here is a listing
of options to pursue:

♦ Private Health Insurance- Most
health insurance policies cover
mental health care cost.

♦ Community Mental Health
Centers- often offer services for
free or on a sliding fee scale.

♦ Religious Organizations- Many
churches, synagogues, and other
religious agencies offer pastoral
counseling.

If you have Medicare or Medicaid,
mental health services are covered.

For more information contact the
following organizations:

♦ *National Mental Health Services*,
Knowledge Exchange Network,

, P.O. Box 42557, Washington, DC 20015; 800-789-2647; TDD: 866-889-2647; {www.mental health.org}.

♦ *American Association of Pastoral Counselors*, 9504-A Lee Highway, Fairfax. VA 22031; 703-385-6967; {www. aapc.org}.

♦ *American Self-Help Clearinghouse*, Saint Clares Hospital, 100 E. Hanover Ave., Cedar Knolls, NJ 07927; 973-326-6789; {www.mentalhelp. net/selfhelp}.

♦ *National Alliance for the Mentally Ill*, Colonial Place Three, 2107 Wilson Blvd., Suite 300, Arlington, VA 22201; 800-9506264; {www.nami.org}.

♦ *National Empowerment Center*, 599 Canal St., Lawrence, MA 01840; 800-769-3728; {www. power2u.org}.

♦ *National Mental Health Consumers Self-Help Clearinghouse*, 1211 Chestnut St., Suite 1207, Philadelphia, PA 19107; 800-553-4539; {www. mhselfhelp.org}.

Financial Help For Caregivers

The Alexandria Division of Social Services offers financial benefits for caregivers of children and adolescents with disabilities. Check your local, city, county or state for financial benefits for which you may qualify.

Free Contraceptives

Well there is not going to be a big "Free Condoms Come and Get'em" sign, but the federal government does provide family planning services under the Title X program. Services are delivered through a network of 4,600 community-based clinics that include

state and local health departments, hospitals, university health centers, Planned Parenthood affiliates, independent clinics and public and non-profit agencies. These clinics provide contraceptive services, infertility services, pregnancy tests, test and treatment for sexually transmitted diseases, and more. Publications are available on a variety of topics, and include titles such as *What You Should Know About The Male Condom, What You Should Know About The Pill*, and *What You Should Know About Abstinence*.

Contact Office of Population Affairs Clearinghouse, P.O. Box 30686, Bethesda, MD 20824; 301-654-6190; {http://opa.osophs.dhhs.gov}. For publications, call 866-640-PUBS.

Free Health Care For Seniors And The Disabled

Over 16,000 seniors live in centers operated by the Salvation Army, as do 1,600 disabled adults. The Salvation Army operates hospitals and clinics throughout the world to provide healthcare for those in need. They even provide homes for those recently discharged from the hospital and need more recovery time.

Contact the Salvation Army Office near you, or Salvation Army National Headquarters, 615 Slaters Lane, P.O. Box 269, Alexandria, VA 22313; 703-684-5500; {www.salvation army.org}.

Low-Cost Health Care For Native Americans

The Indian Health Service provides healthcare services to over 1.5 million Native Americans and Alaskan Natives at a reduced charge. Services include hospital, medical and dental care, environment health and sanitation services, outpatient services, mobile clinics, public health nurses, and preventive care, including immunizations. They cover approximately 60% of the costs.

The website provides links to local area offices and facilities. To receive these services you must be a member of a federally recognized tribe.

Contact Indian health Service, 801 Thompson Ave., Suite 400, Rockville, MD 20852; 301-443-3024; Help Desk: 888-830-7280; {www.ihs.gov}.

Abortions Starting At $250

Some of the 850 Planned Parenthood clinics offer abortions during the first 14 weeks of pregnancy starting at $225 for those not covered by health insurance. In some cases they even have special funds to help women pay for services.

To investigate what your local clinic offers, call 1-800-230-PLAN. Contact Planned Parenthood Federation of America, 434 West 33rd Street, New York, NY 10001; 212-541-7800, Fax:

212-245-1845; {www.plannedparent hood.org}. There is another consumer hotline that can also handle your abortion related questions: Contact The National Abortion Federation, 1755 Massachusetts Ave., NW, Suite 600, Washington, DC 20036; 800-772-9100 or in Canada 800-424-2282; {www. prochoice.org/}.

$$ To Pay Your Alcohol Rehab Bills

Treatment of alcohol abuse can cost you thousands of dollars. The Salvation Army has 152 homes and centers for the treatment of those suffering from alcoholism, as well as many other drug rehabilitation programs.

Contact the Salvation Army Office near you, or Salvation Army National Headquarters, 615 Slaters Lane, P.O. Box 269, Alexandria, VA 22313; 703-684-5500; {www.salvation army.org}.

468 Sources To Pay Emergency Expenses

Not sure where to turn or what resources exist for you? Bravekids.org has put together a resource directory of 468 sources for financial and other types of assistance for those with disabled children or adults or low-income families in need. It could be anything from paying your utility bill to respite care or medical expenses. Check out {www.bravekids. org}.

Free Health Care For Moms and Kids

Are you pregnant or the parent of young children? Do you have a child with special needs? Free maternal and child health services available include prenatal care, well-child care, dental services, immunizations, family planning, vision and hearing screenings, and much more. Each state has some latitude as to how they spend the money. The Maternal and Child Health Division of your state Department of Health is responsible for administering the funds.

Federal law requires that all states provide Medicaid to pregnant women and children through the age of six whose income does not exceed 133% of the poverty line. Many states have additional benefits for children and programs for children with special needs. The following are examples of states that have extended Medicaid coverage:

☐ Minnesota: covers everyone with income below 225% of the federal poverty line, or about $50,000 for a family of four.

☐ Vermont: all children under eighteen with family incomes below 300% of the federal poverty line, or about $54,000 for a family of four.

☐ Washington: all children to age eighteen with family incomes 100% of federal poverty line, or about $15,020 for a family of four.

To find out more about the programs available in your state, call the local department of health, or the state Department of Health and the Maternal and Child Health Hotlines. Your state representative can keep you updated regarding new legislation.

$200 Worth of Free Immunizations For Your Kids, No Matter What Income

Twenty-two percent of children are not protected from chicken pox, polio, diphtheria, mumps, whooping cough, German measles, tetanus, spinal meningitis, and hepatitis B. An increasing number of children are exposed to diseases in day-care

settings and elsewhere. Almost any child, no matter what their income, can receive free or very low cost immunizations in their local area. Contact your county office of health, your state Department of Health; or call the National Immunization Information Hotline at 800-232-4636; {www.cdc.gov/nip}.

$5.00 For STD Tests

If you are worried that you may have contracted a Sexually Transmitted Disease (STD) or even HIV, you can get tested and even treated for free or for very low cost at one of your local public health clinics, or other public and private clinics. Contact your county office of health, or your state Department of Health. For more help in identifying local help, contact STD Hotline at 800-227-8922; {www.cdc. gov/nchstp/dstd/dstdp.html}; National AIDS Hotline at 800-342-AIDS; {www.cdcnpin.org}; or National Herpes Hotline at 919-361-8488; {www.ashastd. org/hrc}.

Discount Card And Extra $600 Toward Prescriptions For Seniors

There is help for seniors to pay for the ever-growing costs of prescription drugs. Qualifying individuals receive a discount card as well as an additional $600 to help with the purchase of prescriptions. Contact the Centers for Medicare and Medicaid Services, 7500 Security Boulevard, Baltimore, MD 21244-1850; 877-267-2323; {www. cms.hhs.gov/discountdrugs/overview.a sp}.

Vouchers for FREE Mammograms

The Actors' Fund's Phyllis Newman Women's Health Initiative (PNWHI) provides vouchers for FREE mammograms for members of the entertainment community. Other health-related services are available. Contact: The Actors' Fund of America, 729 Seventh Avenue, 10th Floor, New York, NY 10019; 212-221-7300, ext. 143; Fax: 212-764-0238; {www.actors fund.org/human/social/newman.html}.

FREE Pharmaceuticals

This foundation offers needy persons FREE pharmaceutical products on a non-discriminatory basis. Giving is on a national basis. Contact: Janssen Ortho Patient Assistance Foundation, Inc., 1 Johnson & Johnson Plaza, New Brunswick, NJ 08933; 800-652-6227; {www.janssen.com/ourproducts/pap.js p}.

Money for Those in Need of Health or Education Services

Grants are awarded to the needy elderly whose other sources of income are inadequate. The majority of those receiving grants are experiencing hardship and require health, economic, or educational assistance. Contact: Alfred I. DuPont Foundation, Inc., 4600 Touchton Road, E., Building 200, Suite 120, Jacksonville, FL 32246; 904-232-4123. {http://jpl. coj.net/sites/alpha.html}

Grants & Loans for Safe Abortions

Hersey Abortion Assistance Fund helps women to pay for their abortions through grants and loans. These women include those with no health insurance or insurance which will not cover abortion, minors, and low-income women. Contact: Pro-Choice Resources, 3249 Hennepin Ave. S., Ste. 255, Minneapolis, MN 55408; 612-825-2000; Fax: 612-825-0159; {www.birdsandbees.org/aboutUs.shtm l}.

FREE Surgeries for Women of Domestic Violence

The Massachusetts Eye and Ear Infirmary R.O.S.E. Partnership funds six surgeries each year for facial reconstruction to women who have suffered injury to the face due to violence. Assistance includes pre- and post-operative care deemed necessary to patients selected by The R.O.S.E. Fund. Contact: The R.O.S.E. Fund, Inc., 175 Federal St., Ste. 455, Boston, MA 02110; 617-482-5400; Fax: 617-482-3443; {www.rosefund.org/ programs/ReconSurgery.asp}.

More than $20,000 for Plastic Surgery Research

The foundation seeks to develop and support the domestic and international education, research and public service activities of plastic surgeons. There are three basic grant awards: 1) Basic Research Grants for basic science research; 2) Research Fellowship Grants, to encourage research and academic career development; and 3) Smile Train Cleft Research Initiative, for healthcare professionals to perform meritorious research projects in the treatment or care of people with cleft lip and palate. Contact: Plastic Surgery Educational Foundation, 444 E. Algonquin Road, Arlington Heights, IL 60005; 847-228-9900 or 888-4-PLASTIC; {www.plasticsurgery.org/ PSEF}

$20,000 for Nurses to Conduct Research

The Research and Model Demonstration Project Grants offer one-year grants. The Principal Investigator or Project Director must be a registered nurse. Applicants are encouraged to conduct research related to SCI nursing practice. Contact: American Association of Spinal Cord

Injury Nurses (AASCIN), 75-20 Astoria Blvd., Jackson Heights, NY 11370-1177; 718-803-3782; Fax: 718-803-0414; {www.aascin.org}

$100,000 to Support People with Medical Condition

The National Ataxia Foundation is dedicated to improving the lives of persons affected by ataxia through service, education and research. Contact: National Ataxia Foundation, Inc., 2600 Fernbrook Lane, Ste. 119, Minneapolis, MN 55447-4752; 763-553-0020; Fax: 763-553-0167; {www.ataxia.org/}.

FREE Hearing Aids for Children

This Foundation provides Miracle-Ear hearing aids to needy hearing-impaired children, aged 16 or younger. The child must be: a resident of the United States; in a family with an income level that does not allow the family to receive public support; and in a family committed to intervention, rehabilitation, and necessary follow-up services. Contact: Miracle-Ear Children's Foundation, 5000 Cheshire Ln. N., Ste. 1, Plymouth, MN 55446-3715; 800-234-5422; {www.miracle-ear.com/resources/children_request. asp}

Financial Assistance for Those who Need Heart Surgery

The Larry King Cardiac Foundation (LKCF) was established to provide funding for life-saving treatment for individuals who would otherwise be unable to receive the treatment and care they need. Eligible patients must meet the following minimum criteria: US citizens or have a legal right to be in the US; do not have financial resources to pay for the procedures themselves; and be free of any criminal conviction. Contact: The Larry King Cardiac Foundation, 15720 Crabbs Branch Way, Suite D, Rockville, MD 20855; 866-302-5523; {www.lkcf.org}.

Money to Help Children with Cancer

The National Children's Cancer Society provides direct financial assistance for medical and non-medical expenses related to treatment for children with cancer. Contact: National Children's Cancer Society, Inc., 1015 Locust Bldg., Ste. 600, St. Louis, MO 63101-1323; 314-241-1600 or 800-5-FAMILY; Fax: 314-241-1996; {www. children-cancer.com}.

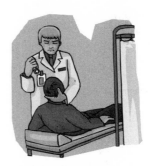

DISCOUNT DRUG PROGRAMS

Help can be just a phone call away. Several states have special drug programs that give huge discounts to seniors and others who are ineligible for Medicaid and who don't have private insurance. For example, seniors in New Jersey can get their prescriptions for only $5, and in Vermont they can get them for as little as $1 or $2.

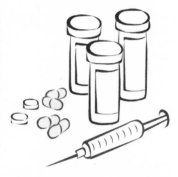

Often all it takes is a phone call and filling out a simple form. You will have to meet income eligibility, but you can make upwards of $23,000 a year and still be eligible in New York, for example. If your state is not listed below, contact your state Department of Aging, but also check out the free drug programs sponsored by the drug manufacturers themselves.

Alabama
Alabama Department of Senior Services
SenioRx
770 Washington Avenue
RSA Plaza Suite 470
Montgomery, AL 36130
334-242-5743
800-AGE-LINE
www.adss.state.al.us/SeniorRx.htm
Eligibility Requirements
- You must be at least 60 years old
- You must have no prescription drug coverage
- You must have a chronic medical condition
- You must be a legal resident of Alabama

- Your annual household income must be less than $18,620 for 1 person and $24,980 for 2 people.

Medication Assistance
Senior Prescription Drug Program
Franklin Primary Health Center
1303 Dr. Martin Luther King Jr. Avenue
Mobile, AL 36603
251-432-4117
www.mobilecounty.org/news/news-seniorprescription.htm
Senior citizens in some areas of Mobile County can participate in the County's Senior Prescription Drug Program. The program provides medication assistance for low-to-moderate income seniors, who are 62 or older and have no prescription drug

coverage. Individuals living within the City of Mobile are not eligible for this county program.

Alaska
Chronic and Acute Medical Assistance
Division of Public Assistance
350 Main Street
PO Box 110640
Juneau, AK 99811-0640
800-211-7470
www.hss.state.ak.us/dhcs/CAMA/defa
ult.htm
Eligibility Requirements
- be in the age range of 21 years to 64 years
- have a covered medical condition
- have no third party resources to cover treatment of that condition
- have very limited financial resources
- be a US Citizen

Prescription drugs and medical supplies are limited to 3 prescriptions per month and no more than a 30-day supply of any drug.

"SeniorCare Rx" Pharmaceutical Assistance Program
The SeniorCare Senior Information Office
3601 C Street, Suite 310
Anchorage, AK 99503-5984
907-269-3680
800-478-6065 (statewide)
Fax: 907-269-3688
http://health.hss.state.ak.us/dsds/senior
caresio.htm
Seniors receive a cash benefit of $120 per month to help with basic needs such as food, housing and medication. In a program implemented in April 2004, seniors who qualify for the Senior Assistance Program and who are not receiving comprehensive Medicaid prescription drug coverage will be provided a choice – between the new SeniorCare prescription drug

subsidy of $1,600 a year or to continue to receive the Senior Assistance Program cash assistance of $1,440 a year. Together with the $600 Medicare subsidy to begin this spring, these eligible seniors opting for the SeniorCare prescription drug benefit will have a combined drug subsidy of $2,200 a year.
Eligibility:
- Minimum age: 65
- Income: Under $16,815 a year (individual), under $23,419 per year (couple)

Arizona
RxAmerica
c/o Arizona CoppeRx Card
Prescription Discount Program
P.O. Box 22690
Salt Lake City, UT 84112-0690
888-227-8315
www.rxamerica.com/az_discount_hom
e.htm?page=mem
Eligibility Requirements
- Be 65 or older
- Be an Arizona resident
- Qualify for SSDI
- Enrollment is free and automatic.

Arizona Drug Discount Program
Plan administrator: Rx America
PBM Facility address:
221 N Charles Lindbergh Dr.
Salt Lake City, UT 84116
888-227-8315
www.rxamerica.com/press_az_discoun
t.html
Savings typically range from 10% to 55% from the overall retail price. Your actual discount may be more or less, depending on the medication and the pharmacy you use.

Eligibility:
Medicare enrollees, 65 and over or disabled. Discounts only. $9.95 enrollment fee.

CoppeRx Card
Plan administrator: Rx America
PBM Facility address:
221 N Charles Lindbergh Dr.
Salt Lake City, UT 84116
888-227-8315
www.rxamerica.com/press_az_discoun
t.html,
www.governor.state.az.us/global/presc
ription_discounts.htm
Will replace Arizona Drug Discount
Program (Rx America) in early 2005.
Savings typically range from 10% to
55% from the overall retail price. Your
actual discount may be more or less,
depending on the medication and the
pharmacy you use.

Eligibility:
Medicare enrollees, 65 and over or
disabled. No enrollment fee.

Arkansas
Arkansas Healthcare Access Foundation
PO Box 56248
Little Rock, AR 2215-6248
800-950-8233
http://users.aristotle.net/~ahcaf
Eligibility Requirements
- You must be an Arkansas Resident.
- You must be uninsured.
- Your income level must be within 100% of the Federal Poverty Guidelines.

Patients apply to their County
Department of Human Services or
Health Unit. After approval, the patient
contacts the pharmaceutical company

using the toll-free numbers that are
supplied. Participating pharmaceuticals
are Johnson & Johnson, Glaxo
SmithKline, and Pfizer.

Prescription Drug Access Improvement Act
This program is not yet operational.
Funding might be implemented in
2005.

Arkansas Department of Human
Services
Donaghey Plaza West
Slot S201
P.O. Box 1437
Little Rock, AR 72203-1437
501-682-8650
Pays for two prescriptions per month
for qualified individuals.
Eligibility:
65 and older. Annual income under
$9,310 for any individual covered by
the plan, $18,620 for married couple,
for 2004 (would provide benefit of 2
prescriptions per month, only after
federal approval is received)

California
800-510-2020
Eligibility Requirements
- Have a Medicare card

Cost
- You can take your Medicare card to any pharmacy that fills Medi-Cal (California's Medicaid) prescriptions. You will be charged the Medi-Cal rate plus a 15 cent processing fee.

Golden Bear State Pharmacy Assistance Program
Dept. of Health Services
P.O. Box 997413
Sacramento, CA 95899-7413
Medi-Cal 916-657-1280
www.dhs.ca.gov/mcs/mcpd/MBB/cont
racting/sb393/default.htm

Discounts up to 100 percent will vary based on income level.

Eligibility:
Medicare recipients, 65 and older or disabled. No income limit. (Requires negotiated manufacturer rebates to achieve larger discounts)

Connecticut
Conn PACE
P.O. Box 5011
Hartford, CT 06102
800-423-5026
www.connpace.com
Eligibility Requirements
- You must be 65 years old or older, or 18 and older with a disability.
- You must have lived in Connecticut for six months.
- Your income cannot exceed $20,800 if you are single, and $28,100 if you are married.
- You may not have an insurance plan that pays for all or a portion of each prescription, a deductible insurance plan that includes prescriptions, or Medicaid.

Cost
- You pay a $30 one time registration fee.
- You pay $16.25 for each prescription.
- You must get generic drugs whenever possible, unless you are willing to pay the difference in price.

Citizens Health Card
Citizens for Citizens
99 Black Falcon Ave.
Boston, MA 02210
800-563-5479
508-679-0041
www.citizensenergy.com
Discounts for prescriptions are available to uninsured or underinsured

citizens who are not eligible for public programs at participating pharmacies.

Cost
- $12 per year for individuals and $28 per year for families

Delaware
Delaware Prescription Drug Assistance Program
EDS DPAP
P.O. Box 950
New Castle, DE 19720
302-577-4900
800-996-9969, ext. 17
www.state.de.us/dhss/dss/dpap.html
Eligibility Requirements
- You must be resident of Delaware
- You must be at lest 65 years old or qualify for Social Security Disability
- Your income cannot exceed 200% of the Federal Poverty Level

Cost
- You pay $5 or 25% of the cost of the prescription, whichever is greater.

Nemours Senior Pharmaceutical Assistance
1801 Rockland Road
Wilmington, DE 19803
302-651-4403
800-842-1900
www.nemours.org
Eligibility Requirements
- You must be a citizen of Delaware
- You must meet financial qualifications

Cost
- Members pay 20% of the drug's cost for each prescription.

District of Columbia
DC Healthcare Alliance
1025 15th Street, NW
Washington, DC 20005
202-842-5809
www.chartered-
health.com/Alliance.htm
Eligibility Requirements
- You must live in the District of Columbia
- You must have no health insurance
- Your income must be at or below 200% of the Federal Poverty Level

Cost
- Membership in the Alliance is free for qualifying D.C. residents. Prescriptions must be from the list of qualifying drugs.

Florida
Silver Saver
1317 Winewood Boulevard
Building 3, 1st Floor, Suite 101
Tallahassee, FL 32399-0700
888-419-3456
www.floridahealthstat.com/silversaver.shtml
With this program, $160 will be put in your Silver Saver account (the balance is held in Medicaid's computer system). Each time you fill a prescription, the amount will automatically be deducted from your account.

Eligibility Requirements
- You must be a Florida resident.
- You must be 65 years or older.
- You must be eligible for Medicare
- Your income must be between $679.01 and $918.00 for an individual, and between $908.01 and $1,232 for a couple.

Costs
- A $2 co-payment is required for generic prescriptions.
- A $5 co-payment is required for brand name drugs that are on Medicaid' Preferred Drug List.
- A $15 co-payment is required for brand name drugs that are not on the list.
- Your doctor must call and request a pre-approval from Medicaid on the prescriptions.

Prescription Discount Program
Agency for Health Care Administration
2727 Mahan Drive
Tallahassee, FL 32308
850-487-4441
888 419-3456
www.floridahealthstat.com/publications/prescripaffordbroch112100.pdf
Drug discount program. Recipients received a nine percent discount on the wholesale price after paying a $4.50 dispensing fee.

Eligibility:
Any Medicare beneficiary, no age or income limit.

Georgia
Georgia Partnership for Caring Foundation
P.O. Box 450987
Atlanta, GA 31145-0987
678-578-2920
800-982-4723
www.gacares.org
Eligibility Requirements
- You must be a resident of Georgia
- You must be uninsured
- Your family income must be at or below 125% of the Federal Poverty Level

Cost
- Prescription drugs are dispensed by participating pharmacy in the Georgia Partnership for Caring Foundation network at no charge

Savings of up to 20%
Twiggs County
County Commissioner
P.O. Box 202, County Courthouse
Jeffersonville, GA 31044-0202
478-945-3629
https://naco.advancerx.com/advpcsrx_
MemberSite/index.jsp
All residents of Twiggs County are eligible to participate in the county's Prescription Drug Discount Program. Twiggs Rx is free and available to all county residents, regardless of age, income or existing health insurance. Simply present the card at a participating pharmacy and save an average of 20% on prescription drugs. Best of all there is no enrollment form or membership fee. Members are also eligible for higher discounts on particular medications, as well as a mail service program which offers an average savings of 50% on a 3-month supply of select medications.

Hawaii
Hawaii Rx Plus Program
P.O. Box 700220
Kapolei, HI 96709-0220
808-692-7999
www.hawaiirxplus.com/
Eligibility Requirements
- You must be a resident of Hawaii
- You do not have all of your drugs paid for by insurance
- Your household income does not exceed 350% of the Federal Poverty Level

Costs
- Consumers can expect to pay 10-15% off of the average wholesale price of a drug

Illinois
Pharmaceutical Assistance Program
Illinois Department of Revenue
P.O. Box 19021
Springfield, IL 62794
800-624-2459
www.revenue.state.il.us/circuitbreaker/
Eligibility Requirements
- You must be 65 years of age or older, or over 16 and totally disabled, or a widow or widower who turned 63 before spouse's death.
- You must be a resident of Illinois.
- Your income must be less than $21,218 for individuals; $28,480 for couples.
- You must file a Circuit Breaker claim form.

Cost
- This program provides grants to help pay for prescriptions. Your grant is figured by a formula using the amount you paid in property tax or mobile home tax and the amount of your total income.
- You must choose the generic brand when available, unless you are willing to pay the difference in price.

Senior Care
Illinois Department on Aging
P.O. Box 19021
Springfield, IL 62794-9021
800-252-8966
www.seniorcareillinois.com
Eligibility Requirements
- You must be a resident of Illinois.
- You must be 65 years or older.
- If you are single, your income must not exceed $18, 620 a year.

If you are married, your income must not exceed $24,980 a year.

Costs

- SeniorCare pays up to $1,750 per person per year, with either no co-pays or a low co-pay. After that, you pay 20% of the cost of each prescription plus any co-pays.
- Seniors pay 10% co-payment for each covered prescription drug with a $1,200 maximum per benefit period.

Illinois Rx Buying Club
P.O. Box 94858
Chicago, IL 60690-4858
866-215-3462
http://www.state.il.us/aging/3hot/phar m-assist_irs.htm
The Illinois Rx Buying Club provides discounts of 5 to 50 percent on all prescription drugs approved by the FDA and available through participating pharmacies and a mail-order option.

Eligibility:
Senior citizens and disabled. No income limits.

Prescription Savings!!
Sangamon County Department of Public Health
ATTN: Sangamo Scripts
2501 North Dirksen Parkway
Springfield, IL 62702
217-535-3100
www.co.sangamon.il.us/events/Sanga moScripts.pdf
Sangamo Scripts, a pharmaceutical discount program is available for any Sangamon County resident over the age of 18 who is not covered by Public Aid though children under 18 can be covered by a parent or guardian under the plan. There is no cost and the average savings per prescription.

Indiana
Hoosier Prescription Drug Program
P.O. Box 6224
Indianapolis, IN 46206
866-267-4679 (toll-free)
www.IN.gov/fssa/hoosierrx
Eligibility Requirements

- You must be 65 years or older
- You must be a permanent resident of Indiana
- You do not have prescription drug insurance
- Your income must be $1,068 or less a month if you are single; and $1,426 per month or less if you are married.
- You can pick up application forms at your local pharmacy, Area Agency on Aging, Social Security office, of Office of Family and Children.

Cost

- Eligible seniors will receive a HoosierRx Drug Card that will give them 75% off the price of their prescriptions.
- For those seniors that also have a Medicare Drug Discount Card, you may use both cards when you purchase prescriptions.

Iowa
Iowa Prescription Drug Corporation
1231 8th Street, Suite 232
West Des Moines, IA 50265
866-282-5817
www.iowapriority.org/default.asp
Eligibility Requirements

- You must be a resident of Iowa.
- You must be eligible for Medicare
- You cannot be receiving Medicaid.

Cost

- There is a $20 annual fee.

- Once you have your card, you will receive a discount on all prescriptions. The discount varies per prescription.

Kansas
Kansas Department of Aging
New England Bldg.
503 S. Kansas
Topeka, KS 66603
785-296-4986
800-432-3535
Senior Pharmacy Assistance Program
www.agingkansas.org/kdoa/programs/
pharmassistprog.htm
Eligibility Requirements
- You must be a Kansas resident.
- You must be 65 years of age.
- You must be a current beneficiary of the Medicare Savings Program.
- You must not be covered under a private prescription insurance plan that pays for any part of your prescription costs.
- You must not be eligible for or enrolled in any other local, state, or federal prescription program such as Medicaid or VA prescription assistance;
- You must not have voluntarily canceled a local, state, federal, or private prescription drug program within six months of application to this program.

Costs
- The program will reimburse you for a portion of your prescription costs. They will not exceed 70% of out-of-pocket prescription drug costs. The maximum reimbursement per individual is limited to $1,200 annually.

20% off Prescription Drugs
Sedgwick County Health Department

1900 E. Ninth St.
Wichita, KS 67214
316-660-7300
www.sedgwickcounty.org/healthdept/
Free prescription drug discount cards are available to help Sedgwick County residents save money at participating pharmacies. The cards are designed for people who don't have prescription drug coverage, but they're available to anyone. The cards will offer an average of 20 percent off on commonly prescribed prescriptions and an average of 50 percent off three-month supplies of generics ordered through a mail service. The cards can be used at more than 70 pharmacies in Sedgwick County, and there are no income or age requirements, or claim forms to file.

Save 20 to 50% on Prescription Drugs
Harvey County Department of Health
800 N. Main, P.O. Box 687
Newton, KS 67114
316-284-6806
www.harveycounty.com/
Save money on your prescription purchases by using the free Harvey County Prescription Discount Card. There are no forms to fill out and everyone is eligible. Save an average of 20% off the pharmacies regular price prescribed prescriptions and an average savings of 50% on 3-month supplies of select generics through mail service.

Kentucky
Health Kentucky, Inc.
12700 Shelbyville Road
Louisville, KY 40243
502-254-4214
www.healthkentucky.org
Eligibility Requirements
- You must be a Kentucky resident
- You must be uninsured

- Your income must be at or below 100% of the Federal Poverty Level
- Resource limit of $2,000

Cost
- Participating physicians write prescriptions from the list of available medications. The prescription can be filled at one of 500 participating pharmacies for free.

Louisiana
Louisiana SenioRx Program
P.O. Box 61
Baton Rouge, LA 70821-0061
225-342-7100
www.louisianaseniorx.org
Eligibility Requirements
- You must be 60 years old or older
- You must have an income below $27,930 for a single, $37,470 for a two-person household
- You must have any insurance for prescriptions
- You must have a chronic illness taking prescribed daily medications for the condition
- You have not voluntarily cancelled any prescription drug program in the past 6 months

Costs
- SenioRx is a counseling service for seniors and does not directly supply medications. Their trained staff will help you apply for pharmaceutical company programs. This service is free of charge.

Maine
Elderly Low-Cost Drug Program
Department of Human Services
11 State House Station
Augusta, ME 04333

800-262-2232
207-287-9200
www.state.me.us/dhs/beas/medbook.htm#lcd
Eligibility requirements
- You must be a Maine resident.
- You may not be receiving SSI payments.
- Your income may not exceed $17,232 if you live alone; $23,112 if you are married or have dependents.
- You must be 62 years of age or older; or be at least 19 years of age and disabled.
- If you spend at least 40% of your income on prescriptions, your income limits will be 25% higher.

Cost
- Each drug will cost $2 plus 20% of the price.

Maine Rx Plus
Department of Human Services
11 State House Station
Augusta, ME 04333
800-262-2232
207-287-9200
www.state.me.us/dhs/beas/medbook.htm
Eligibility requirements
- You must be a resident of Maine.
- You must meet the following maximum monthly income guidelines:
- Single: $2,716; Family of 2: $3,643; Family of 3: $4,571; Family of 4: $ $5498.
- You may be eligible if your out-of-pocket expenses are more than 5% of your household income; or if your out-of-pocket medical expenses are more than 15% of your household income.

Costs
- You may get discounts of 15% to 60% off the retail prices. The greatest discounts are for generic drugs.

Rx Cares For ME
877-RxForME
www.rxcaresforme.org/
Rx Care For ME is an online resource to search for patient assistance programs. Patients simply fill out an online form and receive a listing of programs for which they may be qualified.

Maryland
Maryland Pharmacy Assistance Program
P.O. Box 386
Baltimore, MD 21203-0386
410-767-5397
800-226-2142
www.dhmh.state.md.us/mma/mpap
Eligibility requirements
- For anyone in the state who cannot afford their medications. Income requirements vary, so it is best to call. For a single person, income cannot exceed $10,800; for married couples, $12,492.

Cost
- Your co-pay is $2.50 for generic and $7.50 for certain brand names.

Maryland Pharmacy Discount Program
Eligibility Requirements
- You must receive Medicare.
- Your monthly income must be below $1,358 for a single person and below $1,822 for a couple.

Costs
- Eligible recipients pay 65% of the State's reduced cost, plus a $1 processing fee.

- There are no monthly premiums.

MEDBANK of Maryland, Inc.
P.O. Box 42678
Baltimore, MD 21284
410-821-9262
www.medbankmd.org
Eligibility Requirements
- You must be a Maryland resident
- You must have no other prescription coverage
- You must be ineligible for any entitlement programs like Medicaid
- You must meet financial guidelines

Cost
- Participating physicians write prescriptions from the list of available medications. The Medbank representative identifies Patient Assistance Programs, completes required applications.

21% average savings per prescription
ScriptSave
Anne Arundle County Health Department
3 Harry S. Truman Parkway
Annapolis, MD 21401
410-222-7095
ScriptSave
www.scriptsave.com
The Anne Arundel County Health Department offers county residents ScriptSave prescription discount cards. The program is available to all residents regardless of age and there are no enrollment fees. The average discount with the card is about 21% off each prescription.

Savings of up to 20%
Montgomery County Executive
Douglas M. Duncan

Executive Office Building
101 Monroe Street, 2nd Floor
Rockville, MD 20850
240-777-2500
TTY: 240-777-2544
www.montgomerycountymd.gov/mcgt
mpl.asp?url=/content/PIO/mont_rx.asp
Montgomery County offers all
residents to participate in the county's
Prescription Drug Discount Program.
Montgomery Rx is free and available
to all Montgomery County residents,
regardless of age, income or existing
health insurance. Simply present the
card at a participating pharmacy and
save an average of 20% on
prescription drugs. There is no
enrollment form or membership fee.
Members are also eligible for higher
discounts on select medications and
inject able drugs, as well as, a mail
service program which offers an
average savings of 50% on a 3-month
supply of select medications.

Massachusetts
Prescription Advantage Plan
P.O. Box 15153
Worchester, MA 01615
800-AGE-INFO
www.800ageinfo.com

Eligibility Requirements
- You must be 65 years or old or
  have a qualified disability
- You must be a Massachusetts
  resident

Cost
- Monthly premium for the plan
  varies for $0-$82 per month
  depending upon your income.
  The co-payment also varies for
  $5-$25 depending upon income.
- After you pay $2,000 or 10% of
  your gross annual household
  income (whichever is less)
  toward your Prescription

Advantage deductible and
co-payments, the entire cost of
your prescription drugs,
including the co-payments are
covered for the remainder of the
year.

Citizens Health Card
Citizens for Citizens
88 Black Falcon Avenue
Center Lobby, Suite 342
Boston, MA 02210
800-563-5479
617-338-6300
www.citizensenergy.com
Discounts for prescriptions are
available to uninsured or underinsured
citizens who are not eligible for public
programs at participating pharmacies.

Cost
- $12 per year for individuals and
  $28 per year for families

MassMedLine
Massachusetts College of Pharmacy
and Health Sciences
19 Foster Street
Worchester, MA 01608-1705
866-633-1617
www.massmedline.com
Massachusetts residents can speak
directly to specialists that can answer
questions about the medications they
take and provide information about
programs sponsored by pharmaceutical
companies that provide free, low cost
or discounted medications.

Aggregate Purchasing Law
Executive Office of Elder Affairs
One Ashburton Place, Fifth floor
Boston, MA 02108
617-727-7750
800-243-4636
www.800ageinfo.com/
Not in operation. Delayed by executive
branch. Program would supply rebates

from manufacturers on the cost of drugs.

Eligibility:
State agency to coordinate combined purchasing for Senior Pharmacy Assistance enrollees, Medicare and Medicaid, state workers, uninsured and underinsured people.

Michigan
Elder Prescription Insurance Coverage
3850 Second Street, Suite 201
Wayne, MI 48184-1755
866-747-5844
www.miepic.com
Eligibility Requirements
- You must be a Michigan resident for at least 3 months
- You must be age 65 or older
- Your annual income must be at or below 150% of the federal poverty level.
- You may not be receiving prescription drug benefits through any other insurance, except Medicare.

Cost
- Modest co-pay depending upon income, plus a $25 annual fee.

Wayne County Discount Program
Health and Community Services Administrative Office
3850 Second Street, Suite 201
Wayne, MI 48184-1755
866-896-3450
Eligibility Requirements
- You must be a resident of Wayne County.
- You must be at least 60 years old.

Costs
- Discounts vary on generic and brand name prescriptions.

MiRx Prescription Savings Program
Michigan Department of Community Health
Sixth Floor, Lewis Cass Building
320 South Walnut Street
Lansing, MI 48913
866-755-6479
www.michigan.gov/mdch/0,1607,7-132--100833--,00.html
Application:
http://www.michigan.gov/documents/
MiRx_brochure_150dpi_103392_7.pdf
Beneficiaries of the MiRx Card program will save as much as 20 percent off the retail prices they would normally pay as a cash customer.

Eligibility:
No minimum age. Income levels slide depending on family size (1= $27,930 to 8= $94,050). No enrollment fee.

Receive 25% off Prescription Drugs
Washtenaw County Prescription Plan
Jean Higgins
55 Towner, Bldg 1, Room 121
Ypsilanti, MI 48197
734-544-6886
Fax 734-544-6705
www.ewashtenaw.org/government/dep
artments/public_health/ph_wcpp.html
The Washtenaw County Prescription Plan (WCPP) is a discount prescription drug program for County residents of all ages who have limited, exhausted, or no prescription drug coverage. There are no income or age restrictions. WCPP helps County residents to buy prescription drugs at a discount off of the full retail price. Discounts may range from 5-25%. Many pharmacies in Washtenaw County participate.

Medications 20-30% Off
OLHSA Oakland County
196 Cesar E. Chavez Avenue
P.O. Box 430598
Pontiac, MI 48343-0598

517-546-8500
www.olhsa.org/liv_prescriptions.asp
Livingston county residents 60 years
of age or older can obtain a discount
prescription card. This group discount
is offered through the Ingham Health
Plan Corporation and applies to most
medicines, excluding over-the-counter
drugs and has no enrollment costs. The
program allows participants to save an
average of 20-30% off regular
prescription drug prices at
participating pharmacies.

**Prescription Drug 25% Off Retail
Price**
Barry-Eaton Discount Prescription
Eaton County
1045 Independence Blvd.
Charlotte, MI 48813
517-541-2614
www.eatoncounty.org/prescription.htm
Any resident of Barry or Eaton
counties who does not have other drug
coverage can participate in the Barry-
Eaton Discount Prescription Plan. The
program is a way for people without
prescription coverage to purchase
prescription drugs at lower prices at
their pharmacy. There is no cost for
the card and covered with the
exception of the over-the-counter
drugs and experimental medications.

Discounts as High as 70%
The Jackson County Prescription
Discount Plan (JCPDP)
Jackson County Health Department
1697 Lansing Ave.
Jackson, MI 49202
517-788 – 4420
Fax: 517-788 – 4373
www.co.jackson.mi.us/hd/jcpdp.htm
The Jackson County Prescription
Discount Plan is a way for people
without prescription coverage to
purchase prescription drugs at lower
prices from their pharmacy. Any
resident of Jackson County who does

not have drug coverage may
participate and there is no cost for the
JCPDP card or for enrolling in the
program. People who present a JCPDP
card at a participating pharmacy can
expect to save about 25 percent off the
retail price. Saving will typically be
between 5 and 25 percent with
discounts at times as high as 70%,
though not typical.

Minnesota
**Minnesota's Prescription Drug
Program**
Department of Human Services
444 Lafayette Rd., N
St Paul, MN 55155
651-296-8517
800-657-3659
www.dhs.state.mn.us/main/groups/hea
lthcare/documents/pub/dhs_id_006258
.hcsp
Eligibility Requirements
- Must be age 65 or older, or
  disabled and enrolled in
  Medicaid.
- Must be a Minnesota resident for
  six months
- Have income at or below 120%
  of federal poverty guidelines
  (currently $951 a month for one
  person and $1,269 a month for a
  married couple)
- Have liquid assets of $10,000 or
  less for one; $18,000 or less for
  married couple
- Be enrolled in either Qualified
  Medicare Beneficiary (QMB) or
  Service Limited Medicare
  Beneficiary (SLMB).

Cost
- The Prescription Drug Program
  pays for necessary prescription
  drugs after enrollees pay the first
  $35 monthly deductible. If no
  medications are purchased that
  month, there is no $35 cost. For

more information contact your local county human services agency.

Mississippi
Discounts as High as 70%
The Jackson County Prescription Discount Plan (JCPDP)
Jackson County Health Department
1697 Lansing Ave.
Jackson, MI 49202
517-788-4420
Fax: 517-788-4373
www.co.jackson.mi.us/hd/jcpdp.htm
The Jackson County Prescription Discount Plan is a way for people without prescription coverage to purchase prescription drugs at lower prices from their pharmacy. Any resident of Jackson County who does not have other drug coverage may participate and there is no cost for the JCPDP card or for enrolling in the program. People who present a JCPDP card at a participating pharmacy can expect to save about 25 percent off the retail price. Saving will typically be between 5 and 25 percent with discounts at times as high as 70%, though not typical.

Missouri
Senior Rx Program
P.O. Box 208
Troy, MO 63379
800-375-1406
www.dhss.mo.gov/MoSeniorRx/
Eligibility Requirements
- You must be at least 65 years old.
- You must have been a resident of the State for at least 12 months.
- You may not receive Veterans Administration pharmacy benefits or have prescription insurance that is equal to or greater than this program.
- You must not be enrolled in Medicaid.

- An individual must not have an income that is greater than $17,000 and a married household must not have an income above $25,000.

Cost
- Enrollment fee is $25 or $35 per member, depending on household income.
- Deductible of $250 or $500 per member, depending on household income.
- You pay 40% of the cost of eligible prescriptions.
- The maximum annual benefit is $5,000 per member per year.

Montana
Prescription Drug Expansion Program
Department of Public Health and Human Services
111 N Sanders, Room 301/308
PO Box 4210
Helena, MT 59604
800-551-3191
www.dphhs.state.mt.us/
Not yet operational
Offer discounts on prescription drugs for Medicaid members.

Eligibility:
- Minimum age: 62 (disabled 18 and over)
- Maximum annual income of $18,620 for eligible individuals, regardless of spouse's income.

Nebraska
Prescription Drug Savings!!
Dawes County
451 Main Street
County Courthouse
Chadron, NE 69337-2697
308-432-0102
www.co.dawes.ne.us/

Free prescription drug discount cards are available to help Dawes County residents save money at participating pharmacies. The cards are designed for people who don't have prescription drug coverage, but they're available to anyone regardless of income or age. The program offers an average of 20 percent off on commonly prescribed prescriptions and an average of 50 percent off three-month supplies of generics ordered through a mail service. The cards can be used at many participating pharmacies throughout Dawes County and requires no claim forms.

20%-50% Savings on Prescription Drugs
Keith County
511 N Spruce
P.O. Box 149, County Courthouse
Ogallala, NE 69153-0149
308-284-4726
Fax: 308-284-6277
www.co.keith.ne.us/
Keith County wants to help its residents save money on their prescription drugs by offering prescription drug discount cards. The cards are designed for people who don't have prescription drug coverage, but they're available to anyone regardless of income or age. The program offers an average of 20 percent off on commonly prescribed prescriptions and an average of 50 percent off three-month supplies of generics ordered through a mail service. The cards can be used at many participating pharmacies throughout Keith County and require no claim forms.

Nevada
Senior Rx
1761 E. College Parkway
Building B, Suite 113
Carson City, NV 89706-7954
800-262-7726
www.nevadaseniorrx.com
Eligibility Requirements
- Age 62 and older
- Nevada resident for at least one year
- Not eligible for full Medicaid with prescription benefits
- Household income not over $22,434 for a single person and $29,205 for married couples

Cost
- You pay a co-pay of $10 per generic drug. Senior Rx provides up to $5,000 in benefits per year.

New Hampshire
New Hampshire Prescription Drug Discount Program
New Hampshire Division of Elderly & Adult Services
129 Pleasant Street
Concord, NH 03301-3857
888-580-8902
www.dhhs.state.nh.us/DHHS/BEAS/assist-prescription-drug.htm
This discount card program is for New Hampshire residents age 65 and over who enroll in the program. A discount card is used at participating pharmacies for discounts up to 15% on brand name medications and up to 40% on generic medications. Currently, there are **no** financial eligibility requirements and no membership fees. Mail order is also available.

New Hampshire Bridge Program
Foundation for Healthy Communities
125 Airport Road
Concord, NH 03301
603-225-0900
www.healthynh.com/fhc/initiatives/access/medicationbridge.php
The goal of the program is to help eligible uninsured and underinsured

patients of all ages to receive needed prescription medications from pharmaceutical companies' Patient Assistance Programs. They help residents access medications by helping them find programs.

New Jersey
Pharmaceutical Assistance to the Aged and Disabled (PAAD)
Senior Gold Prescription Discount Program
P.O. Box 725
Trenton, NJ 08625
800-792-9745
609-588-7048
www.state.nj.us/health/seniorbenefits/seniorgolddiscount.htm

Eligibility Requirements
- You must be a New Jersey resident.
- Your income must be less than $20,437 if you are single, or less than $25,058 if you are married. Income can be $10,000 higher and you could qualify for Senior Gold.
- You must be at least 65 years of age, or receiving Social Security Disability.
- Drugs purchased outside the state of New Jersey are not covered, nor any pharmaceutical product whose manufacturer has not agreed to provide rebates to the state of New Jersey.

Cost
- Senior Gold members have a $15 copay plus ½ of the remainder of the cost of the drug.

50% Discount
Camden County Drug Discount Prescription Program
GSPO Provider Service Corp
P.O. Box 4190
Hamilton, NJ 08610

866-792-6226
www.co.camden.nj.us/RX/
If you are a resident of Camden County, New Jersey then you are eligible to participate in the county's Drug Discount Prescription Program. The program is designed to provide Camden County residents with savings of up to 10% to 50% on prescription medications. There are no income requirements, no exclusions for pre-existing condition and no age restrictions. All that is required is a completed application form, proof of residency and a small annual fee of $20 per household ($40 for 3 years). The Camden County Prescription Drug Discount Program is accepted at thousands of participating pharmacies, both local and nationwide.

50% Off Regular Retail Prescription Prices
Cape May County Prescription Savings Program
GSPO Provider Services Corp.
P.O. Box 4190
Hamilton, NJ 08610
800-633-0037
www.co.cape-may.nj.us/FCpdf/PSPBrochure.pdf
Cape May County Prescription Savings Program is available to all Cape May County residents, regardless of your age or income. For an annual fee of $20 per year or $40 for 3 years, you will receive a Cape May County Prescription Savings Card providing up to 10% to 50% off regular retail prescription prices. There are no age requirements, no income requirements and no exclusions for pre-existing conditions.

Save 10% to 50% On Prescription Medications
Atlantic County Resident Prescription Savings Program

GSPO Provider Services Corp.
P.O. Box 4190
Hamilton, NJ 08610
800-633 0037
www.aclink.org/Admin/Main/pres_sav
ings.asp
The Atlantic County Resident
Prescription Savings Program provides
Atlantic County residents with savings
of up to 10% to 50% on prescription
medications. All residents of Atlantic
County and their dependents living in
the same household are eligible, there
are no income requirements, and there
are no exclusions for pre-existing
conditions. For a small annual fee, you
will receive an Atlantic County
Resident Prescription Savings Card
which provides special discounted
pricing on prescription medications for
all members of your household.

New Mexico
New Mexico SenioRx
866-244-0882
www.nmrhca.state.nm.us/spdp/
Eligibility Requirements
- You must be a resident of New
  Mexico
- You must be 65 years of age or
  older

Cost
- There is no enrollment fee
  required to participate
- You can expect savings of
  between 13-19% off brand names
  drugs and 50-55% off of generic
  drugs. Actual discounts may
  vary.

**20%-50% Savings on Prescription
Drugs**
San Miguel County
500 West National, County
Courthouse
Las Vegas, NM 87701-0000
505-425-9333

Fax: 505-425-7019
www.smcounty.net/
Residents in San Miguel County can
save money on their prescription drugs
through the county's prescription drug
discount program. The discount cards
are designed for people who don't have
prescription drug coverage, but they're
available to anyone regardless of
income or age. The program offers an
average of 20 percent off on
commonly prescribed prescriptions
and an average of 50 percent off three-
month supplies of generics ordered
through a mail service. The cards can
be used at many participating
pharmacies throughout San Miguel
County and require no claim forms.

New York
Elderly Pharmaceutical Insurance
Coverage EPIC
P.O. Box 15018
Albany, NY 12212
800-332-3742
518-452-6828
www.health.state.ny.us/nysdoh/epic/fa
q.htm
Eligibility Requirements
- You must be 65 or older.
- You must reside in New York
  State.
- Your income must not exceed
  $35,000 if you are single; or
  $50,000 if you are married.
- You are not eligible if you
  receive Medicaid benefits.

Cost
- You pay between $3-$20 per
  prescription depending upon the
  prescription cost.
- There are two plans for EPIC.
  You can pay an annual fee
  depending upon your income to
  qualify right away. The annual
  fee ranges from $8 to over $300,
  which can be paid in

installments. The EPIC Deductible plan is that you pay no fee, but you pay full price for your prescriptions until you spend the deductible amount. The deductible amount also varies by income and starts at $530.

UP to 50% off Medications
RocklandRx
Rockland County Office of the County Executive
11 New Hempstead Rd.
New City, NY 10956
845-638-5122
www.co.rockland.ny.us/
Rockland County of New York provides a prescription discount program with no annual fee to all of its residents regardless of their age or income. The RocklandRx prescription discount card gives an average price cut of 20 percent off and as much as 50 percent off the cost of commonly prescribed medications, including brand name and generic drugs. The card is accepted at 56 Rockland pharmacies and more than 54,000 pharmacies nationwide.

Save Up to 15% on Brand Name and 44% on Generics
The RxChoice Drugstore Savings Club
Monroe County Department of Human and Health Services
111 Westfall Road
Rochester, NY 14620
585-274-6298
Fax: 585-274-6296
www.monroecounty.gov/org30.asp
Monroe County has partnered with The RxChoice Drugstore Savings Club, a prescription drug discount card with 2 million members nationwide. This plan is opened to any senior who is a resident of Monroe County, New York – regardless of income and does not currently have prescription drug coverage. All enrolled seniors receive a Monroe County-RxChoice Card, which can be presented at most retail pharmacies for a discount on all prescription drugs.

50% Prescription Drugs
NassauRx prescription discount card
Office of the Nassau Comptroller
240 Old Country Road
Mineola, NY
516-571-2386
www.co.nassau.ny.us/comptroller/index.html
The new NassauRx prescription discount card is available to Nassau residents free of charge. With the NassauRx card, any family member can get discounts of an average of 20 percent off – and as much as 50 percent off – the cost of commonly prescribed prescription medications. Any county resident, regardless of age, income or existing health insurance, may use the card. Currently, the card is accepted at more than 90 percent of Nassau pharmacies and at more than 54,000 nationwide. There are no claim forms to fill out and no annual fees to pay, simply present your card with your prescription at any participating pharmacy.

Save up to 50% off Your Medications
UlsterRx
5999 South Park Avenue, No. 248
Buffalo NY, 14075
800-780-8738
Fax: 1-800-771-9180
www.ulsterrx.com/
Ulster County residents can participate in a discount drug card program that allows its members access to affordable prescription drugs through a national network of participating pharmacies. Members can expect to save between 10 and 50 percent on their prescriptions, depending on the

type of medication you need and where you purchase it. The card can be used at neighborhood pharmacies, through mail order or, for the greatest savings, purchase prescriptions through a Canadian pharmacy. All residents of Ulster County are eligible to enroll and enrollment fees are nominal. The annual cost for a single membership is $15, while the annual cost for a family membership is $26.

Reduced Prescription Drugs Prices
TompkinsRx
Tomkin County Health Department
401 Harris B. Dates Drive, Biggs B
Ithica, NY, 14850
877-321-2652
https://tompkins.advancerx.com/advpc
srx_MemberSite/index.jsp
The TompkinsRx card was endorsed by the Tompkins County Legislature on December 21, 2004 to help uninsured and underinsured residents reduce the cost of prescription drugs. Simply present your card at a participating pharmacy and save an average of 20% on prescription drugs. No enrollment form, no membership fee.

20% off Prescription Drugs
County Executive
22 Market. St.
Poughkeepsie, NY 12601
845-486-2000
Fax 845-486-2021
www.dutchessny.gov/CountyGov/Dep
artments/CountyExecutive/CEIndex.ht
m
Free prescription drug discount cards are available to help Dutchess County residents save money at participating pharmacies. The cards are designed for people who don't have prescription drug coverage, but they're available to anyone regardless of age or income.

The cards will offer an average of 20 percent off on commonly prescribed prescriptions and an average of 50 percent off three-month supplies of generics ordered through a mail service. The cards can be used at many participating pharmacies throughout Dutchess County, and there are no claim forms to file.

North Carolina
Office of the Governor
NC Senior Care Program
P.O. Box 10068
Raleigh, NC 27605-5068
866-226-1388
919-733-4534
www.ncseniorcare.com/index.htm
Eligibility Requirements
- Single applicants must have an annual income of $23,275 or less, and $31,225 or less if married.
- Age 65 and older.

Senior PHARMAssist
123 Market Street
Durham, NC 27701-3221
919-688-4772
www.seniorpharmassist.org/
Eligibility Requirements
- You must be a Durham County resident
- You must be 65 years of age or older

Cost
- Seniors who qualify for financial assistance receive a prescription card to purchase approved medicines. The participant pays $8 per prescription.
- Seniors that do not qualify for financial assistance, can receive information from PHARMAssist about alternative prescription assistance programs and local short-term funding programs.

Ohio

Ohio Department of Aging
50 W. Broad Street, 9th Floor
Columbus, OH 43215-3363
866-311-6446
www.goldenbuckeye.com/buckeye.ht
ml

Eligibility Requirements
- You must be an Ohio resident
- You must be 60 years of age or older or 18-59 if Medicare-certified disabled
- You must be ineligible for any other prescription coverage

Cost
- Patient pays a negotiated price for medications

Rx for Ohio
172 East State Street, Suite 410
Columbus, OH 43215
877-RxOhio
www.rxforohio.org
Rx for Ohio is a service for Ohioans that are in need of prescription assistance programs. The web site will help you search for programs that meet your needs.

Ohio's Best Rx
Ohio Department of Job and Family Services
Office of Family Stability
145 South Front Street, 2nd Floor
Columbus, OH 43215
614-466-9783
www.ohiobestrx.com

Eligibility Requirements
- You must be an Ohio resident
- You must be 60 years old or older
- Your income must be 250% of the Federal Poverty Level if you are under the age of 60
- You must be ineligible for prescription coverage

Cost
- There is no cost to participant for the program
- Prescription prices will vary

Prescription Drugs at Reduced Cost
Stark County Prescription Assistance Network
1320 Mercy DR. NW, Mercy Hall
Canton, OH 44708
330-458-4272
Fax: 330-580-4793
www.rxforohio.org/assistance/stark/
The Stark County Prescription Network is funded by 3 non-profit foundations to assist those in the community who fall in to the 200% poverty level. Patients who receive care and prescriptions from private physicians will be assisted through the Network's voucher program; pharmaceutical company patient assistance programs (PAP) and may buy medications through MedShare which offers drugs at reduced cost.

Oregon

Senior Prescription Drug Assistance Program
Oregon Department of Human Services
500 Summer St. NE E25
Salem, OR 97301-1098
503-945-6530
www.dhs.state.or.us/seniors/aging/spd
ap_info.htm
The Senior Prescription Drug Assistance Program (SPDAP) allows members of the program to purchase prescription drugs from participating pharmacies at the State Medicaid rate. $50 annual fee, provides discount not to exceed state Medicaid prescription rates.

Eligibility:
- Minimum age: 65

☐ Maximum annual income of $17,223 for individuals.

Pennsylvania
PACE Card
(Pennsylvania Pharmaceutical Assistance
Contract For The Elderly)
Pennsylvania Department of Aging
555 Walnut St., 5th Floor
Harrisburg, PA 17101
717-787-7313
800-225-7223
www.aging.state.pa.us/aging/cwp
Eligibility Requirements
• You must be 65 or older.
• Your income cannot exceed $14,500 if you are single; $17,700 for married couples.
• You must also live in the state for at least 90 days.

Cost
• You pay a $6.00 co-payment for each generic prescription. You may not purchase drugs out of state.
• You pay a $9.00 co-payment for each brand name prescription.
• PACE limits drug amounts to no more than a 30-day supply or 100 pills. There are no vacation supplies allowed.

PACENET
Eligibility Requirements
• Eligibility is the same as PACE above except for the income limits. A single person's total income can be between $14,500 and $23,500. A couple's combined total income can be between $17,700 and $31,500.

Costs
• You must meet a $40 monthly deductible, which is cumulative if it is not met each month. Once you meet the $40 deductible each month, you will pay an $8 co-payment for each generic prescription and a $15 co-payment for each brand name prescription.

Rhode Island
Rhode Island Pharmaceutical Assistance to the Elderly (RIPAE)
Rhode Island Department of Elderly Affairs
35 Howard Ave.
Cranston, RI 02920
800-322-2880
401-462-4000
www.dea.state.ri.us/socialservices.htm
Eligibility Requirements
• You must be a Rhode Island resident.
• You must be 65 years old.
• Your income must not exceed $17,155 if you are single; $21,445 if you are married.
• You can not have any other prescription drug coverage.

Cost
• Members pay 40% of the cost of prescription drugs used to treat certain illnesses.
• For incomes for single $21,535 and married $26,919, you pay 70%. For incomes for single $37,687 and married $43,070, you pay 85%.

Citizens Health Card
Citizens for Citizens
88 Black Falcon Avenue, Suite 342
Boston, MA 02210
800-214-5697
www.citizensenergy.com
Discounts for prescriptions are available to uninsured or underinsured citizens who are not eligible for public programs at participating pharmacies.

Cost
- $12 per year for individuals and $28 per year for families

Rx for Rhode Island
877-743-6779
http://rxforri.org/index.html
Rx4RI is a program that connects qualified, low-income people with discount prescription drugs, direct from the pharmaceutical manufacturer. The web site will help you search for programs that meet your needs.

South Carolina
SILVERRxCARD
1801 Main Street
P.O. Box 100101
Columbia, SC 29202-3101
877-239-5277 (toll-free)
http://southcarolina.fhsc.com/beneficia ries/SILVERxCARD/documents.asp
Eligibility Requirements
- Applications are available at local government offices, pharmacies, libraries, senior centers and Council on Aging offices.
- Must be 65 or older
- Resident of South Carolina for past six months
- Have no other prescription drug coverage
- Have income of $18,620 or less if single or $24,980 or less if married.

Costs
- You must pay $500 deductible before the plan begins to pay benefits
- Once you meet your deductible, you pay $10 co-pay on generic drugs at $15 co-pay on Brand drug.
- You will pay a $21 co-payment for prior authorization drugs.

- You may not be enrolled in both the Medicare Prescription Drug Plan and the SILVERRx Card.

Communicare
P.O. Box 186
Columbia, SC 29202-0186
800-763-0059
803-933-9183
www.commun-i-care.org

Eligibility Requirements
- You must be a South Carolina resident
- You must not be eligible for any prescription coverage
- You must fall within Communicare income guidelines
- You must fall into and document one of the following
  1. Currently employed
  2. Currently receiving unemployment compensation
  3. Currently receiving Social Security Retirement benefits
  4. Currently receiving Social Security Disability benefits or Workmen's Compensation

Cost
- $20 non-refundable application processing fee
- A patient must have a prescription written by a licensed physician and sent to our Central Fill Pharmacy.

South Dakota
Save 20% on Prescription Drugs
Brookings County Commission
314 6th Avenue
Brookings, SD 57006
605-696-8205
Fax 605-696-8208
www.brookingscountysd.gov

Brookings County Prescription Drug Discount Program offers county residents the opportunity to save an average of 20 percent off the retail price of commonly prescribed prescription drugs. All residents, regardless of age, income or existing coverage, may use the cards as often as people need and with no enrollment form or registration fee. but they may not be used in conjunction with another discount or prescription program. All local pharmacies except Wal-Mart participate in the program.

20%-50% Savings on Prescription Drugs

Davison County
200 East 4th Avenue
County Courthouse
Mitchell, SD 57301-2631
605-995-8608
Fax: 605-995-8618
www.davisoncounty.org/
DavisonCounty helps its residents save money on their prescription drugs by offering prescription drug discount cards. The cards are designed for people who don't have prescription drug coverage, but they're available to anyone regardless of income or age. The program offers an average of 20 percent off on commonly prescribed prescriptions and an average of 50 percent off three-month supplies of generics ordered through a mail service. The cards can be used at many participating pharmacies throughout Davison County and require no claim forms.

Tennessee
TennCare Rx program

Tennessee Department of Finance & Administration
Bureau of Tenncare
729 Church Street
Nashville, TN 37247

TennCare Information Line 800-669-1851
This program is not yet operational.

Eligibility:
Program for "individuals lacking Rx insurance coverage" -details to be specified.

Texas
State Prescription Drug Program

HHSC Headquarters
4900 N. Lamar Blvd.
Austin, TX 78751-2316
512-424-6500
512-424-6597 (TDD)
Not yet in operation. Postponed due to lack of funds. Details of what will be covered have not been determined.
Eligibility:
Medicare dual-eligibles and others; upper limit to be determined by Commission

Vermont
VScript Program

103 South Main St.
802-241-2880
Waterbury, VT 05676
800-250-8427
Eligibility Requirements
- You must be a resident of Vermont.
- You must be at least 65.
- You may not have income in excess of 175% of the federal poverty guidelines. For singles, $16,292; for couples, $21,857. Vscript Expanded has income requirements of $20,947 for singles and $28,102 for couples. The Vhap Program has income of $13,965 for singles and $18,735 for couples. The Vscript and Vscript Expanded are for maintenance prescriptions only. The Vhap program is for both

short-term and long-term prescriptions.
- You may not be in a health insurance plan that pays for all or a portion of the applicant's prescription drugs.

Cost
- There will be a co-payment requirement of $1 or $2 for Vscript and Vhap. Vscript Expanded copay is 50% of the cost of the drug.

The Vermont Medication Bridge Program

c/o RAVNAH
P.O. Box 787
Rutland, VT 05702-0787
866-VTPHARM
www.ravnah.org/vtpharm.htm
The Vermont Bridge Program provides needy patients in Vermont access to necessary prescription medications. The 866 phone number will direct Vermont patients to available programs.

VHAP Pharmacy - Vermont Health Access Program

Office of Vermont Health Access
312 Hurricane Lane
Williston, VT 05495
802 879-5900
800-529-4060 (in state)
800-250-8427 (out of state)
Fax: 802 879-5962
www.dsw.state.vt.us/districts/ovha/ovh a8.htm
Covers acute care and maintenance drugs. Discount varies based on income levels.

Eligibility:
- Minimum age: 65
- Maximum annual income of $13,368 for individuals and $17,988 for married couples.

Disabled: Recipients of disability benefits through SS or Medicare.

VSCRIPT Expanded

Office of Vermont Health Access
312 Hurricane Lane
Williston, VT 05495
802 879-5900
800-529-4060 (in state)
800-250-8427 (out of state)
Fax: 802 879-5962
www.dsw.state.vt.us/districts/ovha/ovh a8.htm
Only covers maintenance drugs. Discount varies, based on income levels.

Eligibility:
- Minimum age: 65
- Maximum annual income of $20,947 for individuals and $28,102 for married couples.

Healthy Vermonters (Plus) Discount Program

Office of Vermont Health Access
312 Hurricane Lane
Williston, VT 05495
802 879-5900
800-529-4060 (in state)
800-250-8427 (out of state)
Fax: 802 879-5962
www.dsw.state.vt.us/districts/ovha/ovh a8.htm
Includes a Medicaid waiver with 2% state payment toward cost of drugs. Not operational following adverse, 2002 federal ruling.

Eligibility:
- Minimum age: None.
- Maximum annual income of $37,240 for individuals over 65 and $49,960 for married couples over 65. For all others, $27,930 for individuals and $37,470 for married couples.

Washington
Rx Washington discount plan
Washington Health Care Authority
676 Woodland Square Loop SE
Lacey, WA 98503
http://rx.wa.gov/rx.shtml
800-227-5255
Negotiated discounts between 15% and 25% discounts on all prescription drugs.

Eligibility:
☐ Minimum age: 50 (disabled over 19)
☐ Maximum annual income of $27,936 for individuals and $37,470 for married couples.

West Virginia
Gold Mountaineer Discount Card
The West Virginia Bureau of Senior Services
1900 Kanawha Boulevard, East
Holly Grove, Building #10
Charleston, WV 25305-0160
304-558-3317
877-987-3646
www.state.wv.us/seniorservices
Eligibility Requirements
• You must be a West Virginia resident.
• You must be at least 60 years old.

Costs
• The card allows a discount for most prescriptions used by seniors. The cost is the Average Wholesale Price minus 13% or the pharmacy's usual and customary price, whichever is lower. For most generic drugs: Maximum Allowable Cost Pricing, which is approximately Average Wholesale Price minus 60%, or the pharmacy's usual & customary price whichever is lower.

Rx for West Virginia
877-WVA-Rx4U
www.rxforwv.org
Rx4WV is a program that connects qualified, low-income people with discount prescription drugs, direct from the pharmaceutical manufacturer. The web site will help you search for programs that meet your needs.

20%-50% Savings on Prescription Drugs
Ohio County
1500 Chapline Street
City County Building
Wheeling, WV 26003-3553
304-234-3628
Fax: 304-234-3827
wvweb.com/cities/wheeling/
Ohio County residents can save money on their prescription drugs by enrolling in the county's prescription drug discount program. The discount cards are designed for people who don't have prescription drug coverage, but they're available to anyone regardless of income or age. The program offers an average of 20 percent off on commonly prescribed prescriptions and an average of 50 percent off three-month supplies of generics ordered through a mail service. The cards can be used at many participating pharmacies throughout Ohio County and require no claim forms.

Wisconsin
SeniorCarex
Department of Health and Family Services
PO Box 6710
Madison, WI 53707-0710
608-266-0554
800-657-2038
www.dhfs.state.wi.us/seniorCare/index.htm
Eligibility Requirements
• You must be a Wisconsin resident.

- You must be 65 years or older.
- You must meet one of the different level income requirements.

Costs
- You pay a $30 annual enrollment fee per person.
- Your co-payment depends on your income level. For the first level, the annual maximum income is $14,896 per individual and $19,984 per couple. With that, there is no deductible and the co-payment is $5 for generic drugs and $15 for brand name drugs. Maximum income amounts for Level 2a are $14,897 to $18,620 per individual and $19,985 to $24,980 per couple. The deductible for that level is $500 and then the same co-payments as above. Level 2b has an $800 deductible and after that is met, the cost is the same co-payment described above. The income levels are $18,621 to $22,344 per individual and $24,981 to $29,976 per couple annually.

Wyoming
Prescription Drug Assistance Program
Department of Health/ Medicaid
Hathaway Bldg., Room 147
2300 Capitol Ave.
Cheyenne, WY 82002
307-777-7531
800-442-2766
http://wyequalitycare.acs-inc.com/
Prescription drug assistance of up to 15 percent off the wholesale price for the elderly. Benefits determined by income level.

Eligibility:
- No age limit.
- Maximum annual income of $9,310 and no more than $1,000 in resource, with home and one vehicle exempt. Enrollees with income under $9,310 are eligible regardless of spouse's income.

REAL ESTATE

No matter where you live in the United States, you can find over 150 money programs to buy property or fix up property just in your city. This is what we are able to find for our clients in our customized real estate research service. But there is nothing magical about finding all of these programs. It just takes hard work and a basic knowledge of where these programs might be hiding.

Here are the main sources to contact for identifying money programs for real estate:

1. Find Federal Money Programs For Real Estate
Anyone selling you information about federal programs on real estate has to get the information from this source. It's printed every six months by the federal government, and is the major source of all federal programs. You can do a free search identifying all the federal real estate programs by going on the web to {http://www.cfda.gov}. The book is also available in almost every public library and for sale from the U.S. Government Printing Office {www.gpo.gov}.

2. Find State Money Programs For Real Estate
Every state has offices that provide financing for buying and fixing up homes and for real estate investing. Call your State Capitol Operator located in your state capital, or go to {http://www.govengine.com/} and look for your state housing office for information about all their programs. You

can find a listing of State Housing Finance Agencies at the National Council of State Housing Agencies website at {www.ncsha.org}.

3. Find Local Government Programs For Real Estate

Contact your city and county officials. Almost every local jurisdiction has money for housing and real estate. Many have money for closing costs, down payments, repairs and even rental assistance. It will take some effort but it's worth the time. You can also locate your local and county government offices on the web at {http://www.govengine. com/localgov/index.html}.

4. Find Money From Non-Profit Organizations for Business

There are thousands of local and national nonprofits groups that help homeowners and real estate investors. They can be groups that offer down payment money, closing cost money, and even free technical assistance. It may take a considerable amount of time to find them all. Your local library can be of help or your local elected officials listed below.

The following organizations can also be helpful in tracking down non-profit organizations:

☐ The Foundation Center of New York City maintains a database of all foundations who provide money to non-profit organizations or individuals. Their information is available on the web at {http://fdncenter.org} or from their participating libraries by contacting 212-620-4230.

☐ The Guidestar company in Williamsburg, VA also maintains a database of foundations and they can reached at 757-229-4631 or at {www.guidestar.com}. Much of their database is accessible for free on the web.

Money and Help To Buy Real Estate
Or Pay Your Rent or Mortgage

 The federal government supports over 1,000 local non-profit organizations that will help homeowners, real estate investors or even renters with any kind of programs they may have with buying real estate or even holding on to it. To find offices near you, contact the U.S. Department of Housing and Urban Development Housing Counseling Center Locator, 800-569-4287 or 800-217-6970 or {http://www.hud.gov/offices/hsg/sfh/hcc/hcc_home.cfm}.

Find Your Local Community Action Agency
There are over 1,000 local non-profit offices that can help you take advantage of basic money programs to purchase or fix up real estate. They offer people help to locate and use government programs or other money from non-profit organizations. To find a community action agency near you, contact Community Action Partnership, 1100 17th St NW Suite 500, Washington, DC 20036 202-265-7546, Fax: 202-265-8850, {info@communityaction partnership.com}; {www.communityactionpartnership.com}.

More Help In Identifying Real Estate Programs
For help identifying more money programs, contact the Office of Community Planning and Development at 800-998-9999 or {http://www.comcon.org}.

We have a book that identifies many of these money sources called "Free Money For Real Estate." Call 1-800-955-POWER or see {http://lesko.com/home/}. We also offer customized real estate research service for any city in the country, see {www.howtogetagrant.com/25grremr61}.

Main Sources of Housing

Four federal government agencies handle most of the federal government's housing programs. Don't let this limit you, but these are the best places to start:

U.S. Department of Housing and Urban Development, 451 7th St., SW, Washington, DC 20410; {www.hud.gov}.

Rural Housing Service, U.S. Department of Agriculture, Room 5037, South Building, 14th St., and Independence Ave., SW, Washington, DC 20250; 202-720-4323; {www.rurdev.usda.gov}.

Bureau of Indian Affairs, Office of Tribal Services, MS 4660 MIB, 1849 C St., NW, Washington, DC 20240; 202-308-3667; {www.doi.gov/bureau-indian-affairs.html}.

U.S. Department of Veterans Affairs, Washington, DC 20420; 202-273-7355; 800-827-1000; {www.va.gov}.

Free Money For Closing Costs and a Down Payment

Houston has a program that offers $4,000 in down-payment and closing costs through their First-Time Homebuyers Program.

Iowa offers up to $2,750 in grants for a down-payment. You can be earning up to $65,000 a year and still be eligible for the money in their Down Payment/Closing Cost Grant Program.

Many cities, like Minneapolis, will offer interest free loans, called Equity Participation Loans, for up to 10% of the cost of the home. You pay back the money when you sell the house.

Programs vary from state to state and city to city. Contact your city government, your county government, and your local community development office to learn about local programs. If you have trouble locating your local community development office, the following organizations may be able to help:

National Association of Housing and Redevelopment Officials, 630 Eye St, NW, Washington, DC 20001; 202-289-3500; 877-866-2476, Fax: 202-289-8181; {www.nahro.org}

Information Center, Office of Community Planning and Development, P.O. Box 7189,

Gaithersburg, MD 20898; 800-998-9999, Fax: 301-519-5027; {www.comcon.org}. Also be sure to contact your state housing office listed in the Appendix.

Free Housing Books

☐ *A Consumer's Guide to Mortgage Settlement Costs*

☐ *Home Mortgages: Understanding the Process and Your Right to Fair Lendings*

☐ *A Consumer's Guide to Mortgage Refinancings*

☐ *Looking for the Best Mortgage: Shop, Compare, Negotiate*

☐ *Consumer Handbook on Adjustable Rate Mortgages*

☐ *A Consumer's Guide to Mortgage Lock-Ins*

For your copies, contact Board of Governors of the Federal Reserve System, Publications Fulfillment, MS-127, Washington, DC 20551; 202-452-3245; Fax: 202-728-5886; {www.federalreserve.gov/}.

WOW!...The Government Will Pay My Mortgage"

You'd never have thought to ask, would you?

There are now programs that will make your mortgage payments for you when you get into financial trouble. For example, Pennsylvania law, 35 P.S. § 1680.401 et seq., states it will provide "*mortgage assistance*

payments to homeowners who are in danger of losing their homes through foreclosure and through no fault of their own and who have a reasonable prospect of resuming mortgage payments within the prescribed time frame." Pennsylvania calls it the ***"Homeowners' Emergency Mortgage Assistance Program."***

One of the best ways to find out if there are programs like this in your area is to contact the local HUD approved Housing Counseling agencies. To find your closest agency, contact your state housing office listed in the Appendix, the Housing Counseling Center locator at 1-800-569-4287; {www.hud.gov/offices/hsg/sfh/hcc/hcc_home.cfm}, or Housing Counseling Clearinghouse, P.O. Box 9057, Gaithersburg, MD 20898; 888-466-3487; Fax: 703-734-0067; {www.hudhcc.org}.

If your local agency doesn't have money to pay your mortgage, they will certainly help you work out other arrangements with your mortgage company.

Free Mortgage Publications

The Federal Trade Commission understands this, so they have compiled several brochures to get you started. Some of the titles include *Home Financing Primer*, *Mortgage Servicing*, *Mortgage Discrimination*, and more.

To receive your copies, contact Public Reference, Room 130, Federal Trade Commission, 600 Pennsylvania Ave., NW, Washington, DC 20580; 202-326-2222; 877-FTC-HELP; {www.ftc.gov}.

Make Money Going To Housing Classes

A HUD-approved housing counseling agency in Philadelphia offers $1,000 in settlement costs to certain people who attend pre-purchase house counseling sessions. A counseling agency in Boston offers new home buyers access to special low down-payment mortgages if they attend pre-housing classes.

There are over 350 HUD-approved counseling agencies that offer free classes and help in housing related issues including:

The Best Way To Buy And Finance A Home
Is A Reverse Mortgage For You?
Foreclosure and Eviction Options
The Best Way To Finance A Home Fix-Up

These non-profit agencies are trained and approved by the U.S. Department of Housing and Urban Development (HUD).

To find your closest agency, contact your State housing office listed in the Appendix, the Housing Counseling Center locator at 1-888-466-3487; {www.hud.gov/hsgcoun.html}, or Housing Counseling Clearinghouse, P.O. Box 9057, Gaithersburg, MD 20898; 888-466-3487, Fax: 703-734-0067.

"Get The Lead Out" And Get Your House Or Apartment Painted For Free

If you are living in a house or apartment that was built before 1978, you, or even your landlord, may be eligible for grant money and other assistance to make sure that you do not suffer the effects of lead poisoning from lead-based paint.

Chips or dust from this type of paint can be highly dangerous to humans, especially children. The U.S. Department of Housing and Urban Development spends over $60 million a year helping home owners and apartment owners eliminate the problems that may be caused by lead paint.

Contact your state department of housing listed in the Appendix to see if your state has money for lead paint removal.

How Lead Paint Can Affect Your Kids

Houses and apartments built before 1978 may contain lead contaminated surface dust and paint chips, which, if consumed by children, can result in reduced intelligence, behavioral problems, learning disabilities, and even permanent brain damage.

Government sponsored programs can help you inspect your home for lead paint and even get a blood test for your children for potential problems. To find out more about these programs or the effects of lead-based paint, contact the following:

National Lead Information Center, 422 South Clinton Avenue, Rochester, NY 14620; 800-424-LEAD; Fax: 585-232-3111; {www.epa.gov/lead/nlic.htm}.

Office of Lead Hazard Control, U.S. Department of Housing and Urban Development, 451 7th Street, SW, Room P3206, Washington, DC 20410; 202-708-1112; Fax: 202-708-1455; {www.hud.gov/offices/lead}.

Home Repair Programs

Here are a few *HOME REPAIR* programs we found that were available at the time we were doing research. Things change, but make sure to contact local agencies to see what may be available to you!

$4,000 Grant To Paint Your Home: That's what Canton, Ohio offers to very low-income residents — grants to paint their house or put on new siding. They feel that an investment like this improves the value of all the properties in the area.

Sunnyvale, California offers some of their residents $400 in grant money to paint their homes. And if you're over 60 or have a disability, you can get a $1,200 grant.

See if your city or state offers a program like this.

City of Sunnyvale
Housing Division
City Hall
456 West Olive Avenue
P.O. Box 3707
Sunnyvale, CA 94088
408-730-7250
http://Sunnyvale.ca/Departments/Community+Development

Tacoma Community Redevelopment Authority
747 Market St., Room 1036
Tacoma, WA 98402
253-591-5236
www.cityoftacoma.org

Housing Program Manager
City of Canton
218 Cleveland Ave., SW, 5th Floor
Canton, OH 44702
330-489-3040
www.cityofcanton.com/citygov/ecdev
dept/genrepair.html

Minneapolis Community Development Agency
Crown Roller Mill
105 Fifth Ave. S, Suite 200
Minneapolis, MN 55401
612-673-5095
Fax: 612-673-5100
www.mcda.org

Los Angeles Housing Department
1200 West 7th Street
Los Angeles, CA 90017
213-808-8888
866-557-7368
www.lacity.org/LAHD

Department of Housing and Community Development
300 W. Washington St., Room 315
P.O. Box 3136
Greensboro, NC 27402
336-373-2349
Fax: 336-412-6315
www.ci.greensboro.nc.us/HCD/

Metropolitan Development and Housing Agency
701 S. 6th St.
Nashville, TN 37202
615-252-8590
www.nashville.gov/mdha

Department of Community Development
Neighborhood Conservation Services Division
602 Robert D. Ray Drive
Des Moines, IA 50309
515-283-4787
www.ci.des-moines.ia.us/departments/cd/

Low-Income Weatherization Program
Housing Authority and Community
Services Agency
177 Day Island Rd.
Eugene, OR 97401
541-682-3755
Fax: 541-682-3411
www.hacsa.org

Cut Your Rent By 50%

Studies show that people with less
income pay a higher portion of their
salary on housing than people in
higher income categories. It is not
unusual for a single mom to pay 70%
of her salary in rent.

The government has a program called
Section 8 Rental Assistance Program
that offers vouchers and direct
payments to landlords. This will, in
turn, cut your rent down to only 30%
of your income.

Of course, there are income
requirements for this program. For
example, in Arlington Country, VA, a
one-person household with an income
of $23,000 qualifies for the program.
Arlington County also has housing
grant rental assistance for low-income
elderly, disabled, and working families
with children. Some of these programs
have waiting lists, but it could be
worth the wait.

To apply for these federal programs,
contact your state housing authority
listed in the appendix, your local
housing authority, or a community
services agency. If you have trouble
getting the help you need, you can
contact Information Center, Office of
Community Planning and
Development, P.O. Box 7189,
Gaithersburg, MD 20898; 800-998-
9999, Fax: 301-519-5027; {www.
comcon.org}.

Free Money To Fix Up Your Home

States, cities, and counties, as well as
local community development
agencies are providing grants, loans,
and even supplies and technical
assistance for homeowners who want
to fix up the inside or outside of their
homes. Many of these have income
requirements you must meet. Others
offer forgivable loans if you stay in the
house a certain number of years. Here
are some examples of what
communities are offering to their
residents:

Sunnyvale, CA: $2,000 grant for
disabled homeowners to fix up anything through the Home Access Grant
Program.

Houston, TX: loans and grants for
major repairs through their Housing
Assistance Program for the Elderly and
Disabled.

Tacoma, WA: Up to $3,500 loan at 0%
interest with no monthly payments
through the Major Home Repair
Program.

Minneapolis, MN: $15,000, no interest,
and no payments until you sell in their
Deferred Rehabilitation Loans.

Baton Rouge, LA: $20,000 grant to fix up your home through the Housing Rehabilitation Grant Program.

Los Angeles, CA: Free help with roofing, plumbing, electrical and heating work, painting, deadbolt locks, smoke alarms, screens, windows, and yard maintenance for seniors or disabled persons through the Handy Worker Program.

Michigan: $1,000 to $10,000 at zero interest, to be paid back when you sell your home through the Rehabilitation Assistance Program.

Nashville, TN: $18,000 at 3% to fix up your home.

Lane County, OR: offers grants for weatherization assistance for weatherstripping, storm doors and windows, and insulation.

Des Moines, IA: offers emergency repair loans.

Greensboro, NC: has low interest loans for people with incomes over $30,000 and $8,500 grants for people with incomes up to $20,000.

Programs vary from state to state and city to city. Contact your city government, your county government, and your local community development office to learn about local programs.

If you have trouble locating your local community development office, the following organizations may be able to help:

☐ National Association of Housing and Redevelopment Officials, 630 Eye St., NW, Washington, DC 20001; 202-289-3500, 877-

---

$ & Help To Fix-Up A Home For A Senior

The Home Modification Action Project at:

http://www.usc.edu/ go/hmap/index.html

866-2476, Fax: 202-289-8181; {www.nahro.org}

☐ Information Center, Office of Community Planning and Development, P.O. Box 7189, Gaithersburg, MD 20898; 800-998-9999, Fax: 301-519-5027; {www.comcon.org}

Also be sure to contact your state housing office listed in the Appendix.

Your Rich Uncle Will Cosign A Loan To Buy or Fix Up a Home

Both the U.S. Department of Housing and Urban Development (HUD) and the Rural Housing Service of the U.S. Department of Agriculture offer loan guarantees to lending agencies around the county. A loan-guarantee assures the lending agency that the government will pay for the loan if you can't.

In addition, the Rural Housing Service has a direct loan program that provides loans to lower income families to buy, build, repair, renovate, or relocate their home. This is called the Section 502 Program.

To investigate the programs available in your area, contact your local HUD office listed in the blue pages of your telephone book, or U.S. Department of Housing and Urban Development (HUD), 451 7th Street, SW, Washington, DC 20410; 202-708-1112, 800-245-2691; {www.hud.gov}.

To find your local Rural Housing Service, look in the blue pages of your telephone book, or contact Single Family Housing Programs, USDA Rural Housing Service, Room 5037, South Building, 14th St. and Independence Ave., SW, Washington, DC 20250; 202-720-4323; {www.rurdev.usda.gov/}.

In addition, you may contact your state housing office located the Appendix.

Money For Seniors And Those With A Disability To Buy or Fix Up A Home

The city of Houston offers $5,000 fix up money for the disabled and elderly in their Emergency Repair Program. Minneapolis offers home repair grants of $10,000 to people with disabilities who have incomes under $18,000. Nebraska has a special low interest loan program to help people with disabilities buy a home.

The Rural Housing Service of the U.S. Department of Agriculture offers special grants through their Section 504 program of up to $7,500 if you're over 62, and need to fix up your home. Programs vary from state to state and city to city, and obviously, many have eligibility requirements.

Contact your city government, your county government and your local community development office to learn about local programs. If you have trouble locating your local community development office, contact *National Association of Housing and Redevelopment Officials*, 630 Eye St., NW, Washington, DC 20001; 202-289-3500, 877-866-2476, Fax: 202-289-8181; {www.nahro.org}, or *Information Center, Office of Community Planning and Development*, P.O. Box 7189, Gaithersburg, MD 20898; 800-998-9999, Fax: 301-519-5027; {www.comcon.org}.

To find your local *Rural Housing Service*, look in the blue pages of your telephone book, or contact Single Family Housing Programs, USDA Rural Housing Service, Room 5014-S, Mail Stop 0701, 1400 Independence Ave., SW, Washington, DC 20250-0701; 202-690-1533; TTY: 800-877-8339; Fax: 202-690-0500; {www.rurdev.usda.gov/}. In addition, you may contact your state housing office listed in the Appendix.

Money To Buy Or Fix Up a Mobile Home

The city of Sunnyvale, Ca will lend you up to $7,500 at 0-5% interest for a mobile home. New York State offers loans to help you buy a mobile home park or the land your mobile home sits on through their *Manufactured Home Cooperative Fund Program*. And the U.S. Department of Agriculture has what is called *Section 504 funds* that allow loans of up to $20,000 to fix a mobile home or to move it from one site to another.

Here is how to contact the major programs for manufactured (mobile) homes.

VA-Guaranteed Manufactured Home Loan

Contact your local office of the Department of Veterans Affairs, or U.S. Department of Veterans Affairs,

810 Vermont Avenue, Washington, DC 20420; 800-827-1000; {www.va.gov/about_va/programs.htm}.

FHA Insured Title I Manufactured Home Loan

Contact your local office of Housing and Urban Development listed in the blue pages of your telephone book, or your state housing office listed in the Appendix, or the Housing Counseling Clearinghouse, 451 7th Street, SW, Washington, DC 20410; 202-708-1112; TTY: 202-708-1455; {www.hud.gov}

Section 504 Rural Housing Loans and Grants

To find your local Rural Housing Service, look in the blue pages of your telephone book, or contact Single Family Housing Programs, USDA Rural Housing Service, Room 5014-S, 1400 Independence Ave., SW, Washington, DC 20250-0701; 202-690-1533; TTY: 800-877-8339; Fax: 202-690-0500; {www.rurdev.usda.gov/}.

Free Houses

Well, maybe they're not free, but they can cost you as little as a few hundred dollars a month. And maybe they're not in good shape, but many of the programs will also offer you a low interest loan to fix up the house.

Some states refer to the program as an *Urban Homesteading Act*. The idea of the program is that the government gets you a home for next to nothing and you agree to live there for a certain number of years.

Minnesota has a program. Baltimore had a very active program for many years. Davenport, Iowa purchases homes, completely rehabs them, and then offers the houses in a lottery each May. You must get a mortgage, but your monthly payments are under $400 a month for a completely rebuilt house!

There are some states, like Alaska, that still offer wilderness land for homesteading. Because the houses are so cheap, there is usually a lottery for eligible buyers. Contact your city government, your county government and your local community development office to learn about local programs.

If you have trouble finding your local community development agency, the following organizations may be able to help. These organizations do not have funds, but may be able to help you locate local agencies.

- National Association of Housing and Redevelopment Officials, 630 Eye St., NW, Washington, DC 20001; 202-289-3500, 1-877-866-2476, Fax: 202-289-8181; {www.nahro.org}

- Information Center, Office of Community Planning and Development, P.O. Box 7189, Gaithersburg, MD 20898; 800-998-9999; Fax: 301-519-5027; {www.comcon.org}

You can also contact your state housing office located in the Appendix.

Free Legal Help For Renters and Home Buyers

It's illegal for landlords, realtors, bankers and others to discriminate against you because of your race, religion, sex, family status, or handicap. Landlords also have rules to follow in dealing with you as a tenant. With the proper free help you can find out how to:

- Stop paying the rent if your toilet doesn't work.
- Get the government to sue your landlord for discriminating against your child.
- Break a lease and not pay a penalty.
- Get your eviction stopped.
- Force a bank to give you a loan for a new home.
- Get your landlord to widen your doorways to fit your wheelchair.
- Get a third party to fight your landlord for you.

To file a complaint or to learn more about your rights in dealing with landlords and people in the housing industry, contact any of the following:

- ☐ Your state housing office
- ☐ Your state Attorney General's office in the Appendix
- ☐ Fair Housing and Equal Opportunity, U.S. Department of Housing and Urban Development, Room 5204, 451 Seventh St, SW, Washington, DC 20410; 800-669-9777; {www.hud.gov/complaints/ housediscrim.cfm}.

Use Your Sweat as a Down Payment and Get a No-Interest Loan

One of the biggest providers of this type of program is the non-profit organization called Habitat for Humanity. You've probably seen them in the news with Ex-President Jimmy Carter helping them build houses. They have even received government money to help support their program.

The typical arrangement is for people with incomes between $9,000 and $30,000. You and your family work an average of 300 to 500 hours building your home or other people's homes, and in return you get a home with no down-payment and a very low mortgage payment.

Because people provide free labor to build the home, you only pay about $60,000 for a $100,000 home, and you get the money interest free. A typical bank loan can cost you over $700 per month, but through this program you pay only about $200 a month.

Other local or national organizations may run similar programs in your area, with or without government financing. To find programs in your area, you can contact:

Habitat for Humanity International, 121 Habitat Street, Americus, GA 31709; 229-924-6935; {www.habitat. org}. To find a local affiliate, call 229-924-6935, ext. 2551 or ext. 2552; Fax: 229-924-0577.

Information Center, Office of Community Planning and Development, P.O. Box 7189, Gaithersburg, MD 20898; 800-998-9999, Fax: 301-519-5027/5622; TDD: 1-800-483-2209; {www.comcon.org}.

Staying Clear Of Deadly Radon Gases

Nowadays when you buy a home, you often have a radon level reading taken, but what do the numbers mean?

The *National Radon Information Hotline* has a free brochure that explains what radon is, how to test for it, and more.

There is also a Radon FIX-IT Program operated by the Consumer Research Council, a nonprofit consumer organization that provides free guidance and encouragement to consumers who are trying to fix their homes that have elevated radon levels. The Program operates from noon to 8 p.m. EST and has information on reducing elevated radon levels, referrals to experts, and names of contractors who are qualified to help.

For more information, contact National Radon Information Hotline at 800-767-7236 (SOS-RADON) and the Radon Fix-It Program at 800-644-6999; or Indoor Air Quality Information Clearinghouse, IAQ Info, P.O. Box 37133, Washington, DC 20013; 800-438-4318; {www.epa.gov/iaq/iaqinfo.html}.

Is Your Drinking Water Safe?

According to the National Consumer Water Survey, 75% of those surveyed have concerns about the quality of the water they drink. Many people are purchasing bottled water or water purification devices for drinking water, but is it a wise use of your money?

The *Safe Drinking Water Hotline* can answer any question or concern you may have regarding drinking water, and can provide you with publications such as: *Is Your Drinking Water Safe?*, *Home Water Testing*, *Home Water Treatment Units*, *Bottled Water* fact sheet, and more. Contact Safe Drinking Water Hotline, U.S. Environmental Protection Agency, 401 M St., SW, Washington, DC 20460;

$83,000 / YR Income and The Government Considers You Needy?

Many of the government housing programs, especially the grant and low interest programs, may have income requirements. But don't let a good salary stop you from investigating the opportunities. The first time home buyer program in Illinois has income requirements that go up to $83,000.

800-426-4791; {www.epa.gov/OGWDW}.

Volunteers Will Fix Up Your (Or Your Mom's) Home For Free

Many service organizations have begun to organize community service days, where the town is beautified along with certain homes in need of repair.

Christmas in April is a national organization with over 185 affiliates that gather together volunteers to help rehabilitate the homes of low-income homeowners. The work is done for free with the goal being to provide a safe and secure home for those in need.

An example of a program in the Dallas area is the Volunteer Home Repair and Weatherization Program. This program provides home repairs that improve the health, safety, and energy efficiency of a home for low-income homeowners.

Contact your city government, your county government and your local community development office to learn about local programs.

In the Dallas area, contact Volunteer Home Repair and Weatherization Program, Center for Housing Resources, 3103 Greenwood, Dallas, TX 75204; 214-828-4390, Fax: 214-828-4412; {www.chrdallas.org}

How To Save Up To $650/Year On Fuel Bills

The average family spends close to $1300 a year on their home's utility bills, and a large portion of that energy is wasted. By using a few inexpensive energy efficient measures, you can reduce your energy bills by 10% to 50%.

With the publication, *Energy Savers: Tips on Saving Energy and Money at Home*, you can go step by step through your home to learn energy saving tips. Topics covered include insulation/ weatherization, water heating, lighting, appliances, and more. There is even a major appliance shopping guide that explains the energy labels on appliances and shows you how to choose the best one for you.

The Energy Efficiency and Renewable Energy Clearinghouse can answer your questions on all these topics and has publications and easy to understand fact sheets. Contact the Energy Efficiency and Renewable Energy Clearinghouse, Mail Stop EE-1,

Department of Energy, Washington, DC 20585; 800-363-3732, 202-586-9220; {www.eere.energy.gov/}.

Get Money For Down Payments And Closing Costs Here

The following are examples of financial assistance programs offered by states, cities and counties at the time we were doing our initial research for this book. Be aware that these programs are constantly changing and all have some form of eligibility requirements, but don't let that stop you! New ones are added and old ones may be discarded.

To be sure that you are aware of all the programs available in your area, contact your state office on housing (listed in the Appendix), your city housing office, your county housing office, as well as any local community development offices that may be in your area. If you need help locating your community development office, the following may be of assistance: National Association of Housing and Redevelopment Officials, 630 Eye St., NW, Washington, DC 20001; 202-289-3500, 877-866-2476; Fax: 202-289-8181: {www.nahro.org}.

- *Houston*: $3,500 to help with a down payment and closing costs in the First-Time Homebuyers Program.
- *Iowa*: 5% of your mortgage in grant money for a down payment and closing costs through Down Payment/ Closing Cost Grant Program.
- *Minneapolis, MN*: $3,000 at 0% interest due when you sell the home
- *Michigan*: $5,000 at 0% interest and no monthly payments

- *Baton Rouge, LA*: $10,000 at 0% interest and no payments for 20 years through Home Buyers Assistance Program.
- *Georgia*: $5,000 for a down payment at 0% interest through Own HOME Program.
- *Hawaii*: $15,000 loans at 3% for down payments, but you only pay interest for the first 5 years in the Down Payment Loan Program.
- *Kansas*: You only need $500 and Kansas will assist with down payment, closing costs, and legal fees in First Time Homebuyers Downpayment Assistance Program.
- *Maine*: Buy a house with only $750, and finance your down payment at 0% through Down Home Program.
- *La Miranda, CA*: 10% loan for down payment for first time homebuyers in the Down Payment Assistance Program.
- *Tacoma, WA*: A $5,000 loan for your down payment and settlement costs in Down Payment Assistance Program.
- *Indianapolis, IN*: Put 1% down and your closing costs go into a 2nd mortgage in Good Neighbor II Loan Program.
- *Los Angeles, CA*: 2% forgivable loan for closing costs money, plus $35,000 loan for repairs with no payments for 30 years or until the house is sold through Home WORKS! Program.
- *New York State*: 0% down payment in Low Down Payment, Conventional Rate Program.
- *Walnut Creek, CA*: Get a second mortgage for half of the closing costs and 2% of down payment with nothing due until you sell or refinance.

Who Qualifies As A First Time Homebuyer?

Most government programs define a first time homebuyer as someone who has not owned a home during the past 3 years or who is legally separated or divorced.

How To Keep Your Air Clean Of Asbestos, Carbon Monoxide, and Second Hand Smoke

You don't need to hire some high priced consultants to find how to keep the air in your home clean of pollution and other toxic substances. The Indoor Air Quality Information Clearinghouse is the expert on all forms of indoor air pollution. They have publications and information on second hand smoke, asbestos, carbon monoxide, air cleaners, and more. You can contact them at Indoor Air Quality Information Clearinghouse, IAQ Info, 600 Maryland Ave., SW, Washington, DC 20024-2520; 800-484-1307; {www.epa.gov/iaq/iaqinfo.html}.

Free Nutrition Counseling and Classes

Nutrition counseling, menu planning, cooking instruction and comparison shopping is available from your local County Cooperative Extension Service. Group instruction is free of charge, but persons requesting individual lessons are asked to pay for the lesson materials.

They also help neighborhoods establish and maintain community gardens, which provide fresh vegetables to area residents. To find an office near you, look in the blue pages of your local telephone book under county government for County Cooperative Extension Service, or contact the state lead office listed in the Appendix.

Government Foreclosed Homes At Bargain Prices

No, they are not giving away the kitchen sink, but you may be able to find some good deals nonetheless. The government sells foreclosed homes all across the country, and even in your neighborhood. You don't need to know someone to get in on these deals. All are sold through real estate agents.

Contact your agent, ask about government repossessed homes and they can do a search for you. These are not just HUD homes, but also those from the VA, Fannie Mae, IRS, Federal Deposit Insurance Corporation, and more.

I want to be able to say that they give you these houses at 50% off, but I can't. Most want fair market value, but the government does not want to carry the real estate taxes for all these houses either. You can make a deal that works out best for everyone.

For more information, contact HUD USER, P.O. Box 23268, Washington, DC 20026-3268; 800-245-2691; TDD: 800-245-2691; Fax: 202-708-9981; {www.huduser.org} (Note: this website has links to all the major government home sale programs); U.S. Department of Veterans Affairs, 810 Vermont Ave., NW, Washington, DC 20420; 800-827-1000; {www.va.gov}.

Free Housing Experts

The HUD website includes text of over 20 helpful guides, such as: *How To Buy a Home, How to Get A Mortgage*, and *Hud-approved Lenders*, as well as listings of government homes for sale. These are not just HUD homes, but

also those from the Department of Veteran Affairs, General Services Administration, and more. Although the houses are not steals, you can find some great deals. For housing information, call HUD USER, P.O. Box 23268, Washington, DC 20026-3268; 800-245-2691; TDD: 800-245-2691; Fax: 202-708-9981; {www.huduser.org}.

$2,000 Grants or 2% Interest Loan To Fix Up Your Home

A family of 4 can be making close to $30,000 year and still be eligible for a 2% interest loan from local Community Action Agency. Some agencies also offer grants or are aware of other local organizations that provide grants. There are about 1,000 of them around the country to help neighborhoods.

To find an agency near you, contact Community Action Partnership, 1100 17th St., NW, Suite 500, Washington, DC 20036, 202-265-7546; Fax: 202-265-8850; {www.communityaction partnership.org}.

Free Weatherization, Fuel Bills, and Rent for Incomes Up to $50,000

If you are within a certain income and need help paying your heating bills, need money to make your house more energy efficient, or need funds for urgent repairs, call your local Community Action Agency. There are about 1,000 of them around the country to help neighborhoods. They will also come out and check if your home or apartment needs to be more energy efficient.

To find an agency near you, contact Community Action Partnership, 1100 17th St., NW, Suite 500, Washington,

DC 20036; 202-265-7546; Fax: 202-265-8850; {www.communityaction partnership.org}.

Also, your local utility can provide you with or refer you to other programs in your area to analyze your energy usage, recommend energy saving measures, provide fuel and utility assistance to retain or restore service, establish payment discounts based on income and usage, or establish affordable payment plans if you are in arrears. Contact your local utility company to take advantage of these services.

Free Furniture

The Community Action Agency in Albany, New York offers free furniture for those with a need because of fire or other hardship reasons. Other agencies offer free furniture if you are moving into a Community Action Agency's affordable housing or housing units operated by the agency. See if your local agency offers free furniture. There are about 1,000 of them around the country to help neighborhoods.

To find an agency near you, contact Community Action Partnership, 1100 17th St., NW, Suite 500, Washington, DC 20036; 202-265-7546; Fax: 202-265-8850; {www.communityaction partnership.org}.

50% Discount On a New Heating System

The California Energy Commission offers residences and small businesses up to 50% of the cost of a new heating or air conditioning system if it meets their standards for "emerging renewable technologies," like solar heating, and more. Their program is

called Emerging Renewables Buy-Down Program.

To learn more, contact California Energy Commission, Media and Public Communications Office, 1516 Ninth St., MS-29, Sacramento, CA 95814; 800-555-7794; outside CA; 916-654-4058; {www.consumerenergy center.org}. Check with your state utility commission in the Appendix to see if your state offers similar programs.

$2,500 to Pay Your Insulation Bills

Storm windows, insulation, and even weatherstripping can help reduce your heating and cooling bills. The U.S. Department of Energy offers the Weatherization Assistance program.

As many as 20-30 million people are eligible for this program; everyone from homeowners to renters, from those who live in single or multi-family housing to those who lie in mobile homes. Each state varies on who is eligible for these services, but typically a family of four can make $24,000 and still qualify. Preference is given to persons over 60, those with disabilities and families with children. If you receive Supplemental Security Income or Temporary Assistance to Needy Families, you are automatically eligible.

You must apply through your state weatherization agency. States allocate dollars to nonprofit agencies for purchasing and installing energy-related repairs, with an energy audit being the first step to determine what is necessary. The average grant is $2,500.

For more information on eligibility and where to apply in your state, contact Weatherization Assistance Programs Branch, EE44, U.S. Department of Energy, 1000 Independence Ave., SW, Washington, DC 20585; 800-DIAL-DOE; Fax: 202-586-4403; {www. eren.doe.gov/buildings/home_weatheri zing.html}.

$2,800 To Pay Your Heating Bill

Even if you are not approved for the U.S. Department of Energy's Weatherization Assistance Program, you might still be eligible for short-term assistance on your utility bill for the Low-Income Home Energy Assistance Program (LIHEAP). Funded by the U.S. Department of Health and Human Services, LIHEAP serves low-income families by offering heating and cooling subsidies, energy crisis intervention to assist in weather-related and fuel supply shortages and household energy-related emergencies, such as utility shutoffs. The amount of money and eligibility for this program varies from state to state, so you need to contact your state LIHEAP coordinator to learn how to apply.

Contact Office of Community Services, Division of Energy Assistance, Administration for Children and Families, U.S. Department of Health and Human Services, 370 L'Enfant Promenade, SW, 5th Floor West, Washington, DC 20447; 202-401-9351; toll-free 888-294-8662; {www.acf.dhhs.gov/programs/liheap}.

States Will Pay Your Property Taxes

Or pay part of the amount. Almost all states have some type of property or homestead tax exemption for the elderly and disabled, and often those with low incomes or veterans. How the program operates varies from state to state, with some states offering a reduced tax rate off of a percentage of the home's value. Other states offer a property tax deferral program for the elderly, where the state would pay the homeowner's property taxes. This would be considered a loan, and the equity would be the value of the home. The loan would be repaid when the home was sold or the homeowner dies. Contact your state or county tax office to see what your area offers. For further help, check online at {www.taxsites.com/agencies.html}

$328 a Month Towards Rent

In some parts of the country, a family of four can make up to $61,700 and still qualify for this program! The U.S. Department of Housing and Urban Development (HUD) offers a variety of rental assistance under the Section 8 Program. Public housing was established to provide decent and safe rental housing for eligible low-income families, the elderly, and persons with disabilities. Public housing comes in all sizes and types, from scattered single family houses to high-rise apartments for elderly families. There are approximately 1.3 million households living in public housing units, managed by some 3,300 housing agencies.

In addition to public housing, there are many different voucher programs designed to assist very low-income families, the elderly, and the disabled to afford decent, safe, and sanitary housing in the private market. Participants are often able to find their own housing, including single-family homes, townhouses and apartments. The Vouchers are administered locally by public housing agencies (PHAs). A family that is issued a housing voucher is responsible for finding a suitable housing unit of the family's choice where the owner agrees to rent under the program. A housing subsidy is paid to the landlord directly by the PHA on behalf of the participating family. The family then pays the difference between the actual rent charged by the landlord and the amount subsidized by the program. Under certain circumstances, if authorized by the PHA, a family may use its voucher to purchase a modest home. A voucher holder must pay 30% of its monthly adjusted gross income for rent and utilities.

Contact the resource center through their toll-free number at 1-800-955-2232 from 9:00 a.m. to 6:00 p.m., Eastern Standard Time (EST) daily Monday through Friday.

U.S. Department of Housing and Urban Development
451 7th Street S.W.
Washington, DC 20410

202-708-1112
TTY: 202-708-1455
www.hud.gov

Having Trouble Getting the House or Apartment you Want?

Federal law prohibits housing discrimination based on your race, color, national origin, religion, sex, family status, or disability. If you have been trying to buy or rent a home or apartment and you believe your rights have been violated, you can file a fair housing complaint. There are several ways to file a complaint; you can file a complaint online at {www.hud.gov/complaints/housediscrim.cfm}; you can call 1-800-669-9777 toll free; or you can print out a form online, complete it, and drop it off at your local HUD office or mail it to the Office of Fair Housing and Equal Opportunity.

Office of Fair Housing and Equal Opportunity
Department of Housing and Urban Development
Room 5204
451 Seventh St. SW
Washington, DC 20410-2000
www.hud.gov/offices/fheo/index.cfm

You can also file a complaint in writing. Your letter should include the following information:

☐ Your name and address
☐ The name and address of the person your complaint is about
☐ The address of the house or apartment you were trying to rent or buy
☐ The date when this incident occurred
☐ A short description of what happened

Then mail it to the Fair Housing Hub closest to you.

Federal Law May Save You Hundreds of Dollars Each Year

Private Mortgage Insurance (PMI) is a monthly premium that you are required to pay if you put less than a 20% down payment on a home. It protects the lender if you default on the loan. The Homeowners Protection Act of 1998 establishes rules for automatic termination and borrowers cancellation of PMI on home mortgages. PMI can end up costing you thousands of dollars during a loan. Check your annual escrow account statement or call your lender to find out exactly what it costs you each year. This act is applicable for certain mortgages signed on or after July 29, 1999 for the purchase, initial construction, or refinance of a single-family home. It does not apply to government-insured FHA or VA loans or to loans with lender-paid PMI.

To receive information from the Federal Trade Commission on the removal of PMI, contact Federal Trade Commission, Public Reference, 600 Pennsylvania Ave., NW, Washington, DC 20580; 877-FTC-HELP (382-4357); {www.ftc.gov}.

House Rich, But Cash Poor

A Reverse Mortgage is a type of home equity loan that allows you to convert some of the equity in your home into cash while you retain ownership. This works like a traditional mortgage, but in reverse. So, instead of making a house payment each month, you receive a payment from your lender. Depending on the type of Reverse Mortgage and the lender, you can take the money in a lump sum, in monthly advances, through a line-of-credit, or a combination of the three. Most Reverse Mortgages do not require any repayment of principal, interest, or servicing fees, for as long as you live in your home. These loans are called rising-debt loans for that reason. The money you get from this type of loan can normally be used for any reason, including paying housing expenses like taxes, insurance, fuel, and maintenance costs.

If you would like a current list of lenders that participate in the FHA-insured program, sponsored by the Department of Housing and Urban Development (HUD), or additional information on reverse mortgages, write to:
AARP Home Equity Information Center
601 E Street, NW
Washington, DC 20049
or visit their website at,
{www.aarp.com}.

For additional information, contact:
National Center for Home Equity Conversion
360 N. Robert, #403
Saint Paul, MN 55101
651-222-6775
Fax: 651-222-6797

You can also contact the Federal Trade Commission (FTC) for information about Reverse Mortgages. Contact Federal Trade Commission, Public Reference, 600 Pennsylvania Ave., NW, Washington, DC 20580; 877-FTC-HELP (382-4357); {www.ftc.gov}.

Short-Term Rent Money

Many city and states offer short-term rent assistance for those in danger of losing their homes or who need help with the security deposit. This is usually only for assistance lasting one to six months.

Often an unexpected car repair or hospitalization, can send a family into a financial crisis situation, so rental assistance programs were begun to help address this need, hoping to stabilize a family. Who qualifies for these programs varies from place to place and where this money is located can also be a challenge. The first place you should check is with your local Social Services Department, local housing programs, or with the welfare office.

Contact your local authorities to see what may be available to you in your area.

Emergency Rent Money

Need rent money in a hurry or you could lose your house or apartment? Close to half the states offer some type of emergency assistance to help prevent homelessness. These programs sometimes focus on exclusively on families or those of very low-income. Who operates these programs also varies from place to place. The first place you should check is with your local Social Services Department, local housing programs, or with the welfare office.

Free Money For Your Downpayment

Here is a program that will give you 5% of the downpayment costs for your new home. This program is open to everyone, not just first time home buyers, and the homes can be valued at up to $300,700!

Funds for this program do not need to be repaid and come from funds raised through the AmeriDream Charity. You must purchase a home from a builder or seller who has enrolled their home in the program. Over 4,500 people become homeowners each month through the AmeriCream Downpayment Gift Program.

To learn more contact AmeriDream Charity, 18310 Montgomery Village Ave., Suite 300, Gaithersburg, MD 20879; 301-977-9133; toll-free 866-263-7437; {www.ameridream.org}.

Pay Your Mortgage, Downpayment, or Closing Costs

Trouble in the house? HUD may be able to help. Layoffs and threatened unemployment causes many homeowners to worry about making their mortgage payments. HUD provides a list of HUD-approved housing counseling agencies! HUD funds housing counseling agencies throughout the country that can give you advice on buying a home, renting, defaults, foreclosures, credit issues, reverse mortgages and working with lenders. Some even offer money to pay your mortgage payments till you get back on your feet. Just contact the agency nearest to you or call 1-888-466-3487. Homeowners with problems that could result in default of their mortgage or foreclosure on their property need to contact a HUD-approved housing counseling agency immediately.

The Housing Counseling Clearinghouse (HCC) operates a toll-free, 24-hour a day automated voice response system that provides homeowners and homebuyers referrals to local housing counseling agencies toll-free at 1-800-569-4287.

The Housing Counseling
Clearinghouse
P.O. Box 10423
McLean, VA 22102
888-466-3487 (toll-free)
TDD: 703-734-1444
Fax: 703-734-7929
www.hud.gov/offices/hsg/sfh/hcc/hccp
rof14.cfm

For those homeowners with FHA mortgages, another resource also exists. The goal of HUD's National Servicing Center is to help FHA homeowners by working with lenders to find creative solutions to avoid foreclosure.

Department of Housing and Urban
Development
National Servicing Center
500 W. Main Street, Suite 400
Oklahoma City, OK 73102
888-297-8685 (toll-free)

U.S. Department of Housing and Urban Development (HUD) Programs

Moving To Opportunity

Moving to Opportunity for Fair Housing (MTO) is a 10-year research demonstration that combines tenant-based rental assistance with housing counseling to help very low-income families move from poverty-stricken urban areas to low-poverty neighborhoods. One of the advantages that tenant-based rental assistance has over subsidized housing projects and public housing is that it allows the recipient to choose modestly priced private housing in neighborhoods that can offer ample educational, employment, and social opportunities. Five public housing authorities (Baltimore, Boston, Chicago, Los Angeles, and New York City) administer this demonstration project.

Households chosen for the demonstration's experimental group receive housing counseling and vouchers for rental housing in areas with less than 10 percent poverty. For more information contact your local HUD office or check out the program online at {www.hud.gov}.

Let The Government Help You Buy Your Home

Home ownership vouchers assist first-time homeowners with their monthly home ownership expenses. The home must pass an initial housing quality standards inspection conducted by the Public Housing Agency (PHA) and an independent home inspection before the PHA may approve the purchase by the family.

PHAs may choose to administer a home ownership program, but are not required to do so. The PHA may impose limits on the size of this program, or limit use of the option to certain purposes. However, PHAs must provide home ownership assistance when required as a reasonable accommodation to a family with a disabled person.

There are low-income requirements. The qualified monthly income of the family who will own the home must not be less than the Federal minimum hourly wage multiplied by 2,000 hours (currently $10,300). Except in the case of an elderly household or a family with a disabled person, welfare assistance is not counted in determining whether the family meets this requirement. There may be other eligibility requirements. (14.871 Section 8 Housing Choice Vouchers).

If you are interested in applying for a voucher, contact the local public housing agency (starting on page 365) or HUD office near you or check out the program online at {www.hud.gov/offices/pihprogramcs/hcv/index.cfm}.

Money to Buy, Fix Up Or Refinance A Home

Did you find a great house that is need of repair? Rather than get a mortgage for the house and another for the rehab, you can combine them into one with the U.S. Department of Housing and Urban Development's (HUD) 203(k).

Section 203(k) insures mortgages covering the purchase or refinancing and rehabilitation of a home that is at least a year old. A portion of the loan proceeds is used to pay the seller, or, if a refinance, to pay off the existing mortgage, and the remaining funds are placed in an escrow account and released as rehabilitation is completed. The cost of the rehabilitation must be at least $5,000.

Section 203(k) insurance enables home buyers and homeowners to finance both the purchase (or refinancing) of a house and the cost of its rehabilitation through a single mortgage, or to finance the rehabilitation of their existing home. Section 203(k) insured loans can finance the rehabilitation of the residential portion of a property

that also has nonresidential uses; they can also cover the conversion of a property of any size to a one- to four-unit structure. Applications must be submitted to the local HUD Field Office through an FHA approved lending institution. 8,000 homes took advantage of this funding. The budget for this program is $900,000,000. (14.108 Rehabilitation Mortgage Insurance 203k). For more information contact your local HUD office or check out the program online at {www.hud.gov/improvements/index.cfm}.

$48,000 To Buy A Mobile Home

For those in the market for a manufactured home, the U.S. Department of Housing and Urban Development (HUD) has a guaranteed loan program to help insure mortgage loans made by private lending institutions to finance the purchase of a new or used manufactured home. The program insures lenders against loss from default on loans of up to $48,600. The program is authorized under Title I. 865 people used this funding last year. The budget for this program is $71,000,000. (14.110 Manufactured Home Loan Insurance-Financing Purchase of Manufactured Homes as Principal Residences of Borrowers).

For more information contact your local HUD office or check out the program online at {www.hud.gov}; or Home Mortgage Insurance Division,

U.S. Department of Housing and Urban Development, 451 7th St., SW, Room 9272, Washington, DC 20410; 202-708-2121; {www.hud.gov/prog desc/manuf13.cfm}.

$2,000,000 To Build or Rehabilitate Condominiums

With their amenities and ease of maintenance, condominiums can offer some households an appealing alternative to traditional home ownership. Under Section 234(d), HUD insures mortgage loans made by private lenders to finance the construction or rehabilitation of condominium projects. Section 234(d) insures mortgages issued to developers of condominium projects for 10-40 years or three-quarters of the property's remaining economic life, whichever is less. The maximum amount of the mortgage varies according to the size of the unit and the type of structure. There are also loan-to-replacement cost limits and debt service limits.

To be eligible for HUD insurance, a condominium project must contain at least four dwelling units. The units may be in detached, semi-detached, row, walk-up, or elevator structures. (14.112 Mortgage Insurance for Construction or Substantial Rehabilitation of Condominium Projects 234d).

For more information contact your local HUD office or check out the program online at {www.hud.gov}; or Home Mortgage Insurance Division, U.S. Department of Housing and Urban Development, 451 7th St., SW, Room 9272, Washington, DC 20410; 202-708-2121; {www.hud.gov/prog desc/condo14.cfm}.

$277,000 To Help Purchase a 2-4 Family Unit

The government wants you to own a home, so they have created this great mortgage insurance program. Down payment requirements can be low; many closing costs can be financed; and some fees are limited.

Through this program, HUD's Federal Housing Administration (FHA) insures mortgages made by qualified lenders to people purchasing or refinancing a home of their own. FHA's mortgage insurance programs help low- and moderate-income families become homeowners by lowering some of the costs of their mortgage loans. FHA mortgage insurance also encourages lenders to make loans to otherwise creditworthy borrowers and projects, by protecting the lender against loan default on mortgages for properties that meet certain minimum requirements--including manufactured homes, single-family and multifamily properties, and some health-related facilities. (14.117 Mortgage Insurance-Homes 203B).

For more information contact your local HUD office, contact the FHA Mortgage Hotline at 1-800-HUDSFHA, or check out the program online at {www.hud.gov/buying/insured.cfm}.

$300,000 For People Whose Homes Were Hurt By A Disaster

If you lost your home due to a major disaster, the U.S. Department of Housing and Urban Development (HUD) has developed a program to help you get back into a home. They even made it easier by requiring no down payment. The borrower is eligible for 100 percent financing, including closing costs.

Through Section 203(h), the Federal Government helps victims in Presidentially designated disaster areas recover by making it easier for them to get mortgage loans and become homeowners or reestablish themselves as homeowners. Section 203(h) program allows the Federal Housing Administration (FHA) to insure mortgages made by qualified lenders to victims of a major disaster who have lost their homes and are in the process of rebuilding or buying another home. (14.119 Mortgage Insurance- Homes for Disaster Victims 203h).

For more information contact your local HUD office, contact the FHA Mortgage Hotline at 1-800-HUDSFHA, or check out the program online at {www.hud.gov/buying/insured.cfm}.

Money For Low to Moderate Income Families Hurt by a Disaster or Urban Renewal

One of the many barriers facing low- and moderate-income home buyers is that lenders have often regarded mortgage loans for comparatively small amounts as unprofitable, the servicing and other administrative costs were thought to outweigh the potential profits. This program increases home ownership opportunities for low- and moderate-income families by insuring small mortgage loans and thus reducing the lender's risk. Traditionally, this program has been targeted to assist displaced persons, although it is used in other situations as well.

This program insures mortgage loans made by private lenders to finance the purchase, construction, or rehabilitation of low-cost, one- to four-family housing. (14.120 Mortgage Insurance- Homes for Low and Moderate Income Families 221d2). For more information contact your local HUD office, contact the FHA Mortgage Hotline at 1-800-HUDSFHA, or check out the program online at {www.hud.gov/buying/index.cfm}.

$200,000 To Help Purchase A Home On 2.5 Acres

Are you looking to buy or build a home on property in a rural area? Through Section 203(i) HUD's Federal Housing Administration (FHA) insures mortgages made by qualified lenders to individuals purchasing homes in outlying areas, where lack of a normal market could make resale in case of default difficult. FHA's mortgage insurance programs help low- and moderate-income families become homeowners by lowering some of the initial costs of their mortgage loans.

FHA mortgage insurance also encourages lenders to make loans to otherwise creditworthy borrowers. Insured loans may be used to finance the purchase of proposed, under-construction, or existing one-family housing, or new farm housing on 2 1/2 or more acres adjacent to an all-weather public road. 1,300,000 loans were made through this program. The budget for this program is $139,000,000,000. (14.121 Mortgage

Insurance- Homes in Outlying Areas 203i). For more information contact your local HUD office, contact the FHA Mortgage Hotline at 1-800-HUDSFHA, or check out the program online at {www.hud.gov}.

Money for Homes in Urban Renewal Areas

Do you want to purchase or rehabilitate a home in an urban renewal area? Many lenders are reluctant to extend mortgages in these circumstances. One of the many barriers facing low- and moderate-income home buyers is that lenders have often regarded mortgage loans for comparatively small amounts as unprofitable, the servicing and other administrative costs were thought to outweigh the potential profits.

This program increases home ownership opportunities for low- and moderate-income families by insuring small mortgage loans and thus reducing the lender's risk. This program insures mortgage loans made by private lenders to finance the purchase, construction, or rehabilitation of low-cost, one- to four-family housing. (14.122 Mortgage Insurance- Homes in Urban Renewal Areas 220). For more information contact your local HUD office, contact the FHA Mortgage Hotline at 1-800-HUDSFHA, or check out the program online at {www.hud.gov/offices/hsg/mfh/progdesc/progdesc.cfm}.

$100,000 To Buy or Fix Up Houses In Older Areas Of A Town

Many people want to buy homes in older areas where lenders are reluctant to loan for the home purchase. Section 223(e) provides mortgage insurance to enable people to purchase or rehabilitate housing in older, declining urban areas.

Section 223(e) can be used only to supplement other HUD mortgage insurance programs. HUD's Federal Housing Administration (FHA) administers mortgage insurance programs that help low- and moderate-income families become homeowners by lowering some of the initial costs of their mortgage loans. (14.123 Mortgage Insurance- Housing in Older, Declining Areas 223e).

For more information contact your local HUD office, contact the FHA Mortgage Hotline at 1-800-HUDSFHA, or check out the program online at {www.hud.gov}.

$1,000,000 For Investors to Develop Co-Ops

The U.S. Department of Housing and Urban Development has created a program to encourage the building of cooperative apartments. Section 213 insures mortgage loans to facilitate the construction, substantial rehabilitation, and purchase of cooperative housing projects. Each member shares in the ownership of the whole project with the exclusive right to occupy a specific unit and to participate in project operations through the purchase of stock.

Section 213 enables nonprofit cooperative housing corporations or trusts to develop or sponsor the development of housing projects to be operated as cooperatives, and also allows investors to provide good quality multifamily housing to be sold to nonprofit corporations or trusts upon completion of construction or rehabilitation. 170 units were developed last year. (14.126 Mortgage Insurance-Cooperative Projects 213).

For more information contact your local HUD office or check out the program online at {www.hud.gov/offices/hsg/mfh/progdesc/progdesc.cfm}; or Office of Multifamily Housing Development, U.S. Department of Housing and Urban Development, Washington, DC 20410; 202-708-1142.

$10,000 To Buy Your House From Long Term Ground Lease

For those homeowners whose homes are on long-term ground leases, there is a program to help you buy your home. The U.S. Department of Housing and Urban Development (HUD) has a loan guarantee program to help finance the purchase of the home. (14.130 Mortgage Insurance-purchase by Homeowners of Fee Simple Title From Lessors 240). For more information contact your local HUD office or check out the program online at {www.hud.gov}.

$60,000 for Renters, Homeowners or Investors to Improve Their Property

Help exists for those that want to improve their homes. Under Title I, HUD insures lenders against most losses on home improvement loans. The Federal Housing Administration (FHA) makes it easier for consumers to obtain affordable home improvement loans by insuring loans made by private lenders to improve properties that meet certain requirements.

This is one of HUD's most frequently used loan insurance products. Title I loans may be used to finance permanent property improvements that protect or improve the basic livability or utility of the property--including manufactured homes, single-family and multifamily homes, nonresidential structures, and the preservation of historic homes. The loans can also be used for fire safety equipment. 7,562 people improved their homes through this program. The budget for this program is $109,000,000. (14.142 Property Improvement Loan Insurance For Improving All Existing Structures and Building of New Nonresidential Structures Title I).

For more information contact your local HUD office, contact the FHA Mortgage Hotline at 1-800-HUDSFHA, or check out the program online at {www.hud.gov/offices/hsg/sfh/title/ti_home.cfm}; or call HUD Customer Service for brochure and list of lenders at 800-767-7468.

Government Backed Graduated Mortgage Payments

Don't think you have enough money to afford mortgage payments? Section 245 enables a household with a limited income that is expected to rise to buy a home sooner by making mortgage payments that start small and increase gradually over time. Section 245 insures mortgages for first-time (and other) buyers who have low and moderate incomes--and who thus cannot meet standard mortgage payments--but who expect that their income will increase substantially in the next 5-10 years.

Potential homeowners who are considering using a graduated-payment mortgage to purchase a home must remember that their monthly payments to principal and interest will increase each year for up to 10 years, depending on which of five available plans they select. (14.159 Section 245

Graduated Payment Mortgage Program). For more information contact your local HUD office, contact the FHA Mortgage Hotline at 1-800-HUDSFHA, or check out the program online at {www.hud.gov}.

$100,000 To Help Buy A Mobile Home and A Mobile Home Lot

Sometimes banks charge a very high interest for a manufactured home and lot, but the U.S. Department of Housing and Urban Development (HUD) offers a loan guarantee program to make it more affordable. This program insures mortgage loans made by private lenders to buyers of manufactured homes and the lots on which to place them.

Title I insurance may be used for loans of up to $64,800 for a manufactured home and lot and $16,200 for a lot only. The lot must be appraised by a HUD-approved lender. The dollar limits for combination and lot loans may be increased up to 85 percent in designated high-cost areas. The maximum loan term is 20 years for a single-module home and lot, 25 years for a multiple module home and lot, and 15 years for a lot only. 1,500 homes used this program last year. The budget for this program is $52,000,000. (14.162 Mortgage Insurance-combination and Manufactured Home Lot Loans Title I).

For more information contact your local HUD office or check out the program online at {www.hud.gov/offices/hsg/sfh/title/ti_home.cfm}; or call HUD Customer Service at 800-767-7468 for brochure.

$200,000 To Help Buy A Home In An Area Affected By A Base Closing

Buying a home in an area hurt by defense cutbacks can be difficult. The U.S. Department of Housing and Urban Development (HUD) offers the 238c program to help families undertake home ownership in military impacted areas.

HUD insures lenders against loss on mortgage loans. These loans may be used to finance the purchase of proposed, under construction, or existing one- to four-family housing, as well as to refinance indebtedness on existing housing. (14.165 Mortgage Insurance-Homes-Military Impacted Areas 238c). For more information contact your local HUD office or check out the program online at {www.hud.gov}.

Money to Buy A Home Using Increased Equity Payments

There is help for those on limited incomes. Section 245(a) enables a household with a limited income that is expected to rise to buy a home sooner by making mortgage payments that start small and increase gradually over time. The increased payments are applied to reduce the principal owed on the mortgage and thus shorten the mortgage term.

Section 245(a) works by helping first-time buyers and others with limited incomes—particularly young families, who expect their income to rise but may not yet be able to handle all of the up front and monthly costs involved in home buying—to tailor their mortgage payments to their expanding incomes and buy a home sooner than they could with regular financing. However, this program adds an innovative twist to this basic product: growing equity mortgages (GEMs) enable the homeowner to apply scheduled increases in monthly payments to the outstanding principal balance of their mortgage and thereby to considerably shorten the term of the mortgage. This reduced term and the faster repayment of principal make GEMs more attractive to lenders and investors than other fixed-rate investments. (14.172 Mortgage Insurance- Growing Equity Mortgages GEM).

For more information contact your local HUD office or check out the program online at {www.hud.gov}.

Uncle Sam Will Co-Sign An Adjustable Rate Mortgage

Here is a way to start with a low monthly mortgage rate. Section 251 insures home purchase or refinancing loans with interest rates that may increase or decrease over time, enabling consumers to purchase or refinance their home at a lower initial interest rate. Under this FHA-insured mortgage product, the initial interest rate and monthly payment are low, but these may change during the life of the loan. FHA uses 1-year Treasury Constant Maturities Index to determine interest rate changes. The maximum amount the interest rate may increase or decrease in any one year is 1 percentage point.

Over the life of the loan, the maximum interest rate change is 5 percentage points from the initial rate. Down payment requirements can be low.

Many closing costs can be financed. 100,000 loans will be available this year. (14.175 Adjustable Rate Mortgages). For more information contact your local HUD office, contact the FHA Mortgage Hotline at 1-800-HUDSFHA, or check out the program online at {www.hud.gov}.

Reverse Mortgages For Seniors

Stop being house rich, but cash poor. The Home Equity Conversion Mortgage program enables older homeowners to withdraw some of the equity in their home in the form of monthly payments for life or a fixed term, or in a lump sum, or through a line of credit.

The Home Equity Conversion Mortgage Program (HECM) can enable an older home owning family to stay in their home while using some of its built up equity. The program allows such a household to get an insured reverse mortgage — a mortgage that converts equity into income. Because older persons can be vulnerable to fraudulent practices, the program requires that persons receive free reverse mortgage housing counseling from a HUD-approved reverse mortgage counseling agency before applying for a reverse mortgage. FHA insures HECM loans to protect lenders against loss if amounts withdrawn exceed equity when the property is sold. HECM can be used by homeowners who are 62 years of age and older. 15,000 loans will be made this year. (14.183 Home Equity Conversion Mortgages 255).

For more information contact your local HUD office or check out the program online at {www.hud.gov/offices/hsg/sfh/hecm/hecmhome.cfm}.

Money to Make Your Home Energy Efficient

The Energy Efficient Mortgages Program (EEM) helps home buyers or homeowners save money on utility bills by enabling them to finance the cost of adding energy-efficiency features to new or existing housing as part of their FHA-insured home purchase or refinancing mortgage. Up to $200 of the cost of an energy inspection report may be included in the mortgage. EEM can be used to make energy-efficient improvements in one- or two-unit existing and new homes. Contact your local HUD office or check out the program online at {www.hud.gov/offices/hsg/sfh/eem/eemhome.cfm}.

Money For Members Of The Armed Services

Section 222 enables members of the Coast Guard and National Oceanic and Atmospheric Administration on active duty to purchase a home that is partially subsidized by the respective service.

Section 222, allows the Department of Transportation (DOT) and the Department of Commerce (DOC) to pay the FHA mortgage insurance premium on behalf of service members on active duty under their jurisdictions. The mortgages may finance single-family dwellings and condominiums insured under standard HUD home mortgage insurance programs. Contact the FHA Mortgage Hotline at 1-800-HUDSFHA, or check out the program online at {www.hud.gov}.

Home Ownership For Everyone

★ HOPE I helps low-income people buy public housing units by providing funds that nonprofit organizations, resident groups, and other eligible grantees can use to develop and implement home ownership programs. HOPE I grants can be used to fund a wide range of home ownership activities that help public housing residents develop the skills, the resources, the partnerships, and the strategies they will need to buy their housing units.

HOPE I Program Fact Sheet available from the Resident Initiatives Clearinghouse, 1-800-955-2232. For more information contact your local HUD office or check out the program online at {www.hud.gov}.

Buy Your Public Housing Unit

The Section 5(h) home ownership program offers Public Housing Agencies (PHA) a flexible way to sell public housing units to low-income families.

Section 5(h) helps low-income families purchase homes through an arrangement that benefits both the buyer and the public housing agency (PHA) that sells the unit. Section 5(h) works for PHAs as well: it permits public housing authorities to sell individual units and developments that may, due to their location or configuration, no longer be efficient to operate--while HUD continues to service the debt.

See Fact Sheet: Section 5(h), available from the Resident Initiatives Clearinghouse, 1-800-955-2232. For more information contact your local HUD office or check out the program online at {www.hud.gov}.

Money to Build or Rehabilitate A Trailer Home Park

Section 207 Program insures mortgage loans to facilitate the construction or substantial rehabilitation of multifamily manufactured home parks. Section 207 promotes the creation of manufactured home communities by increasing the availability of affordable financing and mortgages. (14.127 Mortgage Insurance-Manufactured Home Parks 207). Contact your local HUD office or check out the program online at {www.hud.gov}. For more information contact your local HUD office, contact the FHA Mortgage Hotline at 1-800-HUDSFHA, or check out the program online at {www.hud.gov/offices/hsg/sfh/eem/eemhome.cfm}; or Office of Multifamily Development, U.S. Department of Housing and Urban Development, Washington, DC 20410; 202-708-1142.

Money to Buy a Hospital

The Federal Housing Administration helps hospitals access affordable financing for capital projects. You can use the money for construction financing, refinancing, modernization, remodeling, equipment, or expansion. To be considered for insurance, a hospital must meet certain minimum eligibility requirements. (14.128 Mortgage Insurance- Hospitals 242).

Contact your local HUD office, contact the FHA Mortgage Hotline at 1-800-HUDSFHA, or check out the program online at {www.hud.gov}; or Office of Insured Health Care Facilities, U.S. Department of Housing and Urban Development, Washington, DC 20410; 202-708-0599; {www.hud.gov/progdesc/hlthprog.html}.

Money to Buy A Nursing Home

Section 232 insures mortgage loans to facilitate the construction and substantial rehabilitation of nursing homes, intermediate care facilities, board and care homes, and assisted-living facilities. Section 232/223(f) allows for the purchase or refinancing with or without repairs of existing projects not requiring substantial rehabilitation. Section 232 insures mortgage loans to facilitate the construction and substantial rehabilitation of nursing homes, intermediate care facilities, board and care homes, and assisted-living facilities. (14.129 Mortgage Insurance-Nursing Homes, Intermediate Care Facilities and Board and Care Homes 232). Contact your local HUD office, contact the FHA Mortgage Hotline at 1-800-HUDSFHA, or check out the program online at {www.hud.gov/offices/hsg/sfh/eem/eemhome.cfm}; or Office of Multifamily Development, U.S. Department of Housing and Urban Development, Washington, DC 20410; 202-708-1142; forms can be found at {www.hudclips.org}.

Money to Buy Your Co-op

If you would like to buy a co-op, then the U.S. Department of Housing and Urban Development will assist you with a loan guarantee. They want to make available, good quality, new housing for purchase by individual members of a housing cooperative. (14.132 Mortgage Insurance-Purchase of Sales-Type Cooperative Housing Units 213 Sales). Contact your local HUD office or check out the program online at {www.hud.gov}; forms can be found at {www.hudclips.org}.

$150,000 To Purchase A Condominium

The U.S. Department of Housing and Urban Development has a program that insures the loan for a person who purchases a unit in a condominium building.

Condominium ownership, in which the separate owners of the individual units jointly own the development's common areas and facilities, is one particularly popular alternative. Insurance for condominiums, such as is provided through Section 234(c), can be important for low- and moderate-income renters who wish to avoid being displaced by the conversion of their apartment building into a condominium. (14.133 Mortgage Insurance-Purchase of Units in Condominiums 234c).

Contact your local HUD office, contact the FHA Mortgage Hotline at 1-800-HUDSFHA, or check out the program online at {www.hud.gov/ buying/ index.cfm}.

Money For Investors, Builders And Developers To Refinance Their Projects

Section 207/223(f) insures mortgage loans to facilitate the purchase or refinancing of existing multifamily rental housing. Properties requiring substantial rehabilitation are not eligible for mortgage insurance under this program. HUD permits the completion of non-critical repairs after endorsement for mortgage insurance. (14.134 Mortgage Insurance-Rental

Housing; 14.155 Mortgage Insurance or Refinancing of Existing Multifamily Housing Projects).

Contact your local HUD office, contact the FHA Mortgage Hotline at 1-800-HUDSFHA, or check out the program online at {www.hud.gov/ offices/hsg/mfh/progdesc/progdesc.cf m}; or Office of Multifamily Development, U.S. Department of Housing and Urban Development, Washington, DC 20410; 202-708-1142; forms can be found at {www.hudclips.org}.

$5,000,000 For Investors to Develop Housing For Seniors, Moderate Income Families And People With Disabilities

Section 221(d)(3) and 221(d)(4) insures mortgage loans to facilitate the new construction or substantial rehabilitation of multifamily rental or cooperative housing for moderate-income families, elderly, and the handicapped. Single Room Occupancy (SRO) projects may also be insured under this section.

Both programs assist private industry in the construction or rehabilitation of rental and cooperative housing for moderate-income and displaced families by making capital more readily available. (14.135 Mortgage Insurance-Rental and Cooperative Housing for Moderate Income Families and Elderly 221d3 and 221d4). Contact your local HUD office, contact the FHA Mortgage Hotline at 1-800-HUDSFHA, or check out the program online at {www. hud.gov/offices/hsg/mfh/progdesc/pro gdesc.cfm}; or Office of Multifamily Development, U.S. Department of Housing and Urban Development,

Washington, DC 20410; 202-708-1142; forms can be found at {www.hudclips.org}.

Money For Investors and Nonprofits To Develop Housing For Seniors

The Section 231 insures mortgage loans to facilitate the construction and substantial rehabilitation of multifamily rental housing for elderly persons (62 or older) and/or persons with disabilities.

Insured mortgages may be used to finance the construction, rehabilitation, and purchase of detached, semidetached, walk-up, or elevator type rental housing designed for elderly occupancy or handicapped individuals consisting of eight or more rental units. (14.138 Mortgage Insurance- Rental Housing for the Elderly 231). Contact your local HUD office, contact the FHA Mortgage Hotline at 1-800-HUDSFHA, or check out the program online at {www.hud.gov/offices/hsg/mfh/progd esc/progdesc.cfm}; or Office of Multifamily Development, U.S. Department of Housing and Urban Development, Washington, DC 20410; 202-708-1142.

Money to Develop Rental Housing In Urban Areas

Section 220 insures loans for multifamily housing projects in urban renewal areas, code enforcement areas, and other areas where local governments have undertaken designated revitalization activities. Section 220 insures lenders against loss on mortgage defaults. (14.139 Mortgage Insurance-Rental Housing in Urban Renewal Areas 220 Multi-family).

Contact your local HUD office, contact the FHA Mortgage Hotline at 1-800-HUDSFHA, or check out the program online at {www.hud.gov/offices/hsg/mfh/progdesc/progdesc.cf m}; or Office of Multifamily Development, U.S. Department of Housing and Urban Development, Washington, DC 20410; 202-708-1142.

$2,000,000 To Fix Up Multifamily Units

Section 241(a) insures mortgage loans to finance repairs, additions, and improvements to multifamily rental housing and health care facilities with FHA insured first mortgages or HUD-held mortgages.

Insured mortgages finance repairs, additions, and improvements to multifamily projects, group practice facilities, hospitals, or nursing homes already insured by HUD or held by HUD. (14.151 Supplemental Loan Insurance-Multifamily Rental Housing 241a).

Contact your local HUD office, contact the FHA Mortgage Hotline at 1-800-HUDSFHA, or check out the program online at {www.hud.gov/offices/hsg/mfh/progdesc/progdesc.cf m}; or Office of Multifamily Development, U.S. Department of Housing and Urban Development, Washington, DC 20410; 202-708-1142.

$4,000,000 To Build or Fix Up Housing For Seniors

The Section 202 program helps expand the supply of affordable housing with supportive services for the elderly. It provides very low-income elderly with options that allow them to live independently but in an environment that provides support activities such as cleaning, cooking, transportation, etc.

HUD provides interest-free capital advances to private, nonprofit sponsors to finance the development of supportive housing for the elderly. (14.157 Supportive Housing For The Elderly 202).

Contact your local HUD office or check out the program online at {www.hud.gov/offices/hsg/mfh/progd esc/progdesc.cfm}; or Office of Housing Assistance and Grants Administration, U.S. Department of Housing and Urban Development, Washington, DC 20410; 202-708-2866; {www.hud.gov/progdesc/2eldrl14.cfm}; forms can be found at {www.hudclips.org}.

Money To Finance Coop Buildings

The purpose of FHA's mortgage insurance programs is to encourage lenders to make mortgage credit available to borrowers who would not otherwise qualify for conventional loans on affordable terms and to residents of disadvantaged neighborhoods.

Section 203(n) helps with a financing structured to meet the needs of persons who are buying a corporate certificate and occupancy certificate, the instruments that enable them to own a share of and live in a cooperative housing project. The program insures a loan to purchase an apartment in a residential cooperative--which can be a detached or semidetached building, a rowhouse, or a multifamily building. (14.163 Mortgage Insurance- Single Family Cooperative Housing 203n). Contact your local HUD office, contact the FHA Mortgage Hotline at 1-800-HUDSFHA, or check out the program online at {www.hud.gov}.

Money to Developers In Financial Trouble

The U.S. Department of Housing and Urban Development has a program that provides loans to restore or maintain the physical and financial soundness, to assist in the management and to maintain the low-to moderate-income character of certain projects assisted or approved for assistance under the National Housing Act or under the Housing and Urban Development Act of 1965.

Flexible Subsidy funds can be lent to eligible projects in an amount based on the project's total needs. It may be used to correct physical deficiencies resulting from deferral of regular maintenance; to reduce deficiencies in replacement reserve funds; and to fund operating deficits. Eligible owners are nonprofits, with existing loans from HUD under the Section 202 program. Public bodies do not qualify for this program. (14.164 Operating Assistance For Troubled Multifamily Housing Projects).

Contact your local HUD office or check out the program online at {www.hud.gov/offices/hsg/mfh/progd esc/progdesc.cfm}; or Office of Housing Assistance and Grants Administration, U.S. Department of Housing and Urban Development, Washington, DC 20410; 202-708-2866.

$500,000 If You Can't Make A Profit On Your Apartment Building

Section 223(d) helps avoid insurance claims on HUD-insured multifamily mortgages by insuring separate loans to cover operating losses. Section 223(d) insures two-year operating loss loans that covers operating losses during the first 2 years after completion (or any other 2-year period within the first 10 years after completion) of multifamily rental projects with a HUD-insured first mortgage. (14.167 Mortgage Insurance- Two Year Operating Loss Loans, 223d).

Contact your local HUD office or check out the program online at {www.hud.gov/offices/hsg/mfh/progd esc/progdesc.cfm}; or Office of Multifamily Development, U.S. Department of Housing and Urban Development, Washington, DC 20410; 202-708-1142.

$1,000,000 To Build or Fix Up Housing For People With Disabilities

HUD provides funding to nonprofit organizations to develop rental housing with the availability of supportive services for very low-income adults with disabilities, and provides rent subsidies for the projects to help make them affordable. The Section 811 program allows persons with disabilities to live as independently as possible in the community by increasing the supply of rental housing with the availability of supportive services.

The program also provides project rental assistance, which covers the difference between the HUD-approved operating costs of the project and the tenants' contribution toward rent. (14.181 Supportive Housing For Persons With Disabilities 811).

Contact your local HUD office or check out the program online at {www.hud.gov/offices/hsg/mfh/progd esc/progdesc.cfm}; or Office of Housing Assistance and Grants Administration, U.S. Department of Housing and Urban Development, Washington, DC 20410; 202-708-2866; forms can be found at {www.hudclips.org}.

Money To Help Rid Low-Income Housing Of Drug Related Crime

HUD has put together a program to help reduce or eliminate drug-related crime and related problems in and around the premises of federally assisted low income housing. They want to encourage owners of such housing to develop a plan for addressing the problems of drug-related crime and they offer grants to help owners carry out their plans. Money can be used for increased security, training of tenant patrols, drug intervention activities and drug treatment programs. (14.193 Federally Assisted Low-Income Housing Drug Elimination).

Contact your local HUD office or check out the program online at

{www.hud.gov}; or Office of Housing Assistance and Grants Administration, U.S. Department of Housing and Urban Development, Washington, DC 20410; 202-708-2866.

$400,000 To Help Operate A Homeless Shelter

The Supportive Housing Program is designed to develop supportive housing and services that will allow homeless persons to live as independently as possible. Eligible applicants are States, units of local government, other governmental entities such as PHAs, and private nonprofits.

Transitional housing is one type of supportive housing used to facilitate the movement of homeless individuals and families to permanent housing. Permanent housing for homeless persons with disabilities is another type of supportive housing, as is safe havens for homeless individuals with serious mental illness currently residing on the streets who may not yet be ready for supportive services. (14.235 Supportive Housing Program).

Contact your local HUD office or check out the program online at {www.hud.gov/offices/hsg/mfh/progd esc/progdesc.cfm}; or Office of Special Needs Assistance Programs, Community Planning and Development, U.S. Department of Housing and Urban Development, 451 7th St., SW, Washington, DC 20410; 202-708-4300.

Money To Rid Low-Income Housing of Drug Related Crime

Low-income housing units can be effected by drugs and crime. To combat this problem, the U.S.

Department of Housing and Urban Development (HUD) offers a grant program called the New Approach Anti-Drug Program (formerly Safe Neighborhood Grants Program). This program uses a comprehensive, coordinated neighborhood/community-based approach to eliminate drug-related and other crime problems on the premises and in the vicinity of low-income housing, which may be privately or publicly owned and is financially supported or assisted by public or nonprofit private entities. (14.312 New Approach Anti-Drug Grants).

Contact your local HUD office or check out the program online at {www.hud.gov}; or Program Analysts, Office of Housing Assistance and Grant Administration, U.S. Department of Housing and Urban Development, 451 7th St., SW, Room 6146, Washington, DC 20410; 202-708-2866, ext. 5787; Super-NOFA Information Center at 800-HUD-8929.

Loans to Investors, Builders, Developers of Affordable Housing

Section 542(b) encourages the development and preservation of affordable housing. The program provides insurance and reinsurance for multifamily housing projects whose loans are originated, underwritten, serviced, and disposed of by a Qualified Participating Entity (QPE) and/or its approved lenders. (14.189 Qualified Participating Entities Section 542b).

Contact your local HUD office or check out the program online at {www.hud.gov/offices/hsg/mfh/progd esc/progdesc.cfm}; or Office of Multifamily Development, U.S.

Department of Housing and Urban Development, Washington, DC 20410; 202-708-1142.

$7 Million For Investors, Builders and Developers To Build Houses And Apartments

Section 542(c) enables the U.S. Department of Housing and Urban Development (HUD) and State and local housing finance agencies (HFAs) to provide new risk-sharing arrangements to help those agencies provide more insurance and credit for multifamily loans. Section 542(c) provides credit enhancement for mortgages of multifamily housing projects whose loans are underwritten, processed, serviced, and disposed of by HFAs. HUD and HFAs share in the risk of the mortgage.

Eligible mortgagors include investors, builders, developers, public entities, and private nonprofit corporations or associations may apply to a qualified HFA. (14.188 HFA Risk Sharing Pilot Program). Contact your local HUD office or check out the program online at {www.hud.gov/offices/hsg/mfh/ progdesc/progdesc.cfm}; or Office of Multifamily Development, U.S. Department of Housing and Urban Development, Washington, DC 20410; 202-708-1142.

Money to Build Or Renovate Single Room Occupancy Units

Section 221(d)(3) and 221(d)(4) program insures mortgage loans for multifamily properties consisting of single-room occupancy (SRO) apartments. It is aimed at those tenants who have a source of income but are priced out of the rental apartment market. SRO projects generally require assistance from local governing bodies or charitable organizations in order to reduce the rents to affordable levels. Each SRO apartment can have its own kitchen or bathroom facilities, or these facilities may be shared by several apartments. Apartments can be designed to allow for more than one occupant. (14.184 Mortgage Insurance for Single Room Occupancy Projects).

Contact your local HUD office or check out the program online at {www.hud.gov/offices/hsg/mfh/progd esc/progdesc.cfm}; forms can be found at {www.hudclips.org}.

Money to Pay for Help

If you provide Section 8 (or Section 202) housing to low-income people, you can apply for grant funds to provide support services to the elderly or disabled residents. The goal is to keep these people in their own homes as long as possible by providing supportive services as needed. This service provider can offer case management services, monitor the assistance the residents receive, and act as an advocate for the resident in dealing with community service providers. (14.191 Multi-family Housing Service Coordinators)

Contact your local HUD office or contact Office of Housing Assistance and Grants Administration, Office of

Multifamily Housing Programs, Department of Housing and Urban Development, Washington, DC 20410; 202-708-2866; {www.hud.gov/progdesc/8coord.cfm}.

Keep Rent Affordable

Housing subsidy contracts are expiring on thousands of privately owned multifamily properties with federally insured mortgages. Many of these contracts set rents at amounts higher than those of the local market. As these contracts expire, the Market-to-Market program will reduce rents to market levels and will restructure existing debt to levels supportable by these rents. (14.197 Multifamily Assisted Housing Reform and Affordability).

Contact your local HUD office or check out the program with Charles Williams, Director, Office of Multifamily Housing Assistance Restructuring, Suite 4000, 1280 Maryland Ave., SW, Washington, DC 20024; 202-708-0001; {www.hud.gov/omhar}.

$2,500,000 To Provide Housing For AIDS Patients And Their Families

The Housing Opportunities for Persons with AIDS program provides funds for a variety of services including: counseling, information and referral services; acquisition, rehabilitation, and conversion of property to provide housing and services; new construction of housing; short-term rent, mortgage, and utility payments to prevent homelessness; supportive services such as health, mental health, day care, nutrition services, and more; operating costs for housing; and much more. HOPWA funds have helped many communities establish strategic AIDS

housing plans, better coordinate local and private efforts, fill gaps in local systems of care, and create new housing resources. (14.241 Housing Opportunities for Persons with AIDS (HOPWA)).

Contact your local HUD office or check out the program with David Vos, Director, Office of HIV/AIDS Housing, Community Planning and Development, Department of Housing and Urban Development, 451 Seventh St., SW, Room 7212, Washington, DC 20410; 202-708-1934; 800-877-8339; {www.hud.gov/offices/cpd/aidshousing}.

$4,000,000 For Your Nonprofit To Help People Buy Homes

The Self-Help Homeownership Opportunity Program provides funds to nonprofit organizations that have experience in providing self-help housing homeownership programs. Money can be used for land acquisition and infrastructure improvements and may not exceed $10,000 per dwelling. (14.247 Self-Help Homeownership Opportunity Program-SHOP).

Contact Office of Affordable Housing Programs, Community Planning and Development, Department of Housing and Urban Development, 451 7th St., SW, Washington, DC 20410; 202-708-2684; {www.hud.gov/progdesc/cpdindx.html}.

$450,000 To Make An Apartment Building Assisted Living

If you are a nonprofit and own a multi-family housing development for seniors and the disabled, you are eligible to apply for funds to convert some or all of the dwelling units into an Assisted Living Facility (ALF) for the frail elderly. These facilities are designed to accommodate the frail elderly and people with disabilities who can live independently but need assistance with activities of daily living. ALFs must provide support services such as personal care, transportation, meals, housekeeping, and laundry. (14.314 Assisted Living Conversion for Eligible Multifamily Housing Projects (ALCP).)

Contact your local HUD office or contact Office of Grant Policy and Management, Department of Housing and Urban Development, Room 6138, 451 Seventh Street, SW., Washington, DC 20410; 202-708-3000; {www.hud.gov/offices/hsg/mfh/progdesc/alcp.cfm}.

Help People Keep Their Homes

Sometimes money is tight and people get into a financial mess. You can help them straighten out their finances and keep their homes by providing counseling to homeowners, homebuyers, perspective renters, and tenants. Grants are available to HUD-approved local housing counseling agencies, HUD approved national and regional intermediaries, and to State housing finance agencies. Grants provide a variety of housing counseling services, including single family home buying, homeownership, mortgage default, HECM, rental, and rental delinquency under HUD and

other programs. (14.169 Housing Counseling Assistance Program).

Contact your local HUD office or Program Support Division, Office of Insured Single Family Housing, Department of Housing and Urban Development, 451 7th Street, SW, Washington, DC 20410; 202-708-0317; {www.hud.gov/offices/hsg/sfh/hcc/hcc_home.cfm}.

$10,000 Grant to Make Your Home Healthier

The purpose of the Healthy Homes Initiative is to develop, demonstrate and promote cost effective, preventive measures to correct multiple safety and health hazards in the home environment that produce serious diseases and injuries in children. This program focuses on demonstration projects that implement housing assessment, maintenance, renovation, and construction techniques to identify and correct housing-related illness and injury risk factors. Eligible applicants include: not-for-profit institutions, for-profit firms (for-profit firms are not allowed to profit from the project), and State and local governments (14.901 Healthy Homes Initiative Grants).

Contact your local HUD office or contact Ms. Ellen Taylor, Planning and Standards Division, Office of Healthy Homes and Lead Hazard Control, Department of Housing and Urban Development, 451 Seventh Street, SW, Room P3206, Washington, DC 20410; 202-755-1785, extension 116; {www.hud.gov/offices/lead}.

Buy A HUD Foreclosed Multi-Family Property

The U.S. Department of Housing and Urban Development sometimes needs to sell multifamily housing projects that are owned by the Department or are subject to a mortgage held by the Department. The property can be sold with tenant-based Housing Choice Vouchers provided to eligible tenants. The property can also be sold with a grant for the rehabilitation of the property if the new owners meet certain requirements. The multi-family housing project can also be sold to the highest bidder. (14.199 Multifamily Property Disposition).

To learn about possible foreclosure sales, contact a Realtor or Marc Harris, Department of Housing and Urban Development, Office of Housing, Multifamily Housing Programs, Office of Asset Management, Room 6160, 451 7th Street, SW., Washington, DC 20410; 202-708-0614, ext. 2680; {www.hud.gov/progdesc/multindx.cfm}.

Get A $100,000 Home For $1 Plus Fix Up Money

Single family homes that are acquired in foreclosure actions by the Federal Housing Administration (FHA) are eligible for sale to local governments across the nation for $1 plus closing costs when the properties have been listed for at least six months and remain unsold. Local governments buying HUD properties for $1 plus closing costs may sell or rent them to low- and moderate-income families, to first-time homebuyers, or to groups that will use the properties to provide services such as child- care centers, domestic abuse shelters, job training centers, etc. (14.313 Dollar Home Sales).

Contact your local HUD office or contact Asset Management and Disposition Division, 451 7th Street, SW, Washington, DC 20410; 202-708-1672; {www.hud.gov/offices/hsg/sfh/reo/reo_home.cfm}.

50% Discount For Law Enforcement Officers To Buy A Home

The Officer Next Door (OND) program helps make this goal a reality by making homeownership faster and more affordable for Law Enforcement Officers.

Law enforcement officers may purchase HUD-owned single unit properties located in designated revitalization areas at a 50 percent discount off list price. You must be a full-time, sworn law enforcement officer who is "employed full-time by a Federal, state, county or municipal government; or a public or private college or university." Officers must agree to occupy homes as their sole residence for a period of 3 years. OND property is listed at the following website {http://www.hud.gov/offices/hsg/sfh/reo/homes.cfm} and sold exclusively over the Internet. Properties are single family homes located in revitalization areas. Properties available through the program are marked with a special Office Next Door button.

You may also buy a home from a government agency or a nonprofit organization that bought the home from HUD. When an agency or nonprofit buys the house, HUD expects the full discount to be passed on to you. . To make a HUD home even more affordable, you may apply for an FHA-insured mortgage with a downpayment of only $100 and you may finance all closing costs. If the home you want to purchase needs repairs, you may use FHA's 203(k) mortgage program. (14.198 Officer Next Door Sales Program).

Contact your local HUD office or check out the program online at {www.hud.gov/offices/hsg/sfh/hsgsingle.cfm}. Information is also available from the HUD HELP line at 800-569-4287.

$5,000,000 to Start A Homeless Shelter

The Emergency Shelter Grant Program provides funds for programs designed to improve the quality of emergency shelters and transitional housing for the homeless, make available additional shelters, meet the costs of operating shelters, and provide essential social services to homeless individuals. States, cities, and counties can receive funds, and then these fund can be distributed to nonprofits. (14.231 Emergency Shelter Grants Program ESG).

Contact your local HUD office or John Garrity, Director, Office of Special Needs Assistance Programs, U.S. Department of Housing and Urban Development, 451 7th St., SW, Room 7262, Washington, DC 20410; 202-708-4300; {www.hud.gov/offices/cpd/homeless/programs/esg/index.cfm}.

Money to Pay Mortgages, Rents, Or Utility Payments In Emergencies

Funds are available for food and feeding related expenses, such as transportation of food and food preparation and serving equipment. Money can also be used for mass shelter and rent/mortgage and/or utility

assistance for one month only. The (83.523 Emergency Food and Shelter National Board Program- Emergency Food and Shelter).

Contact Curtis Carleton, Federal Emergency Management Agency, Preparedness, Training and Exercises Directorate, Washington, DC 20472; 202-646-4535; or Sharon Bailey, Director, Emergency Food and Shelter Program, 701 North Fairfax Street, Suite 310, Alexandria, VA 22314; 703-706-9660; {www.fema.gov}.

Grants To Pay Rents For People With Disabilities Or Chronic Illnesses

The Shelter Plus Care Program provides rental assistance, in connection with supportive services funded from sources other than this program, to homeless persons with disabilities (mentally ill, chronic alcohol or drug problems, or AIDS) and their families. The rental assistance can be through tenant-based, sponsor-based, project-based, or single room occupancy. States, local governments, or public housing agencies can apply for the funds. (14.238 Shelter Plus Care).

Contact your local HUD office or John Garrity, Director, Office of Special Needs Assistance Programs, U.S. Department of Housing and Urban Development, 451 7th St., SW, Room 7262, Washington, DC 20410; 202-708-4300; {www.hud.gov/progdesc/cpdindx.html}.

Money For Housing Research

Housing issues and programs change as needs change, and research is required to find out what works best. The U.S. Department of Housing and

Urban Development offers research funds to researchers, research organizations, state and local governments, academic institutions, and nonprofits. The funds are to carry out research, demonstration and program evaluation and monitoring projects of high priority and pre-selected by the Department to improve the operations of the Department's programs. (14.506 General Research and Technology Activity).

Contact Assistant Secretary for Policy Development and Research, Department of Housing and Urban Development, 451 7th Street SW., Washington, DC 20410. Attention: Budget, Contracts, and Program Control Division; 202-708-1796; {www.huduser.org}.

Help the Hispanic Community

Grants are available to help Hispanic-Serving Institutions of higher education (HSIs) expand their role and effectiveness in addressing community development needs in their localities, including neighborhood revitalization, housing, and economic development. Only nonprofit institutions of higher education are eligible for funds. (14.514 Hispanic-Serving Institutions Assisting Communities).

Contact Armand Carriere in the Office of University Partnerships, Office of Policy Development and Research, 451 7th Street SW., Washington, DC 20410; 202-708-3061, extension 3181; {www.hud.gov/grants}.

Local Colleges Get Money to Fix Up Your Home

Money is available to assist Historically Black Colleges and Universities (HBCUs) expand their

role and effectiveness in addressing community development needs in their localities, including neighborhood revitalization, housing, and economic development. The HBCU program also encourages greater citizen participation in the local/neighborhood planning process. (14.520 Historically Black Colleges and Universities Program).

Contact Ophelia Wilson, Office of University Partnerships, Office of Policy Development and Research, Dept. of Housing and Urban Development, 451 7th Street, SW., Washington, DC 20410; 202-708-3061, extension 4390. Fax: 202-708-0309; {www.oup.org}.

$3 Billion In Grants To Fix Up Homes In Cities

Community Development Block Grant money is available to metropolitan cities to help them provide decent housing and expand economic opportunities for low to moderate income residents. Recipients may undertake a wide range of activities directed toward neighborhood revitalization, economic development, and provision of improved community facilities and services. Entitlement communities develop their own programs and funding priorities as long as programs/activities conform to the statutory standards and program regulations. Community-based development organizations may carry out neighborhood revitalization, community economic development or energy conservation projects to further achieve the national objectives of the CDBG program. (14.218 Community Development Block Grants/ Entitlement Grants).

Contact Entitlement Communities Division, Office of Block Grant Assistance, Community Planning and Development, 451 7th Street, SW., Washington, DC 20410; 202-708-1577; {www.hud.gov/offices/cpd/index.cfm}.

$5 Million In Grants To Fix Up Homes In Small Towns

The Small Cities Program provides funding for the development of viable urban communities by providing decent housing, a suitable living environment, and expanding economic opportunities, principally for persons of low and moderate income. Small Cities develop their own programs and funding priorities. It could be acquisition, rehabilitation or construction of certain public works facilities and improvements, clearance, housing rehabilitation, code enforcement, direct assistance to facilitate and expand homeownership among persons of low and moderate income, relocation payments and assistance, administrative expenses, economic development, completing existing urban renewal projects, and certain public services with some restrictions. This program is only available to three counties in Hawaii. (14.219 Community Development Block Grants/Small Cities Program (Small Cities)). Contact State and Small Cities Division, Office of Block Grant Assistance, Community Planning and Development,

Department of Housing and Urban Development, 451 7th Street, SW., Washington, DC 20410; 202-708-1322; {www.hud.gov/offices/cpd/about/cpd_programs.cfm}.

Help to Get The Money

The Community Development Block Grants/Special Purpose Program is designed to help States, units of general local government, Indian tribes and areawide planning organizations to plan, develop and administer local Community Development Block Grant programs. Assistance may be used to transfer skills and knowledge in planning, developing and administering the Community Development Block Grant programs from those individuals and institutions which possess them to eligible block grant entities and affiliated CDBG participants which need them. Project activities show how they will increase the effectiveness with which eligible block grant communities can use CDBG funds to meet community development national and local program objectives. (14.227 Community Development Block Grants/Special Purpose).

Contact Office of Management and Technical Assistance, Community Planning and Development, Department of Housing and Urban Development, 451 7th St., SW., Washington, DC 20410; 202-708-3176; {www.hud.gov/progdesc/cpdindx.html}.

Money to Buy Or Fix Up Houses In The Pacific Islands Or The Virgin Islands

Community Development Block Grant funds provide community development assistance to the Pacific Islands of American Samoa, Guam, the Northern

Mariana Islands, and the Virgin Islands in the Caribbean. Funds have been used for housing rehabilitation, infrastructure and public facilities development, and/or improvements, economic development initiatives, microenterprise/small business creation and/or assistance, and first-time home buyer assistance. (14.225 Community Development Block Grants/Special Purpose Grants/ Insular Areas). Contact Office of Block Grant Assistance, Community Planning and Development, Department of Housing and Urban Development, 451 7th St., SW, Washington, DC 20410; 202-708-1322; {www.hud.gov/offices/cpd/about/cpd_programs.cfm}.

$570,000,000 For Local Communities to Fix Up Your House

Section 108, the loan guarantee provision of the Community Development Block Grant program, is one of the most potent and important public investment tools that HUD offers to local governments. It allows them to transform a small portion of their CDBG funds into federally guaranteed loans large enough to pursue physical and economic revitalization projects that can renew entire neighborhoods. Such public investment is often needed to inspire private economic activity, providing the initial resources or simply the confidence that private firms and individuals may need to invest in distressed areas. Units of general local government are eligible for funds. (14.248 Community Development Block Grants-Section 108 Loan Guarantees (Section 108)).

Contact Financial Management Division, Room 7180, Community Planning and Development, Department of Housing and Urban Development, 451 7th Street, SW., Washington, DC 20410; {www.hud.gov/offices/cpd/about/cpd_progra ms.cfm}.

Help For Native Alaskans and Hawaiians

Alaska Native Institutions (ANIs) of higher education and Native Hawaiian Institutions (NHIs) of higher education can enhance their role and effectiveness in addressing community development needs in their localities, including neighborhood revitalization, housing, and economic development, by applying for this grant program. Cities, counties, towns, and villages can benefit from this program. (14.515 Alaska Native/Native Hawaiian Institutions Assisting Communities).

Contact Armand Carriere in the Office of University Partnerships, Office of Policy Development and Research, 451 7th Street, SW., Washington, DC 20410; 202-708-3061, extension 3181; {www.oup.org}.

Help for Public Housing

Revitalization Grants enable Public Housing Agencies (PHA) to improve the living environment for public housing residents of severely distressed public housing projects through the demolition, substantial rehabilitation, reconfiguration, and/or replacement of severely distressed units; revitalize the sites on which severely distressed public housing projects are located and contribute to the improvement of the surrounding neighborhood; and more.

HOPE VI Demolition Grants enable PHAs to expedite the demolition of obsolete and/or severely distressed public housing units. Any subsequent new construction or revitalization of any remaining units must be funded from other resources. Up to 15 percent of a grant may be used for Community and Supportive Services programs. Only Public Housing Agencies operating public housing units are eligible to apply. (14.866 Demolition and Revitalization of Severely Distressed Public Housing (HOPE VI)).

Contact Assistant Secretary for Public and Indian Housing, Deputy Assistant Secretary for Public Housing Investments, Office of Urban Revitalization, Department of Housing and Urban Development, Washington, DC 20410; 202-401-8812; {www.hud.gov/hopevi}.

Money for Public Housing

The Capital Fund provides funds annually to Public Housing Agencies (PHAs) for capital and management activities, including modernization and development of public housing. The funds may be used for the development, financing and modernization of public housing developments and for management improvements. The funds may not be used for luxury improvements, direct

social services, costs funded by other programs, and ineligible activities as determined by HUD on a case-by-case basis. Only Public Housing Agencies are eligible to apply for funds. (14.872 Public Housing Capital Fund (CFP)).

Contact Assistant Secretary for Public and Indian Housing, 451 7th St., SW, Washington DC 20410; 202-708-0950; {www.hud.gov/progdesc/pihindx.html}.

50% Discount For Teachers K-12 To Buy A Home

The Teacher Next Door Initiative is designed to strengthen America's communities by encouraging public and private school teachers to live in low and moderate income neighborhoods. Teachers (State-certified in grades Kindergarten through 12th grade) may purchase HUD-owned single unit properties located in designated revitalization areas at a 50 percent discount off list price. Teachers must agree to occupy homes as their sole residence for a period of 3 years. (14.310 Teacher Next Door Initiative). Contact Asset Management and Disposition Division, 451 7th Street SW, Washington, DC 20410; 202-708-1672; {www.hud.gov/offices/hsg/sfh/reo/reo_home.cfm}.

Free Help to Complain to A Mobile Home Manufacturer

Manufactured home construction and safety standards have been established to protect the quality, durability, safety and affordability of manufactured homes; to facilitate the availability of affordable manufactured homes and to increase home ownership for all Americans; to provide for the establishment of practical, uniform, and, to the extent possible, performance-based Federal construction standards for manufactured homes; to encourage innovative and cost-effective construction techniques for manufactured homes; and to protect residents of manufactured homes with respect to personal injuries and the amount of insurance costs and property damages in manufactured housing. Any purchaser of a manufactured home built on or after June 15, 1976, for residential use is automatically covered by the program. (14.171 Manufactured Home Construction and Safety Standards (Manufactured Housing)).

Contact Office of Single Family Housing (HU), Office of Consumer and Regulatory Affairs (HUC), Manufactured Housing and Standards Division (HUCM), Room 9152, Department of Housing and Urban Development, Washington, DC 20410; 202-708-6409; Fax: 202-708-4213; Toll-free consumer hotline (leave message only): 800-927-2891; {www.hud.gov/progdesc/snglindx.html}.

More Money to Help Fair Housing

The government funds the Equal Housing Agency, but money is also available to develop, implement, carry out, or coordinate programs or activities designed to obtain enforcement of the rights granted by the Fair Housing Act or by substantially equivalent State and local fair housing laws. Financial assistance

is provided for specialized projects conducted by State and local fair housing agencies certified by HUD as "substantially equivalent." (14.408 Fair Housing Initiatives and Administrative Enforcement Initiative Program (FHIP & AEI)).

Contact Lauretta A. Dixon, Director, FHIP/FHAP Support Division, Office of Programs, Office of Fair Housing and Equal Opportunity, Department of Housing and Urban Development, 451 7th Street, SW., Room 5234, Washington, DC 20410; 202-708-0800, ext. 7051; {www.hud.gov/progdesc/fheoindx.html}.

Help People Learn Their Rights

Financial assistance is provided for specialized projects conducted by public or private entities to inform the public concerning rights and obligations under the Fair Housing Act or State or local laws that provide rights and remedies for alleged discriminatory housing practices. State and local governments; public or private nonprofit organizations or institutions and other public or private entities that are formulating or carrying out programs to prevent or eliminate discriminatory housing practices are eligible for funds. (14.409 Fair Housing Initiatives Program (FHIP) Education and Outreach Initiative (FHIP & EOI)).

Contact Lauretta A. Dixon, Director, FHIP/FHAP Support Division, Office of Fair Housing and Equal Opportunity, Department of Housing and Urban Development, 451 7th Street, SW., Room 5224, Washington, DC 20410; 202-708-0800, ext. 7051; {www.hud.gov/progdesc/fheoindx.htm l}.

Nonprofits Can Help With Fair Housing

Money is available to nonprofits to develop, implement, carry out, or coordinate programs or activities designed to obtain enforcement of the rights granted by the Fair Housing Act or by State and local fair housing laws. Financial assistance is provided for projects conducted by private nonprofit fair housing enforcement organizations that are formulating or carrying out programs to prevent or eliminate discriminatory housing practices. Only private nonprofit fair housing enforcement organizations are eligible for funds. (14.410 Fair Housing Initiatives Program (FHIP) Private Enforcement Initiative (FHIP & PEI)).

Contact Lauretta A. Dixon, Director, FHIP/FHAP Support Division, Office of Fair Housing and Equal Opportunity, Department of Housing and Urban Development, 451 7th Street, SW., Room 5234, Washington, DC 20410; 202-708-0800, ext. 7051; {www.hud.gov/progdesc/fheoindx.html}.

Help Those In Need

To address the needs of public housing residents, supportive services, resident empowerment activities and/or assisting residents in becoming economically self- sufficient are necessary. The primary focus of the program is on "welfare to work" and on independent living for the elderly and persons with disabilities. Grant funds may be used for both economic development and supportive services activities, organizational development, mediation, including the employment of service coordinators/ case managers. Those eligible to apply include Public and Indian Housing (PHAs/IHAs), and Tribally Designated Housing entities

(TDHEs), resident management corporations, resident councils or resident organizations (including nonprofit entities supported by residents). (14.870 Resident Opportunity and Supportive Services (ROSS)).

Contact Customer Services and Amenities Division, Office of Public and Assisted Housing Delivery, Public and Indian Housing, Department of Housing and Urban Development, Room 4224, 451 Seventh Street, SW., Washington, DC 20410; 202-708-4214; {www.hud.gov/progdesc/pihindx.html}.

Money For Teens To Learn To Build Or Fix Up Houses

The Youthbuild program ·provides funding assistance for a wide range of multi-disciplinary activities and services to assist economically disadvantaged youth. The opportunities are designed to help disadvantaged young adults who have dropped out of high school to obtain the education and employment skills necessary to achieve economic self-efficiency and develop leadership skills and a commitment to community development in low income communities.

Grant funds can be used to fund eligible educational and supportive services and activities composed of basic skills development, and counseling, referral and support services. Funds can also be used for architectural and engineering fees, construction, rehabilitation, acquisition, operating expenses and replacements reserves. Those eligible to apply for funds include public and private nonprofit agencies, state or local housing agencies, or state and local units of government. (14.243 Opportunities for Youth- Youthbuild Program).

Contact Jackie Williams-Mitchell, Director, Office of Rural Housing and Economic Development, Department of Housing and Urban Development, 451 7th Street SW., Washington, DC 20410, Room 7137; 202-708-2290; {www.hud.gov/progdesc/cpdindx.html }.

$2,000,000 Grant To Provide Single Room Occupancy Units

Grants are available to rehabilitate residential properties, so that when finished they will contain multiple single room dwelling units. Public Housing Agencies and private nonprofit organizations are eligible to apply for funds. (14.249 Section 8 Moderate Rehabilitation Single Room Occupancy).

Contact John D. Garrity, Deputy Director, Office of Special Needs Assistance Programs, Community Planning and Development, Department of Housing and Urban Development, Room 7262, 451 7th Street, SW., Washington, DC 20410; 202-708-4300; {www.hud.gov/prog desc/cpdindx.html}.

Grants To Local Communities To Provide Money To Buy Or Fix Up Homes And To Pay Rent

In general, under the HOME Investment Partnerships Program, HUD allocates funds to eligible State and local governments to strengthen public-private partnerships and to expand the supply of decent, safe, sanitary, and affordable housing. Participating jurisdictions may use HOME funds to help renters, new homebuyers or existing homeowners, with primary attention for very low-income and low-income families. (14.239 HOME Investment Partnership Program).

The HOME program is implemented through State and local governments called participating jurisdictions. Participating jurisdictions may be States or units of general local government, including consortia and urban counties. HOME participating jurisdictions have a great deal of flexibility in designing and managing their HOME programs. HUD's Office of Affordable Housing Programs Office administers the HOME program.

HUD Office of Affordable Housing
Office of Community Planning and Development
451 7th Street, SW
Washington, DC 20410

202-708-2470
TTY: 800-877-8339

$5,000 To Get Rid Of Lead Paint In Your Home

Lead poisoning can be very dangerous, but even more so in children. Lead-Based Paint Hazard Control grants provide assistance to State, Tribal, and local governments in developing programs for the identification and control of lead-based paint hazards in privately-owned housing that is owned by or rented to low- or very-low income families. Applicants eligible for Hazard Control Grants are States, Tribes, or units of local government. (14.900 Lead-Based Paint Hazard Control in Privately-Owned Housing).

Contact Hazard Control Grants: Matthew E. Ammon, Director, Lead Hazard Control Grants Division, Office of Lead Hazard Control, Department of Housing and Urban Development, 451 Seventh Street, SW., Room P-3206, Washington, DC 20410; 202-755-1785 ext. 158; {www.hud.gov/progdesc/leadindx.htm l}.

70% Discount On Rent

In order to best assist very low-income families in obtaining decent, safe, and sanitary rental housing. Vouchers are available to increase the housing choice for families. The Section 8 Rental Voucher Program provides housing assistance payments to participating owners on behalf of eligible tenant. Housing assistance payments are generally 70% of the rent with the family paying 30% of their income. Public Housing Agencies apply for these vouchers which are then given to low-income families. (14.871 Section 8 Housing Choice Vouchers). Contact Office of the

Public and Assisted Housing Delivery, Department of Housing and Urban Development, Washington, DC 20410; 202-708-0477; {www.hud.gov/prog desc/pihindx.cfm}.

Low Cost Flood Insurance

Through the National Flood Insurance Program, property owners may buy flood insurance at a premium rate that is generally lower than a normal actuarial rate. Maximum amounts for coverage are $35,000 for a single family home, $100,000 for all other residential structures, plus $10,000 per dwelling unit for contents. (83.100 Flood Insurance Program). Contact Federal Insurance Administration, FEMA, Washington, DC 20472; 202-646-3429; 888-FLOOD29; {www.fema.gov}.

Nonprofits Can Buy HUD Foreclosures At 30% Off Fair Market Value

The U.S. Department of Housing and Urban Development (HUD) needs to do something with the properties they acquire through foreclosures. They sell many to interested buyers on a competitive basis, but they also sell to nonprofit organizations and local governments at a discount. These organizations can purchase the properties for 10-30% off the fair market value. The nonprofit or local government must agree that the home will be used in conjunction with a home ownership plan. (14.311 Single Family Property Disposition).

Contact Asset Management and Disposition Division, Office of Single Family Housing, U.S. Department of Housing and Urban Development, Washington, DC 20410; 202-708-1672; {www.hud.gov/offices/hsg/sfh/reo/reo_home.cfm}.

$500 Per Month To Help Pay Your Rent

In order to make good quality rental housing available to low-income families at a cost they can afford, the U.S. Department of Housing and Urban Development makes payments to owners of approved HUD-insured and non-insured multifamily rental housing projects to supplement the partial rental payments of eligible tenants. Assistance covers the difference between the tenant's payment and the basic market rental. The tenants payment is usually 30% of their income, the HUD pays the other 70%. Eligible sponsors include nonprofits or other investors. (14.149 Rent Supplements- Rental Housing for Lower Income Families) and (14.856 Lower Income Housing Assistance Program- Section 8 Moderate Rehabilitation (Section 8 Housing Assistance Payments Program for Very Low Income Families- Moderate Rehabilitation)) for Public Housing Agencies.

Contact Director, Office of Multifamily Housing Management, Department of Housing and Urban Development, Washington, DC 20410; 202-708-3730; {www.hud.gov/progdesc/multindx.cfm}.

U.S. Department of Agriculture Programs

The Rural Housing Service (RHS) is an agency of the U.S. Department of Agriculture (USDA) and offers programs to assist individuals, developers and nonprofits. The goal is for you to live in a clean safe place. Programs include homeownership assistance, housing rehabilitation and preservation, rental assistance, farm labor housing and more. Typically these programs are limited to rural areas, usually having a population of no more than 20,000 people. Read on to see how you can make your dream a reality!

Many of the programs include a five-digit number in the description. The number refers to the Catalog of Federal Domestic Assistance, which is a publication that lists all the government money programs. You can search the catalog online at {www.cfda.gov}, and it is also available in most public libraries.

For more information or to learn about different programs, you can contact the Rural Housing Service of the U.S. Department of Agriculture at:

Rural Housing Service
U.S. Department of Agriculture
Room 5037, South Building
14th Street and Independence Ave., SW
Washington, DC 20250
202-720-4323
www.rurdev.usda.gov

$7,000 for a Bathroom/Kitchen

Money is available to help those in rural areas install basic services to make their homes more habitable. Grant funds may be used to connect service lines to a residence, pay utility hook-up fees, install plumbing and related fixtures, i.e. a bathroom sink, bathtub or shower, commode, kitchen sink, water heater, outside spigot, or bathroom, if lacking.

These grants are available to households who own and occupy the dwelling, and are available only in Arizona, California, New Mexico, and Texas. This program is called Individual Water and Waste Grants.

Contact your state, area or local Rural Development office or contact Single Family Housing, Direct Loan Division, U.S. Department of Agriculture, Washington, DC 20250; 202-720-1474; {www.rurdev.usda.gov}.

$200,000 to Buy or Fix Up Homes In the Country

The Farm Labor Housing Loan and Grant program provides capital financing for the development of housing for domestic farm laborers. 1% loans and grants are provided to buy, build, improve, or repair housing for farm laborers, including persons whose income is earned in aquaculture (fish and oyster farms) and those engaged in on-farm processing.

Funds can be used to purchase a site or a leasehold interest in a site; to construct housing, day care facilities, or community rooms; to pay fees to purchase durable household furnishings; and to pay construction loan interest. Loans are for 33 years at 1% interest, except as noted above. Grants may cover up to 90% of development costs. (10.405 Farm Labor Housing Loans and Grants).

Contact your state, area or local Rural Development office or contact Multi-Family Housing, U.S. Department of Agriculture, Washington, DC 20250; 202-720-1604; {www.rurdev.usda.gov}.

$15,000 Grant For Owners or Developers In Small Towns To Fix Up Their Homes

The Housing Preservation Grants program provides funds to repair or rehabilitate individual housing, rental properties, or co-ops owned and/or occupied by very low- and low-income rural persons. Housing Preservation

Grant assistance is available from grantees to assist very-low and low-income homeowners to repair and rehabilitate their homes.

Assistance is also available to rental property owners to repair and rehabilitate their units providing they agree to make such units available to very-low and low-income families.. (10.433 Rural Housing Preservation Grants).

Contact your state, area or local Rural Development office or contact Multi-Family Housing, U.S. Department of Agriculture, Washington, DC 20250; 202-720-1600; {www.rurdev.usda.gov}.

$50,000 To Fix Up Your Home After A Natural Disaster

The Rural Housing Service assists homeowners to meet emergency needs resulting from a natural disaster. Money is only available to the extent that funds are not provided by the Federal Emergency Management Agency (FEMA).

Applicants must own and occupy the home in a rural area. Loan recipients must have sufficient income to repay the loan. Grant recipients must be 62 years of age or older and be unable to repay a loan for that part of the assistance received as a grant. The applicant's income for a loan may not exceed the very low-income limit. (10.444 Direct Housing — Natural Disaster Loans and Grants Section 504).

Contact your state, area or local Rural Development office or contact Single Family Housing, U.S. Department of Agriculture, Washington, DC 20250; 202-720-1474; {www.rurdev.usda. gov}.

$2,700 A Year For Rent

Rural Rental Assistance Payments help people with very low and low incomes, the elderly, and persons with disabilities if they are unable to pay the basic monthly rent.

Tenants in Rural Housing contribute 30% of their adjusted income, and the Rural Housing Service pays the rest of the rental rate. Prospective tenants can contact their local rural housing office to see what apartments participate in this program. Landlords can contact the local Rural Housing office to learn how they can qualify to participate in this program.

Contact your state, area or local Rural Development office or contact Multi-Family Housing, U.S. Department of Agriculture, Washington, DC 20250; 202-720-1600; {www.rurdev.usda. gov}.

$27,500 In Grants And Loans To Fix Up Your Home

That is the amount of money you can get to repair your rural home through the Section 504 Rural Housing Repair and Loan program. These low interest long-term loans helped over 4,000 homeowners use this money to fix up their homes. This program is limited to

very low income homeowners. The Very Low-Income Housing Repair program provides loans and grants to very low-income homeowners in rural areas to repair, improve, or modernize their dwellings or to remove health and safety hazards. Grant funds are only available to homeowners aged 62 or older who cannot repay a Section 504 Loan. This includes repairs or replacement of heating, plumbing or electrical services, roof or basic structure as well as water and waste disposal systems, and weatherization. Loans of up to $20,000 and grants of up to $7,500 or more are available. Grant funds may be used only to pay for repairs and improvements resulting in the removal of health and safety hazards. (10.417 Very Low-Income Housing Repair Loans and Grants (Section 504 Rural Housing Loans Grants)).

For more information Director, Single-Family Housing Processing Division, Rural Housing Service, Department of Agriculture, Washington, DC 20250; 202-720-1474; {www.rurdev.usda.gov}.

$100,000 Direct Loans To Buy or Fix Up Homes In The Country

Rural Housing Service provides financing for individuals and families who cannot obtain credit from other sources to purchase homes in rural areas. Applications are received at USDA offices. Funds may be used to purchase suitable existing homes, new site build homes, approved modular units, and new manufactured units from an approved dealer/contractor. Funds may also be used to repair or remodel homes, or to make the home accessible and usable for persons who are developmentally disabled.

Loans may be made for up to 100% of the appraised value of the site and the home. Maximum repayment period is 33 years, or under certain conditions, 38 years. Downpayment is not required if your net assets do not exceed $7,500. (Section 502 Direct Loan Program- 10.410 Very Low to Moderate Income Housing Loans).

Contact your state, area or local Rural Development office or contact Single Family Housing, Direct Loan Division, U.S. Department of Agriculture, Washington, DC 20250; 202-720-1474; {www.rurdev.usda.gov}.

$105,000 Guaranteed Loan To Buy Or Fix A House

Through USDA's Guaranteed Rural Housing Loan Program, low and moderate income people can qualify for mortgages even without a down-payment. Loans may be for up to 100% of appraised value. Mortgages are 30-year fixed rate. Guaranteed loans can be made on either new or existing homes. Homes must be located in rural areas (USDA can determine eligible areas). (Section 502 Guaranteed Loan Program- 10.410 Very Low to Moderate Income Guaranteed Housing Loans).

Approved lenders under the Single Family Housing Guaranteed Loan program include:
- Any State housing agency;
- Lenders approved by:
  - HUD for submission of applications for Federal Housing Mortgage Insurance or as an issuer of Ginnie Mae mortgage backed securities;
  - the U.S. Veterans Administration as a qualified mortgagee;
  - Fannie Mae for participation in family mortgage loans;
  - Freddie Mac for participation in family mortgage loans;
  - Any FCS (Farm Credit System) institution with direct lending authority;
  - Any lender participating in other USDA Rural Development and/or Consolidated Farm Service Agency guaranteed loan programs.

Contact your state, area or local Rural Development office or contact Single Family Housing, Direct Loan Division, U.S. Department of Agriculture, Washington, DC 20250; 202-720-1474; {www.rurdev.usda.gov}.

Want To Help Build Your Country Home?

Here is a chance for you to put in some sweat equity and build the home of your dreams. The Section 502 Mutual Self-Help Housing Loan program is used primarily to help very low- and low-income households construct their own homes. The program is targeted to families who are unable to buy clean, safe housing through conventional methods.

Families participating in a mutual self-help project perform approximately 65 percent of the construction labor on each other's homes under qualified supervision.

If families cannot meet their mortgage payments during the construction phase, the funds for these payments can be included in the loan. Maximum repayment period is 33 years, or under certain conditions, 38 years. (Section 502 Mutual Self-Help Loan Program- 10.410 Very Low to Moderate Income Housing Loans).

Contact your state, area or local Rural Development office or contact Single Family Housing, Direct Loan Division, U.S. Department of Agriculture, Washington, DC 20250; 202-720-1474; {www.rurdev.usda.gov}.

$1,000,000 To Purchase Or Fix Up Rental Housing

Rural Rental Housing Loans are direct, competitive mortgage loans made to provide affordable multifamily rental housing for very low-, low-, and moderate-income families; the elderly; and persons with disabilities. This is primarily a direct mortgage program, but its funds may also be used to buy and improve land and to provide necessary facilities such as water and waste disposal systems.

In new Section 515 projects, 95 percent of tenants must have very low incomes. In existing projects 75 percent of new tenants must have very low incomes. Very low-, low-, and moderate-income families; the elderly; and persons with disabilities are eligible for tenancy of Section 515-financed housing.

Loans can be made to individuals, trusts, associations, partnerships, limited partnerships, State or local public agencies, consumer cooperatives, and profit or nonprofit corporations. (10.415 Rural Rental Housing Loans).

Contact your state, area or local Rural Development office or contact Multi-Family Housing, U.S. Department of Agriculture, Washington, DC 20250; 202-720-1600; {www.rurdev.usda. gov}.

Money To Build Rental Units

The Rural Housing Service guarantees loans under the Rural Rental Housing Guaranteed loan program for development of multi-family housing facilities in rural areas of the United States. Loan guarantees are provided for the construction, acquisition, or rehabilitation of rural multi-family housing. Occupants must be very- low, low- or moderate-income households, elderly, handicapped, or disabled persons with income not in excess of 115% of the area median income.

The average rent of all units is 30% of 100% of the median income of the surrounding area (adjusted for family size). The terms of the loans guaranteed may be up to 40 years, and the loans must be fully amortized.

The program is limited to rural areas. An applicant must be: A citizen of the United States or a legally admitted alien for permanent residence in the United States; a nonprofit organization such as a local government, community development group or American Indian tribe, band, group, or nation (including Alaskan Indians, Aleuts, Eskimos, and any Alaskan native village); or a for-profit corporation.

Eligible lenders are those currently approved and considered eligible by the Federal National Mortgage Association, the Federal Home Loan Mortgage Corporation, the Federal Home Loan Bank members, or the Department of Housing and Urban Development for guaranteed programs supporting multifamily housing. State Housing Finance Agencies may also be considered eligible lenders. Other lenders have the opportunity to enter into a correspondent bank relationship with approved lenders in order to participate in the program. (10.438 Section 538 Guaranteed Rural Rental Housing Program).

Contact your state, area or local Rural Development office or contact Multi-Family Housing, U.S. Department of Agriculture, Washington, DC 20250; 202-720-1604; {www.rurdev.usda.gov}.

$400 Per Month To Help Pay Rent In Small Towns

The Rural Rental Assistance Payments are made to developers who operate low-income housing. These payments are used to reduce the rents paid by residents whose rents exceed 30 percent of their income. (10.427 Rural Rental Assistance Payments).

Contact Director, Multi-family Housing Portfolio Management Division, Rural Housing Service, Department of Agriculture, Washington, DC 20250; 202-720-1600; {www.rurdev.usda.gov}.

Money For Conserving the Water and Soil During an Emergency

The Emergency Conservation Program provides assistance to rehabilitate eligible farmlands. These funds are made available without regard to a Presidential emergency disaster designation.

To be eligible the applicant must have suffered a natural disaster that if untreated would impair or endanger the land. Money can be used for debris removal, fence restoration, grading and shaping of farmland, water conservation, and more. (10.054-Emergency Conservation Program).

Contact your state or local Rural Development office or contact U.S. Department of Agriculture, Farm Service Agency, Stop 0513, 1400 Independence Ave., SW, Washington, DC 20250; 202-720-6221; {www.fsa.usda.gov}.

Money To Improve Your Water and Soil

The Conservation Reserve Program encourages farmers to plant long-term resource-conserving covers to improve soil, water, and wildlife resources. This is a voluntary program that offers annual rental payments, incentive payments, and annual maintenance payments for certain activities, and cost-share assistance to establish approved cover on eligible cropland. (10.069- Conservation Reserve Program).

Contact your state or local Rural Development office or contact U.S. Department of Agriculture, Farm Service Agency, Stop 0513, 1400 Independence Ave., SW, Washington, DC 20250; 202-720-6221; {www.fsa.usda.gov}.

Loans to Help Your Country Property Recover From an Emergency

The Farm Service Agency provides emergency loans to help producers recover from production and physical losses due to drought, flooding and other natural disasters. Emergency loan funds may be used to restore or replace essential property, any all or part of production costs associated with the disaster year, pay essential family living expenses, refinance certain debts, and more. Farmers and ranchers must have suffered at least a 30% loss of crop production or a physical loss to livestock, livestock products, real estate, or chattel property. (10.404- Emergency Loans).

Contact your state or local Rural Development office or contact U.S. Department of Agriculture, Farm Service Agency, Stop 0520, 1400 Independence Ave., SW, Washington, DC 20250; 202-720-1632; {www.fsa. usda.gov}.

Money To Fix Up An Abandoned Coal Mine

Approximately 1.1 million acres exists of abandoned coal-mined land and are need of reclaiming. Money is available to protect people and the environment from the adverse effects of past coal mining practices, and to promote the development of soil and water resources of unreclaimed mined lands. (10.910- Rural Abandoned Mine program).

Contact your state or local Rural Development office or contact Deputy Chief for Natural Resources, Conservation Programs, Natural Resources Conservation Service, U.S. Department of Agriculture, P.O. Box 2890, Washington, DC 20013; 202-720-1873; {www.nrcs.usda.gov}.

Money For Farmers and Ranchers to Improve Water and Soil

Many farmers face serious threats to soil, water, and related natural resources. The Environmental Quality Incentives Program provides technical, financial, and educational assistance to address these concerns in an environmentally beneficial and cost-

effective manner. The program works primarily in priority areas where significant natural resource programs exist. All activities must be carried out according to a conservation plan. (10.912- Environmental Quality Incentives Program).

Contact your state or local Rural Development office or contact Deputy Chief for Natural Resources, Conservation Programs, Natural Resources Conservation Service, U.S. Department of Agriculture, P.O. Box 2890, Washington, DC 20013; 202-720-1868; {www.nrcs.usda.gov}.

$400,000 Grants To Build Homes In Small Towns

In order to expand the supply of affordable housing and access to economic opportunities in rural areas, grants are available that can be used for capacity building, and support for innovative housing and economic development activities for these programs. Local, rural, nonprofit organizations, community development corporations, Federally recognized Indian Tribes, State Housing Financing Agencies and State Community and Economic Development Agencies are eligible for funds. (14.250 Rural Housing and Economic Development).

Contact Jackie Williams-Mitchell, Director, Office of Rural Housing and Economic Development, Community Planning and Development 451 7th St., SW., Rm. 7137, Washington, DC 20410; 202-708-2290; {www.hud.gov/ rhed.html}.

$750,000 To Buy A Farm

Loans are available to assist eligible farmers, ranchers, and aquaculture operators, including farming cooperatives, corporations, partnerships, and joint operations, through the extension of credit and supervisory assistance. Loans can be used so people can become owner-operators of not larger than family farms; make efficient use of the land, labor, and other resources; carry on sound and successful farming operations; and enable farm families to have a reasonable standard of living. Loan funds may be used to: enlarge, improve, and buy family farms; provide necessary water and water facilities; provide basic soil treatment and land conservation measures; and more. Those eligible to apply for the loan must be U.S. citizens or permanent residents, and have the necessary education and/or experience to operate a family farm. (10.407 Farm Ownership Loans).

Contact Department of Agriculture, Farm Service Agency, Director, Loan Making Division, Ag Box 0522, Washington, DC 20250; 202-720-1632; {www.fsa.usda.gov}.

Buy Some Land

Funds are provided to assist public or private nonprofit organizations in providing sites for housing, to acquire and develop land in rural areas that will be subdivided as building sites and sold on a cost development basis to families eligible for low and very low income loans, cooperatives, and broadly based nonprofit rural rental housing applicants. Money can also be used for water and sewer facilities, needed landscaping, walks, parking areas, and driveways. Those eligible for loans include private or public nonprofit organizations that will provide the developed sites to qualified borrowers on a cost of development basis in open country and towns of 10,000 population or less and places up to 25,000 population under certain conditions. (10.411 Rural Housing Site Loans and Self-Help Housing Land Development Loans (Section 523 and 524 Site Loans)).

Contact Director, Single-Family Housing Processing Division, Rural Housing Service, Department of Agriculture, Washington, DC 20250; 202-720-1474; {www.rurdev.usda.gov}.

$300,000 Grant To Help Families Build Part Of Their Own House

Funds are available in the form of Self Help Technical Assistance Grants that will provide financial assistance to qualified nonprofit organizations and public bodies that will aid needy very low and low-income individuals and their families to build homes in rural areas by the self help method. Any State, political subdivision, private or public nonprofit corporation is eligible to apply. Section 523 Grants are used to pay salaries, rent, and office expenses of the nonprofit organization.

Eligible organizations may use technical assistance funds to hire the personnel to carry out a technical assistance program for self-help housing in rural areas; to pay necessary and reasonable office and administrative expenses; to purchase or rent equipment such as power tools for use by families participating in self-help housing construction; and to pay fees for training self-help group members in construction techniques or for other professional services needed. (10.420 Rural Self-Help Housing Technical Assistance (Section 523 Technical Assistance)).

Contact Director, Single-Family Housing Processing Division, Rural Housing Service (RHS), Department of Agriculture, Washington, DC 20250; 202-720-1474; {www.rurdev. usda.gov}.

Free Housing Counseling Services For Families In Small Towns

Many organizations want to help low-income rural families obtain adequate housing. These objectives can be accomplished through the establishment or support of housing delivery and counseling projects run by eligible applicants. Uses of grant funds may include: development and implementation of a program of technical and supervisory assistance; payment of reasonable salaries of professional, technical, and clerical staff actively assisting in the delivery of the project; payment of office expenses; payment of administrative costs; and payment of reasonable fees for necessary training. Technical and Supervisory Assistance Grants may be made to public or private nonprofit corporations, agencies, institutions,

organizations, Indian Tribes, and other associations. (10.441 Technical and Supervisory Assistance Grants).

Contact Rural Housing Service (RHS), USDA, 14th Street and Independence Avenue SW., Washington, DC 20250; 202-720-1474; {www.rurdev.usda.gov}.

$20,000 Grant To Prepare A Loan Package For An Apartment Building

Getting the paperwork in order often takes time and skill. Grants are available to package single family housing applications for very low- and low-income rural residents who wish to buy, build, or repair houses for their own use and to package applications for organizations wishing to develop rental units for lower income families. Grants reimburse eligible organizations for part or all of the costs of conducting, administering, and coordinating an effective housing application packaging program. local governments, and private nonprofit organizations. (10.442 Housing Application Packaging Grants (Section 509 Grants)).

Contact Director, Single Family Housing Processing Division, Rural Housing Service, Department of Agriculture, Washington, DC 20250; 202-720-1474; {www.rurdev.usda.gov}.

Other Agencies

In addition to the U.S. Department of Housing and Urban Development and the Rural Housing Service of the U.S. Department of Agriculture, there are several other agencies that offer special housing programs. The Bureau of Indian Affairs offer a variety of grants and loan programs to Native

Americans, Alaskan Indians, Aleuts, Eskimos, and others to help fill a need for adequate housing. These programs include block grants to communities to provide facilities and improve housing stock, as well as guaranteed loan programs to help people purchase or rehabilitate their homes. The U.S. Department of Veteran Affairs also offers loan guarantee programs to veterans or surviving spouses, in addition to grants to help veterans adapt their homes for a disability.

Many of the programs listed include a five-digit number in the description. The number refers to the Catalog of Federal Domestic Assistance, which is a publication that lists all the government money programs. You can search the catalog online at {www.cfda.gov}, and it is also available in most public libraries.

For more information or to learn about different programs, you can contact:

Bureau of Indian Affairs
Office of Tribal Services
MS 4660 MIB
1849 C St., NW
Washington, DC 20240
202-308-3667
www.doi.gov/bureau-indian-
affairs.html

U.S. Department of Veterans Affairs
Washington, DC 20420
202-273-7355
800-827-1000
www.va.gov

$55,000 To Help Build or Fix Up A Home For Native Americans

Native American homeowners that are living in homes in need of major repairs can get assistance from the federal government. The resources of the Bureau of Indian Affairs' Housing Improvement Program (HIP) eliminates substantially substandard housing for very low income eligible Native Americans living in approved tribal service areas. Grants allow for renovations, repairs, or additions to existing homes. The program will even build an entire house when there is no other available program to meet the need in the immediate or near future. It is restricted to use within reservations and approved tribal service areas. Individual members of Federally recognized Indian tribes in need of housing assistance who are unable to obtain assistance from any other source, and who meet the eligibility criteria of the HIP regulations can apply. (15.141 Indian Housing Assistance)

For more information, the Office of Tribal Services, Human Services, Bureau of Indian Affairs, MS 4660 MIB, 1849 C St., NW, Washington, DC 20240; 202-208-3667; {www.doi. gov/bia/tservices/hip/housing.htm}; {www.doi.gov/bureau-indian-affairs.html}.

Grant To Native American Communities To Fix Up Homes

The federal government wants to assist Native American tribes and Alaska Native villages to develop viable communities. Block grants are available to improve the housing stock, provide community facilities, make infrastructure improvements, and expand job opportunities by supporting the economic development of communities. Applicants may include any Native American tribe, band, group, nation, or tribal organization, including Alaska Indians, Aleuts, and

Eskimos, and any Alaska Native village that is eligible for assistance under the Indian Self-Determination and Education Assistance Act or which had been eligible under the State and Local Fiscal Assistance Act of 1972. (14.862 Indian Community Development Block Grant Program). Contact your local HUD Office of Native American Programs (ONAP) Area Office, or the Denver Office of Native American Programs, U.S. Department of Housing and Urban Development, Suite 3990, 1999 Broadway, Denver, CO 80202; 800-561-5913; {www.hud.gov}.

Money For Native Americans To Fix Up A Home

Grants are given to American Indian tribes in a way that recognizes their right to self-govern. Block grants are provided to the tribes with approved Indian Housing Programs, on an annual basis. The tribes and Alaska Native villages determine who will receive the grant. The funding serves the housing needs of low-income American Indians and Alaska Natives. Eligible affordable housing activities must include developing or supporting rental or ownership housing or providing housing services to benefit low-income Indian families on Indian reservations and other Indian areas. (14.867 Indian Housing Block Grant). Contact the appropriate HUD Office of Native American Programs; or Office of Native American Programs, Denver Program Office, 1999 Broadway, Suite 3390, Denver, CO 80202; 800-561-5913; {www.hud.gov}.

$150,000 To Help Native Americans Buy A Home

Buying a home has just got easier for Native Americans! This program is a guarantee mortgage loan program made through private financial institutions to benefit Native Americans. Mortgage loans can be made for the purchase or rehabilitation of an existing home, construction of a new home, or refinance of a current mortgage. The applicant must be a Native American, or an Indian Housing Authority or Tribe, who may then rent the home to a Native American. (14.865 Indian Housing Indian Loan Guarantee Program).

Check out the program at {www.codetalk.fed.us/loan184.html}; or for more information, contact Director, Office of Loan Guarantee, National Office of Native American Programs, 1999 Broadway, Suite 3390, Denver, CO 80202; 800-561-5913; {www.hud.gov}.

Money For Native American Communities To Build Affordable Housing

Most of the native land of American Indians is held in trust by the federal government and must receive federal approval before a lien can be placed on the property. Because of this, many lenders have not been willing to make home loans to individual Native Americans. This program offers a loan guarantee to private sector lenders who make home mortgage loans to eligible borrowers for homes located in Indian Country. The applicant must be a federally recognized Indian tribe or Tribally Designated Housing Entity that is either a beneficiary or recipient of Indian Housing Block Grants (IHBG) funds. (14.869 Title VI Federal Guarantees for Financing Tribal Housing Activities).

Contact Director of the Office of Loan Guarantee, National Office of Native American Programs, 1999 Broadway,

Denver, CO 80202; 800-561-5913; {www.hud. gov}.

$48,000 Grant For Veterans To Adapt Their Home For A Disability

Severely disabled veterans can get help to purchase a home that is adapted to meet their special needs. The program uses grant money to provide 50% of the cost of the adapted house, land and allowable expenses. The money may be used to construct a suitable home, remodel an existing home, or to reduce the outstanding mortgage on an adapted home already owned by the veteran.

This program is for veterans with a permanent, total, and service-connected disability due to: (1) loss or loss of use of both lower extremities, (2) which includes (a) blindness in both eyes, having only light perception, plus (b) loss or loss of use of one lower extremity; or (3) loss or loss of use of one lower extremity, together with (a) residuals of organic disease or injury, or (b) the loss or loss of use of one upper extremity which so affect the functions of balance or propulsion as to preclude locomotion without the aid of braces, crutches, canes, or a wheelchair. The maximum grant amount is $48,000; the maximum amount for adaptation and/or equipment for the veterans home is $9,250. (64.106 Specially Adapted Housing for Disabled Veterans).

Contact your nearest Regional VA Office or Department of Veterans Affairs, Washington, DC 20420; 202-273-7355; 800-827-1000; {www.va.gov}.

$150,000 To Help Veterans and Unmarried Spouses of Veterans to Buy or Fix Up A Home

Veterans can get more liberal financing terms to purchase their homes. This program is available to veterans, certain service personnel, and certain unmarried surviving spouses of veterans. Home loans may be guaranteed or secured by the VA for the purchase, refinance, construction, or improvement of homes. Veterans must get a Certificate of Eligibility from their local Veterans Office. (64.114 Veteran Housing Guaranteed and Insured Loan).

Contact your local Veterans Office or check out the program; or contact the Department of Veterans Affairs, Washington, DC 20420; 202-273-7390; 800-827-1000; {www.va.gov}.

$33,000 For Disabled Veterans To Fix Up A Home

If your home still needs more alterations after using the Specially Adapted Housing for Disabled Veterans grant, this program will help. Disabled Veterans who are eligible for the Specially Adapted Housing grant mentioned above may be eligible for a direct loan from the Veterans Administration. The funds are to be used for additional assistance in adapting the veteran's home to their special needs. To be considered for the loan, the veteran must meet the requirements for the grant, a loan must be necessary to supplement the grant, and home loans from a private lender cannot be available in the area where the property is located. The maximum amount of the loan is $33,000. (64.118 Veterans Housing Direct Loan for Certain Disabled Veterans).

Contact your local Veterans Affairs field office; or contact the Department of Veterans Affairs, Washington, DC 20420; 202-273-7390; 800-827-1000; {www.va.gov}.

$20,000 For A Manufactured Home

Whether you have a lot for a manufactured home, or are looking for both, the VA can give you assistance to make that happen. Veterans, service persons, and certain unmarried surviving spouses of veterans can get help to obtain credit for the purchase of a manufactured home. The terms of the loan will be more liberal than those that are available to non-veterans. The guarantee is for the purchase of a new or used manufactured home and/or to purchase or improve a lot to place a manufactured home. (64.119 Veterans Housing Manufactured Home Loans).

Contact your local Veterans Benefits Administration field office; or the Department of Veterans Affairs, Washington, DC 20420; 202-273-7390; 800-827-1000; {www.va.gov}.

$541,000 To Help Homeless Vets

The creation of the Homeless Veterans Comprehensive Service Programs Act of 1992 provides funding to public and nonprofit entities so that they may deliver supportive services and housing for homeless veterans. The grant money may be used to acquire, renovate or alter facilities, and to provide per diem payment, or in-kind assistance, to those that provide these services. Applicants eligible for grants include public and nonprofit private entities with the capacity to effectively administer a grant; which demonstrate that adequate financial support will be available to carry out the project; and which agree to and demonstrate capacity to meet the applicable criteria and requirements of the grant program. The average range of financial assistance is $12,610 to $541,000. (64.024 VA Homeless Providers Grant & Per Diem Program). Contact the Program Manager, VA Homeless Providers Grant and Per Diem Program, Mental Health Strategic Healthcare Group (116E), Department of Veterans Affairs, 810 Vermont Avenue, NW, Washington, DC 20420; 202-273-8966; 877-322-0334; {www.va.gov}.

Houses For $1

Did you know your community can buy homes for $1.00? Through HUD's Dollar Homes initiative, single-family homes acquired in FHA foreclosure actions are eligible for sale to local governments across the nation for $1 plus closing costs when the properties have been listed for at least six months and remain unsold. Local governments buying HUD properties for $1 plus closing costs may sell or rent them to low- and moderate-income families, to first-time homebuyers, or to groups that will use the properties to provide services to the community such as child-care centers, shelters, job training centers, etc. To locate homes in your community, contact your local HUD office, or the U.S. Department of Housing and Urban Development, 451 7th Street S.W., Washington, DC 20410; 202-708-1112; {http://www.hud.gov/offices/hsg/sfh/reo/goodn/dh mabout.cfm}. {http://12.46.245.173/pls/portal30/CATALOG.PROGRAM_

TEXT_RPT.SHOW?p_arg_names=pr
og_nbr&p_arg_values=14.313}.

Grants of up to $15,000 for Housing Projects

$15,000 grants for housing/shelter and rehabilitation purposes. Focuses primarily in the Washington DC area, and New York. Contact The Sulica Fund, Inc., 4902 Montgomery Avenue, Bethesda, MD 20816-3020; 301-907-4453.

Grants Over $10,000 for Homebuyers

Grants of up to $10,600 to homebuyers in California; amount depends on income, home purchase price and mortgage loan type. Contact American Home Buyers Alliance Foundation, 15585 Monterey Rd., Suite E, Morgan Hill, CA 95037; 408-776-8815, ext. 15; {http://www.americanhome buyersalliance.org/}.

Work for a Non-Profit and Get Money for a New Home

The Employee Matching Gifts Program matches contributions of $25 to $10,000 (per employee, per year) from full-time, retired, permanent part-time employees, and non-employee directors of any 501(c)(3) non-profit organization, excluding the United Way. The first $500 is matched on a two-to-one basis. Contact Fannie Mae Foundation, 4000 Wisconsin Avenue, N.W., N. Tower, Suite 1, Washington, DC 20016-2804; 202-274-8057 or 202-274-8000; Fax: 202-274-8100; {http://www.fanniemaefoundation.org }; {grants@fanniemaefoundation.org}.

5% Down Payment Gift

American Family Funds helps prospective homebuyers who have worked in the same field for two years and have no recent history of late bill payments purchase a home with little or no money down. Administered by the Dove Foundation, the Down Payment Gift Program provides an average of 3 to 5 % of the purchase price of single-family homes, condos, and multi-family units. Any individual who pre-qualifies for a loan that allows charitable gift contributions can apply for an AFF gift through their financial institution and real estate agent. Sellers and builders must agree to pay a service fee ($750 maximum) plus the gift amount, which is applied to the Dove Foundation's gift pool. Benefits to enrolled property sellers include an increase in the number of buyers able to purchase the home at or close to list value. There are no set maximums on gift amount. Seller must pay gift plus $750 maximum charge. Contact American Family Funds, Inc.; 3720 Airport Boulevard., Suite C, Mobile, AL 36608; 251-344-1084; {www.americanfamilyfunds.com}.

Get 6% of the Price of Your New Home

Financial assistance gifts offered by the Nehemiah Foundation help both first-time and repeat homebuyers purchase new and existing houses. Down payment or closing cost assistance comes in the form of gift funds ranging from 1% to 6% of the final contract sales price. In Nehemiah's program, there is no cost to buyers, no repayment of gift money, no income or asset limitation, and no geographical restriction. The program benefits homebuyers nationwide. To be eligible, an individual or family must use a mortgage product that accepts gift contributions and must be the primary occupant of the home to be bought. The Foundation is part of the Nehemiah Corporation of America, a non-profit community development firm focused on homeownership and affordable housingContact Nehemiah Corporation of America; 1851 Heritage Lane, Suite 201, Sacramento, CA 95815; 877-634-3642; {www. getdownpayment.com}.

Money for Your New Home in One Hour

The Neighborhood Gold Down Payment Assistance Program helps families purchase a home in the neighborhood of their choice with no money down. Neighborhood Gold works with The Buyers Fund, Inc. a non-profit organization, to provide prospective homeowners with gift money to cover down payment requirements and closing costs. To receive a grant, a buyer should work with a lender to obtain a mortgage that allows down payments in the form of a charitable gift. If a buyer is approved for a loan, he or she can receive Neighborhood Gold gift funds, regardless of income level. The mortgage professional fills out the grant application, and will receive a gift letter from us within ONE HOUR. Neighborhood Gold has local representatives who can offer assistance in the application process and answer any questions before, during and after the home buying process. As part of the grant, Neighborhood Gold offers a the Mortgage Payment Protection Plan, which covers up to six months of payments and may make it easier for a

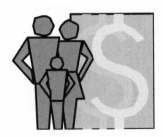

program participant to attain mortgage financing for the home of their dreams. National Contact Neighborhood Gold, Inc.; 3575 North 100 East, Suite 275, Provo, UT 84604; 888-627-3023; {www.neighborhoodgold.com}.

$30,000 Gifts for Homebuyers

The Home Down Payment Gift Foundation gives homebuyers presents of up to $30,000 to assist with home purchases. The gift program is aimed at low- to moderate-income buyers. Gifts generally range between three to six percent of the final home sale price, up to $30,000. Applications are available online, and the Foundation promises an answer in 24 hours. In order to qualify, a buyer needs to purchase a house that has been enrolled in the program; the foundation will aid the seller in the enrollment process. The seller is also required to make a donation to the Foundation based on the purchase price of the home (generally, gift amount plus fee of 3.75% of price), to be used to fund other gifts. Gift funds are wired to the closing agent 24 hours prior to closing. The maximum gift amount is $30,000 or 6%. Seller pays gift amount plus fee 3.75% of price. Contact The Home Down Payment Gift Foundation, Inc.; 1700 Rockville Pike, Suite 400, Rockville, MD 20852; 888-856-4600; {www.homedownpayment.org}.

Making Dreams into Reality...with a Down Payment Gift of 5%

Certain homebuyers are eligible to receive a financial "gift" from Gaithersburg-based AmeriDream, Inc. A qualifying buyer can receive 5% of the purchase price of a home to cover down payment or closing costs... and the homeowner does not have to repay the amount. A buyer submits a gift program application through a qualified lender and the gift money is wired to his or her settlement agent on the day of closing. The gift amount is based on the price of the home purchased, as well as the fee amount a seller is willing to pay to have his or her home enrolled in the program. The program covers single-family homes priced under $333,700 and multi-unit dwellings priced under $641,650 that have been enrolled in the Gift Program by the property's builder or seller.

Contact AmeriDream, Inc.; 18310 Montgomery Village Avenue, Third Floor, Gaithersburg, MD 20879; 866-263-7437; {www.ameridream.org}.

$22,500 for Closing Costs

The Genesis Foundation gives to individuals and families as much as $22,500 to cover the down payment and closing costs associated with buying a home of their own. No cash investment on the part of the homebuyer is required. Genesis's down payment program sets no geographic boundaries on homes and no income restrictions on buyers. A buyer is automatically qualified for a gift from Genesis if they purchase a participating home and have obtained mortgage financing through an eligible loan program. To receive a gift, a buyer and his or her mortgage lender needs only to fill out the Gift Funds Request Form, and the buyer and seller need to sign a Gift Letter. All forms and program guidelines are available online.

Contact The Genesis Foundation; 8834 N. Capital of Texas Hwy., Suite 110, Austin, TX 78759; 512-231-0270; {www.thegenesisprogram.org}; {support@thegenesisprogram.org}.

Homes for All Gives 7% to Homebuyers

The affordable housing charity Homes For All provides families with down payment assistance grants of up to 7% of a home's purchase price. Homes For All has opened its program to first and repeat homebuyers of all income levels and to homes across the country. Program participants need to have an acceptable credit history and the financial ability to make mortgage payments. For a home to be eligible, a seller or builder needs to sign an agreement with Homes For All that a fee equal to the down payment gift plus a service fee will be paid to the organization upon settlement. Homes For All assists buyers in getting their chosen homes enrolled in the program. All applications are available online. Contact Homes For All, Inc.; 13180 North Cleveland Avenue, Suite 136, North Fort Myers, FL 33903; 941-656-4633; {www.ezdownpayment.com}.

Family Home Provides Gift Money to Families

Families looking to purchase a home that is under $166,000 can look to Family Home Providers to provide up to 3% of the home's price to put towards a down payment or closing costs. The home can be in the community of the homebuyer's choice, and can be a new home, existing house, condo or town home. To qualify, a buyer must work with a lender that has been approved by the organization and obtain an approved FHA mortgage. The mortgage lender works directly with Family Home Providers on the gift application process. Under this program, a home seller or builder has to pay the organization the amount of the gift plus a service fee of $400 after closing. Separate applications for new homes and resold homes are available on line. Program is based in the Atlanta-area, but gifts are available nationwide. Contact Family Home Providers, Family Home Providers, Inc.; 6030 Bethelview Road, Suite #202, Cumming, GA 30040; 770-887-4578; {www.familyhomeproviders.org}.

$20,000 Down Payment Gifts for Homebuyers at a Lower Price for Sellers

A down payment grant from the Horizon Community Finance Fund can amount to as much as $20,000 or ten percent of a home's purchase price. To qualify, the buyer must be approved with a loan that allows gift funds and the seller must agree to pay the gift amount plus a service fee of no more than $699 at closing to The Horizon Fund. What is required is an application completed by the mortgage lender, a signed Horizon gift letter, and a terms and conditions document signed by both seller and buyer.

Contact The Horizon Community Finance Fund; 39178 10th Street West, Suite F, Palmdale, CA 93551; 800-348-8888; {www.thehorizonfund.org}.

10% Grants to Lower Income Homebuyers

The GiftAmerica Program (GAP) provides qualifying homebuyers with grants of up to 10% of a home's purchase price to cover closing costs associated with the purchase of a home. The buyer does not need to be a first-time homebuyer, and there are no maximum income restrictions. To qualify, a prospective homeowner must be approved for a mortgage home loan program that allows for charitable gift contributions. To be considered for the program, a home must be enrolled in the GiftAmerica Program by the seller or property builder. Enrolled sellers agree to contribute the gift amount plus $500 to GiftAmerica after settlement; in exchange, the seller may attract more qualified buyers for the home and receive a tax deduction for the contribution. All application forms are available on-line and can be faxed to GiftAmerica when completed. Completed applications are processed in only 48 hours!

Contact GiftAmerica, Inc.; P.O. Box 676, Clarksburg, MD 20871-0676; 301-231-0028; {www.giftamerica.org}.

Fast, Easy, NO Money Down Assistance

Apollo Housing deems its Down Payment Assistance Program to be the fastest and easiest program out there. Prospective homebuyers who have been approved for a mortgage that allows for down payment assistance need only have their lender fill out and fax in a grant application. Those approved for loans are automatically qualified to receive a grant. Additionally, the home of your dreams needs to be enrolled with Apollo by the seller or builder. At closing, a fee is deducted from the home purchase price received by the seller, an amount which is tax deductible as a selling expense. Assistance fees are $295 for a new house and $375 for a resold home, and can be paid by the buyer, seller or lender. The program is administered in conjunction with the public charity Alta Crossing, Inc. Grants top out at 6% of home purchase price; buyer does not have to put money down. Sellers and builders contribute no more than total of gift amount and $375. Contact Apollo Housing, LLC; 877-313-3485; {www.apollohousingllc.com}.

Get Your New Home for NO Money Down With a $40,000 Gift

Homebuyers can get a gift of up to $40,000 to cover home purchase costs from the Newsong Buyers Assistance Program. The grant can cover the full down payment amount – an individual does not need to put any money down to buy a home. The Newsong gift program places very few restrictions on program participation. To qualify, a prospective client needs to obtain from a lender a mortgage that accepts down payment funding in the form of a charitable gift. Not every home is eligible – the seller or builder must agree to register the property with Newsong and to donate the gift amount plus a small administrative fee to Newsong. Buyers who are approved for loans are automatically eligible to receive up to $25,000. Average gift amounts are between $5,000 and $15,000. Application procedures are simple for the prospective homebuyer: simple mortgage and realtor referral forms, gift applications, and instructions, program details and process guidelines are all online. And decisions on funding amounts are made the same or following business day! Contact Newsong Buyer's Assistance; 8022 South Memorial, Suite 200, Tulsa, OK 74133; 918-254-6999; {www.buyers-assistance.com}.

Charity Partners with Homebuyers to Pay Down Payment Costs

Partners in Charity will give prospective homebuyers a financial gift of up to 10 % of their home's purchase price to cover down payment and closing costs. Under the homebuying program, Partners in Charity will supply a two to ten percent down payment, depending on a family's needs, without requiring any second mortgage or lien or future repayment of any monies. Gifts are not limited to first-time home purchases and can be used for condos, town homes or single-family houses. The current homeowner must agree to the Partners in Charity program terms, including the payment of the gift amount plus a service fee at closing. Program participants are required to undergo homebuyer counseling. Initial applications are available on line, as is a mortgage application form. Contact:Partners In Charity, Inc.; 10 East Main Street, Suite 114, East Dundee, IL 60118; 800-705-8350; {www. partnersincharity.org}.

Get Up To 15% of Your Home's Purchase Price

The organization provides closing cost assistance grants to prospective buyers who are able to contribute between three and five percent of a home's purchase price. There is no preset limit on the maximum amount of funding that a participant can receive from BuyersGrant; grants are typically between one and 15 % of a home's purchase price. An applicant needs to be pre-qualified for a mortgage that accepts gift down payment funds. BuyersGrant points applicants to FHA loans and conventional mortgages that offer as much as 97% financing to a buyer. For the latter, BuyersGrant may supply the remaining three percent, enabling the buyer to retain his required three percent as reserved assets. BuyersGrant offers multiple programs and administers grant programs for other nonprofits. Its main program is open to homebuyers who have not owned or had an ownership interest in residential property over the past three years. Additionally, the seller of the house being purchased must agree to pay BuyersFund a fee at closing. Applications may be obtained by contacting BuyersGrant. Maximum gift amount is 15%; buyer must be able to put 3 to 5% down. Maximum fee charge to sellers is gift amount plus greater of 1% or $750. Contact BuyersGrant, Inc.; P.O. Box 271447, Flower Mound, TX 75027-1447; {www.buyersgrant.com}; {mail@buyersgrant.com}.

Closing Cost Gifts Up to $10,000

A New Horizon will gift up to $10,000 to a homebuyer towards the purchase of a home. The gift funds can be used for down payment and/or closing costs, making it possible for a buyer to purchase a home with zero money out of pocket. The buyer need only qualify for an FHA, VA or conventional mortgage that allows for gift contributions. New Horizon offers a loan pre-qualification service online. The group works with a network of affiliated mortgage lenders, or a buyer may select a lender who agrees to participate in the program. The lender works with New Horizon to complete the gift application process. Sellers must pay to A New Horizon a minimum of the gift amount plus $595. $10,000 or 5% is the limit on gift funding; buyer need not put any money down. MINIMUM charge to sellers is $595 plus gift. Contact Carmen Accardi; A New Horizon; 500 Fairway Drive, Suite 208, Deerfield Beach, FL 33441; 800-556-1548 ext.1227; {www.anewhorizon.org/services/dpa.html}; {CAccardi@anewhorizon.org}.

Contribute 1%, Get 5% towards Your New Home

The Global Gift Program supplies to homebuyers monetary gifts of up to 5% of a home's purchase price. In exchange for an increased pool of potential buyers, participating home sellers pay the gift amount as well as service fee of no more than $500 to Global Gift. Gifts are typically 3%, and, in combination with mortgage financing, allow buyers to contribute as little as 1% towards the purchase of their choice of homes. Buyers must obtain a single-family mortgage loan with a mortgage lender to qualify. The organization offers a streamlined one-page application, which is available on line, and has local representatives who will meet with applicants and have the authority to approve gift funds. Global Gift will provide approval in three hours in many cases. Contact Global Gift; P.O. Box 6856, Albuquerque, NM 87197-6856; 505-250-4706; {www.globalgift.info/Programs.htm}.

A Home IS Affordable... With a $10,000 Gift

The Affordable Housing Alliance, an organization dedicated to developing affordable housing options, provides grants to individuals and families to be used towards the purchase of a home. Gifts of up to 5% of a home's purchase price, with a maximum of $10,000, are given. To be eligible for the program, a prospective buyer must be looking to purchase an "Eligible Home" and obtain mortgage financing from a lender that is registered with the Affordable Housing Alliance program. An eligible home is defined as one that is being sold by an owner/builder who has agreed to pay a $500 service fee, to donate to the Alliance the grant amount received by the homebuyer, and to other defined terms. Unlike most programs, grant monies received by a homebuyer can be used to pay off other debts, as well as for down payment and closing costs. Another benefit to homebuyers: Those who know they will need financial assistance, but who have not yet found the perfect property or obtained a mortgage may apply for and reserve a grant for up to a year. The grant maximum is the lesser of 5% of home price or $10,000. Flat charge to sellers is total of gift amount and $500 fee. Contact The Affordable Housing Alliance; 10318 4th Avenue West, Everett, WA 98204; 425-353-7131; {www.housinggrants.org/sellers.htm}.

Qualify For a Mortgage and Get Free Down Payment Money

The Down Payment Assistance Program administered by the Agape Economic Development Corporation features monetary gifts of up to 5% of a home's purchase price. A participating homebuyer is required to provide 1% of the purchase price of the new home, and Agape will fund the balance of down payment and closing costs up to the 5% level. Assistance is contingent upon a seller's agreement to pay a fee and the availability of grant money in Agape's revolving fund. A service fee of $950 must be paid by the buyer, seller or the lender. The home's seller must also give to Agape between 2 to 5% of the purchase price. Guidelines and

requirements for all participants are outlined on Agape's website; all required paperwork and sample documents can be downloaded as well. Buyers must also complete an approved Homeownership course as a prerequisite to receiving the gift funds. After the closing of the home sale, Agape will wire the agreed upon gift amount to closing agent within three days. Grant assistance up to 5% is provided, with buyer required to contribute additional 1% of home purchase price. Seller pays maximum of 5%, additional charge of $950 to be paid by seller, buyer or lender. Contact Agape Economic Development, Inc.; 17339 Barnhill Cerritos, CA 90703; 562-924-9655; {www.homeloan assistance.com/program.htm}.

$15,000 Gifts… Plus $1,000 More If Gift Is Delayed!

Homebuyers working with Alpha Assistance Inc. can receive as much as $15,000 to put towards the purchase of a new home. The organization also makes a funding guarantee – if the gift amount is not received on time at closing, the buyer gets additional $1,000. Requirements for participation are that the buyer must qualify for a mortgage that accepts charitable donation and must purchase a home from a seller that agrees to pay to Alpha the down payment gift amount plus a $750 service charge. The program applies to single-family homes, condos, town homes, mobile homes, and multifamily properties of up to four units. Additional benefits to a participating homebuyer include a free online homeownership course (not required), a free home warranty plan, and a free mortgage protection plan, all available at the buyer's option. Forms, guidelines and program brochures are available online. Other programs administered by Alpha Assistance include a scholarship program and project to build and donate homes to needy families. Gift maximum is $15,000, with no money towards purchase required from buyer. Sellers required to pay gift plus $750 service fee. Contact Alpha Assistance, Inc.; P.O. Box 2573, Desoto, TX 75123; 877-684-7268; {www.alphaassistance. com}.

Extra $10,000 Can Mean a Home with No Money Down

The Homeownership Program run by the American Assistance Corporation (AAC) can benefit those looking to sell their homes, as well as homebuyers, by increasing the number of people able to afford the property. By agreeing to pay a $650 service fee plus the amount of an AAC buyer grant, a home for sale can be purchase by a homebuyer that has access to down payment funding provided by AAC. Grants of up to $10,000 enable prospective homebuyers to make the purchase with little or no money down. To be eligible for an AAC gift, a buyer must qualify for an FHA mortgage or any loan that allows for charitable gifts. Three forms are required to get the process rolling: a Gift Letter and Gift Request Form filled out by the mortgage lender and the buyer, and the seller's Participating Home Agreement. All forms are available online and may be faxed to AAC. Gift approval can take as little as two hours. The organization does not require the use of any particular lender or real estate agent, and offers assistance for every step of the process. The maximum gift amount is the lesser of 5% or $10,000; buyer can put no money down. Total cost to sellers is gift amount plus $650. Contact American Assistance Corporation; 2800 E. Plano Pkwy., Suite 300, Plano, TX 75074; 972-423-

0394; {www.american-assistance .com}; {admin@american-assistance. com}.

Lower Income Homebuyers Get Money to Build a NEW Home

Gifts of 3% of a home's sale price are supplied by AmeriHomes to homebuyers who lack sufficient funds to cover down payment and/or closing costs for immediate home purchase. AmeriHome's Home Equity Assistance Program is specifically designed for NEW homes only; resold properties are not eligible for purchase. Gift money is paid over a four to ten month time period, as a home is being built, and takes the form of mortgage payment assistance. Specifically, for the designated period, AmeriHome will pay a homebuyer's EXISTING rental or mortgage payments, enabling the buyer to save for the down payment on the NEW home being built. The buyer is required to deposit the saved amounts in an escrow account. To qualify, a homebuyer must meet the following criteria: household income must exceed $25,000; credit history must be acceptable for past two years; and there cannot have been any judgments, accounts in collections or bankruptcy filings for the previous two years. It costs a homebuyer $150 to apply. AmeriHome works with lenders directly to obtain a mortgage on behalf of a buyer. Builders must agree to pay a $500 commitment fee (and the gift amount). An AmeriHome consultant will contact buyers after filling out a simple information form regarding address, employment, desired home location and price, and income. The program is for new homes only. Contact AmeriHomes, Inc.; 421 Coventry Drive, Nashville, TN 37211; 888-446-6382; {www.free-down-payment-program.com}.

6% Gifts with No Strings Attached and No Money Down

A gift from the Amiya Institute means that a homebuyer can get their perfect home for no money down. The nationwide Buyers Aid Gift Fund provides grants of up to 6% of a home's purchase price. Any homebuyer is eligible to receive Amiya's down payment gifts. Those interested need to fill out a short online application form to obtain a Gift Fund Pre-Qualification Certificate. This certificate will help a client's mortgage lender find a suitable financing package for the home selected. The home's seller must agree to deduct from the final purchase price the amount of the gift plus a $540 administrative and wiring fee. All forms are available online to be faxed to Amiya. Contact Amiya Institute; 7100 Hayvenhurst Avenue, Suite #320, Van Nuys, CA 91406; 888-846-3750; {www.homebuyaide.com}; {www.homebuyersaid.org}; {info@homebuyersaid.org}.

Gifts of Gold -- $18,000 for Your New Home

Buyer's Dream consists of a down payment assistance program offering gifts of up to $18,000... or more on a case-by-case basis! The money may be used for closing costs or, unlike many programs, to buy down a mortgage rate. Buyers are eligible for the program by qualifying for a loan that accepts gift funds from a non-profit organization and by purchasing a home in which the seller agrees to pay a service fee to The Buyer's Dream Fund after the home closes. For all gifts under $10,000 the fee to sellers is the gift amount plus $495. Applicants can receive referrals to lenders, realtors and builders who are already

participants in Buyer's Dream, or, if a participant is already working with someone, Liberty Gold will contact them to coordinate the process. The application, gift request letters, and seller's participation form can be printed directly from Liberty Gold's website. Final forms can be submitted as late as 24 hours before closing. $18,000 is the general gift limit; no money down required by the buyer. Seller is charged gift amount plus $450. Contact Liberty Gold, Inc. and The Buyer's Dream Fund, Inc.; Waterstone Professional Building, 14077 Cedar Road, Suite 201. Cleveland, OH 44118; 216-320-0870; {www.libertygold.org}.

Down Payment Assistance Up to 5% of a Home's Price

Since its inception in 1994, C-CAP LLC has assisted more than 5,000 households in attaining homeownership through its down payment assistance program. The C-CAP Gift program operates in a way different from many programs: gift amounts are determined by how much a seller is willing to contribute. As a general guideline, gifts up to 5% of a home's purchase price are automatically accepted; for amounts over 5%, a homebuyer's mortgage lender should call for approval. Application and required forms are available online, to be completed by the lender, and signed by the buyer and seller. CCAP also offers a separate grant program specifically designed for low- to moderate-income families in Wisconsin. No set gift limit, but need approval for gifts over 5% of purchase price. Charge to seller is determined at seller's option. Contact C-CAP LLC; 259 West Broadway, Suite 100, Waukesha, WI 53186; 800-590-1745; {www.c-cap.com}.

Customized Down Payment Grants Up to $25,000

Consumer Debt Solutions grants operates a private gift trust fund, and will provide grants of up to $25,000, depending on a participant's needs. To be eligible, a prospective homebuyer should have available assets of LESS than $15,000 and qualify for a mortgage that accepts charitable gift donations. Unique to this program is the treatment of fees normally paid by the seller. A buyer must obtain a commitment from ANY party (family member, the home seller, private corporation, any person or organization) to "replenish" CDS's trust fund by the amount of the grant provided by CDS; the required pledge letter is available online. To apply, CDS first recommends that a prospective buyer register online with the program, and then obtain their credit reports in an effort to clear up problems. After securing a qualifying mortgage, the lender will work with CDS on the full gift application package. Participants must attend a free homebuyer education webcast offered by CDS. Lenders and buyers should contact CDS to have appropriate forms faxed to them. Maximum gift is $25,000; buyer must have less than $15,000 in cash reserves. Gift amount can be repaid by ANY third party. Contact Consumer Debt Solutions, Inc.; 158 Vineyard Avenue, Highland, NY 12528; 845-691-9697; {www.cdsgrants.com}.

Lenders Help Homebuyers Get Up to $24,000!

Gift funds of up to $24,000 are available to homebuyers from the Community Housing Assistance Program of America (CHAPA). The program is designed for people who can afford and qualify for a mortgage, but lack the liquid assets to pay for down payment and closing costs. A chosen mortgage lender determines a homebuyer's eligibility for the program and fills out the gift application paperwork on his or her behalf. Gift amount is determined by need; generally, gifts range from 3 to 6% of a home's purchase price. CHAPA will reserve gift funds for accepted buyers as all paperwork is completed for the gift, a buyer's mortgage financing and the home sale transaction. Mortgage lenders benefit from the program as well: for each mortgage and gift package processed, CHAPA will donate $100 in the lender's name to the charity of choice; the money accumulated on the lender's behalf is used for community grants. Gifts generally range from 3 to 6%, with a $24,000 maximum. Seller pays gift amount plus administrative fee. Contact CHAPA Homebuyer Gift Program; National Administration Office, 504 North 4th Street, Suite 202, Fairfield, IA 52556; 888-218-0180; {www.chapagifts.org}.

Home Purchases Made Possible Through Free 3% Gifts

Cornerstone Ministries' Home Buyer Grant Program will provide up to 3% of a home's purchase price to be used for down payment and/or closing costs. If combined with a mortgage product that features 97% financing (such as an FHA mortgage), the buyer need not contribute any money upfront. However, to obtain down payment assistance from Cornerstone, a buyer must have liquid asset reserves of at least 1% of the home's purchase price. Any property is eligible, provided that its seller enters into a Home Registration Agreement with Cornerstone that requires a payment of the gift amount plus 0.7% of the home's final purchase price. A buyer qualifies for the program by qualifying for a mortgage product that accepts charitable donations for down payment and by verifying the necessary currency reserves. Necessary forms are available online and may be faxed to Cornerstone. Maximum gift is 3% of home price and buyer must have at least 1% in liquid assets. Maximum cost to seller is 3.7% of home purchase price. Contact Cornerstone Ministries; P.O. Box 836961, Richardson, TX 75083; 972-497-9590; {www.cornerstonegrant.org}.

3% Down Payment Gifts Equals a New Home for Many

The Center of Resources for Economic Education and Development administers a down payment assistance program that enables qualifying homebuyers to purchase a home for no money down. Individuals who qualify for a gift fund-accepting mortgage are automatically eligible for CREED's Buyer's Assistance program provided that the seller of the house agrees to enroll in the program and pay to CREED 3% of the home's purchase price and a $370 administrative fee. Gifts are typically 3% and max out at $25,000, with exact amounts determined by the organization based on a home's purchase price. CREED will refer applicants to realtors and mortgage lenders who routinely use down payment assistance programs in client transactions. Application materials to be filled out by lenders,

sellers, and homebuyers can be printed from the CREED website. Gifts typically are 3%; buyer funds not required. The seller's service fee is 3% plus $370. Contact The Center of Resources for Economic Education and Development, Inc.; 66 W. Harding Ave, Ste C9, Cedar City, UT 84720; 435-865-9727; {www.creedinc.org}.

Down Payment Gifts Up to 6% for Low- to Moderate-Income Families

The down payment assistance program offered by the Curtilage Fund is available to low- to moderate-income families. Homebuyers whose household income is less than 115% of the area median income are eligible to receive from Curtilage a monetary gift of up to 6% of a home's purchase price. To apply, a prospective homebuyer must qualify for an FHA mortgage loan. As many FHA loans offer 97% financing, the average Curtilage down payment gift is 3%.... which means a buyer pays NO money down for a new home! Gift application forms are to be filled out by a real estate professional, and are available online. Maximum gift amount is 6%. Buyers must meet income guidelines; no cash reserves or payment due required. Seller must pay gift amount plus $700 for existing homes or $500 for new homes.

Contact 136 South Main Street, Suite A-200, Salt Lake City, UT 84101;

801-532-4669; {www.curtilage.org/buyer.php}.

Deep Pockets Help Homebuyers Cover Down Payment Costs

The Deep South Community Development Corporation provides down payment assistance to homebuyers in all 50 states. The DSCDC Down Payment Assistance Program provides gift money to prospective homebuyers who qualify for a mortgage product that allows for charitable gift funding.

Different from many programs, Deep South advises buyers to approach a home seller and request that he or she increase the home's purchase price by the amount of the gift desired plus the required 1% service fee. This enables the seller to get full asking price without any deductions at closing, and may result in a higher gift amount to the buyer. However, the program requires that a buyer contribute in earnest money 1% of the home's purchase price. Deep South permits the buyer to use a co-signer. Seller participation form and the gift application to be filled out by a buyer's mortgage lender are available online and may be faxed to DSCDC. Gift amount is seller's contribution less 1% service fee; recommended that seller increase the house purchase price to cover contribution. Buyer is required to have 1% earnest money. Contact Deep South Community Development Corporation; 2964 Ember Drive, Suite 116, Decatur, GA 30034; 866-262-1943; {www.dsr downpayment.com}.

Foundation Grants Housing Funds Up to $25,000

Homebuyers looking to purchase a single-family home or a one- to four-unit property can get a gift of up to $25,000 to cover down payment and closing costs. The Del Sol Foundation's Down payment Gift Program requires that a program participant obtain an participating mortgage plan and provides a list of mortgage lenders and brokers who have standing relationships with the organization. The buyer's mortgage must be a maximum insured loan. Required from a home seller is an agreement to pay the down payment gift amount plus a fee of $950 after the closing. Under the Del Sol program, a buyer is required to contribute 1% of his or her money towards the down payment or closing costs. The organization also offers educational courses to homebuyers at its Homeownership Center in California. Del Sol's programs are focused on California.

Gift maximum is $25,000 and buyer must pay 1% of home's purchase price. Seller must deduct from proceeds the gift amount plus $950. Contact Del Sol Foundation, Inc.; 11428 Paramount Boulevard, Downey, CA 90241; 562-858-3765; {www.delsolfoundation.org}.

24-Hour Approval of Free 6% Down Payment Gift

A homebuyer who realizes that he or she lacks sufficient assets to afford a down payment on a new home can turn to The Down payment Assistance Foundation for funding of up to 6% of the home's purchase price, with amounts that typically range from 3 to 6%. Funding is provided by the organization to the buyer as a gift, not to be repaid. The buyer works with a mortgage professional to obtain a qualifying mortgage (FHA is recommended) and to request the appropriate down payment gift amount from the Foundation. NO money down or cash reserves are required from the buyer. The gift is contingent upon a seller's willingness to pay the amount of the gift plus a fee not to exceed 1%. A gift request form and the seller's enrollment form can be printed from The Downpayment Assistance Foundation's website. The Foundation needs only 24 hours to approve and provide gift funding. Buyer can receive funding of up to 6% with no down payment contribution required on his or her part. Seller pays maximum of gift amount plus 1% fee. Contact the Down Payment Assistance Foundation, Inc.; 117 Oakwind Pointe, Acworth, GA 30101; 770-966-1001 or 866-255-4711; {www.dpaf.com}.

Program Offers Down Payment Gifts to Suit Buyer's Needs

Though its programs target Latino populations, the Down Payment Fund Gift Program is open to all homebuyers, regardless of race, income level, or geographic location. The program offers gifts of unrestricted amounts to be used to fund the down payment and closing costs associated with purchasing a home; amount is determined by mortgage financing and buyer need. Program requirements include: the buyer must obtain a mortgage that allows for a portion or all of a down payment to come from a charitable gift (not limited to FHA mortgages); the buyer must purchase a home that has

been (or now will be) enrolled in the Down Payment Fund program; and the seller must agree to pay to the Fund the gift amount plus a $600 service fee. A spotless credit record is not required, and the homebuyer does not have to put any money into the transaction or have a certain level of cash reserves. Monies are wired to the closing or escrow agent when the home sale is finalized. NO set limits on gift amounts. NO buyer contribution or reserves required. Seller must pay gift amount and $600 fee. Contact The Down Payment Fund; 315 West Mill Plain Boulevard, Suite 210, Vancouver, WA 98660; 800-620-2239; {www.thedownpaymentfund.com}.

$20,000 Grant Helps Buyers Move in Now

The DPA Alliance and QuickDown.com offer to qualifying homebuyers gifts of up to $20,000 to help homebuyers move into a home of their own. Participants do not have to be first time buyers, meet income restrictions, have a set amount of cash reserves, or pay any of their own money towards closing costs (if mortgage financing allows). They do have to qualify for a mortgage product that allows gift funding to be used. And they do have to purchase a home enrolled in the QuickDown program by the seller or builder. The seller is required to pay the amount of the down payment gift, as well as a fee of $700 for existing houses or $450 for newly built homes. The fee can be adjusted down by 10% (to $630/$405) if it would mean saving the transaction. Participation requires a completed Gift Application and a Cooperating Home Agreement, both are available online. Maximum gift is $20,000; zero down purchases are possible. Seller pays gift plus maximum fee of $700, which can be negotiated down to $630. Contact QuickDown.com User Support; 3214 North University Avenue # 604, Provo, UT 84604; 866-321-3696; {www.quickdown.com}.

Help to Buy Your Dream Home

The DreamHome Foundation will grant up to 5% of the purchase price of a home priced up to $300,000 to cover a homebuyer's down payment and closing costs. Grant monies come from an existing pool of funds created from donations made by participating home sellers and builders. All DreamHome transactions must involve a participating seller – one who agrees to pay to the Foundation the amount of the grant given for the home sale plus an additional grant contribution of $795. The sales contract must contain an addendum outlining the seller's contribution commitment. A collection of forms required from the buyer, lender and seller, as well as a number of sample documents and graphic program presentations are available online. DreamHome promises to process grant requests within two hours of receipt and to have all gift money available at closing. Buyers can receive a grant of up to 5% of a home's purchase price (amount could be increased under certain conditions). Seller must donate back gift amount plus $795. Contact DreamHome Foundation; 4880 S.W. Meadows Road, Suite 300, Lake Oswego, OR 97035; 888-801-6400; {www.dream homefoundation.net}.

Down Payment Gifts Up to 10% plus Free Mortgage Protection

The Dreamhouse Fund offers homebuyers monetary gifts to pay for the down payment on a new home plus a free 12-month Mortgage Protection Plan. The Dreamhouse gift amount is typically 3 to 6% of home price, if using an FHA mortgage program, but can be as much as 10% if the home seller is willing to donate that amount to the Dreamhouse Fund. To participate in the program, a prospective homebuyer needs to work with a lender to obtain a qualifying mortgage. After determining the needed gift fund amount based on the mortgage-financing program obtained, the lender then submits a grant application. The chosen home needs to be sold by a seller that has enrolled in the program, or agrees to pay the costs associated with enrolling. Sellers are required to pay the down payment grant amount and an additional amount ranging from $695 to $850. Dreamhouse not only helps buyers get into their dream house, but also helps them stay in it: all participating homebuyers receive 12 months of mortgage insurance protection free, with the option of renewing the policy at a discounted rate thereafter. Gifts up to 10%, depending on mortgage and corresponding needs of buyer. Seller pays maximum of grant plus $850. Contact The Dreamhouse Fund; 9450 SW Commerce Circle #460 Wilsonville, OR 97070; 503-582-0706; {www.dreamhousecharity.com}.

Gifts of 6% Can Cover All Closing Costs

Dreammaker Charity is a dream for both buyers and sellers looking to participate in a down payment assistance program. Qualifying buyers receive gifts of up to 6% of a home's contract sale price to be used for the down payment or closing costs. For sellers, Dreammaker charges only a $250 processing fee on top its required "replenishment" of the gift amount.

Builders pay only a $195 fee for newly constructed houses. The amounts are paid to the funding arm of the Dreammaker program, International Housing Solutions, Inc. It is open to any homebuyer who qualifies for an FHA-approved mortgage and finds a home offered by a seller or builder who is willing to work with Dreammaker. Application instructions are available online, and lenders can access materials upon registering and logging in to the website. It also offers a free credit scoring service, a quick solution for those who want to switch to Dreammaker from another program and a customer service department available by phone. Buyers can get gifts up to 6%. Sellers must pay gift plus $250; builders pay gift plus $195 for newly built houses. Contact Dreammaker Charity/GiftFUNDER; 424 N. 7th Street, Suite 200, Sacramento, CA 95814; 800-894-1444; {www.dreammakerprogram.com}.

Free Money for Homebuyers with Government Loans

Any individual or family who has qualified for an FHA or VA mortgage loan has also automatically qualified for an Esther Foundation Down Payment Grant. Used in conjunction with this mortgage plan, an Esther gift enables a buyer to purchase a home with no money downThe seller or builder of the desired home must, however, agree to pay to Esther the amount of the grant as well as a contribution fee of only $395. Half of this fee is donated to charities. Esther provides on its website a list of approved wholesale lenders, as well as a network of lenders, realtors, home builders and closing agents that can help a homebuyer to benefit from its program. All lenders must register with the Esther Foundation in order to

request a gift on behalf of a homebuyer. The Foundation administers a separate closing cost grant program designed for homebuyers using conventional, FHA or VA mortgages. Gift amounts are dependent on mortgage. Buyer must obtain FHA or VA mortgage and is not required to put any money down. Seller contribution is grant amount plus $395. Contact The Esther Foundation; 1716 North Meadowlark Road, Orem, UT 84097; 866-937-8437; {www.esther.ws}.

FREE Down Payment Assistance Of Up to 9% Of a Home's Sales Price

The Esther Foundation will provide to qualifying individuals a grant of up to 9% of a home's purchase price to cover the closing costs associated with buying the home they've waited for. "Qualifying" under this program entails qualifying for a mortgage product that allows for the use of charitable gift funds. How the program works: The grant basically allows a home's seller to pay the transaction closing costs to and through the Esther Foundation. The full amount of the grant is then considered a charitable donation and is fully tax deductible for the seller. An additional service fee of $395 (not tax deductible) also must be paid by the seller. How a homebuyer can participate: The buyer locates a home whose seller agrees to the program requirements; within 24 hours prior to closing, the buyer and lender submit the one-page Closing Cost Grant Request to the Esther Foundation; the grant money is wired to the escrow agent at the time of closing. The maximum grant is 9% of purchase price; no contribution from the buyer is required and any qualifying mortgage plan is acceptable. Seller pays grant amount (fully tax deductible), plus very low $395 additional fee.

Contact The Esther Foundation; 1716 North Meadowlark Road, Orem, UT 84097; 866-937-8437; {www.esther.ws}.

Free Services for Homebuyers – Plus Free Down Payment Money

The Foundation for Housing Assistance (FFHA) down payment assistance program provides grants to homebuyers of up to 5% of a home's purchase price, and works directly with real estate agents, sellers, and lenders to minimize a buyer's work. The majority of grants are equal to 3%. Buyers must pay $25 to apply for a grant. A buyer must work through a mortgage professional to obtain a qualifying mortgage; FFHA provides applicants with a list of preferred lenders after a buyer submits an initial enrollment form. Buyers must also agree to pay the full asking price of an enrolled home. For a home to be eligible for and enrolled in the program, its seller must not only agree to pay 4% of the home price to FFHA after closing (the 3% grant plus a 1% service fee), but also to supply a 1-year home owner warranty on the property. Registration and seller enrollment

forms are available online and can be sent electronically to FFHA. Grant maximum is 5%. Seller must pay 4%, plus provide a one-year warranty on the home.

Contact Foundation For Housing Assistance; 1387 Marlowe Avenue, Suite 12, Cleveland, OH 44107; 216-521-4663; {www.ffha. net}.

Families Can Get Down Payment Gifts Up to $40,000

Families interested in purchasing a home that is priced under $400,000 may be eligible to receive up to 10% of the price (or $40,000!) from the Foundation For Life Enhancement. The foundation's nationwide Homebuyers Financial Assistance Program provides down payment and closing cost grants to individuals who have qualified for an FHA mortgage or conventional loan that allows for charitable gift contributions. The grant can be used to cover the full down payment amount, letting many homebuyers move in without putting any money down. There are no cash reserve requirements for the buyer. To apply for a grant, a buyer and seller must enter into a contract that includes an addendum confirming that the home seller will pay to the Foundation For Life Enhancement the amount of the grant plus a service fee equal to 1% of home price. Although grant processing can take as little as 24 hours, the Foundation for Life Enhancement recommends that the Grant Application and signed contract addendum sent for processing as early as possible. All grant monies are wired to the title company before closing. The maximum buyer's grant is $40,000, or 10% of homes priced under $400,000. Buyer need not put any money down. Seller pays grant plus additional 1% fee.

Contact Foundation for Life Enhancement, Inc./Homebuyers Financial Assistance Program; P.O. Box 670386, Dallas TX 75367; 800-493-5156; {www.homegrants.net}.

$15,000 Can Help You Get the Keys to a New Home

The Key Grant Program is a national down payment assistance program administered by the Franklin Foundation that provides homebuyers with gifts of up to $15,000 to use towards the purchase of a home. To participate, a buyer must be able to qualify for a loan that allows a financial gift to be used as part or the entire down payment. Homes purchased through the Key Grant Program must be owner-occupied, but buyers do not need to be first-time homebuyers. The seller of the home being purchased must agree to participate in the Franklin Foundation's Key Grant Program by making a contribution equal to the amount of the buyer's grant, plus a service fee of $500.00. To request gift funding, three forms are required and all are available online: a Participating Home Agreement (for the seller to fill out); a Buyer Application; and a Gift Letter (to be completed by lender and buyer). All three forms should be faxed together. Within 24 hours prior to the closing date, the Franklin Foundation will wire the down payment funds to the closing attorney. Buyer can put no money down and get a gift of $15,000 maximum. Seller

pays back gift amount plus $500. Contact The Franklin Foundation, Inc.; 18401 Woodfield Road, Suite G, Gaithersburg, MD 20879; 800-506-3616; {www.keygrant.org}.

A No-Strings Attached Down Payment Gift of 6% -- Never to Be Repaid

Down payment gifts of up to 6% of a home's sales price are available to eligible homebuyers through the Futures Home Assistance Program. The program is based on qualification for a mortgage product that accepts financial gifts as down payments and the agreement of a home's seller to participate in the program, and not on a buyer's income or geographic location. Seller's fees are low: only $295 on top of the gift amount needs to be paid by a seller to Futures after closing. A buyer can apply online through his or her mortgage lender for gifts up to 6%; requests for greater amounts must be done manually. Required application materials include a Funds Request Form and a contract addendum containing the seller's participation agreement. Futures also offer a free online homeownership education course. The maximum gift is 6%. Seller pays gift plus $295 fee. Contact Futures Home Assistance Program; 675 Southcrest Pkwy., Suite 100, Stockbridge, GA 30281; 800-672-4055; {www.onlinewithfutures.org}.

GIK Gives as Much as $30,000 to Homebuyers

To qualify for as much as a $30,000 down payment or closing cost grant from the GIK (Giving in Kindness) Foundation, a homebuyer need only qualify for an approved mortgage program offered by a GIK approved lender. The mortgage must accept all or a portion of a down payment in the form of a charitable gift. GIK gifts top out at 10% of a home's purchase price, or $30,000, whichever is less. The program can be used with new or re-sale homes, condos, townhomes, and manufactured or modular homes, as long as the property will be the primary residence of the buyer. The seller of the home must agree to the program terms, which include an after-closing payment to GIK of the amount of the gift plus a fee equal to either 1% or $950, whichever is less, if the buyer has obtained an FHA mortgage, or, for conventional mortgages, a maximum of $1500. Although a gift from GIK may result in a "no money down" purchase for the buyer, the organization details additional costs that will be incurred with the purchase of the home, including inspection and appraisal fees. A mortgage lender must first register with GIK, and receive approval, before submitting required application forms. Gift requests, applications, and seller agreement forms are all available online. Top grant is lesser of 10% or $30,000; no money down transactions are possible, but non-closing costs will be incurred. Seller fees are gift plus a maximum fee of $1500. Contact Giving in Kindness Foundation, Inc.; 888-645-4438; {www.gikfoundation.com}.

Fast, Easy, Free Down Payment Money Up to 10%

The only requirement for participation in the Downpayment Assistance Program, administered jointly by the Harford Food Bank and the Homestead Trust, is that the buyer qualifies for an eligible loan program that allows gift funds from a charity and purchases a Harford Food Bank Participating Home. The lender or homebuilder fills out the program application at any point up to two hours before settlement, and the seller pays the gift

price, plus a $500 service fee. Furthermore, the Harford Food Bank does not require the homebuyer to put money down or have cash reserves in order to qualify for gift funds. The maximum gift amount is 10% with no cash reserve or buyer contribution required. Seller pays gift amount plus $500. Contact Homestead Trust; 3450 Ellicott Center Drive, Ellicott City, MD 21043; 410-480-1967; {www.homesteadtrust.org}.

Home Gift USA Lives Up to Its Name Through 6% Grants

The down payment gift money program administered by Home Gift USA is divided into two branches: one for homebuyers who take out an FHA mortgage, and the other for those who obtain conventional mortgage financing for their new home. The FHA track allows homebuyers to buy a property with no money down and features gifts of up to 6%. Homebuyers who have obtained a conventional mortgage that allows for charitable gift funds can get from Home Gift USA a grant of up to 10% of a home's purchase price. For both programs, qualification for a mortgage means qualification for the gift program. Buyers must choose a home that has been, or will now be, registered as a participating home by the home's builder or seller. For the FHA program, sellers are charged a low fee of $325 on top of the gift amount, but this fee is lowered to $300 if the buyer attends free homeownership classes. Transactions involving conventional mortgages require a fee of 0.25%, with a $325 minimum. Interested homebuyers need to work through their lenders to apply for the Home Gift USA program. Applications can be submitted electronically or manually via fax or mail. Home Gift must receive all materials 48 hours prior to closing. Gift maximum for buyers with FHA mortgages is 6%, and with conventional mortgages 10%. Seller pays gift amount plus maximum of $325 for FHA, or 0.25% with all other mortgage types. Contact Home Gift USA Charities; P.O. Box 608144, Orlando, FL 32860; 866-691-GIFT(4438); {www.homegiftusa.org}.

Zero Investment Purchases Made Possible with 7.5% Down Payment Gifts

A homebuyer does not have to put any money down to get a new house if he or she uses the financial assistance offered by the Home Buyers Assistance Foundation. Its down payment gift program provides qualifying individuals and families with non-repayable gifts of up to 7.5% of a home's sale price, provided the monies are used for down payment and closing costs. Paperwork is minimized for the buyer: required forms are completed by the buyer's realtor and/or lender. However, prior to participation, a buyer must qualify for a mortgage that accepts down payment funds from charitable gifts. The program is available for homes nationwide; however the seller of the chosen property must agree to pay to the Foundation the gift amount plus a $400 gift service fee. 7.5% is the maximum gift amount for buyers, while sellers pay gift plus $400. Contact Home Buyers Assistance Foundation; 288 South Main Street, Suite 300, Alpharetta, GA 30004; 866-521-HBAF; {www.hbaf.org}.

Homebuyer Gifts Up to 20% for Down Payment or Debt Payoff

HomeGrants USA and the New Home Gallery offer financial assistance options including funding for down payment assistance, closing costs, credit repair, credit reduction, interest rate buy downs, pre-paid costs, and debt collection pay-offs, all as allowed by the Lender of buyer's choice. HomeGrants offers gifts of 3 to 20% of a home's contract sales price, to be used in combination with FHA, VA, and conventional loan programs that allow for use of charitable gift funding. The organization promises a custom-fit program – tailoring the gift amount to the buyer's need. HomeGrants operates nationwide. Its funding may be used on any price range home, either new or existing. There is no charge to apply. To be eligible, an individual or family must qualify for an approved mortgage plan and find a home whose seller is willing to participate in the HomeGrants program. Participating sellers commit to paying the amount of the buyer's gift as well as a low $350 service fee. Gift applications are completed by the lender of the homebuyer's choice; a buyer is not limited to a list of "approved" lenders. All needed forms may be downloaded and faxed to HomeGrants. The organization lessens the burden on the homebuyer further by working directly with the mortgage lender, realtor or builder. Additionally, for those who cannot now qualify for a mortgage due to existing credit problems, HomeGrants also offers credit counseling. The HomeDreams program works with prospective buyers to resolve credit issues so that loan qualification – and homeownership – can become a reality sooner rather than later.

Customized gift amounts, up to 20%. No cash required from buyer. Seller pays gift plus $350. Contact HomeGrants USA/The New Home Gallery; 11901 Brinley Avenue, Suite

100, Louisville, KY 40243; 866-NHG-FUND; {www.homegrantsusa.org}.

Down Payment Gifts Up to $35,000 Give Hope to Prospective Buyers

Individuals hoping to move into a new home can turn to Buyer's Hope for help to pay down payment and closing costs they could not otherwise afford. The program, part of the Home Ownership Foundation, offers gift money for the purchase of homes that have been enrolled in the program by a builder or seller. Exact gift amounts are determined after a buyer qualifies for an approved FHA or conventional mortgage and the mortgage lender requests funds from Buyer's Hope. Absolute maximum for gifts is $35,000. In order for a prospective homebuyer to benefit from the program, the seller of the chosen home must commit to pay to Buyer's Hope the gift amount plus a fee of 1%. The fee is not to exceed $1000. The seller's agreement and gift applications are available online. Buyer's Hope promises to have funds available within 24 hours. Gift amounts determined after application. Seller's contribution maximum is gift amount plus $1000.

Contact Buyer's Hope; 142 Timber Creek Drive, Cordova, TN 38018; 888-240-7283; {www.buyershope.com}.

5% Closing Costs Gifts Through Your Mortgage Lender

Prospective homebuyers can receive up to 5% of a home's sale price as a free gift for participating in Home Ownership Providers down payment assistance program. The gift can be used to pay for closing costs and/or the down payment required to purchase a new house. The only requirement for program qualification is obtaining eligible mortgage financing – any plan that accepts charitable gifts as part or all of a down payment. Home Ownership Providers works directly with a buyer's lender or real estate professional on the gift process and paperwork.As with almost all down payment assistance programs, the receipt of gift money is dependent on the participation of a home's seller. The seller must agree to pay the amount of the gift, plus a service fee. The program is centered in and geared towards homes in the Atlanta area. The maximum gift is 5%. Seller's contribution is gift amount plus approximately $375. Contact Home Ownership Providers, Inc.; 2265 Roswell Road, Suite 100, Marietta, GA 30062; 800-HOP-9911; {www.hop-downpayments.org}.

$25,000 in Down Payment Assistance for Homebuyers with Mortgages

The Homebuyer Gift Charity offers a down payment gift program that offers the following benefits to prospective buyers: non-repayable gifts of approximately 3% of a home's purchase price, but can be up to $25,000; no out-of-pocket money required for purchase; both FHA and conventional mortgages allowing for gifts are eligible; no first-time buyer restrictions; and only three forms required for processing. The costs of participation on the part of the seller are the gift amount plus a service fee. A seller's assist will be a maximum of 6% of the home's purchase price if the seller gets a 3% gift using an FHA mortgage. Forms are available on line. Homebuyer Gift Charity needs at least seven days to process a gift. Monies are wired directly to the settlement company of the day of closing. Gifts up to $25,000; no money down. Seller's maximum contribution is 6%. Contact Homebuyer Gift Charity; 724-834-6065; {www.homebuyergift charity.org}.

Mortgage Help...And 5% Down Payment Gift Money

The Homebuyer's Assistance Fund Program will give an individual or family the down payment -- up to 5% of the purchase price - so that they can become homeowners. Buyers must qualify for a loan that allows Gift Funds and must purchase their home from a builder or seller who has enrolled his or her home in the Homebuyer's Assistance Fund Program. The cost for an enrolled seller is the amount of the gift plus a $900 service fee. The program features a tiered system that determines a buyer's gift amount based on the seller's level of participation: buyers are eligible to receive up to 5% of the home's purchase price if the seller has enrolled in the Gold Program; up to 3% with the Silver Program; and up to 2% if the seller is classified as Bronze. After a buyer qualifies for a mortgage loan and has chosen an enrolled home, his or her mortgage lender requests the appropriate gift amount from the Homebuyer's Assistance Fund. Forms for the seller and for the buyer and lender to complete are available on line. The program is associated with MortgagesMadeEZ, which offers

mortgage pre-qualification and loan comparison services online. Gifts max out at 5%, with no buyer contribution required. Seller determines level of contribution, with a maximum cost of 5% of home price plus $900.

Contact Homebuyer's Assistance Fund / MortgagesMadeEz.com; 7247 N. Stagecoach Drive, Park City, UT 84098; 888-776-6912; {www. mortgagesmadeez.com}.

Use 9% Down Payment Gifts to Pay off Existing Debts

Use of the monetary gifts provided by the New Life Family Housing Group is not limited to down payments; a prospective homeowner can also use the money to pay off existing debts or for prepaid. New Life provides gifts of up to 9% of a home's sale price and requires no cash investment on the part of a buyer. A buyer qualifies for the program when he or she qualifies for a single-family mortgage loan that allows a charitable organization to provide gifts funds toward closing costs and down payment requirements. However, the purchase must be of a Certified Home – one whose seller agrees to pay the required fee of between $495 and $650 and to donate the gift amount to New Life and its partner, the Homeownership Foundation of America. The monies are deducted from the seller's proceeds at the close of escrow. All three forms required for participation in the New Life program – the Home Grant Application and the Gift Letter for the buyer and the seller's Certified Home Agreement -- are available online and may be faxed to New Life. The organization promises to provide funding within 24 hours if necessary. The maximum gift is 9%, with buyer allowed to put no money down. Seller contributes maximum of $650 plus gift amount. Contact New Life Family Housing Group, Inc.; 8725 Loch Raven Boulevard, Suite 203, Towson, MD 21286; 888-860-3679; {www.new lifefamily.com/newlife/faq.html}.

$15,000 Down Payment Gifts From the "HART"

The Housing Action Resource Trust (HART) aims to increase homeownership opportunities for those that can afford a mortgage payment but cannot come up with the immediate funds required for a down payment on a new house. To this end, HART offers gifts of up to $15,000 to cover the upfront costs associated with a home purchase, i.e. down payment, closing costs, pre-paid and rate buy-downs. An added benefit – HART promises a response on a gift request within 8 hours. The program is available nationwide, to all individuals and families regardless of income, and for resale and newly constructed houses. Any costs? Only for the seller, who must agree to pay to HART the amount of the buyer's gift. This agreement should be an addendum to the home contract. A unique feature of this program is that the associated transaction fee of $350 for new homes, or $500 for resale, can be paid by or split between the seller, buyer, lender or realtor. The seller is not required to shoulder the entire fee. Buyers who have found a home and a mortgage lender can request a gift online. HART also enables buyer to find and apply for a home loan online through its website. Gift requests and letters are to be submitted by the lender on behalf of the buyer. Gifts up to $15,000 can be used for down payment or other eligible uses. Seller pays gift amount. Fee of $350/$500 can be split among parties to the transaction. Contact Housing Action Resource Trust, Inc.; 8711 Monroe Court, Suite A, Rancho Cucamonga, CA 91730; 888-820-HART; {www. hartprogram.com}.

Non-Denominational Homebuying Grants

The Individual Freedom Ministries Church (IFMC) provides down payment assistance to all qualifying homebuyers, regardless of income, location or faith. The gift funds distributed by IFMC Gift Program vary according to the buyer's needs, with the actual amount determined by what the seller is willing to contribute. IFMC lays down some requirements for prospective buyers: first, they must qualify for a mortgage product that allows for gift funds to be used as down payment (it recommends FHA); second, they must purchase an IFMC Participating Property; and third, they must have at least 1% of the home's purchase price in cash reserves. For a property to be eligible, its seller must sign an agreement detailing the contribution (amount is at the seller's discretion) he or she will make to IFMC upon closing of the home sale. Buyers apply through their lender, who must first register with and be approved by IFMC. All forms are available online, with electronic submission possible. Gift funds are wired to the closing agent within 48 hours of settlement. Gift amounts and seller contributions are determined by seller. Buyer must have 1% in cash reserves. Contact IFMC Gift Program; P. O. 4166, Enterprise, FL 32725; 866-375-3636; {www.ifmcgift.com}.

Use 5% Gifts to Buy a Home without Investing Your Money

Although primarily for residents of metropolitan Detroit, homebuyers in other areas can benefit from the JVS Down Payment Assistance Program. JVS provides gift money to homebuyers, allowing them to purchase a home with essentially no "out of pocket" costs. The gift can be used to purchase any new or existing home provided that the purchase price does not exceed set limits determined by location. Gifts are determined by need and by the seller's agreed upon contribution, but are generally less than 5% of a home's price. Sellers must register their homes and agree to pay a fee to JVS based on the gift amount plus a service charge; seller's can choose to pay between 2.75 and 5.75% of a home's purchase price. Participating home agreements for sellers and builders are available online. Forms to be completed by lenders for the homebuyer and for the involved title company can also be accessed and printed from the JVS website. Gifts vary by need, zero down transactions allowed. Seller maximum contribution is 5.75% of purchase price. Contact JVS / Down Payment Assistance Program; 248-233-4242; {www.jvsdownpayment.org}.

Reserve Gift Funds of Up to $25,000 Today

Homes are available for no money down, thanks to the help of Jordan Ministries' DPGift Program. A seller who has enrolled his or her home in the program (and agreed to repay to Jordan the amount of the gift plus a processing fee) can attract more eligible buyers by advertising the zero down payment benefit. The seller's fee is $500 for gifts under $10,000, and $750 for any other amount. To be eligible to receive a DPGift of as much as $25,000, a homebuyer must first choose an enrolled home and then qualify for a mortgage plan that accepts charitable gifts to satisfy down payment requirements. To enroll, a buyer will complete a DPGift Application Form. Upon approval, he or she will receive an approval letter and Funds Reservation Certificate from DPGift via e-mail. The buyer should bring this form to a realtor or lender, who will assist in completing the gift transaction and the home purchase. Seller enrollment form, Gift Application and Gift reservation forms are available online to fax to DPGift. Gifts up to $25,000 enable no money down purchases. For gifts under $10,000, seller pays gift plus $500; for $10-25,000 gifts, charge is gift amount plus $750. Contact DPGift.org / Jordan Ministries, Inc.; 5415 Shakespeare Drive, Dover, FL 33527; 813-787-6023; {www.dpgift.org/pages/831026/index.htm}.

Approval for 6% Down Payment Gifts in 30 Minutes

Fair Housing Assistance and Ken-Ray Inc. works directly with lenders, brokers, investors, realtors and title companies to provide down payment assistance to people who qualify for a home loan and to ensure that adequate funds are available in escrow prior to the closing of a home sale. A Buyer must qualify for a loan that allows Gift Funds to be used for a down payment and closing costs. Gifts of up to 6% of a home's purchase price are automatically approved in almost all cases; requests for amounts over 6%

are subject to review. A buyer may receive the full amount of the down payment as a gift, and retain some of his or her own funds in the bank! Once Ken-Ray receives the required application materials, it promises an answer within 30 minutes, and funding within 24 hours if needed. The purchase must be of a home whose seller or builder has agreed to the program's participation requirements; namely, the repayment of the gift amount plus a service fee. The fee is 0.75% for all 3 and 5% gifts, with a maximum fee of $900; fees for larger gift amounts are determined on a case-by-case basis. Newly built homes are eligible for the program, with Ken-Ray providing builders and developers with bulk discounts on repayment costs. A grant application and sample letters are available online. Grants of up to 6% (maybe more on approval), with no cash requirement is available for buyers. Maximum charge to sellers is gift plus $900. Contact Fair Housing Assistance/Ken-Ray Inc.; 1784 S. 290 E., Orem, UT 84058; 800-626-1163; {www.fairhousingassistance.com/lenders.html}.

No Set Limits on Down Payment Assistance from Keystone

Keystone Grants, Inc. provides qualifying homebuyers with gifts of free money to cover the down payment and closing costs attached to the purchase of a new home. The Keystone Plan includes a detailed plan of action for an interested homebuyer, from first pre-qualifying for a mortgage programs that allows the use of gift funds, to choosing an affordable home through a realtor, to approaching a seller about participating in the Keystone Plan and making an offer, to, lastly, completing gift applications and receiving funding. NO cash reserves or payment is required on the part of the buyer. The home's seller must agree to pay to Keystone the amount of the gift and a fee of $800 for resold homes and $600 for new homes. Required documents include the seller's Keystone Plan Property Enrollment Form, an addendum to the home sales contract, mortgage originator sign-up form (required to access gift requests), and gift request and letters to be completed by the lender and signed by the buyer. Keystone promises to have funding available for a closing that is only 24 hours away! No set limit on gifts – determined by mortgage and buyer's need. Seller must pay gift amount plus $800 ($600 for new homes). Contact Keystone Grants, Inc.; 11441 South State Street, Suite A-374, Draper, UT 84020; 888-785-7526; {www.keystoneplan.org/home buyers.php}.

$30,000 Down Payment Grants Help Home Sellers, Too

While the Main Street Foundation (MSF) offers buyers down payment gifts of up to $30,000, it also promises that sellers participating in its program will usually net as much if not more for their home than without MSF. Down payment grants can enable buyers to pay the full asking price of a home. Sellers pay to MSF the grant amount plus a fee, but that amount is generally equal to or less than the amount a seller would have to reduce the home's price to sell on the open market. The seller must pay the gift amount plus a service fee of $750 or 1% of purchase price, whichever is less. Grants to buyers generally average around 3 to 5%. The buyer must use an approved mortgage professional and qualify for an approved loan. To enroll, a Participating Home Agreement and MSF Gift Request form need to be faxed to the organization. Forms are online for electronic submission. In most cases, MSF will fax back an approval letter the same day! Gifts generally equal 3% of purchase price, with no money down required. Sellers gift plus maximum fee of $750. Contact Main Street Foundation, Inc.; 320 North Clayton Street, Lawrenceville, GA 30045; 866-678-1977; {www.getadownpayment. com/id3.html}.

6% Gifts Help Homebuyers Say "Mi Casa"

Mi Casa, organizations dedicated to increasing minority homeownership for the Latino Community, administers a gift program to assist homebuyers with the down payment and closing cost required to purchase a property. The program is open to individuals and families across the country, regardless of race, ethnicity or income level. The maximum gift that may be received from the Mi Casa program is 6% of the contract sales price of the home being purchased. A buyer is not required to put down any money of his own, or have a set level of cash reserves. Homebuyers do need to purchase a home enrolled in the Mi Casa program and obtain financing through a loan program that allows charitable organizations to provide gift funds to a buyer for use towards their down payment and/or closing costs, such as FHA. A home is enrolled when its seller makes a commitment to pay to Mi Casa the down payment gift amount received by the home's buyer, a fee of the lesser of $650 or 1%, and a wire transfer fee of $20. All required forms are available online. Mi Casa was founded by the League of United Latin American Citizens. Gifts up to

6% of home purchase price. Seller pays maximum of gift plus $670. Contact 8834 N. Capital of Texas Hwy., Suite 110, Austin, TX 78759; 512-795-8522; {www.lulacmicasa. org}.

Lower-Income Buyers Have Access to Free Down Payment Money

Low- to moderate-income homebuyers unable to pay the down payment and closing costs required to move into a new home can look to the Mid-West Housing Authority for financial assistance. The organization provides gift funding to individuals and families looking to purchase a home that is priced under $240,000. The average gift is 3% of purchase price.

To take advantage of Mid-West's down payment program, homebuyers must first find a home enrolled in the Down Payment Assistance Program, then be approved for a mortgage that allows for a charitable organization to provide gift funds, and finally, submit a request for these gift funds at least 48 hours prior to settlement. Sellers participating in the program have agreed to pay to Mid-West a fee equaling the gift amount plus 1% upon closing. Necessary seller, buyer and lender forms and a sample contract language are online, and must be returned at least 48 hours prior to closing. A buyer's down payment gift will be provided directly to the settlement agent at closing. Homes must be priced below $240,000, with average gift set at 3%. Seller pays gift amount plus 1%.

Contact Mid-West Housing Authority; 1442 East Primrose Street, Suite 200, Springfield, MO 65804; 866-239-1515; {www.mid-westhousing.com}.

$25,000 Down Payment Gifts for Homes across the US

Families that dream of owning a home of their own can turn to the National Home Foundation (NHF) for down payment gifts of up to $25,000. Gifts do not have to be repaid, and are available for buyers who qualify for a single-family mortgage loan that permits the use of charitable gift funds for the down payment. There are no cash reserve or minimum payment requirements placed by NHF on the buyer – only what may be specified in the particular mortgage obtained.

The program is designed for low- to moderate-income homebuyers, and properties must be priced at below $300,700 (or $578,150 for multi-unit dwellings). The home can be anywhere in the US, as long as the seller agrees to participate in the NHF program and deduct from sale earnings the amount of the buyer's gift and a "donation" that is determined on a case by case basis; the required Seller Participation form can be printed off of the NHF website. Only two forms are required and can be faxed or sent electronically: The seller's participation agreement and the buyer's Down payment Gift Application. How it works: Within 24 hours of receiving the homebuyer Application, a written approval is issued. On or before the closing date, NHF will wire the funds to the closing office. Following the closing, the seller's donation fee will be wired to NHF by the closing agent from the proceeds of the home sale.

Gifts up to $25,000 with no cash or payment required from buyer; maximum allowable home price is $300,700. Total cost to seller is determined on case-by-case basis. National Home Foundation, Inc.; 15200 Shady Grove Road, Suite 350, Rockville, MD 20850; 301-840-3844; {www.national homefoundation.org}.

Get Up to 6% of a Home's Price…for Free

National Home and the JW Hansen Community Foundation teamed up to offer free down payment money to qualified homebuyers across the country. The National Home Down Payment Gift Program supplies buyers with up to 6% of a home's sale price to be used towards down payment and closing costs only. No money down is required from the buyer, however, as many gifts average at 3%, a buyer may need to supplement any difference resulting from the requirements of the particular mortgage obtained. A homebuyer qualifies for the program by qualifying for a mortgage that accepts gift funds and by choosing a home that has been enrolled as a participating home by the seller. As a participant, the seller must agree to pay the amount of the gift. A fee of $800 for existing homes priced over $100,000, 0.75% for those under that amount, or $650 for new homes can be paid by the seller, buyer or lender. Required forms for the homebuyer and lender are generated once a mortgage lender registers and logs into National Home's online system. Seller participation forms are available online. National Home also makes it easy for a buyer to reserve funding immediately – a reservation form can be filled out and submitted electronically. The maximum gift is 6%, with no money down purchases allowed. Seller must pay gift amount. Maximum fee of $800 can be paid by seller, buyer or lender. Contact National Home; 4811 Chippendale Drive, Suite 602, Sacramento, CA 95841; 888-487-4663; {www. nationalhome.org}.

If You Have Only $2,000, You Can Get the Home of Your Dreams NOW

For families that can afford to contribute $2000 towards the purchase of a new home, the National Housing Foundation pledges to help supplement the remainder of down payment and closing costs. The foundation's down payment assistance program is open to families whose household income is less than 115% of the area median income. Amount of gifts depends on a buyer's need and chosen mortgage plan. Program participation depends on the buyer's ability to meet detailed selection criteria, which is described fully on the foundation's website. The program requires that the buyer work with a lender and realtor that has been designated a National Housing Foundation Community Partner; the organization will make referrals to interested buyers. Another requirement is pre-qualifying for an approved

mortgage plan, which the partner lender will work on. Additionally, the home purchased must be enrolled with the National Housing Foundation, and its seller must agree to pay the gift amount plus a 0.75% service fee. Finally, the buyer is required to attend homeownership education classes. The Foundation will aid buyers in meeting all requirements and in the gift application process. Required forms and applications are available online. If there is no regional office of the National Housing Foundation in a buyer's area, the organization recommends use of the Nehemiah down payment assistance program. Buyer must contribute $2000, gift amount determined by need and mortgage plan. Seller pays gift amount plus 0.75% of home's purchase price.

Contact National Housing Foundation, Inc.; 943 N. Plum Grove, Suite A, Schaumburg, IL 60173; 888-395-3100; {www.nationalhousing.org/ menu/downpayment.html}.

3 to 5% Closing Cost Coverage

The North American Housing Foundation supplies homebuyers with gifts of 3% or 5% of a home's price to be used for down payment and/or closing costs. The gifts do not have to be repaid. To qualify, a buyer must pre-qualify for a mortgage that accepts charitable gift funds for down payment costs; FHA mortgages are preferred. Additionally, the homebuyer must make a cash investment of 1% of the home's price. A certificate of completion from an approved homeownership education class is also required. Finally, the homebuyer needs to work with a seller who agrees to pay to NOAH the gift amount (3 or 5%) plus a service fee of 1% of the home's sales price. The seller must sign a participation agreement. A grant application and gift letter for the buyer and lender to complete may be printed from NOAH's website and faxed to the organization upon completion. If accepted, gift funds will be wired to the closing agent. The gift maximum is 5% and buyer must make cash investment of 1%. Seller pays gift amount plus 1% service fee. Contact The Noah Program; P.O. Box 14583, Spokane, WA 99214-0583; 509-928-8310; {www.noahprogram.org}.

Families Get Help to Move in With No Money Down

The Positive Alternatives Down Payment Assistance Gift Program administered by Family Grants LLC works to make it possible for families to purchase a home with zero money down. The program features down payment and closing cost gifts of either 3% or 5%; gifts of higher amounts up to $25,000 may be possible if approved by a lender, the home's seller, and Family Grants. Requirements for participation on the part of the buyer include pre-qualifying for a mortgage program that allows for a down payment gift and purchasing a property whose seller has agreed in writing to the terms and conditions of the Positive Alternatives program. The seller must commit to pay to Family Grants the amount of the down payment gift plus a fee of either ½% or $650, whichever is less. Both new and resale homes are eligible. All forms for seller, buyer, realtor and lender are available online. Gift letters are usually faxed to an accepted applicant within two hours, with funds available the same day if the request is received before lunch! Gifts are 3 or 5% of purchase price, or more upon approval. No cash investment or reserves are required. Seller maximum

cost is gift plus $650. Contact Family Grants, LLC; 26211 Equity Dr. Suite B, Daphne, Alabama 36526; 251-625-8666 –OR- Positive Alternatives; 965 E. 5600 SO., Salt Lake City, UT 84121-1025; 877-625-8666; {www.familygrants.com}.

Individualized Down Payment Gifts of Up to $25,000

The Su Casita Program supplies grants to qualified homebuyers to enable them to purchase Su Casita eligible properties throughout the United States. The gift amount by Su Casita is set according to the particular loan program obtained by the buyer. The maximum gift provided is $25,000. A buyer is not required to put any money into the home transaction. Funds provided to buyers by Su Casita are a gift -- no lien is recorded against the home and there is no repayment for the gift funds.

Gift Funds can be used for a down payment, closing costs, to buy down mortgage rates, or for prepaid expenses. There are no income restrictions, first-time buyer qualifications, or geographic limitations set on a prospective homebuyer. The buyer must purchase a Participating Home, for which a seller has signed a commitment form to pay to Su Casita the gift amount and a service fee equal to 1% of the home's purchase price. Applications and gift forms are completed by the buyer's mortgage lender, who will determine the exact gift amount based on the home loan obtained. Funds are wired to the closing agent, who must register with Su Casita before the date of closing. Gifts cannot be reserved ahead of time: all forms and mortgage confirmations must be completed.

Required forms are available online. Gifts are determined by mortgage type, capped at $25,000, with no money down purchases a part of the program. Sellers commit to pay gift amount plus 1%. Contact Su Casita, Inc.; 2928 Manor Road, Austin, TX 78722; 888-562-8869; {www.vlender.com/r/rort}.

Qualified Buyers Get the Gift of Down Payments... Plus 10 Free Trees!

Sustainable Living Foundation (SLF) is committed to making home ownership attainable for all by providing down payment assistance to people in need. A gift of up to 5% of the purchase price can be put toward the down payment or closing costs in connection with the home purchase. The SLF Down Payment Gift Program can be used with any mortgage loan program that allows gift funds and is open to repeat and first-time homebuyers. Qualification for an eligible loan qualifies the buyer for a gift from SLF. The SLF application process requires from lenders only 2 forms (both available online) for each gift request. There are no application or registration requirements for Lenders and Real Estate Agents. Settlement or closing Agents are asked to complete a one-time general information form. A buyer must purchase an enrolled home to receive gift funds. Builders/Sellers can enroll their homes in the program by completing the online Seller Enrollment Form, which includes details on a required fee equal to the gift amount plus $400. Sellers have the option of choosing from three gift participation levels: 2%, 3% or 5% of the home's purchase price. An added bonus for homebuyers: They receive 10 free trees with each home purchased through our gift program and can choose from a variety of flowering, oak or spruce trees. Top gift is 5%. Seller pays gift amount plus $400. Contact Sustainable Living Foundation; 618 Kenmore Avenue, Suite 2A, Fredericksburg, VA 22401; 540-373-6277; {www.sustainable livingfoundation.org}.

Lenders Can Help Get $10,000 Down Payment Gifts for Homebuyers

The United American Housing and Education Foundation makes it easy for homebuyers: Purchase a home from a builder or seller who has agreed to participate in its Alliance Housing Assistance program and be approved for a mortgage that allows for gift funds, and a buyer is eligible to receive a gift of up to $10,000 or 5% of the sales price, whichever is lower. To make it even simpler, the organization provides a list of participating sellers and mortgage lenders on its website. There is no cash investment required on the part of the buyer. The cost to sellers and builders to participate is only $285 on top of the gift amount. Three forms are required: the seller's Service Fee Agreement, a Gift Funds Request and a Gift Letter. A buyer's mortgage lender has all forms completed and signed appropriately by the buyer, seller and closing agent. The three forms can be downloaded from the United American Housing and Education Foundation's website. Funds are wired to the closing agent up to 72 hours prior to closing. The maximum gift is the lesser of $10,000 or 5%. Seller pays gift and only $285 fee.

Contact United American Housing and Education Foundation / Alliance Housing Assistance Program; 6110 Pinemont, Suite 125, Houston, TX

77092;   713-353-0425;   {www.
allianceassistance.org}.

Mission POSSIBLE: Buying a Home With 5% Gift and NO Money Down

World   Mission's   EquityGrants
program gives down payment funds to
a prospective homebuyer –up to 5 % of
the purchase price if the homebuyer
has obtained a government FHA or
VA loan, and 10 % or more for
conventional mortgages. To take
advantage of EquityGrants gifts, a
buyer needs to (1) qualify for an
eligible mortgage with a lender and (2)
either get the seller or builder to
participate in the program, or find one
who is already participating. The
organization can refer interested
individuals to participating sellers,
builders and mortgage professionals.
The seller must agree to pay a service
fee in order to participate. This fee
equals the gift amount and a
processing fee of 0.75% of the home's
price; the processing fee will never
exceed $750. How a buyer can join the
EquityGrants program: After a buyer is
approved for the loan and has signed
the contract for the purchase of a
home, his or her real estate
professional requests gift funds by
completing for the online application
form. EquityGrants sends the down
payment money directly to the closing
company just prior to closing. All
forms must be completed, signed and
received at least 24 hours prior to
closing. Gifts are capped at 5% for
FHA mortgages and generally at 10%
for conventional. Sellers fee is capped
at $750 (plus gift amount).

Contact Equity Grants; 1701 Porter
SW, Suite 6, Wyoming, MI 49509;
866-872-3722;
{www.equitygrants.com}.

Affordable Homebuying of a Different Stripe: 3% Gifts

The Zebra Project pledges to make its
down   payment   gift   program
exceedingly easy for homebuyers.
There are no income, asset or
citizenship requirements, no warranty
required on resale homes, and no pre-
purchase counseling required. The
maximum amount of a gift is 3% of a
home's purchase price. The buyer can
use the funds for the following
purposes: to cover all or a portion of a
down payment; to buy down a
mortgage interest rate; to pay off
required pre-paid items such as
property taxes; or to satisfy any debts
in collection that are part of a
mortgage's underwriting conditions.
Although primarily aimed at first-time
homebuyers, the Zebra program also
serves the needs of single parent
families, displaced spouses, and any
family who does not have the funds to
purchase a home they are truly in need
of. To qualify, a homebuyer must
obtain an eligible mortgage that
features 97% LTV (97% financing) –
Zebra prefers to work with FHA
mortgages – and obtain a signed
commitment from the property's seller
to pay to Zebra the amount of the gift
plus a 0.75 or 1% service fee. All
application and agreement forms are
available online and must be submitted
at least 48 hours prior to closing. Gifts
are wired directly to the closing agent.
Gifts are 3% maximum, with no buyer

cash investment required. Sellers pay gift amount plus top fee of 1%. Contact The Zebra Project, Inc.; 1950 North Park Place, Building 500, Atlanta, GA 30339; 770-226-9300; {www.zebraproject.org}.

Get Half Your Home For Free???

The Housing Down Payment Assistance Program offered by NetLogis Caritas provides qualifying homebuyers across the country with financial gifts to be used to cover the down payment and closing costs requirements associated with buying and moving into a new property, or to buy down the rate on an approved mortgage product (FHA, some sub-prime mortgages, or certain rural property loans).

The buyer needs to qualify for a mortgage that allows for gift contributions and to get the seller of the home to agree to NetLogis's participation requirements. The seller must sign an agreement that he or she will pay to NetLogis the amount of the buyer's grant plus a fee generally equal to 1% of a home's price. In exchange, the buyer may deduct the grant amount for tax purposes, and, according to the organization, expect to increase the pool of qualified buyers by 500%. Note, however, that the 1% administrative fee does not have to be paid by the seller; the buyer, lender or realtor can also pay it. The buyer needs to meet certain debt and household income ratio requirements, which can be equated using a calculation provided on the NetLogis website. NetLogis will help buyers find a mortgage professional and match them with a local real estate agent. Application forms for sellers, buyers and lenders are available online. NetLogis offers approvals within 24

hours and funding within 3 days. Gifts of up to 50% allow no money down transactions. Seller must pay grant amount. 1% administrative fee can be paid by seller, buyer, lender or realtor. Contact NetLogis; 981 Exchange Tower, Montreal, Quebec, Canada H4Z 1K1; 514-736-1324; {www.netlogis.com}.

Network of Down Payment Providers Helps Homebuyers

The Community Housing and Development Corporation (CHDC) provides down payment grant and gift funding for programs administered by several different companies. Links to the following organizations and programs can be found on CHDC's website: the Halo Program; Homebuyers Gift Inc.; Responsible Homeownership, Inc.; Hosanna Housing Program; National Housing Assistance Program; family Home Providers; and AllFund Gift Program. Programs are virtually identical, with most based in Las Vegas. Some down payment gifts from these programs may enable a buyer to purchase with no money down. A home must be enrolled in the respective program in order for the buyer to receive gift funds. The same CHDC companies make up the membership of the Housing Alliance of Nonprofit Downpayment Providers. Contact Community Housing and Development Corporation; 4550 W. Oakey Boulevard, Las Vegas, NV 89102; 800-734-3633; {www.community housingdevelopment.org}.

Elderly, Disabled and Low-Income Families Receive FREE Home Revitalization

Working with an extensive network of volunteers, Rebuilding Together provides home rehabilitation and preservation for those who are elderly, disabled or low-income homeowners. In addition to major rehabilitation projects, this organization provides emergency year-round services in most areas. Disabled homeowners can receive assistance in building ramps, installing grab bars while other homes are repainted, cleaned and weatherized. All repairs are FREE to the homeowner; labor and many of the supplies are donated. The agency also hosts a National Rebuilding Day the last Saturday of April in which major rehabilitation efforts are carried out. A national non-profit organization, Rebuilding Together has affiliates in over 865 cities and towns across the U.S. working to rehabilitate houses and non-profit facilities. National

Contact Rebuilding Together, 1536 Sixteenth Street, N.W., Washington, D.C. 20036-1042; 202-483-9083; 202-483-9081; {http://www.rebuilding together.org}; {cinadc@aol.com}; {info@rebuildingtogether.org}.

Your House with Handicap Access

The difficulty of navigating through their own home can leave a disabled person stranded without the help of a caretaker. United Cerebral Palsy Association addresses this vital concern by providing free home modification for more than 400 low-income, disabled Austinites each year. UCP's Architectural Barrier Removal Program allows residents greater mobility by widening doorways and installing wheelchair accessible showers and toilets. The wheelchair ramps built by UCP make a world of difference to disabled clients. Transit services for the disabled will not pick up a resident unless they have a ramp accessible entrance, leaving some disabled people literally trapped in

their homes. New ramps and railings make street access easy. UCP services allow disabled residents to move freely about their homes and enjoy a greater degree of independence and privacy. FREE home modifications for low-income disabled persons. Contact United Cerebral Palsy (UCP) National, 1660 L Street, NW, Suite 700, Washington, D.C. 20036; 800-872-5827 or 202-776-0406; Fax: 202-776-0414; {http://www.ucp.org}.

Non-Profit Groups and Realtors Buy Housing That Helps Residents

Neighborhood Reinvestment Corporation, local NeighborWorks® organizations and Neighborhood Housing Services of America make up the Neighbor Works system, which has successfully built healthy communities for 25 years. The three elements work together to create new opportunities for residents while improving communities. Although these programs are mostly for groups and not individuals, you should contact them anyway because they could lead you to specific people who can help individuals. For more information on programs, go to their website or call them at the number below. They offer housing opportunities for residents, nation-wide. Contact Neighborhood Reinvestment Corporation, 1325 G Street, NW, Suite 800, Washington, D.C. 20005-3100; 202-220-2300; Fax:

202-376-2600; {www.nw.org/network/home.asp}.

$10,000 Grants to Buy a Home & Other Financing Options

Eligible homebuyers that are willing to be educated on homeownership and on the responsibilities of living on a balanced budget may qualify for up to $10,000 or more in grants to help them pay down payment and/or closing costs and any other qualifying items. Grants do not need to be repaid by the homebuyer. The Home Grants program is for those people who: are just beginning their search; have or have not begun working with a real estate agent; have or have not yet found that perfect house; have or have not begun working with a financial institution regarding the financing of the home; and are interested in purchasing a home that is "for sale by owner." Additionally, for those grantees who are in need of these services, HAC can also coordinate and provide the following: complete home loans at competitive interest rates via participating financial institutions that participate in the program and support this non-profit organization; and if the homebuyer has not yet decided on real estate agent, HAC can refer grantees to a local real estate agent who is qualified to handle a home search based on the Home Grant request. All individuals who wish to receive a Home Grant must complete the program's educational courses to qualify for the Home Grants program. Grants up to $10,000 or more for down payment, closing costs or other homebuying-related costs are available.

Contact Housing Assistance Corporation, 1324 South Eastern Avenue, Las Vegas, NV 89104; 702-385-3973; Fax: 702-385-4055; {http://www.housingassistance.org/buyer.htm}.

Special Loans to Help Build a Brand New Home

American Home Partners offers special construction loan financing packages to individuals and families earning more than $35,000. With its subsidiary Home Partners Credit Corporation, the organization will finance up to 95% for the purchase of land and 100% for the materials, labor and related costs for building a new home. American Home Partners does not require a buyer/builder to make payments during construction, so there is no need to worry about paying rent and paying off the building loan at the same time. The term of the construction loan is 12 months, generally with a 10.9% interest rate and a 13.58% APR; interest accrues during construction. The homebuyer is required to invest time and effort, not money. He or she serves as Project Manager during home construction, arranging for permits and inspections, soliciting bids, selecting and scheduling subcontractors and generally overseeing the building of a new home. American Home Partners provides the home plans, arranges for supply and materials delivery, issues checks for subcontractors, and provides monthly statements that detail budget and loan balance figures. The program also helps participants apply for and obtain a mortgage. A pre-qualification form is available online; a pre-qualification review costs $10. They offer 95% financing for construction of a new home; buyer serves as building project manager. Contact 20 Realty Drive, Cheshire, CT 06410; 800-343-2884; {www.americanhomepartners.net}.

$5,000 for Choosing the Right Realtor to Manage a Home Sale or Purchase

SmartMove offers cash rebates based on the price of a house that is bought or sold; the program is open to both homebuyers and sellers nationwide. Gifts range from $100 to $5,000. The program is geared towards companies and organizations, who register for FREE to become SmartMove members, for use by employees; some single customers may also be eligible for the cash rebate program. A buyer or seller is NOT eligible if currently registered in another cash back real estate program, receiving employer reimbursement for real estate services, or already committed to a real estate firm by listing agreement, buyer broker agreement, or ratified sales contract. A SmartMove coordinator will connect participants with a partner real estate professional. If interested, enroll easily on the SmartMove website. Maximum $5000 rebate for buying or selling a home through an enrolled agent; buyer must enroll in program – typically through employer. Contact SmartMove; 800- 645-6560 or 703-359-1831; {www.smartmove. com}.

No Money Down Mortgages at Your Fingers

Low Cost Lenders specializes in locating the best, most affordable mortgages to suit a homebuyer's needs. By filling out an online questionnaire, a prospective buyer will immediately receive the names of 4 local lenders who offer loan products that offer comparable mortgage plans. The service is not limited to only mortgages for home purchases. Low Cost Lenders will connect clients with institutions that offer refinancing, home equity loans, home improvement

loans, debt consolidation loans, equity credit lines, land purchase loans, and financing for new home construction. The service is free and there is no obligation to those who fill out and submit a loan finder questionnaire. This is a referral service only – connects prospective buyer with mortgage lenders. Contact Low Cost Lending, Inc.; Canoga Park, CA; 800-449-9744; {www.best-mortgages.us}.

VERY Low Prices on Historic Homes and Properties

The National Trust For Historic Preservation offers an on-line service for homebuyers and investors looking to purchase and rehabilitate distressed historic homes and properties. FOR SALE: Properties At Risk is a list of historic properties and properties at risk which are for sale at a greatly reduced rate, or even for FREE, if the buyer commits to restoring the property. The service provides a picture, property description, sale price and all contact information needed to inquire about purchasing. Listings are updated online as they come. Looking to sell a distressed property? For Sale: Properties At Risk will advertise your home or property online for only $10 per month. Visit {www.nationaltrust. org/historic_homeowner/buying_sellin g/distressed_properties.html} to view the latest list of properties for sale or to find out how to list a home or other property you are looking to sell.

Homeownership Made Possible for Those with Debt Problems

CreditWorks is a mortgage loan product that helps people who are working to resolve debt and credit problems buy a home. CreditWorks is currently available through a national initiative by the National Foundation for Credit Counseling, Freddie Mac and local credit counseling agencies, including the Consumer Credit Counseling Service of Greater Atlanta (CCCS). This initiative helps people burdened with excessive debt and impaired credit become eligible for a market-rate mortgage faster than would otherwise be possible. To take advantage of CreditWorks, potential borrowers must take affirmative steps to improve their credit by participating in a Debt Management Program and participating in homebuyer pre- and post-purchase counseling. The program enables potential borrowers to qualify for a market-rate home mortgage loan, even with very low credit scores, in only 12 months. Benefits of the program include easier mortgage qualification with no maximum housing expense-to-income ratio, the use of funds for a down payment from a variety of sources, including extended family members, Individual Development Accounts and other sources, and the use of premium financing to cover closing costs, financing costs and prepaids/escrows. Eligible properties include 1-unit primary residences, including single-family dwellings, condominiums and Planned Unit Developments, and approved manufactured homes. There are no income limits for participation in CreditWorks. Contact Consumer Credit Counseling Services, Housing Department, 100 Edgewood Avenue, Suite 1800, Atlanta, GA 30303.

ATTN: CreditWorks Program; 866-616-3716; {www.cccsinc.org}; {housing@cccsinc.org}.

Union Members Save Big When Buying Homes

The AFL-CIO works to increase homeownership opportunities for working families through its Hit Home program. The program is an initiative among the AFL-CIO Housing Investment Trust, Countrywide Home Loans and Fannie Mae. Hit Home facilitates the home buying and refinance process by offering: homeownership education; cost-saving measures, such as a free appraisal and credit report; and the Working Family Mortgage, which allows homeowners to build up home equity faster and cuts interest costs by scheduling automatic electronic deductions to match the payment schedules of each individual borrower. Program participants can save up to hundreds of dollars off closing costs. They have access to apply for Countrywide's wide selection of competitively priced home loans including zero down payment and low down payment programs to make qualifying faster and easier. Mortgage loans feature a flexible payment schedule and up to thousands of dollars in interest savings over the life of the loan. All members of AFL-CIO affiliated unions and the UBC are eligible to participate in the Hit Home program. The AFL-CIO and Countrywide Home Loans offers a dedicated toll-free number (1-866-HIT-HOME) that puts interested members directly in touch with a trained bilingual representative for the program. Contact AFL-CIO Housing Investment Trust, 1717 K Street, NW, Suite 707, Washington, D.C. 20036; 202-331-8055; Fax: 202-331-8190; {aflcio-hit.com}; {info@aflcio-hit.com}.

Foundation Grants and Funding for Housing

The Allstate Foundation partners with local organizations throughout the Southeast to offer a range of programs designed to assist community residents. The Foundation is active in funding housing assistance initiatives. In the Housing Rehabilitation program, Allstate partners with the Neighborhood Reinvestment Corporation/Neighborhood Housing Services to provide funds to homeowners for rehabbing and enhancing their homes. Funds are also used to educate future homeowners on how to save, purchase and insure their first home. The Allstate Foundation also awards grants to nonprofit organizations to fund projects that promote safe and vital communities and economic empowerment, including those that result in improved and more accessible housing to community residents. For information on Allstate Foundation's grant program, see {http://www.allstate. com/community/PageRender.asp?Page =foundationfunding.htm}.

To inquire about Allstate and partner activities in your area, contact Nancy Lemke, Field Corporate Relations Manager, Allstate Foundation, at 678-589-6095. To apply for a grant, contact Executive Director, The Allstate Foundation, 2775 Sanders Road, Suite F4, Northbrook, IL 60062-6127; 847-402-5502; {www.allstate.com}; {allfound@allstate.com}.

Big Bucks for Home Projects

Bank of America Community Development Banking (CDB) is actively involved in developing and financing affordable housing in communities across the country. Bank of America CDB works in partnership with community-based organizations to maximize the positive impact on the community and to act as a catalyst for reinvestment in moderate-income communities. Developers and other organizations active in the production and improvement of affordable housing and homeownership opportunities can turn to Bank of America for financing and potential partnering. Projects and initiatives include more than $2 billion in loans and investments for the construction and rehabilitation of single-family and multifamily affordable housing; the development of several low- and mixed income housing communities; low-income housing tax credit investments in housing projects; and many more services. To find out more about Bank financing and funded developments or about how the Bank of America can help with your real estate investment, contact {https:// www.bankofamerica.com/community/i ndex.cfm?template=contact_us_here& contact_returnto=%2Fcommunity}.

Contact Bank of America, Community Development Banking, 10 Light Street, 19th Floor, MD4-302-19-02, Baltimore, MD 21201; 888-488-9802; {www.bankofamerica.com/ community}.

$50,000 Grants to Fund Housing Projects

The Ludwick Family Foundation provides grants to non-profit public charities to fund projects that provide a significant public benefit. Grant amounts range for $5,000 to $50,000, with the Foundation awarding between 20 and 25 grants per year. The foundation tends to provide grants for tangible types of items that assist a program or project, rather than funding the program itself. Grants may be used to support the purchase of new property, vehicles or equipment, equipment replacement and modernization, improvements to facilities, and educational materials. Recent foundation grants have been awarded to organizations throughout the US, with a number focusing on housing. Recent grantees and projects include the purchase of equipment and scaffolding for the construction of affordable housing in Alabama (Auburn University's Rural Studio), property renovations for Habitat of Humanity offices in South Dakota, and improvements to transitional housing facilities in Orange County, CA. Contact Ludwick Family Foundation, P.O. Box 1796, Glendora, CA 91740; 626-852-0092; Fax: 626-852-0776; {www.ludwick.org}; {ludwickfndn@ludwick.org}.

$25,000 Grants for Affordable Housing Construction

The Home Depot Foundation provides grants to nonprofit organizations to support the construction of affordable housing and housing-related programs and services. The Foundation considers requests for both operating and programmatic support. Money is awarded to high-performing organizations that are successfully constructing, rehabilitating and/or preserving quality affordable housing for low-to-moderate income families are helping to make the dream of home ownership a reality for many people. Grants typically range from $5,000 to $25,000. In addition to actual construction projects, the Home Depot Foundation is interested in partnering with organizations that help to build the capacity of nonprofit developers and that support innovation in the field. Informational FAQ's on the grant program are available at

{www.homedepotfoundation.org/hfus/enus/faq.html}. To see if your project and organization is eligible for a Home Depot grant and to access an online application, take the Eligibility Quiz offered on the Foundation's website; see {www.homedepotfoundation.org/hfus/enus/eligibility.html}.

Contact The Home Depot Foundation, 2455 Paces Ferry Road, Atlanta, GA 30339; 770-384-3889; Fax: 770-384-3908; {www.homedepotfoundation.org/}; {hd_foundation@homedepot.com}.

Unable to Qualify for a Mortgage? Now You Can!

The Neighborhood Assistance Corporation of America (NACA) offers very low-interest, flexible mortgages, often with NO down payment requirements, to homebuyers across the country. The NACA program focuses on families who could not access conventional financing, borrowers that have credit problems, or no credit history, and borrowers that do not have substantial savings or income. NACA works with low and moderate income buyers for as long as it takes to qualify for a mortgage, provides hands-on assistance throughout the buying process, and also provides post-purchase services that may include financial assistance with mortgage payments, if needed. The organization offers a comprehensive home buying education and counseling at many of its office locations. Mortgage financing is available for one to four family properties, condos and co-ops. These may be existing homes, new construction, or manufactured homes. A special program for the purchase of homes needing renovations is also offered (see below). Mortgage interest rates are one point below market. Loans feature flexible underwriting terms. To be eligible for a NACA mortgage, a borrower must meet income guidelines, attend homebuyer education, and purchase a home that meets price limitsContact Neighborhood Assistance Corporation of America, 3607 Washington Street, Boston, MA 02130; 888-297-5568; {www.naca.com}.

Low-Interest Home Loans to Buy and Renovate a House

The Purchase and Rehabilitation Program offered by the Neighborhood Assistance Corporation of America enables homebuyers to address their home renovation or rehabilitation needs before moving into their new home. The purchase price and cost of the rehab work is included in one mortgage with one monthly payment. This helps ensure homebuyers that they won't be saddled with unexpected renovation costs after they purchase their home. Repairs crucial to the integrity of a home such as replacing outdated heating systems, upgrading electrical, and repairs to the structure due to termite damage, plus certain other improvements, can be addressed through the Purchase and Rehabilitation Program. Under the Purchase/Rehab option, if a participant is making substantial repairs and cannot live in the property during the

rehab, he or she will not have to make a mortgage payment for a period of up to 6 months! NACA requires that all repairs be undertaken by an approved Rehabilitation Specialist, and will provide direct referrals. The program is aimed at low- to moderate-income homebuyers, borrowers who are unable to secure traditional financing due to credit or other issues, and those without significant savings and/or incomes. Contact NACA to find out more about the program and about the requirements for participation. Contact Neighborhood Assistance Corporation of America, 3607 Washington Street, Boston, MA 02130; 888-297-5568; {www.naca.com}.

Funding for Affordable Housing Development – From Start to Finish

The Housing Assistance Council (HAC) operates several loan funds that provide vital seed money to rural housing developers. Community-based, nonprofit organizations, housing development corporations, self help housing sponsors, farm worker organizations, cooperatives, Indian tribes, public agencies, units of local government, public utility districts, and small business and minority contractors are all invited to apply for the predevelopment, site acquisition, site development and/or construction loan products. The Housing Assistance Council's loan fund provides low-cost financing to developers of affordable housing in rural communities nationwide. Funds are currently available at 5.0% interest. Funded projects must aim to improve housing and living standards for rural, low- and very low-income households, such as creation of subdivisions and new single- or multi-family housing units, rehabilitation of existing units, and improved water and waste water disposal systems in rural communities. The proposed projects must be located in areas, which are rural in character, with a preference for projects located in towns with populations of less than 25,000. If you are interested in applying for HAC loan funds, please contact Stephen Grant, Loan Fund Program Assistant, at 202-842-8600, ext. 128, for information regarding application criteria and to request an application packet. Contact Housing Assistance Council, 1025 Vermont Avenue, N. W., Suite 606, Washington, D.C. 20005, Attention: Loan Fund Division; {www.rural home.org}.

Loans for Self-Help Housing Program Providers and Projects

The Housing Assistance Council provides loan funds through the HUD Self-Help Homeownership Opportunity Program (SHOP) to self-help housing providers pay for land acquisition and infrastructure improvement for the development of self-help units. The homebuyer family must contribute a significant amount of sweat equity towards the construction of the dwelling. Loan funds are made available through a competitive application process and cannot exceed $10,000 per lot. SHOP loans are at 0% interest with a 1% service fee charged to cover HAC closing costs. Up to 80% of the SHOP loan may be forgiven when the borrower has satisfied the conditions of the loan agreement. The forgivable portion may become a grant for the group to establish its own revolving loan fund for future site acquisition and development of self-help housing or to provide direct subsidies to participating homebuyer families.

If you are interested in applying for an HAC/SHOP loan, please contact Stephen Grant, Loan Fund Program Assistant, at 202-842-8600, ext. 128, for information regarding application criteria and to request an application packet. Contact Housing Assistance Council, 1025 Vermont Avenue, N. W., Suite 606, Washington, D.C. 20005, Attention: Loan Fund Division; {www.ruralhome.org}.

$1 Million Loans to Housing and Other Non-Profits

The Nonprofit Finance Fund (NFF) makes loans to non-profit organizations, including housing and development groups, to finance the organizations' property and space needs, operations, and certain other costs. Loans generally max out at $1 million, but financing up to $2 million will be considered. NFF loans can be used for facilities projects, acquisition of space, new construction, renovation/leasehold improvements, relocation, related soft costs, and equipment needs, among other things. NFF will also provide working capital based on a borrower's cash flow needs, a sound business plan and solid track record, and will provide bridge loans for anticipated funding commitments. NFF targets and approves loans to organizations that are financially equipped to use debt as a strategic tool, not as an emergency stopgap measure. Particularly, borrowers should have been in existence as 501(c)(3) tax-exempt entities for at least three years and have an annual budget that meets guidelines. Contact Nonprofit Finance Fund, 70 West 36th Street, 11th Floor, New York, NY 10018; 212-868-6710; Fax: 212-268-8653; {http://www.non profitfinancefund.org/location.asp?aut oId=42}; {NA@nffusa.org}.

Grants for Non-Profit Housing Organizations

The Fannie Mae Foundation awards grants to support the development of affordable housing, preservation, and for homeownership counseling efforts in communities having residents of mixed income levels. The Foundation also provides research grants to support its mission and strategic priorities. While many grants are awarded by soliciting proposals from organizations with the demonstrated ability to create strong partnerships with the Foundation, Fannie Mae also sets aside an amount of grant funding to be awarded through a competitive process. Projects and organizations that are targeted for grant funding include those that: Increase the Affordable Housing Supply and/or Increase Sustainable Homeownership and Build Individual and Community Wealth. Contact Fannie Mae Foundation, 4000 Wisconsin Ave., NW, North Tower, Suite One, Washington, D.C. 20016-2804; 202-274-8000; Fax: 202-274-8100; {http://www.fanniemaefoundation.org/grants/grants_for_organizations.shtml}; {grants@fanniemaefound ation.org}.

Profitable Tax Credits Available for Investors

Raymond James Tax Credit Funds offers services in tax credit syndication, which offers investors the opportunity to profit from low income housing tax credits. Raymond James Tax Credit Funds sponsors investments in apartment properties that qualify for low-income housing tax credits. Benefits to investors include an increased after-tax income, through both tax credits that directly reduce tax liability over a 10 to 12 year period, and tax losses that decrease taxable income over 15 years.

Additionally, investors provide a benefit to the community by increasing the stock of quality affordable housing. Contact Raymond James Tax Credit Funds, 880 Carillon Parkway, Department 11V00, St. Petersburg, FL 33716; 727-567-1000 or 800-438-8088; Fax: 727-567-8455; {www.rjtcf.com/}; {lauren.godwin@raymond james.com}.

Free Voice Mail for the Homeless

Community Voice Mail (CVM) is a national non-profit organization that offers free voicemail to homeless people, thus providing a way for potential employers, social service agencies and relatives to contact them. This service also enables the homeless to apply for a job without having to tell a prospective employer they have no permanent place to live. The program started in 1991 in Seattle and has grown to 34 cities in 19 states, helping more than 47,000 people find jobs and housing last year. Community Voice Mail gives each homeless person a phone number and each records a message. The numbers cannot be used for outgoing calls, but people can check their messages from any regular or pay phone. The service costs the soup kitchen or homeless shelter as little as $7 per number per month. Community Voice Mail numbers are distributed based on demonstrated financial need, lack of reliable phone service, or pursuit of a goal for work, housing, healthcare, or safety from domestic violence. Once these goals are achieved, CVM recycles the phone number to the next available subscriber. Contact Community Voice Mail National Office, 2901 Third Avenue, Suite 100, Seattle, WA 98121; 206-441-7872; Fax: 206-443-3755; {http://www.cvm.org/index. htm}; {info@cvm.org}.

Up to $715,000 for Affordable Housing Development

ICE's principal lending goes to community land trusts, limited equity cooperatives, and community-based nonprofit organizations creating housing that is permanently affordable to people with lower incomes. Funds from the RLF are commonly used to finance land acquisition and the acquisition, construction and rehabilitation of housing. The types of loans included in the RLF are: 1) Construction Loans (Rehabilitation) up to $715,000 for projects like affordable housing developments with special emphasis placed on those that are part of a land trust or are otherwise designed to be permanently affordable. Housing may be a cooperative, affordable rental, lease-to-purchase, or affordable for-sale housing. Loan terms range from six to 24 months, based on a construction completion schedule; interest only monthly until completion, principal upon completion or sale of residences; 2) Mini-Permanent Loans (Balloon) up to $500,000 for the same project-types as the Construction Loans. Terms are typically three to five years with an amortization period of 10–30 years; 3) Permanent Mortgage Loans from $100,000 up to $715,000. These loans are fully amortizing loans (length to be determined based on fund availability,

up to a maximum of 30 years); 5) Bridge Loans for property acquisition or project financing, secured by real estate where an identifiable repayment source is acknowledged and assigned Up to $250,000 for project/ financing secured by real estate OR up to $100,000 for working capital secured by receivable (a minimum loan amount of $5,000) is available with terms of six to 12 months, based on projected receivable payment; and 6) Facilities Loans up to $715,000 for the construction and/or permanent financing of facilities for organizations that create affordable housing for people with lower incomes, with special emphasis placed on those that are part of a land trust. Contact Institute for Community Economics, Inc., 57 School Street, Springfield, MA 01105-1331; 413-746-8660; Fax: 413-746-8862; {http://www.iceclt.org/ loanfund/}; {http://www.iceclt.org/ loanfund/loanapply.html}; {rlf@iceclt.org}; {info@iceclt.org}.

Technical Assistance for Affordable Housing Developers

The Institute for Community Economics (ICE) provides technical assistance to community-based organizations working to promote community control of local land and to develop permanently affordable housing. Priority for technical assistance is given to community land trusts (CLTs) and groups that want to establish CLTs. Direct technical assistance to both urban and rural groups is provided through site visits, telephone and email consultation, and regional and national trainings and conferences. Direct assistance is supported by a range of introductory and technical publications. Organizations seeking technical assistance should contact Liz Wills at the information below. Contact Liz Wills, Director of Technical Assistance, Institute for Community Economics, Inc., 57 School Street, Springfield, MA 01105-1331; 413-746-8660, ext. 119; Fax: 413-746-8862; {http://www.iceclt.org/clt/ice techassist.html}; {Liz@iceclt.org}.

Emergency Rent and Mortgage Money

Provides families with emergency money to pay rent or mortgage payments to avert eviction thus enabling them to keep their residence. This program is only open to families of Jefferson Parish, Louisiana. If you find that you need assistance, contact the Jefferson Community Action Programs, 1221 Elmwood Park, Blvd, Suite 402, Jefferson, LA 70123: 504-736-6900; {www.jeffparish.net/index. cfm?DocID=1179}.

Mortgage Assistance

Mortgage assistance can be given to avoid foreclosure if the individual or family can reasonably expect to pay the mortgage in the future. The purpose of this program is to prevent homelessness. This program is no cost to the participant. Residents of Grant, Adams and Lincoln Counties are eligible for this assistance.

If you need emergency help with your mortgage, contact the North Carolina Community Action Council, 903 West Third Ave, Moses Lake, WA 98837; 509-765-9206; {www.nccac.net/Emergency. htm}.

Emergency Mortgage Assistance

The Emergency Food and Shelter Assistance programs is utilized to assist individuals and families in need of emergency assistance with issues regarding payment of utility bills, rent and mortgage payments and also provides temporary shelter and food. This assistance is only open to area residents of Miami-Dade, Florida. Service is available at the following Community Centers: Liberty City Community Enrichment Center, 305-756-2830; Goulds Community Enrichment Center, 305-223-2121; Accion Community Enrichment Center, 305-547-7713. Information about this program can be accessed online at {www.miamidade.gov/CAA/ health.asp}.

$5,000 To Help Pay Your Mortgage

The National Alliance to End Homelessness offers financial assistance to pay past due rent, mortgage or contract to prevent eviction or foreclosure. The Program is open to individuals, families and youth in Aitkin, Carlton, Chisago, Isanti, Kanabec, Mille Lacs and Pine Counties in Minnesota. If you need some help with your living expenses to prevent foreclosure, contact the Community Services Department, Lakes & Pines Community Action Council, 1700 Maple Avenue East, Mora. MN 55051; 320-679-1800; {www.endhomelessness.org/best/actio ncouncil.htm}.

Pay Your Back Mortgage Payments

Rental and mortgage payments are available to households in danger of becoming homeless through unforeseen circumstances. Clients are expected to match the balance of the payment. If a client has exhausted all avenues to pay any balance due, the agency shall consider the legitimacy of a request to pay the entire balance. Citizens of St. Tammany Parish, Louisiana are eligible for this program. If you live in the St. Tammany, contact the St. Tammany Parish, Dept of Community Action, Suite 310, 520 Old Spanish Trail, Slidell, LA 70458; 985-646-2090; {www.stpgov.org/departments/caa/caa-new-pro.html}.

$1,000 A Month To Pay Your Mortgage

If you live in Wisconsin and receive a WHEDA loan, you get an added benefit for a fee of $150. Then if you lose your job, you will have payment protection. It's called the Mortgage Guardian program and it will pay your mortgage for up to 6 months. Check with your state housing association to see if you are eligible for a similar program. For additional information, contact the Wisconsin Housing and Economic Development Authority (WHEDA), 201 W. Washington Avenue, Suite 700, Madison, WI 53703; 608-266-7884, 800-334-6873; {www.wheda.com/Cat_SFL/guardian.asp}.

Free Mortgage Money, Living Expenses and Scholarships

The American Legion is an organization dedicated to supporting members of the military service and their families currently serving on active duty. Volunteers are available to shop for groceries, baby-sit, mow the lawn, fix motor vehicles and other household chores. Grants are available for shelter, food, clothing, medical and dental care. The Temporary Financial Assistance may be able to help your family in an emergency. Assistance starts at the local level. To apply, check your local telephone directory for a Post near you. You can also contact them at 800-504-4098 or {familysupport@legion.org}, {www.legion.org/activeduty/index.php?content=ad_financialassist}.

$60,000 If Your Mortgage Payments Are Over 60 Days Due

The Pennsylvania Housing Finance Agency offers to state residents, a loan program designed to protect citizens who, through no fault of their own, are financially unable to make their mortgage payments and are in danger of losing their homes to foreclosure. Participants in the Homeowners' Emergency Mortgage Assistance Program receive loans to help bring delinquent payments current. Continuing monthly assistance may be available as well. Total financial assistance maximum is $60,000, or 24 months of payments. Participants are expected to contribute $25 per month for payments during the term of the loan. The home must be located in Pennsylvania and be owner-occupied. The program also has other eligibility requirements. To see if you qualify, contact the Pennsylvania Housing Finance Agency, 211 North Front Street, P.O. Box 15530, Harrisburg, PA 17105-5530; 800-342-2397; {www.phfa.org/programs/hemap/index.htm}.

FREE MONEY FOR ARTISTS, WRITERS, DANCERS, POETS, MUSICIANS, ACTORS, ETC

Artists don't have to be struggling if they know how to use the system. If you cannot find what you need in the programs presented in this chapter you should also investigate the following.

1) *Federal Government Money Programs For Artists*
   These are the two most important federal agencies that offer money for artists.
   - National Endowment Of the Arts
     Washington, DC
     202-682-5400
     http://arts.endow.gov

   - National Endowment of the Humanities
     Washington, DC
     202-NEH-1121
     www.neh.gov

2) *More Federal Government Money Programs For Artists*
   You can always stay up to date on programs from the federal government by checking out the Catalog of Federal Domestic Assistance. This book is available at your local public library or the U.S. Government Printing Office (www.gpo.gov). You can also search the contents of this book for free on the web at {www.cfda.gov}.

3) *Sell Your Art To The Government*
   There are many government offices which purchase artists freelance work. For help in finding out how to sell your services to the government you can contact one of the 1,000

offices all over the country called Small Business Development Centers. They will help you tackle any business problem you. All their services are free or for very little cost. Contact 800-8-ASK-SBA; {www.sba. gov/sbdc/sbdcnear.html}.

4) Find State Money Programs For Artists

Every state has money for artists. Look for your state office of the Arts or the state arts commission. You can find them by dialing 411 and asking for your state capitol operator or by going to {www.govengine.com}.

5) Money From Foundations For Artists

The following are the major sources of information for finding grants from non-profit organizations.

> The Foundation Center
> 79 Fifth Avenue
> New York, NY 10003
> 212-620-4230
> www.fdncenter.org

They have a database of over 75,000 non-profit organizations that give out grants. This database is accessible on the web for a fee or you can go into one of the Foundation Center libraries around the country and use their database for free. You can call their office and they will tell you what libraries in your area have these directories. The Foundation Center also gives short courses on topics like "How to Search for Grant Money", or "How to Write a Grant". Don't pay thousands of dollars for courses on these subjects when you can get it from one of the best for a very reasonable price.

- Guidestar
  4801 Courthouse Street
  Suite 220
  Williamsburg, VA 23188
  757-229-4631
  www.guidestar.org

Guidestar has a similar database to The Foundation Center, but do not offer training and classes.

$10,000 To Teach Art To Kids

The Arts in Education program offers grants to strengthen arts education in the school curriculum. The program awards two grants, one to Very Special Arts and the other to the John F. Kennedy Center for the Performing Arts. VSA supports projects for disabled people in the arts and the Kennedy Center provides educational activities that emphasize the importance of the arts in education. Funding is used for educator training and activity development. Contact the U.S. Department of Education, Improvement Programs, 400 Maryland Ave., S.W., Rm. 3C126, FB-6, Washington DC 20202-6140; 202-260-2487; {www.ed.gov/programs/artsed/index.html}.

$ To Produce A Radio Show

Did you know that Radio One started out as a small business that received venture capital funding? The New Markets Venture Capital Program is a business funding program designed to promote economic development and the creation of job opportunities for individuals living in low-income areas. Recipients use funds to make equity capital investments in smaller enterprises located in low-income geographic areas. Contact the New Markets Venture Capital Program, 409 3rd Street, NW, Suite 6300, Washington, DC 20416; 202-205-6510; {www.sba.gov/INV}.

$5,000 For A Writers Workshop

Get money to start your own writers' workshop. Through the National Endowment for the Arts' Challenge America program, the Writers' Colony at Dairy Hollow received support for readings and workshops. Find out how your group could be the next to receive support. Contact the National Endowment for the Arts, 1100 Pennsylvania Ave. NW, Washington D.C., 20506; {www.arts.endow.gov/}.

$10,000 For Storytelling

Share the great tradition of storytelling with others. Through the NEA's Challenge America program, the California Indian Storytelling Association will bring together storytellers from four states to meet and share their stories. Contact the National Endowment for the Arts, 1100 Pennsylvania Ave. NW, Washington D.C. 20506; {www.arts.endow.gov/}.

$23,000 For Photo Exhibit

Looking for funding to exhibit your art? Through the National Endowment for the Arts' Challenge America program, the Sixth Street Photography Workshop will produce a photography exhibit entitled *Stories of the City*.

How can you be next? Contact the National Endowment for the Arts, 1100 Pennsylvania Ave. NW, Washington D.C. 20506; {www.arts.endow.gov/}.

$7,500 To Play Your Piano

Ever dreamed of playing in a music festival? The National Endowment for the Arts' Challenge America program is offering grant support for the three-day Crestone Music Festival in CO. Contact the National Endowment for the Arts, 1100 Pennsylvania Ave. NW, Washington D.C. 20506; {www.arts.endow.gov/}.

$ To Create A Crafts Website

Are you a skilled crafter who would like to share your talent? The National Endowment for the Arts' Challenge America program is currently providing support to launch a new website. For your chance to share your passion with others, contact the National Endowment for the Arts, 1100 Pennsylvania Ave. NW, Washington D.C. 20506; {www.arts.endow.gov/}.

$ For A Tap Dance Festival

Have a love and a talent for dance? Through the National Endowments for the Arts' Heritage & Preservation grant program, American Tap Dance Foundation is receiving support for the Tap City Festival. Find out how your feet could earn you funding, contact the National Endowment for the Arts, 1100 Pennsylvania Ave. NW, Washington D.C. 20506; {www.arts.endow.gov}.

$15,000 To Teach Writing

Have an idea for teaching writing, art, or music? Through the National Endowment for the Arts' Learning in the Arts program, grant support for the Merging of Cultures project has been awarded. Contact the National Endowment for the Arts, 1100 Pennsylvania Ave. NW, Washington D.C. 20506; {www.arts.endow.gov}.

$20,000 To Write A Novel

Dream of writing the great American novel, but the demands of the real world keep you from picking up a pen? The National Endowment for the Arts' Literature Fellowship program encourages the production of new work by affording writers the time and means to write. Each literature fellow receives a $20,000 award. Contact the National Endowment for the Arts, 1100 Pennsylvania Ave. NW, Washington D.C. 20506; {www.arts.endow.gov}.

$ To Produce A New Play

Think you might be the next Tom Stoppard or Sam Shepard? The National Endowment for the Arts' Services to Arts Organizations and Artists program is supporting the Continued Life Fund, an initiative that provides production stipends to theaters committed to presenting sequential productions of a new play. Find out how you can get funding for the world premiere of your play. Contact the National Endowment for the Arts, 1100 Pennsylvania Ave. NW,

Washington D.C. 20506; {www.arts.endow.gov}.

$200,000 To Make An Independent Film

Independent films are one of the hottest commodities in the movie world today. The Independent Television Service was established by Congress to fund and present innovative public television programs. ITVS offers an Open Call, which is an open invitation to independent producers to propose single public television programs on any subject. Applicants must be independent producers, who own the copyright of their production, have artistic, budgetary and editorial control of their project, and are not regularly employed by a public or commercial broadcast entity or film studio. Contact the Independent Television Service, 501 York Street, San Francisco, CA 94110; 415-356 8383; {www.itvs.org/producers}.

$25,000 For Performing Artists To Perform Overseas

Get your artwork the exposure it deserves. The Fund for U.S. Artists at International Festivals and Exhibitions awards grants to performing artists and organizations that have been invited to participate in international festivals. Contact the Cultural Programs Division Staff, Bureau of Educational and Cultural Affairs, U.S. Department of State, SA-44, 301 4th Street, SW, Suite 568, Washington, D.C. 20547; 202-619-4779; {http://exchanges.state.gov/education/citizens/culture/}.

$20,000 To Produce A Film

Did you know that through the Miller Brewing Company you can make your business dreams come true? Through the Miller Urban Entrepreneurs Business Grant Competition, individuals have received funding for their film company, and other endeavors. Entrepreneurs have the chance to vie for $20,000 and $2,500 business grants. A team of national judges select the grant awardees based upon the business plans developed and submitted by individuals age 21-30 years old. Contact the Miller Brewing Company, 3939 W. Highland Blvd, Milwaukee, WI 53208; 414-931-2000; {www.millerbrewing.com/inthecommunity/urban/businessGrant.asp}.

$5,000 To Dream Big

Want to realize your dreams while you are still young? Through the Start Something program, a 12 year old staged a concert and a 15 year old held a judo tournament. This innovative program helps young people ages 8 to 17 identify and achieve their dreams. Students can participate as part of a class or other group, or on their own through the web site. Scholarships can be used for almost anything that will help take kids toward a positive dream or goal. Examples include music lessons, sports camps, special educational programs, travel, and equipment. Contact Start Something, P.O. Box 59214, Minneapolis MN, 55459; 800-316-6142; {http://startsomething.target.com}.

$6,000 To Start A Hip-Hop Magazine

What do a hip-hop magazine, a backpack design company, and a skin care salon have in common? They are all micro businesses funded through the Micro Business Development Corporation. MBD offers economic opportunities and business growth by providing access to variety of resources. MBD is a Colorado non-profit organization providing micro enterprise support services. This is for Colorado entrepreneurs. Check with your local Economic Development Association to see what your area may offer. Contact the MicroBusiness Development Corporation, 3003 Arapahoe St., Suite 112A, Denver, CO 80205; 303-308-8121; {www.microbusiness.org}.

$5,000 to Make Comic Books

The Foundation offers financial assistance to fully committed, self-publishing comic book creators and qualified charitable and non-profit organizations. The purpose is to assist comic book creators with some of the costs in self-publishing their work. Contact Xeric Foundation, 351 Pleasant St., PMB 214, Northampton, MA 01060-3900; 413-585-0671; {www.xericfoundation.com}.

$500 To Teach Ceramics

Want to put your artistic talents to work, but not sure where to start? Here's the answer you have been looking. Through the Dorchester Bay Economic Development Corporation small business loan, you can get the funds you need to make your business dreams a reality. The program awarded ten small business loans totaling $132,300 in the past year. This is only for businesses in the Dorchester Bay area. Check with your local Economic Development Association to see what your area may offer. Contact Dorchester Bay Economic Development Corporation, 594 Columbia Rd., Dorchester, MA 02125; 617-825-3522; {www.dbedc.com}.

Free Art Exhibits

Want to learn more about medieval art? Or maybe teach your kids a thing or two about Monet? Through the National Gallery of Art Loan Program, you can get educational material on the Gallery's collections and exhibitions, free of charge. The program is open to individuals, schools, colleges, and libraries across the Nation. Check out the easy-to-use website for ordering your materials. Contact the Department of Education Resources, National Gallery of Art, 2000B South Club Drive, Landover, MD 20785; {www.nga.gov/resources}.

Actors Get $40 to Buy Shoes

The Conrad Cantzen Memorial Shoe Fund offers entertainment professionals up to $40, once in a twelve month period for shoes costing no more than $80. Contact The Actors' Fund of America, 729 Seventh Avenue, 10th Floor, New York, NY 10019; 212-221-7300, ext. 146; Fax: 212-764-0238; {www.actorsfund.org/human/social/cantzen.html}.

$300,000 to Make a Film

The primary focus of funding is independent documentary film. Grant awards for production typically range from $50,000 to $300,000 and provide partial support for documentary series and individual independent films. Contact John D. and Catherine T. MacArthur Foundation, 140 S. Dearborn St., Ste. 1100, Chicago, IL 60603-5285; 312-726-8000; Fax: 312-920-6258; {www.macfound.org}.

$25,000 to Educating the Public on Modern Art

This foundation provides grants to individuals, in-kind gifts, internship funds, scholarship funds to educate the public about modern art and modernism and the art of Robert Motherwell. Contact Dedalus Foundation, Inc., c/o Hecht & Co., PC, 111 W. 40th Street, New York, NY

10018; {www.moma.org/education/internships_dedalus.html}.

Grants of $100,000 or More for Songwriters

The funds are provided to preserve and enhance the legacy of Johnny Mercer as well as providing educational programs for music appreciation, assisting in the development of songwriters, and enhance the general appreciation of American popular music. Contact The Johnny Mercer Foundation, c/o Prager and Fenton, 675 3rd Avenue, New York, NY 10017; 212-382-2790; {www.johnny mercerfoundation.org/}. Application Address: The John Mercer Foundation, 234 W. 44th St., Ste. 901, New York, NY 10036; 212-835-2299.

Music Teachers and Others: Grants, Scholarships and Funds for You!

Over $2.0 million is available through this foundation to provide scholarship aid grants to accredited colleges and universities in the field of music, to increase music education and to popularize the teaching of music as a profession. Grants to individuals limited to providing emergency aid to worthy music teachers in need. Contact The Presser Foundation, 385 Lancaster Ave., No. 205, Haverford, PA 19041; 610-658-9030.

Grants from $500 up to $56,500 for Art Scholars

Grant awards are available to art scholars so that they can go to Los Angeles to study at the Rifkind Center for German Expressionist Studies. Giving is done primarily to the arts, especially art museums. Contact Robert Gore Rifkind Foundation, 1301 Schuyler Road, Beverly Hills, CA

90210; 310-275-0959; {www.lacma. org/info/resource/rifkind.htm}.

$30,000 Grants for Artists

This national giving foundation awards up to $30,000 in an effort to promote artistic development. Grants are given to individuals interested in media and communications and the visual arts. Contact The Penny McCall Foundation, Inc., c/o Jennifer McSweeney Reuss, 163 E. 81st St., Apt. 10A, New York, NY 10028; Fax: 212-988-9714; {pennymccallfnd@ aol.com}.

$2,500 to Dance, Act, or Take Pictures

The Puffin Foundation Ltd. makes grants that encourage emerging artists in the fields of art, music, theater, dance, photography, and literature whose works due to their genre and/or social philosophy might have difficulty being aired. Grants range from $1,000 to $2,500. Contact Puffin Foundation Ltd., 20 East Oakdene Avenue, Teaneck, NJ 07666-4111; {www. puffinfounda tion.org/}.

$24,000 for Racing Club Employees

Grants of up to $24,000 are given to economically disadvantage indigent employees of turf and racing clubs. Contact The Jockey Club Foundation, 40 E. 52nd Street, New York, NY 10022-5911; {www.tjcfoundation. org/}.

$10,000 to Develop Your Art

Grants ranging from $4,000 to $10,000 are awarded to artists who have dedicated their lives to developing their art, regardless of their level of commercial success. Artists must have been working in a mature phase of their art for at least 20 years. The

Emergency Assistance Program is intended to provide interim financial assistance to qualified artists whose needs are the result of an unforeseen, catastrophic incident, and who lack the resources to meet that situation. Contact: Adolph and Esther Gottlieb Foundation, Inc., 380 West Broadway, New York, NY 10012; 212-226-0581; Fax: 212-226-0584; {http://www.gott liebfoundation.org}.

Artists Live Rent-FREE for One Month

The Foundation maintains the William Flanagan Memorial Creative Persons Center (better known as "The Barn") in Montauk, on Long Island in New York, as a residence for writers, painters, sculptors and composers. The Center is open from June 1st to October 1st. Residencies are for one month periods of time. The standards for admission are, simply, need and talent. Contact: Edward F. Albee Foundation, 14 Harrison St., New York, NY 10013; 212-226-2020; {www.pipeline.com /%7Ejtnyc/albeefdtn.html}.

Grants for Radio & Television Professionals

This foundation provides grants in time of personal or family crisis for radio and television professionals. The foundation provides anonymous financial grants to those who, through no fault of their own, are in acute need due to critical illness, advanced age, death of a spouse, an accident or other serious misfortune. Contact: Broadcasters' Foundation, 7 Lincoln Ave., Greenwich, CT 06830; 203-862-8577; Fax: 203-629-5739; {www.br oadcastersfoundation.org/index.html}.

$27,000 in Emergency Aid for Artists

Grants from $500 up to $27,000 are provides for visual artists and their families. Financial aid is available through the Emergency Funding Grant Program to support professional artists and their families in the event of illness, distress, disability, or bereavement. Contact Artists Fellowship, Inc., c/o Salmagundi Club, 47 5th Avenue, New York, NY 10003; 646-230-9833; {www.artists fellowship.com/financial.html}.

$2,000 Grants for Pop/Rock Latin Songwriters

The ASCAP Foundation and Heineken USA Incorporated offers grants to Pop/Rock songwriters residing in one of the three greater metropolitan areas of Boston, Chicago and New York; and to Latin songwriters living in Miami or Los Angeles. These $2,000 grant programs are designed to assist up-and-coming Pop/Rock Latin songwriters with career advancement. Contact The ASCAP Foundation Heineken USA, ASCAP Foundation, One Lincoln Plaza, New York, NY 10023-7142; 212-621-6219; {www. ascapfoundation.org}.

$100,000 for Film Producers

The America at a Crossroads initiative provides grants to fund the production of films related to post-9/11 America. Grant amounts top out at $100,000 and can be used for film research and development, production and/or distribution. Individual film producers are eligible for grant funding. Contact Corporation for Public Broadcasting, 401 Ninth Street, NW, Washington, DC 20004-2129; 202-879-9600; {www.cpb.org/tv/funding/crossroads}.

High School Seniors Get $1,500 to Study Art or Art History

Awards grants of $1,500 each to graduating seniors who intend to further their studies in fine arts or art history at an accredited college, university, or art school. Foundation started by renowned Modern artist Robert Motherwell. Contact Dedalus Foundation, 555 W. 57th St., Ste. 1222, New York, NY 10019; {www.dedalusfoundation.org}.

$1,000 for Pianists

The Scholarship Program for Young American Pianists offers $1,000 scholarships awarded on competitive basis to outstanding young American pianists, especially those who demonstrate a special affinity for the interpretation of Chopin's music. Contact The Chopin Foundation, 1440 79th Street Causeway, Suite 117, Miami, FL 33141; 305-868-0624; Fax: 305-868-5150; {www.chopin.org}.

$5,000 for Composers

The American Music Center provides grants of up to $5000 to composers to help them realize their music in performance, and in some cases, on a recording. Grants are project-based, for a specific work and specific event associated with the work, such as a performance, reading or recording. Contact American Music Center, Anna Smith, Manager of Grantmaking Programs, RE: CAP Application, 30 West 26th Street, Suite 1001, New York, NY 10010-2011; 212-366-5260, ext. 29; {www.amc.net/}.

Money for Young Artists

Scholarship and fellowship grants are awarded to emerging young artists in theater, dance and film to help them realize their career goals. Grantees must be nominated by their school or organization. Contact: Princess Grace Foundation USA, 150 East 58th Street, 25th Floor, New York, NY 10155; 212-317-1470; Fax: 212-317-1473; {www.pgfusa.com}.

Grants for Emerging Playwrights

Provides grants to emerging playwrights. Grants are available directly to an individual through a residency at New Dramatists, Inc. in New York. Playwrights may submit applications independently and do not have to be nominated. Contact Princess Grace Foundation USA, 150 East 58th Street, 25th Floor, New York, NY 10155; 212-317-1470; Fax: 212-317-1473; {www.pgfusa.com}.

$6,000 for Women Artists

Artist Enrichment program provides grants to feminist artists and arts organizations to be used for artistic development, artist residencies, the exploration of new areas or techniques, and the creation of new art. Art Meets Activism program provides grants to feminist social change artists and arts organizations for projects. This is for Kentucky women artists. Contact Kentucky Foundation for Women, 1215 Heyburn Building, 332 West Broadway, Louisville, KY 40202-2184; 502-562-0045; Fax: 502-561-0420; {www.kfw.org/}.

Up to $2,000 for Women Musicians or Music Educators

Provides grants to women who are composers, music educators, musicologists, and performers. The mission of the Fund is to seek out women's music projects from women of ethnic, cultural, and racial diversity and especially the work of lesbians. Contact The PatsyLu Music Fund, Open Meadows Foundation, P.O. Box 150-607, Van Brunt Station, Brooklyn, NY 11215-607; 718-768-2249; {www.openmeadows.org/}.

Published Writers Get $15,000

Grants of approximately $15,000 to developing writers who have published at least one book of fiction or a collection of short stories published in literary and/or commercial publications. Contact The Sherwood Anderson Foundation, C/O Michael M. Spear, Foundation Co-President, 216 College Road, Richmond, VA 23229; 804-282-8008; {http://oncampus.richmond.edu/academics/journalism/sahome.html}.

Grants for Artists in Financial Need

Two separate grant programs for artists in financial need: 1) Grants for painters, sculptors, and printmakers who have worked at least 20 years on their art, and are in current financial need to support their work; and 2) Emergency grants of up to $10,000 for painters, sculptors, and printmakers who are in current financial need which is the result of a recent emergency occurrence such as a fire, flood or medical emergency. Contact Adolph and Esther Gottlieb Foundation, Inc., Sara Ross, Grants Manager, 380 W. Broadway, New York, NY 10012-5115; 212-226-0581; Fax: 212-226-0584; {www.gottliebfoundation.org/}.

$20,000 for Contemporary Music Composers

Provides grants through a commissioning program for composers and their orchestras and chamber groups that have a record of excellence in the performance of contemporary music. Contact Koussevitzky Music Foundation, Inc., c/o Brown Raysman LLP, 900 Third Avenue, New York, NY 10022; 212-895-2367; Fax: 212-895-2900; {www.koussevitzky.org/}; {info@koussevitzky.org}.

$10,000 to Support Media Projects

This foundation offers funding that supports independent media projects in post-production that address the economy, class issues, poverty, women, war and peace, race, and labor. Contact Center for Alternative Media and Culture, P.O. Box 0832, Radio City Station, New York, NY 10101; 212-977-2096; {www.mediarights.org/workshop/prod_workshop/dyn_res_list2.php}.

1,000 Grants to Write Fiction

The Arch and Bruce Brown Foundation awards yearly grants to writers in three rotating disciplines: Theatre, Full-length Fiction, and Short

Stories. All works submitted must present the gay and lesbian lifestyle in a positive manner and be based on, or inspired by, a historic person, culture, event, or work of art. The Foundation also offers grants to production companies to offset expenses in producing gay-positive theatrical works based on history. Contact Arch and Bruce Brown Foundation, PMB 503, 31855 Date Palm Drive, Suite 3, Cathedral City, CA 92234; {www. aabbfoundation.org}.

Artists Get $1,500 to Finish Their Media and Film Art Works

Finishing Funds provides artists with grants up to $1,500 to help with the completion of electronic media and film art works which are currently in progress. Eligible forms include a variety of media. Work must be innovative, creative and approach the various media as art forms; all genres are eligible, including experimental, narrative and documentary art works. Individual artists can apply directly to the program and do not need a sponsoring organization. Applicants must be residents of New York State; students are not eligible. Contact Electronic and Film Arts Grants Program, Experimental Television Center, 109 Lower Fairfield Rd., Newark Valley, NY 13811; 607-687-4341; Fax: 607-687-4341; {www. experimentaltvcenter.org/}.

$1,000 to Fund Events for Independent Media Artists

Presentation Funds provides grants to not-for-profit organizations throughout New York State. The program seeks to encourage events which increase understanding of and appreciation for independent media work in all areas of the State. Events must be open to the public; courses, classes and workshops with limited enrollments are not eligible. The intention of this program is to provide partial assistance; organizations must also provide additional support for the event. Publicly supported educational institutions are not eligible. Contact Electronic and Film Arts Grants Program, Experimental Television Center, 109 Lower Fairfield Rd., Newark Valley, NY 13811; 607-687-4341; Fax: 607-687-4341; {www. experimentaltvcenter.org/}.

$2,000 Per Project to Strengthen Artistic Activities

The Media Arts Technical Assistance Fund is designed to help non-profit media arts programs in New York State stabilize, strengthen or restructure their media arts organizational capacity, services and activities. The Fund will provide up to $2,000 per project to organizations which receive support from NYSCA's. Contact Electronic and Film Arts Grants Program, Experimental Television Center, 109 Lower Fairfield Rd., Newark Valley, NY 13811; 607-687-4341; Fax: 607-687-4341; {www. experimentaltvcenter.org/}.

Grants to Produce Films in New York City & Los Angeles

This Foundation offers grants and other incentives to individuals who produce films or videos in New York City or L.A. The programs are as follows: The Roy W. Dean New York City Film Grant, The Roy W. Dean Los Angeles Video Grant, and The Roy W. Dean Los Angeles Film Grant. Contact From the Heart Productions, Attn: Roy W. Dean Film and Video Grants, 1455 Mandalay Beach Road. Oxnard, CA 93035-2845; 866-689-

5150; {www.fromtheheartproduc tions.com/grant}.

Writers: Grants up to $1,500

Grants of up to $1,000 are given to U.S. or Canadian poets, fiction writers, and non-fiction writers "whose work addresses women's concerns or speaks for peace and justice from a feminist perspective." Contact Money for Women / Barbara Deming Memorial Fund, P.O. Box 630125, Bronx, NY 10463; {www.lgbtfunders.org/lgbt funders/dstate.htm#Money%20for%20 Women}.

$50,000 Grant to Film in New Zealand

The New Zealand film grant is for all residents of New Zealand. If you are a resident living abroad, you can enter but you must film in New Zealand. Contact From the Heart Productions, Attn: Roy W. Dean Film Grant, 1455 Mandalay Beach Road. Oxnard, CA 93035-2845; 866-689-5150; {www. fromtheheartproductions.com/grant-nz.shtml}.

$15,000 to Promote Social Change through Media Production

The Paul Robeson Fund for Independent Media, a program of the New York City-based Funding Exchange, supports media activism and grassroots organizing by funding the pre-production and distribution of social issue film and video and radio projects. The fund is interested in projects that address critical social and political issues. The primary purpose of the fund is to support independent media productions that are not only compelling politically and artistically but will also be used as tools for progressive social change activism and organizing. Contact Funding Exchange, 666 Broadway, Suite 500, New York, NY 10012; 212-529-5300 or 212-529-5356, ext. 307; Fax: 212-982-9272; {www.fex.org/grantmaking. shtml#robeson}.

$10,000 for Native American Artists

The Kookyangw Fund was created to provide financial support, encouragement, and exposure to emerging Native American graphic and visual artists. The goals of the fund are to increase knowledge, awareness and understanding of Native American arts; to encourage aesthetic expression by promoting the use of high-technology tools by Native American artists; and to enable their participation in the profession. (The Kookyangw Fund is currently NOT accepting applications, check the website for updates.) Contact First Nations Development Institute, 2300 Fall Hill Ave., Ste. 412, Fredericksburg, VA 22401; 540-371-5615; Fax: 540-371-3505; {www. firstnations.org}.

$5,000 Cash Awards for Women Filmmakers

The Film Finishing Fund offers cash awards to support independent and non-profit women filmmakers in completing documentary, dramatic, educational, animated, or experimental films or videos which promote equal opportunities for women, enhance media images of women, and influence prevailing attitudes and practices regarding and on behalf of women. Contact Women in Film Foundation, 8857 W. Olympic Blvd., Ste. 201, Beverly Hills, CA 90211; 310-657-5154; Fax: 323-463-0963; {www.wif.org/info_page.cfm?id=11}.

Grants to Help Publish History of Art Books

The Millard Meiss Publication Grants award grants for the purpose of subsidizing book length scholarly manuscripts in the history of art and related subjects that have been accepted by a publisher on their merits, but cannot be published in the most desirable form without a subsidy. Contact College Art Association, 275 7th Ave., 18th Floor, New York, NY 10001-6708; 212-691-1051; Fax: 212-627-2381; {www.collegeart.org}.

Gap Funding for Artists who Have Recently Graduated

The Professional Development Fellowships help MFA, terminal MA and Ph.D. students bridge the gap between graduate study and professional careers. By offering support at this critical juncture in scholars' and artists' careers, the Association makes timely degree completion more viable and employment opportunities more

accessible. Each fellow receives support over a period of two years. Contact College Art Association, 275 7th Ave., 18th Floor, New York, NY 10001-6708; 212-691-1051; Fax: 212-627-2381; {www.collegeart.org}.

Emergency Funds for Artists up to $8,000

The Craft Emergency Relief Fund is a nonprofit organization making loans and small grants to professional craft artists experiencing career-threatening illness, accident, fire, theft, or natural disaster. CERF is a small revolving fund with loans ranging from $500 to $8,000 and grants up to $1,000. Services include referrals to craft suppliers who have agreed to offer discounts on materials and equipment to craft artists eligible for CERF funds, and booth fee waivers with certain craft show producers. Contact Craft Emergency Relief Fund, Inc., P.O. Box 838, Montpelier, VT 05601-0838; 802-229-2306; Fax: 802-223-6484; {www.craftemergency.org/cerfloan.doc}.

Grants of $1,500 to Aid Artists Worldwide

Aid to Artisans offers practical assistance to artisans world-wide, working in partnerships to foster artistic traditions, cultural vitality and community well-being. Aid to Artisans makes approximately 50 modest grants each year to craft-based associations worldwide. Typically, these grants range from $500 to $1,500 and are used to help these groups purchase much needed equipment and materials to improve or increase their craft production. Contact Aid to Artisans, 331 Wethersfield Avenue, Hartford, CT 06114; 860-677-1649; Fax: 860-676-2170; {www.aidtoartisans.org/what/grants.html}.

Financial Assistance for Artists Living with HIV/AIDS

Visual AIDS provides direct services to artists living with HIV/AIDS. The Visual AIDS Artist Material Grants are awarded to Visual AIDS active members, who are low income artists in need of financial assistance in obtaining materials for their artwork. Contact Visual AIDS, 526 W. 26th St. # 510, New York, NY 10001; 212-627-9855; Fax: 212-627-9815; {www.visualaids.org}; {visaids@earthlink.net}.

$1,000 to Help Artists Pay Bills

Change, Inc. provides emergency grants up to $1,000 for artists in all disciplines needing help with rent, medical expenses, utility bills, fire damage, etc. Students are not eligible for Change, Inc. Contact Change, Inc., Box 54, Captiva, FL 33924; 212-473-3742; {www.bronxarts.org/art_residencies.asp}; {www.sunshineartist.com/magazine/dreary_days.htm}.

Emergency Funds for American Indian Artists

The Indian Artist Disaster Relief Fund provides funds for American Indian artists who have suffered losses through death, long-term illness or other tragedy. Contact Indian Artist Disaster Relief Fund, Arizona Indian Arts Alliance (AAIA), Box 250, Tumacacori, AZ 85640; 520-398-2226; {www.indianartistsofamerica.com/}.

$12,000 Grants for Visual Artists

The Grants Program for Individuals in the Visual Arts offers grants of up to $12,000 to visual artists whose work can be viewed advantageously through slides. This program has been suspended until 2006. Contact The Elizabeth Foundation for the Arts, P.O. Box 2670, New York, NY 10036; 212-563-5855; Fax: 212-563-1875; {www.efa1.org/}; {grants@efal.org}.

Low-Rent Studios for Artists in New York City

The EFA Studio Center program provides subsidized artists' studios in New York City. This program was established to help visual artists develop their careers and achieve financial self-sufficiency. Contact The Elizabeth Foundation for the Arts, P.O. Box 2670, New York, NY 10036; 212-563-5855; Fax: 212-563-1875; {www.efa1.org/}; {grants@efal.org}.

Fellowships for Poets, Writers, and Visual Artists

The center seeks to give talented individuals the opportunity to engage in the process of discovery. There are two kinds of fellowships available through this Foundation: The Visual Arts Fellowship, which is available to artists in any of the visual arts media, however, facilities may limit certain types of work; and the Writing Fellowship, which offers fellowships to fiction and poetry writers of merit. Contact Fine Arts Work Center in Provincetown, Inc., 24 Pearl Street, Provincetown, MA 02657-1504; 508-487-9960; Fax: 508-487-8873; {www.fawc.org}; {info@fawc.org}.

$50,000 Grants for Contemporary Art

Grants are awarded annually to outstanding or unusually promising artists and arts organizations that create, present, or support work of an imaginative, contemporary nature. Funding is given in the areas of dance, music, performance art/theater, poetry, and the visual arts. Some additional funding is available to organizations and to individuals through a discretionary grants program for urgent situations related to their work. The foundation biennially awards the John Cage Award for Music by a formal nomination process. Contact Foundation for Contemporary Performance Arts, Inc., 820 Greenwich Street, New York, NY 10014; 212-807-7077; Fax: 212-807-7177.

$2,000 for Professional Artists

This Foundation gives primarily to professional artists, 25 years of age or older, working in paint and to arts organizations serving these artists. Individual artists must submit (6) 35mm color slides of the highest quality, representing permanent work in the visual arts. Contact Sam and Adele Golden Foundation for the Arts, c/o Mark Golden, 188 Bell Road, New Berlin, NY 13411; 607-847-8158; Fax: 607-847-8158; {www.golden foundation.org}.

Up to $350,000 for Writers

The Literary Program supports the creation of exceptional poetry and prose written originally in the English language and to increase the audience for contemporary literature. The foundation honors writers whose work reflects and changes our understanding of the world. Contact Lannan Foundation. 313 Read St., Santa Fe, NM 87501; 505-986-8160; Fax: 505-986-8195; {www.lannan.org}.

$50,000 for Dissertations on American Art

The Luce Foundation awards fellowships to doctoral candidates working on dissertations in American art. Funds are used solely to advance completion of the student's

dissertation. Contact The Henry Luce Foundation, Inc., 111 W. 50th St., Ste. 4601, New York, NY 10020; 212-489-7700; Fax: 212-581-9541; {www.h luce.org/4disfm.html}.

$1,000 Grants for Sculptors

Grants ranging from $350 up to $1,000 are provided to encourage the creation and appreciation of sculpture throughout the U.S.; one award given annually to a sculptor for outstanding ability as well as commitment to sculpture. Contact National Sculpture Society, Inc., 237 Park Ave., New York, NY 10017; 212-764-5645; Fax: 212-764-5651; {www.nationalsculp ture.org/scholarships.asp}.

$30,000 for Working Artists in Need

The Pollock-Krasner Foundation's dual criteria for grants are recognizable artistic merit and demonstrable financial need, whether professional, personal or both. The Foundation encourages applications from artists who have genuine financial needs that are not necessarily catastrophic. Grants are intended for a one-year period of time. The Foundation will consider need on the part of an applicant for all legitimate expenditures relating to his or her professional work and personal living, including medical expenses.

The maximum grant amount is $30,000. Contact The Pollock-Krasner Foundation, Inc., 863 Park Ave., New York, NY 10021; 212-517-5400; Fax: 212-288-2836; {www.pkf.org/grant.html}.

Up to $35,000 for Photographers

The W. Eugene Smith Grant in Humanistic Photography is presented annually to a photographer whose past work and proposed project, as judged by a panel of experts, follows the tradition of W. Eugene Smith's compassionate dedication exhibited during his 45-year career as a photographic essayist. Contact W. Eugene Smith Memorial Fund, Inc., c/o Intl. Ctr. of Photography, 1133 Ave. of the Americas, New York, NY 10036; 212-857-0038 or 212- 857-0000, ext. 138; {www.smithfund.org}.

$10,000 for Individual Artists

Tanne Awards recognize prior outstanding achievement by individual artists who have demonstrated exceptional talent and creativity but have limited financial resources or have difficulty obtaining funding. The awards are intended to enrich the recipient's artistic life and are unconditional. Grants range from $5,000 up to $10,000. Contact Tanne Foundation, c/o Grants Mgmt. Associates, 77 Summer Street, Boston, MA 02110; 617-426-7172; Fax: 617-426-5441; {www.tannefoundation. org/}; {mjenney@grantsmanagement. com}.

More Money for Artists of All Kinds

The Louis Comfort Tiffany Foundation awards grants in painting, sculpture, printmaking, photography, video and craft media. Emerging American artists and craftspeople are recognized every two years by a series of monetary grants. The awards go to the artists whose work shows promise, but who have not yet received widespread critical or commercial recognition. Contact The Louis Comfort Tiffany Foundation, c/o Artists Space, 38 Greene St., 3rd Fl., New York, NY 10013; {http://louis comforttiffanyfoundation.org/grants_p rogram.html}.

$500 Plus Artists Can Live & Work on a Farm

Selected artists from all over the country spend two weeks to one month living and working in excellent facilities located within a short walk from the farm. The Artist-in-Residence facility is primarily available for one artist at a time although two artists working collaboratively may be in residence together. Artists will be given a monthly stipend of $500 to offset the cost of food, travel, supplies or other related needs. (A collaborative team will receive one stipend.) Artists are responsible for their own personal living expenses, travel, supplies, long distance telephone charges and for any other expenses relating to the cost of producing work that may be incurred while in the program. Contact Weir Farm Trust, Inc., 735 Nod Hill Road, Wilton, CT 06897; 203-761-9945; Fax: 203-761-9116; {www.nps.gov /wefa}; {evanswft@optonline.net}.

Artists Work Outdoors & Get $500!

The Weir Farm Trust invites professional visual artists to apply to the Visiting Artists Program at Weir Farm National Historic Site. The program will begin in the summer and continue for one year. Housing and studio space are not provided for this program - rather artists use Weir Farm as an "open air" studio. A $500 honorarium to help cover travel expenses or supplies is available. The purpose of the Visiting Artists program, is to give selected artists the opportunity to create a cohesive body of work based on each artist's personal interpretation of Weir Farm. Contact Weir Farm Trust, Inc., 735 Nod Hill Road, Wilton, CT 06897; 203-761-9945; Fax: 203-761-9116; {www. nps.gov/wefa}; {evanswft@optonline. net}.

Holographic Artists Get $10,000 Support Grants

This Foundation sponsors a yearly Holography Award Program, selecting from 4-8 art holographers a year for a grant of $10,000. The Foundation also supports activities that further the art of holography. The funding supports fine art holography only; organizations must show that they have additional sources of support; only established programs are funded. Contact The Shearwater Foundation, Inc., c/o Joseph Arnold, 12 E. 86th St., Apt. 1539, New York, NY 10028-0516.

$15,000 for Musical Theatre Artists

The Jonathan Larson Performing Arts Foundation provides financial assistance and encouragement to emerging composers, lyricists and book writers, as well as non-profit producing companies with a commitment to developing and supporting the work of new musical theatre projects and musical theatre artists. The Foundation is one of the few places that individual creative artists in the performing arts can go to apply for direct financial support. Contact Jonathan Larson Performing Arts Foundation, Inc., c/o Nancy

Kassak Diekmann, P.O. Box 672, Prince St. Station, New York, NY 10012; 212-529-0814; Fax: 212-253-7604; {www.jlpaf.org/}; {JLPAF@ jlpaf.org}.

$5,000 Scholarships for Design Students and Others

The Worldstudio Foundation provides scholarships to minority and economically disadvantaged students who are studying the design/arts disciplines in colleges and universities in the United States. Scholarship recipients are selected not only for their ability and their need, but also for their demonstrated commitment to giving back to the larger community through their work. Basic scholarships are awarded in the amount of $1,000, $1,500 and $2,000. One or two awards are also given each year in the amount of between $3,000 and $5,000 at the jury's discretion. These awards are paid directly to your school to be applied toward your tuition. In addition, Honorable Mention prizes are awarded. Contact Worldstudio Foundation, Inc., 225 Varick St., 9th Floor, New York, NY 10014; 212-366-1317; Fax: 212-807-0024; {www. worldstudio.org}; {scholarships@ worldstudio.org}.

Up to $30,000 for Music Composers

Commissioning Music/USA is available both to consortia and to individual organizations. Organizations may form a consortium to commission one or more composers to write works which the participating groups will perform or present a total of six times. Recognizing that emerging composers may not have access to the resources necessary to put together a consortium, Meet The Composer also accepts applications from individual organizations, which will perform or present the work a total of four times. Individual organizations may only apply on behalf of one composer. Grants range from $5,000 to $30,000. Contact Meet The Composer, Inc., 75 Ninth Ave., Ste. 3RC, New York, NY 10011; 212-645-6949; Fax: 212-645-9669; {www.meetthecom poser.org}; {metrevino@meetthe composer.org}.

$5,000 to Compose Music

Meet The Composer has created *Global Connections* to create support for composers to share their work with a global community. *Global Connections* helps ensure that international audiences see and hear the impressive and creative range of work offered by today's living composers. Grants will range from $500 to $5,000. Contact Meet The Composer, Inc., 75 Ninth Ave., Ste. 3RC, New York, NY 10011; 212-645-6949; Fax: 212-645-9669; {www. meetthecomposer.org}; {metrevino@ meetthecomposer.org}.

Get $100,000 to Join an Orchestra!

A partnership program of the American Symphony Orchestra League and Meet The Composer, *Music Alive* offers support for composer residencies with professional and youth orchestras of all sizes. There are two types of *Music Alive* composer residencies: the Short Term Residencies offer support for residencies of two to eight weeks within one season; the Extended Residencies offer support for multi-year, full-season residencies of up to three years. Funding amounts range from $7,000 to $28,000 for Short Term Residencies, and from $30,000 up to $100,000 per year for Extended

Residencies. Contact Meet The Composer, Inc., 75 Ninth Ave., Ste. 3RC, New York, NY 10011; 212-645-6949; Fax: 212-645-9669; {www. meetthecomposer.org}; {metrevino@ meetthecomposer.org}.

$1,000 to Perform Music

The Meet The Composer Fund, the founding program of Meet The Composer, awards grants that enable composers to participate actively in performances of their work. Participation may include performing, conducting, speaking with the audience, presenting workshops, giving interviews, and coaching rehearsals. Awards will range from $250 to $1000 per composer and will be based on the amount of the composer's activity related to the proposed event. Contact Meet The Composer, Inc., 75 Ninth Ave., Ste. 3RC, New York, NY 10011; 212-645-6949; Fax: 212-645-9669; {www. meetthecomposer.org}; {metrevino@ meetthecomposer.org}.

$25,000 for Young Artists to go to College

The Arts Recognition and Talent Search (ARTS) allows 17 and 18 year-old artists to apply for college scholarships. The most accomplished applicants are chosen to participate in the final adjudication process known as ARTS Week, a series of performances, master classes, seminars and readiness held in Jan. in Miami,

FL. These 125 awardees have the opportunity to earn cash awards of up to $3,000 each and be named Presidential Scholar in the ARTS. Artists in the categories of dance, jazz, film and video, music, photography, theater, visual arts, voice, and writing are eligible. Contact National Foundation for Advancement in the Arts, 800 Brickell Ave., Ste. 500, Miami, FL 33131; 305-377-1140; Fax: 305-377-1149; {www.ARTSawards. org}; {info@nfaa.org}.

Fellowships, Housing & $1,000 for Visual Artists

The Fellowships in the Visual Arts program is conducted in collaboration with the Corcoran Gallery of Art in Washington, D.C., and provides a six-month residency that is renewable for two years. Each fellow receives round-trip transportation to Miami, FL; housing and studio space in Miami Beach; $1,000 monthly stipend; and funds for supplies. At the end of the residency, the Corcoran Gallery of Art hosts an exhibit and publishes a catalog of the show for distribution to museums, art dealers, curators and galleries. Contact National Foundation for Advancement in the Arts, 800 Brickell Ave., Ste. 500, Miami, FL 33131; 305-377-1140; Fax: 305-377-1149; {www.ARTSawards.org}; {info@nfaa.org}.

$200 to Meet Artists' Expenses

The Astral Career Grants of up to $200 are awarded to meet modest expenses in response to external opportunities requiring timely action by an artist. Grants are only available in the fields of music and dance. The grant does not cover funds for medical care or general living support. Applicants must be U.S. citizens or permanent residents, and cannot be full-time students. Contact National Foundation for Advancement in the Arts, 800 Brickell Ave., Ste. 500, Miami, FL 33131; 305-377-1140; Fax: 305-377-1149; {www. ARTSawards.org}; {info@nfaa.org}.

Financial Awards for Published Gay, Lesbian and Transgender Literature

The Lambda Literary Awards recognize and honor the best in lesbian, gay, bisexual and transgender literature. Contact Lambda Literary Foundation, P.O. Box 73910, Washington, D.C. 20056-3910; 202-462-7924; Fax: 202-462-5264; {www. lambdalit.org}; {llf@lambdalit.org}.

Up to $250,000 to Make Videos for T.V.

Grant for programs that take creative risks, explore complex issues and express points of view seldom seen on commercial or public television by reflecting voices and visions of underrepresented communities and address the needs of underserved audiences, particularly minorities and children. Grants range from $20,000 up to $250,000. Contact Independent Television Service, 501 York Street, San Francisco, CA 94110; 415-356-8383; Fax: 415-356-8391; {www. itvs.org}; {itvs@itvs.org}.

Over $8,000 for High School Film Students

A&E awards grants and scholarships to K-12 students and teachers. There are two different award programs under this Foundation: 1) the A&E Classroom Program, which awards $500 to K-12 teachers that demonstrate creative classroom uses for A&E and History Channel programming; and 2) History Channel Awards in which A&E annually awards 3 scholarships of $5,000 to high school students and 5 grants of $3,000 and a school video library to teachers participating in the National History Day competition. Contact A & E Television Networks Corporate Giving Program, P.O. Box 1610, Grand Central Station, New York, NY 10163-1610; 212-210-1400; {www.historychannel.com/classroom/awards.html}; {www.aande. com}.

$1,000 + Publication to Write About Museums

The Brooking Paper on Creativity in Museums is a writing competition that awards a $1,000 to an author with notable examples of creativity, innovation, and imagination in museum operations. The winning paper will be published in Museum News. Contact American Association of Museums, 1575 Eye St., N.W., Ste. 400, Washington, DC 20005-1105; 202-289-1818; Fax: 202-289-6578; {www.aam-us.org}.

Museum Professionals Get $1,000 for Excellence

The Nancy Hanks Memorial Award for Professional Excellence awards a certificate of $1,000 stipend to be used in furtherance of the honoree's professional development with less than ten years in the field. Application for the award must be made by the nominee's director. The presentation takes place during the AAM annual meeting. Contact American Association of Museums, 1575 Eye St., N.W., Ste. 400, Washington, DC 20005-1105; 202-289-1818; Fax: 202-289-6578; {www.aam-us.org}.

$1,200 per Month Plus Travel Costs for Performers, Artists, Writers, Filmmakers

The Artist Fellowship Program provides residencies of four to eight

weeks at the AAS library for creative and performing artists, writers, filmmakers, and journalists to conduct historical research. Recipients receive $1,200/month stipends plus a travel allowance. Successful applicants are those whose work is for the general public rather than for academic or educational audiences. Contact American Antiquarian Society, 185 Salisbury Street, Worcester, MA 01609-1634; 508-755-5221; Fax: 508-754-9069; {www.americanantiquarian. org}; {cfs@mwa.org}.

$1,000 per Month to Research & Write on American Culture

Short-Term Fellowships provides support for one to three months' residence in the Society's library at stipends of $1,000 per month. Open to individuals engaged in scholarly research and writing in any area of American history and culture through 1876. Currently there are nine short-term fellowships available. For a complete list of the different programs offered, Contact American Antiquarian Society, 185 Salisbury Street, Worcester, MA 01609-1634; 508-755-5221; Fax: 508-754-9069; {www. americanantiquarian.org}; {cfs@mwa. org}.

Scholarships for Vocal Arts Students

SOS offers vocal arts scholarships to students at the National Foundation for Advancement in the Arts and at local universities in Southern California including UCLA, USC and Cal State Northridge. Additional scholarships to selected music schools and universities nationwide are currently in development. Contact Society of Singers, Inc., 6500 Wilshire Blvd., Ste. 640, Los Angeles, CA 90404; 323-653-7675 or 866-767-7671; Fax: 323-653-7675; {www.singers.org/default. htm}; {sos@singers.org}; {help@ singers.org}.

$3,000 for Published Works in Science by Adults, Children, Journalists, Broadcasters

The Science Writing Award in Physics and Astronomy for articles, booklets, or books intended for children preschool to 15 years of age offers awards for works published between Jan. and Dec. of the previous year. Winning authors receive a $3,000 prize, a Windsor Chair, and a testimonial. Applicants must be physicists, astronomers, or members of AIP or its affiliated societies. Contact American Institute of Physics, Inc., 1 Physics Ellipse, College Park, MD 20740-3843; 301-209-3100; Fax: 301-209-0843; {www.aip.org/aip/writing}; {aipinfo@aip.org}.

$5,000 to Write a Book on War

An annual award consisting of $5,000 and a 24k gold-framed citation of achievement honoring the best fiction set in a period when the United States was at war. It recognizes the service of American veterans and military personnel and encourages the writing and publishing of outstanding war-related fiction. Contact American Library Association, 50 E. Huron Street, Chicago, IL 60611-2795; 800-545-2433; Fax: 312-944-0379; {www.ala.org}; {ala@ala.org}.

Awards for Anyone to Write a Novel

This foundation offers several award programs, which are for authors or publishers of books for everyone. Non-fiction, fiction, poetry, children's picture books, and young adult literature are subjects included in the awards. For a complete list of the different programs offered, contact ALA directly. Contact American Library Association, 50 E. Huron Street, Chicago, IL 60611-2795; 800-545-2433; Fax: 312-944-0379; {www.ala.org}; {ala@ala.org}.

Up to $20,000 to Create Dance Performances

The Dance: Creation to Performance program awards a three-year initiative in amounts of $20,000, $15,000, $10,000 and $5,000 each year. Artists applying for a grant must be a U.S. citizen or permanent resident, have been a permanent resident of California for at least two years at the time of application, and have demonstrated experience in presenting concert choreography, dance/theater, or traditional dance forms to the public. Contact Dance/USA, 1156 15th St., N.W., Ste. 820, Washington, DC 20005-1726; 202-833-1717; Fax: 202-833-2686; {www.danceusa.org}; {asnyder@danceusa.org}.

High School & College Students: up to $10,000 for Essay Writing

Awards are given in three categories of essay writing: 9th and 10th graders write on Rand's novelette "Anthem", with prizes ranging from $30 to $2,000; 11th and 12th graders write on Rand's novel "The Fountainhead", with prizes ranging from $50 to $10,000; and undergraduate students write on Rand's novel "Atlas Shrugged", with prizes ranging from $400 to $5,000. Contact Ayn Rand Institute/The Center for the Advancement of Objectivism, 2121 Alton Pkwy., Ste. 250, Irvine, CA 92606-4926; 949-222-6550; Fax: 310-306-4925; {www.aynrand.org}; {mail@aynrand.org}. Application address for individuals: The Ayn Rand Institute, P.O. Box 6099, Inglewood, CA 90312.

Financial Assistance for Rhythm and Blues Musicians

The foundation provides emergency financial assistance and career recognition awards to artists and practitioners of rhythm and blues music who worked and/or recorded rhythm and blues music in the 1940's, 50's, and 60's. There are two programs providing assistance and recognition: 1) the Doc Pomus Financial Assistance Grant Program that supports the current and specific financial needs of legendary artists; and 2) the Pioneer Awards Program that recognizes legendary artists whose lifelong contributions have been instrumental in the development of rhythm and blues music. Awards recipients are nominated by foundation trustees, advisory board and artist steering committee, and past Pioneer Award honorees, and are selected by the board of trustees. Contact The Rhythm and Blues Foundation, Inc., 555 Madison Ave., Ste. 793, New York, NY 10022-3301; 212-833-5406; Fax: 212-833-4094; {www.rhythm-n-blues.org/}.

Up to $5,000 for Music Students

The organization seeks to promote and raise the standard of music, including history, composition, performances, appreciation and criticism, and to aid and recognize those learning or serving in the field of music. The organization offers a variety of grants and scholarships to universities, colleges and individuals. Individual grants and scholarships range from $500 up to $5,000. Contact Sigma Alpha Iota Philanthropies, Inc., 34 Wall St., Ste. 515, Asheville, NC 28801-2710; 828-251-0606; Fax: 828-251-0644; {www.sai-national.org}; {nh@sai-national.org}.

Financial Assistance for Barbershop Quartet Singers

The organization provides music education for members and support for leadership of other chapters. Any individual, quartet, or chorus in the

Evergreen District can apply to the trustees to use the Bud Leabo Memorial Fund. Contact Society for the Preservation & Encouragement of Barbershop Quartet Singing in America (also known as SPEBSQSA - Evergreen District), 4241 21st Ave. W., No. 100, Seattle, WA 98199; 206-282-3883; {www.evg.org/default.asp}; {support@evg.org}.

Up to $7,500 for Young Professional Singers

Through annual auditions in New York the foundation gives a number of $7,500 cash awards to gifted singers in the early stages of professional careers, to be used for any career-related purpose. Winners may also receive role preparation assistance for a period of five years, to help defray expenses incurred in musical, dramatic, vocal, and language coaching for specific professional engagements. The number of awards given each year varies according to the resources of the foundation. Contact William Matheus Sullivan Musical Foundation, Inc., P.O. Box 189, Kent, CT 06757; 860-927-3572 or 518-668-4064; Fax: 860-927-1680; {www.sullivanfoundation. org}; {info@sullivanfoundation. org}.

$2,500 for Scientific Journal Writing

The objective of the Journal of Bone and Joint Surgery Resident Journal Club Grants is to support journal club activities for orthopaedic residents. Participation in this program is open to existing and new journal clubs. The program will enhance residency training by providing educational information on managing an effective journal club, and will teach residents how to evaluate current scientific literature. Grants of $2,500 per program are available. Contact Orthopaedic Research Education Foundation, 6300 N. River Rd., Ste. 700, Rosemont, IL 60018-4238; 847-698-9980; Fax: 847-698-7806; {www. oref.org}; {wurth@oref.org}.

Money to Study Archaeology in the Maya Region

This Foundation offers field research grants in support of archaeological field research in the Maya Region. Contact Ahau Foundation, Inc., 1003 Tramway Ln. N.E., Albuquerque, NM 87122-1316; 505-797-2428; {Peter Ahau@aol.com}. Application address: 13158 Candelaria Rd. N.E., Albuquerque, NM 87112; 505-856-3424.

Up to $3,500 for Playwrights

This Foundation awards grants of $1,000 to $3,500 in support of individual playwrights (and other writers and artists). Criteria are merit and need. Contact Ludwig Vogelstein Foundation, Inc., P.O. Box 510, Shelter Island, NY 11964-0510.

$35,000 for Emerging Writers

The Whiting Writers Awards are given annually to ten emerging writers in fiction, nonfiction, poetry and plays. The awards, of $35,000 each, are based on accomplishment and promise. Candidates are proposed by nominators from across the country. Winners are chosen by a selection committee, a small group of recognized writers, literary scholars, and editors, appointed annually by the Foundation. The Foundation does not accept applications to the Writers' Program. Contact Mrs. Giles Whiting Foundation, 1133 Ave. of the Americas, 22nd Floor, New York, NY 10036-6710; 212-336-2138; {www. whitingfoundation.org}.

Money for Creative Writers

The foundation supports writers in all disciplines and attempts to highlight the importance of writers in the society as well as their contributions to the worldwide community. This foundation awards to writers in the categories of playwriting, screenplay, original sitcom, original TV drama, novel, short fiction, children's picture book and poetry. Contact The Writers Foundation, Inc., 3936 Semoran Blvd., No. 368, Orlando, FL 32822; 407-679-3777; {www.writersfoundation.com}; {info@writersfoundation.com}.

$10,000 for Artists to Travel to Europe or Russia

Project grants enable U.S. artists, curators and presenters to implement projects in Central Europe, Russia and Eurasia with grants ranging from $2,000 to $10,000. Cooperative arts projects resulting in the creation of new work or those that establish a mutually beneficial exchange of ideas and expertise among artists, curators and arts organizations are eligible to apply. Contact CEC ArtsLink, Inc., 12 West 31st Street, 4th Floor, New York, NY 10001; 212-643-1985; {www. cecip.org/}; {al@cecartslink.org}.

Up to $9,000 to Write Poetry

This organization offers 12 awards and prizes to professional and student poets. The awards range from $250 up to $9,000 and are as follows: 1) the Writer Magazine/Emily Dickinson Award, which awards $250 in honor of the memory and poetry of Emily Dickinson, for a poem inspired by Dickinson though not necessarily in her style; 2) the Cecil Hemley Memorial Award, which grants $500 for a lyric poem that addresses a philosophical or epistemological concern; 3) the Lyric Poetry Award of $500 for a lyric poem on any subject; 4) the Lucille Medwick Memorial Award, which awards $500 for an original poem in any form on a humanitarian theme; 5) the Alice Fay Di Castagnola Award offering $1,000 for a manuscript-in-progress of poetry or verse-drama; 6) the Louise Louis/Emily F. Bourne Student Poetry Award, which grants $250 for the best unpublished poem by a student in grades 9 through 12 from the United States; 7) the George Bogin Memorial Award of $500 for a selection of four or five poems that use language in an original way to reflect the encounter of the ordinary and the extraordinary and to take a stand against oppression in any of its forms; 8) the Robert H. Winner Memorial Award, which awards $2,500 in acknowledgment of original work being done in mid-career by a poet who has not had substantial recognition, and it is open to poets over forty who have published no more than one book; 9) the Norma Farber First Book Award of 500 for a first book of original poetry written by an American and published in either a hard or soft cover in a standard edition during the calendar year; 10) the William Carlos Williams Award, which offers between $500 and $1,000 for a book of poetry published by a small press, non-profit, or university press; 11) the Frost Medal, which awards $2,500 for distinguished lifetime service to American poetry; and 12) the Shelley Memorial Award, which awards between $6,000 and $9,000 to a living American poet, selected with reference to his or her genius and need. There may be entry fees associated with each submission. Contact Poetry Society of America, 15 Gramercy Park, New York, NY 10003-1705; 212-254-9628; {www. poetrysociety.org/}.

Money for Actors to Go to School

The John L. Dales Scholarship Fund helps qualified Guild members and their children reach their educational potential by providing more than a million dollars in scholarships for study at accredited institutions of higher learning. An applicant may receive up to five scholarships. Grants range from $3,000 to $5,000. Contact The Screen Actors Guild Foundation, 5757 Wilshire Blvd., 7th Floor, Los Angeles, CA 90036; 323-549-6649; Fax: 323-549-6710; {www.sagfoun dation.org}; {dlloyd@sag.org}.

Grants To Actors to Help Pay for Health Care

The Foundation's Catastrophic Health Fund provides grants to eligible Guild members and their dependents that suffer from catastrophic illness or injury and are unable to afford the Guild Health Plan's Self-Pay Program. The Fund ensures that every eligible Guild member and his or her family can depend on continued health benefits when they need them most. Contact The Screen Actors Guild Foundation, 5757 Wilshire Blvd., 7th Floor, Los Angeles, CA 90036; 323-549-6649; Fax: 323-549-6710; {www.sagfoundation.org}; {msmith@sag.org}.

Emergency Assistance for Actors

The Foundation provides funds for the aid, relief and care of needy, sick, indigent and aged Guild members. When assistance is needed, it is given quickly and compassionately, always maintaining strict confidentiality and dignity for each recipient. Contact The Screen Actors Guild Foundation, 5757 Wilshire Blvd., 7th Floor, Los Angeles, CA 90036; 323-549-6649;

Fax: 323-549-6710; {www.sagfoun dation.org}; {msmith@sag.org}.

FREE Rent & Utilities for Artists to Go to New Mexico

The Foundation's purpose is to provide a quiet haven where artists may pursue their creative endeavors without pressure to produce while they are in residence. Artists can live in the fully furnished apartments for a period of up to three months rent-free and utility-free. No spouses, children or pets are permitted to reside at the Foundation during the period of a residence grant. Artists are responsible for purchasing and preparing their own meals, paying their own travel expenses and providing their own working material. Contact: The Helene Wurlitzer Foundation of New Mexico, P.O. Box 1891, Taos, NM 87571; 505-758-2413; Fax: 505-758-2559; {hwf@ taosnet.com}.

$50,000 to Write a Civil War Book

The Lincoln Prize at Gettysburg College shall be awarded annually for the finest scholarly work in English on the era of the American Civil War. The $50,000 Prize will generally go to a book but in rare instances an important article or essay might be honored. The Prize is intended chiefly to encourage outstanding new scholarship, but a lifetime contribution to the study of Lincoln, or the American Civil War soldier, may qualify for the award.

Contact The Lincoln and Soldiers Institute, Campus Box 435, Gettysburg, PA 17325. Application address: c/o Tina Grim, 233 N. Washington St., Gettysburg, PA 17325; 717-337-6590; {www. gettysburg.edu/academics/cwi/lincoln_ prize/graphics/about1.html}.

$1,000 Travel Money for Food Writers

The IACP Foundation has a travel grant program for professional food writers whose research requires or will benefit from access to the holdings of specific libraries with significant culinary collections in the U.S. Applicants must demonstrate that they are under contract for a book, magazine or newspaper article. The average stipend is $1,000 but may vary according to the proposal. Contact The International Association of Culinary Professionals Foundation, 304 W. Liberty St., Ste. 201, Louisville, KY 40202-3068; 502-587-7953; Fax: 502-589-3602; {www.iacpfoundation. com/}; {kkelty@HQTRS.com}.

$20,000 for Pianists And Music Students

The Murray Dranoff Foundation, Inc. provides prizes and awards for pianists and music students who perform chamber music. It sponsors piano competitions and awards prizes for these competitions ranging from $20,000 to $200. Contact The Murray Dranoff Foundation, Inc., 180 N.E. 39th St., Ste. 207, Miami, FL 33137; 305-572-9900; Fax: 305-572-9922; {www.dranoff2piano.org}.

Help for Actors and Others with AIDS

Broadway Cares/Equity Fights AIDS is a foundation that provides assistance to people living with AIDS/HIV. Projects include providing food, shelter, transportation, emergency financial aid, emotional/practical support systems, and nonreimbursable medical expenses. Contact Broadway Cares/Equity Fights AIDS, 165 W. 46th St., Ste. 1300, New York, NY 10036; 212-840-0770; Fax: 212-840-0551; {www.bcefa.org}; {info@bcefa .org}.

Emergency Funds for Writers with AIDS

The PEN American Center, Inc. provides financial support to writers and others in the publishing industry through several awards programs and with emergency funds made available to published professional writers and editors for unexpected financial and HIV/AIDS-related crisis situations. In especially urgent cases the PEN Writers Fund can release up to $200 within 24 hours. Contact PEN American Center, Inc., 568 Broadway, Ste. 401, New York, NY 10012-3225; 212-334-1660; Fax: 212-334-2181; {www.pen.org}; {PEN@pen.org}.

Grants for Jewish Artists

The Adi Foundation of Florida, Inc. administers the Adi Prize for Jewish Expression in Art and Design. Artist must be over 18 years old and are allowed one submission. Collaborations between artists are permitted. Contact Adi Foundation of Florida, Inc., c/o Yaffa Dermer, 2525 Flamingo Pl., Miami Beach, FL 33140-4318. Application address: c/o The Hebrew University of Jerusalem, Humanities Dept, Mt. Scopus, Jerusalem 91905, Israel. Phone: 02-6235235; Fax: 02-6243131; {www. adifoundation.co.il/index_eng.php}.

Up to $80,000 for Artists

Arts International, Inc. provides grants to help identify, develop, and circulate new artwork crossing borders worldwide. Grants range from $1,000 to $80,000 to support a variety of art-related projects and activities, including projects that foster cultural understanding between the Islamic world and the U.S. Contact Arts International, Inc., 526 W. 26th St., Suite 516, New York, NY 10001; 212-924-0771; Fax: 212-924-0773; {www.artsinternational.org}; {info@artsinternational.org}.

$10,000 Scholarships for Songwriters and Musicians
BMI Foundation, Inc. encourages the creation, performance and study of music through awards, scholarships, internships, grants, and commissions. Funding includes: the Jazz Composition Prize of $3,000; general grants to music organizations; the John Lennon Scholarship for Songwriters and Composers which consists of one $10,000 scholarship, and two $5,000 scholarships to young songwriters 15-25; and the Peermusic Latin Scholarship, which awards a $5,000 scholarship for the best song or instrumental work in any Latin genre. Contact BMI Foundation, Inc., 320 W. 57th St., New York, NY 10019-3705; 615-401-2411; {www.bmifoundation.org}.

$10,000 to Promote American Dance
Capezio/Ballet Makers Dance Foundation, Inc. provides funding for dance-related organizations. It offers the Capezio Dance Award, which annually awards $10,000 to an individual, company, or organization that has made a significant contribution to American dance. Contact Capezio/Ballet Makers Dance Foundation, Inc., 1 Campus Rd., Totowa, NJ 07512; 973-595-9000; {www.capezio dance.com}.

$200,000 for Arts Achievements
The Dorothy and Lillian Gish Prize is an annual prize of $200,000 for lifetime achievement in the arts to an individual who has made an outstanding contribution to the beauty of the world and to mankind's enjoyment and understanding of life. Contact Edward L. Jones, V.P., The Dorothy and Lillian Gish Prize, c/o JPMorgan Chase Bank, 345 Park Ave., 4th Fl., New York, NY 10154; 212-464-2305; Fax: 212-464-2305; {jones_ed_1@ JPMorgan.com}.

$25,000 for Puppet Theatre
The Jim Henson Foundation provides grants to develop and encourage the creative art of puppetry in the United States. Emphasis is on contemporary puppet theater for adults, with some focus on new works suitable for family audiences. Giving activities include $44,762 for 12 grants to individuals ranging from $25,000 to $358. Contact The Jim Henson Foundation, 584 Broadway, Ste. 1007, New York, NY 10012; 212-680-1400; Fax: 212-680-1401; {www.hensonfoundation.org}; {email: info@hensonfoundation.org}.

Money for Playwrights and Arts Management Students
The John F. Kennedy Center for the Performing Arts nurtures new works and young artists, and serves the nation as a leader in arts education. The

Center provides grants to nonprofit professional American theater companies, including production grants of $10,000, and development grants of $2,500. For both the production and development grants funds may be used for creative support, actor support, and production support. In addition, playwright grants are awarded to winning playwrights. Also, arts management and arts education interns receive a stipend of $800 per month to help defray housing and transportation costs. Contact John F. Kennedy Center for the Performing Arts, 2700 F St., N.W., Washington, DC 20566-0001; 202-416-8603; Fax: 202-416-8205; {www.kennedy-center.org}.

$7,016 for Needy Professional Musicians

The Musicians Foundation, Inc. helps professional musicians by providing emergency financial assistance in meeting current living, medical and allied expenses. The Foundation does not award scholarships, loans, or composition grants. Contact Musicians Foundation, Inc., 875 6th Ave., Ste. 2303, New York, NY 10001; 212-239-9137; Fax: 212-239-9138; {www.musiciansfoundation.org}; {info@musiciansfoundation.org}.

$5,000 for Young, Aspiring Artists

The Netherland-America Foundation promotes understanding and better relations in the U.S. and the Netherlands through cultural, educational, and philanthropic activities. It awards cultural grants ranging between $500 and $5,000 to young, beginning and aspiring artists in both the visual and performing arts, and a separate $6,000 award to young Dutch or American musicians. It also provides educational grants and fellowships to U.S. students studying in the Netherlands. Contact The Netherland-America Foundation, 82 Wall St., Ste. 1101, New York, NY 10005; 212-825-1221; Fax: 212-825-9105; {www.thenaf.org/}; {info@The NAF.org}.

$50,000 to Promote Opera

Opera America, Inc. seeks to promote opera as exciting and accessible to individuals from all walks of life. Awards ranging from $50,000 to $5,000 are available for audience development, repertoire development and artist development. Contact Opera America, Inc., 1156 15th St., Ste. 810, Washington, DC 20005-1704; 202-293-4466; Fax: 202-393-0735; {www.operaamerica.org}; {frontdesk@opera america.org}.

$25,000 for Education, Arts, and the Environment

The New Earth Foundation provides grants for wide variety of innovative programs related to education, social services, the arts, communication, and the environment. The foundation typically funds programs connected with newer and smaller non-profit organizations. It may consider programs for children and youth, garden and other such programs if they show that they reach outside the norm in their vision and approach and are innovative and effective. Programs must demonstrate a practical means of planning and implementation. Grants available to individuals working under the umbrella of an established non-profit organization. Contact New Earth Foundation, 2940 Southwest Drive, Suite 4A, Sedona, AZ 86336; 928-204-1151; {www.newearthfoundation.org/neweath/home.cfm}; {director@newearthfoundation.org}.

$1,000 for Puppeteers

The Puppeteers of America Endowment Fund gives to members of Puppeteers of America, Inc. for projects related to their work in puppetry. Contact Len Gerwick, Puppeteers of America Endowment Fund, 115 Calvert Ave., West Babylon, NY 11704; 631-587-0194; {www.puppeteers.org/}; {len@gerwick puppets.com}.

Money for Classical Music Composers

REC Music Foundation promotes new classical music composers, primarily through the development of new computer tools. Contact REC Music Foundation, c/o Robert E. Crawford, Jr., 61 Crestwood Dr., Clayton, MO 63105; {www.recmusicorg/siteindex. html}; {recrawfo@recmusic.org}.

$70,000 for Education and the Arts

The Wallace Foundation provides grants for developing effective educational leaders to improve student learning; providing informal learning opportunities for children and families in communities; and increasing participation in the arts. Contact The Wallace Foundation, 2 Park Ave., 23rd Fl., New York, NY 10016; 212-251-9700; {www.wallacefunds.org}; {wrdf@wallacefunds.org}.

Grants for the Arts, Education, Environment, and Science

The Lifebridge Foundation, Inc. was established for the purpose of supporting organizations and individuals who, through cultural, education, and/or scientific means, are "dedicated to creating bridges of understanding among all people by bringing to realization the concepts of one humanity and the interconnectedness of all life." The foundation funds a wide variety of projects relating to the arts, education, the environment, science, and world goodwill. Contact The Lifebridge Foundation Inc., P.O. Box 793, Times Square Station, New York, NY 10108; 212-757-9711; Fax: 212-757-0246; {www.lifebridge.org/mission.htm}; {info@lifebridge.org}.

Over $1.0 Million for Film Video, and Media Artists

This foundation provides grants and project funding for independent film and video makers and other media artists who have little likelihood of being supported through traditional funding sources. They offer several grant categories. Contact them to see if they can help you with your artistic venture. Film Arts Foundation, 145 Ninth Street, San Francisco, CA 94103; 415-552-8760; {www.filmarts. org}.

Up to $5,000 for Film Production Projects

The Frameline for the Horizons/ Frameline Film & Video Completion Fund provides grants to lesbian, gay, bisexual and transgender film and video makers. Completion funds include post-production for films and videos, including sub-titling and video-to-film transfer. Contact Frameline,

145 Ninth Street, Suite 300, San Francisco, CA 94103-2636; 415-703-8650; Fax: 415-861-1404; {www.frameline.org/}, {info@frameline.org}.

Artists Receive Funding to Promote Their Work

The Jerome Foundation makes grants to support the creation and production of new artistic works by emerging artists, and contributes to the professional advancement of those artists. The Jerome Foundation supports programs in dance, literature, media arts, music, theater, performance art, the visual arts, multidisciplinary work and arts criticism. It provides financial assistance to non-profit arts organizations that support emerging creative artists who are residents of Minnesota and New York City; artists receive direct support from funded programs. Contact The Jerome Foundation, 125 Park Square Court, 400 Sibley Street, St. Paul, MN 55101-1928; 651-224-9431; Fax: 651-224-3439; {www.jeromefdn.org}.

$1,400 for Artistic Endeavors

The Artist Trust has provided more than $2.2 million in direct grant support to 1,112 Washington State promising musicians, writers, visual and craft artists, playwrights, choreographers, composers, performers and filmmakers. The GAP Program provides support for artist-generated projects, which can include

the development, completion or presentation of new work. GAP awards are open to artists of all disciplines. Contact Artist Trust, 1835 12th Avenue, Seattle, WA 98122-2437; 206-467-8734; Fax: 206-467-9633; {www.artisttrust.org}.

$20,000 Grants to be Artistic

Creative Capital provides grants to artists in four disciplines: visual arts, film/video arts, performing arts, and emerging art fields. They are looking for innovative and unique projects. Initial grants range from $5000 to $20,000, with grantees eligible for additional funding of more than $20,000 for a number of purposes. Applicants must be a U.S. citizen or permanent resident, at least 25 years old and have 5 years of professional working artist experience. Contact Creative Capital, 65 Bleecker Street, 7th Floor, New York, NY 10012; {http://creative-capital.org/what wedo/}, {info@creative-capital.org}.

Photography Grants up to $5,000

The Aaron Siskind Foundation provides grants of up to $5,000 to photographers using still-photography based media. Grant awards are based upon quality of work and the promise of future achievement. Funds must be used to support the artist's creative endeavors. Contact Aaron Siskind Foundation, c/o School of Visual Arts, MFA Photography, 209 East 23rd Street, New York, NY 10010; 609-348-5650; {www.aaronsiskind.org}; {info@aaronsiskind.org}.

$10,000 to Create and Display Artwork in the U.S.

Provides grants to artists in the amounts ranging from $500 to $10,000 for the production and display of interactive artworks in communities and venues across the United States and around the globe. Targets innovative interactive art: projects designed to be touched, handled, played with, and moved through in a public arena; art that solicits a collaborative response from its audience, even as it encourages collaboration between artists. Contact the Black Rock Arts Foundation, 1900 Third Street, 2nd Floor, San Francisco, CA 94107; 415-626-1248; {www. blackrockarts.org}, {info@blackrock arts.org}.

DISABILITIES

According to the Census Bureau, about 1 in 5 Americans have some kind of disability and 1 in 10 have a severe disability. Disability is no respecter of age, sex or race, but nevertheless, the likelihood of having a disability increases with age. More than three-quarters of Americans age 22-64 with disabilities do not receive public assistance. Americans with disabilities are at a critical disadvantage compared to other Americans, according to a survey from the National Organization on Disability. A Harris Poll found:

- ◆ 35% of people with disabilities reported being employed full or part time.
- ◆ Three times as many disabled people live in poverty.
- ◆ People with disabilities remain twice as likely to drop out of high school
- ◆ The disabled are twice as likely to have inadequate transportation.

Over 43 million Americans have disabilities of one kind or another, and many dream of supporting themselves with good paying jobs. The Federal Government has stepped in and funded programs across the country to help the disabled reach their goals by providing them with all kinds of services to get them on their way. The help available ranges from free information services, self help groups, free legal aid, free money for education, job training, transportation, equipment and mobility aids. And if you are denied aid, there are several free sources of legal help that can get you what you deserve.

If you do not find what you need in this section, you can investigate the following:

1. ***Check out the website {www.disability.gov}***
   DisabilityInfo.gov is the federal government's gateway to disability-related information and resources. You can find information on employment, housing, health, income support, technology, transportation and independent living.

2. ***State Vocational Rehabilitation Offices***:
   State Vocational Rehabilitation offices are the main entry point for services within your state. Services differ from state to state, but they can provide medical information, vocational training, adaptive equipment, business assistance, counseling, and more. To locate your state vocational office contact your state operator or check out the website {www.govengine.com}, or a listing can be found at {www.jan.wvu.edu/SBSES/ VOCREHAB.HTM}.

3. ***Financial Aid For People With Disabilities***:
   This is a free report written by the American Council on Education and provides a wealth of information on how to fund a college education. It takes you step-by-step through the financial aid process, explaining the types of aid available and what you will be expected to pay. What is great about this report is that it explains how to make sure that disability expenses are covered and what government agencies fit into the financial aid process. It details how disability benefits can be protected while in college and provides a list of scholarship information for those with disabilities. This report is available through the Education Resources Information Center (ERIS) at 800-LET-ERIC (538-3742) or online at {www.eric.ed.gov}.

4. ***Find All Federal Government Money Programs For Disabilities***

They are described in a book called the *Catalog of Federal Domestic Assistance*. This book is available at your local public library or the U.S. Government Printing Office {www.gpo.gov}. You can also search the content of the book for free on the web at {www.cfda.gov}.

5. Another great resource for information is the ***Council for Exceptional Children***.

Topics covered include all aspects of education and development of children with disabilities, current research, links to resources and more. Contact Council for Exceptional Children, 1110 N. Glebe Rd., Suite 300, Arlington, VA 22201; 888-CEC-SPED; 703-620-3660; {www.cec.sped. org}.

Free Job Training, Help And Money for the Disabled
We cannot emphasize enough the help that is available from your state. We have known people who have gotten $11,000 to start a business at home and $15,000 to finish a degree because they were suffering from low self-esteem. Terri Handshoe got her college education paid for, as well as had an interpreter and books covered during schooling. Sandy Smith got a $3,000 custom designed telephone system which allowed her to work for a major hotel chain. You can receive:

- Medical examinations and treatment
- Vocational evaluation, training and placement
- Assistive devices
- Transportation
- Occupational equipment
- Rehabilitation engineering
- Student services
- Financial assistance

☐ Housing assistance
☐ Home retrofitting

Your state Vocational Rehabilitation offices want to keep you a productive member of society, and they will do what it takes to get you on your way. If you are denied any of these services, you have several places you can turn for help. The first stop is your state Client Assistance Program. They will help you learn your rights and handle the appeal to get you what you need. They can take your appeal process from the first stages, all the way to the U.S. Supreme Court if necessary and it won't cost you a penny. Make sure you carefully read through the introduction and contact the programs listed below to learn more about what benefits are available to you, as well as your rights.

People Who Will Help You Find The Money

Disability Information

The clearinghouse responds to inquiries, provides referrals, and gives out information about services for individuals with disabilities at the national, state, and local levels. Free publications include:

- *Pocket Guide to Federal Help for Individuals with Disabilities*
- Brochure: *America needs us all, people with disabilities learning and earning.*
- *Clearinghouse on Disability Information* fact sheet

Contact Office of Special Education and Rehabilitation Services, U.S. Department of Education, 400 Maryland Ave., SW, Washington, DC 20202-7100; 202-245-7468; {www.ed.gov/about/offices/list/osers/index.html}.

Higher Education and Adult Training for People With Handicaps

The Higher Education and Adult Training for People with Handicaps (HEATH) Resource Center is a clearinghouse and information exchange center for resources on postsecondary education programs and the disabled. Topics include educational support services, policies, procedures, adaptations, and opportunities on American campuses, vocational-technical schools, adult education programs, independent living centers, and other training organizations after high school. Another clearinghouse, National

Information Center for Children and Youth with Disabilities, handles the concerns of younger disabled persons through secondary school. Contact George Washington University, HEATH Resource Center, 2121 K Street, NW, Suite 220, Washington, DC 20037; 202-973-0904, 800-544-3284; {www.health.gwu.edu}.

ERIC Clearinghouse on Disabilities and Gifted Education

Topics cover all aspects of the education and development of children with disabilities, those who are gifted or both; including identification, assessment, intervention, and enrichment information. Contact The Council for Exceptional Children, 1110 N. Glebe Rd., Suite 300, Arlington, VA 22201-5704; 888-CEC-SPED, 703-620-3660, TTY: 866-915-5000; {www.cec.sped.org/}.

National Association of Rehabilitation Providers and Agencies

A private membership organization of rehabilitation agencies and professionals. Refer inquiries to members. Contact National Association of Rehabilitation Providers and Agencies, 12100 Sunset Hills Road, Suite 120, Reston, VA, 20190-3221; 703-437-4377, Fax: 703-435-4390; {www.naranet.org/}.

National Clearinghouse of Rehabilitation Training Materials

This Clearinghouse can supply rehabilitation training materials in print or on video. Contact National Clearinghouse of Rehabilitation Training Materials, Oklahoma State University, 206 W. Sixth Street, Stillwater, OK 74078-4080; 800-223-5219, 405-744-2000; {www.nchrtm.okstate.edu}.

National Dissemination Center for Children with Disabilities

The Clearinghouse is an information and referral center that provides information on disabilities and disability related issues, as well as referrals to a wide network of specialists from agencies and organizations across the nation. They focus on children and youth ages birth to 22. Contact National Information Center for Children with Disabilities, P.O. Box 1492, Washington, DC 20013-1492; 800-695-0285, 202-884-8200; {www.nichcy.org/}.

National Rehabilitation Association

A private membership organization of professionals, vendors and suppliers of rehabilitation services, consumers and family members, students and professors. Contact National Rehabilitation Association, 633 South Washington St., Alexandria, VA 22314; 703-836-0850, 703-836-0849 (TDD); {www.nationalrehab.org}.

ABLEDATA

National database containing information on assistive technology and rehabilitation equipment for persons with disabilities. Contains more than 25,000 products from over 2,700 manufacturers and distributors. Publications include the *Assistive Technology Directory*; *ABLEDATA thesaurus*; *ADA Source book*; Fact sheets and computer guides. ABLEDATA, 8630 Fenton St., Suite 930, Silver Spring, MD 20910; 800-227-0216, TTY: 301-608-8912; {www.abledata.com}.

Rehabilitation Information Hotline

The National Rehabilitation Information Center, a library and information center on disability and rehabilitation, collects and disseminates the results of federally funded research projects. NARIC also maintains a vertical file of pamphlets and fact sheets published by other organizations. NARIC has documents on all aspects of disability and rehabilitation including, physical disabilities, mental retardation, psychiatric disabilities, independent living, employment, law and public policy and assistive technology. National Rehabilitation Information Center (NARIC), 4200 Forbes Blvd., Suite 202, Lanham MD 20706; 800-346-2742, 301-459-5900, TTY: 301-459-5984, Fax: 301-562-2401; {www.naric.com}.

Free Money for the Disabled Who Have Worked in the Past

If you're disabled and expect to be so for at least one year, and have worked long enough and recently enough under Social Security, you may be eligible for Social Security Disability Insurance Benefits (DIB). If you are found entitled to DIB, you will receive a monthly check in an amount based on your prior earnings.

If you start back to work after receiving DIB, the Social Security Administration will evaluate your work activity. You can earn $830 a month and remain eligible for benefits. These amounts will be adjusted annually based on increase in the national wage index. Social Security offers the disabled two programs, Social Security Disability Insurance and Supplemental Security Income.

Social Security Disability Insurance pays benefits to you and certain members of your family if you have worked long enough and paid Social Security taxes. Supplemental Security Income pays benefits based on financial need.

You can use their online Benefits Eligibility Screening Tool Kit to help determine which programs you are eligible to receive benefits. Benefits usually continue until you are able to work again on a regular basis. There are however, special rules called "work incentives" that can provide continued benefits as you head back to work. Their Disability Starter Kit provides adults and children with help getting ready for your disability interview or online application. Social Security Administration, 6401 Security Blvd., Baltimore, MD 21235-0001; 800-772-1213, TTY: 800-325-0778; {www.ssa.gov}.

Free and Low Cost Medical Insurance For the Disabled Who Have Worked In the Past

If you qualify for the Disability Insurance Benefits (DIB) described above, and have been receiving these payments for at least two years, you will also qualify to receive Medicare Part A for free which provides insurance coverage for hospitalization.

You can also receive Medicare Part B for a monthly premium of $78.20. This

provides insurance coverage for your doctor visits and testing services. This is the same Medicare coverage those over 65 receive. Remember, there are deductibles and limits of coverage. For instance, doctor visits are covered after you meet the $110 deductible for the year, after which Medicare will pay 80% of the approved rate, and you are responsible for the other 20%. To apply for this medical insurance or to receive the *Medicare Handbook* which provides detailed information on coverage, contact Medicare Hotline Health Care Finance Administration, 7500 Security Blvd., Baltimore, MD 21244-1850; 877-267-2323, TTY: 866-226-1819, 410-786-3000; {http://cms.hhs.gov}.

Cash For Dependents Of the Disabled

Social Security Administration Hotline 800-772-1213
If you are eligible for Disability Insurance Benefits (DIB) described above, your dependents (wife, husband, children, or and in some cases, grandchildren) may also be eligible for payments on your record. To find out if your dependent is eligible, contact the hotline listed above.

Money For The Disabled Who Have Not Worked In The Past

If you are disabled but have not done enough work under Social Security for Disability Insurance Benefits (DIB), you may still be eligible to receive Supplemental Security Income (SSI) benefits if your income and resources are low enough. Contact Social Security Administration, 6401 Security Blvd., Baltimore, MD 21235-0001; 800-772-1213, TTY: 800-325-0778; {www.ssa.gov}.

What To Do When Benefits Are Denied

If you are denied any of the above mentioned Social Security cash benefits — which often happens regardless of the disability or its severity — you can get free legal help to appeal the Social Security Administration's decision on your application. Contact your state or local Department of Welfare and request the name and address of the nearest Legal Services Corporation (LSC) program, and also contact your nearest State Client Assistance Program (CAP) office. Both programs offer low income individuals free legal help and representation in appealing application decisions.

The CAP program will either provide you with free legal help and representation for your appeal or they will help you find such aid. Unlike legal help offered under the Legal Services Corporation, CAP services are not determined by your income. On the chance that neither of these agencies are able to help you, contact the Disability Rights Education and Defense Fund (DREDF) at {www.dredf.org} or 510-644-2555.

Free Information for Employers Who Hire the Handicapped

The Job Accommodation Network (JAN) brings together free information about practical ways employers can make accommodations for employees and job applicants with disabilities. The Network offers comprehensive information on methods and available equipment that have proven effective for a wide range of accommodations, including names, addresses, and phone numbers of appropriate resources. They also provide information regarding the Americans with Disabilities Act 800-232-9675. Job Accommodation Network (JAN), West VA University, P.O. Box 6080, Morgantown, WV 26506-6080; 800-526-7234 (V/TTY), 304-293-7186, Fax: 304-293-5407; {http://janweb.icdi.wvu.edu}. {jan@jan.wvu.edu}.

Free Money for Education and Job Training

If your disability stops you from being able to keep a full time job or from being able to competitively look for a job, your state's Office of Vocational Rehabilitation (OVR) can help. OVR can give you up to $6,000 each year for job training or education. You can use this grant money, which you do not have to repay, to cover any expenses related to your training or education, including tuition and fees, travel expenses, books, supplies, equipment (computers, motorized wheelchairs, etc.), food allowances, tutoring fees, photocopies, and so on. Contact your state's Office of Vocational Rehabilitation.

Help For the Handicapped to Find or Create a Job

Your state Office of Vocational Rehabilitation (OVR) also acts as an employment agency for the disabled and can contact employers for you who have looked favorably on hiring the disabled in the past. OVR will act as a liaison between you and a prospective employer and help them create a job for you by providing needed disability-related job equipment, provide needed transportation or other mobility equipment, or by providing any other help you might need to be able to work at a job for which you're qualified. For example, OVR has provided books in Braille and Braille-to-speech

conversion equipment, and computer-robotics equipment that have allowed disabled individuals to work at a variety of jobs. Contact your state's Office of Vocational Rehabilitation.

Help For the Handicapped Already On the Job

If you are working and become disabled or handicapped, your state Office of Vocational Rehabilitation (OVR) can provide you with the equipment, transportation, education, training and other help you might need to keep your job. For example, many times an unexpected disability can put someone in a wheelchair. OVR may be able to provide you with a motorized wheelchair so you can continue in your current job. Contact your state Office of Vocational Rehabilitation for more information.

Medical Help For the Disabled/Handicapped

Your state Office of Vocational Rehabilitation can pay for (or help you pay for) any medical testing or treatment that is expected to help you, as a handicapped or disabled individual, have a more healthy, prosperous and independent life. Contact your state Office of Vocational Rehabilitation for more information.

What To Do When OVR Benefits Are Denied

The first place to start when your state Office of Vocational Rehabilitation denies you handicap or disability benefits is your nearest state Client Assistance Program (CAP) office. CAP is a free information, referral, and legal service that helps disabled or handicapped individuals appeal a denial by OVR (or another agency). For a variety of reasons, it is not uncommon for a disabled individual to be turned down for services by OVR even when he/she is in fact eligible to receive them. It is often helpful to get a photocopy of Chapter 34 of the *Code of Federal Regulations of the U.S. Department of Education* from your local or county library. These are the federal guidelines that each state OVR must follow when determining eligibility. This part of the code is only a few pages in length and can help you explain to the Client Assistance Program officer why you believe you are eligible even though you've been denied. CAP can take your appeal process from the first stages all the way to the U.S. Supreme Court if necessary — and it won't cost you a penny.

A CAP Specialist can help in many ways by:
♦ Providing assistance and advocacy services to help you resolve any
♦ problems you may have in applying for or receiving rehabilitation services;
♦ Explaining your rights and your responsibilities throughout the rehabilitation process;
♦ Helping you to communicate your concerns to DORS staff;
♦ Giving you accurate information on rehabilitation programs and services;
♦ Explaining DORS policies and procedures to you;
♦ Helping you when a service has been denied or when you are not satisfied with a service provided;
♦ Providing legal services when necessary to represent you in a formal hearing; and
♦ Providing information about your employment rights under the Americans with Disabilities Act.

It is also sometimes helpful to contact the state Office of Vocational Rehabilitation (OVR) itself and make the executive director aware of your circumstances. When it appears that progress via CAP is stalled or has been dragging on for months, it can also be very helpful to contact the regional commissioner of the Rehabilitation Services Administration (RSA), a branch of the Office of Special Education Programs of the U.S. Department of Education. RSA is responsible for overseeing and funding the state OVR agencies and is generally receptive to a short explanatory phone call and letter from those who believe they can clearly show that they have been wrongly denied OVR services. If they think you've got a case, they'll contact the OVR in question and make sure that they review your application more favorably.

Contact the U.S. Department of Education, Office of Special Education and Rehabilitative Services, RSA, Washington, DC 20202: 202-245-7468, and ask for the address and phone number of the regional commissioner for the ED-OSERS-RSA office serving your area, or check the website {www.ed.gov/about/offices/list/osers}.

Free Legal Help and Information Services For the Handicapped

If you think you've been wrongly denied benefits or discriminated against because of a disability or handicap, the Client Assistance Program (CAP) will help you fight for your rights when you're denied various types of disability benefits from any disability program. They will help you directly and/or put you in contact with the agencies that can help you. Contact your local CAP office.

More Free Legal Help for the Disabled

A national nonprofit law and policy center, the Disability Rights Education and Defense Fund (DREDF) can provide you with direct legal representation and act as co-counsel in cases of disability based discrimination. They also seek to educate legislators and policy makers on issues affecting the rights of people with disabilities.

Contact Disability Rights Education and Defense Fund (DREDF), 2212 Sixth St., Berkeley, CA 94710; 510-644-2555; {www.dredf.org}.

Help to Start a Business

If you dream of owning your own business, but need a little help, call the Small Business Administration (SBA). The SBA can help you think through your business plan, and give you some direction to help your business grow. Contact SBA Answer Desk, 6302 Fairview Rd., Suite 300, Charlotte, NC 28210; 800-8-ASK-SBA, TTY: 703-344-6640; {www.sba.gov/answerdesk. html}, {answerdesk@sba.gov}.

Plan for Achieving Self-Support (PASS)

Many people with disabilities want to work, and you're probably one of them. But maybe you need to go back to school before you can get a job. Or, maybe you'd like to start your own business, but you don't have the money. Whatever your work goal may be, a PASS can help you reach it. A PASS lets you set aside money and/or other things you own to help you reach your goal. For example, you could set aside money to start a business or to go to school or to get training for a job.

Your goal must be a job that will produce sufficient earnings to reduce your dependency on Supplemental Security Income (SSI) payments. A PASS is meant to help you acquire those items, services or skills you need so that you can compete with able-bodied persons for an entry level job in a professional, business or trade environment. If you have graduated from college or a trade/technical school, they usually consider you capable of obtaining such a position without the assistance of a PASS. You can contact your local Social Security office to find out whether a PASS is appropriate for you.

5 States Give Money For Disability Insurance

California Disability Insurance

California State Disability Insurance (SDI) is a partial wage-replacement insurance plan for California workers. The SDI program is State-mandated, and funded through employee payroll deductions. SDI provides affordable, short-term benefits to eligible workers who suffer a loss of wages when they are unable to work due to a NON WORK-RELATED illness or injury, or a medically disabling condition from pregnancy or childbirth. The majority of California employees, approximately 12 million workers, are covered by the SDI program. Disability is defined as any mental or physical illness or injury which prevents you from performing your regular or customary work. This includes elective surgery; illness or injury resulting from pregnancy, childbirth, or related conditions; or inability to work due to a written order of quarantine from a state or local health officer. California Disability Insurance, Employment Development Department, 800 Capitol Mall, MIC 83, Sacramento, CA 95814; 800-480-3287, 800-563-2441 TTY; {www.edd.ca.gov/direp/diind.htm}.

Hawaii Temporary Disability Insurance

The state of Hawaii Temporary Disability Insurance (TDI) provides wage replacement benefits for non-work related illness or injury. Workers must have been in covered employment with any Hawaii employer for at least 14 weeks with 20 or more hours each week and earned at least $400 during a 52 week period. You may obtain a claim from your employer. Contact State of Hawaii Department of Labor and Industrial Relations, Disability Compensation Division, Temporary Disability Insurance, P.O. Box 3769, Honolulu, HI 96812-3769; 808-586-9161; {http://dlir.state.hi.us/}, {http://dlir.state.hi.us/forms/dc_1.pdf}.

New Jersey Temporary Disability Benefits

Under the New Jersey Temporary Disability Benefits Law, cash benefits are payable when you cannot work because of sickness or injury NOT caused by your job. Workers who become disabled within 14 days of their last day of work in covered New Jersey employment may be covered for disability insurance under the State Plan. Contact New Jersey Department of Labor, Division of Temporary Disability Insurance, P.O. Box 387, Trenton, NJ 08625-0387; 609-292-7060; {www.state.nj.us/labor/tdi/tdiindex.html}.

New York State Insurance Fund

The New York State Insurance Fund (NYSIF) is a non-profit agency of the State of New York consisting of The Disability Benefits Fund, which insures against disabling off-the-job sickness or injury sustained by employees. Employers with one or more employees are subject to the provisions of the New York State Disability Benefits Law. The law provides for the payment of cash benefits to employees who become disabled because of injuries or sicknesses which have no connection to their employment, and for disabilities arising from pregnancies. workers' compensation cases, the cost of medical treatment is borne by the insurance carrier. Contact New York State Insurance Fund, Office of Temporary and Disability Assistance, 225 Oak Street, Buffalo, NY 14203; 866-NYSIFDB; {www.nysif.com/disability/aboutdisabilitybenefitsPol.asp}.

Rhode Island Disability Insurance

If you become ill or injured in Rhode Island and a doctor's examination shows that you cannot work for at least 7 consecutive days, you should apply for TDI benefits as soon as possible. To file for Temporary Disability Insurance (TDI), simply complete a TDI application form and mail it to

Rhode Island Department of Labor and Training. Be sure to print or write carefully and answer all the questions completely and accurately. You can get an application form at any office of the Rhode Island Department of Labor and Training. You can also call 401-462-8420 to have an application sent directly to you. You can download an application at {www.dlt.ri.gov/tdi}. To be eligible for TDI, you must meet certain medical and earnings requirements. If you suffer a non-work related disability, apply for benefits. The office will determine if you qualify based on all facts relating to your claim and notify you as quickly as possible. Contact Rhode Island Department of Labor and Training, Temporary Disability Insurance, P.O. Box 20070, Cranston, RI 02920; 401-462-8420, Fax: 401-462-8466; {www.dlt.ri.gov/tdi}.

Free Pet Care At Veterinary Teaching Hospitals

The International Association of Assistance Dog Partners (IAADP), a cross-disability advocacy organization, provides information on veterinary teaching hospitals and what they offer

disabled clients with assistance dogs. After surveying 26 hospitals, the IAADP found nineteen hospitals which have adopted official policies to reduce the cost of health care for assistance dogs.

Other veterinary teaching hospitals provide funds for indigent clients or offer help on a case by case basis. Contact the International Association of Assistance Dog Partners (IAADP), 38691 Filly Drive, Sterling Heights, MI 48310; 586-826-3938; {www.iaadp.org}; {info@iaadp.org}.

More Health Care Assistance For Disabled Clients With Assistance Dogs

Bayer, Fort Dodge Animal Health, Friskies, and Nutramax Laboratories, in cooperation with the International Association of Assistance Dog Partners (IAADP), provides grants to subsidize the veterinary care of assistance dogs. Grants are available for disabled clients unable to pay for expensive procedures required to treat and keep their dogs in full working condition. Membership in IAADP is required to apply for the subsidized vet care. Members also qualify for the following: a free AVID microchip and registration in PETtrac; free enrollment in the AKC Companion Recovery program; an Emergency Recovery Kit; plus various publications, brochures and newsletters. Veterinarians who are working with an IAADP member in need of subsidized pet care should call the Bayer Animal Hospital at 800-422-9874. Contact International Association of Assistance Dog Partners (IAADP), 38691 Filly Drive, Sterling Heights, MI 48310; 586-826-3938; {www.iaadp.org}; {info@iaadp.org}.

Assistance Dogs and Training Provided Free of Charge to the Blind (Valued at $5,700)

Pilot Dogs, Inc.

Pilot Dogs, Inc. is an organization providing guide dogs to the blind. The organization not only provides their trained dogs free of charge, they also provide four weeks of training so that the new owner is equipped to fully utilize and care for his or her new dog. The dog, the transportation to and from the Pilot Dog training school, the room and board during the four weeks of training and all necessary equipment are provided free of charge. Pilot Dogs pays for the $5,700 service. Contact Pilot Dogs, Inc., 625 West Town St., Columbus, OH 43215; 614-221-6367; Fax: 614-221-1577; {www.pilotdogs. org/}.

The Guide Dog Foundation for the Blind

The Guide Dog Foundation for the Blind, Inc. offers free guide dogs to legally blind individuals of high school age or older. Individuals who qualify for the program travel to New York for 25 days of training with their new guide dogs. The training and transportation to and from the school are also provided free of charge. The free travel applies to applicants residing in the U.S., as well as those from Canada and Mexico. Contact the Guide Dog Foundation For The Blind, 371 East Jericho Turnpike, Smithtown, NY 11787; 800-548-4337; 631-930-9000; Fax: 631-361-5192; {www. guidedog.org}.

Southeastern Guide Dogs

Any legally blind person, 16 or older may apply for a free guide dog from Southeastern Guide Dogs, Inc. Also included free of charge are the 26-day training course (with room and board) and the dog harness. Southeastern Guide Dogs makes a lifetime commitment to the dog and its new owner and provides follow-up visits each year or as often as necessary. There is an outreach program where those who qualify, can receive in-home training. The training with this program lasts 2 weeks. If you live in the North or South Carolina areas, call the outreach center at 704-721-5000. For those in the Georgia area, call 404-814-0650, and all others should call the main office at 800-944-3647. Contact Southeastern Guide Dogs, Inc., 4210 77th St. East, Palmetto, FL 34221; 941-729-5665; 800-944-DOGS (3647); Fax: 941-729-6646; {www. guidedogs.org}.

$15,000 Service Dogs Available Free Of Charge

Support Dogs, Inc. offers free service dogs to eligible individuals with disabilities. The standard skills of the service dogs include opening heavy doors, loading wheelchairs into vehicles, pulling wheelchairs up inclines and over long distances, retrieving dropped or distant objects, and other tasks of daily living. The service dogs fall into the following categories: Street Certified, Certified Facility, Home Certified and Certified Home-Based, and Pediatric Companion. Support Dogs has programs that cover three different assistance areas; Service, TOUCH (Therapy), and Pediatric. Contact Support Dogs, Inc., 11645 Lilburn Park Road, St. Louis, MO 63146; 314-997-2325; {www.supportdogs.org}.

Canine Companions

Canine Companions for Independence (CCI) is a nonprofit organization that provides trained service and hearing dogs and continued support to people with disabilities who want to increase their independence with the aid of a dog. People interested in receiving a dog must pay a $100 training fee, which covers everything the dog will take home. Contact CCI, National Headquarters, P.O. Box 446, Santa Rosa, CA 95402; 800-572-2275; 707-577-1770; 866-224-3647; TDD: 707-

577-1756; {www.caninecompanions. org}.

Canine Working Companions

A regional group serving New York State is Canine Working Companions providing specially trained dogs to assist people with disabilities. They also work diligently to educate the public about the rights of the disabled with companion assistance animals. They are funded through donations and memberships. The dogs are raised and trained by the organization. There is a $25 application fee. They serve the state of New York except for the city of New York and the Buffalo areas. Contact Canine Working Companions, P.O. Box 2128, Syracuse, NY 13220-2128; 315-656-3301; {www. canineworkingcompanions.org}.

Assistance Dogs for the Disabled

"PAWS with a Cause" is a national charitable and non-profit organization, which trains dogs to assist the disabled. Since 49 million Americans are disabled in some way — and only

3% of the disabled are blind — these animals are more than just "seeing eye dogs." They are trained to help individuals with cerebral palsy, muscular dystrophy, spinal cord injuries, epilepsy, hearing impairment, vision loss and a host of other disabilities.

A disabled person seeking an assistance dog sends an application to PAWS, which then assesses the needs of the applicant. Once an applicant is accepted into the program, PAWS begins the fund-raising process to secure the financial support needed for the training of the assistance dog. Recipients of assistance dogs are not charged a fee of any kind; they are only encouraged to take an active role in the fund-raising process. Once the training is complete, full ownership of the assistance dog is transferred to the disabled recipient.

If you are not disabled but want to help this commendable cause, you can enroll in the Foster Puppy Program to raise a puppy until it begins its assistance training. Contact PAWS WITH A CAUSE, National Headquarters, 4646 South Division, Wayland, MI 49348; 800-253-PAWS; 616-877-7297; Fax: 616-877-0248; {www.pawswithacause.org}.

Trained Dogs - Valued at $12,000 - Given Free To Disabled Youth

Disabled children ages 12 and older can now discover why dogs are called "man's best friend." Trained assistance dogs can aid seriously disabled children- those with muscular dystrophy, cerebral palsy, spina bifida, as well as other disabilities- in opening and closing doors, pulling wheelchairs, pushing elevator buttons, alerting a parent at night, or going for help in an emergency.

Loving Paws Assistance Dogs is a non-profit organization, which trains and provides dogs to care for disabled children. Although the trained dogs are valued at $30,000 each, recipients are asked to pay only a small application fee and the dog is given free of charge.

Contact Loving Paws Assistance Dogs, P.O. Box 12005, Santa Rosa, CA 95406; 707-586-0798; Fax: 707-586-0799; {www.lovingpaws.com}; {info@lovingpaws.com}.

372 Sources To Pay Emergency Expenses
Not sure where to turn or what resources exist for you? Bravekids.org has put together a resource directory that lists over 372 sources for financial and other types of assistance for those with disabled children or adults or low-income families in need of help. It could be anything from paying your utility bill to respite care or medical expenses. Contact {www.bravekids. org}.

Financial Benefits For Caregivers
The Alexandria Division of Social Services offers financial benefits for caregivers of children and adolescents with disabilities. Check your local, city, county or state Department of Social Services for financial benefits for which you may qualify if you care for someone who is disabled.

Business Help To The Disabled
People with disabilities and chronic health conditions are starting businesses at twice the rate as non-disabled people. This is due to the fact

that the unemployment rate for the disabled is at a staggering 70%! Self-employment can provide the flexibility and adaptations necessary for you to be a success. The U.S. Small Business Administration provides millions of dollars each year to support the initiatives of micro businesses. Check with the SBA office closest to you for more information about services available through SBA. To reach that office either call 1-800-U-ASK-SBA or log on to www.sba.gov. In addition, state vocational rehabilitation programs and other government and private organizations provide a variety of services to aspiring entrepreneurs with disabilities. The Main source of information is the Small Business and Self-Employment Service (SBSES) of the Office of Disability Employment Policy of the U.S. Department of Labor. This office provides information, counseling and referrals about self-employment and small business ownership opportunities. You can learn about starting and managing a business, disability issues such as social security and PASS plans, and more. All this information is free. Contact Small Business and Self-Employment Service, Job Accommodation Network, P.O. Box 6080, Morgantown, WV 26506; 800-526-72234; {www.jan.wvu.edu/SBSES}.

$30,000 For Job Seekers With Disabilities
The Federal Government has funded programs around the country to help people with disabilities get and keep jobs. The programs include money for education, job training, living expenses, transportation, equipment and mobility aids. Contact your state Office of Vocational Rehabilitation and the Client Assistance Programs

located in your state capital. There are also some programs at the Social Security Administration at 800-772-1213; {www.ssa.gov}. Contact: Clearinghouse on Disability Information, Office of Special Education and Rehabilitation Services, U.S. Dept. of Education, Room 3132 Switzer Bldg., Washington, DC 20202; 202-205-8241; {www.ed.gov/offices/OSERS/index.html}.

Extra $1,000 For Seniors and Disabled

Each year over 3 million eligible seniors and people with disabilities fail to apply for a little-known program that will give them over $1,000 extra in their Social Security check. That's how much the government deducts for Medicare Part B payments. The program is called Qualified Medicare Beneficiaries Plan, or Specified Low-Income Medicare Beneficiaries Plan. To learn more contact your local Social Security Office at 800-772-1213. You can also contact the Medicare Hotline and request the publication Guide to Health Insurance for People with Medicare. Contact Medicare Hotline at 800-MEDICARE or online at {www.medicare.gov}.

Cheap Health Insurance For Disabled Workers

A change in the Balanced Budget Act of 1997 allows states to offer Medicaid to individuals who are working and who have a disability. Prior to this, states could only offer Medicaid to people with disabilities who were NOT working. The income limit goes up to $40,000 a year. Contact your state Department of Health to identify your Medicaid office. You can also check out the website of the Bazelon Center at {www.bazelon.org}.

$10,000 To Buy A Van or Talking Computer

People with disabilities now have a place to turn to learn everything they need to know about how the latest technology can improve their lives. It can be a specially equipped van, a talking computer, a special kitchen or eating aid, or adaptive toys for children. A project funded by the U.S. Department of Education called Technical Assistance Project has an office in each state that can provide information services, equipment loan programs, funding information, and loans. Contact your state Office of Social Services or Vocational Rehabilitation. Contact Rehabilitation Engineering and Assistive Technology Society of North America (RESNA), 1700 North Moore St., #1540, Arlington, VA 22209; 703-424-6686; 703-524-6639 (TTY); {www.resna.org}.

Get $15,000 In Work Incentive Assistance For Disabled Beneficiaries

Did you know you can get deductions to your income that increase your benefits? Maybe you received a free computer or have work done for free by a friend for your business. These and other items or services can actually help you to sustain or increase your benefits. Find out how by contacting the Social Security

Administration, Office of Public Inquiries, Windsor Park Building, 6401 Security Blvd., Baltimore, MD 21235; 800-772-1213; {www.ssa.gov/work/ResourcesToolkit/workincentive schart.html#IRWE}.

$$$ To Attend College With A Disability

Funding provides students with disabilities a quality postsecondary education. The Demonstration Projects to Ensure Students With Disabilities Receive a Quality Higher Education support technical assistance and professional development activities for faculty and administrators in institutions of higher education to improve their ability to provide a quality postsecondary education for students with disabilities. Grantees in the program will develop innovative, effective, and efficient teaching methods and other strategies to enhance the skills and abilities of postsecondary faculty and administrators in working with disabled students. Grantees will also disseminate information from their grant activities to other institutions of higher education. Contact the U.S. Department of Education, OPE, 1990 K St., N.W., Washington, DC 20006-8526; 202-502-7808; {www.ed.gov/programs/disabilities/index.html}.

$210,000 To Hire Employees With Disabilities

The Projects with Industry program supplies grants for private industry to provide job training and placement, as well as career advancement services, to create and expand job and career opportunities for individuals with disabilities. Contact the U.S. Department of Education, OSERS, 400 Maryland Ave., S.W., Rm. 5006, PCP, Washington, DC 20202-2647; 202-

245-7569; {www.ed.gov/programs/rsapwi/index.html}.

$8,000 Toward Independent Living Services For The Blind

Through the U.S. Department of Education, state agencies can apply to receive an average of $498,000 toward independent living services for older individuals with severe blindness. Funding is to be used to provide such things as eyeglasses and other visual aids, services and equipment to enhance mobility and self-care, training in Braille, teaching services in daily living activities. Contact the U.S. Department of Education, OSERS, 400 Maryland Ave., S.W., Rm. 5055, PCP, Washington, DC 20202-2741; 202-245-7273; {www.ed.gov/programs/rsailob/index.html}.

Free Sign Language Training

Through the Rehabilitation Services Administration, up to $160,000 in funding is available to organizations to train interpreters for the deaf. Contact the U.S. Department of Education, OSERS Rehabilitation Services Administration, 400 Maryland Ave., S.W., Washington, DC 20202-2736; 202-205-9393, 202-401-3664 TDD; {www.ed.gov/about/offices/list/osers/index.html}.

Up to $2,000 for Disabled Youths to Volunteer

Win up to $2,000 to fund a project for National Youth Service Day and beyond! The Clay Aiken Able to Serve Awards program offered by Youth Service America and The Bubel Aiken Foundation provides grants up to $1,000 each to young people, between the ages of 5 and 22 with developmental disabilities to plan and carry out service and/or volunteer projects. An additional $1000 may be awarded for projects that continue beyond the National Youth Services Day timeframe. Contact Clay Aiken

ABLE to SERVE Awards, Youth Service America, 1101 15th Street, NW, Suite 200, Washington, D.C. 20005; 202-296-2992; Fax: 202-296-4030; {www.ysa.org/awards/award_ grant.cfm}; {info@ysa.org}.

EDUCATION

Every year of education means an average of an extra $200,000 worth of life time earnings. And education is the key to competing in our fast changing society and staying productive throughout your entire life. So go get more education no matter how much you have now, and here's the money to do it.

There is no way that this book, or any other directory of scholarships, can contain every single scholarship available no matter what they say. There are tens of thousands of scholarships available for higher education and they keep adding and changing as we speak. The book that we produce that has the most on scholarships is "Free Money To Change Your Life" and is available at 1-800-955-POWER or {www.lesko.com}.

The programs listed below are a collection of the more useful scholarships and money programs available for people of any age to go to college either full or part time.

If you do not find what you need in this section you can find additional scholarships by investigating the following:

1) ***Find All Federal Government Money Programs For Education......***
They are described in a book called the Catalog of Federal Domestic Assistance. This book is available at your local public library or the U.S. Government Printing Office {www.gpo.gov}. You can also search the contents of this book for free on the web at {www.cfda.gov}.

2) *Find All State Money Programs For Education...*

There are close to 400 programs worth almost $3 billion dollars in financial aid available through all 50 states. Did you know that there are state money programs which:
Pay for a singing degree?

- ◆ Give you money to study wildlife?
- ◆ Give you $2000 to go to vocational school?
- ◆ Pay for your nursing, teaching or law degree?
- ◆ Give you $7000 to study marine sciences?

Every state has grants and other money available for higher education. Look for the state office of higher education. You can find them by dialing 411 and asking for your state capitol operator or by going to the web at {www.govengine.com} and clicking on your state.

3) *Find Money For College If You Are Over 55*

If you are over 55 you will certainly be eligible for most of the programs listed below, but you should also be aware that there are special programs for seniors starting at age 55 or 60. These programs are at most state supported colleges and community colleges and they offer courses and even degrees for free or for a very low cost. Contact all the state supported colleges in your area for their requirements.

4) *Find All The Non-Government Money Programs*

There are dozens of scholarship directories available including this one. And because one directory cannot possibly have everything, it is better to have a collection of scholarship directories, but this can become too expensive. So, you can go to your local library as they have the latest edition of enough directories that can help you, or you can go into a local large bookstore that has a coffee shop and buy a cup of $3.00 coffee and spend an afternoon at the bookstore looking thru all the books. You are only going to get a few scholarships out of any one book. Copy down the info and do your follow up. This way, for the price of a cup of coffee, you have access to hundreds of dollars worth of directories. Most of these big book stores have big comfy chairs to encourage you to spend time there using their books. Such a deal.

5) *Free Research To Find More Money*
This is a free information clearinghouse that has free research either on the web or on the phone on any education topic. For example, you can search for information sources on topics such as scholarships or financial aid for graduate students. What do you have to lose? It's FREE. Contact: Education Resources Information Center (ERIC), 800-LET-ERIC (538-3742), {www.eric.ed.gov}.

No job is safe anymore. Companies seem to hire and fire for no reason at all. But if you get fired and have the right education and training you can go across the street and get a better job than the one you lost. Education is power.

$50,000 To Go Back To College

No matter what your age, it is never to late to go back to school. There are actually more people on college campuses today over 35 than there are 18 and 19 year olds. And if you are 55 or 60, there are over 350 colleges where you can go back to school for free or next to nothing. It is the best investment of your time and money you can make in this country. All the good jobs require brainpower. The more brainpower you have, the more money you are worth in the job market. A friend of mine recently completed her masters and increased her salary by $12,000 per year. That is a minimum of an extra $12,000 per year for the next 30 years of her working life: $360,000. You cannot make anywhere near that kind of return on your investment on Wall Street, at your bank, or even in real estate. To find money for college check the following: 1) For all federal money programs, look at a book called the Catalog of Federal Domestic Assistance, published by the U.S. Government Printing Office and available in most public libraries, on online at {www.cfda.gov}. 2) For state money programs, contact your state department of higher education located in your state capital, and 3) For private and foundation scholarship money, go to a good book store or a public library and look at four or five of the biggest scholarship books you can find. No one source has everything, so check as many as you can and apply everywhere.

Get Your GED At Age at 94

If Cecil Smith of California can get his GED when he was 80 years old after he dropped out of junior high school, anyone can do it. The National Institute for Literacy is a government organization that will find you free help in preparing and taking your High School Equivalency Diploma tests. You can search for help near you online at {www.literacydirectory.org}, or call them at 1-800-228-8813.

Get Your GED

Bill Cosby, Mary Lou Retton, and 10 million other people famous and not so famous have obtained their GED. GED stands for General Educational Development, and consists of tests in five different areas. Once you pass these tests, you earn your GED diploma, which is the equivalent of a high school diploma. GED tests are given all across the U.S. You can contact your local Board of Education to learn about the tests and any adult education classes they may offer to prepare you. You can also contact the GED Information Hotline at 800-62-MY-GED. The tests are administered by American Council on Education, CALEC, One Dupont Circle, NW, Suite 250, Washington, DC 20036; 202-939-9490; {www.acenet.edu/calec/ged}.

350 Colleges You Can Go To For Free If You're 55-60

Believe it or not, more than 350 colleges and universities all across the country have special programs for seniors who are interested in going back to school. This often means free or low-cost tuition, discounts on fees and books, and even special deals on housing. Anyone interested should contact the school they wish to attend to find out how to apply for a discount

or waiver. Some limitations and restrictions may apply.

$37,000 Per Year To Get A Grad Degree

Through the STAR (Science to Achieve Results) fellowship program, get your graduate degree in a variety of environmental disciplines, including engineering, public health, and ecological sciences. You can have your tuition paid and have a nice stipend to live on! Contact the U.S. Environmental Protection Agency, Ariel Rios Building, 1200 Pennsylvania Avenue, NW, Washington, D.C. 20460; 202-564-6923; {http://es.epa.gov/ncer/rfa/current/2004_grad_fellow.html}.

$48,000 Per Year To Get A Grad Degree

Through the U.S. Department of Homeland Security (DHS) Graduate Fellowship program, get your graduate degree in the physical, biological, social, or behavioral sciences — including science policy, engineering, mathematics, or computer science. Have your tuition covered and have money to live on! You must have career and employment goals aligned with the mission and objectives of the DHS, but you are not required to accept a position with them following graduation. Contact the U.S. Department of Homeland Security, 245 Murray Drive, SW., University

Programs, Washington, DC 20528; 202-282-8000; {www.orau.gov/dhsed/04grad.htm}.

$22,000 Per Year To Get A Degree

Through the U.S. Department of Homeland Security (DHS) Undergraduate Scholarships for Rising Juniors program, get your degree in the physical, biological, social, or behavioral sciences — including science policy, engineering, mathematics, or computer science. The program will pay you tuition and give you money to live on! You must have career and employment goals aligned with the mission and objectives of the DHS, but you are not required to accept a position with them following graduation. Contact the U.S. Department of Homeland Security, 245 Murray Drive, SW., University Programs, Washington, DC 20528; 202-282-8000; {www.orau.gov/dhsed/04ugrad.htm}.

$1,000 Scholarships For Two Students In Every High School

Find out how high school students can get $1,000 toward college through the Presidential Freedom Scholarship for outstanding service to the community. All they need to do is volunteer 100 hours of their time within a one year period. To apply, contact Presidential Freedom Scholarships, 1150 Connecticut Avenue, NW, Suite 1100, Washington, DC 20036; 866-291-7700; {www.nationalservice.org/scholarships/}.

$20,000 A Year To Study Health-Related Research

Through the National Institutes of Health (NIH) Undergraduate Scholarship Program, eligible undergraduates will receive $20,000 a year in grants, invaluable research experience, and a guaranteed position with the renowned NIH after graduation. To find out how you can be a recipient, contact NIH, Office of Loan Repayment and Scholarship, 2 Center Drive, Room 2E24, MSC 0230, Bethesda, MD 20892-0230; 888-352-3001; {http://ugsp.info.nih.gov/exesumfaq.htm}, {http://12.46.245.173/pls/portal30/CATALOG.PROGRAM_TEXT_RPT.SHOW?p_arg_names=prog_nbr&p_arg_values=93.187}.

$7,000 + Spending Money To Study Health Care

The Nursing Workforce Diversity project provides student stipends, pre-entry preparation, and retention activities. Stipends are $250 per month to eligible full-time project students. Scholarships are limited to a maximum of $7,000 per student per year for upper division nursing students. Contact the Division of Nursing, U.S. Department of Health and Human Services, 5600 Fishers Lane, Room 9-35, Rockville, Maryland 20857; 301-443-5688; {http://12.46.245.173/pls/portal30/CATALOG.PROGRAM_TEXT_RPT.SHOW?p_arg_names=prog_nbr&p_arg_values=93.178}.

$1,200 And Air Fare For D.C. Interns

The Morris K. Udall Native American Congressional Internship program offers Native American or Alaskan Native students ten-week internship in Washington, D.C., working full-time in congressional offices or federal agencies. The program provides airfare to and from Washington, D.C., lodging at George Washington University, and per diem to cover meals, transportation and incidentals. In addition, a $1,200 stipend at the conclusion of the internship is awarded. Contact The Morris K. Udall Foundation, 130 South Scott Avenue, Tucson, AZ 85701-1922; 520-670-5529; {www.udall.gov}. {http://12.46.245.173/pls/portal30/CATALOG.PROGRAM_TE XT_RPT.SHOW?p_arg_names=prog_nbr&p_arg_values=85.402}.

$24,000 To Study Environmental Policy

The Morris K. Udall Fellowship Program awards two Ph.D. dissertation fellowships of $24,000 to students whose work is in the areas of environmental public policy or environmental conflict resolution. Recipients must be in the final, writing year of their Ph.D. work and must submit a copy of their dissertation to the Udall Foundation at the end of the award year. Contact the Morris K. Udall Dissertation Fellowship Program, South Scott Avenue, Tucson, AZ 85701-1922; 520-670-5609; {www.udall.gov}, {http://12.46.245.173/pls/portal30/CATALOG.PROGR AM_TEXT_RPT.SHOW?p_arg_name s=prog_nbr&p_arg_values=85.401}.

$5,000 To Study The Environment

The Morris K. Udall Scholarship Program awards grants to young Americans pursuing environmental careers and to Native Americans and Alaska Natives pursuing careers in health care and tribal public policy. All applicants must be sophomores or juniors attending college. The Udall Foundation awards approximately 80 scholarships of up to $5,000 (and 50 scholarships of $350 to honorable mention recipients). Scholarship recipients are eligible for one year of support per application year. Contact the Morris K. Udall Scholarship Program, 130 South Scott Avenue, Tucson, AZ 85701-1922; 520-670-5529; {www.udall.gov}. {http://12.46.245.173/pls/portal30/CATALOG.PRO GRAM_TEXT_RPT.SHOW?p_arg_na mes=prog_nbr&p_arg_values=85.400}

$7,000 To Study Math and Science

The Barry M. Goldwater Scholarship Program is a merit-based grant awarded to college sophomores and juniors who are pursuing a career in mathematics, the natural sciences, or engineering. Each scholarship covers eligible expenses for tuition, fees, books, and room and board, up to a maximum of $7,500 annually. See {www.act.org/goldwater}. Barry M. Goldwater Scholarship And Excellence In Education Foundation, 6225 Brandon Avenue, Suite 315, Springfield, VA 22150-2519; 703-756-6012. {http://12.46.245.173/pls/portal30/CATALOG.PROGRAM_TE XT_RPT.SHOW?p_arg_names=prog_nbr&p_arg_values=85.200}.

$26,000 To Attend Any College

The Harry S. Truman Scholarship Program is a $26,000 merit-based federal grant awarded to college juniors who are preparing for a career in public service. The Foundation seeks candidates who have extensive records of public and community service, are committed to careers in government or elsewhere in public service, and have outstanding leadership potential and communication skills. Contact the Harry S. Truman Scholarship Foundation, 712 Jackson Place, NW Washington, DC 20006; 202-395-4831; {www.truman.gov}, {http://12.46.245.173/pls/portal30/CATALOG.PROGRAM_TEXT_RPT.SHOW?p_arg_names=prog_nbr&p_arg_values=85.001}.

Free Tutoring For College

Through Early Intervention and Scholarships, the GEAR UP Program (Gaining Early Awareness and Readiness for Undergraduate) encourages low-income students to obtain their high school diploma and encourages and prepares them to attend an institution of higher education. Funding is available to local education agencies. Contact GEAR UP, Office of Postsecondary Education, Department of Education, 1990 K Street, NW, Washington, DC 20006-8524; 202-502-7676; {www.ed.gov/programs/gearup/index.html}, {http://12.46.245.173/pls/portal30/CATALOG.PROGRAM_TEXT_RPT.SHOW?p_arg_names=prog_nbr&p_arg_values=84.334}.

Free Adult Learning Classes

The National Institute for Literacy is a national resource for adult education and literacy programs that offers a range of educational and instructional

classes and tutoring. They offer free literacy classes, free training for obtaining your GED, help with learning disabilities, and teach reading, spelling, and math. Contact National Institute for Literacy, 1775 I Street, NW; Suite 730, Washington, DC 20006-2401; 202-233-2025; {www.nifl.gov}.

$40,000 Per Year For Graduate School

The Scholarship For Service program provides scholarships to graduate students that fund the costs for books, tuition, and room and board while attending an approved institution. Participants also receive stipends of up to $12,000. In exchange, students agree to work for the Federal Government for a period equivalent to the length of the scholarship or one year, whichever is longer. Contact the Scholarship For Service Program Office, 8610 Broadway, Suite 305, San Antonio, TX 78217-6352; {www.sfs.opm.gov/ScholarshipMain.asp}.

$32,000 Per Year Toward College Expenses

Scholarship For Service program provides scholarships to undergraduate students that fund the costs for books, tuition, and room and board while attending an approved institution of higher learning. Participants will also receive stipends of up to $8,000. While still in school, students will also serve a paid internship. In exchange, students agree to work for the Federal Government for a period equivalent to the length of the scholarship or one year, whichever is longer. Contact the Scholarship For Service Program Office, 8610 Broadway, Suite 305, San Antonio, TX 78217-6352; {www.sfs.opm.gov/ScholarshipMain.asp}.

$55,000 Toward Ph.D. Research in Urban Planning

The HUD Urban Scholars Fellowship Grant provides financial assistance to recent Ph.D.s with academic appointments at institutions of higher education to undertake research on topics of interest to HUD. The fellowship assists with the costs incurred in the timely completion of a research project, including salary for two summers, graduate assistants to work on the research project, computer software, and travel expenses. Contact the Office of University Partnerships, U.S. Department of Housing and Urban Development, Room 8110, 451 7th Street, SW, Washington, DC 20410; 202-708-3061 ext 3852; {www.oup.org}, {http://12.46.245. 173/pls/portal30/CATALOG.PROGR AM_TEXT_RPT.SHOW?p_arg_name s=prog_nbr&p_arg_values=14.518}.

$10,000 Grants for High School Seniors

The Frederick B. Abramson Memorial Foundation Scholarships are awarded to economically disadvantaged public high school seniors in Washington DC. These scholarships are available to help them defer college expenses at a four-year accredited institution. Contact Scholarship Committee, The Frederick B. Abramson Memorial Foundation, 1050 Connecticut Avenue, N.W., Suite 200, Washington, DC

20036; 202-828-5120; {http://www. abramsonfoundation.org/scholarship/in dex.shtml}.

$10,000 to Attend Medical School

This foundation makes annual grants to students with inadequate financial resources. Students must be third or fourth year medical students in attendance at medical schools in states east of or contiguous to the Mississippi River. Grants will not exceed $10,000. Contact Joseph Collins Foundation, c/o Willkie Farr & Gallagher, 153 East 53rd Street, New York, NY 10022; {http://medschool.slu.edu/sfp/index.ph tml?page=extrascholarships&cat=extra muralprograms#Joseph%20Collins%2 0Foundation}.

Up to $100,000 for Surgical Education

Grants ranging from $25,000 up to $100,000 will be awarded to support innovative research and education projects and programs which will advance surgical education in North America. Giving is done nationwide to ASE members as well as to members of other national surgical associations. Association for Surgical Education Foundation, P.O. Box 19655, Springfield, IL 62794-9655; 217-545-3835; {www.surgicaleducation.com/ asefounda/cesert.htm}.

$9,500 Fellowships for Jewish Students

Wexner Graduate Fellowships cover all tuition expenses and required fees plus a generous living stipend. Fellowships are granted for a two-year period and may be renewed. Giving is done nationwide. Fellowships are awarded to North Americans who are college graduates and who plan to pursue a career in the Jewish community. Contact Wexner

Foundation, 6525 W. Campus Oval, Ste. 110, New Albany, OH 43054; 614-939-6060; Fax: 614-939-6066; {www.wexnerfoundation.org}.

$5,000 for Teachers and Other Educators

This Foundation provides grants of up to $5,000 directly to teachers and other educators to facilitate specific projects and the teacher's work in the classroom, school, district, and community. The Education Foundation is most interested in projects that seek to improve student achievement through geographic literacy, use of new technologies, the understanding of diverse cultures and the promotion stewardship of natural and cultural resources. Contact National Geographic Society Education Foundation, 1145 17th Street N.W., Washington, D.C. 20036-4688; {www.nationalgeographic.com/education/teacher_community/get_grant.html}.

$50,000 to Attend Graduate School

The Graduate program awards approximately 45-50 scholarship grants worth up to $50,000 each to college seniors or recent graduates to attend graduate or professional programs. You must be nominated by the Jack Kent Cooke Foundation representative. Contact Jack Kent Cooke Foundation, 44115 Woodridge Parkway, Suite 200, Lansdowne, VA 20176-5199; 800-498-6478, 703-723-8000; Fax: 703-723-8030; {www.jackkentcookefoundation.org}, {jkc@jackkentcookefoundation.org}.

Education Grants for Family Members of 9/11 Victims

September 11th Program provides grants to dependents and spouses of people killed or permanently disabled in the attacks on the Pentagon and the World Trade Center, the crash of United Airlines Flight 93 in Pennsylvania, and the September and October 2001 anthrax attacks for undergraduate study at any two-year, four-year, technical, or trade school in the United States. Contact Jack Kent Cooke Foundation, 44115 Woodridge Parkway, Suite 200, Lansdowne, VA 20176-5199; 703-723-8000; Fax: 703-723-8030; {www.jackkentcooke foundation.org}, {jkc@jackkentcooke foundation.org}.

Up to $30,000 to Study Longer

The Undergraduate Transfer program awards scholarship grants in amounts up to $30,000 each to students and recent alumni from community colleges or two-year institutions that transfer to and will pursue bachelor's degrees at four-year institutions. Applicants must be U.S. citizens with a 3.5 grade point average from their community college. Contact Jack Kent Cooke Foundation, 44115 Woodridge Parkway, Suite 200, Lansdowne, VA 20176-5199; 800-498-6478, 703-723-8000; Fax: 703-723-8030; {www.jackkentcookefoundation.org}; {jkc@jackkentcookefoundation.org}.

$3,000 Grants for Sports Journalism Studies

The Freedom Forum and the National Collegiate Athletic Association (NCAA) provide $3,000 scholarship grants to college juniors who have career goals in sports journalism and major in journalism or have experience in campus sports journalism. Contact Freedom Forum, Inc., 1101 Wilson Blvd., Arlington, VA 22209-2248; 703-528-0800; {www.freedomforum.org/}; {news@freedomforum.org} or The NCAA Leadership Advisory

Board, P.O. Box 6222, Indianapolis, IN 46206-6222; 317-917-6477; {www.ncaa.org/about/scholarships.ht ml}.

Up to $2,000 for High School Seniors for Academic Achievement

The Best Buy Children's Foundation awards scholarship grants ranging from $1,000 to $2,000 to 3 graduating high school seniors in each U.S. Congressional District and the District of Columbia. Scholarship recipients are selected based on community service and academic achievement and must be entering an accredited U.S. university, college or technical school. Contact Best Buy Children's Foundation, Best Buy World Headquarters, P.O. Box 9312, Minneapolis, MN 55440; {http://com munications.bestbuy.com/communityr elations/Scholarship.asp}, {Com munityRelations@BestBuy.com}.

$5,000 to Pay for College Housing or Tuition

The Christermon Foundation, the non-profit arm of the Beverage Alcohol Industry, awards scholarship grants ranging from $1,500 to $5,000 to children, grandchildren or legal guardians of persons currently proprietor of, or employed full-time with, an individual or company holding a valid California liquor license. This includes restaurants, hotels, retail and wholesale grocery establishments, drug store operations, convenience stores, wineries, breweries, airlines, etc. Grants can be used towards tuition and housing at a college or university. Contact Christermon Foundation, 9 Orchard Road, Suite 100, Lake Forest, CA 92630; 949-837-5291; Fax: 949-837-9481; {www.christermon.com/}, {information@cfsc.occoxmail.com}.

$60,000 Scholarship Grants for Outstanding College Students

The Foundation offers scholarship grants of $3,000 per year up to 4 years to students who are affiliated with footwear, leather or related industries. Scholarship awards are based on academic record, personal promise, character and financial need and are renewable for 4 years of undergraduate study. "Super Scholarship" Grants of up to $15,000 per year (renewable for 4 years) are available to exceptional students. Contact Two/Ten International Footwear Foundation, 1466 Main Street, Waltham, MA 02451; 781-736-1503, 800-FIND-210; {www.twoten.org}, {scholarship@twoten.org}.

Get ALL Four Years of College Paid For!

The Jackie Robinson Foundation awards four-year scholarship grants to African Americans high school seniors who are outstanding students and have a financial need. Program also offers hands-on mentoring and leadership development, bringing graduation rate of students receiving funding to a very high 92%. Contact Jackie Robinson Foundation, 3 West 35th Street, 11th Floor, New York, NY 10001; 212-290-8600; Fax: 212-290-8081; {www. jackierobinson.org/}, {requests@jackierobinson.org}.

Money to Go to School in Nebraska

Scholarships are available to Nebraska students who are or will be attending a Nebraska state college or two year college or trade school in Nebraska and have at least a 2.5 grade point average. Scholarships are provided for up to five years for a four-year college or up to three years for two-year schools or until graduation. Contact The Buffett Foundation, P. O. Box 4508, Decatur, IL 62525; 402-451-6011; {www.buffettscholarships.org/}, {buffettfound@aol.com}.

Money to Learn a Foreign Language

Blakemore Freeman Language Grants are awarded for one year of advanced language study in East or Southeast Asia. Students studying Chinese, Vietnamese, Tibetan, Japanese, Indonesian, Thai, Korean, Khmer, Burmese and/or Malaysian are eligible for funding. The Foundation also offers "Refresher Grants" to professors, language professions and others for advanced language study. Contact The Blakemore Foundation, 1201 Third Avenue, Suite 4800, Seattle, WA 98101-3266; 206-359-8778; Fax: 206-359-9778; {www.blakemorefoundation.org/about.htm}, {blakemore@perkinscoie.com}.

Scholarships up to $28,000 for Gay & Lesbian Students

A Point Scholarship covers tuition, books, supplies, room and board, transportation and living expenses, and is set up with the individual college to meet the needs of the Point Scholar. Individual scholarship amounts range from $5,000 to $28,000 per year. All Point Scholars sign a Contract of Excellence, agreeing to maintain at least a 3.5 GPA, support The Point

Foundation's (TPF) vision, speak at TPF events, maintain contact with the TPF Board of Trustees, and give back to the LGBT community through completion of an individual service project. This is a national award program for undergraduate, graduate and post-graduate students. Contact Point Foundation, P.O. Box 261111, Lakewood, CO 80226; 866-33-POINT; {www.thepointfoundation.org}; {tim@thepointfounation.org}.

$10,000 Scholarships for Young Adults

The Susan G. Komen Breast Cancer Foundation College Scholarship Award Program assist students who have lost a parent to breast cancer, offering college scholarships of up to $10,000 a year, over a four-year period, to young adults (graduating high school to age 25). Contact Susan G. Komen Breast Cancer Foundation, 5005 LBJ Freeway, Suite #250, Dallas, TX 75244; 972-855-1616; {www.komen.org/intradoc-cgi/idc_cgi_isapi.dll?IdcService=SS_GET_PAGE&nodeId=562}.

Over $37,000 Fellowships for Law Students

This Foundation offers fellowships to graduating law students to work in public interest organizations. The salary for the Fellowships is currently

$37,500 and pays all fringe benefits. Fellowships are awarded for one year, with the expectation of renewal for a second year. Contact Skadden Fellowship Foundation, Four Times Square, New York, NY 10036; 212-735-2956; {www.sasmf.com/fellows/default.html}.

Over $25 Million for College Students

Awards are presented to well-rounded, college-bound high school students with highly developed ethics and goals. Selection of Coca-Cola Scholars is based on a number of factors, with special emphasis on each individual's character, personal merit, and background. National Scholars receive $20,000 and Regional Scholars receive $4,000 over a four-year period. Contact Coca-Cola Scholars Foundation, Inc., P.O. Box 442, Atlanta, GA 30301-0442; 404-733-5420, 800-306-2653; Fax: 404-733-5439; {www.coca-colascholars. org}.

$1,000 to Research in Iranian Studies

This Foundation gives grants of $1,000 to individuals in support of research in Iranian studies, including an award for best dissertation and publication of a quarterly journal. Contact the Foundation for Iranian Studies, Inc., 4343 Montgomery Ave., Suite 200, Bethesda, MD 20814-4401; 301-657-1990; Fax: 301-657-1983; {www.fis-iran.org/prize.htm}.

Over $12,500 for Women to go to School

The R.O.S.E. Fund offers four programs. The R.O.S.E. Scholarship acknowledges women and children who are survivors of abuse through a scholarship of up to $10,000 to be used toward any college or university in

New England. The R.O.S.E. Scholarship at Pine Manor College annually awards one Pine Manor student who is or will be enrolled in a minimum of twelve credits per semester. The R.O.S.E. Scholarship at UMASS Boston annually awards two $2,500 scholarships to current or future UMASS Boston students who are or will be enrolled in a minimum of nine credits per semester. The R.O.S.E. Continuing Education Grants Program provides grants from $200 to $1,000 to be used toward education or work related training. Applicants must be nominated and they go to classes or school in New England. Contact The R.O.S.E. Fund, Inc., 175 Federal Street, Suite 455, Boston, MA 02110; 617-482-5400; Fax: 617-482-3443; {www.rosefund.org/programs/scholars hip.asp}, {rosefund@ici.net}.

$1,500 Grant for Girls to Study Sports in Graduate School

The Dorothy Harris Endowed Scholarship offers full-time female graduate students in physical education, sports management, sports psychology, or sports sociology a $1,500 scholarship to attend an accredited graduate school in the fall. Contact the Women's Sports Foundation, Eisenhower Park, East Meadow, NY 11554; 516-542-4700, 800-227-3988, Fax: 516-542-4716; {www.womenssportsfoundation.org}.

Internships + $5,000 for African American Women

The Jackie Joyner-Kersee/Ray Ban Minority Internship gives women of color an opportunity to gain experience in a sports-related career and interact in the sports community. Applicants may be undergraduates, college graduates, graduate students, or women in career change. Internships include $4,000 to $5,000 in stipends. Contact Women's Sports Foundation, Eisenhower Park, East Meadow, NY 11554; 516-542-4700, 800-227-3988, Fax: 516-542-4716; {www.womens sportsfoundation.org}.

$5,000 Grants for African American Sports Women

The Zina Garrison/Visa Minority Internship offers women of color internship opportunities in sports-related careers and stipends of up to $5,000. Applicants may be in school to apply. Contact Women's Sports Foundation, Eisenhower Park, East Meadow, NY 11554; 516-542-4700, 800-227-3988; Fax: 516- 542-4716; {www.womenssportsfoundation.org}.

$5,000 For You or Your Team

The GoGirlGo! Ambassador Awards Program awards 9th through 12th grade girls who make a difference in the lives of girls in their communities with grants of up to $5,000. If you are on a team that makes a difference, your team can also apply. Contact Women's Sports Foundation, Eisenhower Park, East Meadow, NY 11554; 516-542-4700, 800-227-3988, Fax: 516-542-4716; {www.women ssportsfoundation.org}.

$750 Grants for Graduate Students

The Kathleen Stitt Award provides $500 to selected graduate students enrolled full-time in a M.S. or Ph.D.

program at an accredited college or university, or to faculty members employed at an accredited college or university. Contact Child Nutrition Foundation, 700 S. Washington St., Suite 300, Alexandria, VA 22314; 703-739-3900; Fax: 703-739-3915; {www.asfsa.org/continuinged/assistan ce/stitt/}.

$2,500 For Research To School Nutrition Association Members

The Hubert Humphrey Research Grant is available to active members of the School Nutrition Association at the graduate or post-graduate level. Awards are for a minimum of $2,500 for research which is consistent with the Associations platform. Contact Child Nutrition Foundation, 700 S. Washington St., Suite 300, Alexandria, VA 22314; 703-739-3900; Fax: 703-739-3915; {www.asfsa.org/continuing ed/assistance/stitt/}.

$2,500 For Foodservice Research

This grant is for School Nutrition Association members who want to conduct academic or non-academic research applicable to local or state-level foodservice programs. Contact Child Nutrition Foundation, 700 S. Washington St., Suite 300, Alexandria, VA 22314; 703-739-3900; Fax: 703-739-3915; {www.asfsa.org/continuing ged/assistance/stitt/}.

$200 To Pay For The GED

The GED Jump Start Scholarship provides money to Child Nutrition Association members for GED classes, study materials, test fees, child care and transportation. Contact Child Nutrition Foundation, 700 S. Washington St., Suite 300, Alexandria, VA 22314; 703-739-3900; Fax: 703-

739-3915; {www.asfsa.org/contin uinged/assistance/stitt/}.

Free Tuition, Fees and Books

If you are or your parent is a current member of the School Nutrition Association and you are interested in pursuing a school foodservice-related field, this scholarship may be for you. The Nancy Curry Scholarship offers tuition, fees and books for the winning recipient. Applicants must enter an accredited institution and should have a GPA of 3.0 or above on a 4.0 scale. One scholarship is awarded yearly. Contact Child Nutrition Foundation, 700 S. Washington St., Suite 300, Alexandria, VA 22314; 703-739-3900; Fax: 703-739-3915; {www.asfsa.org/ continuingged/assistance/stitt/}.

$150-$1,000 For Foodservice Education

If you are or your parent is a current member of the School Nutrition Association and you are interested in pursuing a school foodservice-related field, this scholarship may be for you. The Schwan's Food Service Scholarship offers $150-$1,000 awards that are renewable for up to four years. Contact Child Nutrition Foundation, 700 S. Washington St., Suite 300, Alexandria, VA 22314; 703-739-3900; Fax: 703-739-3915; {www.asfsa.org/ continuingged/assistance/stitt/}.

Money For School Food Service Graduate School

If you are a current member of the School Nutrition Association and you are interested in continuing your school foodservice-related field at the graduate level, this scholarship may be for you. The Professional Growth Scholarship covers tuition, fees and books only and is renewable for up to four years. Contact Child Nutrition

Foundation, 700 S. Washington St., Suite 300, Alexandria, VA 22314; 703-739-3900; Fax: 703-739-3915; {www.asfsa.org/continuinged/assistan ce/stitt/}.

Over $25,000 for Arc Welding and Engineering Design Scholars

This Foundation provides programs with awards up to $25,000 to encourage educational development in the field of arc welding and engineering design. The sponsored award programs are: Arc Welding Awards for Students, Pre-professional Design Competition for Engineering and Technology, and Professional Design Competition. Contact The James F. Lincoln Arc Welding Foundation, 22801 St. Clair Avenue, Cleveland, OH 44117-1199; 216-481-4300; {www.jflf.org/awards/ default.asp}.

$2,000 for Students Studying in Restaurant or Food Service Programs

Undergraduate Merit Scholarship for College Students provides $2,000 awards for undergraduate students pursuing a certificate, associate degree, or bachelor's degree in a restaurant/ foodservice-related program. Applicants must have a minimum 2.75 GPA, have completed at least one term of a two- to four-year degree program, and have a minimum of 750 hours of work experience in the restaurant and hospitality industry. Contact the

National Restaurant Association Educational Foundation, (formerly National Institute for the Food Service Industry), 175 W. Jackson Blvd., Suite 1500, Chicago, IL 60604-2702; 800-765-2122, 312-715-1010; Fax: 312-715-0807; {www.nraef.org}.

High School Seniors Get $2,000 to Study Restaurant & Hospitality

The Undergraduate Merit Scholarship for High School Seniors offers $2,000 for high school seniors who have demonstrated a commitment to both postsecondary foodservice education and a career in the restaurant and hospitality industry. Applicants must have a minimum 2.75 GPA and must have performed at least 250 hours of foodservice-related work. Contact the National Restaurant Association Educational Foundation, (formerly National Institute for the Food Service Industry), 175 W. Jackson Blvd., Suite 1500, Chicago, IL 60604-2702; 800-765-2122, 312-715-1010, Fax: 312-715-0807; {www.nraef.org}.

Up to $75,000 for Research

The Getty Scholar and Visiting Scholar Grants are awarded yearly to scholars, artists or writers working on projects related to a specific theme designated by the institution. Getty Scholars are in residence for a year and receive a maximum stipend of $75,000, an office, research assistant, airfare to Los Angeles, an apartment, and health benefits. Visiting Scholars are in residence for three months and receive a maximum stipend of $10,500, an office, research assistant, airfare to Los Angeles, and an apartment. Contact J. Paul Getty Trust, 1200 Getty Center Drive, Suite 800, Los Angeles, CA 90049-1685; 310-440-7320; Fax: 310-440-7703; {www.

getty.edu/grants/research/scholars/scholars.html}.

Up to $22,000 for Pre- and Postdoctoral Fellowships

Pre-doctoral and Postdoctoral Fellowships provide support for emerging scholars to complete work on projects related to the Getty Research Institute's annual theme. Recipients are in residence at the Getty Research Institute, where they pursue research to complete their dissertations or to expand them for publication. Pre-doctoral fellowship applicants must have advanced to candidacy and expect to complete their dissertations during the fellowship period. Both fellowships provide an office at the Research Institute, airfare to Los Angeles, an apartment in the Getty scholar housing complex, and health benefits. Contact the J. Paul Getty Trust, 1200 Getty Ctr. Dr., Suite 800, Los Angeles, CA 90049-1685; 310-440-7320; Fax: 310-440-7703; {www.getty.edu/grants/research/scholars/pre_post_fellows.html}.

Over $31,000 to Fund Research in Conservation

The Conservation Guest Scholar Program at the Getty Conservation Institute supports new ideas and perspectives in the field of conservation, with an emphasis on the visual arts—including sites, buildings, and objects—and the theoretical underpinnings of the field. These grants are for established conservators, scientists, and professionals who have attained distinction in conservation and allied fields. Conservation Guest Scholars are in residence at the Getty Center for three to nine consecutive months. A monthly stipend of $3,500 is awarded, prorated to the actual dates of residency, up to a maximum of

$31,500. In addition to the stipend, the grant also includes a workstation at the Conservation Institute, research assistance, airfare to Los Angeles, an apartment in the Getty scholar housing complex, and health benefits. Contact J. Paul Getty Trust, 1200 Getty Ctr. Dr., Suite 800, Los Angeles, CA 90049-1685; 310-440-7320; Fax: 310-440-7703; {www.getty.edu/grants /research/scholars/conservation.html}.

$2,500 to Help You Become a Veterinarian!

The AAEP has collaborated with the American Live Stock Insurance Company (ALSIC) to offer scholarships to 4th-year veterinary students who have indicated a strong desire to pursue a career in equine medicine at schools nationwide. Eight $2,500 scholarships are awarded annually. Contact the American Association of Equine Practitioners, 4075 Iron Works Pkwy, Lexington, KY 40511-8462; 859-233-0147; Fax: 859-233-1968; {www.aaep.org}.

$15,000 to Study Equine Medicine

Research funds are offered to graduate veterinarians at institutions with graduate training programs pertaining to the horse. Applicants must be in equine-based residency graduate training programs, and they or their faculty advisor must be AAEP members. The foundation allocates a total of $40,000 annually for these scholarships. Typically, two to six individuals receive scholarships in amounts ranging from $3,500 to $10,000, but the Research Committee will consider proposals of up to $15,000. Contact the American Association of Equine Practitioners, 4075 Iron Works Pkwy, Lexington, KY 40511-8462; 859-233-0147; Fax: 859-233-1968; {www.aaep.org}.

Fellowship up to $75,000 for Theological Research

The Henry Luce III Fellows in Theology provides five fellowships of up to $75,000 for salary and benefit replacement and, if needed, funds for direct research expenses to full-time faculty of member schools of the Association. Awards will be made on a competitive basis for research projects that demonstrate special promise of quality, significance for theological education, and applicability to the life of faith communities and contemporary society. Fellows are for one year and must leave all academic responsibilities. Contact the Association of Theological Schools in the U.S. & Canada, 10 Summit Park Dr., Pittsburgh, PA 15275-1103; 412-788-6505; Fax: 412-788-6510; {www.ats.edu}.

Theological Grants

The ATS Lilly Theological Research Grants program offers three grants. Faculty Sabbatical Grants offers up to five faculty members up to $25,000 each during leave. The Theological Scholars Grants offers ten grants of up to $10,000 each for research separate from leave. The Research Expense Grants offers ten grants of up to $5,000 each for well-designed research projects. Project proposals must be at least six consecutive months in length to be considered. Contact the Association of Theological Schools in the U.S. & Canada, 10 Summit Park

Dr., Pittsburgh, PA 15275-1103; 412-788-6505; Fax: 412-788-6510; {www.ats.edu}.

Truck Stop Employees Get $2,500 to go to School

The Bill Moon Scholarship offers twelve $2,500 scholarships to truck stop industry employees or their dependents. Students who plan on enrolling on a full-time basis in postsecondary studies at an accredited school are eligible. Contact The NATSO Foundation, 1737 Kings Street, Suite 200, Alexandria, VA 22314; 888-275-6287, 703-549-2100; Fax: 703-684-9667; {www.natsofoundation.org}.

$250 for Completed Research

The Larry Metcalf Exemplary Dissertation Award is a $250 award given in odd-numbered years for research completed in pursuit of the doctoral degree which makes a significant contribution to research in the field. The research must be outstanding in the areas of problem statement, analysis of related literature, methods and procedures, analysis of data, and discussion of results. Contact the National Council for the Social Studies, 8555 16th St., N.W., Ste. 500, Silver Spring, MD 20910; 301-588-1800; Fax: 301-588-2049; {www.ncss.org}.

Up to $1,000 to Help Pay for Your Tuition and Books

The foundation provides educational grants to members for educational purposes to assist in paying for tuition and books. Grants range from $100 up to $1,000. If you are a member, contact the Alpha Epsilon Pi Foundation, Inc., 8815 Wesleyan Rd., Indianapolis, IN 46268-1171; 317-876-1913; Fax: 317-876-1057; {www.aepi.org}; {office@aepi.org}.

$5,000 Educational Grants

The foundation provides grants for arthritis research, and also gives grants to Alpha Omicron Pi Fraternity, Inc., for educational purposes. Grants range from $750 up to $5,000. Contact Alpha Omicron Pi Foundation, 5390 Virginia Way, Brentwood, TN 37024-0395; 615-370-0920; {www.aoiifoundation.org}.

Law Students Receive up to $34,500 for Research & More

Fellowships are awarded to junior scholars who have completed all requirements for their Ph.D. within the past two years, or who are currently in the final stages of completing their dissertations, in order to encourage original and significant research on law, the legal profession, and legal institutions. Fellows receive a $30,000 stipend, fringe benefits for 12 months, and up to $3,500 for research support. Relocation expenses of up to $1,000 may also be reimbursed. In addition, Summer Research Fellowships for Minority Undergraduate Students are awarded to four sophomore or junior minority undergraduates interested in graduate study in the social sciences. Students must have a 3.0 GPA. A $3,600 stipend is provided for each student. Contact the American Bar Foundation, 750 N. Lake Shore Dr., Chicago, IL 60611; 312-988-6500; Fax: 312-988-6579, 312-988-6611; {www.abf-sociolegal.org}; {fellowships@abfn.org}.

$50,000 to do Research at Postdoctoral Level

ACLS Fellowships provide awards to individual scholars at the postdoctoral level to pursue research in the humanities and social sciences. The program offers up to $50,000 for Full Professor and equivalent, $40,000 for Associate Professor and equivalent, and $30,000 for Assistant Professor and equivalent (also includes New York Public Library Fellowships) for six to twelve months of research leave between July and February. Contact the American Council of Learned Societies, 633 Third Avenue, New York, NY 10017-6795; 212-697-1505; Fax: 212-949-8058; {www.acls.org}.

Tuition Fees Paid with $22,500 Grants

The Henry Luce Foundation/ACLS Dissertation Fellowship Program in American Art offers fellowships of $22,500 for a one-year term. The fellowships may be carried out in residence at the fellow's home institution, abroad, or at another appropriate site for research. An applicant must be a candidate for a Ph.D. to be granted by a department of art history in the U.S. Contact the American Council of Learned Societies, 633 Third Avenue, New York, NY 10017-6795; 212-697-1505; Fax: 212-949-8058; {www.acls.org}.

Over $14,000 for Graduate Students

The Graduate Scholarship Competition offers full-time graduate students in communication sciences and disorders up to 10 scholarship awards. They include: up to seven general graduate student scholarships for master's or doctoral study at $4,000 per award; one $2,000 graduate student scholarship giving priority to a student with a disability; one $4,000 graduate student scholarship giving priority to a student who is a racial/ethnic minority and a U.S. citizen; and one $4,000

graduate student scholarship giving priority to an international/minority student studying in the U.S. Contact the American Speech-Language-Hearing Association Foundation, 10801 Rockville Pike, Rockville, MD 20853; 301-897-5700; Fax: 301-571-0457; {www. ashfoundation.org}.

$5,000 to Study Human Speech

The Research Grant in Speech Science awards new researchers a $5,000 grant. The grant is designed to further research activities of new investigator. It can be used to initiate new research or to supplement an existing research project. Funds may be requested for a variety of purposes; for example, equipment, subjects, research assistants, or research-related travel. Contact the American Speech-Language-Hearing Association Foundation, 10801 Rockville Pike, Rockville, MD 20853; 301-897-5700; Fax: 301-571-0457; {www.ashfoun dation.org}.

$2,000 to Research Child Language Development

The Student Research Grant in Early Childhood Language Development awards graduate or postgraduate students in communication sciences and disorders a $2,000 research grant in the area of early childhood language development. Contact the American Speech-Language-Hearing Association Foundation, 10801 Rockville Pike, Rockville, MD 20853; 301-897-5700; Fax: 301-571-0457; {www.ashfoun dation.org}.

Research Grants of $2,000 for Speech Studies

The Student Research in Clinical or Rehabilitative Audiology awards graduate or postgraduate students in communication sciences and disorders a $2,000 research grant in audiology. Contact the American Speech-Language-Hearing Association Foundation, 10801 Rockville Pike, Rockville, MD 20853; 301-897-5700; Fax: 301-571-0457; {www.ashfound ation.org}.

$10,000 Research Grant for Speech, Language, and Hearing

The New Century Scholars Research Grants offers $10,000 to individuals in teacher-investigator careers in higher education or at research institutes or laboratories. If you are in the speech, language and hearing field, contact the American Speech-Language-Hearing Association Foundation, 10801 Rockville Pike, Rockville, MD 20853; 301-897-5700; Fax: 301- 571-0457; {www.ashfoundation.org}.

$5,000 For Professionals to Conduct Research in Audiology

Scientists that have earned their latest degree in communication sciences within the last 5 years are eligible for the Investigator Research Grant. $5,000 grants are awarded to pursue research in audiology or speech-language pathology. Contact the American Speech-Language-Hearing Association Foundation, 10801 Rockville Pike, Rockville, MD 20853; 301-897-5700; Fax: 301-571-0457; {www.ashfoundation.org}.

More Money to do Research

The foundation provides grants for proposals that promise to increase understanding of the causes, manifestations, and control of violence, aggression, and dominance. The foundation awards research grants to individuals for individual projects in

the range of $15,000 to $30,000 a year for periods of one or two years. Contact The Harry Frank Guggenheim Foundation, 527 Madison Avenue, New York, NY 10022; 212- 644-4907; Fax: 212-644-5110; {www.hfg.org}.

$15,000 to Study Violence and Aggression

Dissertation Fellowships are awarded each year to individuals who will complete the writing of the dissertation within the award year on subjects related to violence, aggression and dominance. These fellowships of $15,000 each are designed to contribute to the support of the doctoral candidate to enable him or her to complete the thesis in a timely manner. Contact The Harry Frank Guggenheim Foundation, 527 Madison Avenue, New York, NY 10022; 212-644-4907; Fax: 212-644-5110; {www.hfg.org}.

$3,000 Grants for Medical Studies

The Foundation's Grant Program considers proposals for original study on projects concerned with parapsychology. Grants are available for scientists, universities, laboratories and individuals conducting research on extrasensory perception, psychokinesis and related phenomena. Awards are available as follows: The Eileen J. Garrett Scholarship for undergraduate and graduate study of parapsychology; The Frances P. Bolton Fellowship for post-doctoral writing in parapsychology; The D. Scott Rogo Award for Parapsychological Literature for writers with a book project in parapsychology; and The Charles T. Tart and Judith A. Tart Student Incentive Award for undergraduate and graduate students conducting research. Grants range from $500 up to $3,000. Contact the Parapsychology Foundation, Inc., P.O. Box 1562, New York, NY 10021-0043; 212-628-1550; Fax: 212-628-1559; {www.parapsychology.org}; {info@parapsychology.org}.

Grants of $50,000 to Study Dermatology

This program awards $50,000 grants annually to individuals to foster the career development of young research investigators working in the field of dermatology and cutaneous biology. The research must be focused on a categorical skin disorder or specific skin function. Contact American Skin Association, Inc., 346 Park Ave. S., New York, NY 10010; 212-889-4858 or 800-499-SKIN; Fax: 212-889-4959; {www. americanskin.org}.

$3,600 Scholarship for Worldwide Unity

The Scholarship Grant Fund awards a maximum grant of $1,200 per year over a three-year period of $3,600 to ITAA members in any country who has been a member for one year prior to making application. Grants may be considered for training in transactional analysis, including training fees, tuition for ongoing training or selected workshops, room and board, books and supplies, contract filing fees and both oral and written exam fees. Contact Eric Berne Fund of the International Transactional Analysis Association, c/o Rosa Krauscz, 436 14th St., Ste.

1301, Oakland, CA 94612-2710; 510-625-7720; Fax: 510-625-7725; {www. itaa-net.org}, {itaa@itaa-net.org}.

$25,000 + Tuition for Education & Defense of the U.S.

The Foundation's Graduate Fellowship award, is based on merit, consists of a cost-of-education allowance and a personal-support stipend. Hertz Fellows therefore have no costs for any ordinary educational costs, regardless of their choice among tenable schools. The stipend, paid over the nine-month academic year, is $28,000. The Fellowship award is renewable annually for up to five years. Fellows must attend one of the foundation's tenable schools, or must petition the foundation to include a school that he/she desires to attend. Contact Fannie and John Hertz Foundation, 2456 Research Drive, Livermore, CA 94550; 925-373-1642; Fax: 925-373-6329; {www.hertz foundation.org}, {askhertz@aol.com}.

Awards of $1,000 for Theses in the Physical Sciences

The Doctoral Thesis Prize offers students that have done their work on the application of the physical world to submit their thesis. Early in the summer of each year, members of the committee examine the Ph.D. dissertations completed by Hertz Fellows during the preceding academic year for their overall excellence and pertinence to high-impact applications of the physical sciences. Each Thesis Prize winner receives an honorarium of at least $1,000. Contact Fannie and John Hertz Foundation, 2456 Research Drive, Livermore, CA 94550; 925-373-1642; Fax: 925-373-6329; {www. hertzfoundation.org}, {askhertz@aol.com}.

$35,000 Grants for Clinical Research of Psychoanalysis

The Award may be made to one or more persons who has published or contributed in a significant or major way to clinical psychoanalysis or psychoanalytical research. The Award may also be made to one or more educational or scientific organizations which sponsor the development of methodology in psychoanalysis or which create new interest in that field and which are located in an eligible country. Contact Mary S. Sigourney Award Trust, P.O. Box 10206, Bainbridge Island, WA 98110; 206-842-1097; {www.sigourney.org/default.aspx}.

Up to $18,000 in Grants for Outdoor Medical Studies

The Charles S. Houston Award is given annually to one or two students who have submitted research proposals most likely to result in a substantive contribution to the field of wilderness and environmental medicine. The research is usually conducted over the course of a summer, approximately three months. The amount of the award is up to $5,000. The Annual WMS Research Training Grant offers a grant of up to $6,000 to a resident or fellow of an accredited American or Canadian medical training program, or to a doctoral candidate at an American or Canadian university. The WMS

Herbert N. Hultgren Grant offers a grant of up to $7,000 to a Wilderness Medical Society member. Contact Wilderness Medical Society, 5390 N. Academy Boulevard, Suite 310; Colorado Springs, CO; 80918; 719-572-9255; Fax: 719-572-1514; {www.wms.org/}.

Up to $15,000 for Physical Therapy Students

The Mary McMillan Doctoral Scholarship provides assistance to physical therapists with an outstanding potential for doctoral studies in their first year of their doctorate. Scholarships are available for full-time or part-time be licensed physical therapists students who have been accepted by a doctoral program. Up to six McMillan Doctoral Scholarships in the amount of $5,000 each can be awarded. Contact The Foundation for Physical Therapy, Inc., 1111 N. Fairfax Street, Alexandria, VA 22314; 703-684-2782, 800-875-1378; Fax: 703-706-7343; {www.apta.org/Foundation}; {foundation@apta.org}.

$30,000 for Physical Therapy Fellows

The New Investigator Fellowship Training Initiative (NIFTI) Fellowship funds doctoral physical therapists as developing researchers and improve their competitiveness in securing external funding for future research. Fellowships are for $30,000 annually for salary and fringe benefits and are paid directly to the institution. The fellowship is for one year. Contact The Foundation for Physical Therapy, Inc., 1111 N. Fairfax Street, Alexandria, VA 22314; 703-684-2782, 800-875-1378; Fax: 703-706-7343; {www.apta.org/Foundation}; {foundation@apta.org}.

$40,000 to Test Physical Therapy Methods

Research Grants are available for $40,000 research grants on evaluating the effectiveness of physical therapist interventions. The principal investigator must be a licensed physical therapist. Contact The Foundation for Physical Therapy, Inc. 1111 N. Fairfax Street, Alexandria, VA 22314; 703-684-2782, 800-875-1378; Fax: 703-706-7343; {www.apta.org/Foundation}; {foundation@apta.org}.

$40,000 for Young Doctors

Fellowship Awards of $50,000 are granted to young post-doctoral investigators in the early stages of their careers. Awards are for a one-year period; a second year of funding may be considered. All applicants must have a M.D. or Ph.D. or equivalent. Research Grants are also available. Contact Huntington's Disease Society of America, Inc., 158 W. 29th St., 7th Floor, New York, NY 10001-5300; 212-242-1968, 800-345-HDSA; Fax: 212-239-3430; {www.hdsa.org}; {rgraze@hdsa.org}; {llacy@hdsa.org}.

Money to Become a Librarian

The American Library Association is committed to promoting and advancing the librarian profession. The ALA and its units provide more than $300,000 annually for study in a master's degree in library and information studies from an ALA accredited program, or for a master's degree in school library media program that meets the ALA curriculum guidelines for a National Council for Accreditation of Teacher Education (NCATE) accredited unit. Several scholarships and fellowships are offered. Contact American Library Association, 50 E. Huron Street, Chicago, IL 60611-2795; 800-545-2433; {www.ala.org}; {ala@ala.org}.

Up to $25,000 for Jewish Educators

The Covenant Awards for Exceptional Jewish Educators allow educators working in any setting to receive Covenant Awards, including professionals working in day schools, camps, informal programs, Hillel programs, family and adult programs, and other kinds of educational endeavors. Each award carries with it a prize of $20,000 for the educator and an additional $5,000 for the educator's home institution. Educators at any stage of their careers with significant achievements in the field of Jewish education are eligible candidates. Contact The Covenant Foundation, 1270 Avenue of the Americas, Suite 304, New York, NY 10020; 212-245-3500; Fax: 212-245-0619; {www.covenantfn.org}; {info@covenantfn.org}.

Up to $10,000 in Grants for Pharmacy Students & Faculty

This foundation offers a variety of grants, fellowships and scholarships for students and faculty of pharmacy. The "Gateway To Research" Scholarship Program, provides awards of up to $5,000 to undergraduate and graduate students. The First Year Graduate School Scholarships include: Kappa Epsilon-First Year Graduate Fellowship offers $4,000 to final year pharmacy students; Phi Lambda Sigma First Year Graduate Scholarship awards $7,500 to Phi Lambda Sigma senior pharmacy students; Rho Chi-Schering Plough Scholarship awards $7,500 outstanding Rho Chi members in their senior year. The Pre-doctoral Fellowships awards up to $6,000 to students that have completed three semesters of graduate study. The AFPE Clinical Post-Pharm. Fellowships in the Biomedical Research Sciences awards $27,500 fellowships to Pharm.D.-level clinical pharmacists. The New Investigators Program for Pharmacy Faculty provides up to $10,000 to new faculty members to assist in establishing a research program. Contact American Foundation for Pharmaceutical Education, 1 Church Street, Suite 202, Rockville, MD 20850; 301-738-2160; Fax: 301-738-2161; {www.afpenet. org}; {info@afpenet.org}.

$10,000 for Physicists in the U.S.

The Prize for Industrial Applications of Physics awards $10,000 prizes by nomination only to U.S. residents and individuals who have worked primarily in U.S.-based industry, in recognition of outstanding contributions to the industrial applications of physics. Recipients also receive a certificate and a travel allowance to receive the prize. Contact American Institute of Physics, Inc., 1 Physics Ellipse, College Park, MD 20740-3843; 301-209-3034; Fax: 301-209-0843; {www.aip.org/aip/writing}; {aipinfo@aip.org}.

$6,000 for Costs Associated with Research

The Franklin program is designed to help meet the costs of travel to libraries and archives for research purposes, the purchase of microfilm, photocopies or equivalent research materials, the costs associated with fieldwork, or laboratory research expenses. Franklin grants are made for non-commercial research. They are not intended to meet the expenses of attending conferences. Applicants are

expected to have a doctorate, or to have published work of doctoral character and quality. American citizens and residents of the United States may use their Franklin awards at home or abroad. Foreign nationals must use their Franklin awards for research in the United States. Applicants who have received Franklin grants may reapply after an interval of two years. Funding is offered up to a maximum of $6000. Contact American Philosophical Society, 104 S. 5th Street, Philadelphia, PA 19106-3387; 215-440-3429; {www.amphilsoc.org/grants/franklin.htm}; {eroach@amphilsoc.org}.

$1,200 per Month to Research in APS Library

The American Philosophical Society Library offers short-term residential fellowships for conducting research in its collections. The fellowships are open to both U.S. citizens and foreign nationals who are holders of the Ph.D. or the equivalent, Ph.D. candidates who have passed their preliminary examinations, and independent scholars. Applicants in any relevant field of scholarship may apply. The stipend is $2,000 per month, and the term of the fellowship is a minimum of one month and a maximum of three months. Contact American Philosophical Society, 104 S. 5th Street, Philadelphia, PA 19106-3387; 205-440-3443; {www.amphilsoc.org/grants/resident.htm}; {eroach@amphilsoc.org}.

$3,000 to Research Native American Languages and More

The Phillips Fund of the American Philosophical Society provides grants for research in Native American linguistics, ethnohistory, and the history of studies of Native Americans, in the continental United States and Canada. Grants are not made for projects in archaeology, ethnography, psycholinguistics, or for the preparation of pedagogical materials. The grants are intended for such extra costs as travel, tapes, films, and consultants' fees, but not for general maintenance or the purchase of books or permanent equipment. The average award is about $2,200; grants do not exceed $3,000. Contact American Philosophical Society, 104 S. 5th Street, Philadelphia, PA 19106-3387; 215-440-3429; {www.amphilsoc.org/ grants/phillips.htm}; {eroach@a mphilsoc.org}

Get $75,000 for Three Years for Scientific Research

The Career Development Awards encourage a commitment to scientific research in orthopaedic surgery. Candidates must have completed a residency in orthopaedic surgery and demonstrated a sustained interest in research and excellence in clinical training. Budget may include salary support. Awards of up to $75,000 per year for three years, conditional upon annual review, will be considered. Contact Orthopaedic Research Education Foundation, 6300 N. River Rd., Suite 700, Rosemont, IL 60018-4238; 847-698-9980; Fax: 847-698-7806; {www.oref.org}; {wurth@ oref.org}.

Get $15,000 for Your Research Interests

The objective of the Resident Research Awards is to encourage development of research interests for residents and fellows in approved orthopaedic programs. Grants of $15,000 are offered to be used over a twelve month

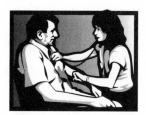

timeframe to cover research expenses but not salary or travel. Contact Orthopaedic Research Education Foundation, 6300 N. River Rd., Suite 700, Rosemont, IL 60018-4238; 847-698-9980; Fax: 847-698-7806; {www.oref.org}; {wurth@ oref.org}.

$20,000 for Medical Students to Further Their Careers

The Orthopaedic Research and Education Foundation sponsors a Medical Student Summer Orthopaedic Research Fellowship. Medical students with an interest in orthopaedics are eligible to apply. The medical student needs to identify an investigator with an ongoing orthopaedic research project who is willing to accept the student as a research assistant. OREF will provide $2,500 as salary support for the student, payable directly to the institution. This program is intended to be a summer research fellowship. Contact Orthopaedic Research Education Foundation, 6300 N. River Rd., Suite 700, Rosemont, IL 60018-4238; 847-698-9980; Fax: 847-698-7806; {www.oref.org}; {wurth@ oref.org}.

Nurses: $15,000 or More for Research

The Nursing Research Grants Program encourages the research career development of all nurses, but special interest is given to beginning and experienced nurse researchers. Beginning researcher should be a nurse who has no more than three research-based publications in referenced journals and has received as principal investigator, no more than $15,000 in extramural funding in one particular research area. Experienced researcher should be a nurse who has more than three research-based journal publications and has received more than $15,000 as principal investigator, in research funding since their degree. Contact American Nurses Foundation, Inc., 8515 Georgia Avenue, Suite 400 West, Silver Springs, MD 20910; 800-274-4ANA; {www.ana.org/anf}; {anf@ana.org}.

Medical Students Get up to $4,000 to Better the Public

The foundation provides financial assistance to students enrolled in recognized schools or institutions of medical education and to promote the betterment of public health through financial support of scientific and medical research. The Health Literacy Grant Program provides $500 to $4,000 for programs that promote clearer communication between patients and their physicians and other healthcare providers. The Seed Grant Research Program awards $1,500 to $2,500 to medical students and residents to help them conduct small projects in applied and clinical research. Contact the American Medical Association Foundation, 515 N. State Street, Chicago, IL 60610; 800-262-3211 ext 4750, 312-464-4543; {www.ama-assn.org}.

$3,000 for Law Students to Finish School

The Alia Herrera Memorial ATLA Auxiliary Scholarship is a $3,000 scholarship available to students entering their second or third year of law school and to law students who

have the equivalent of one year to complete their studies. Only law students who are student members of the law school student section of ATLA, law students attending law schools in the San Francisco area and law students who are children of ATLA members may apply. Contact the Association of Trial Lawyers of America Education Fund, 1050 31st St., N.W., Washington, DC 20007-4409; 202-965-3500, 800-424-2725; {www.atla.org}; {nca@atlahq.org}.

Tuition Assistance up to $1,000 for Minority Law Students

The Richard D. Hailey ATLA Law Student Scholarships offers up to six $1,000 tuition assistance scholarships to first- and second-year African American, Hispanic, Asian American, and Native American and Bi-Racial ATLA law student members based on financial need, a 500-word essay, recommendations, demonstrated commitment to ATLA and its mission, expressed desire to represent victims, and interest and skills in trial advocacy. Contact the Association of Trial Lawyers of America Education Fund, 1050 31st St., N.W., Washington, DC 20007-4409; 202-965-3500, 800-424-2725; {www.atla.org}; {nca@atlahq.org}.

$2,500 Scholarship for Law Students

The ATLA Trial Advocacy Scholarship is a $2,500 scholarship available to second- and third-year ATLA law student members. Contact the Association of Trial Lawyers of America Education Fund, 1050 31st St., N.W., Washington, DC 20007-4409; 202-965-3500, 800-424-2725; {www.atla.org}; {nca@atlahq.org}.

$1,000 for Law Students to Attend Law Convention

The Leesfield/ATLA Law Student Scholarship is a $1,000 scholarship granted to a law student with financial need to allow him/her to attend the ATLA's annual convention. Applicants must be first- or second-year ATLA law student members. Contact the Association of Trial Lawyers of America Education Fund, 1050 31st St., N.W., Washington, DC 20007-4409; 202-965-3500, 800-424-2725; {www.atla.org}; {nca@atlahq. org}.

Four-Year Scholarships for College Students

The Bonner Scholar Program seeks to transform the lives of students at twenty-five specific colleges and universities as well as their campuses, local communities, and nation by providing access to education and opportunities to serve. The Bonner Foundation provides four-year community service scholarships to approximately 1500 students annually. The scholarship serves those individuals who have high financial need and a commitment to service. It is designed to heighten the overall education a Scholar receives by asking students to engage in ongoing service work and helping them develop the tools and the knowledge necessary to make that work meaningful and lasting. Contact The Corella & Bertram Bonner Foundation, Inc., 10 Mercer Street, Princeton, NJ 08540; 609-924-6663; Fax: 609-683-4626; {www.bonner.org}; {info@bonner. org}.

Graduate Students Get Help to Do More Schooling

The K. Patricia Cross Future Leaders Award recognizes students who are committed to developing academic and civic responsibility in themselves and in others. All graduate students planning a higher education career are eligible. Students are to be nominated by a faculty member or administrator and should demonstrate leadership ability or potential for exercising leadership in teaching and learning. The award includes a stipend to attend the National Conference on Higher Education that covers travel, lodging, registration, and a one-year AAHE membership. Contact The American Association for Higher Education, 1 Dupont Circle, Suite 360, Washington, DC 20036-1110; 202-293-6440; Fax: 202-293-0073; {www.aahe.org}; {info@aahe.org}.

$3,000 for Noteworthy Students

The AOA Presidential Memorial Leadership Award honors and recognizes an osteopathic student entering his/her second, third or fourth year of studies who has demonstrated outstanding character, service, and leadership potential in the osteopathic profession. One award of $3,000 will be presented to the recipient awarded during the AOF Honors Ceremony at the AOA Annual Convention and Scientific Seminar. Contact American Osteopathic Foundation (formerly National Osteopathic Foundation), 142 E. Ontario, Ste. 502, Chicago, IL 60611; 312-202-8232 or 800-621-1773, ext. 8232; Fax: 312-202-8216; {www.aof-foundation.org}; {vheck@aof-foundation.org}

$400 to Help with Tuition

The Russell C. McCaughan Education Fund Scholarship provides scholarships to one rising second year student at each of the accredited colleges/schools of osteopathic medicine. Special emphasis is placed on financial need, academic ability, extracurricular activities, and a strong interest in osteopathic principals and philosophy. Scholarships of $400 will be awarded to one student at each of the accredited colleges/schools of osteopathic medicine. Contact American Osteopathic Foundation (formerly National Osteopathic Foundation), 142 E. Ontario, Ste. 502, Chicago, IL 60611; (312) 202-8232 or (800) 621-1773, ext. 8232; Fax: (312) 202-8216; {http://www.aof-foundation.org}; {vheck@aof-foundation.org}

$2,000 to Help You Study Medicine

The Welch Scholars Grant provides monetary aid to students entering their second, third or fourth year of studies at an accredited college/school of osteopathic medicine. Special emphasis will be placed on the financial need and academic achievement of the student. Grants of $2,000 will be awarded to students from each of the colleges/schools of osteopathic medicine who best meet the criteria and have a desire to continue in osteopathic medicine. Contact American Osteopathic Foundation (formerly National Osteopathic Foundation), 142 E. Ontario, Ste. 502, Chicago, IL 60611; (312) 202-8232 or (800) 621-1773, ext. 8232; Fax: (312) 202-8216; {http://www.aof-foundation.org}; {vheck@aof-foundation.org}.

$5,000 for Minority Students

The William G. Anderson, D.O. Scholarship for Minority Students honors an outstanding minority medical student, entering their second, third or fourth year of studies at an accredited college/school of osteopathic medicine, who

demonstrates both academic achievement and outstanding leadership qualities. One scholarship of $5,000 will be presented to the recipient during the AOF Honors Ceremony at the AOA Annual Convention and Scientific Seminar. Contact American Osteopathic Foundation (formerly National Osteopathic Foundation), 142 E. Ontario, Ste. 502, Chicago, IL 60611; 312-202-8232 or 800-621-1773, ext. 8232; Fax: 312-202-8216; {http://www.aof-foundation.org}; {vheck@aof-foundation.org}

$1,000 to Help Pay for Your Education

This Foundation awards over 8,000, $1,000 awards to be used for educational expenses during the first year of college or post-secondary vocational/technical school. Applicants do not have to be employed by Burger King. Candidates must maintain a 2.5 GPA, work an average of 15 hours per week and demonstrate community leadership. Contact The Burger King/McLamore Foundation, Inc., 9300 S. Dadeland Blvd., Miami, FL 33156; 305-378-7355; Fax: 507-931-9168; {www.bkscholars.scholarshipamerica.org/}; {bk@csfa.org}.

$2,000 to Study Islam

FEF, Inc. supports education for Muslim U.S. citizens and permanent residents. The awards are distributed on a need/merit basis up to $2,000 a year. Contact The Fadel Educational Foundation, Inc., P.O. Box 212135, Augusta, GA 30917-2135; 866-705-9495; {http://fadelfoundation.org/}; {afadel@bww.com}.

$10,000 for Muslim Students to Go to School

The Barakat Foundation gives to selected scholars who have already been accepted by the Department of Near Eastern Languages and Civilization, University of Chicago: One scholarship of $10,000 by the Barakat Foundation to a Muslim student accepted for the doctoral program in Islamic archeology for the first year of study. Contact the Assistant Administrator, The Barakat Foundation, 17076 Blackie Road, Salinas, CA 93907; {www.barakat.org/foundation}.

Scholarships of $3,000 for Muslim Students

The AL-AMEEN Scholarship offers one male and one female Muslim undergraduate student a scholarship that provides up to $3,000 per school year for the first year. An additional $3,000 will be provided for the second year. Payments are made before the term starts. This scholarship is for U.S. residents only. Contact Al-Ameen Scholarship, c/o The Muslim Scholarship Fund, Progressive Muslim Scholarship, 14252 Culver Blvd., Suite A714, Irvine, CA 92604; {www.muslimscholarshipfund.org/}.

Up to $3,000 to Help You Go to College

The Roothbert Fund was created to help men and women in need of financial aid to further their education. Scholarships may only be applied to study at an accredited institution based in the United States. The Fund seeks candidates who are "motivated by spiritual values," and works to foster fellowship among them. While the Fund does not emphasize any particular form of religious practice or worship, it seeks to provide support to persons motivated by spiritual values. Grants range from $2,000-$3,000 . Aid is given for the ensuing school year. Contact The Roothbert Fund, Inc., 475 Riverside Drive, Room 252, New York, NY 10115; 212-870-3116; {www.roothbertfund.org}; {mail@roothbertfund.org}.

Grants for Education Projects

The Fellows' Projects Program is for Roothbert Fellows who are no longer on grant are eligible to apply to the Fund for seed money in the form of small grants for individual or group projects taking place within the United States that are consonant with the aims of the founders. Fundamentally, the Fellows Projects Program aims to pay for full or partial costs of: educational or service projects conducted by Fellows for the benefit of others in ways that either extend or fulfill the vocational commitments developed while these Fellows were on stipend, or otherwise embody a continuing expression of Fellows' commitment to the purposes of the Fund; or activities intended to increase Fellows' spiritual awareness or commitment, or to increase their knowledge, skill and other capabilities in ways that fulfill the Fund's purposes. Contact The Roothbert Fund, Inc., 475 Riverside Drive, Room 252, New York, NY 10115; 212-870-3116; {www.roothbertfund.org}; {mail@roothbertfund.org}.

$10,000 for Medical Research for Lesbians

Through the Lesbian Health Fund, the organization awards grants ranging from $500 to $10,000 to support medical research in the areas of: rates and risk factors for cancer, infection, and disease among lesbians; access to the health care system for lesbians; mental health concerns of lesbians and their families; lesbian family issues; and exploration of diversity in the lesbian population. Grants are also awarded to educate health care workers about lesbian health needs, and to educate lesbians about risk reduction, early diagnosis of health problems, and safe insemination techniques. Contact The Gay and Lesbian Medical Association, 459 Fulton St., Ste. 107, San Francisco, CA 94102; 415-255-4547; Fax: 415-255-4784; {www.glma.org}; {info@glma.org}.

$50,000 or More to Study Greek Prehistory

Projects relevant to the history of the Aegean world from the Paleolithic to the first Olympiad are eligible for funding. Projects outside the Aegean must have a direct relationship to Aegean prehistory in order to be considered for funding. Excavation Directors only may also apply for funds for technical archaeological services for publication preparation. Projects which are finished with excavation and are preparing material

for publication are eligible. Grants range from $1,000 to over $50,000. Contact The Institute for Aegean Prehistory, 3550 Market St., Suite 100, Philadelphia, PA 19104; 215-387-4911; {www.archaeological.org/webinfo.php?page=10158&entry=145&search_type=fellowships}.

Research Grants up to $75,000 for Geologists

Students of mineral resources throughout the world may apply to the Society of Economic Geologists for thesis research grants available from the Society of Economic Geologists Foundation and the Society of Economic Geologists Canada Foundation. The purpose of the grants is to provide partial support of master's and doctoral thesis research for graduate students. Individual grants usually range from $500 to $3,000, or equivalent, but larger awards may be made. Contact the Society of Economic Geologists Foundation, Inc., 7811 Shaffer Parkway, Littleton, CO 80127; 720-981-7882; Fax: 720-981-7874; {www.segweb.org/StudentGrants.htm}, {seg@segweb.org}.

Up to $10,000 to Study Food

Culinary Scholarships and grants ranging from $500 to $10,000 are given for basic, continuing and specialty education courses in the U.S. and abroad. Awards are tuition credit and cash. There are a number of scholarships and grants available at locations throughout the world. Contact The International Association of Culinary Professionals Foundation 304 W. Liberty St., Suite 201, Louisville, KY 40202-3068; 502-581-9786 ext. 264; Fax: 502-589-3602; {www.iacpfoundation.com/}.

Organizations giving Scholarship/ Education grants to members of military or children:

☐ Contact: 82nd Airborne Division Association Educational Fund, 3310 Boone Trail, Fayetteville, NC 28306-2136; 910-822-4534; Fax: 910-425-0244; {www.82nd association.org}.

☐ Contact: AAAA Scholarship Foundation, Inc., 755 Main Street, Suite 4D, Monroe, CT 06468-2830; 203-268-2450; Fax: 203-268-5870; {www.quad-a.org}; {aaaa@quad-a.org}.
This Foundation offers scholarships for Army Aviation Association of America members and selected dependents.

☐ Contact: Aerospace Education Foundation, 1501 Lee Highway, Arlington, VA 22209; 703-247-5839; Fax: 703-247-5853; {www.aef.org}; {rkay@aef.org}
The Foundation provides grants/scholarship assistance to Air Force personnel and spouses.

☐ Contact: Intrepid Foundation, One Intrepid Square, West 46th Street & 12th Avenue, New York, NY 10036; 212-957-7024; {www.intrepidmuseum.org},{dw inters@intrepid-foundation.org}.
This Foundation provides scholarships to children of veterans and service members who were lost in Iraq.

☐ Contact: Marine Corps -- Law Enforcement Foundation, PO Box 37, Mountain Lakes, NJ 07046; 877-606-1775; Fax: 973-625-9239; {www.mc-lef.org}; {info@mc-lef.org}.
Financial aid is available for disabled children of Marines as is scholarship assistance to children of Marines and Federal law enforcement personnel whose parent dies on duty.

☐ Contact: Marine Corps Scholarship Foundation, P.O. Box 3008, Princeton, NJ 08543-3008; (800) 292-7777; Fax: (609) 452-2259; {www.marine-scholars.org}; {mcsf@marine-scholars.org}.
This Foundation provides scholarships to children of current/former Marines, and children of Navy Corpsmen that served with the Marines, who pursue collegiate or VoTech education.

☐ Contact: Military Officers Association of America Scholarship Fund, 201 North Washington Street, Alexandria, VA 22314; 800-234-6622; Fax: 703-549-2311; {www.moaa.org}.
Provides interest free loans and grants to children of enlisted and officers for college education.

☐ Contact: Seabee Memorial Scholarship Association, PO Box 6574, Silver Spring, MD 20916; 301-570-2850; {www.seabee.org}; {smsa@erols.com}.
Provides children and grandchildren of Seabees with financial assistance for college

☐ Contact: SEAL - Naval Special Warfare Foundation, PO Box 5965, Virginia Beach, VA

23471; 757-363-7490; Fax: 757-363-7491; {www.nswfoundation org}; {info@nswfoundation. org}.
Scholarships/grants for children of Navy SEALs.

☐ Contact: Special Operations Warrior Foundation, P.O. Box 14385, Tampa, FL 33690; 813-805-9400; Fax: 813-805-0567; {www.specialops.org}; {warrior@specialops.org}.
Provides four year or vocational college scholarship grants to children surviving Special Operations personnel killed in operational or training missions.

$2500 for Medical Sonographers

The SDMS Educational Foundation provides grants, scholarships, and financial awards for students, researchers, and professionals in the field of diagnostic medical sonography. Medical sonography students must have a minimum GPA of 2.5 to be eligible for this financial assistance. Financial support to individuals ranges from approximately $295 to $2500. Contact Society of Diagnostic Medical Sonography, 2745 Dallas Pkwy., Suite 350, Plano, TX 75093-8730; 214-473-8057; Fax: 214-

473-8563; {www.sdms.org/default. asp}, {foundation@sdms.org}.

$2,000 Scholarships and Grants for Wildlife Preservation

The Rocky Mountain Elk Foundation, Inc. provides financial support for the preservation of elk and other wildlife. Grants are awarded for undergraduate wildlife management scholarships, conservation education, and related programs. Scholarship applicants must be junior or senior undergraduates in a recognized wildlife program. The Wildlife Leadership Award provides $2,000 for winning applicants. Contact the Rocky Mountain Elk Foundation, Inc., 2291 W. Broadway, P.O. Box 8249, Missoula, MT 59807; 406-523-4550, 800-CALL-ELK ext. 520; {www. elkfoundation.org/}.

Funding for International Studies

The Institute of International Education, Inc. provides grants, scholarships, and fellowships that enable outstanding men and women to study, conduct research, and receive practical training outside their own countries. Contact the Institute of International Education, Inc., 809 United Nations Plaza, New York, NY 10017-3380. 212-883-8200; Fax: 212-984-5452; {http://www.iie.org/}.

Scholarships for All Kinds of Students; Grants for Career Training, Parent Training, and At-Risk Individuals

The ESA Foundation provides a wide variety of scholarships to students of varying backgrounds, areas of study, and geographic locations. Each state chapter offers a number of scholarship programs for high-school seniors through undergraduates. Contact the

ESA Foundation, P.O. Box 270517, Fort Collins, CO 80527; 970-223-2824; Fax: 970-223-4456; {www.esaintl.com/esaf/}.

Scholarships for Gifted Students

The Malone Scholars are top-level students chosen by one of several private secondary schools throughout the country to receive scholarships that are funded through Malone Family Foundation scholarship endowments. The selected schools may offer scholarships based on merit and need to gifted students. Contact The Malone Family Foundation, 12300 Liberty Boulevard, Englewood, CO 80112; {www.malonefamilyfoundation.org/index.html}.

$20,000 College Scholarships for Financially Needy High School Seniors

The Farris Foundation offers the Farris Scholar Award, which is a four-year scholarship of up to $20,000 that can be used to obtain an undergraduate degree in any field of study. The objective of the Farris Scholars Program is to make a college education possible for a deserving student who otherwise might not be able to attend college. The scholarship is open to high school seniors at selected high schools across the country. The scholarship is based on need, community service, personal career goals, leadership, academics and citizenship. Contact The Farris Foundation, Inc., P.O. Box 304, Lawrenceville, GA 30046-0304; 770-962-4448; Fax: 770-962-4430; {www.farrisfoundation.org/scholarships.html}, {info@farrisfoundation.org}.

$2,000 Fellowships for Etruscan Studies

The Etruscan Foundation offers fellowships for up to $2000 each, designed to help defray the costs of student participation in a field school or in archaeological fieldwork at ancient sites in Italy. These fellowships are available to current graduate students at accredited North American colleges and universities. These scholarships are not limited to work on Etruscan sites; applications for archaeological work at any ancient site in Italy are welcome. Contact The Etruscan Foundation, Ms. Gwen Dwyer, c/o Grants Management Associates, 77 Summer Street, 8th Floor, Boston, MA 02110-1006; 617-426-7080, ext. 301; Fax 617-426-7087; {www.etruscanfoundation.org/programs.html}.

Grants and Fellowships for Women

The American Association of University Women Educational Foundation provides fellowships and grants to women who are U.S. citizens or permanent residents for educational, project, and professional support. The foundation offers several types of funding, including American Fellowships, Career Development Grants, Community Action Grants, Eleanor Roosevelt Teacher Fellowships, and Selected Professions Fellowships. Contact the American Association of University Women Educational Foundation, 1111 16th St. N.W., Washington, DC 20036-4873; 202-728-7602; 800-332-AAUW; {www.aauw.org}.

$10,000 Scholarships for Emergency Nurses

The Emergency Nurses Association offers undergraduate, graduate, and doctoral scholarships ranging from $2,000 to $10,000. Contact the Emergency Nurses Association Headquarters, Foundation & Development, 915 Lee Street, Des Plaines, IL 60016-6569; 847-460-4100, 800-900-9659 ext. 4100; Fax: 847-460-4004; {www.ena.org/foun dation/grants/}.

$10,000 Scholarships for Environmental Studies

The National Fish and Wildlife Foundation funds projects to conserve and restore fish, wildlife, and native plants. One of these, the Budweiser Conservation Scholarship Program, is a competitive scholarship program to support and promote innovative research or study that seeks to respond to today's most pressing conservation issues. This program awards a minimum of ten scholarships of up to $10,000 each to cover either graduate or undergraduate students' expenses for tuition, fees, books, room and board and other direct expenses related to their studies. Another award provided by NFW is the Guy Bradley Award, which is presented to outstanding individuals in the field of wildlife law enforcement. Recipients receive a check for $1,000, and a donation of $1,000 is made in the recipient's name to the wildlife project(s) of his or her choice. Contact National Fish And Wildlife Foundation, 1120 Connecticut Avenue,

NW, Suite 900, Washington, DC 20036; 202-857-0166; Fax: 202-857-0162; {http://www.nfwf.org/ programs/budscholarship.htm}, {http://www.nfwf.org/programs/guy_b radley.htm}.

$7,000 Scholarships, Fellowships, and Grants for Polish Americans

The Kosciuszko Foundation awards scholarships, fellowships, and grants for a variety of educational programs related to Poland. U.S. citizens of Polish descent and non-Polish Americans majoring in Polish studies are eligible for many of these programs. Scholarships range from $1,000 to $7,000, and provide educational support for eligible undergraduate, graduate, and medical school students. Contact The Kosciuszko Foundation, Inc., 15 East 65th Street, New York, NY 10021; 212-734-2130; Fax: 212-628-4552; {http://www.kosciuszkofoundation.org /EDScholarships_list.html}.

$20,000 Grants for Anthropological Research

The Leakey Foundation provides grants for research into the environments, archeology, and human paleontology; the behavior, morphology, and ecology of the great apes and other primate species; and the behavioral ecology of contemporary hunter-gatherers. The majority of the Foundation's General Research Grants to doctoral students are in the $3,000-$12,000 range; however, larger grants, especially to post-doctoral students and senior scientists, may be funded up to $20,000. Contact Grants Officer, The Leakey Foundation, P.O. Box 29346, 1002A O'Reilly Avenue, San Francisco, CA 94129-0346; 415-561-

4646; Fax: 415-561-4647; {www.
leakeyfoundation.org/grants/g2.jsp},
{grants@leakeyfoundation.org}.

$$$ For Institutions That They Can Pass On to You

$45,000 To Teach Business

The Centers for International Business
Education program provides funding
to schools of business for curriculum
development, research, and training on
issues of importance to U.S. trade and
competitiveness. The average award
for individual institutions is $370,000,
which will be used for such services as
establishing an advisory council and
locating appropriate faculty to meet the
objectives of this program. Contact the
U.S. Department of Education, OPE,
Office of Higher Education Programs,
1990 K St., N.W., Washington, DC
20006-8500; 202-502-7628;
{www.ed.gov/programs/iegpscibe/inde
x.html}. {http://12.46.245.173/pls/
portal30/CATALOG.PROGRAM_TE
XT_RPT.SHOW?p_arg_names=prog_
nbr&p_arg_values=84.220

$$$ For Qualified College Students Toward Post-Baccalaureate Achievement

Through the Ronald E. McNair Post-
Baccalaureate Achievement program,
institutions of higher education receive
funding to prepare eligible
undergraduates for doctoral studies.
Services provided by the program
include research opportunities,
mentoring, summer internships,
tutoring, academic counseling,
assistance in obtaining student
financial aid, and assistance in
securing admission and financial aid
for enrollment in graduate programs.
Eligible participants are low-income,
first-generation college students and
students underrepresented in graduate

education for graduate study. Contact
the U.S. Department of Education,
OPE Higher Education Programs,
Federal TRIO Programs, 1990 K
Street, N.W., 7th Floor, Washington,
DC 20006-8510; 202-502-7600;
{www.ed.gov/programs/triomcnair/ind
ex.html}. {http://12.46.245.173/pls/
portal30/CATALOG.PROGRAM_TE
XT_RPT.SHOW?p_arg_names=prog_
nbr&p_arg_values=84.217}.

$30,000 In Graduate Assistance in Areas of National Need

The U.S. Department of Education
offers funding for fellowships to
graduate academic departments,
programs, and units of institutions of
higher education. The fellowships,
awarded by the funded institution, are
for superior graduate students with a
financial need, who plan to teach or do
research in academic areas of national
need. These areas include biology,
chemistry, computer and information
science, engineering, geological
science, mathematics, and physics.
Contact the International Education
and Graduate Programs Service, Office
of Postsecondary Education,
Department of Education, 400
Maryland Ave., SW., Washington, DC
20202-5247; 202-502-7638; {www.
ed.gov/programs/iegpsgaann/index.ht
ml}, {http://12.46.245.173/pls/portal
30/CATALOG.PROGRAM_TEXT_R
PT.SHOW?p_arg_names=prog_nbr&p
_arg_values=84.200}.

$$$ For A Degree In Physical Therapy

Through the Rehabilitation Training
Program, grants are provided for
training in fields directly related to the
vocational and independent living
rehabilitation of individuals with
disabilities, such as rehabilitation

medicine and physical and occupational therapy. Contact the Rehabilitation Services Administration, Office of Special Education and Rehabilitative Services, Department of Education, 400 Maryland Avenue, SW., Washington, DC 20202-2649; 202-245-7458; {www.ed.gov/students/college/aid/rehab/index.html}, {http://12.46.245.173/pls/portal30/CATALOG.PROGRAM_TEXT_RPT.SHOW?p_arg_names=prog_nbr&p_arg_values=84.129}.

$$$ For First Generation College Students

The TRIO Upward Bound program awards funds to generate skills and motivation necessary for success in education beyond high school among high school students from low-income families, high school students from families in which neither parent holds a bachelors degree, and low-income, first-generation military veterans who are preparing to enter postsecondary education. Funds are used to support a residential summer program and academic year program, and to pay stipends to students. Contact the U.S. Department of Education, OPE, Higher Education Programs, Federal TRIO Programs, 1990 K Street, N.W., 7th Floor, Washington, DC 20006-8510; 202-502-7600; {www.ed.gov/programs/trioupbound/index.html}, {http://12.46.245.173/pls/portal30/CATALOG.PROGRAM_TEXT_RPT.SHOW?p_arg_names=prog_nbr&p_arg_values=84.047}.

$40,000 For Graduate School

The Perkins Loan is awarded to undergraduate and graduate students with exceptional financial need. This is a campus-based loan program, with the school acting as the lender using a limited pool of funds provided by the

federal government. The maximum annual loan amount limit for an eligible student attending an institution is $6,000 for graduate students or $4,000 for undergraduates. Contact the institution they plan to attend. You can also contact the Office Federal Student Aid, Department of Education, 400 Maryland Avenue, SW., Washington, D.C. 20202-5446; 800-433-3243; {http://ifap.ed.gov}, {http://12.46.245.173/pls/portal30/CATALOG.PROGRAM_TEXT_RPT.SHOW?p_arg_names=prog_nbr&p_arg_values=84.038}.

$$$ To Study A Foreign Language

Through the National Resource Center and Fellowships Program for Language and Area, as well as the Language and International Studies program, academic year and summer fellowships are provided to institutions to assist graduate students in foreign language and either area or international studies. Contact the Office of Postsecondary Education, Department of Education, 400 Maryland Avenue, SW., Washington, DC 20202-5331; 202-502-7688; {www.ed.gov/programs/iegpsnrc/index.html}, {www.ed.gov/programs/iegpsflasf/index.html}, {http://12.46.245.173/pls/portal30/CATALOG.PROGRAM_TEXT_RPT.SHOW?p_arg_names=prog_nbr&p_arg_values=84.015}.

$4,000 To Attend Any College

Through the Federal Supplemental Educational Opportunity Grants program, eligible undergraduate students with demonstrated financial need are eligible for grant assistance to help meet educational expenses. Grants range from $100 to $4,000 per academic year, and students are eligible to receive the grant until they have completed their degree. Contact the educational institution you attend or plan to attend. For additional information, contact Office of Federal Student Aid, Department of Education, 400 Maryland Avenue, SW., Washington, DC 20202-5446; 800-433-3243, {http://ifap.ed.gov}, {http://12.46.245.173/pls/portal30/CATALOG.PROGRAM_TEXT_RPT.SHOW?p_arg_names=prog_nbr&p_arg_values=84.007}.

$30,000 For A Degree In Community Planning

Under the Community Development Work-Study Program, HUD will make grants to institutions of higher education for the purpose of providing assistance to those enrolled in full-time graduate programs in community and economic development, community planning, community management, or other related fields of study. Applicants must be economically disadvantaged and minority students who participate in community development work-study programs. Contact the U.S. Department of Housing and Urban Development, 451 7th Street S.W., Washington, DC 20410; 202-708-1112; {www.oup.org}, {http://12.46.245.173/pls/portal30/CATALOG.PROGRAM_TEXT_RPT.SHOW?p_arg_names=prog_nbr&p_arg_values=14.512}.

$100,000 to Educate on International Affairs

Up to $100,000 is available for individuals who are interested in educating the general public on international affairs. The foundation's current program goals are as follows: 1) Education, including teacher education and liberal arts education; 2) International Peace and Security; 3) International Development; and 4) Democracy. Contact the Carnegie Corporation of New York, 437 Madison Avenue, New York, NY 10022; 212-371-3200; Fax: 212-754-4073; {www.carnegie.org}.

Over $17,000 to Attend a Non-Profit College or University

Provides scholarships funds for students in chemistry, biochemistry, and the biological and medical sciences. Grants made to non-profit colleges/universities to promote research in chemistry and the life science and fund scholarships for in-depth undergraduate research experiences and comprehensive faculty mentoring. Scholarship awards up to $17,600 for two summers and one academic year. Contact Arnold and Mabel Beckman Foundation, 100 Academy, Irvine, CA 92617; 949-721-2222; Fax: 949-721-2225; {www.beckman-foundation.com}.

$35,000 for Education Research

The Spencer Foundation provides several kinds of financial support, including scholarships, grants, employee matching, and fellowships, for research in the field of education. The Foundation does not provide grants to individuals, except those working under the auspices of an institution. Contact The Spencer

Foundation, 875 N. Michigan Ave., Suite 3930; Chicago, IL 60611-1803; 312-337-7000; Fax: 312-337-0282; {www. spencer.org}.

GoGirlGO!

This grant is designed to help non-profit programs throughout the country maximize sports and physical activities for girls in third to eighth grade. The program focuses on an under-served population of girls, particularly economically disadvantaged girls or girls from populations with high incidences of health-risk behaviors. Contact Women's Sports Foundation, Eisenhower Park, East Meadow, NY 11554; 800-227-3988, 516-542-4700; {www.womenssportsfoundation.org}.

Get Loans Directly From Your School

(Federal Direct Loan 84.268)
The Direct Loan Program was begun to provide loans directly to students through schools, rather than through private lenders. Borrowers complete an application, the Free Application for Federal Student Aid (FAFSA), for all Department student financial aid programs. Schools receive the funds and then disburse them to students.

There are four different direct loans: Federal Direct Stafford/Ford Loans are for students who demonstrate financial need; Federal Direct Unsubsidized Stafford/Ford Loans are for students regardless of financial need; Federal Direct PLUS Loans are for parents to pay for their children's education; and Federal Direct Consolidation Loans help combine one or more federal education loans into one loan. For your Free Application for Federal Student Aid, contact Federal Student Aid Information Center, Union Center Plaza, 830 First Street, NE, Washington, DC 20044; 800-433-

3243; {www.ed.gov/DirectLoan/}, {www.studentaid.ed.gov}.

$15,000 For Graduate Students To Study Overseas

(Educational Exchange - Graduate Students 19.400)
Graduate students who would like to spend a year studying overseas can apply for the Fulbright Program, where if accepted, they will receive round trip transportation, tuition, books, maintenance for one academic year in one country, and health insurance. Students apply through the Fulbright program adviser located at their college or university. Contact Institute of International Education, 809 United Nations Plaza, New York, NY 10017; 212-883-5400; {www. iie.org}.

$4,000 Grants For Students Having Trouble Paying Tuition

(Federal Supplemental Education Opportunity Grants 84.007)
The Federal Supplemental Educational Opportunity Grants (FSEOG) are for undergraduate study and range from $100 to $4000 per academic year, with the student eligible to receive a FSEOG for the time it takes to complete their first degree. Students should contact the Financial Aid office

of the school they attend or plan to attend for information regarding application. A student *Financial Aid Handbook* is available. Contact the Federal Student Aid Information Center, P.O. Box 84, Washington, DC 20044; 800-433-3243; {www.studentaid.ed.gov}.

Money For a Foreign Language Degree

(National Resource Centers and Fellowships Program for Language and Area or Language and International Studies 84.015)
The Department of Education has funds to support centers which promote instruction in foreign language and international studies at colleges and universities. In addition, there are graduate fellowships to pursue this course of study in order to develop a pool of international experts to meet our nation's needs. Students must apply to those institutions that received the money. Contact Higher Education Programs, U.S. Department of Education, 1990 K Street, NW, Washington, DC 20006; 202-502-7700; {www.ed.gov/about/offices/list/ope/iegps/index.html}.

Travel Overseas For Your Doctorate Research

(International Overseas Doctoral Dissertation 84.022)
This program provides opportunities for graduate students to engage in full-time dissertation research abroad in modern foreign language and area studies with the exception of Western Europe. Contact International Education Programs Service, Office of Postsecondary Education, U.S. Department of Education, 1990 K Street, NW, 6th Floor, Washington, DC 20006; 202-502-7632; {www.ed.gov/programs/iegpsddrap/index.html}.

Money For Students And Teachers To Travel Overseas

(Overseas Group Projects Abroad 84.021)
The program objective is to help educational institutions improve their programs in modern foreign language and area studies through overseas study/travel seminar group research, advanced foreign language training, and curriculum development. Contact Higher Education Programs, U.S. Department of Education, Office of Post Secondary Education, 1990 K Street, NW, 6th Floor, Washington, DC 20006; 202-502-7624; {www.ed.gov/programs/iegpsgpa/index.html}.

Loans To Go To School

(Federal Family Education Loans 84.032)
Guaranteed loans for educational expenses are available from eligible lenders such as banks, credit unions, savings and loan association, pension funds, insurance companies, and schools to vocational, undergraduate, and graduate students enrolled at eligible institutions. The PLUS program is also available, which allows parents to borrow for their dependent student. Contact the Office of Student Financial Assistance, U.S. Department of Education, Washington, DC 20202; 800-433-7327; {www.ifap.ed.gov/}.

Work-Study Program Pays For School

(Federal Work-Study Program 84.033)
Part-time employment is available to students to help meet education expenses. This program pays an hourly wage to undergraduates. Graduate students may be paid by the hour or may receive a salary. A Student Financial Aid Handbook is available, as is a list of grantee institutions, by

contacting Federal Student Aid Information Center, P.O. Box 84, Washington, DC 20044; 800-433-3243. Contact the Division of Policy Development, Student Financial Assistance Programs, Office of Assistant Secretary for Postsecondary Education, 400 Maryland Ave., SW, Washington, DC 20202; 800-443-3243; {www.ed.gov/programs/fws/index.html}.

Get Help To Study
(TRIO Upward Bound 84.047)
This program generates skills and motivation necessary for success in education beyond high school among low income and potential first-generation college students and veterans. The goal of the program is to increase the academic performance and motivational levels of eligible enrollees. Eligible students must have completed the eighth grade and be between the ages of 13 and 19, enrolled in high school, and need such services to achieve their goal of college. The program provides instruction in reading, writing, study skills, and mathematics. They can provide academic, financial, or personal counseling, tutorial services, information on student financial assistance, assistance with college and financial aid applications, and more.

Contact Margaret Wingfield, Federal Trio Programs, College and University Preparation and Support Team, Office

of Post Secondary Education, U.S. Department of Education, 1990 K Street, NW, 7th Floor, Washington, DC 20006-8510; 202-502-7600; {www.ed.gov/programs/trioupbound/index.html}.

Low-Interest Student Loans
(Federal Perkins Loan Program 84.038)
Low-interest loans are available to eligible post-secondary students with demonstrated financial need to help meet educational expenses. To apply, contact the Financial Aid office of the school you attend or plan to attend. A student Financial Aid Handbook is available, as well as a list of grantee institutions by contacting the Federal Student Aid Information Center, P.O. Box 84, Washington, DC 20044; 800-433-3242; TTY: 800-730-8913. Contact the Division of Policy Development Student Financial Assistance Programs, Office of Assistant Secretary for Postsecondary Education, U.S. Department of Education, 400 Maryland Ave., SW, Washington, DC 20202-5446; 800-433-3242; {www.ed.gov/programs/fp/}.

$2,700 Grants To Go To School
(Federal Pell Grant Program 84.063)
Grants are available to students with financial need to help meet education expenses. Grants may not exceed $2,700 per year, and must be used for student's first bachelors or other professional degree. A Free Application for Federal Student Aid is available from the Federal Student Aid Information Center, P.O. Box 84, Washington, DC 20044; 800-433-3243; {www.studentaid.gov}. Contact Division of Policy Development, Office of Student Financial Assistance,

U.S. Department of Education, 400 Maryland Ave., SW, Washington, DC 20202; 800-433-3243; {www.ed.gov/programs/fpg}.

Aid For Students Who Want To Help The Deaf

(Training Interpreters For Individuals Who Are Deaf and Individuals Who Are Deaf-Blind 84.160)

This program supports projects that train new interpreters and improve the skills of manual, oral, and cued speech interpreters already providing services to individuals who are deaf and individuals who are deaf-blind. Grants are awarded for training, classroom instruction, workshops, seminars, and field placements. Students must apply to those institutions that have received the program money.

For a listing of institutions that received money contact the Office of Special Education and Rehabilitation Services, U.S. Department of Education, 400 Maryland Ave., SW, Washington, DC 20202; 202-205-9393; TTY: 202-401-3664; {www.ed.gov/students/college/aid/rehab/catinter.html}.

Money For Students Interested In Helping People With Disabilities

(Rehabilitation Training 84.129)

This program supports projects that provide new personnel and improve the skills of existing personnel trained in providing vocational rehabilitation services to individuals with disabilities in areas targeted as having personnel shortages. Training grants are provided in fields directly related to the vocational and independent living rehabilitation of individuals with disabilities, such as rehabilitation counseling, independent living, rehabilitation medicine, physical and occupational therapy, speech-language, pathology and audiology, and more. Students must apply to those institutions that have received the program money.

Contact Tim Muzzio at Rehabilitation Services Administration, Office of Special Education and Rehabilitation Services, U.S. Department of Education, 400 Maryland Ave., Washington, DC 20202; 202-245-7458; {www.ed.gov/programs/rsatrain}.

$25,400 Per Year For Graduate Study

(Jacob K. Javits Fellowships 84.170)

This program provides fellowships to individuals of superior ability for graduate study in the fields within the arts, humanities, and social sciences. To apply for these fellowships contact the Federal Student Aid Information Center, P.O. Box 84, Washington, DC 20044; 800-4-FED-AID or Office of Postsecondary Education, U.S. Department of Education, Jacob K. Javits Fellowship Program, 1990 K Street, NW, 6th Floor, Washington, DC 20006; 202-502-7542; {www.ed.gov/programs/iegpsjavits}.

$1,500 Per Year For College

(Robert C. Byrd Honors Scholarships 84.185)

Scholarships are available to exceptionally able students who show promise of continued academic achievement. To apply for this grant award, interested applicants must contact their state educational agency, which administers this program. U.S. Department of Education, Higher Education Programs, 1990 K Street, 6th Floor, Washington, DC 20006-8512; 202-502-7582; {www.ed.gov/programs/iduesbyrd/index.html}.

Money For Graduate Study

(Graduate Assistance In Areas Of National Need 84.200)
Fellowships are available through graduate academic departments to graduate students of superior ability who demonstrate financial need and are able to enhance the capacity to teach and conduct research in areas of national need. Students must apply to those institutions that have received the money. For a listing of institutions that received money contact the office listed below. Contact International Education and Graduate Programs Service, Office of Postsecondary Education, U.S. Department of Education, 1990 K Street, 6th Floor, Washington, DC 20006-8524; 202-502-7638; {www.ed.gov/programs/gaann/index.html }.

Grants For Those Who Have Trouble Paying Tuition

(Ronald E. McNair Post Baccalaureate Achievement 84.217)
This program provides grants to institutions of higher education to prepare low income, first-generation college students and students underrepresented in graduate education for graduate study. Students must apply to those institutions that have received the money. For a listing of institutions that received money contact the office listed below. Contact

U.S. Department of Education, Federal Trio Programs, Office of Postsecondary Education, 1990 K Street, 7th Floor, Washington, DC 20006-8510; 202-502-7600; {www.ed.gov/programs/triomcnair}.

Part-Time Jobs In The Government

(Student Temporary Employment Program 27.003)
The program gives students 16 years of age and older an opportunity for part time temporary employment with federal agencies in order to allow them to continue their education without interruptions caused by financial pressures. Apply for this program through the youth division of the local office of the State Employment Service. Contact the Main State Employment Service office for referral to a local office. Contact Employment Service, Office of Personnel Management, 1900 E St., NW, Washington, DC 20415; 202-606-1800; {www.usajobs.opm.gov/students.asp}, {www.opm.gov/employ/students/index.asp}.

Internships For Graduate Students To Work AT 54 Government Agencies

(Presidential Management Fellows Program 27.013)
The PMF Program is a two-year entry-level employment and career development program designed to attract to the federal civil service men and women with graduate degrees from diverse cultural and academic backgrounds. Nominees for the PMI Program undergo a rigorous, competitive screening process. Agencies designate positions for the PMFs and each establishes its own procedures for considering and hiring PMFs. An application form and more

information can be requested by contacting the Career America Hotline at 912-757-3000. Contact U.S. Office of Personnel Management, 1900 E Street, NW, Washington, DC 20415-1000; 202-606-1800; {www.pmi.opm. gov}.

Money For Nursing Students
(Nursing Student Loans 93.364)
The Nursing Student Loan program provides for long-term, low-interest loans to full-time and half-time financially needy students pursuing a course of study leading to a diploma, associate, baccalaureate or graduate degree in nursing. To apply for this loan, contact the student financial aid office at the school where you intend to apply for admission or where you are enrolled. Contact the Division of Health Careers, Diversity and Development, Bureau of Health Professions, Health Resources and Services Administration, Public Health Service, U.S. Department of Health and Human Services Administration, Parklawn Building, Room 8-34, 5600 Fishers Lane, Rockville, MD 20857; 301-443-4776; {http://bhpr.hrsa.gov/dsa/}.

Money for Health Profession Students
(Health Professions Student Loans 93.342)
The Health Professions Student Loan Program provides long-term, low interest rate loans to full-time financially needy students pursuing a degree in dentistry, optometry, pharmacy, pediatric medicine, or veterinary medicine. Funds are made available to schools for the establishment of revolving student loan funds. To apply for this loan, contact the student financial aid office at the school where you intend to apply

for admission or where you are enrolled. Contact the Division of Health Careers, Diversity and Development, Bureau of Health Professions, Health Resources and Services Administration, Public Health Service, U.S. Department of Health and Human Services Administration, Parklawn Building, Room 8-34, 5600 Fishers Lane, Rockville, MD 20857; 301-443-4776; 888-275-4772; {http://bhpr.hrsa.gov/dsa/}.

Loans For Disadvantaged Health Profession Students
(Loans for Disadvantaged Students 93.342)
Loans for Disadvantaged Students Program provides funding to eligible health professions schools for the purpose of providing long-term, low-interest loans to assist full-time, financially needy, disadvantaged students to pursue a career in allopathic or osteopathic medicine, dentistry, optometry, podiatry, pharmacy, or veterinary medicine. To apply for this loan, contact the student financial aid office at the school where you intend to apply for admission or where you are enrolled. Contact the Division of Health Careers, Diversity and Development, Bureau of Health Professions' Health Resources and Services Administration, Public Health Service, U.S. Department of Health and Human Services Administration, Parklawn Building, Room 8-34, 5600 Fishers Lane, Rockville, MD 20857; 301-443-4776; 888-275-4772; {http://bhpr.hrsa.gov/dsa/}.

Money For Primary Care Students
(Health Professions Student Loans, Including Primary Care Loans 93.342)
The Primary Care Loan Program provides long-term low interest rate

loans to full-time financially needy students pursuing a degree in allopathic or osteopathic medicine. To apply for this loan, contact the student financial aid office at the school where you intend to apply for admission or where you are enrolled. Loans cannot exceed tuition. Contact the Bureau of Health Professions, Health Resources and Services Administration, Public Health Service, U.S. Department of Health and Human Services Administration, Parklawn Building, Room 8-34, 5600 Fishers Lane, Rockville, MD 20857; 301-443-4776; 888-275-4772; {http://bhpr.hrsa.gov/dsa/}.

Money For Faculty Loan Repayments

(Disadvantaged Health Professions Faculty Loan Repayment Program 93.923)
The Faculty Loan Repayment Program provides a financial incentive for degree-trained health professionals from disadvantaged backgrounds to pursue an academic career. The health professional must agree to serve as a member of a faculty of a health professions school, providing teaching services for a minimum of two years, faculty for schools of medicine, nursing, osteopathic medicine, dentistry, pharmacy, pediatric medicine, optometry, veterinary medicine, public health, or a school that offers a graduate program in clinical psychology. The federal government agrees to pay as much as $20,000 on the individual's educational loans.

Contact the Division of Health Careers, Diversity and Development, Bureau of Health Professions, Health Resources and Services Administration, Public Health Service,

U.S. Department of Health and Human Services Administration, Parklawn Building, Room 8-34, 5600 Fishers Lane, Rockville, MD 20857; 301-443-4776; 888-275-4772; {http://bhpr.hrsa.gov/DSA/flrp/index.htm}.

Scholarships For Disadvantaged Health Profession Students

(Scholarships For Health Profession Students From Disadvantaged Backgrounds 93.925)
The Scholarships For Disadvantaged Students program provides funds to eligible schools for the purpose of providing scholarships to full-time financially needy students from disadvantaged backgrounds enrolled in health professions and nursing programs. Funds are awarded to accredited schools of medicine, osteopathic medicine, dentistry, optometry, pharmacy, podiatric medicine, veterinary medicine, nursing (diploma, associate, baccalaureate, and graduate degree), public health, allied health (baccalaureate and graduate degree programs of dental hygiene, medical laboratory technology, occupational therapy, physical therapy, radiologic technology), and graduate programs in clinical psychology.

Contact the student financial aid office at the school where you intend to apply for admission or where you are enrolled. Contact the Bureau of Health Professions, Health Resources and Services Administration, Public Health Service, U.S. Department of Health and Human Services Administration, Parklawn Building, Room 8-34, 5600 Fishers Lane, Rockville, MD 20857; 301-443-4776; 888-275-4772; {http://bhpr. hrsa.gov/dsa/}.

Money For American Indians Who Want To Be Health Care Professionals

(Health Professions Recruitment Program For Indians 93.970)
The program objective is to increase the number of American Indians and Alaskan Natives who become health professionals. Some of the projects funded include the recruitment of American Indians into health care programs, a variety of retention services once students have enrolled, and scholarship support. Students should contact their school directly for assistance. Contact Indian Health Service, Division of Health Professions Support, 801 Thompson Ave., Suite 400, Rockville, MD 20852; 301-443-4242; {www.ihs.gov}.

Health Professions Scholarships For American Indians

(Health Professions Pregraduate Scholarship Program for Indians 93.123)
The program objective is to provide scholarships to American Indians and Alaskan Natives for the purpose of completing pre-graduate education leading to baccalaureate degree in the areas of pre-medicine or pre-dentistry. Contact the Indian Health Service for application information; Indian Health Service, Scholarship Program, 801 Thompson Ave., Suite 120, Rockville, MD 20852; 301-443-6197; {www.ihs. gov}.

Money For American Indians Who Need Extra Studies For Health Care Program

(Health Professions Preparatory Scholarship Program for Indians 93.971)
The program objective is to make scholarships available to American Indians and Alaskan Natives who need to take some extra courses in order to qualify for enrollment or re-enrollment in a health profession school. For application information contact Indian Health Service, Scholarship Program, 801 Thompson Ave., Suite 120, Rockville, MD 20852; 301-443-6197; {www.ihs.gov}.

Scholarships For Health Care Professionals

(Health Professions Scholarship Program 93.972)
This program objective is to provide scholarships to American Indians and Alaskan natives attending health professions schools and who are interested in serving other Indians. Upon completion, scholarship recipients are obligated to serve in the Indian Health Service one year for each year of scholarship support, with a minimum of two years. Contact Indian Health Service, Scholarship Program, 801 Thompson Ave., Suite 120, Rockville, MD 20852; 301-443-6197; {www.ihs.gov}.

Opportunity To Receive College Tuition From NSA

(Stokes Educational Scholarship)
National Security Agency (NSA) will consider any student who meets the requirements below and who chooses a

major in either computer science, electrical or computer engineering, languages or mathematics. Requirements consist of having a minimum SAT score of 1100 and a minimum composite ACT score of 25. Chosen students can receive college tuition, reimbursement for books, year-round salary, summer work and have a guaranteed job with the NSA.

Students must work for NSA for one and a half times their length of study, which is usually about five years. Contact the National Security Agency, 9800 Savage Road, Suite 6779, Ft. George G. Mead, MD 20755-6779; 866-672-4473; {www.nsa.gov/careers/students_4.cfm}.

Health Careers Opportunity Program
(Health Careers Opportunity Program 93.822)
The Health Careers Opportunity Program provides assistance to individuals from disadvantaged backgrounds to obtain a health or allied health profession degree. Grants can be used to identify, recruit, and select individuals from minority and disadvantaged backgrounds for education and training in a health or allied health professions school; facilitate entry of eligible students into such schools; provide counseling or other services designed to assist such individuals in successfully completing their education and training; provide preliminary education for a period prior to entry into the regular course of health or allied health professions education, and more. For a listing of institutions that received money, contact the Division of Health Careers, Diversity and Development, Bureau of Health Professions, Health Resources and Services Administration, Public

Health Services, U.S. Department of Health and Human Services, Room 8A-09, 5600 Fishers Lane, Rockville, MD 20857; 301-443-1348; {http://bhpr.hrsa.gov/diversity/hcop/default.htm}.

Grants for Native Hawaiian Students
(Native Hawaiian Higher Education Program 84.316)
Grants are given to provide full or partial fellowship support for Native Hawaiian students enrolled at two or four year degree granting institutions of higher education. Awards are based on academic potential and financial need. Contact Susana Easton, Higher Education Programs, Office of Postsecondary Education, Department of Education, 1990 K Street, NW, Washington, DC 20006; 202-502-7628; {www.ed.gov/programs/iegps hawaiian}.

Money For Nursing Students To Repay Their Loans
(Nursing Education Loan Repayment Agreements For Registered Nurses Entering Employment At Eligible Health Facilities 93.908)
This program assists in the repayment of their nursing education loans. The program is designed to increase the number of registered nurses serving designated nurse shortage areas. An Applicant Information Bulletin For Registered Nurses is available at the address listed below. Contact Chief, Diversity and Basic Nurse Education Branch, Division of Nursing, Bureau of Health Professionals, Health Resources and Services Administration, 5600 Fishers Lane, Room 9-36, Rockville, MD 20857; 301-443-3232; 866-813-3753; {http://bhpr.hrsa.gov/nursing/loanrepay.htm}.

Scholarships For National Health Service Corps

(National Health Service Corps Scholarship Program 93.288)
The program objective is to provide service-conditioned scholarships to health professions students to assure an adequate supply of physicians, dentists, certified nurse midwives, certified nurse practitioners, and physician assistants in Health Professional Shortage Areas. The scholarship pays for tuition and required fees, books, supplies, and equipment for the year, plus a monthly stipend to students, and a single annual payment to cover the cost of all other reasonable educational expenses. Each year of support incurs one year of service. Contact Division of National Health Service Corps, NHSC Scholarship Program, c/o I.Q. Solutions, 11300 Rockville Pike, Suite 801, Rockville, MD 20852; 301-594-4400; 800-638-0824; {http://nhsc. bhpr.hrsa.gov}.

Money To Train To Be A Professional Nurse

(Professional Nurse Traineeships 93.358)
The program objective is to prepare individuals who have completed basic nursing preparation as nurse educators, public health nurses, nurse midwives, and nurse practitioners, or as other clinical nursing specialists. Money can be used to support a student while they complete the professional nurse traineeships. Students must apply to those institutions that have received the program money. Contact the Division of Nursing, Bureau of Health Professions, Health Resources and Services Administration, Public Health Service, U.S. Department of Health and Human Services, 5600 Fishers Lane, Room 9-35, Rockville, MD 20857; 301-443-6333; {http://bhpr. hrsa.gov/}.

Money For Health Professionals Who Want To Be In Public Health

(Public Health Traineeships 93.964)
The program objective is to help support graduate students who are studying in the field of public health. Grants are given to colleges and universities offering graduate or specialized training in the public health field. Support is limited to the fields of biostatistics, epidemiology, environmental health, toxicology, public health nutrition, and maternal and child health. Students must apply to those institutions that have received the money. Contact the Division of Associated, Dental, and Public Health Professions, Bureau of Health Professions, Health Resources and Services Administration, Public Health Service, Parklawn Bldg., Room 8C-09, 5600 Fishers Lane, Rockville, MD 20857; 301-443-6864; {http://bhpr. hrsa.gov/publichealth/phtrainee.htm}.

Money For Job Safety and Health Training

(Occupational Safety and Health - Training Grants 93.263)
The program objective is to develop specialized professional and

paraprofessional personnel in the occupational safety and health field with training in occupational medicine, occupational health nursing, industrial hygiene, and occupational safety. Students must apply to those institutions that have received the money. Contact the Grants Management Officer, Procurement and Grants Office, Centers for Disease Control and Prevention, 626 Cochrans Mill Road, P.O. Box 1870, Pittsburgh, PA 15236; 412-386-6428, 888-472-6874; {www. cdc.gov/niosh/oep}.

$30,000 To Study The Humanities

(Promotion of the Humanities - Fellowships and Stipends 45.160)
Fellowships and Summer Stipends provide support for scholars to undertake full-time independent research and writing in the humanities. Grants are available for 6 to 12 month fellowships and two months of summer study. Projects may contribute to scholarly knowledge or to the general public's understanding of the humanities. Contact Fellowships and Stipends, Division of Research and Education, National Endowment for the Humanities, 1100 Pennsylvania Ave., Room 318, Washington, DC 20506; 202-606-8400, 800-NEH-1121; {www.neh.gov}.

Money To Repay Loans

(National Health Service Corps Loan Repayment 93.162)
The National Health Service Corps provides for the repayment of educational loans for health professionals who agree to serve in a health manpower shortage area. Priority is given to primary care physicians, dentists, certified nurse midwives, certified nurse practitioners, and physicians' assistants. Money can

be used to repay student loans. The amount of money available per professional is up to $25,000 a year during the first two years of practice and $35,000 for each year after that. Contact the National Health Service Corps Scholarships, Division of Scholarships and Loan Repayments, Bureau of Primary Health Care, Health Resources and Services Administration, Public Health Service, U.S. Department of Health and Human Services, 5600 Fishers Lane, Room 8A-55, Rockville, MD 20857; 301-594-4400; 800-221-9393; {http://nhsc. bhpr.hrsa.gov/join_us/lrp.cfm}.

Money For Health Care Training In Rural Areas

(Interdisciplinary Training For Health Care For Rural Areas 93.192)
This program is designed to help fulfill the health care needs of people living in rural areas. Money is set aside to recruit and retain health care professionals in rural health care settings. Funds can be used for student stipends, postdoctoral fellowships, faculty training, and the purchase or rental of necessary transportation and telecommunication equipment. Money can be used to support health profession students. Students must apply to those institutions that have received the money. Contact the Division of Associated, Dental and Public Health Professions, Bureau of Health Professions, Health Resources

and Services Administration, Room 8C-26, Parklawn Building, 5600 Fishers Lane, Rockville, MD 20857; 301-443-6867; 877-477-2123; {http:// bhpr.hrsa.gov/interdisciplinary/rural.ht ml}.

Get Your Loans Paid Through Indian Health Service

(Indian Health Service Loan Repayment Program 93.164)
To ensure that there are enough trained health professionals, the Indian Health Service provides for the repayment of loans to those professionals who agree to serve in an Indian Health Service Facility. Money can be used for the repayment of student loans. The minimum period of participation is two years, and the maximum loan payment is $20,000 per year. Contact the Indian Health Service, Loan Repayment Program, 801 Thompson Ave., Suite 120, Rockville, MD 20852; 301-443-3369; {www.ihs.gov}.

Money For Disadvantaged Students To Study Nursing

(Nursing Workforce Diversity 93.178)
Schools of nursing can receive financial assistance to meet the costs of projects that increase nursing education opportunities for individuals from disadvantaged backgrounds. Money can be used for counseling, preliminary education of students, and to support a student. Students must apply to those institutions that have received the money. Contact the Division of Nursing, Bureau of Health Professions, Health Resources and Services Administration, Public Health Services, U.S. Department of Health and Human Services, Room 8C-26, Parklawn Building, 5600 Fishers Lane, Rockville, MD 20857; 301-443-6880; {http://bhpr.hrsa.gov}.

Money To Train To Become A Nurse Anesthetist

(Nurse Anesthetist Traineeships 93.124)
Registered nurses can receive money to become nurse anesthetists through this program that provides funds for a maximum 18-month period of full-time study. Nurses must complete 12 months of study in a nurse anesthetist program. Students need to apply to those institutions that have received the money. Contact the Division of Nursing, Bureau of Health Professions, Health Resources and Services Administration, Public Health Service, U.S. Department of Health and Human Services, Room 9-36, 5600 Fishers Lane, Rockville, MD 20857; 301-443-5787; {http://bhpr.hrsa.gov}.

Money To Study The Break Up Of The USSR

(Program for Study of Eastern Europe and the Independent States of the Former Soviet Union 19.300)
The program is designed to sustain and strengthen American expertise on the Commonwealth of Independent States, Georgia, the Baltic countries, and countries of Eastern Europe by supporting graduate training; advanced research; public dissemination of research data, methods, and findings; contact and collaboration among government and private specialists; and first hand experience of the (former) Soviet Union and Eastern European countries by American specialists, and more. Funds are given to nonprofit organizations and institutions of higher learning who act as intermediaries. Students must apply to those institutions that received the money. Contact the Eurasian and East European Research and Training Program, INR/RES, U.S. Department

of State, 2201 C St., NW, Room 2251, Washington, DC 20520; 202-736-4572; {www.state.gov/}.

Money To Study Food

(Food and Agricultural Science National Needs Graduate Fellowship Grants 10.210)

These grants are to be used to encourage outstanding students to pursue and complete a graduate degree in an area of the food and agricultural sciences for which there is a national need for development of scientific expertise. Money can be used to support a student completing a graduate, masters, or doctorate degree. Students must apply to those institutions that received the money. Contact the Grants Program Manager, Office of Higher Education Programs, CSREES, U.S. Department of Agriculture, 1400 Independence Ave., SW, Stop 2251, Washington, DC 20250-2251; 202-720-7854; {www.reeusda.gov}.

Money To Study Community Planning and Development

(Community Development Work-Study Program 14.512)

The Community Development Work-Study Program makes grants to institutions of higher education to provide assistance to economically disadvantaged and minority students. Students take part in community development work-study programs while they are enrolled full-time in graduate or undergraduate programs with that major. Students must apply to those institutions that received the money. Contact the U.S. Department of Housing and Urban Development, Community Planning and Development, Office of University Partnerships, 451 7th St., SW, Room 8106, Washington, DC 20410; 202-708-3061, 800-877-8339; {www.hud.gov/progdesc/cdwsp.cfm}.

Money To Study Housing Issues

(Doctoral Dissertation Research Grant Program 14.516)

The program objective is to encourage doctoral candidates to engage in policy related housing and urban development research and to assist them in its timely completion. Money can used to support Ph.D candidates. Students can request an application package from the address listed below or by calling HUD USER at 800-245-2691. For additional information, contact Armand Carriere, Office of University Partnerships, U.S. Department of Housing and Urban Development, 451 7th St., SW, Room 8106, Washington, DC 20410; 202-708-3061; {www.huduser.org}, {www.oup.org/about/ddrg.html}.

Money For Members Of Indian Tribes To Go To College

(Indian Education-Higher Education Grant Program 15.114)

The program objective is to provide financial aid to eligible Indian students to enable them to attend accredited institutions of higher education. Members of an Indian tribe may be eligible for these grants to supplement the total financial aid package prepared by their college financial aid officer. Contact Bureau of Indian Affairs, Office of Indian Education Programs, Room MS-3512-MIB, U.S. Department of the Interior, 1849 C Street, NW, Washington, DC 20240-0001; 202-208-6123; {www.oiep.bia.edu}.

Money For Criminal Justice Majors

(Criminal Justice Research and Development - Grant Research Fellowships 16.562)

The program objective is to improve the quality and quantity of knowledge about crime and the criminal justice system, and increase the number of persons who are qualified to teach in collegiate criminal justice programs, to conduct research related to criminal justice issues, and to perform more effectively within the criminal justice system. Students can receive a fellowship for a year.

Detailed information can be received by requesting the NIJ Research Plan from the National Criminal Justice Reference Service, Box 6000, Rockville, MD 20850; 800-851-3420. Contact the NCJRS Research and Information Center, 2277 Research Blvd., Rockville, MD 20850; 301-519-5063; {www.ojp.usdoj.gov/nij/}.

$3,000 A Year To Be A Merchant Marine

(State Marine Schools 20.806)

The program objective is to train merchant marine officers in State Marine Schools. You can receive $3,000 per year to train to be a merchant marine officer at a designated State Marine School. In exchange for this incentive payment program, you must commit yourself to a minimum of five years duty to the Maritime Administration. You must also remain in a reserve unit of an armed force for a minimum of eight years. Students need to apply to one of the State Marine Schools. Contact the Office of Maritime Labor and Training, Maritime Administration, U.S. Department of Transportation, 400 7th St., SW, Washington, DC

20590; 202-366-5755; 800-996-2723; {www.marad.dot.gov}.

All Expenses Plus $558 A Month To Be A Merchant Marine

(U.S. Merchant Marine Academy – Kings Point 20.807)

This program trains merchant marine officers while they attend the Merchant Marine Academy in Kings Point, NY. Students receive training, subsistence, books, quarters, uniforms, medical care, and program travel without cost. In addition, the student will receive a monthly wage from their steamship company employer.

Contact Office of Maritime Labor and Training, Maritime Administration, U.S. Department of Transportation, 400 Seventh St., SW, Washington, DC 20590; 202-366-5484; 800-996-2723; {www.marad.dot.gov}.

Money For Disabled Veterans To Go To College

(Vocational Rehabilitation For Disabled Veterans 64.116)

The program objective is to provide all services and assistance necessary to enable service-disabled veterans and service persons hospitalized pending discharge to achieve maximum independence in daily living and, to the maximum extent possible, to become employable and to obtain and maintain suitable employment. The fund provides for the entire cost of tuition, books, fees, supplies, and other services to help the veteran live. Students must obtain an application from any Veterans Affairs office or regional office. Contact Veterans Benefits Administration, Department of Veterans Affairs, Washington, DC 20420; 202-273-7419, 800-827-1000; {www.va.gov}.

Money For Social, Behavioral, And Economic Sciences Students

(Social, Behavioral, and Economic Sciences 47.075)
The program objective is to promote the progress of the social, behavioral, and economic science; to facilitate cooperative research activities with foreign scientists, engineers, and institutions and to support understanding of the resources invested in science and engineering in the U.S. Funds are provided for U.S. scientists and engineers to carry out studies abroad, to conduct research, to engage in joint research projects with foreign counterpart organizations, and to support international scientific workshops in the U.S. and abroad. Students must contact the Assistant Director, Social, Behavioral, and Economic Research, National Science Foundation, 4201 Wilson Blvd., Suite 935Arlington, VA 22230; 703-292-5111; {www.nsf.gov}.

Money For Spouses And Children Of Deceased Or Disabled Veterans To Go To School

(Survivors and Dependents Educational Assistance 64.117)
The program provides partial support to those seeking to advance their education who are qualifying spouses, surviving spouses, or children of deceased or disabled veterans who, as a result of their military service, have a permanent and total (100 percent) service connected disability, or a service personnel who have been listed for a total of more than 90 days as currently Missing in Action, or as Prisoners of War. Spouse, surviving spouse, or child of a deceased or disabled veteran can receive monthly payments to be used for tuition, books, subsistence, for courses, training, or college. Benefits may be awarded for pursuit of associate, bachelor, or graduate degrees at colleges and universities, as well as study at business, technical, or vocational schools. Contact Department of Veterans Affairs, Central Office, Washington, DC 20420; 202-273-7132, 800-827-1000; {www.gibill.va.gov}.

Money For Retired Veterans To Go To School

(All-Volunteer Force Educational Assistance 64.124)
Honorably discharged veterans can take advantage of the Montgomery GI Bill Active Duty benefits, which provides funds to pursue professional or vocational education, and even covers correspondence courses.

Veterans can receive a monthly stipend while attending school, with the amount varying depending upon date of entry into the service and length of service. Additional information and application materials are available through any regional Veterans Affairs office. Contact Department of Veterans Affairs, Central Office, Washington, DC 20420; 202-273-7132, 800-827-1000; {www.gibill.va.gov}.

Volunteer And Earn Money To Pay For School

(AmeriCorps 94.006)
AmeriCorps program provides meaningful opportunities for people to serve their country in organized efforts, fostering citizen responsibility, building their community, and providing education opportunities for those who make a serious commitment to service. Stipends can be used to support the person while they volunteer. Health care and childcare benefits may also be provided. Participants will also receive an education award, which may be used to pay for higher education or for vocational training, and may also be used to repay any existing student loans. Contact the Corporation for National and Community Service, 1201 New York Avenue, NW, Washington, DC 20525 202-606-5000, ext. 474; {www.americorps.org}, {www.nationalservice.org/}.

Fellowships for Creative Writers and Translators

(Promotion of the Arts-Grants to Organizations and Individuals 45.024)
The National Endowment for the Arts provides grants to support Literature Fellowships, Fellowships for Creative Writers, Fellowships awarded to writers of poetry, fiction, and creative nonfiction to allow them to devote time to writing, research, travel, and to advance their writing careers. Contact National Endowment for the Arts, 1100 Pennsylvania Ave., NW, Washington, DC 20506; 202-682-5400; {www. arts.gov}.

Scholarships for Minorities

(Higher Education Multicultural Scholars Program 10.220)
This program is designed to increase the ethnic and cultural diversity of the food and agricultural scientific and professional work force, and to advance the educational achievement of minority Americans. Money is given to colleges and universities that have a demonstrable capacity to attract, educate, and graduate minority students for careers as agriscience and agribusiness professionals. Contact the National Program Leader, Education Programs, CSREES, U.S. Department of Agriculture, Stop 2251, 1400 Independence Ave., SW, Washington, DC 20250; 202-720-1973; {www. reeusda.gov}.

Money For Vietnam Veterans To Go To School

(Post-Vietnam Era Veterans' Educational Assistance 64.120)
Post-Vietnam veterans who entered the Armed Services between 1977 and 1985 may be eligible for funds to obtain a college degree or vocational training. Through this program, the government matches $2 for every $1 the serviceman contributes. Contact your local or regional Veterans Affairs office for additional information or application materials. Contact Department of Veterans Affairs, Central Office, Washington, DC 20420; 202-273-7132, 800-827-1000; {www.gibill.va.gov}.

Free Money for College

Scholarships abound if you know where to look. Some samplings include:

- $2,500 for Young Composers
- Scholarships for Mature Women
- $4,000 for Gardening Students
- $1,500 for Women over Age 35
- $5,000 for Broadcasters
- $1,500 for Veterinarian Students
- $2,500 for Architecture Majors

- $5,000 for Pharmacy Students
- $10,000 for Legally Blind Students
- $5,000 for Journalists
- $4,000 for Physical Therapists

Where do you find these kinds of scholarships? Everywhere! Some great starting places include:

General Financial Aid Information Websites

FinAid
http://www.finaid.org

The Financial Aid Resource Network
http://www.theoldschool.org

Employers

If you have a job, ask your own human resources department if they offer scholarships or tuition reimbursement programs. If you are still in high school, have your parents ask their employers.

Professional or Social Organizations

Of what professional or social organizations are you or your parents members? 4H, JayCees, Lions Club? Association for Internet Addiction?

If you or your parents are a member of an organization, ask them and see if they offer any kind of scholarships. If you are NOT a member of any organizations, the next thing to check with is organizations that represent what you are planning on studying. Many such organizations offer scholarships to students who are studying what they support, even if you are not a member.

Labor Unions

Are you or your parents a member of a union? All the major labor unions offer scholarships for members and their dependent children (AFL-CIO, Teamsters, etc.)

Church

Check with your church. Your local parish may or may not have any scholarships for their members, but the diocese or headquarters may have some available. And if you have been very active in your local church, they may be able to help you in other ways.

High School

If you are still in high school, it is very important that you speak with your guidance counselor or administration office and ask about scholarships that are available to students at your school.

College

If you are already attending college, or are planning on attending, the financial aid office at your college can be an excellent resource for scholarships and financial aid. You will also find applications for most of the state and federal level aid programs available at your financial aid office.

And if that weren't enough, scholarship books abound. We did a quick recent review of some of the more interesting options and found the following list. Most of these should be available in your local library, as well as at the bookstore.

- *8 Steps to Help Black Families Pay for College: A Crash Course in Financial Aid* by Thomas LaVeist and Will LaViest, Random House, 2003.

- *Financial Aid for Asian Americans 2003-2005,* Reference Service Press.

- *The Scholarship Almanac,* Peterson's/Thompson Learning, 2004.

- *The College Blue Book: Scholarships, Fellowships, Grants and Loans,* Macmillan Information, 2004.

- *Scholarships, Fellowships and Loans,* Bellman Publishing Company, 2004.

- *The College Board Scholarship Handbook 2004* by College Board, College Entrance Examination Board, 2001.

- *Chronicle Financial Aid Guide 2003-2004: Scholarships and Loans for High School Students, College Students, Graduates, and Adult Learners,* Chronicle Guidance Publishing, 2003.

- *College Financial Aid for Dummies* by Herm Davis and Joyce Lain Kennedy, Hungry Minds Publishing, 1999.

- *The Complete Scholarship Book: The Biggest, Easiest Guide for Getting the Most Money for College by Fastweb.com,* Sourcebook Trade, 2000.

- *Directory of Financial Aid for Women, 2003-2005* by Gail Ann Schlachter, Reference Service Press, 2003.

- *Get Free Cash for College* by Kelly Y. Tanabe, Supercollege Publishing, 2003.

- *How to Go to College Almost for Free* by Benjamin R. Kaplan, Harper Resource, 2002.

- *Scholarships 2003 (Scholarships (Kaplan))* by Gail Schlachter, R. David Weber and Douglas Bucher, Kaplan, 2002.

- *The Scholarship Book 2004* by Daniel Cassidy, Prentice Hall Press, 2004.

- *Winning Scholarships for College: An Insider's Guide* by Marianne Ragins, Holt, 2004.

Free Money for Federal Employees and Their Families To Go To College

Over $2.75 million in college scholarships is awarded exclusively to federal and postal employees and their family members. The Federal Employee Education Assistance Program (FEEA) scholarship applications are available from January through March each year. You can get an application online at their web site.

Eligible applicants include current civilian federal and postal employees with at least three years of federal service and their dependent family members (children and spouses). Employee applicants may be part-time students; dependents must be full-time. For more information send a self-addressed, stamped #10 business envelope to: FEEA Scholarships, Suite

200, 8441 W Bowles Ave, Littleton, CO 80123-9501; 303-933-7580; {www.feea.org/scholarships.shtml}.

Save Your Money

Don't spend money on something you can do yourself! Many scholarship search services will charge you $300 and guarantee you that they will find you a certain number of scholarships for which you MAY qualify. You can do that yourself and save the $300 for your college textbooks. Search for scholarships on the web using any of these search engines for FREE!

Free Scholarship Information Service
{www.freschinfo.com}

The Scholarship Page
{www.scholarship-page.com}

FastAid
{www.fastaid.com}

Princeton Review
{www.princetonreview.com}

Go College
{www.gocollege.com}

FastWEB
{http://fastweb.monster.com}

ASIS Arkansas Scholarship Information Service
{www.arkansasscholarshipconnection.org}

College Planning Web Site
{http://collegeplan.org}

College Net
{www.collegenet.com}

OSAD Scholarship Search
(online study abroad directory)
{www.umabroad.umn.edu}

Arkansas Student Loan Authority
{www.asla.state.ar.us}

STUDENT LOAN FORGIVENESS

Wouldn't it be great if someone offered you FREE money to help pay off your student loans? Well guess what, there is money and it's waiting for you!!! Amazingly, there are numerous programs offered by employers, non-profit organizations, universities, and the state and federal government that will give you money, solely to pay off your student loans.

According to a national study done in 2002, the average student loan debt for students who completed a four-year degree was $18,900. This is a 66 percent increase since 1997. Those students who attended a public four-year college averaged $17,100 and those who attended a private four-year college averaged $21,200.

bit of debt! But don't fear, there is a way to ease your payments and it's called a student loan forgiveness program.

Loan forgiveness programs may be the answer to your loan worries. Here's how they work: You provide a public service that helps those in need--teaching underprivileged children, building homes for low-income families, giving health care or legal services to the disadvantaged--and, in return, the program cancels all or part of your educational loan debt.

These programs are real, they work and they are being taken advantage by many people. We have stories from many professionals who applied and received financial assistance to help them pay off their burdensome loan.

You're probably asking yourself how to start finding a program that is right for you. To help make this process easier for you, an array of loan forgiveness programs have been sorted into nine categories:

1. Volunteer/Non-Profit: Programs listed in this category will largely require work to be performed through volunteer work such as the Peace Corps and Americorps.

2. Teachers/Education: This section includes programs designed to attract teachers and the educational community to underprivileged areas.

3. Universities: Unbeknownst to many graduates but various loan forgiveness programs are offered through universities. This section will describe the programs offered and lists them by the name of the University.

4. Specialty Employment: This area lists programs for individuals who work in certain geographic locations and the child care industry.

5. Employers: Believe it or not there are some employers who are willing to help you pay off your student loan. This segment lists their names and contact information.

6. Medical: This sector covers numerous programs intended for persons employed within the medical field such as doctors, nurses, dentists and so forth.

7. Legal: This section pertains to loan forgiveness programs geared toward recruiting attorney in to areas to help the underprivileged

8. Specialty Legal: Many states and employers are willing to help attorneys with their loan burdens. This section lists state by state agencies willing to help if the attorney does a certain amount of work for the disadvantaged.

Each category will describe the program, list the requirements, and provide contact information. A word of advice, read through all of the categories, especially *Medical,* as this category covers several areas in the medical field, such as nurses, doctors, and dentists. Also many of these programs can be helpful in directing you to other areas of monetary aid such as grants and so forth.

Now that you know about these programs, the only thing standing between you and paying off or significantly reducing your student loans is to start applying. Good Luck!

Volunteer/ Non Profit

$4,725 To $7,400 To Help Pay Off Student Loans

Americorps will reward you with $4,725 to spend on your college debts, and a stipend of up to $7,400 just for joining their volunteer program for one year. If you successfully complete one full-time term of service you will be eligible for an award of $4,725, complete one part-time term of service and you will be eligible for an award of $2,362.50. If you are in a short-term program, such as a summer program, you will be eligible for a "reduced part-time" award -- usually $1,000 or less. Contact the Corporation for National and Community Service Headquarters, 1201 New York Avenue, NW, Washington, D.C. 20525; 202-606-5000; {www.americorps.org/}.

Pay Off $4,725 Of Your Student Loans Through Volunteer Work

VISTA (Volunteers in Service to America) will pay off $4,725 of your loans if you join in on their cause for at least 1,700 hours. Participants are eligible to receive either an education award or end-of-service stipend of $1,200. Contact the Corporation for National and Community Service Headquarters, 1201 New York Avenue, NW; Washington, D.C. 20525; 800-942-2677; {www.americorps.org/joining/benefits.html}.

Military

Serve Your Country And Slash $10,000 Off Your Student Loans

If you join the Army Reserve or the National Guard after graduation, you can receive up to $10,000 to pay off your student loans. Contact the United States Army Reserve Command (USARC), 1401 Deshler Street, S.W., Fort McPherson, GA 30330-2000; 800-359-8483; {www4.army.mil/USAR/home/index.php}.

$65,000 College Loan Repayment

The Army College Loan Repayment program allows participants to pay off federally insured student loans when they enlist in the Army, in a qualifying job. To be eligible, applicants must enlist for three years on Active Duty or six years in the Army Reserve and their loan status must not be in default. For Active Duty Soldiers, participants can receive up to $65,000 to repay college loans. For Army Reserve Soldiers, individuals can receive up to $20,000 to repay college loans. Contact the United States Army at 800-872-2769; {www.army.com/}.

Let The Navy Help You Pay Off Up To $65,000 Of Your Student Loans

The Navy will pay for up to $65,000 of loans acquired from a post–secondary education for college students and graduates who qualify. To be eligible for the program the loan cannot be in default and it must be the applicant's first enlistment. The LRP is available to all active Navy enlisted positions! Contact the U.S. Navy at 800-872-6289; {www.navy.com/jsp/explore/education/summary.jsp?cid=4&pid=5}

.

$10, 000 Available For You!!

The College Loan Repayment Program (CLRP) is a program created for all non-prior service persons considering enlistment in the U.S. Air Force. If you have taken some college courses and have accumulated debt, this great program may be for you. Participants must sign up for this program when signing the enlistment contract. Under CLRP repayment maximum is $10,000 per recruit. Contact Air Force Personnel Center, Randolph AFB, TX 78150; 800-346-3374 ext 2; {www.airforce.com/index_fr.htm}.

Pennsylvania Soldiers Collect $2,500

A one-time student loan forgiveness benefit of up to $2,500 can be yours if you served in the Armed Forces, in an active duty status, between September 11, 2001, and December 31, 2005. The Armed Forces Loan Forgiveness Program recognizes the bravery, dedication, and loyalty of our servicemen and women who served in the aftermath of September 11, 2001, for our nation. Contact the Pennsylvania Higher Education Assistance Agency, PA State Grants and Special Programs, 1200 N 7th St, Harrisburg, PA 17102-1444; 800-233-0557; {www.pheaa.org/loanforgiveness/armed_forces.shtml}.

Teachers/ Education

Receive $5000 To Help Pay Off Student Loans While Making A Difference

The Federal Teacher Loan Forgiveness Program offers individuals who teach full-time for five consecutive complete academic years, in certain elementary and secondary schools serving low-income families, forgiveness of up to a combined total of $5,000 in principal and interest of their Direct Loan and/or Federal Family Education Loan Programs (FFELP) loans. Contact American Education Services AES/PHEAA, Attn: Loan Discharge, 1200 N. 7th Street, Harrisburg, PA 17102-1444; 800-692-7392, 717-720-2676; {www.aessuccess.org/manage/cant_make_payment/Federal_Teacher_Loan_Forgiveness.shtml}.

$9,900 Loan Forgiveness Award!!!!

The Quality Early Education Loan Forgiveness program offers monthly student loan debt assistance to graduates working in Pennsylvania, in the field of Early Childhood Education. If you are eligible, the program will forgive up to one-sixth of your qualifying loan debt annually, not to exceed the maximum of $3,300 per year for three years or the program's $9,900 maximum benefit. Contact the Pennsylvania Higher Education Assistance Agency, PA State Grants and Special Programs, 1200 N 7th St, Harrisburg, PA 17102-1444; 800-233-0557; {www.pheaa.org/}.

$6000 Of Student Loan Forgiveness!!

Teachers for New Hampshire[SM] provides financial assistance in the form of a variable-interest rate, forgivable loan, covering up to 50 percent of the direct costs (tuition and fees) and the cost of books for the program, not to exceed a cumulative maximum of $6,000. Individuals who meet the application criteria are eligible to apply on an annual basis. Repayment of this loan will be forgiven for individuals who are employed as full-time teachers for three years following completion of their teacher preparation program. Contact New Hampshire Higher Education Loan Corporation, P.O. Box 2111, Concord, NH 03301; 800-330-0787; {www.teachersforNH. org}.

Extra Money!! $2,500 Per Year To Repay Undergraduate Loans

Due to a critical Teacher shortage in Florida, the Florida Department of Education is offering Teachers forgiveness of their student loans. If you are a Florida teacher and you are certified in a critical teacher shortage subject area contact The Office of Student Financial Assistance, 1940 North Monroe Street, Suite 70, Tallahassee, FL 32303-4759; 888-827-2004; {www.firn.edu/doe/osfa/cts lffactsheet.htm}.

$10,000 Of Student Loan Forgiveness

The Missouri Advantage Repayment Incentive Option (MARIO) will provide up to $10,000 in student loan forgiveness for college students who graduate with a math or science degree and go to work for a Missouri life science related company. The program offers up to $2,500 in loan forgiveness for every year the student works at a Missouri life science company for a maximum of four years. Contact Capitol Building, Room 216, Jefferson City, MO 65101; 573-751-3222; {www.mohela.com/Misc/Info/Newsrel

ease%20Bob%20Holden%20Life%20 Science%20forgiveness.htm}.

Mississippi Residents $$4000 Per Year Loan Forgiveness

The William Winter Teacher program is specifically designed to increase the supply of teacher educators for public schools in Mississippi. Awards are made on an annual basis with priority given to renewal students. Program participation is limited to 4 years or $8,000. Contact the Mississippi Student Financial Aid Office, 3825 Ridgewood Road, Jackson, MS 39211-6453; 800-327-2980; {www.ihl. state.ms.us/financialaid/Contact.html}, Email: {sfa@ihl.state.ms.us}.

$5000 Forgivable Loan $$$$$$

This program offers 2-3 forgivable loans annually to assist and encourage promising engineering graduate students to pursue careers in teaching at the college level. Upon completion of the doctoral degree, one year's loan will be forgiven for each year the recipient teaches. This program is renewable for up to three years. This offer is open to all citizens of North America (U.S., Canada, and Mexico). The applicant must hold an undergraduate degree from an engineering program at an accredited school. Contact SAE Washington Office, 1828 L Street NW, Suite 905, Washington, DC 20036; 202-463-7318; {www.sae.org/students/doc schol.htm}, Email: {scholarships@ sae.org}.

$5000 For Minority Teachers!!!

Receive up to $5000 annually if you are an African-American, Asian-American, Native American, or

Hispanic college junior or senior working toward teacher certification. Participants must teach 3 or 5 years in Arkansas to have the amount received forgiven. Contact the Arkansas Department of Higher Education, 114 East Capitol Ave, Attn: Minority Teachers Scholarship, Little Rock, AR 72201; 501-371-2050, 800-54-STUDY; {www.arkansashighered.com/mteachers.html}.

New Mexico Graduates Receive $25,000

The New Mexico Commission on Higher Education has created a loan-for-service program designed to increase the number of ethnic minorities and women available to teach in an academic discipline in which ethnic minorities and women are demonstrably underrepresented in New Mexico public colleges and universities. If eligible the maximum award is $25,000 per year. Contact the New Mexico Commission on Higher Education, 1068 Cerrillos Road, Santa Fe, NM 87505; 505-476-6500; {www.nmche.org/collegefinance/mino ritydoc.asp}.

$25000 A Year To Become A North Carolina Teacher

The Prospective Teacher Scholarship Loan program provides $2500 per academic year for individuals on their way to teacher licensure or to licensure in special services areas, including school psychology, school counseling, speech/language pathology, audiology, and library/media services. The loans are provided for a maximum of four years or the minimum number of years required earning licensure based on the entry-level degree. Recipients are obligated to teach one year in a North Carolina school for each year of assistance they receive. Contact the

Center for Recruitment and Retention, Division of Human Resource Management, Department of Public Instruction, 301 N. Wilmington St., Raleigh, NC 27601; 919-807-3369; {www.ncpublicschools.org/scholarshi ps/ptsl.html}, Email: {scholars@dpi. state.nc.us}.

100% Student Loan Forgiveness!!

If you are a teacher and have served full time in a public or nonprofit elementary or secondary school system as a teacher in a school serving students from low-income families; or special-education teacher, including teachers of infants, toddlers, children, or youth with disabilities; or teacher in the fields of mathematics, science, foreign languages, or bilingual education, or in any other field of expertise determined by a state education agency to have a shortage of qualified teachers in that state, you may qualify for cancellation (discharge) of up to 100 percent of a Federal Perkins Loan. Contact The Office of Federal Student Aid, Federal Perkins Loan Teacher Cancellation Program, Union Center Plaza, 8 31st Street, Washington D.C. 20202; 800-433-3243; {http://studentaid.ed.gov/PORTALSWebApp/students/english/c ancelperk.jsp?tab=repaying}.

$5000 Student Loan Forgiveness

You might be able to have up to $5,000 of your Stafford Loans canceled if you are teaching in a low-income school and you are a new borrower. A new borrower is one who has no outstanding FFEL or Direct Loan balance. To qualify you must work as a full-time teacher for five consecutive years in an elementary or secondary school that has been designated as a "low-income" school. Contact The Office of Federal Student Aid Federal Perkins Loan Teacher Cancellation Program, Union Center Plaza, 8 31st Street, Washington D.C. 20202; 800-433-3243; {http://studentaid.ed.gov/PORTALSWebApp/students/english/cancelstaff.jsp?tab=re paying}.

Kansas Teachers $$$$$$ Loan Forgiveness

The Wichita Public Schools wanted to increase the diversity in the teaching staff, so they began The Grow Your Own Teacher program. To participate in this program and receive loan forgiveness, you must sign a Statement of Commitment and Intent to teach letter. Each participant is obligated to begin teaching full-time, in his/her area of licensure, with the Wichita Public Schools the first semester immediately following graduation and continuing for a period of three consecutive years. Participants involved in the program for less than four years will have a pro-rated teaching obligation. Contact GYOT Program, 201 N Water, Room 932, Wichita, KS 67202-1292; 316-973-4504 Fax: 316-973-4629; {www.us d259.com/jobs/gyot.htm}, Email: {mwhisman@usd259.net}.

Iowa Teachers Receive $9000 Loan Forgiveness

Current Iowa teachers are eligible to receive benefits from the Iowa Teacher Shortage Forgivable Loan Program.

The conditions for eligibility are individuals who currently teach and are continuing their academic studies in designated shortage areas and individuals who currently teach in shortage areas with conditional licensure and are pursuing certification in the shortage area are eligible for forgivable loans. Contact the Iowa College Student Aid Commission, Attn: Iowa Teacher Shortage Forgivable Loans, 200 Tenth Street, Des Moines, IA 50309; 800-383-4222.; {www.iowacollegeaid.org/lo ans/teacher_shortage_NEW04.html}, Email: {info@iowa collegeaid.org}.

South Carolina Wants To Reduce Your Student Loans By $5000

Your student loans can be cancelled by up to $5000/year. You can take advantage of this program by teaching in the South Carolina public schools, in an area of critical need. For this program, students may have their loan canceled at a rate of 20% per year of teaching in critical subject areas or critical geographical locations in South Carolina specified by the SC Loan Corporation. Students who teach in both a critical subject area and a critical geographical area may have their loan canceled at a rate of 33 1/3% per year. Contact The Office of Financial Aid, 119 Tillman Hall, Rock Hill, SC 29733; 803-323-2189; {www.winthrop.edu/finaid/types/teach er.htm}.

$10,000 Loan Forgiveness

This forgivable loan program is available to Wisconsin residents interested in becoming teachers of the visually impaired or orientation and mobility instructors. Eligible undergraduate, graduate or students willing to work in this field could be eligible to receive up to $10,000 per year for up to four years. In order to qualify, participants must be a licensed teacher of the visually impaired or an orientation and mobility instructor in a Wisconsin school district, the Wisconsin Center for the Blind and Visually Impaired or a cooperative educational service agency. For each of the first two years of full-time teaching, 25% of the loan is forgiven each year. For the third year of full-time teaching, the remaining 50% is forgiven. Contact the Higher Educational Aids Board, Post Office Box 7885, Madison, WI 53707-7885; 608-267-9865; {http://heab.state.wi.us/pres0801.html}, Email: {HEABmail@heab.state.wi.us}.

Universities

$$$$ For You>>> CSU Forgivable Loan Program

The Forgivable Loan/Doctoral Incentive Program (FLP) is a competitive program that provides loans to a limited number of full-time doctoral students at accredited universities. The Program provides loans of up to $10,000 per year. Participants may borrow a maximum of $30,000 over a five-year period. Contact The California State University, Office of the Chancellor, 401 Golden Shore, Long Beach, CA 90802-4210; 562-951-4000; {www.calstate.edu/HR/FLP/}.

100% Loan Forgiveness For Notre Dame Graduates

This program is designed for J.D. graduates of Notre Dame Law School who are working in or have accepted positions in qualifying employment, expect to have an annual income below $50,000, and owe principal on

eligible loans, may apply for loan repayment assistance. To qualify, an eligible graduate must have personally incurred, while enrolled at Notre Dame Law School, need-based loans totaling $10,000 or more to finance the cost of the graduate's legal education. Contact M. Catherine Roemer, CPA Assistant Dean for Law School Administration, Notre Dame Law School, 102 Law School, Notre Dame, IN 46556-0780; 574-631-6891; {www.nd.edu/~ndlaw/LoanAssist/description.html}, Email: {Roemer.8@nd.edu}.

$$$$ Baker University Loan Forgiveness!!!!! $$$$

Students who complete a bachelor's degree at Baker University's College of Arts and Sciences may be eligible for the school's loan forgiveness program. The Challenge Loan program becomes available beginning a student's sophomore year. The funds start out as a loan, but are forgiven if you graduate from Baker. Contact Baker University, P.O. Box 65, Baldwin City, KS 66006-0065; 913-594-6451; {www.bakeru.edu/}.

$8000 Per Year For Fordham University Law School Graduates

The Fordham Loan Repayment Assistance Program (LRAP) is available to JD alumni, beginning with the class of 2003, who borrowed federal and/or private educational loans approved by Fordham, who are working full time in law-related positions in 501(c) (3) non-profit organizations and have "qualifying incomes" below $47,600. Repayment assistance for the educational loans will be in the form of a Fordham LRAP loan of up to $8,000 per year for up to five years. Contact Fordham Law School, 33 West 60th Street, 2nd

Floor, New York, NY 10023; 212-636-6815; {http://law.fordham.edu/htm/falrap.htm}, Email:{financialaid@law.fordham.edu}.

Receive 100% Loan Forgiveness From Brooklyn Law School

The Brooklyn Law School. will extend a loan to a graduate for the first year of his or her participation in the LRAP Program. The Law School will forgive the entire amount of the LRAP Loan immediately upon satisfactory completion of the first full year of participation. To receive this 100% loan forgiveness, the participant must be in good standing for the complete year with regard to all LRAP eligibility requirements. Interest will accrue at the rate of 5% per annum, but will also be forgiven along with the principal upon completion of the first year. Contact Brooklyn Law School Office of Financial Aid, 250 Joralemon Street, Brooklyn, NY 11201; 718-780-7915; {www.brook law.edu/admissions/tuitionandaid/lrap. php#forgiveness}.

Free Tuition And Living Expenses!!!

The forgivable loan program offered by Tyndale University College and Seminary permits qualifying students to receive a loan to pay for part or all of their tuition and living expenses. If certain conditions are met, the entire loan may be forgiven at the end of the academic year. To qualify for the program, students must demonstrate financial need, and they are encouraged to solicit donations to the FLP fund. Contact Tyndale University College & Seminary, Office of Financial Aid, 25 Ballyconnor Court, Toronto, Ontario, Canada M2M 4B3; 416-226-6620; {www.tyndale.ca/fina id/flp.php}, Email: {info@ tyndale.ca}

$$ Interest Free Forgivable Loan- Redeemer University

If you are a prospective or current student of Redeemer University you may be eligible to obtain interest free forgivable loans. This is a loan program whereby qualifying students receive a loan to pay for part or all of their tuition and related costs for the academic year. If certain conditions are met the entire loan may be forgiven after the end of the academic year. To qualify for the program students must demonstrate financial need. Contact Redeemer University College, Office of Financial Assistance, 777 Garner Road East, Ancaster, ON Canada L9K 1J4; 905-648-2131, 800-263-6467; {www. redeemer.on.ca/}.

$$$$$$$$ For Student Loan Repayment- Stanford University

Stanford University offers Loan Forgiveness Program designed to help attorneys. By pursuing a public interest career Stanford graduates are eligible for benefits for up to ten years after they receive their JD. After they meet the income and employment qualifications for three years, participants become eligible for cancellation of 25 percent of their LRAP loans; after four years, 50 percent; and after five to ten years, 100 percent!! Contact the Stanford Law

School, Attn Faye Deal, Associate Dean for Admissions and Financial Aid Crown Quadrangle, 559 Nathan Abbott Way, Stanford, CA 94305-8610; 650-723-0302; {www.law. stanford.edu/students/admits/lrap/} Email: {fdeal@stanford.edu}

$3500 Loan Forgiveness-Franklin Pierce Law Center

This program is for eligible law school graduates of the Franklin Pierce Law Center. Applicants are eligible to receive up to an annual maximum of $3,500 from the Phinney Fund for up to five years after graduation if they remain in qualifying public interest employment. Awards are made to individuals with the greatest debt and the lowest income. Contact The Franklin Pierce Law Center, Two White Street, Concord, NH 03301; 603-228-1541; {www.piercelaw.edu/finan/loan.htm}.

American University 100% Loan Forgiveness

If you are alumni of the American University Washington College of Law you may be entitled to have all of your student loans eradicated. The Public Interest Loan Repayment Assistance Program (PILRAP) helps relieve economic burden imposed by educational debt by providing loan repayment assistance for JD graduates who work in full-time non-profit, government or other employment in which the graduate is engaged in serving under-represented or traditionally marginalized populations. Contact the Washington College of Law, Attn: Stephanie Sullivan Assistant Director, Public Interest Specialist, 4801 Massachusetts Avenue, NW, Washington, DC 20016; 202-274-4000; {www.wcl.ameri can.edu/finaid/pilrap.cfm#contact}, Email: {pilrap@wcl.american.edu}.

50% Of Your Loans Paid Off!!!

If you are a graduate or undergraduate student attending an accredited engineering school and majoring in the metallurgy, minerals, or materials science fields then you may be eligible to receive loan forgiveness of half your student loans. The WAAIME Scholarship Loan Fund Program requires eligible students to only pay back 50 percent of the loan amount with no interest. Contact WAAIME, 345 East 47th Street, New York, NY 10017; 212-705-7692; {www.metsoc. org/Students/tmscomp.asp#waaime}.

George Washington Law School Graduates Receive $8000 Loan Forgiveness

This program is to assist law school graduates working in public interest employment loan forgiveness of up to $8000 per year. The George Washington Law School Loan Reimbursement Assistance Program requires that all applicants graduated in 1990 or later, must work approximately 30 or more hours/week in a legal public interest job, and your gross annual salary minus your annual law loan repayments is equal to or less than $37,000. Contact The George Washington University Law School, 2000 H Street, NW, Washington, DC 20052; 202-994-6261; {www.law. gwu.edu/pubint/lrap.asp}.

Georgetown Graduates 100% Loan Forgiveness!!!

This Program is to help JD graduates in pursuing careers in the field of public interest law. The Georgetown University Law Centers Loan Repayment Assistance Program offers eligible participants 100% forgiveness. To qualify applicants must be JD graduates from the class of 1996 and beyond. Contact the Financial Aid Office/LRAP Committee, Georgetown University Law Center, 600 New Jersey Ave., N.W., Washington, D.C. 20001; 202-662-9080; {www.law. georgetown.edu/finaid/lrap/}.

NYU Graduates Full Loan Repayment

NYU School of Law graduates pursuing careers in public service or with not-for-profit organizations following graduation are eligible to receive to have their debt burden paid in full or part by NYU. Contact the Office of Student Financial Services, New York University School of Law, 245 Sullivan Street, Suite 400, New York, NY 10012-1301; 212-998-6050; {www.law.nyu.edu/depts/financialaid/l rap/moreinfo.html}.

$3000 Loan Repayment Assistance From Seattle University

This program is open to all graduates of the Seattle University School of Law. Graduates who choose full time public interest legal careers and are licensed attorneys may be eligible to receive up to $3000 of forgiveness. The qualifying income limit is a maximum of $45,000 annually and the graduate must remain in qualifying public interest employment for at least one year. Contact the Office of Financial Aid, Seattle University of Law, 901 12th Avenue, Seattle, WA

98122-1090; 206-398-4250; {www. law.seattleu.edu/financialaid/lrap?mod e=standard}.

Up To $21,250 Medical School Loan Forgiveness From University Of Arizona

This program offers the University of Arizona Medical Students loan forgiveness of up to $21,250 per year with a maximum of four years. Each participant is required to a two year service commitment at a board approved location. Contact Maggie Gumble, University of Arizona College of Medicine, Financial Aid Office, PO Box 245026 Tucson, AZ 85724-5026; 520-626-7145; {www. medicine.arizona.edu/financial_aid/am slp.html}.

Specialty Employment

Work In Alaska And Have Your Loans Forgiven!!!!

The Michael Murphy Loan is available to individuals who wish to study law enforcement, law, probation and parole, penology, or other related fields are eligible to work off one-fifth per year or 100% of their loans. To be eligible the applicant must work as a State Trooper (or related law enforcement official) in Alaska. Contact Lt. of Recruitment, Alaska State Troopers, 5700 East Tudor Road, Anchorage, AK 99507; 907-269-5511; {http://alaskadvantage.state.ak.us/page /110}.

Up To 100% Loan Forgiveness For Child Care Workers

This program offers child-care providers an opportunity to pay off up to 100 percent forgiveness of their total eligible Stafford subsidized and unsubsidized loans. To qualify for the child care provider loan forgiveness demonstration program, a borrower must be a new borrower, have received an associate or bachelor's degree in the field of early childhood education, and after receiving that degree, have worked full-time for at least two consecutive years. Contact KHEAA, P.O. Box 798, Frankfort, KY 40602-0798; 800-928-8926; {www.kheaa.com/fed_ccplf.html}.

Attention Agricultural Graduates, $10,000 Of Loan Forgiveness Is Waiting For You!!

If you are an agriculture or veterinary medicine graduate who helps operate a family farm or practice veterinary medicine that includes agricultural animals in Pennsylvania you are eligible for a maximum award of $10,000 in loan forgiveness payments. Contact the Agriculture Education Loan Forgiveness Program, P.O. Box 8114, Harrisburg, PA 17105-8114; 717-720-2800; {www.pheaa.org/loan forgiveness/Agriculture_Education_Loan_Forgiveness_Program.shtml}.

Employers

Free $$$$$ To Pay Off Federally Insured Student Loans

The U.S. Federal Government has established a student loan repayment program which authorizes agencies to repay certain types of federally insured student loans as a recruitment or retention incentive for highly qualified personnel. If you qualify, an agency may agree to provide student loan repayment benefits of up to $10,000 per calendar year, subject to a

cumulative maximum of $60,000 per employee. Contact The Office of Personnel Management, 1900 E Streets NW, Washington, DC 20415-1000; 202-606-1800; {www.opm.gov/oca/PAY/StudentLoan/index.asp}.

$100 Forgivable Loan

Members of the Pennsylvania Association of Extension 4-H Agents are eligible for one or more of Chapter Forgivable Loans in the amount of $100.00 for graduate study and professional improvement. This forgivable loan is available to active members and Cooperative Extension employees with at least two years service and who expect to join Epsilon Sigma Phi when they become eligible. Contact the College of Agricultural Sciences at Penn State University, 217 Ag Administration, University Park, PA 16802; 814-865-2541; {www.extension.psu.edu/pae4ha/Opportunities.htm}, Email: {BedfordExt@psu.edu}.

$500 Loan Forgiveness

Members of the Pennsylvania Association of Extension 4-H Agents are eligible for one forgivable loan in the amount of $500.00. This forgiveness may be awarded annually to an active member for professional improvement and advanced studies leading to a graduate degree. Contact the College of Agricultural Sciences at Penn State University, 201 Ag Administration, University Park, PA 16802; 814-865-254; {www.

extension.psu.edu/pae4ha/Opportunitie
s.htm}, Email: {BedfordExt@psu.
edu}.

Medical

Pennsylvania Nurses Receive $12,500 To Pay Off Nursing School Loans!!

To help recruit and retain qualified
nurses in Pennsylvania, the "Nursing
Loan Forgiveness for Healthier
Futures" program was created to help
struggling nurses repay their student
loans. By working for a participating
Pennsylvania health care organization,
after graduation from an approved
nursing education program, you may
receive student loan forgiveness for up
to 25 percent (a maximum of $12,500)
of your eligible debt over a three-year
period. Contact the American
Education Services, Nursing Loan
Forgiveness for Healthier Futures
Program, Lender School Team, PO
Box 2461, Harrisburg, PA 17105-
2461; 800-859-5442; {www.pheaa.
org/loanforgiveness/healthier_futures.s
html}.

Hospital Workers Available Student Loan Forgiveness

This program provides a forgivable
loan if you are enrolled in a
professional-level degree, certificate,
or diploma program. You must be full-
time, in a shortage health care or
related occupational field, at an
accredited educational institution or
teaching hospital. The loan is
"forgiven" if you work for a specified
period of time in an upgraded position
for a TUF-contributing Employer, after
completing your program of study.
Contact 1199SEIU/ League,
Employment Training & Job Security
Headquarters, 330 west 42nd Street,

New York, NY 10036; 212-643-9340;
{www.1199etjsp.org/HospitalWorker/
HW_ForgiveLoan.htm}.

$20,000 Loan Forgiveness!!!!!

This program is for health worker
participants who will enter into a
service contract for two years with the
Indian Health Service, a Federal health
program for American Indians and
Alaska Natives. All health professions
are eligible to apply to the Loan
Repayment Program however special
consideration is given to nurses, nurse
practitioners, mental health and
physician priority medical specialties.
The LRP will pay an additional 20
percent annually to the Internal
Revenue Service (IRS) to offset the
increased tax liability incurred by the
participant. Contact The Indian Health
Service Loan Repayment Program,
Twin brook Metro Plaza -- Suite 100A,
12300 Twin brook Parkway,
Rockville, MD 20852; 301-443-3396;
{www.ihs.gov/GeneralWeb/HelpCente
r/CustomerServices/loan.asp}.

$35,000 Loan Forgiveness Available To Clinical Researchers

In exchange for a two-year
commitment of clinical research, The
National Institutes of Health will repay
up to $35,000 per year of your
qualified educational debt, pay an
additional 39% of the repayments to
cover your Federal taxes, and may
reimburse state taxes that result from
these payments. To participate, you
must be a U.S. citizen (or U.S. national
or permanent resident) and have a
M.D., Ph.D., and Psy.D. Pharm. D.,
D.O., D.D.S., D.M.D., D.P.M., D.C.,
N.D., or equivalent doctoral degree
from an accredited institution. Contact
the National Institutes of Health

(NIH), 9000 Rockville Pike, Bethesda, MD 20892; 866-849-4047; {http:// lrp.info.nih.gov/about/lrp-clinical.htm}.

Up To $21,250 Medical School Loan Forgiveness

This program offers the University of Arizona Medical Students loan forgiveness of up to $21,250 per year with a maximum of four years. Each participant is required to a two year service commitment at a board approved location. Contact Maggie Gumble, U. of Arizona College of Medicine, Financial Aid Office, PO Box 245026 Tucson, AZ 85724-5026; 520-626-7145; {www.medicine.arizona.edu/financial_aid/amslp.html}.

Health Professionals Receive Up To $70,000 Loan Forgiveness

This program is opened to all US Citizens licensed to practice in CO. Applicants must have qualified debt incurred as a result of health professions education, must agree to practice F/T in HPSA for a minimum of 2 years, and must be employed by a public or private non-profit agency in a HPSA area. The Colorado Health Professions Loan Repayment Program will award up to $70,000 in qualified educational debt per provided over a maximum rate of $20,000 per year for the first 2 years and variable thereafter. Contact UCHSH, Colorado AHEC Program, P.O. Box 6508, Mail Stop F433, Aurora, CO 80045-0508; 303-724-0030, Fax: 303-315-0891; {www.uchsc.edu/ahec/ rp/index.htm}.

$90,000 Loan Repayment Assistance

This program is opened for Osteopathic Physicians only - 3rd year resident or beyond. Participants must agree to practice in primary care and work in a shortage area for four years. The Student Community Primary Care Initiative (SCPCI) will pay up to $90,000 of student loan debt to loans of the physician's choice. Contact SCPCI/Financial Aid Office, Attn. Charlene Marinaro, Program Coordinator, 3200 Grand Avenue, Des Moines, IA 50312; 515-271-1671; {www.dmu.edu/coms/ scpci.htm}.

Up To $30,000/Year For M.D's, D.O's, and PH.D's

If you are a Medical Doctor and willing to sign a contract committing two years of full-time primary care clinical services in a public or nonprofit entity located in a Federally-designated Health Professional Shortage Area (HPSA) in Iowa, you can receive up to $30,000 of loan forgiveness. The Iowa PRIMECARRE Loan Repayment Program requires that all applicants be a US citizen, licensed to practice in Iowa, and have Medical education-related debts. Contact Bureau of Health Care Access, Attn: Patricia Kehoe, PRIMECARRE Coordinator, 321 E. 12th Street, 5th Floor, Des Moines, IA 50319; 515-281-7689, 800-308-5986; {www.idph.state.ia. us}.

Up To $20,000/Year For D.D.S

If you are a Dentist and willing to sign a contract committing two years of full-time primary care clinical services in a public or nonprofit entity located in a Federally-designated Health Professional Shortage Area (HPSA) in Iowa, you can receive up to $20,000 of loan forgiveness. The Iowa PRIMECARRE Loan Repayment Program requires that all applicants be a US citizen, licensed to practice in Iowa, and have Medical education-related debts. Contact Bureau of Health Care Access, Attn: Patricia Kehoe, PRIMECARRE Coordinator, 321 E. 12th Street, 5th Floor, Des Moines, IA 50319; 515-281-7689, 800-308-5986; {www.idph.state. ia.us}.

Up To $15,000/Year For Health Professionals

If you are a Physician Assistant, Nurse Practitioner, Certified Nurse Midwife, Clinical Psychologist, Clinical Social Worker, or Psychiatric Nurse Specialist and willing to sign a contract committing two years of full-time primary care clinical services in a public or nonprofit entity located in a Federally-designated Health Professional Shortage Area (HPSA) in Iowa, you can receive up to $15,000 of loan forgiveness. The Iowa PRIMECARRE Loan Repayment Program requires that all applicants be a US citizen, licensed to practice in Iowa, and have Medical education-related debts. Contact Bureau of Health Care Access, Attn: Patricia Kehoe, PRIMECARRE Coordinator, 321 E. 12th Street, 5th Floor, Des Moines, IA 50319; 515-281-7689, 800-308-5986; {www.idph.state. ia.us}.

$$$$ Knock Off $25,000 Of Your Medical School Loans

The National Health Service Corps can help you reduce your student loans by $25,000!! Fully trained health professionals who commit to work in a community of great need are eligible to compete for repayment of their loans. In addition to loan repayment, these clinicians receive a competitive salary, some tax relief benefits. Contact NHSC, 5600 Fishers Lane, Park lawn Building, Rockville, MD 20857; 800-221-9393; {http://

nhsc.bhpr.hrsa.gov/join_us/}, Email: {nhsc@hrsa.gov}.

Rural Physicians Obtain $13,000 Per Year Of Loan Forgiveness

This program is offered to first, second, or third year primary care medical residents who plan to practice full-time in a designated rural area in Minnesota Selected participants are eligible for four years of loan forgiveness. During each year that a participant serves as a physician in a designated rural area for a minimum of 30 hours per week for up to four years, the ORHPC will pay directly to the participant an annual lump sum (approximately $13,000). Contact the Minnesota Department of Health, Office of Rural Health and Primary Care, Attn: Loan Forgiveness Program Officer, P.O. Box 64975, St. Paul, MN 55164-0975; 800-366-5424, 651-282-6302; {www.health.state.mn.us/ divs/chs/loan.htm}.

Registered Nurses Receive $150 Per Month

Full-time Registered Nurses can receive up to $150 per month to help assist with the monthly payment of their Nursing Student Loan. This loan program will remain in effect for as long as the RN is a full-time employee or until the loan is satisfied. Contact the North Philadelphia Health System, Human Resources Dept Nurse Recruiters, 8th St & Girard Ave, Philadelphia, PA 19130; 215-787-2052; {www.nphs.com/HR/prg_ loan.htm}, Email: {jobs@nphs.com}.

25% Of Your Student Loans Forgiven!!!

The Nursing Student Loan Forgiveness Program provides financial assistance to eligible nurses in repaying student loans incurred while obtaining a Florida license. Eligible nurses may have 25% of their outstanding student loan(s) paid annually, for a maximum of four years. The maximum payment is $4,000 per year. Contact the Florida Department of Education, Office of Student Financial Assistance, 1940 North Monroe Street, Suite 70, Tallahassee, FL 32303-4759; 407-328-2474, 888-827-2004; {www.scc-fl.edu/nursing/scholarships/loan-forgiveness.htm}.

$13,000 Lump Sum Student Loan Forgiveness

This program is offered to first, second or third year primary care medical residents who plan to practice full-time in an underserved urban area in Minnesota. Selected participants are eligible for four years of loan forgiveness. During each year that a participant serves as a physician in an underserved urban area for a minimum of 30 hours per week for up to four years, the ORHPC will pay directly to the participant an annual lump sum (approximately $13,000). Contact the Minnesota Department of Health, Office of Rural Health and Primary Care, Attn: Loan Forgiveness Program Officer, P.O. Box 64975, St. Paul, MN 55164-0975; 800-366-5424, 651-282-6302; {www.health.state.mn.us/divs/chs/loan.htm}.

$15,000 Loan Forgiveness Paid Directly To You!!!

This program is offered to individuals attending a program of study designed to prepare them to become a licensed dentist. Selected participants are eligible for up to four years of loan forgiveness. There is a minimum service obligation of three years. Each year a participant must deliver service totaling 25 percent of their yearly

patient encounters to public program or sliding fee scale patients. In turn, the ORHPC will pay directly to the participant an annual lump sum (approximately $15,000 as of 5/1/04.) Contact the Minnesota Department of Health, Office of Rural Health and Primary Care, Attn: Loan Forgiveness Program Officer, P.O. Box 64975, St. Paul, MN 55164-0975; 651-282-6302, 800-366-5424; {www.health.state.mn.us/divs/chs/dentist.htm}.

$23,000 Loan Forgiveness For Dental Workers

This program offers Dentists up to $23,000 per year of loan forgiveness if they have at least 30% patient population enrolled in Maryland's Medical Assistance Program (MMAP). You must be a Maryland resident and you must have graduated from an accredited US dental school. Contact The Maryland Higher Education Commission, 839 Bestgate Road, Suite 400, Annapolis, MD 21401; 410-767-7899; {www.mhec.state.md.us/financialAid/ProgramDescriptions/prog_larpdent.asp}.

$$$$$ Loan Forgiveness $$$$$

This program is offered to individuals currently attending a program of study designed to prepare the individual for service as a midlevel practitioner. Selected participants are eligible for up to four years of loan forgiveness. For each year that a participant serves as a midlevel practitioner in a designated rural area for a minimum of 30 hours per week, the ORHPC will pay directly to the participant an annual lump (approximately $6,000). Contact the Minnesota Department of Health, Office of Rural Health and Primary Care, Attn: Loan Forgiveness Program Officer, P.O. Box 64975, St. Paul, MN 55164-0975; 800-366-5424, 651-282-6302; {www.health.state.mn. us/divs/chs/loan.htm}.

Calling All Minnesota Nursing Students!! Receive $3,000 Per Year Of Loan Forgiveness

This program is offered to individuals currently attending a program of study designed to prepare the individual to become either a registered nurse, RN or a licensed practical nurse, LPN. Individuals must plan to practice full-time in a nursing home or Intermediate Care Facility for Persons with Mental Retardation or Related Conditions (ICFMR) in Minnesota after completion of their educational program. Selected participants are eligible for up to four years of loan forgiveness. For each year that a participant serves as a RN or LPN in a nursing home or ICF/MR for an average of 30 hours per week, the ORHPC will pay directly to the participant an annual lump sum

(approximately $3,500). Contact the Minnesota Department of Health, Office of Rural Health and Primary Care, Attn: Loan Forgiveness Program Officer, P.O. Box 64975, St. Paul, MN 55164-0975; 800-366-5424, 651-282-6302; {www.health.state.mn.us/divs/chs/loan.htm}.

Ethnic

$5000 For Armenian Ancestors

This fund provides forgivable loans of up to $5,000 to worthy students regardless of age, gender, or level of education or training To be eligible for the W.E.D. Educational Fund the applicant must be a citizen of the United States, of Armenian ancestry, show need for financial assistance, demonstrate academic and/or technical excellence in their chosen field and pursue studies or training in the United States or Canada. Contact The William Ervant Doctor Educational Fund at Saint Mary Armanian Church, P.O. Box 39224, Washington, DC 20016; 202-693-1440; {www.wedfund.org}.

Legal

100% Loan Forgiveness For JD Graduates!!!!

If you are alumni of the American University Washington College of Law you may be entitled to have all of your student loans eradicated. WCL implemented the Public Interest Loan Repayment Assistance Program (PILRAP) that helps relieve economic burden imposed by educational debt by providing loan repayment assistance for JD graduates who work in full-time non-profit, government or other employment in which the graduate is engaged in serving under-represented or traditionally marginalized populations. Contact the Washington College of Law, Attn: Stephanie Sullivan Assistant Director, Public Interest Specialist, 4801 Massachusetts Avenue, NW - Washington, DC 20016; 202-274-4000; {www.wcl. american.edu/finaid/pilrap.cfm#contac t}, Email: {pilrap@wcl.american.edu}.

$7500 For Maryland Government Employees!!

Maryland residents which provide public service in state or local government or nonprofit agencies in Maryland may receive up to $7500 per year of loan forgiveness. You must have graduated from a college in Maryland or from a law school. You must be employed full-time in state or local government or in a nonprofit organization in Maryland and your employer must help low income, underserved residents or underserved areas in the state. Your gross salary cannot exceed $50,000 and, if married, your combined salaries cannot exceed $110,000. Contact The Maryland Higher Education Commission, Office of Student Financial Assistance, 839 Bestgate Road, Suite 400, Annapolis, MD 21401; 410-260-4546, 800-974-1024; {www.mhec.state.md.us/ financialAid/ProgramDescriptions/pro g_larp.asp}.

NYU Graduates Full Loan Repayment

NYU School of Law graduates pursuing careers in public service or with not-for-profit organizations following graduation are eligible to receive to have their debt burden paid in full or part by NYU. Contact the Office of Student Financial Services, New York University School of Law, 245 Sullivan Street, Suite 400, New

York, NY 10012 1301; 212-998-6050; {www.law.nyu.edu/depts/financialaid/l rap/moreinfo.html}.

$3000 Loan Repayment Assistance

This program is open to all graduates of the Seattle University School of Law. Graduates who choose full time public interest legal careers and are licensed attorneys may be eligible to receive up to $3000 of forgiveness. The qualifying income limit is a maximum of $45,000 annually and the graduate must remain in qualifying public interest employment for at least one year. Contact the Office of Financial Aid, Seattle University of Law, 901 12th Avenue, Seattle, WA 98122-1090; 206-398-4250; {www. law.seattleu.edu/financialaid/lrap?mod e=standard}.

$24,000 Of Loan Forgiveness For Florida Attorneys

The Florida Bar Foundation is offering up to $6000 per year in loan repayment assistance. To qualify applicants and participants must be employed on a full-time basis by a Foundation funded legal assistance for the poor grantee; Receiving an annual salary of not more than $40,000, and be admitted to The Florida Bar by the end of the first year after having been selected as a participant. Contact The Florida Bar Foundation, 109 East Church Street, Orlando, FL 32801; 407-843-0045, 800-541-2195; {www.flabarfndn.org}, Email: {PDoyle@Flabarfndn.org}.

New York Attorneys Receive $25,000

Attorneys in New York are eligible to apply for up to $5000 per year of student loan forgiveness. The New York State Bar requires all applicants to have a law degree, be employed in the state of New York, demonstrate educational debt, and fall within a salary limitation. Contact the Student Loan Assistance for Public Interest (SLAPI), New York State Bar Association, One Elk Street, Albany, NY 12207; 518-463-3200; {www. nysba.org/slapi}.

$28,000 Loan Assistance From North Carolina

The North Carolina Legal Educational Assistance Foundation offers attorneys up to $7000 per year of loan forgiveness. To qualify applicants must have graduated within 10 years from an ABA accredited law school, Work full-time in a law-related public service job in North Carolina, have an Eligibility Determination Income, must not be in default on any loan, and make the full loan payment each month. Contact the North Carolina Legal Education Assistance Fund (NCLEAF), 6070-J Six Forks Road, Raleigh, NC 27609-8611; 919-845-6089, {www.ncleaf.org}, Email: {ncleaf@intrex.net}.

Texas Attorneys Receive Up To $6000

Texas attorneys are eligible to receive up to $1200 per year from the Texas Access to Justice Commission. To qualify for these program applicants must work full time for any legal service which is a recipient of TEAJF or work for a non profit agency. Contact the Texas Lawyers Care/State

Bar of Texas, Texas Access to Justice Commission, P.O. Box 12487, Austin, TX 78711; 800-204-2222 ext. 2155, 512-463-1463 ext. 2155; {www.texas atj.org/ProgramsServices/StudentLoan Repaymen11A6/index.asp}.

$25,000 Loan Repayment Assistance From Washington

The Washington State Bar Association has approved an LRAP that will be administered through the Washington State Bar Foundation. The program will likely begin taking applications from its first round of participants in 2005. Loan repayment assistance will be $5,000/year per program participant for a maximum of 5 consecutive years. Contact Paula Littlewood, Deputy Director of the Washington State Bar Association, 2101 Fourth Avenue, Suite 400, Seattle, WA 98121-2330; 206-443-9722, 800-945-9722; {www. wsba.org/info/contact.htm}.

Specialty Legal

If you are an attorney and work for Legal Services, Disability Rights or a Legal Aid organization, you may qualify to receive a substantial amount of student loan forgiveness. To qualify, employees must meet certain qualifications and practice in underprivileged areas. For more information on each program please check a list of eligible companies at {www.equaljusticeworks.org}:

EXPENSES

The programs described in this section are mostly for your day-to-day living expenses, like food, telephone or just extra money to pay off anything, like your credit card bills. This section should not preclude you from looking into other sections of the book, because they too can help with expenses, especially expenses for

certain situations. For example, prescription drug or doctor bills would be covered under Health and your rent or mortgage would be under Housing.

When you contact a government office for help, please don't just use the word "grant" when asking about available money programs. I know this is the most common term used by people seeking help, but you cut yourself out of a lot of suitable programs. Programs are established using all kinds of names including grants, direct payments, loans you don't have to pay back, assistance payments, vouchers, or even services. So when you are looking for this kind of money try not to use the word "grants" and just use the word "assistance". This way you are more likely to find **all** the possible programs that can help you.

Yes, you are right. There are income requirements for some of these programs. But remember every program has a different requirement. And even if they have an income requirement, it may be different for different parts of the country. And if the program says it is only for people with low income, you may be shocked that what the government considers low income. It can be as much as $35,000 or more for some of the basic programs and I have even seen income requirements going up to $80,000 for some housing programs in the New York area. And remember, by contacting the right bureaucrat there can always be exceptions to the rules.

You can't stop if you don't find what you need in the programs below. Space precludes us from listing the thousands more that are available and publishing deadlines prevent us from having the latest. So here is where you can turn to continue your work in getting what you need.

1. **Find More Federal Money Programs**
   Look at a book called the *Catalog of Federal Domestic Assistance*. It contains all the federal government programs that give out money. This book is available at your local public library or the U.S. Government Printing Office {www.gpo.gov}. You can also search the contents of this book, by key word or government department, for free on the web at {www.cfda.gov}.

2. **Find More State Money Programs**
   Every state government has dozens of money programs that help people pay their expenses. The problem is that there is never one central place to look. You have to go agency by agency, or department by department and search for what is available. Some good departments to start are health, agriculture, commerce, and social services. You can find them by dialing 411 and asking for your state capitol operator or by going to the web at {www.govengine.com} and clicking on your state.

3. **Find More Local City and County Programs**
   Start looking at every local city and county government for programs that might help. If you don't know where to go, you can call 411 and ask for the mayor's office or the office of the county executive. Just tell them you are looking for programs that might provide financial assistance to residents.

You can also go to {www.govengine.com} and under each state there will be a listing of all cities and counties. Click on those of interest and start searching for programs.

4. ***Find More Money From Non-Profit Organizations***
There are 2 major sources for finding money from these groups:

A. The Foundation Center of New York City maintains a database of all foundations who provide money to non-profit organizations or individuals. Their information is available on the web at {http://fdncenter.org} or from their participating libraries by contacting 212-620-4230 (or they are also listed on the website).

B. The Guidestar company in Williamsburg, VA also maintains a database of foundations and they can reached at 757-229-4631 or at {www.guidestar.com}. Much of their database is accessible for free on the web.

5. ***Volunteer Organizations***
There are a number of national volunteer organizations around the country that offer grants and other free services to solve problems for people in their community. The Lions Club awarded over $340 million in grants since they started, and the Kiwanis Clubs give out over $100 million every year.

Find your local club for each of the organizations below and contact them for information on their programs. If they do not have an on going program that specifically suits you, you can ask if you send a letter of request for their consideration.

It can't hurt to ask. We've used these clubs in this way to help people in our "Show Me The Money Contest".

These organizations run programs that offer money for:
- day care services
- summer camp
- scholarships
- travel
- free eye glasses
- cataract surgeries
- health problems
- travel
- medical equipment, and
- money for emergencies

☐ Kiwanis International
3636 Woodview Trace
Indianapolis, IN 46268-3196
USA
317-875-8755
http://www.kiwanis.org
find a local Kiwanis club
http://www.kiwanis.org/clubloc/

☐ United States Junior Chamber
P.O. Box 7
Tulsa, OK 74102
1-800-JAYCEES
http://www.usjaycees.org/
find a local Jaycees chapter
http://www.usjaycees.org/chapter_links.htm

☐ Lions Clubs International
300 W 22nd Street
Oak Brook, IL 60523
630-571-5466 ext 356
http://www.lionsclubs.org/
630-571-5466 ext 356

find a local lions club
http://www.lionnet.com/united_states.html

6. *Find Money For Emergencies*

There are a number of national groups that provide free money and services thru a network of local offices. Check each of the groups below and see what their local offices have to offer.

☐   Catholic Charities USA
     1731 King St., #200
     Alexandria, VA 22314
     703-549-1390
     www.catholiccharitiesinfo.org

Over 14,000 local organizations offer a variety of services for many different community problems including child care, elderly services, emergency financial services, rental assistance, and more. To find an office near you go to their main web site and see "Need Assistance? Find A Local Agency?" and put in your state.

☐   Salvation Army National Headquarters
     615 Slaters Lane
     P.O. Box 269
     Alexandria, VA 22313
     703-684-5500
     www.salvationarmyusa.org/

Families in need can receive a wide range of services including utility assistance, transitional housing emergency food, clothing, and more. For an office near you, contact the headquarters above or {http://www.redshield.org/}.

7. *Find a Local Non-Profit With Money and Services*

The United Way is a national organization that raises money for thousands of local non-profit organizations who offer money and services to people in their community. Your local United Way can identify non-profits in your area that may offer the resources or services you are looking for. Contact:

☐ United Way of America
701 North Fairfax St.
Alexandria, VA 2314
703-836-7112
www.unitedway.org

to find a local chapter go to the web site and enter your zip code under "Find A Local United Way."

8. *Find Your Local Community Action Agency*

Over 1,000 local non-profit offices offer free money and help to improve your life in almost any area. Although these agencies do get money from the federal government they also get money from other sources, and as a result, no two of these offices are exactly alike. But most all of them help in the area of employment, bill paying, child care and self employment. The following is a sample of programs you will find when you contact an office near you. Along with the program, we also identify the local agency providing this program. These programs are specific to these areas. Check with your local office to see what they offer.

Get a $3 grant for every $1 you save
Community Action Partnership {http: //www.managingmymoney.com/}

$10,000 no interest, no payment, forgivable loans for home repairs
CFS Economic Opportunity Corporation
{http://www.advant.com/ cefs/energy.htm}

Buy a home with only $1,000
CEFS Economic Opportunity Corporation {www.advant.com/ cefs/homebuy.htm}

$3,000 grant to fix your furnace
CEFS Economic Opportunity Corporation
{http://www.advant.com/ cefs/ihwap.htm}

$25,000 no interest, no payment, forgivable loan for home fix-up
CEFS Economic Opportunity Corporation
{http://www.advant.com/ cefs/rehab.htm}

$2,000 to pay heating bills
CEFS Economic Opportunity Corporation
{http://www.advant.com/ cefs/liheap.htm}

Free Cars, if you pay repairs and registration
CAP Agency Shakopee, MI {http:// www.capagency.org/pages/service.htm}

Free Crisis Nursery, up to 73 hours of overnight care and 10 days day care
CAP Agency Shakopee, MI {http:// www.capagency.org/pages/service.htm}

Eviction Prevention
TEAM, Inc Derby, CT {http://www. teamcaa.org/housing.htm}

$10,000 to start a business
Community Action Program, Inc of Western Indiana
{http://www.capwi. org/new_page_9.htm}

$700 for child care
Community and Family Services, Inc. Portland, IN
{www.comfam.net/ pages/childcare.html}

$350 for an air conditioner
City of Des Moines, Iowa {http://www.ci.des-moines.ia.us/
departments/CD/Comm%20Serv/L-
I%20Assist%20Programs.htm}

$1,000 To Repair Furnace
City of Des Moines, Iowa {http://www.ci.des-moines.ia.us/
departments/CD/Comm%20Serv/L-
I%20Assist%20Programs.htm}

$45/month for pre-school
Mid-Sioux Opportunity, Inc., Remsen, IA {http://www.mid-
siouxopportunity.org/ ccr/community_
resources/empowerment.html}

To find a community action agency near you go to:
{http://www.communityactionpartnership.com/about/links/map.a
sp} or contact Community Action Partnership, 1100 17th St NW
Suite 500, Washington, DC 20036; 202-265-7546; Fax: 202-
265-8850; {info@communityactionpartnership.com}; {www.
communityactionpartnership.com}.

If your local agency doesn't have what
you need, ask for names of other
organizations who might be able to help.

You live in America and pay taxes. You
have a right to know about and use these
programs. If you run into a road block, don't let a little negative
feedback stop you. Try the next program, and then the next. And

then start looking for more. This country has so much to offer, but you have to find it.

$2,000 A Month To Pay Your Mortgage While You Are Looking For Work

There are now programs that will make your mortgage payments for you when you get into financial trouble. One of the best ways to find out if there are programs like this in your area is to contact the local HUD approved Housing Counseling agencies. To find your closest agency, contact your state housing office, or the Housing Counseling Center locator at 800-569-4287; {www.hud.gov/hs gcoun.html}; or Housing Counseling Clearinghouse, P.O. Box 10423, McLean, VA 22102; 800-217-6970.

Free Credit Repair

The Federal Trade Commission has many publications to get you on the road to good credit and can also tell you your rights in dealing with collection agencies. Contact Public Reference, Room 130, Federal Trade Commission, Washington, DC 20580; 877-FTC-HELP; {www.ftc.gov}; You can also get free counseling at your local County Cooperative Extension Service listed in the government section of your phone book under County Government. Or contact one of the non-profits that can help with your debt: National Foundation for Credit Counseling, 801 Roeder Rd., Suite 900, Silver Spring, MD 20910; 800-388-2227; {www.nfcc.org}; or Credit Counseling Center of America, P.O. Box 830489, Richardson, TX 75083; 800-493-2222; {www.cccamerica.org}. Remember that these non-profits get money from credit card companies so they are not likely to explain your bankruptcy options to you.

Get Extra $6,000 If You Cannot Work

If you don't qualify for Social Security, or if your benefits are very low, you may qualify for Supplemental Security Income (SSI). This program was established to help poor seniors over 65 and the blind and disabled meet basic living expenses. To find out more about the program contact your local Social Security office or contact the Social Security hotline at 800-772-1213 or online at {www.ssa.gov}.

$500 In Free Emergency Money

If you need emergency money to pay a bill, or for housing, training, health care, or just additional support, these organizations can be of service and they are likely to have an office near you. Community Action Agencies: nearly 1,000 agencies around the country receive funds from the Community Services Block Grant to offer education, counseling, employment, training, and more. To locate an agency serving your area contact National Community Action Partnership, 1100 17th St., NW, Washington, DC 20036; 202-265-7546; {www.communityactionpartner ship. com}.

Extra $1,000 For Seniors and Disabled

Each year over 3 million eligible seniors and people with disabilities fail to apply for a little-known program that will give them over $1,000 extra in their Social Security check. That's how much the government deducts for Medicare Part B payments. The program is called Qualified Medicare

Beneficiaries Plan, or Specified Low-Income Medicare Beneficiaries Plan. To learn more contact your local Social Security Office at 800-772-1213. You can also contact the Medicare Hotline and request the publication Guide to Health Insurance for People with Medicare. Contact Medicare Hotline at 800-MEDICARE or online at {www.medicare.gov}.

50% Discount On Phone Service

Under the Federal Communication Commission's Link-up America and Lifeline programs, low-income households seeking telephone service are given a 50% discount on local connection charges, and may be able to pay installment payments on the remaining charge. To learn more contact your local telephone company.

10% to 100% Off Eyeglasses

Pearle Vision Centers offers 50% off either the lenses or frames when you purchase a complete set of glasses to people 50-59; 60% off to those 60-69; and so on until seniors reach 100 and they are given 100% off either the lenses or frames when they purchase a complete set of glasses. Lens Crafters and Eye Glass Factory also offer discount programs. Now it makes seeing clearly less costly.

$800 for Food

The Food Stamp Program was designed to help low-income families buy the food they need to stay healthy and productive. The amount of Food Stamps you get each month is determined by the number of people in your family and by the household income. Look in the blue pages of your telephone book under "Food Stamps," "Social Services," or "Public Assistance." You can also find more information by contacting U.S. Department of Agriculture, Food and Nutrition Service, 3101 Park Ctr., Dr., Park Office Center Bldg., Alexandria, VA 22302; 703-305-2276; {www.fns.usda.gov/fncs}.

$2,000 To Pay Your Heating Bills

Storm windows, insulation, and even weatherstripping, can help reduce your fuel bill. Families can receive assistance to weatherize their homes and apartments at no charge if you meet certain income guidelines. States allocate dollars to nonprofit agencies for purchasing and installing energy-related repairs, with the average grant being $2,000 per year. Contact your state Energy Office or the Weatherization Assistance Programs Branch, EE44, U.S. Department of Energy, 1000 Independence Ave., SW, Washington, DC 20585; 202-596-4074; {www.eere.energy.gov/weather ization}.

Make $500 Turning In Annoying Telephone Solicitors

The Federal Communications Commission's Consumer Protection Act says that you can collect $500 or more from telephone solicitors if they call two or more times within a 12 month period after you tell them to stop; they call you with a pre-recorded voice message to your home; they call you at home before 8am or after 9 pm; and more. For more information contact Federal Communications Commission, Common Carrier Bureau, Consumer Complaints, Mail Stop 1600A2, Washington, DC 20554; 888-CALL-FCC; {www.fcc.gov/cgb/con sumerfacts/tcpa.html}.

$700 Off Your Utility Bills

The legislature in Massachusetts passed a law giving discounts up to $700 on heating bills for families making up to $30,000, along with up to 40% discount on electric bills, $108 off telephone bills, and $100 off oil bills. Contact your state's Public Utilities office to find out about special discounts on your gas, electric, cable or telephone service in your state.

Free Legal Help To Fight Your Credit Card Company

If you are having trouble with your credit card company, remember that they are regulated by a banking institution. Different banks are governed by different agencies, but all take complaints and make efforts to assist customers. Your state Banking Commissioner handles complaints dealing with state chartered banks. For banks with the word "national" or "N.A." in its name contact Comptroller of the Currency, Compliance Management, U.S. Department of the Treasury, 250 E St., SW, Washington, DC 20219; 202-874-4900; 800-613-6743; {www.occ.treas.gov}. For Savings and Loans contact Office of Thrift Supervision, U.S. Department of the Treasury, 1700 G St., NW, Washington, DC 20552; 202-906-6000; 800-842-6929; {www.ots.treas. gov}. For FDIC Insured contact Federal Deposit Insurance Corporation, Office of Consumer Affairs, 550 17th St., NW, Room F-130, Washington, DC 20429; 877-ASK-FDIC; {www.fdic.gov}.

Free Legal Help To Fight The IRS

The Taxpayer Advocate administers the Problem Resolution Program (PRP) that has the authority to cut through red tape. They will keep you informed of your case's progress. PRP can usually help with delayed refunds, unanswered inquiries, and incorrect billing notices. For more information request Publication 1546, The Taxpayer Advocate Service of the IRS. To get in contact the program, call the IRS at 800-829-1040; {www.irs.gov}.

The Government Owes You Money

You may not know it, but there may be money sitting and waiting for you in government offices. It may be because of an old utility deposit you forgot about or an IRS check that was sent to an old address. Find out if there is hidden money for you at these government offices: National Association of Unclaimed Property Administrators, P.O. Box 7156, Bismarck, ND 58507; {www. unclaimed.org}; contact the IRS at 800-829-1040; {www.irs.gov}; U.S. Department of Housing and Urban Development, P.O. Box 23699, Washington, DC 20026; {www.hud. gov/refunds/index.cfm}; Veterans Affairs at 800-827-1000; {www.va. gov}; or Social Security at 800-772-1213; {www.ssa.gov}.

Get $540 To Buy Fresh Fruit

Seniors making up to $22,000/ year can get as much as $540 to buy fresh fruit and vegetables from road side stands. Through the little-known Senior Farmers' Market Nutrition Program, seniors in 40 states can have the government help buy their produce. Find out how much your state can give you to buy food. Contact the USDA Food and Nutrition Service, 3101 Park Center Drive, Room 926, Alexandria, VA 22302; {www.fns.usda.gov/fncs}. To locate your State office go to {www.fns.usda.gov/wic/SeniorFMNP/SFMNPcontacts2004.htm}.

Get $25,000 Toward Hotels, Rental Assistance, And Home Repair For Disaster Victims

A victim of disaster and not sure how you are going to pay the mountain of expenses? Through FEMA's Individual Assistance Program, you could be eligible for $25,000 of assistance. FEMA will help pay for hotel stays, apartment rental, home repair or even new construction. Don't miss out on the help you need and deserve. Contact FEMA at 800-621-FEMA (TTY: 800-462-7585) and register. {http://www.fema.gov/rrr/inassist. shtm}.

$14,800 in Grant Money For Disaster Victims

Has your family been part of a major disaster? Through FEMA, you can get up to $14,800 in grant money to help get you back on your feet. The money will cover real and personal property, medical and dental bills, as well as many other expenses. To find out more, contact the Department of Homeland Security 245 Murray Drive, S.W. Washington, D.C. 20528; (202) 282-8000; {http://12.46.245.173/pls/portal30/CATALOG.PROGRAM_TE

XT_RPT.SHOW?p_arg_names=prog_nbr&p_arg_values=97.035}.

Free Boat Safety Inspections And Boating Classes

Do your own online boat inspection and then have the Coast Guard do one for you for free! Sign up for free classes and even download water safety booklets online. For more information on these free services, go to the U.S. Coast Guard Auxiliary's website {http://www.cgaux.org/cgauxweb/public/pubframe.htm}.

$5,000 Yearly for Certain WWII Vets

If you meet the criteria set by SSI, you could receive over $5,000 a year in benefits. Contact the Social Security Administration, Office of Public Inquiries, Windsor Park Building, 6401 Security Blvd., Baltimore, MD 21235; 800-772-1213; {http://www.ssa.gov/pubs/10157.html}. For additional information visit {http://12.46.245.173/pls/portal30/CATALOG.PROGRAM_TEXT_RPT.SHOW?p_arg_names=prog_nbr&p_arg_values=96.020}.

$2,500 Grants for Everyone

This foundation is dedicated to making a difference in the communities where employees, franchisees, and customers of Jack in the Box restaurants work and live. Its primary charitable partner is Big Brothers Big Sisters, as well as the United Way and local nonprofit organizations in the headquarters city of San Diego in the areas of youth, education, and human services. Hardship grants are made to company employees in need. Giving is on a national basis. Contact Jack in the Box Foundation, c/o Tax Department, 9330 Balboa Avenue, San Diego, CA

92123-1516; {http://www.jackinthe box.com/foundation/}

Tax Free Income, Transportation Expenses, And Free Physicals To Help Seniors

Through the Senior Companion Program, work as a volunteer for the elderly while getting compensated for your time! Benefits include an hourly tax-free wage, transportation expenses, free physicals, and free meal. Make a difference and make money too! For more information, contact the Senior Corps at 800-424-8867 or TTY 800-833-3722; {http://www.seniorcorps. org/joining/scp/}.

Over $6,000 Grants for Older Women

This foundation provides grants to economically disadvantaged women over the age of 65. Grants are generally awarded up to $6,000, but could be more. This is a national grant program. Contact Sarah A. W. Devens Trust, c/o Rice, Heard & Bigelow, Inc., 50 Congress St., Ste. 1025, Boston, MA 02109; 617-557-7509; {axs@riceheard.com}.

Over $11,000 Grants for People in Need

Grants to individuals as well as employee matching gifts are awarded

to needy individuals who are economically disadvantaged. Its goals are to prevent homelessness, promote self-sufficiency and to enhance community services. Giving is on a national basis in areas of company operations. Contact Washington Group Foundation (formerly Morrison Knudsen Corporation Foundation), P.O. Box 73, Boise, ID 83729; 208-386-5201; {http://wwwwgint.com/ washington_foundation_how.html}; {marlene.puckett@wgint.com}. Application Address: Washington Group Foundation, 1 Morrison Knudsen Plaza, Boise, ID 83729.

Grants & Other Financial Assistance for Employees

Over $20.0 million is available to disperse as financial assistance for individuals who work or have retired from Abbott Laboratories. Grants, loans, financial education and counseling services are provided due to financial hardships. Assistance is awarded to employees and retirees worldwide. Contact The Clara Abbott Foundation, 200 Abbott Park Rd., D579/AMJ37, Abbott Park, IL 60064-3537; {http://clara.abbott.com}.

$5,000 for Heroism

This foundation awards medals and monetary awards to civilians within the U.S. and Canada who demonstrated voluntary heroism in saving or attempting to save the lives of others. Maximum award amount is $5,000. Grant monetary assistance, including scholarship aid, is also given to awardees and to the dependents of those who have lost their lives or who have been disabled in such heroic manner. This amount can be up to $3,500. Contact Carnegie Hero Fund Commission, 425 6th Ave., Ste. 1640, Pittsburgh, PA 15219-1823; 412-281-

1302 or 800-447-8900; Fax: 412-281-5751; {http://www.carnegiehero.org/}; {carnegiehero@carnegiehero.org}.

Money for Women in Massachusetts

Provides grants to economically disadvantaged elderly Protestant women in Massachusetts. Contact Laura A. Burgess Fund, c/o Fleet Private Clients Group, P.O. Box 6767, Providence, RI 02940-6767. Application Address: Laura A. Burgess Fund, c/o Fleet National Bank, 100 Federal St., Boston, MA 02110; 617-434-4644.

Financial Help for Former Jockeys and Horse Grooms

Provides financial assistance grants to help individuals who were at one time employed by or associated with the thoroughbred industry. Grants are provided to injured former jockeys and exercise riders, retired grooms and hot walkers, spouses of deceased industry personnel, ill backstretch workers and their families who are facing financial need. Contact The Jockey Club Foundation, 40 E. 52nd St., New York, NY 10022-5911; {http://www.tjc foundation.org/}.

Financial Assistance for Daughters of Deceased Railroaders

This foundation provides limited financial assistance to daughters of railroad employees who die (the cause need not be work-related) while in the employ of a railroad in the United States. Funding is provided to encourage each girl to pursue her education. In order to qualify for a grant of financial assistance from the Foundation, the girl must live in the home of the surviving parent or guardian, maintain a good health

program, receive satisfactory academic grades and is encouraged to participate in religious services of her faith. Eligibility of the daughter is also dependent upon the parent remaining unmarried. This supplement to family income is to be used in its entirety for the benefit of the girl. The Foundation also provides certain health care benefits to the daughter. Contact The John Edgar Thomson Foundation, c/o The Rittenhouse Claridge, 201 S. 18th Street, Suite 318, Philadelphia, PA 19103; 215-545-6083; {http://www. utu.org/DEPTS/PR-DEPT/ DAUGHTER.HTM}.

$5,000 for Emergency Situations in Women's Rights

The Urgent Action Fund provides small grants up to $5,000 to support strategic interventions that take advantage of opportunities to advance women's human rights. The Fund supports "urgent actions" that cannot wait for a month or six weeks or six months. Grantmaking categories include: situations of armed conflict, escalating violence or politically volatile environments; precedent-setting legal or legislative action; and protection of women's human rights defenders. Individuals and organizations can apply for this national funding program. Contact Urgent Action Fund for Women's Human Rights, P.O. Box 1287, Boulder, CO 80306-1287; 303-442-2388; Fax: 303-442-2370; {www. urgentactionfund.org}; {urgentact@ urgentactionfund.org}.

Grants to Aid Victims of Violence

The New England Patriots' R.O.S.E. Award offers a cash award to a female victim of violent crime who is working to overcome her adversities. The award is meant to help her continue in her journey toward regaining her self-esteem and rebuilding her life. Cash awards vary according to funding availability. Contact The R.O.S.E. Fund, Inc., (formerly Ryka Rose Foundation), 175 Federal St., Ste. 455, Boston, MA 02110; 617-482-5400; Fax: 617-482-3443; {http://www.rose fund.org}; {rosefund@ici.net}.

Achievement Award + Cash Award for Charity

The Heinz Family Foundation R.O.S.E. Achievement Award recognizes a woman survivor of violence for her work and achievements in the area of ending violence against women. The recipient's choice of non-profit organization receives the cash award.

Contact The R.O.S.E. Fund, Inc., (formerly Ryka Rose Foundation), 175 Federal St., Ste. 455, Boston, MA 02110; 617-482-5400; Fax: 617-482-3443; {http://www.rosefund.org}; {rosefund@ici.net}.

Grants up to $7,500 for Social Services and Medical Needs

Grants range from $1,000 to $7,500 for support of social services, higher education, music, museums, and medical needs. This foundation gives on a national basis. Contact The

Chazen Foundation, P.O. Box 801, Nyack, NY 10960; {http://www.cha zenscholar.com/project.php3}; {scho larprogram@chazenscholar.com}.

Financial Assistance to Victims of Natural Disaster

The fund provides monetary and non-monetary relief to individuals in the U.S. and Canada who are victims of disasters such as hurricanes and earthquakes. Contact Teamster Disaster Relief Fund, 25 Louisiana Ave., N.W., Washington, DC 20001; 202-624-6871; {http://www.teamster.org}.

$3,000 Matching Funds for Employees

The Foundation will match active BearingPoint employee and board of director's contributions to eligible non-profit organizations at 100%, up to a limit of $3,000 total per donor per fiscal year. Full-time & part-time active US & Canadian BearingPoint employees who work 1,000 hours or more in a year and board of director's members are eligible to participate in the matching gift program. Contact BearingPoint, Inc. Corporate Giving Program (formerly KPMG Consulting, Inc. Corporate Giving Program), c/o BearingPoint Charitable Foundation, 106 Allen Road, Liberty Corner, NJ 07938; 908-607-2300; {http://www.bearingpoint.com/about_us/philanthro py/rand_blazer.html}; {us-kcingiving program@kpmg.com}; {us-becom munitysupp@BearingPoint.net}.

Financial Assistance for Employees in Need

Through the Corporate Giving Program, BearingPoint coordinates emotional and financial support for employees impacted by traumatic or catastrophic events, giving employees a place to turn when they are in need. BearingPoint does not accept unsolicited grant proposals from outside organizations. All requests for funding and support are generated by BearingPoint employees. Contact BearingPoint, Inc. Corporate Giving Program (formerly KPMG Consulting, Inc. Corporate Giving Program), c/o BearingPoint Charitable Foundation, 106 Allen Road, Liberty Corner, NJ 07938; 908-607-2300; {http://www .bearingpoint.com/about_us/philanthro py/rand_blazer.html}; {us-kcingiving program@kpmg.com}; {us-becom munitysupp@BearingPoint.net}.

Help for the Elderly and Needy, and for Catholic Organizations

St. Benedict's Charitable Society provides relief assistance to elderly, infirm, and needy people for basic living, medical and funeral expenses; it also provides support for Catholic churches, organizations and scholarship funds. Contact Margaret Kuehmstedt, Treas., St. Benedict's Charitable Society, 1663 Bristol Pike, Bensalem, PA 19020-5702; 215-244-9900.

Employees Volunteer to Get Cash Rewards

WAVE is a volunteer program that helps Fannie Mae and Fannie Mae Foundation employees find volunteer opportunities and provide incentives for employees to participate in volunteer activities. Employees can receive up to 10 hours of paid leave per month to perform community service. The WAVE program also features a grants program called Dollars for Doers which matches employee volunteer hours with cash grants to the organizations for which they volunteer. The Employee

Matching Gifts Program is another component of WAVE, which matches personal financial contributions by employees, up to $10,000 per year.

Contact Fannie Mae Foundation, 4000 Wisconsin Ave. N.W., N. Tower, Ste. 1, Washington, DC 20016-2804; 202-274-8066 or 202-274-8057 or 202-274-8000; Fax: 202-274-8100; {http:// www.fanniemaefoundation.org}; {grants@fanniemaefoundation.org}.

Up to $25,000 for Those in Need

This Foundation offers support for Christian churches, and educational, missionary, and welfare programs and also awards grants to needy individuals. Grants range from $5,000 up to $25,000. Contact Agape Fund, 800 Middlebrook Road, Prescott, AZ 86303; {http://www.communioncha pel.org/agape_fund_guidelines.htm}.

Money for Italian Americans

The Italian-American Community Services Agency awards grants to Italian-Americans in financial need and indigent individuals, including senior citizens. Contact Italian-American Community Services Agency (formerly Italian Welfare Agency, Inc.), 678 Green St., San Francisco, CA 94133-3896; 415-362-6423; {http://Italiancommunity services.org/index.htm}; {email: ampierini@italiancommunityservices. org}.

$100 to People with AIDS

Out of the Closet Foundation, Inc. is a foundation that provides financial support and scholarships to AIDS organizations and institutions, which have AIDS programs, with a focus on gay-related issues. Giving activities include $1,000 for 16 grants with a high of $100 and a low of $25. Contact Edward Maloney, Exec. Dir., Out of the Closet Foundation, Inc., P.O. Box 20084, Cherokee Sta., New York, NY 10021; 212-472-3573. Additional address: OOTC Thrift Shop (AIDS Thrift Shop), 220 E. 81st St., New York, NY 10028.

$15,000 to Pay for Child Care

The Child Care and Development Block Grant gives money to states to help families meet their child care needs. Parents may choose from a variety of child care providers, including center-based, family child care and in-home care, care provided by relatives, and even sectarian child care providers. You can even get money to start a day care center! Income qualifications vary from state to state, and each state operates their programs slightly differently.

To find out how to take advantage of this program in your state and to learn the eligibility requirements, contact National Child Care Information Center, 243 Church St., NW, Vienna, VA 22180; 800-616-2242; {http://nccic.org}.

Pay Only $9/wk for Child Care at Local Nonprofits

Local nonprofits around the country get grants from the United Way or other institutions and offer free and sliding scale day care services. The United Way spends about a third of its funds, about $1 billion a year, on programs for children and families.

For example, the Community Partnerships for Children Program in Brockton, MA provides child care for a family of 2 with weekly income of $210 for only $9.00 a week, and families of 4 with income of $1,000 a week can get care for $114 a week per child. There are about 500 local United Way Information and Referral Services around the country that can point you to local groups that can help you solve your child care problems. Look in the phone book for your local United Way agency, or contact United Way of America, 701 N. Fairfax Street, Alexandria, VA 22314-2045; 703-836-7112; {www.unitedway.org}.

Free Pre-School for Your Child

Head Start is preschool that has a great student teacher ratio and all teachers are certified in early childhood development. It prepares the children with school readiness, and research shows that these children enter kindergarten with the skills necessary to succeed. There are income requirements for acceptance into the program, but the program does allow 10% of the students to have higher incomes. And 10% of the program needs to be offered to kids who have a disability. To learn more about Head Start programs near you, contact your local board of education, the state Department of Social Services, or Administration for Children and Families, U.S. Department of Health and Human Services, Head Start Bureau, 370 L'Enfant Promenade, SW, Washington, DC 20201; 202-737-1030; {www.acf.dhhs.gov/programs/hsb}.

Free Child Care For Teens With Disabilities

48 states provide a subsidy to parents who qualify for childcare for children ages 14 to 19 who are physically and/or mentally incapable of self-care. Each state sets their eligibility requirement and the amount of funds they have available for this type of care. To learn what your state has to offer, contact your state Child Care and Development Block Grant lead agency.

Money for Your Child Care Center

Child Care Works is a new partnership between the District of Columbia, eight area banks and three community organizations that make training, grants and loans available to licensed neighborhood day care providers to provide slots for 1,000 children. Maryland and Ohio provide special low-interest loans through their Department of Economic Development to fund child care centers. Even the Child Care and Development Block Grant provides money to develop child care centers and before and after school programs. Contact your state Department of Economic Development or your Child Care and Development Block Grant lead agency.

$4,000 To Pay For Child Care

IRS Publication 503, *Child and Dependent Care Expenses*, outlines the rules covering this benefit and describes how to figure the benefit if your employer covers some of the cost. You may claim up to $3,000 for the care of one child (or $6,000 for two or more). For more information, contact the IRS Information Line at 800-829-1040; or {www.irs.gov}. In addition, 25 states and the District of Columbia offer some type of child care income tax benefit either in the form of credits

or deductions. Contact your state Tax Revenue office to see what your state offers.

Free Tax Help For Seniors

The Tax Counseling for the Elderly program was designed to provide free taxpayer assistance to those ages 60 and above. The staff usually consists of retired individuals associated with nonprofit organizations that receive grants from the IRS to perform this service. Often they provide counseling in retirement homes, neighborhood sites or private houses of the homebound. For information on the Tax Counseling for the Elderly program near you, contact your local IRS office, call the hotline at 800-829-1040; {www.irs.gov}.

Free Copies of Your Credit Report

You can get a free copy of your credit report if:

- you have been denied credit, insurance, or employment within the last 60 days
- you're unemployed and plan to look for a job within 60 days
- you're on welfare, or
- your report is inaccurate because of fraud.

Otherwise they can charge you up to $9 for a copy of your report. For copies of your report, contact the credit reporting agencies listed in the yellow pages of your telephone book, or contact the three major national credit bureaus:

Equifax
PO Box 740241, Atlanta, GA 30374; 800-685-1111; {www.equifax.com}

Experian (formerly TRW)
PO Box 949, Allen, TX 75013; 888-397-3742; {www.experian.com}

Free Money For Everybody

Trans Union

> P.O. Box 2000, Chester, PA 19022; 800-916-8800; {www.transunion.com}

If you have trouble getting satisfaction from a credit reporting agency contact: Consumer Response Center, Federal Trade Commission, CRC-240, Washington, DC 20580; 877-FTC-HELP; {www.ftc.gov}.

$500 Extra for Seniors and Disabled

The state of Pennsylvania offers up to $500 for seniors and people with disabilities who pay property taxes or rent. If you live in Pennsylvania, contact Department of Aging, 555 Walnut St., 5th Floor, Harrisburg, PA 17101; 717-783-1549. If you live elsewhere, contact your state Office on Aging listed in the blue pages of your phone book, or your state Department of Revenue.

Free Gov't Benefits Check Up

The National Council on the Aging offers a service to seniors so that they may find available programs to help them pay for prescriptions, health care, utilities, and other related things. This free service is called Benefits CheckUp and it can be found at {www.benefitscheckup.org}. At the site, a simple and confidential questionnaire is filled out, and then it will check over 1,000 programs to see if any are available based on the information given. This does not require a name, address, phone, or social security number.

Discounts On Your Banking Bills

First Citizens Bank has **Senior Quest Accounts** where customers 60 and over receive unlimited check writing, no per check charge, interest bearing checking, no monthly service charge, free safe deposit box, no ATM fees, free cashier's checks, travelers' checks, and money orders. They even offer special rates on 6 and 12 month CD's, no annual fee credit card, free direct deposit and discount brokerage fees, with some of these services requiring a minimum balance. Other banks offer similar services, with most offering free checks, no minimum balance, and unlimited check writing.

Money For Veterans

The Department of Veterans Affairs hotline can provide you with information on such programs as life insurance, comprehensive dental and medical care, nursing homes, home loan programs, burial services, and more. Contact Department of Veterans Affairs, 810 Vermont Ave., NW, Washington, DC 20420; 800-827-1000; {www.va.gov}.

Christian Scientists Get Free Money

The New Horizons Foundation provides financial assistance to residents of Los Angeles County, CA, who are over 65 years of age and active Christian Scientists. Contact New Horizons Foundation, c/o Gifford & Dearing, 700 S. Flower St., Suite 1222, Los Angeles, CA 90017-4160; 213-626-4481.

Grants and camperships are available through the Sunnyside Foundation, Inc. to underprivileged Christian Science children under the age of 20 who regularly attend Sunday School and are Texas residents. Contact Sunnyside Foundation, Inc., 8222 Douglas Ave., Suite 501, Dallas, TX 75225-5936; 214-692-5686.

$1,000 Extra for Seniors

- Monetary assistance is available for living expenses such as food and medicine through the Sarah A.W. Devens Trust to economically disadvantaged women over age 65 residing in MA. Contact Sarah A.W. Devens Trust, c/o Rice, Heard & Bigelow, Inc., 50 Congress St., Suite 1025, Boston, MA 02109; 617-557-7415.

- Supplemental monthly income is available to elderly indigent residents of the Southeastern U.S. through the Alfred I. duPont Foundation. Contact Alfred I. duPont Foundation, 1650 Prudential Drive, Suite 302, Jacksonville, FL 32207; 904-858-3123.

$2,000 For Being Mugged

Millions of people and their families are victimized by crime every year in the U.S. And to better address the growing belief that the law was better at protecting the rights of criminals than those of the victims, Congress enacted a law to establish a Crime Victims Fund to compensate innocent victims of violent crime. Part of the money is given to help compensate victims or their families for costs relating to such crimes as muggings, sexual crimes, and even murder. Part of the money from these funds is given out to victims as direct cash payments to help compensate for costs related to the violent crimes. Contact the office in your state if you find yourself the victim of a violent crime and need money to help pay for such related costs as medical bills, lost wages, and funeral expenses. For more information you may contact:

- Office for Victims of Crime Resource Center, National Criminal Justice Reference Service, P.O. Box 6000, Rockville, MD 20849; 800-851-3420; 301-519-5500 (8:30 am to 7 pm EST); {www.ncjrs.org}.
- Office for Victims of Crime, U.S. Department of Justice, 950 Pennsylvania Avenue, NW, Washington, DC 20530; 202-514-2601; {www.usdoj.gov/crimevictims.htm}

Extra Money For Indiana Presbyterians

The Frank L. and Laura L. Smock Foundation offers Presbyterian Indiana residents who are ailing, physically disabled, blind, needy or elderly medical and nursing care assistance. Contact Frank L. and Laura L. Smock Foundation, c/o Wells Fargo Bank Indiana, N.A., P.O. Box 960, Fort Wayne, IN 46801-6632; 219-461-6451.

Extra Money For Pittsburgh-Area Jewish Families in Need

Financial assistance is offered to needy Jewish families residing in the Pittsburgh area through the Jewish Family Assistance Fund for living, personal, food and medical expenses. Contact Jewish Family Assistance Fund, 5743 Bartlett St., Pittsburgh, PA 15217-1515; 412-521-3237.

Free Meals At Day Care

Not only does the government offer free lunches for school children, but your younger children can also receive

free meals at day care centers, family day care homes, and more. Child and Adult Care Food Program (CACFP) provides nutritious meals to 2.6 million children and 74,000 adults who receive day care outside of their home.

CACFP reaches even further to provide meals to children residing in homeless shelters, and snacks and suppers to youths participating in eligible afterschool care programs.

CACFP reimburses participating centers and day care homes for their meal costs. It is administered at the Federal level by the Food and Nutrition Service (FNS), an agency of the U.S. Department of Agriculture. The State education or health department administers CACFP, in most States. Programs include:
Child Care Centers
Adult Day Care Centers
Family Day Care Homes
Homeless Shelters
After School Care Programs

Contact FNS Public Information, 3101 Park Center Drive, Room 926, Alexandria, VA 22302; 703-305-2281; {www.fns.usda.gov/cnd/care/cacfp/cacfphome.htm}.

Free Lunches For Students
The National School Lunch Program (NSLP) is a federally assisted meal program administered by the USDA, operating in public and nonprofit private schools and residential child care institutions. It provides nutritionally balanced, low-cost or free lunches to children each school day. The program was established under the National School Lunch Act, signed by President Harry Truman in 1946.

Contact USDA Food and Nutrition Service, 3101 Park Center Drive,

Room 914, Alexandria, VA 22302; 703-305-2286; {www.fns.usda.gov/cnd/Lunch/}.

$700 Food Money for Women & Children
The Women, Infant and Children (WIC) Program's mission is to safeguard the health of low-income

women, infants, and children up to age 5 who are at nutritional risk by providing nutritious foods to supplement diets, information on healthy eating, and referrals to health care. A family of four can make up to $33,485 and still qualify!

WIC foods include iron-fortified infant formula and infant cereal, iron-fortified adult cereal, vitamin C-rich fruit and/or vegetable juice, eggs, milk, cheese, peanut butter, dried beans or peas, tuna fish and carrots.

In addition to the regular WIC program, a majority of the states have chosen to operate the WIC Farmers' Market Nutrition Program (FMNP), established in 1992, it provides additional coupons to WIC participants that they can use to purchase fresh fruits and vegetables at participating farmers' markets.

Contact Supplemental Food Programs Division, Food and Nutrition Service – USDA, 3101 Park Center Drive, Alexandria, VA 22302; 703-305-2746;

Fax: 703-305-2196; {www.fns.usda.gov/fns/}.

Free Food for Seniors

The Nutrition Services Incentive Program (NSIP) is the new name for the United States Department of Agriculture (USDA) cash or commodity program, known as the Nutrition Program for the Elderly (NPE). While there is no means test for participation in this program, services are targeted to older people with the greatest economic or social need, with special attention given to low-income minorities. Since American Indians, Alaskan Natives, and Native Hawaiians tend to have lower life expectancies and higher rates of illness at younger ages, Tribal Organizations are given the option of setting the age at which older people can participate in the program. Contact your state or local Administration on Aging.

National Administration on Aging
Administration on Aging
330 Independence Avenue, SW
Washington, DC 20201
202-619-0724
www.aoa.gov/

Eldercare Locator
800-677-1116
www.eldercare.gov/

USDA Food and Nutrition Service
3101 Park Center Drive
Alexandria, VA 22302
703-305-2060
www.fns.usda.gov/fdd/programs/nsip/

Rich Kids Pay 2 Cents for Pint of Milk

The Special Milk Program (SMP) provides milk to children in schools and childcare institutions that do not participate in other Federal child nutrition meal service programs. The program reimburses schools for the milk they serve. Schools in the National School Lunch or School Breakfast Programs may also participate in the Special Milk Program to provide milk to children in half-day pre-kindergarten and kindergarten programs where children do not have access to the school meal programs.

Contact your local school or the USDA Food and Nutrition Service, 3101 Park Center Drive, Room 914, Alexandria, VA 22302.; 703-305-2286; {www.fns.usda.gov/cnd/Milk/}.

Free Food for Native Americans

The Food Distribution Program on Indian Reservations (FDPIR) is a program that provides commodity foods to low-income households, including the elderly, living on Indian reservations, and to Native American families residing in designated areas near reservations.

Participants on many reservations can choose fresh produce instead of canned fruits and vegetables. Contact the office in your area for more information. Contact Food and Nutrition Service – USDA, Food Distribution Division, 3101 Park Center Drive, Alexandria, VA 22302; 703-305-2888; Fax: 703-305-2420; {www.fns.usda.gov/fdd/programs/fdpir/fdpirhome.htm}.

Free Extra Food

The Commodity Supplemental Food Program (CSFP) works to improve the health of low-income pregnant and breastfeeding women, other new mothers up to one year postpartum, infants, children up to age six, and elderly people at least 60 years of age by supplementing their diets with nutritious USDA commodity foods. Food packages include a variety of foods, such as infant formula and cereal, non-fat dry and evaporated milk, juice, farina, oats, ready-to-eat cereal, rice, pasta, egg mix, peanut butter, dry beans or peas, canned meat or poultry or tuna, cheese, and canned fruits and vegetables.

To check eligibility and availability contact Food and Nutrition Service – USDA, Food Distribution Division, 3101 Park Center Drive, Room 504, Alexandria, VA 22302; 703-305-2888; Fax: 703-305-2420; {www.fns.usda. gov/fdd/programs/csfp/}.

Free Emergency Food
The Emergency Food Assistance Program (TEFAP) is a Federal program that helps supplement the diets of low-income needy people, including elderly people, by providing them with emergency food and nutrition assistance at no cost.

States provide the food to local agencies that they have selected, usually food banks, which in turn, distribute the food to soup kitchens and food pantries that directly serve the public. Contact Food and Nutrition Service – USDA, Food Distribution Division, 3101 Park Center Drive, Alexandria, VA 22302; 703-305-2888; Fax: 703-305-2420; {www.fns.usda. gov/fdd/programs/tefap/}.

Free Food for Kids in the Summer
The Summer Food Service Program (SFSP) was created to ensure that children in lower-income areas can continue to receive nutritious meals during long school vacations, when they do not have access to school lunch or breakfast. Schools, public agencies, and private nonprofit organizations may sponsor the program. Sponsors provide free meals to a group of children at a central site, such as a school or a community center. Contact USDA Food and Nutrition Service, 3101 Park Center Drive, Room 914, Alexandria, Virginia 22302.; 703-305-2286; {www.fns. usda.gov/cnd/Summer/}.

Get $600 For Each Child
The child tax credit is a credit on your taxes up to $600 for each of your children. This will increase in stages up to $1,000 in 2010. To be able to take this credit you must meet certain requirements. The credit is limited to people with an income below a certain modified adjusted gross income level.

The instructions and worksheet needed to figure this credit are included in the 1040 or 1040A tax return packets. If you are claiming an adoption credit, mortgage interest credit, or District of Columbia first time homebuyers credit, you must use Publication 972 from the IRS to figure your child tax credit. You can download that publication and Form 8812, referred to above, from the IRS website at {www.irs.gov} To receive them by Fax-On-Demand, call 703-368-9694 or call 800-TAX-FORM (829-3676) to have them sent by mail or go to {www.irs.gov}.

$4,008 For You and Your Family
The Earned Income Tax Credit (EITC), also known as the Earned Income Credit (EIC) is a Federal income tax credit for low-income working individuals and families. The EITC reduces the amount of taxes

owed. If the credit exceeds the amount of taxes owed, it is possible to get a refund check. The amount of the EITC depends on the size and income of the family. You need publication 596 by calling 800-829-3676; or online at {www.irs.gov}.

Money To Pay For Your Kid's Bills

The Masonic Angel Fund is a special charity designed for children and sponsored by local Masonic Lodges across the country. Funds can be used to fill a wide variety of children's needs, such as a new winter coat, a pair of glasses or shoes, and can even fund scholarships for music or arts instruction. If professional services are needed, for example a doctor or a dentist, the local Lodge may be able to rely on one of their members to donate their services. Referrals for all these services are done through the school system, which helps build a good relationship between the schools and the Masonic Lodge. Currently the Fund is available in 40 Lodges, but the goal is to have it spread to all the Masonic Lodges. For more information on the Fund contact The Masonic Angel Fund, P.O. Box 1389, Orleans, MA 02653; 508-255-8812; {www.masonicangelfoundation.org/go al.htm}.

Free Take Out Meals for Seniors

People 60 and over who are homebound because of illness, incapacity, or disability or who are otherwise isolated can receive hot meals delivered to their home. The program is funded in every state by the Older Americans Act. Contact your local area agency on aging or your state Department on Aging to learn who you need to contact in your area.

You can also contact the Eldercare Locator hotline at 800-677-1116 for more assistance.

Free Money For Members of Armed Services and Vets to Pay Bills

The American Red Cross helps those in need in a variety of ways. If they have been sent to serve with the U.S. military, then members of the armed services and their families can contact the Red Cross for help in cases of emergency. Services they can provide include communicating with family members, emergency financial assistance, counseling and more.

Contact the American Red Cross National Headquarters, 2025 E Street NW, Washington, DC 20006; 202-303-4498; {www.redcross.org/services/afes}.

Free Money For Kids To Go To 79 Camps

The Salvation Army is concerned about the happiness of children, so they operate many children's homes and nurseries. In additions there are 239 camps children can attend as well as over 400 clubs. The Salvation Army wants to offer children a healthy alternative, so they can live their lives to the fullest. Contact the Salvation Army Office near you, or Salvation Army National Headquarters, 615

Slaters Lane, P.O. Box 269, Alexandria, VA 22313; 703-684-5500; {www.salvation armyusa.org}.

Free Summer Camp For Kids With Parents In Prison

Angle Tree camping serves over 10,000 children each summer in week-long Christian camps. Supported by funds from the local churches and the Prison Fellowship, local children of prisoners are identified and given a week's vacation in the outdoors. In addition, Angel Tree provides gifts at Christmas time to children in need. Contact Angel Tree, P.O. Box 1550, Merrifield, VA 22116; 800-55-ANGEL; {www.angeltree.org}.

Money To Put In Your Savings Account

Triple your savings by taking advantage of Individual Development Accounts. These accounts are currently available in 350 communities with more in development. Designed to help low-income people save for a down payment, college, or a small business, funds matched with one dollar from the government and one dollar from private funds. A short course on money management is usually required. To learn more about the program or to see what may be available in your community, contact Corporation for Enterprise Development, 777 N. Capitol St., NE, Suite 800, Washington, DC 20002; 202-408-9788; {www.idanetwork. org}.

372 Sources To Pay Emergency Expenses

Bravekids.org has put together a resource directory that lists over 372 sources for financial and other types of assistance for those with disabled children or adults or low-income families in need of help. It could be anything from paying your utility bill to respite care or medical expenses. Check out {www.bravekids.org}.

Services Available From Veterinary Teaching Hospitals

Veterinary teaching hospitals can be an excellent place to take your pet, and most of them will take new patients directly or as referrals from other veterinarians. But as research and teaching institutions, they have access to a lot more resources than your average veterinary hospital. Many but not all of these hospitals provide services like:

♦ *Free Services and Drugs for People Who Can't Pay*
♦ *Free Medical Treatment for Strays in Need Brought in by Non-owners*
♦ *Free Answers to Questions Over the Telephone*
♦ *Free and Discount Treatment for Companion Animals and Assistance Dogs*
♦ *Discounts for Seniors*

Call to see what services your local Veterinary Teaching Hospital may offer.

Pay for Taxi Service to Work, School or Day Care

One county in Oregon has a program that picks up you and your child, taking your child to day care and you to work. North Carolina has programs where counties are given vans to transport people back and forth to work, with lower fees charged to those in welfare-to-work programs. Mississippi has a program that will pick you up at your house and take you back and forth to work if you are working to get off welfare. Some communities, like Fairfax County in Virginia, maintain a database that helps locate the necessary transportation for work and day care needs. And Kentucky operates an 800 hotline that tries to solve any work-related transportation need.

To start looking for programs like this in your area, contact your local congressman's office or your local social service agency. They won't know about all the programs but can probably give you some starting places. You should also find out about local vanpool and rideshare programs. Your local chamber of commerce or library should have this kind of information for you.

Money for Auto Repairs, Car Insurance, Driver's Ed, or Just a Tank of Gas

There are federal programs as well as state programs to help people with limited incomes keep their vehicles on the road so that they can get back and forth to work, focusing on those trying to get off welfare. Some states will even give you money for driver's education or to pay for a driver's license. The issue, like the programs for free cars, is to **help people make it to work**.

These programs are organized like a patchwork quilt in most areas involving federal, state, county and non-profit organizations.

To start looking for programs like this in your area, contact your local congressman's office or your local Social Services. They won't know about all the programs but can probably give you some starting places. Most branches of the Goodwill Industries have a Wheels to Work program. Other programs can be found by typing in the keywords "Wheels to Work" in an Internet search engine.

Here is just a *SAMPLING* of the Wheels to Work programs that we found:

Workforce Transportation Services
Goodwill Industries of Central Arizona
417 North 16th Street
Phoenix, AZ 85006
602-254-2222
Email: {dcrews@goodwillaz.org}
{www.goodwillaz.org/}

Good News Garage
Rockingham Community Action
7 Junkins Ave.
Portsmouth, NH 03801
603-431-2911
Client Access: 800-556-9300
Email: {w2@rcaction.org}
{www.reaction.org}

Wabash Valley Goodwill Industries, Inc.
2702 South 3rd Street
P.O. Box 2720
Terre Haute, IN 47802
812-235-1827
Fax: 812-235-1397
Email: {office@wvgoodwill.org}
{http://wvgoodwill.org/wtw1.htm}

Goodwill Industries of North Carolina
1235 S. Eugene St.
Greensboro, NC 27406-2393
336-275-9801
Fax: 336-274-1352

Email: {kcaughron@goodwill-cnc.
org}; {www.triadgoodwill.org/}

New Leaf Services
3696 Greentree Farms Dr.
Decatur, GA 30034
404-289-9293

Citrus Cars
Polk Works
205 Main Street, Suite 107
Bartow, FL 33830
863-519-0100
www.polkworks.org

Wheelz 2 Work
Bucks County Housing Group, Inc.
2324 2ⁿᵈ Street Pike, Suite 17
Wrightstown, PA 18940
866-WLZ-2WRK, ext. 15
(866-959-2975, ext. 15)
www.wheelz2work.org

Wheels to Work
Monticello Area Community Action
Agency
1025 Park Street
Charlottesville, VA 22901
434-295-3171
http://avenue.org/macaa/cars.html

Gift of Wheels
The Arc of Find du Lac
500 North Park Avenue
Fond du Lac, WI 54935
920-923-3810
www.geocities.com/arc_of_fdl/index.h
tm

Free Bus Passes

Detroit's **Suburban Mobility
Authority for Regional
Transportation (SMART)** has a
program called "Get a Job/Get a Ride"
that gives a month's worth of free rides
to anyone in the Detroit area who gets
a job. The only requirement is that you
started a new job within the last 30
days. New Jersey will give a free one-

month pass to those on low income
that get a job or are going to training.

Check with your local Chamber of
Commerce, Transit Authority, or your
state Department of Transportation.

Free Seminars on Buying a Car

Don't be intimidated by salesmanship.
The dealer wants your money, so they
don't want you to leave without
signing on the bottom line. Many
different organizations and groups
offer classes on how to buy a car.
Contact your county cooperative
extension service, your local adult
education department, or women's
organizations in your area to see what
they may have to offer.

Free Seminars on How to Fix Up a Car

Many different organizations and
groups offer classes on how to fix a
car. Begin by contacting your local car
insurance company, automobile road
service company, or department of
motor vehicles. I have even seen
classes being offered by automobile
dealerships. Other places to check
include your county Cooperative
Extension Service, your local adult
education department, or women's
organizations in your area. You can

save yourself worry, stress, and money if you are prepared and knowledgeable regarding your car.

Free Car Repairs

Recalls have to be fixed for free and the repair shop didn't know that. To find out about recalls for any car, contact:

❑ **Auto Safety Hotline**, US Dept. of Transportation, NEF-11.2HL, 400 Seventh St., SW, Washington, DC 20590; 888-327-4236; {www.nhtsa.dot.gov/}

❑ The **Consumer Report** people have a searchable database for car recall information. Contact Consumers Union, 101 Truman Ave., Yonkers, NY 10703; 914-378-2000; {consumerreports.org}

Discounts on Buses, Trains and Subways

If you are a senior citizen, you can usually ride most forms of transportation for about half-price. Amtrak and Greyhound offer discounts of 5-15%. Children even get to take advantage of discount programs, with the youngest group often getting a free ride. Check out these websites: {www.amtrak.com}; {www.greyhound.com}. Don't forget to ask about a variety of reduced fare programs, including student and military discounts. Often job training programs will compensate you for your travel, so before you begin training, inquire about support services such as transportation and child care.

Get Free Taxi Rides for Grandma to go to the Doctor

The Eldercare Locator provides access to an extensive network of organizations serving older people at state and local community levels. This service can connect you to information sources for a variety of services including transportation. For more information, contact Eldercare Locator, National Association of Area Agencies on Aging, 1112 16th St., NW, Washington, DC 20024; 800-677-1116 between 9 a.m. and 8 p.m. EST; {www.aoa.gov}.

$195/Mo for Parking Money

Your employer can give you $100 a month to pay for going to work in a bus, van or metro, or give you $195 a month for parking. You get the money tax free, and the employer gets to take a tax deduction. It's called the *Qualified Transportation Fringe Benefit* or *Transit Benefit Program*. Get a copy of IRS Publication 535, *Business Expenses* and show your boss the section entitled "Qualified Transportation Fringe". The publication is available from your local IRS office or from 800-TAX-FORM or from their web site at {www.irs.gov}.

Free Child Safety Seats

There are hospitals that give out free child safety seats as you leave with your new baby, with no questions asked and no income requirements. Local police and fire departments inspect child safety seats to see that they are in proper order and properly installed, and sometimes provide free seats to those whose current equipment is not considered safe. Local organizations, like the Easter Seals Society were part of a federal program that gives out millions of dollars worth of free seats because of a settlement the U.S. Department of Transportation made with General Motors. Other groups will lend you a seat for as little as $5. The state of Minnesota alone has over 225 such programs.

To find a program near you, contact your local police or fire department. Or contact your state information operator listed in the Appendix and ask them for your state office for Highway Safety or Traffic Safety. These national organizations may also be able to give you a local source:

- *National SAFEKIDS Campaign*, 1301 Pennsylvania Ave., NW, Suite 1000, Washington, DC 20004; 202-626-0600; fax 202-393-2072; {www.safekids.org}

- *National Highway Traffic Safety Administration*, U.S. Department of Transportation, 400 Seventh St., SW, Washington, DC 20590; 800-424-9393; {www.nhtsa.dot.gov}

Free Rides to Pick Up a Sick Child at School

Suppose your child is sick at school and needs you in the middle of the day, but you don't have a way to get there because you go to work most days by some other way than using your car. You can probably get a free ride, taxi, or free rental car from the local *"Guaranteed Ride Home Program."*

You can also use the service for most family emergencies if your normal ride falls through, or if you have to work late unexpectedly. Call your local carpool or vanpool service to see if they have a similar program. Most of these programs require that you pre-register, but it is always best to plan ahead for emergencies anyway.

If you do a computer search using the terms (including the quotes) "guaranteed ride home program," you will find a listing of many of the programs offered. You can also contact your state Department of Transportation for starting places.

Cheap Air Fare to See Sick Relatives

When a family member is very ill or has died, families have to make last minute airline reservations. Obviously you lose out on the 21-day advance purchase rates, but almost all airlines offer *bereavement* or *compassion* fares for domestic travel. Generally the fares are available to close family members, and the discount on the full-fare rate varies from airline to airline. Many require that you provide the name of the deceased and the name, address and phone number of the funeral home handling arrangements. In the case of a medical emergency, the name and address of the affected family member and the name, address and phone number of the attending physician or hospital are required. Contact the airline of your choice to learn more about the "Bereavement/Compassion Fares." Full fare rate varies from airline to airline, but you could save up to 50%.

Free Cars and Air Fare to Go on Vacation

Not quite as easy as it sounds, but there are programs out there to help people move their cars. Most of the cars need to be driven across the country and in exchange, many car moving companies offer free gas and airline travel home.

Obviously, you do not get to pick your make and model, and you need to be flexible as to the departure time and destination, but this is one way to see America. Contact local moving companies to see what they have to offer. There is even a website for those interested in having their cars moved at {www.movecars.com}, and they may be able to provide you with information.

Air courier services operate the same way, but you are required to have a valid passport. Most air freight services don't do enough business to send a plane overseas each day. As a courier, you carry a package checked as baggage to an overseas destination. There have been no incidences of contraband problems, and customs is familiar with this service. You deliver the package to a company representative in the customs section of the airport, then you are on your own. In exchange, you get to fly to exotic ports for FREE or cheap. Children are not allowed to accompany couriers.

Contact companies listed in the air courier section of your phone book, do a web search using the terms "air courier service," or contact the Air Courier Association at 800-282-1202; or online at {www.aircourier.org}.

Free Taxi To Take Your Child to a Doctor's Appointment

The Federal Transit Administration provides over $50 million a year to over 1,000 local organizations to provide free non-emergency transportation for people who are elderly or have a disability. But the groups who get this federal money can also provide free transportation services to moms who are in a jam. The regulations state that the vehicles can also be used to "serve the transportation needs of the general

public on an incidental basis." You may have to do some educating to get a local group to give you a ride. Tell them to see Circular FTA C9070, 1D, for Section 5310 Program, Chapter V, Program Management, paragraph 3b. It's available from the U.S. Federal Transit Administration or on the web at {www.fta.dot.gov/library/policy/ circ9070/ chapter5.html}.

To find groups in your area who receive these FTA Section 5310 Grants for Elderly and Persons With Disabilities, contact your state department of transportation or the U.S. Federal Transit Administration, Office of Program Management, Office of Resource Management and State Programs, 400 7th St., SW, Washington, DC 20590; 202-366-4020; {www.fta.dot.gov}.

$200+ to Use Your Car

You can deduct:

- 34 1/2 cents per mile if you use your car for business (IRS Publication 463, Travel Entertainment, Gift, and Car Expenses)

- 14 cents per mile if you use your car during charity work (IRS Instructions for Schedule A, Itemized Deductions)

- 12 cents per mile if you use your car for medical care (IRS Instructions for Schedule A, Itemized Deductions)

- 12 cents per mile if you use your car to move to a new job (IRS Publication 521, Moving Expenses)

These publications are free from your local IRS office, by calling 1-800-829-3676 or download from {www.irs.gov}.

Discounts on Car Rentals

You never should pay full-price for car rentals and there are deals aplenty if you keep your eyes opened. AAA and AARP membership will save you a few bucks, as will many other membership programs. Car rental agencies also often offer discounts to senior citizens. Many times, if you book your flight and car rental at the same time, you can get a discount rate, plus get miles added to your frequent flyer program.

The free brochure, *Renting a Car*, outlines some points to consider and questions to ask when you reserve a rental car. You can learn how to choose a rental car company and understand the terms they use for insurance and charges. Contact Public Reference, Room 130, Federal Trade Commission, Washington, DC 20580; 202-326-2222, 877-FTC-HELP; or online at {www.ftc.gov}.

Free Child Care for AmeriCorp & Vista Workers

Over $10,000,000 a year is paid out to cover child care services for people working with AmeriCorps or VISTA. These programs allow you to tackle community problems on everything from disaster relief to tutoring. National Service jobs also provide a stipend, housing, and even college money; child care is a bonus. Contact Corporation of National Service, 1201 New York Ave., NW, Washington, DC 20525; 202-606-5000; {www.nationalservice.org}.

Free Child Care When Training or Looking For a Job

Welfare reform, called *Temporary Assistance for Needy Families (TANF)*, does more to help people not wind up on welfare. The new program includes free training, education, child care, and transportation assistance necessary to help you obtain employment.

Child care is an important part of the program. Eligibility requirements vary from state to state, so contact your TANF office nearest you to learn what options are available to you. For more information, contact Office of Family Assistance, Administration for Children and Families, 370 L'Enfant Promenade, SW, Washington, DC 20447; 202-401-9215; {www.acf.dhhs. gov/programs/opa/facts/tanf.htm}.

Work for Companies That Offer Free/ Discount Child Care

You may be surprised at the number of daycare centers offering services right inside company office buildings. In fact the federal government may be in the lead as they have over 1,000 child care centers that are sponsored by various governmental agencies. Talk to other moms and dads on the playground, call human resources departments, and even check with your local chamber of commerce. All may be able to direct you to companies providing this benefit. A directory of sites is available for $25 from the Work and Family Connection, 5197

Beachside Dr., Minnetonka, MN 55343; 800-487-7898; {www.work family.com}. Another resource is your local Child Care Resource and Referral Agency, who should be aware of programs in their area. To locate your local referral agency, contact Child Care Aware, 1319 F Street, NW, Suite 500, Washington, DC 20004; 800-424-2246, {www.childcareaware.org}.

Besides child care centers, some employers offer a dependent care assistance plan that allows you to pay for child care out of pre-tax dollars. Other employers offer direct subsidies to offset child care costs.

$2,500 to Help Pay for an Adoption

The National Adoption Foundation (NAF) is a national nonprofit organization dedicated to providing financial support, information, and services for adoptive and prospective adoptive families. They recently announced the expansion of its programs to include home equity loans, as well as unsecured loans and grants for adoption expenses. A grant program to cover adoption expenses is also available on a limited basis for prospective adoptive parents.

Other sources of money for adoption include:

- Ask your employer for employee adoption assistance benefits. Approximately 65 percent of Fortune 500 companies now offer some kind of adoption benefit.

- Take advantage of the new adoption expense tax credit in advance by modifying your income tax withholding to reflect your tax savings when you file your return. This frees up cash for adoption expenses due now.

Contact National Adoption Foundation, 100 Mill Plain Rd., Danbury, CT 06811; 203-791-3811; Fax: 203-791-3801; Email: {info@nafadopt.org}; {www.nafadopt.org/default.asp}. To download an application: {www.nafadopt.org/pdf/adoption.pdf}.

Free Credit Repair

Here are some of the free reports you can get from the Federal Trade Commission dealing with free credit repair:

- *Credit Repair: Self-Help May Be The Best*
- *Knee Deep in Debt*
- *How To Dispute Credit Reporting Errors*
- *How To Deal With Credit Problems*
- *Credit Scoring*

For your copies, contact Consumer Response Center, 600 Pennsylvania Ave., NW, H-130, Federal Trade Commission, Washington, DC 20580; 202-326-2222; 877-FTC-HELP; {www.ftc.gov}.

The following nonprofit and government organizations provide free, or low-fee credit counseling services. You can contact them to find the office nearest you. Some of these offices are financed by the bank and credit card industry, who are biased toward having you pay all your bills without using the bankruptcy option. So be sure that they explain your bankruptcy options.

❑ *National Foundation for Credit Counseling*, 801 Roeder Road, Suite 900, Silver Spring, MD 20910; 301-589-5600; {www.nfcc.org}

❑ Free internet credit counseling services from the nonprofit organization, *Credit Counseling Center of America*, P.O. Box 830489, Richardson, TX 75083-0489; 800-493-2222; {www.cccamerica.org}

❑ *County Cooperative Extension Service*: to find your local office, see the blue pages of your phone book.

$100 to Pay Your Heating Bill

The state of Michigan offers a home heating bill tax credit (that means you pay less in taxes) for people who are low income, receiving public assistance or unemployment.

Call your state department of taxation to learn about tax credits available to you. Michigan Department of Treasury, Lansing, MI 48956; 800-487-7000; {www.michigan.gov/treasury}. To download a 2-page form: {www.michigan.gov/documents/MI_1 040CR7_81085_7.pdf}.

Free Voice Mail Services

If you are unemployed and the phone company cut off your phone, how does a potential employer get in touch with you? Free voice mail. You can get set up with your own personalized greeting, as well as get a security code and instructions on how you can retrieve your messages 24 hours a day. The program is available in over 34 cities and is growing. See if you're

eligible for your area by contacting Community Technology Institute, P2901 Third Avenue, Suite 100, Seattle, WA 98121; 206-441-7872; Fax: 206-443-3755; {www.cvm. org}.

Free Directory Assistance

Directory assistance can cost up to 95 cents per request and an additional 50 cents for the connection. To assist persons with visual, hearing, or other disabilities, local telephone companies offer directory and operator assistance exemptions. Simply request and complete a form from the local telephone company and have your physician complete the appropriate section. When you return the form to the phone company, you'll be eligible for the exemptions. Contact the business office of your local telephone company.

$400/wk When You're Out of Work

Mass lay-offs, base closings, trade agreements, and high unemployment in your state, all affect your ability to find and keep a job. If you are out of work, take advantage of unemployment insurance. All states are required to provide benefits up to 26 weeks and some extend them further. If your state has very high unemployment, you may be eligible for 13 additional weeks of compensation. If you lost your job because of an increase in imports, you may qualify to have your benefits extended up to an extra 52 weeks if you are in a job-retraining program.

Your weekly benefit amount depends upon your past wages within certain minimum and maximum limits that vary from state to state. Many states also will add additional funds depending upon the number of dependents. If you are denied benefits, learn about the appeal process, as your chances of winning are good. Contact your state Unemployment Insurance office listed in the blue pages of your phone book.

$700 for Your Utility Bills
The legislature in Massachusetts passed a law giving discounts up to $700 on heating bills for families making up to $30,000, along with up to 40% discount on electric bills, $108 off telephone bills, and $100 off oil bills. It's in the Massachusetts Budget for FY 99 (Line Item 4403-2110). Also:

☼ **Phoenix, Arizona** offers discounts on utility bills, discounts on phone bills and even help paying utility deposits and heating repairs for low-income residents through the Arizona Public Service Energy Support Program, P.O. Box 53999, Phoenix, AZ 85072-3999; 800-253-9406; 602-371-7171; {www.aps.com}.

☼ **Ameritech in Illinois** gives a 50% plus $10 discount on connection charges and $6.25 off the monthly bill to low-income residents. To sign up, call Ameritech at 888-256-5378; {www.ameritech.com}.

☼ **Ohio** offers reduced or free phone hook up service and possibly $8.00 a month off your phone bill for low-income residents. Contact Public Utilities Commission, 180 E. Broad St., Columbus, OH 43215; 800-686-7826; {www.puco.ohio.gov/ Consumer/PIC/assistance.html}.

Contact your state's utilities office in the blue pages of your phone book to find out about special discounts on your gas, electric, cable or telephone in your state.

Free Private Eye to Find Missing Children
Besides location and investigative services, as well as mediation services for families estranged by parental abduction, you can also get free kidnapping prevention programs and referral and support services. Contact Find-A-Child of America, Inc., P.O. Box 277, New Paltz, NY 12561; 800-I-AM-LOST; 914-255-1848; 800-A-WAY-OUT (for mediation and support); {www.childfindofamerica. org}.

$1,000 While You Wait For Gov't Money
General Public Assistance or just Public Assistance is a welfare program offered in 42 states. This is a program of last resort for people either waiting to qualify for other government programs such as disability benefits, or who do not qualify for any programs, yet need money to live. The program eligibility and benefit levels vary within and across state lines. In some states, this benefit is only available in certain areas. There are strict income and asset levels that you must meet to qualify. Contact your local welfare office, your state Department of Social Service, or your state Temporary Assistance to Needy Families office to

see what your state offers and the eligibility requirements.

Dress For Success For Free

Looking for work and can't afford the right wardrobe? There are about 50 nonprofit organizations around the country that provide women with two separate outfits for free. One can be used to go to an interview and the other can be used once you get the job. The following organization acts as a clearinghouse for similar opportunities around the country. Bottomless Closet, 445 North Wells, Chicago, IL 60610; 312-527-9664; Fax: 312-527-4305; {www.bottomlesscloset.org}.

Career Gear, 120 Broadway, 30th Floor, New York, NY 10271; 212-577-6190; Email: {info@careergear.org}; {www.careergear.org/}. This organization has locations in New York, Michigan, Ohio, and Florida.

Dress for Success, 32 East 31st Street, Suite 602, New York, NY 10016; 212-532-DSNY, ext. 23; Email: {newyork@dressforsuccess.org}; {www.dressforsuccess.org/}. This organization has locations in almost every state and internationally.

StyleWorks, 328 Flatbush Avenue, #350, Brooklyn, NY 11238; 718-398-1264; {www.styleworks.org/}.

Suited For Change, 1712 I Street, NW, Suite B100, Washington, DC 20006-3750; 202-293-0351; {www.suitedforchange.org}.

50% Off Camping Bills For Seniors

Almost all states offer discounts to seniors at state parks. Entrance fees are usually waived for seniors, or states like Illinois offer 50% off camping fees. Eighteen states have no residency requirements to receive the discount, so if you are planning a cross country camping trip, contact the state Parks Department to find out about eligibility criteria. For those wanting to camp in the National Forest, the Golden Age Passport is available to those 62 and over. For $10 you receive free lifetime admission to the parks, plus 50% off on camping and many other services. The Passport is available at all National Forests. 202-238-4200; {http://buy.nationalparks.org/golden.asp}

10% Off Airline Tickets for Seniors

Every airline offers discounts to seniors amounting to usually 10%. What happens, though, is that some of the airlines' special offers may be exempt from the discount. It is best to see what the lowest available rate is and then inquire about the discount.

All the major airlines also offer coupon books for seniors that are four round-trip tickets good for wherever the airline flies. The price of the coupon books is around $540. In many instances, the airline only requires that one person meet the age requirement for a discount, so your companion can receive the lower rate as well.

10-50% Off Hotel Bills for Seniors

Almost all major hotel chains offer discounts from 10-30% off the cost of rooms. Some require that you belong to AARP or AAA, so it is best to call ahead and ask. Three hotel chains, Ramada Inn {www.ramada.com}, Hilton {www.hilton.com} and Red Roof Inns {www.redroof.com} offer special deals to seniors who frequent their hotels. Ramada's Best Years Club charges $15 for a lifetime membership fee. The fee entitles you to 25% off regular two double bed room rates, plus you receive points redeemable for travel and prizes (800-672-6232; available at most Ramadas). Hilton Senior HHonors program charges $50 ($40 annual renewal fee), and seniors receive up to 50% off rooms and 20% off hotel restaurants (800-492-3232). Red Roof has a lifetime Redicard for seniors that costs $10. The card gets you 10% off rooms, plus 3 $5 off coupons for lodging (800-843-7663).

10% Off Your Restaurant Bill

The Early Bird specials can happen all day once you hit a certain age. Many restaurant chains offer special deals for seniors. Most restaurant chains are independently owned and operated, but they usually follow the recommendations from the headquarters. Places like Denny's, Bob Evan's, and International House of Pancakes frequently offer seniors a reduced price menu. Other chains, such as Applebee's, Kentucky Fried Chicken, and Wendy's, often give seniors a 10% discount on their meals.

Free Hunting and Fishing Licenses For Seniors

Practically every state has a special license rate for seniors. States such as Alabama, Alaska, Delaware, Georgia, Kansas, and others do not require that people age 65 and over to carry a fishing and hunting license. Other states offer seniors, on average, half off the cost of licenses. Inquire where you usually purchase these licenses to learn what age you need to be to receive the discount and the specific details.

Free Books on Tape

The National Library Service (NLS) maintains a large collection of books, magazines, journals, and music materials in Braille, large type, and recorded formats for individuals who cannot read or use standard printed materials because of temporary or permanent visual loss or physical limitations. Reading materials and necessary playback equipment for books on record and cassette are distributed through a national network of cooperating libraries. Books in the collection are selected on the basis of their appeal to a wide range of interests. Bestsellers, biographies, fiction, and how-to books are in great demand.

Contact your local library to find out what they have available to you, or you may contact handicapped Readers Reference Section, National Library Service for the Blind and physically Handicapped, Library of Congress, Washington, DC 20542; 202-707-5100; 800-424-8567; {www.loc.gov/nls}.

Take a Free Vacation

"Passport In Time" helps you open a window on the past by allowing you to join activities such as archaeological excavation, site mapping, drafting, laboratory and art work, collecting oral histories, restoration, and much more.

Projects vary in length and there is no registration cost or fee. You may even receive a small stipend to offset your living expenses. Contact Passport In Time Clearinghouse, P.O. Box 31315, Tucson, AZ 85751; 800-281-9176; {www.passportintime.com}.

Free Concert or Theater Tickets

Many music and theater groups offer special programs to older adults in the form of discounted tickets, free concerts, transportation, afternoon teas, and/or daytime events. Contact your state arts group, state Department of Aging or local senior citizens groups to see what is available in your area.

Ca$h for Sharing What You Know

Retired Senior Volunteer Program matches the personal interests and skills of older Americans with opportunities to help solve community problems. RSVP volunteers choose how and where they want to serve - from a few to over 40 hours a week. RSVP makes it easy for older adults to find the types of volunteer service opportunities that appeal to them. RSVP volunteers tutor children in reading and math, help to build houses, help get children immunized, model parenting skills to teen parents, participate in neighborhood watch programs, plan community gardens, deliver meals, offer disaster relief to victims of natural disasters, and help community organizations operate more efficiently. Volunteers receive supplemental insurance while on duty, and receive on-the-job training. Contact National Senior Service Corps, 1201 New York Ave., NW, Washington, DC 20525; 202-606-5000; 800-424-8867; {www.seniorcorps.org}.

$3,000 While Helping Others

Foster Grandparents devote their volunteer service to one population: children with special or exceptional needs. Across the country, Foster Grandparents are offering emotional support to child victims of abuse and neglect, tutoring children who lag behind in reading, mentoring troubled teenagers and young mothers, and caring for premature infants and children with physical disabilities and severe illnesses.

If you meet certain income guidelines and are 60 or older, you may be eligible for this program. You will receive a modest tax free stipend to offset the cost of volunteering, and are reimbursed for transportation, some meals, an annual physical and accident and liability insurance. Contact National Senior Service Corps, 1201 New York Ave., NW, Washington, DC 20525; 800-424-8867; 202-606-5000; {www. seniorcorps.org}.

Cash for Helping Fellow Seniors

Senior Companions reach out to adults, who need extra assistance to live independently in their own homes or communities. Senior Companions assist their adult clients with in basic but essential ways: they provide companionship and friendship to isolated frail seniors, assist with simple chores, provide transportation, and add richness to their clients' lives. Senior Companions serve frail older adults and their caregivers, adults with disabilities, and those with terminal illnesses. If you meet certain income guidelines and are 60 or older, you may be eligible for this program. You will receive a modest tax free stipend to offset the cost of volunteering, and are reimbursed for transportation, some meals, an annual physical and accident and liability insurance. Contact National Senior Service Corps, 1201 New York Ave., NW, Washington, DC 20525; 800-424-8867; 202-606-5000; {www. seniorcorps.org}.

Money to Pay Employees At Your Nonprofit

Do you need people to work for your nonprofit, but don't have the budget?

There are several agencies within the Federal government which provides staffing for a variety agencies. To register your organization for workers paid by the government, contact the Corporation for National and Community Service. They have several programs such as AmeriCorps and the Senior Corps that train and pay for volunteers to serve in a variety of public service agencies. In partnership with non-profit groups, faith-based organizations, schools, and other public agencies, participants in these programs tutor children, build and renovate homes, provide immunizations and health screenings, clean up and preserve the environment, serve on neighborhood crime-prevention patrols, and respond to disasters.

Contact Corporation for National and Community Service, 1201 New York Ave., NW, Washington, DC 20525; 202-606-5000; 877-USACORPS; {www.nationalservice.org}.

Money & Help for Those Who Served

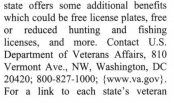

The U.S. Department of Veterans Affairs hotline can provide you with information on such programs as life insurance, comprehensive dental and medical care, nursing homes, home loan programs, burial services, and more. In addition each state offers some additional benefits which could be free license plates, free or reduced hunting and fishing licenses, and more. Contact U.S. Department of Veterans Affairs, 810 Vermont Ave., NW, Washington, DC 20420; 800-827-1000; {www.va.gov}. For a link to each state's veteran

services, check out {www.nasdva. com/}.

Free Fans
Fan Care is a great program sponsored by Virginia Power. If you are a resident of Virginia and 60 or older, you may be eligible for a free fan to help you make it safely through the hot summer. Fans are distributed through the local Area Agencies on Aging.

To learn about eligibility requirements, contact Fan Care, Department for the Aging, 1600 Forest Ave., Suite 102, Richmond, VA 23229; 800-552-3402; 804-662-9333. For those outside of Virginia, contact your state Department of Aging or your state utility commission, both listed in the Appendix to see what they have to offer.

Free Passports for Families of Vets
It's hard to believe that a passport can cost up to $60, but did you know that you can get it free of charge if you are a member of a family visiting an overseas grave site of a veteran? Eligibility for these free passports includes widows, parents, children, sisters, brothers, and guardians of the deceased who are buried or commemorated in permanent American military cemeteries on foreign soil. For additional information, write to the American Battle Monuments Commission, 2300 Clarendon Blvd., Arlington, VA 22201; 703-696-6897; {www.abmc. gov}.

Free Help Finding Lost Loved Ones
When a loved one disappears, those left behind struggle and often spend thousands trying to locate their missing

person. The Salvation Army received over 35,000 requests for assistance, and was able to trace over 10,000 missing persons.

To learn more about the services offered contact the Salvation Army Office near you, or Salvation Army National Headquarters, 615 Slaters Lane, P.O. Box 269, Alexandria, VA 22313; 703-684-5500; {www.salvation armyusa.org}.

Pay Your Bills While You Become An Entrepreneur

It is a dream for many people to own their own business, but often money is a concern. There are different programs to help you pay your bills while you start your business or go through microenterprise training. This applies even if you are receiving Temporary Assistance for Needy Families (TANF), as TANF funds can be used to support you while you are being trained or starting your business.

Contact your state TANF office to see what programs are available in your area. You can also learn about other microenterprise programs by contacting your state economic development office. For other resources and to locate programs in your area, contact:

- Center for Law and Social Policy, 1015 15th St., NW, Suite 400, Washington, DC 20005; 202-906-8000; {www.clasp.org}. See Microenterprise Development and Self-Employment for TANF Recipients in the publications section.

- The Aspen Institute, One Dupont Circle, NW, Suite 700, Washington, DC 20036; 202-736-1071; {http://fieldus.org/directory}.

- Association for Enterprise Opportunity, 1601 N. Kent St., Suite 101, Arlington, VA 22209; 703-841-7760; {www.microenter priseworks.org}.

Job Hunting & Volunteering

Workers are on the move like never before. Nobody is staying in one place. By age 34, the average American worker has held nine jobs, which might mean nine different skill sets. In addition to new job skills, you must have resume, interviewing and other job hunting abilities to find your next exciting career. Volunteering can often turn into part-time or full-time work or give you additional work skills that you may need to find a job. When  you're asked to volunteer say yes, it may just be your next step to a new job.

The programs listed below are a collection of job hunting and volunteer programs available for people looking to volunteer, acquire new job training skills or increase their job hunting tactics.

If you do not find what you need in this section, you can find additional information by checking out the following:

1) ***Find All Federal Government Programs For Job Hunting and Volunteering***
They are described in a book called the *Catalog Of Federal Domestic Assistance*. This book is available at your local library or the U.S. Government Printing Office {www.gpo.gov}. You can also search the contents of this book for free on the web at {www.cfda.gov}.

2) Find Employment And Training Information And Statistics

The Employment and Training Administration provides job training, employment, labor and market information and income maintenance services primarily through state and local programs. They can help you start or advance your career, know your rights as a worker or just answer employment questions. Contact them at {www.doleta.gov} or call them at 877-US-2JOBS.

3) Find All Of Your State Programs For Job Hunting

The Employment and Training Administration can direct you to specific programs in your state to find training for your dream job. All you need to do is click on your state to view a list of resources. Many states offer funds to employers to help them upgrade the skills of their employees. Check it out at {www.doleta.gov/regions/} or {www.dol.gov/contacts/state_of.htm}. You can also look for your state Department of Labor, or Department of Jobs and Family Services by contacting your state capitol operator or going to {www.govengine.gov}.

4) Find All Kinds Of Career And Job Information

If you are 15 and looking for your first job or 80 and looking for a job to help keep you young, CareerOneStop has the web site to help you. They offer electronic tools operating as a federal-state partnership that includes: America's Job Bank, America's Career InfoNet and America's Service Locator. You can find them online at {www.career onestop.org}.

5) Find Volunteer Opportunities Throughout The Country

A great place to start looking for ways you can make a difference by volunteering, is to check out the Federal governments' web site on volunteering. They can show you a variety ways that you can make a difference. Your volunteer search can begin at {www.usafreedomcorps.gov}.

6) Money To Train For A New Job

You are out of work and need to learn some new skills in order to get employed. The Career One Stop can help you. They have information about Federal job training programs, Workforce Investment Act training, apprenticeships and more. Career One Stops can help you do a career and skills assessment to see where you are and where you need to go. They will even help direct you to money sources to pay for the training you need. For more information, check out {www.careeronestop.org}.

7) Help For Divorced Or Widowed Women

Single parents, recently divorced women and women in transition sometimes need a helping hand. Women Work! is an organization whose mission is to help women become self-sufficient. This is accomplished by helping them get the education, training and jobs they need to be successful. Women Work! has over 1,000 programs across the country doing just that. To learn what is offered in your neighborhood, contact Women Work! 1625 K St., NW, Suite 300, Washington, DC 20006; 202-467-6346; 800-235-2732; Fax: 202-467-5366; {www.womenwork.org}.

8) Free Help For Women

Many states have Women's Commission whose job is to advocate with the state legislatures on the role of women. In fact there are over 270 women's commissions at city, county and state levels. Since the Commissions are a link between the government and the private sector, they may be aware of programs and services available to women. A map is available on the website showing where commissions are located. To learn more contact the National Association of Commissions for Women, 8630 Fenton St., Suite 934, Silver Spring, MD 20910; 301-585-8101; Fax: 301-585-3445; {www.nacw.org}.

9) *Free Help Writing Resumes and Job Searching*
A good resume will get you in the door for an interview, but how do you write one? The Career One Stop can help you. They will sit down with you to help you compose the perfect resume, or you can complete the online tutorial to get it done. After that is done, they have a database of over 12 million employers to help you find the perfect job. Look for them at {www.careeronestop.org} or call toll-free 877-US-2JOBS.

$8,000 To Train For A New Job
If you have found yourself on the losing end of a plant closing or mass layoff, apply for money and re-training under the Economic Dislocation and Worker Adjustment Assistance Act. The program is administered by each state, and because of that, the program differs from state to state. Workers can receive classroom, occupational skills, and/or on-the-job training to qualify for jobs in demand. Basic and remedial education, entrepreneurial training, and instruction in literacy or English-as-a-second-language may be provided. For more information, contact your state Department of Labor in the blue pages of your phone book, or contact Employment and Training Administration, U.S. Department of Labor, Room N-5426, 200 Constitution Ave., NW, Washington, DC 20210; 202-693-3580; {www.doleta.gov}.

Free Help To Get A Government Job
The government hires about 400,000 a year no matter what the budget is. The average wage is about $45,000. Only about 20% of the jobs are in Washington, D.C. with the rest scattered throughout the world. Contact the U.S. Office of Personal Management (OPM) USAJobs at 478-757-3000; {www.usajobs.opm.gov} for more information on the best place to start. You should also contact the local office of your Congressman. They can send you information and help you through the process.

Free Resume Writing, On-Line Job Search Training and Free Computers

You can go to a local government office or sometimes a local non-profit organization that is contracted by the federal government to provide the job seeker with free help in resume writing, job interview techniques, or job searching on the internet. They will even let you use free computers to prepare your resume or search the web. To see if there are offices like this near you, contact your state One-Stop Labor Information Center headquarters located in your state capital, or online at {www.doleta.gov/usworkforce/onestop/onestopmap.cfm}.

Making Money With Internships

Government internships are great temporary or part time jobs and they can pay good money. You can make $2,000 a month in the summer learning how Congress works, or earn $550 a week tracking down endangered species for the Department of Interior, or get a part time job at NASA while at school making $12 an hour helping prepare for the next manned space flight. Check out the opportunities at {www.studentjobs. gov}.

Making Money As A Volunteer

There are government volunteer programs like AmeriCorps that can give you up to $5,000 a year for spending money plus room, board, health care and money for college tuition. And others like those at the Fish and Wildlife that offer $25 a day on a 2 week romp in Yosemite observing wildlife. Other programs offer stipends and health care for seniors who want to be Foster Grandparents or to be a Companion to another senior. Contact the local office of your congressman or senator or the Federal Information Center to see if they can direct you to more government volunteer programs 1-866-347-7846; or online at {www.firstgov.gov}.

$$$$$$ Money and Help For Divorced and Widowed Women Job Seekers

Women Work! is a national network of over 1000 programs that provide support networks, skills training, job placement assistance, education and training, workshops, and more designed to help women enter the workforce. To learn what is available in your state, contact Women Work!, National Network for Women's Employment, 1625 K St., Suite 300, Washington, DC 20006; 800-235-2732; {www.womenwork.org}.

$500 Worth of Dress-For-Success Interview Clothes

Looking for work and cannot afford the right wardrobe? There are 50 non-profit organizations around the country that provide women with two separate outfits for free. One can be used to go to an interview and the other can be used to get the job. The following organization acts as a clearinghouse for similar opportunities around the country. Bottomless Closet, 445 North Wells, Chicago, IL 60610, 312-527-9664; {www.bottomlesscloset.org}.

Free Day Care and Car Fare When Training For A New Job

There are a number of programs, mostly at the local level that offer free child care, free transportation and even tuition to go to college or to get training. You may even be eligible to receive money to pay for your books. Programs like these may be hard to identify but are run by either your state or local Social Service Agency or your local One-Stop Labor Information Center {www.doleta.gov/usworkforce/onestop/onestopmap.cfm}. Contact your state capital operator located in your state capital to begin tracking down these programs in your area.

$$$$$$ Money and Help For Ex-Military Job Seeker

If you are a Vet, there are a bunch of programs that will help you search for a new career including the following:

- vocational and educational counseling
- special assistance for vets with disabilities or homelessness
- help with training to be a teacher
- free tutoring for vets in college
- free counseling and money to start a business
- special employment and training programs

Contact Department of Veterans Affairs at 800-827-1000; {www.va.gov}.

Free Legal Help With Bad Employment Agencies and Employment Scams

The Federal Trade Commission (FTC) can help you identify and prosecute any mean people who take advantage of you when you are looking for work or trying to improve your work skills. The following free publications are available:

- *Coping with a Temporary Loss of Income*
- *Choosing a Career or Vocational School*
- *Federal and Postal Job Scams: Tip-offs to Rip-offs*
- *Get-Rich-Quick and Self-Employment Schemes Campaign*
- *Making a Buck: Employment and Work-at-Home Information*
- *Medical Billing Business Opportunity Schemes*
- *OUCH...Students Getting Stung Trying to Find $$$ for College*
- *Out of Work? How to Deal with Creditors*
- *Work-at-Home Schemes*

Contact Public Reference, Room 130, Federal Trade Commission, Washington, DC 20580; 877-FTC-HELP; {www.ftc.gov}. Also contact your State Attorney General's Office located in your state capital, as they will also help you get justice.

Show A Potential Employer How To Get $7,000 To Hire You

Many state governments have programs that offer free money if they hire new employees. Other states will give employers free money to take a new employee and train them in a needed skill, like computers, or in certain occupations like food service. Employers can also get $2,400 from the government for hiring people with disabilities, people who live in certain zip codes, people who received government assistance, ex-felons or even veterans. To find out about programs in your area, contact your state Office of Labor, your state Office of Economic Development and your state Office of Taxation all located in your state capital {www.govengine.com}.

Show Your Boss How To Get Money To Train You For A Better Job

Show your boss how to make you become more productive (and more employable when you leave) by tapping into free government money to upgrade your skills. You can learn computer skills, customer service skills, new technologies or even stress management. See what your state offers and let your boss know about it. Contact your state Office of Labor or Department of Economic Development located in your state capital {www.govengine.com}.

Get More Unemployment Insurance

Laid off workers receive up to $400 per week of Unemployment Insurance while looking for a new job or line of work. In some states you can extend your unemployment benefits if you are participating in a retraining program, lost your job because of imports, or live in a high unemployment area. Check with your local Unemployment Insurance office to see if you qualify for extra money.

Receive a Presidential Award For Volunteering One Hour A Week

The President's Volunteer Service Award is given to deserving adults, kids, and families each year. As little as one hour a week and you could receive recognition from the President of the United States. In addition to the award, you will receive a note of congratulations from the President. Find out how you could earn the bronze, silver, or gold award. Contact President's Volunteer Service Awards, c/o Points of Light Foundation, 1400 I Street, NW Suite 800, Washington, DC 20005; 866-545-5307; {https://

www.presidentialserviceawards.gov/tg/pvsainfo/dspAboutAwards.cfm}.

Seniors Get Paid To Help Community

Low-income seniors can volunteer to serve as mentors, tutors, and caregivers for children and young kids with special needs and can also work in schools, hospitals, and recreation centers in their communities. Volunteers work twenty hours per week, and receive a small paycheck and other benefits. Contact Senior Corps, Corporation for National and Community Service, 1201 New York Ave., NW, Washington, DC 20525; 800-424-8867; {www.cns.gov}.

$4,725 To Help Pay Off Student Loans While Making A Difference

Looking for a little adventure? Or maybe some invaluable work experience? How about making money to help pay the high cost of a college degree? Through AmeriCorps you can do all of that while making a difference. Volunteer part-time or spend a year learning new skills, meeting new people, and exploring a new town – all while earning money to pay off school loans. You can also receive health benefits, child care assistance, and even relocation expenses and income for helping a community in need. Contact AmeriCorps at 800-942-2677 or {www.americorps.org}.

$20,000 To Change Careers

The Transition to Teaching program provides 5-year grants to support efforts to recruit, train, and place individuals in teaching positions and to support them during their first years in the classroom. This program, which strives to ease the shortage of qualified teachers in many of our nation's schools, is seeking mid-career professionals with substantial career experience, as well as recent college graduates. Grants will be awarded to State educational agencies, high-need local educational agencies, and partnership agencies with for-profit or nonprofit organizations. Contact the U.S. Department of Education, OII, Teacher Quality Programs, 400 Maryland Ave., S.W., Rm.5E115, FB-6, Washington, DC 20202; 202-260-0223; {www.ed.gov/programs/transiti onteach/index.html}. {http://12.46.24 5.173/pls/portal30/CATALOG.PROGR AM_TEXT_RPT.SHOW?p_arg_names =prog_nbr&p_arg_values=84.350}.

Part-Time Jobs For College Students

The Federal Work Study Program offers part-time employment to eligible undergraduate and graduate students to help meet educational expenses. The program encourages community service work and work related to each student's course of study. Students earn at minimum the current federal minimum wage, but the amount may be higher, depending on the type of work and the skills required. Contact the institution that you attend or plan to attend. You can also contact the Office Federal Student

Aid, Department of Education, 400 Maryland Avenue, SW., Washington, D.C. 20202-5446; 800-433-3243. {http://12.46.245.173/pls/portal30/CA TALOG.PROGRAM_TEXT_RPT.SH OW?p_arg_names=prog_nbr&p_arg_v alues=84.033}.

$2,000 Per Month As A White House Intern

Through the White House Fellows Program, one-year fellowships are offered in Washington D.C., providing young men and women with Federal government experience early in their careers. Applicants must have the skills to serve at the highest levels of government, show leadership potential, and have a demonstrated commitment to public service. Finalists must undergo comprehensive background investigations for security clearance purposes. The White House Fellowship Program includes an Education Program, enabling fellows to meet with leaders in fields in and outside their respective job assignments, and travel to other U.S. cities, domestic military bases, and foreign countries to participate in public policy discussions. Contact the President's Commission on White House Fellowships, 712 Jackson Place, N.W., Washington, DC 20503; 202-395-4522; {www.whitehousefellows. gov}. {www.usajobs.opm.gov/EI-13.asp}.

$230 per Week for Interns Promoting Child Safety

The Child Welfare League of America Internship Program offers internships to MSW students engaged in a field placement. Internships are available in the fall, spring, and summer and are not compensated. The Everett Public Service Internship Program awards a stipend of $230 per week to interns who have completed at least two semesters of college, be a current undergraduate or graduate student, or recently graduated within the same calendar year as the internship. The Everett Internships are offered during the summer semester. Contact Child Welfare League of America, 440 1st St., N.W., Ste. 310, Washington, DC 20001-2085; 202-638-2952; Fax: 202-638-4004; {http://www.cwla.org}.

Fellowships to Promote Families and Child Welfare

The Casey Children and Family Fellowship Program aims to change youth-serving institutions in states and localities by helping key leaders develop strategic vision, planning ability, organizational understanding, and communication skills. The fellowship explicitly strives to increase the pool of leaders with the vision and ability to frame and sustain major system reforms and community capacity-building initiatives that benefit large numbers of children and families. The fellowship is an intensive 11-month, full-time program for outstanding mid- to senior-level professionals who aspire to leadership positions where they can help shape the future of public, private and nonprofit organizations that have an impact on children and families. Contact The Annie E. Casey Foundation, 701 St. Paul St., Baltimore, MD 21202; 410-547-6600; Fax: 410-547-6624; {http://www.aecf. org}; {webmail@aecf.org}

Nurses Receive Financial Help for Bills

Nurses House financial awards assist with such needs as rent or mortgage payments, food, utilities, telephone and health insurance. When possible, Nurses House attempts to assist applicants in identifying other potential sources of assistance. By providing anonymous help for nurses with serious needs, Nurses House is there to ease the financial strains that accompany misfortune. Awards will vary depending on the applicant's level of need. Contact Nurses House, Inc., 2113 Western Ave., Ste. 2, Guilderland, NY 12084-9501; 518-456-7858; Fax: 518-452-3760; {http://www.nurseshouse.org/}; {mail@NursesHouse.org}.

$10,000 To Train For A New Career

If you have better skills, you can get a better job. This is why the government can offer you up to $10,000 to take a few months off to sharpen up your computer skills, learn to be a chef, or even get any specialized training that will make you more employable for the jobs that are out there now. If you think that specialized training will help you get a better job, contact your state One-Stop Labor Information Center headquarters located in your state capital and they can direct you to a local office to explain how to get this training. Check them out at {www.doleta.gov/usworkforce/onestop/onestopmap.cfm}.

$7,000 Of Retraining If Over 55

The Senior Community Service Employment Program offers part-time training and employment opportunities

for eligible low-income persons 55 years of age and older in a variety of public and private non-profit community service settings, such as senior centers, nutrition programs, social service agencies, and many others. Contact your state Department of Labor or Division of Older Worker Programs, U.S. Department of Labor, Employment and Training Administration, 200 Constitution Ave., NW, Room N4641, Washington, DC 20210; 202-693-3842; {http://www. doleta.gov/seniors}.

Get Paid While You Learn

There are apprenticeship programs all over the country that will provide free on-the-job training, and you will learn while you earn. Why would a company offer to train you for free? Simple- they get a skilled worker that they have trained themselves. Contact your local Job Service office or Bureau of Apprenticeship and Training, U.S. Department of Labor, 200 Constitution Ave., NW, Room N4649, Washington, DC 20210; 202-693-3812; {www. doleta.gov}.

$8,000 For Women And Minorities In Construction

Let the Institute For Social And Economic Development project get you a job in the world of construction. Though this nontraditional employment project designed to create 110 job opportunities over a 30-month period, job placement and apprenticeships for low-income women and minorities in the construction field are being offered. To find out more, contact the U. S. Department of Health and Human Services, Administration for Children and Families, Office of Community Services, Division of Community Discretionary Programs, 370 L'Enfant

Promenade, S.W - 5th Floor West, Washington, D.C. 20447; 202-401-5307; {www.acf.hhs.gov/programs/ocs/dcdp/joli/revised/sum2000.htm}.

$50,000 For Flight Training

Did you know under the GI Bill you can get your teaching certificate, or even receive flight training? Through the All-Volunteer Force Educational Assistance program, a number of programs may be approved for training under the Montgomery GI Bill. The programs include, but are not limited to, courses at colleges and universities leading to associate, bachelor or graduate degrees; flight training; state-approved teacher certification programs; courses leading to a certificate or diploma from business, technical or vocational schools. Separate work-study and tutorial benefits are also available. Contact the Department of Veterans Affairs, Central Office, Washington, DC 20420; 202-273-7132. {http://12. 46.245.173/pls/portal30/CATALOG.P ROGRAM_TEXT_RPT.SHOW?p_arg _names=prog_nbr&p_arg_values=64.1 24}.

$1,200 For Tutoring

Get help with tutoring though the GI Bill. Through the All-Volunteer Force Educational Assistance program, funding is available for individuals to receive tutoring for training programs such as courses at colleges and universities leading to associate, bachelor or graduate degrees; courses leading to a certificate or diploma from business, technical or vocational schools; noncredit preparatory courses necessary for admission to a college; and licensing and certification tests. Contact the Department of Veterans Affairs, Central Office, Washington, DC 20420; 202-273-7132. {http://

12.46.245.173/pls/portal30/CATALO
G.PROGRAM_TEXT_RPT.SHOW?p
_arg_names=prog_nbr&p_arg_values=
64.124}

$400/wk When You Are Out of Work

If you have been laid off or downsized from your job through no fault of your own, then help is available to you. Unemployment compensation is the government's first line of defense against the ripple effects of unemployment. By cash payments made directly to laid off workers, the program ensures that at least a significant portion of the necessities of life, such as food, shelter, and clothing, can be met while a search for work takes place.

The Federal-State Unemployment Insurance Program provides unemployment benefits to eligible workers who are unemployed through no fault of their own, and meet other eligibility requirements. Check to see if you qualify for any additional benefits above and beyond the Unemployment Insurance Program.

Temporary Extended Unemployment Compensation Program

Temporary Emergency Unemployment Compensation (TEUC) provides extra weeks of federally funded unemployment benefits to unemployed workers throughout the country who

have received all regular unemployment benefits available to them.

Extended Benefits Program

Extended Benefits are available to workers who have exhausted regular unemployment insurance benefits during periods of high unemployment. The basic Extended Benefits program provides up to 13 additional weeks of benefits when a State is experiencing high unemployment.

Unemployment Compensation for Federal Employees Program

The Unemployment Compensation for Federal Employees program provides benefits for eligible unemployed former civilian This program is operated under the same terms and conditions that apply to regular State Unemployment Insurance (see State Unemployment Insurance). In general, the law of the State in which your last official duty station in Federal civilian service was located will be the State law that determines eligibility for unemployment insurance benefits.

There is no payroll deduction from a Federal employee's wages for unemployment insurance protection. Benefits are paid for by the various Federal agencies.

Unemployment Compensation for Ex-service Members Program

The Unemployment Compensation for Ex-service members program provides benefits for eligible ex-military personnel. If you were on active duty with a branch of the U.S. military, you may be entitled to benefits based on that service. You must have been separated under honorable conditions. There is no payroll deduction from the service member's wages for unemployment insurance protection. The various branches of the military pay for benefits.

Disaster Unemployment Assistance Program

Disaster Unemployment Assistance provides financial assistance to individuals whose employment or self-employment has been lost or interrupted as a direct result of a major disaster declared by the President of the United States. Before an individual can be determined eligible for Disaster Unemployment Assistance, it must be established that the individual is not eligible for regular unemployment insurance benefits (under any state or federal law).

Supplement Your Retirement

If you are 55 years old or over, have a low-income and having trouble finding a job, the Senior Community Service Employment Program (SCSEP) may be able to help. The federal government provides job and educational training by placing seniors into community and government agency jobs for up to 20 hours a week. The job assignments may include positions at the library, schools, recreation facilities, maintenance and any other services essential for the community. These opportunities may then lead to non-subsidized jobs and higher pay. To learn more about the opportunities in your area check the web site at {www.doleta.gov/Seniors/html_docs/docs/statecontacts.cfm}.

You may also contact National Office: Division of Older Worker Programs, U.S. Department of Labor, Employment and Training Administration, 200 Constitution Ave. NW, Room N-5306, Washington, D.C.

20210; 202-693-3842; {www.doleta.gov/Seniors/}.

Learn New Technical Skills

The business world is in constant need of skilled technical workers, however, foreign workers under the H-1B visa program are filling many of those jobs in the U.S. today. Because of this, the government has set aside millions of grant dollars for companies to train American workers for these technical jobs in hopes to lessen their dependency on skilled foreign workers. Businesses compete for grants to provide technical skills training for workers who have lost their jobs, or who want to upgrade their skills or change occupations. Contact the US Labor Department for additional information at U.S. Department of Labor, 200 Constitution Avenue, NW, N4659, Washington, DC 20210; 202-693-3010; {http://www.doleta.gov/h-1b/}.

Become a Journeyman

Getting a good job does not always mean that you have to go to college or a trade school. There are thousands of apprenticeship programs all over the country and in U.S. territories that will provide free on-the-job training, and best of all you earn while you learn. Apprenticeship training is a system that can train you to be a highly skilled worker to meet the demands of employers competing in a global economy. Generally, apprentices need to be at least 16 years old and the programs can range in time commitment from 1-6 years depending on the chosen field. Program sponsors will pay most of your training costs while at the same time paying you wages that increase as your skill level increases. For the apprentice, this can translate into an educational benefit worth $40,000 to $150,000. Apprenticeships are for everyone; you can be rich, middle class, poor, man or women you just have to be willing to in the time and effort to become an expert at your new career. Programs may be sponsored by employers, a union or even the military and include construction, service, information technology, manufacturing, health care and public utilities apprenticeships.

For local offices and information, look in the blue pages of your phone book for the Bureau of Apprenticeship or the State Apprenticeship Council located in your state, or contact an employer or union engaged in the trade you want to enter. Check the website {www.doleta.gov/atels_bat/sainformat ion.cfm}. To learn who to call in your area, contact National Office: Bureau of Apprenticeship and Training, Frances Perkins Building, 200 Constitution Avenue, NW, Room N4671; Washington, DC 20210; 202-693-2700; {http://www.doleta.gov/atels_bat}.

Free Training and Money if You're Laid Off

If you have been laid off because of a plant closing or downsizing, apply for money and re-training from the government under the Economic Dislocation and Worker Adjustment Assistance Act (EDWAA). This money is not just for big business layoffs but includes long-term unemployed workers with limited job opportunities in their fields including farmers, ranchers and other self-employed persons who become unemployed due to general economic conditions. Under certain circumstances, states may even authorize service for displaced homemakers. The Economic

Dislocation and Worker Adjustment Assistance Act is administered by each state, and because of that, the program differs from state to state. The Governor of each state designates a Dislocated Worker Unit (DWU) that operates and administers the program at the local level to best service their states needs. The programs may include retraining services: retraining classes, on-the-job training, occupational skills, literacy classes and even English as a second language. Readjustment services include outreach, testing and counseling, job search services, including child care and transportation allowances and relocation assistance. Dislocated workers in training who have exhausted all of their unemployment insurance may receive needs-related payments while they finish their training. For additional information, contact your state Department of Labor or the Dislocated Workers Unit by using the blue pages of your local phone book. To learn more about services in your area contact National Office: Office of Adult Services, Division of Adults and Dislocated Workers, U.S. Department of Labor, Room C-5325, 200 Constitution Avenue, NW; Washington, DC 20210; toll-free 877-US-2JOBS; {http://www.doleta.gov/programs/factsht/edwaa.cfm}.

Job Corps

Just because you are a high school drop-out, have a low-income, need additional basic education, are homeless, a runaway or in foster care doesn't mean that you have to settle for a low paying job for the rest of your life. If you are ready to work hard and show commitment, you may be ready to participate successfully in Job Corps and gain the benefits of the program. Job Corps is the nation's largest and most comprehensive residential, education and job training program for at-risk youth, ages 16 through 24. Today, Job Corps continues to serve nearly 70,000 students a year at 118 Job Corps centers throughout the country. Job Corps has provided more than 2 million disadvantaged young people with the integrated academic, vocational, and social skills training they need to gain independence and get quality, long-term jobs or further their education. Job Corps has many career choices including agriculture, construction, food service, business management, health care, engineering, transportation and many more. The culinary arts students not only learn to sauté and broil, they also get to enter exciting Culinary Expos to show off their talents in the food industry. To apply contact a Job Corps counselor at (800) 733-JOBS or apply on line at the web site listed below, or contact U.S. Department of Labor, 200 Constitution Ave., NW, Washington, DC 20210; 800-733-JOBS; {http://jobcorps. doleta.gov/}.

Free Help If You Lose Your Job Because of Increased Imports

As the business world becomes more and more competitive, many US businesses are moving their companies to other parts of the globe. U.S. workers may lose their jobs when this happens. The government however, is willing to help! The President signed into law the Trade Adjustment Assistance Reform Act of 2002 (TAA Reform Act) on August 6, 2002, which provides you with assistance if you lose your job because of increased imports. The Trade Adjustment Assistance Reform Act has consolidated the North America Free Trade Agreement (NAFTA) into the TAA Reform Act. Any worker, no matter what their prior income level, can apply for assistance. The Trade Adjustment Assistance Reform Act of 2002 can help you learn marketable skills to move you on to new and better job opportunities. Workers may be eligible for up to 130 weeks of on-the-job and classroom training; you can receive 78 weeks of income benefits after your unemployment expires; you can receive $1,250 for job search and relocation expenses; health care benefits may also be available. This program is also available to farmers who have been hurt by imports! For more information contact U.S. Department of Labor, Employment and Training Administration, Division of Trade Adjustment Assistance, 200 Constitution Avenue, NW, Room C-5311, Washington, DC 20210; 202-693-3560; {http://www.doleta.gov/ tradeact}.

One-Stop Can Do It All

Are you looking for help in a career change or job skills training? If so, the government may have the help you need. The Workforce Investment Act (WIA), which replaces the Job Training Partnership Act (JTPA), provides a comprehensive workforce system to help Americans find the tools they need to manage their careers and to help U.S. companies find skilled workers. You can find access to job search assistance, career guidance, salary data, training and education resources at your local One-Stop Service Center. The Workforce Investment Act (WIA) is now one of the main government program offering retraining funds to assist job seekers.

Contact your state One-Stop Career Center located in the appendix, check the web site to find the closest office, or contact National Office: Office of Career Transition Assistance, U.S. Department of Labor, 200 Constitution Avenue, NW, Room S-4231, Washington, DC 20210; 202-693-3031; {http://www.doleta.gov/usworkforce/onestop/}; {www.doleta.gov/usworkforce/onestop/onestopmap.cfm}.

Free Job Training

Actually many state Departments of Labor offer a variety of job training programs to help employers train new hires or upgrade the skills of their current workers. Although these programs need to be initiated by the employer with the Labor Department, you can take the initiative and see what they have to offer. Then show your boss how eager you are to learn new skills, at no cost to them!

- California will reimburse you $20 per hour per student for training for mid-level Information Technology positions, as part of the TechForce program of the Employment Development Department.
- Ohio Training Tax Credit Program provides tax credits of up to $100,000 per year to help offset costs of training current workers.

- Pennsylvania offers Customized Job Training grants for specialized job training for existing or new employees; Guaranteed Free Training Program up to $700 per employee; and Critical Job Training Grants for high demand jobs or jobs with a shortage of skilled workers.
- Rhode Island has a Job Creation Grant Fund to offer customized training and an Excellence Through Training Grant Program that provides grants up to $30,000 to upgrade and retrain existing employees.
- Arkansas' Business and Industry Training program will provide financial assistance to companies to recruit new workers, will provide customized training before employment, and will pay for more training once you hire the employee. They also offer the Existing Workforce Training Program which will pay for upgrading the skills of your current employees.

Contact your state Department of Labor listed in the Appendix to see what job training programs or tax credits they may offer to help you get the training or the employees you need.

The Little Extras

We talk about a great many different types of job training programs, but it is worth repeating about certain extras that many of these programs offer. If you have children and are in need of child care in order to seek employment, many of these programs cover those costs. If you find a job in another county or even another state, you may qualify for job relocation assistance. Do you need help getting to the job training site? There may be funds to pay for transportation costs, as well as other supplies need to complete the training program. If you need something special, just ask your job counselor. You may be surprised!

Food Stamps-Not Just For Groceries Anymore!

The Food Stamp Program can do more than just help pay for your monthly food expenses; it can also help you train for a new job. On May 13, 2002, President Bush signed into law, a law that reauthorizes the Food Stamp Employment and Training Program (FSET) until 2007. The U.S. Department of Agriculture requires each state to operate an employment and training program for Food Stamp recipients. The goal of the Food Stamp Employment and Training Program is to help recipients prepare for and become employed. Services may include an individual assessment of work-related strengths and barriers and an Employment Plan designed to help participants obtain or upgrade the skills necessary to gain employment. Job training may also include General Equivalency Diploma (GED), English as a Second Language (ESL), high school diploma or short-term vocational training. FSET services are administered by each state, usually through service providers such as WorkForce Centers, community action agencies and county employment and training providers. To apply for benefits or obtain information, contact your local Food Stamp program. Check your local phone book in the government pages under "Food Stamps". Contact National Headquarters, USDA Food and Nutrition Service, Food Stamp Program, 3101 Park Center Drive,

Room 808, Alexandria, VA 22302; 703-305-2026; {www.fns.usda.gov/fsp}.

On the Road to Independence

All kinds of free help is out there for teenagers in foster care, and young adults who have been raised in foster homes. Signed into law in 1999, the John H Chafee Foster Care Independence Program (CFCIP) offers assistance to current and former foster care youths achieve self-sufficiency. Activities and programs include, but are not limited to help with education, employment, financial management, housing, emotional support and assured connections to caring adults for older youth in foster care as well as youth 18-21 who have aged out of the foster care system. This legislation helps ensure that young people involved in the foster care system get the tools they need to make the most of their lives. Contact your state division of Child and Family Services for information on the Chafee Foster Care Independence Program. Contact Children's Bureau, Administration for Children and Families, Mary E. Switzer Building, 330 C Street, S.W. Washington, D.C. 20201; 202-205-8618; {http://www.acf.hhs.gov/programs/cb/programs/indep_living.htm}.

Tools for Teens

Bottom line: most construction jobs pay well. Many of the today's youths who dropout of school, would prefer a hands-on approach to their education. Young men and women can get experience in construction trades while helping to build and restore affordable housing for low-income and homeless persons through the Youthbuild Program. Youthbuild provides grants to assist high-risk, very low-income youth between the ages of 16-24 to learn housing construction skills and to complete their high school education at the same time. Youthbuild teaches participants how to tear down or rehabilitate old houses and how to build new houses from the ground up. Youthbuild programs offer educational and job training services, leadership training, counseling, living allowances, placement services and even driver's education courses. To obtain additional information, contact the HUD office or check their web site for a program in your area. Contact U.S. Department of Housing and Urban Development, Office of Community Planning and Development, Jackie Mitchell, 451 7th Street, SW, Washington, DC 20410; 202-708-2035; {www.hud.gov/offices/ cpd/economicdevelopment/programs/y outhbuild/index.cfm}; {www.youthbuild.org/}.

One-Stop Career Shopping

Are you tired of your old job? Do you need help training for a new career? Are you ready for a new exciting job? Well, the Department of Labor Employment and Training Administration's Career One-Stop may just be your ticket. Career One Stop is a national online career development resource, which provides internet-based access for Americans, needing job search assistance, career guidance, salary data and training and education resources. You can find jobs from entry level to technical to professional to CEO. In addition to the online program, there are also Comprehensive One-Stop Career Centers located throughout the country. Each community has tailored their system to meet the needs of the citizens in their area. The centers may offer computers, career counseling, workshops and many other services. The number of centers is growing everyday. To locate the Career One-Stop Program go to their web site. For additional information and to locate your closest Career One-Stop Center, go to the service locator web site or refer to the appendix of this book for a listing. Contact U.S. Department of Labor, Frances Perkins Building, 200 Constitution Avenue, NW, Washington, DC 20210; 877-US-2JOBS; 202-693-2700; 877-889-5627 TTY; {www.doleta.gov/usworkforce/ onestop/}; Career One-Stop: {www. careeronestop.org/}; Career One-Stop Center Locator: {www.servicelocator. org/nearest_onestop.asp}.

Earn Money While You Learn

Do you want to start your own business? You can take free business training classes while you collect unemployment benefits. If approved for this training, you may also be eligible for addition money for transportation and child care costs. This program is offered through the Workforce Investment Act (formerly known as the Job Training Partnership Act- JTPA). The goal of this program is to help unemployed people stay gainfully employed, even if it in their own businesses. Local offices are located across the country to help you learn how to properly launch your new business. The toll free number 877-US-2JOBS can help you locate your nearest job training or one-stop career center. You may also contact your local Workforce Investment Act office, or contact Office of Employment and Training Programs, U.S. Department of Labor, 200 Constitution Ave., NW, Room N-4464, Washington, DC 20210; 202-693-3031; 877-US-2JOBS; {www.doleta.gov/uswork force/wia}.

Employment Help for Native Americans

If your ancestors were the some of the first people in our country, the Indian and Native American Program may be able to help you with valuable job skills. The Workforce Investment Act (WIA) provides help to Indians, Alaska Natives, and Native Hawaiians who are economically disadvantaged, unemployed, and underemployed. Grants are distributed to organizations at a local level to provide the best quality of service to its customers. The goal of the program is to expand the occupational, academic, and literacy skills of Indians and Native Americans while enhancing their job prospects. The Workforce Investment Act also authorizes funds to provide employment and training programs for Indian youth on reservations. Contact your local reservation, tribal government or One-Stop Career Center found in the appendix for additional information. You may also contact National Office: U.S. Department of Labor, Frances Perkins Building, 200 Constitution Avenue, NW, Room N-4641, Washington, DC 20210; 202-693-3841; {www.doleta. gov/DINAP}.

Training After the Harvest for Seasonal Farmworkers

We all depend on the fresh fruits and vegetables in our grocery stores and we thank seasonal farmworkers for picking them. The work however does not provide steady income throughout the year for the workers and their families and many migrant and seasonal workers become unemployed. The National Farmworker Jobs Program (NFJP) assists migrant and

other seasonally employed farmworkers and their families, achieve economic self-sufficiency through job training and other related services that address their employment related needs. Services available include skills assessment, basic education, job search, on-the-job training and other related assistance. The Migrant and Seasonal Farmworkers program also has a program to help farmworker youth ages 14 through 21. Contact your local One-Stop Career Center listed in the appendix for additional information. Contact National Office: Division of Seasonal Farmworker Programs, Employment and Training Administration, Room S-4206, 200 Constitution Avenue, NW, Washington, DC 20210; 202-693-3843; {www.doleta.gov/msfw}.

Troubled Teen Training Right in Your Town

Troubled teens may need some guidance and support to get them through to adulthood. The Workforce Investment Act (WIA) provides funds to states and local communities to provide their 14-21 year olds with many opportunities. The program targets youth who are low income, basic skills deficient, drop outs, homeless, a parent or offender that requires additional help in completing their educational program or hold employment. Local Workforce Investment Boards provide eligible youth the following services: tutoring, study skill training, dropout prevention, summer employment opportunities and occupational skill training. The Department of Labor, in conjunction with the Department of Justice, also administers the Going Home: Serious and Violent Offender Reentry Initiative help violent offenders re-enter their communities through job placement and security. To find the program closest to you contact your local One-Stop Career Center listed in the appendix. Contact National Office: U.S. Department of Labor, Frances Perkins Building, 200 Constitution Avenue, NW, Room N-4469, Washington, DC 20210; 202-693-6378; {http://www.doleta.gov/youth_services}.

Grant Money for Youths

Opportunities for youths living in high-poverty communities may be limited simply because of where they live, however the federal government provides millions of dollars every year to the Youth Opportunity Grant (YOG) Program. The Workforce Investment Act authorized the Youth Opportunity Grant program to increase the high school graduation rate, college enrollment rate, and employment rate of youth living in high-poverty communities. The program targets any youth, 14-21, regardless of income, who lives in federally designated zones, enterprise communities, and other high-poverty areas. The Grants are funded annually so you need to check their web site for the most up to date information. Contact National Office: U.S. Department of Labor, Frances Perkins Building, 200 Constitution Avenue, NW,

Washington, DC 20210; 202-693-6378; {http://www.doleta.gov/youth_services/yog.cfm}.

One Strike You're Not Out

Everyone makes mistakes, especially when we are young. That's why the Young Offender Initiative: Demonstration Grant Project was formed. The Department of Labor has funded projects to get youth at-risk of criminal involvement, youth offenders, and gang members between 14 and 24 into long-term employment at wage levels that prevent future dependency and break the cycle of crime and juvenile delinquency. The overall goal is to increase coordination between the One Stop Career System and other local agencies serving youth. To obtain additional information contact your local One-Stop Career Center listed in the appendix. Contact National Office:, U.S. Department of Labor, Frances Perkins Building, 200 Constitution Avenue, NW, Washington, DC 20210; 202-693-6378; {http://www.doleta.gov/youth_services/Program_Services.cfm}.

Job Assistance Close to Home

Help finding a new job may be as close as your own back yard, or at least in your own town. Each state offers programs to get people the training and job counseling they need to earn a steady paycheck. Utilize your state's programs and soon you'll be laughing all the way to the bank! Contact your State Employment Agency to find out about specific programs in your state {www.govengine.com}. Your state may offer free job training, tuition waivers, job listings, resume writing assistance, and maybe even child care during your job search. Don't forget to check the website for a wealth of information.

KIDS

Children are our future and we want to do as much as possible to help them along their way. Child care, education, health issues, and more lead the list. But where do we look to find the answers? There are several good starting places where we can begin the search, keeping in mind that these are only the tip of the iceberg.

1) Find All Federal Government Money Programs For Children....

They are described in a book called the Catalog of Federal Domestic Assistance. This book is available at your local public library or the U.S. Government Printing Office {www.gpo.gov}. You can also search the contents of this book for free on the web at {www.cfda.gov}.

2) Find All State Money Programs For Children...

Every state has money programs to help children. Look for your state offices of health, education, or jobs and family services. You can find them by dialing 411 and asking for your state capitol operator or be going to the web at {www.govenegine.com} and clicking on your state.

3) Find Money For Child Care....

Each state operates a little differently in dealing with child care funds. To learn more about what your state has to offer, you can contact National Child Care Information Center, 243 Church Street, NW, Vienna, VA 22180; 800-616-2242; {http://nccic.org}. They can direct you to resources in your area to apply for child care funds.

4) Find Health Information For Children...
You can search for health information through the National Health Information Center, P.O. Box 1133, Washington, DC 20013; 800-336-4797; {www. health.gov/NHIC}.

5) Find Helpful Educational Information For Children....
The U.S. Department of Education has established a helpful website for parents looking for information on how to help their children succeed in school. Check out {www.ed.gov} to see what they have to offer.

6) Find Programs Available Through the Smithsonian
The Smithsonian offers a wealth of education programs and resources. To learn more about what they offer, check them out on the web at {www.si.edu}.

7) Ask ERIC
The Education Resources Information Center (ERIC) is sponsored by the U.S. Department of Education and produces a wealth of journals and literature on a wide range of educational topics. ERIC use to sponsor clearinghouses on topics like Math and Science, Elementary and Early Childhood Education, Disabilities and Gifted Education, and more. These have lost their funding, although many of the host organizations are continuing in some form. To learn how to access articles or to be referred to a specific contact go to {www.eric.ed.gov} or 800-LET-ERIC. To learn how to contact a clearinghouse, go to {http://www.lib.msu.edu/corby/education/eric/clearinghouseplans.htm}.

$1,200/Month In Day Care Money While You Look For Work

The Child Care and Development Block Grant gives money to states to help families meet their child care needs. Parents may choose from a variety of child care providers, including center-based, family child care and in-home care, care provided by relatives, and even sectarian child care providers. You can even get money to start a day care center! To find out how to take advantage of this program in your state and to learn the eligibility requirements, contact National Child Care Information Center, 243 Church Street, NW, Vienna, VA 22180; 800-616-2242; {http://nccic.org}.

$5,000 Worth of Free Health Care for Kids

Make up to $38,657 and get free health care for your kids. Almost every state now has a Children's Health Insurance Program (CHIPS), which extends medical coverage to many children who may not be covered. Contact your state Department of Health to see what version of the CHIPS program is offered in your area; or call a new government hotline to help locate free health care for kids at 877-KIDS-NOW; 877-543-7669; {www.insure kidsnow.gov}.

$10,000 For Teenagers To Start A Business

The U.S. Department of Agriculture has a program that loans money to kids between the ages of 10 and 21, who live in small towns, to start a business. Some states even run entrepreneur camps or special business training programs for kids. Contact your local Farm Service, or the Farm Service Agency, Loan Marketing Division, Ag Box 0522, Washington, DC 20250; 202-720-1632; {www.fsa.usda.gov}.

$6,000 Worth Of Free Speech Therapy For Pre-Schoolers

You can have your child tested to see if any speech problems are developing and get free speech therapy. It is part of the U.S. Individuals with Disabilities Education Act (IDEA), to make sure that children in need receive special education beginning on their third birthday (in some states it starts at age two). The program is run through your local school district, so check with them first, or your state Department of Education. You can also contact Office of Special Education Programs, U.S. Department of Education, 400 Maryland Avenue, SW, Washington, DC 20202; 202-205-5507; {www.ed.gov/about/offices/list/osers/index.html}.

$675 Million in Uncollected Child Support

No matter what your income, you can get the most powerful organization in the world, your government, to fight for you to establish paternity; set up a court order for child support; track down a missing parent, collect child support; and get the courts to adjust child support orders. There are a few states that may charge you up to $25. Contact your state Child Support Enforcement Office or contact Office of Child Support Enforcement, U.S. Department of Health and Human Services, 370 L'Enfant Promenade, SW, Washington, DC 20447; 202-401-9383; {www.acf.dhhs.gov/programs/cse/}.

$2,000 For Day Care While In College

To support low-income parents attending college, the Child Care Access Means Parents In School program supports campus-based child care services. Awards are used to support or establish child care programs for infants and toddlers, as well as before and after school services to the extent necessary to allow students to pursue a postsecondary education. Contact the U.S. Department of Education, OPE, Higher Education Programs, 1990 K Street, NW, 7th Floor, Washington, DC 20006-8510; 202-502-7642; {www.ed.gov/programs/campisp/inde

x.html}. {http://12.46.245.173/pls/portal30/CATALOG.PROGRAM_TEXT_RPT.SHOW?p_arg_names=prog_nbr&p_arg_values=84.335}.

$10,000 For Student Science Project

The P3 National Student Design Competition for Sustainability will provide grants to teams of college students to research, develop, and design solutions to sustainability challenges. P3 highlights people, prosperity, and the planet, and challenges from a wide range of categories will be considered. The P3 Award will be given to the winner of a national, intercollegiate design competition among interdisciplinary student teams for their research, development, and design solutions to the scientific and technical challenges of sustainability. Grant awards will average $10,000. Contact the U.S. Environmental Protection Agency, Office of Research and Development, Washington, DC; 202-564-1589; {www.epa.gov/ncer}, {http://es.epa.gov/ncer/P3/}.

Money to Educate Children

This foundation provides grant funding in order to help young people, from early childhood through grade 12, prepare to meet the challenges of our changing global society. The foundation primarily supports programs that provide: comprehensive education reform for U.S. urban schools, innovative models for pre-K-12 public school improvement, and innovative work at the university level to improve pre-K-12 education. Contact Lucent Technologies Foundation, 600 Mountain Avenue, Murray Hill, NJ 07974; 908-582-4200; {http://www.lucent.com/news/foundation/}; {foundation@lucent.com}.

Money To Help Families

There is a database of over 400 non-profit and government organizations that was set up to help families who have special needs when they are stuck with a health-related problem. It says it's for kids, but many of the organizations help anyone in need. There are groups that will give out grants like $400 to pay rent, $500 to pay for child care, $800 to spend on camp, or $750 to buy health products. This money is often location specific, so read through carefully. Go to {www.bravekids.org} and take a look.

Funding to Help Families with Sick Children

The First Hand Foundation provides grants to families with children who have health problems. Grants can be used to pay for expenses associated with clinical procedures and treatment, medical equipment and supplies, and expenses associated with families of seriously ill children who must relocate during treatment. Contact First Hand Foundation, c/o Cerner Corporation, 2800 Rockcreek Parkway, Kansas City, MO 64117; 816-201-1569; Fax: 816-571-1569; {http://www.firsthandfoundation.org/grants.asp}.

Grants to Help Children Develop Websites

The Where Fun and Learning Click! Program awards grants for the development of websites for children between the ages of 6 and 12. Websites can focus on Current Events/News, Literature, Sports/ Exercise, Technology and/or Science, U.S. History, Visual or Performing Arts, and/or World culture/history /geography, to name a few. Contact PBS Kids Interactive, 1320 Braddock Place, Alexandria, VA 22314; 703-739-8660;   {www.pbs.org}; {slovato@pbs.org}

$500 for Young Girls to Promote Health and Fitness

Youth Service America, the cosmetics firm BonneBell and the teen magazine CosmoGirl! offers a Born to Lead Grant program. Grants of $500 are available to young ladies between the ages of 13-25 for service and/or volunteer programs that promote the importance of health and fitness of the community, themselves, and their peers. Contact Born To Lead Grant, Youth Service America, 1101 15th Street, NW Suite 200, Washington, D.C. 20005; 202-296-2992; Fax: 202-296-4030;   {http://www.ysa.org/ awards/award_grant.cfm}; {info@ysa.org}.

$500 Grants for Community Service Efforts

Youth Service America and AT&T sponsor the AT&T Cares Youth Service Action Fund, which offers fifty annual grants of $500 each to young people (ages 5-25) and organizations to implement service and/or volunteer projects for National Youth Service Day, the largest service event in the world. Contact AT&T Cares Youth Service Action Fund, Youth Service America, 1101 15th Street, NW, Suite 200, Washington, D.C. 20005; 202-296-2992; Fax: 202-296-4030;   {http://www.ysa.org/ awards/award_grant.cfm}; {AT&TCARES@YSA.org}.

Up to $2,000 for Disabled Youths to Volunteer

The Clay Aiken Able to Serve Awards Program offered by Youth Service America and The Bubel Aiken Foundation provides grants up to $1,000 each to young people, between the ages of 5 and 22 with developmental disabilities to plan and carry out service and/or volunteer projects. An additional $1000 may be awarded for projects that continue beyond the National Youth Services Day timeframe. Contact Clay Aiken ABLE to SERVE Awards, Youth Service America, 1101 15th Street, NW, Suite 200, Washington, D.C. 20005; 202-296-2992; Fax: 202-296-4030;   {http://www.ysa.org/awards/ award_grant.cfm}; {info@ysa.org}.

$2,000 for Activism Projects by Young Women

Provides grants of up to $2,000 to young women 19 and under who propose to develop and lead projects that are focused on activism and social change. Contact The Ellen Dougherty Activist Fund, Open Meadows Foundation, P.O. Box 150-607, Van Brunt Station, Brooklyn, NY 11215; 718-768-2249; {http://www.openmea dows.org/}; {openmeadows@igc.org}.

FREE Computers for Children in Need

The Second Byte Foundation provides computers to disadvantaged children. Awards are based in part, on 100-word essay written by the student on why they should receive this opportunity and how they will benefit from the computer. Kids and families receive computers through schools or other organizations that apply for the program. Contact Second Byte Foundation, 2663 Townsgate Road, Westlake Village, CA 91361; 888-263-

2983; Fax: 805-495-9935; {www.2nd byte.org}; {info@2ndbyte.org}.

$10,000 for Teenagers who Don't Smoke

Lorillard awards grants to students involved with smoking prevention and scholarships to teenagers who choose not to smoke. There are two award programs: TeenH.I.P. Awards, which annually awards 10 $10,000 scholarships to teenagers who choose not to smoke; and TeenH.I.P. Grant Program in which Lorillard annually awards five $10,000 grants to students to create or fund a youth smoking prevention program. Support is given on a national basis. Contact Lorillard Tobacco Company Contributions Program, 72 Green Valley Road, Greensboro, NC 27408; {http://www.lorillard.net}. Application address for TeenH.I.P. Grants: Alex Abraham, Weber Shandwick, Inc., c/o TeenH.I.P. Grant Program, 676 N. St. Clair, Ste. 1000, Chicago, IL 60611; {teenhip@bsmg.com}.

$5,000 for Children to Write a Book

The Schneider Family Book Awards honor an author or illustrator for a book that embodies an artistic expression of the disability experience for child and adolescent audiences. The book must emphasize the artistic expression of the disability experience for children and or adolescent audiences. The book must portray some aspect of living with a disability or that of a friend or family member, whether the disability is physical, mental or emotional. Three annual awards each consisting of $5,000 and a framed plaque, will be given annually in each of the following categories: birth through grade school (age 0–10), middle school (age 11–13) and teens

(age 13–18). Contact American Library Association, 50 E. Huron Street, Chicago, IL 60611-2795; 800-545-2433; Fax: 312-944-0379; {http://www.ala.org}; {ala@ala.org}.

$1,000 for Young Entrepreneurs to Start a Business

Youth Venture provides $1,000 grants to young entrepreneurs to start businesses, clubs, civic-minded organizations, or businesses. Open to those 12 to 20 who want to start a venture that aims at improving their community. Contact Youth Venture, 1700 North Moore Street, Suite 2000, Arlington, VA 22209; 703-527-4126; {http://www.youthventure.org}; {info@youthventure.org}; {http://www.youthventure.org/index.php?tg=addon/6/contact}.

Up to $15,000 for Youth

Sponsored by The Reader's Digest Foundation, the *National Youth of the Year Program is* designed to promote and recognize service to Club and community, academic performance and contributions to family and spiritual life. Clubs select a Youth of the Year who receives a certificate and medallion then enters state competition. State winners receive a plaque and enter the regional competition. Regional winners receive a $5,000 scholarship and enter a national competition held in Washington, DC. The National Youth of the Year receives an additional $10,000 scholarship and is installed by the President of the United States. Contact Boys & Girls Clubs of America, 1230 W. Peachtree St., N.W., Atlanta, GA 30309-3494; 404-487-5700; {http://www.bgca.org}; {info@bgca.org}.

Education Awards for Qualified Teens and Young Adults

This program, the result of a partnership between Boys & Girls Clubs of America and the Corporation for National Service (AmeriCorps), provides education awards to Club members ages 17 and 18 and Club alumni ages 19-24 who serve their Clubs and communities. CLUB Service recognizes young people's service, helps them access higher education opportunities and encourages them to pursue future careers as Club professionals. Contact Boys & Girls Clubs of America, 1230 W. Peachtree St., N.W., Atlanta, GA 30309-3494; 404-487-5700; {http://www.bgca.org}; {info@bgca.org}.

Money for Special Schooling in the U.S. and Canada

The Foundation provides support for Waldorf education in North America Waldorf Education is a developmentally appropriate, balanced education that integrates the arts and academics for children from preschool through twelfth grade, (Grades 10 through 12 are not yet available in Nelson). Waldorf Education encourages the development of each child's sense of truth, beauty, and goodness – an antidote to violence, alienation, and cynicism. Contact The Michael Foundation, Inc., 518 Kimberton Rd., PMB 320,

Phoenixville, PA 19460; Fax: 610-917-0800.

$5,000 for Student Essays about Senior Citizens

The KFC Corporation Contributions Program, through its Colonel's Way Award program, awards grants to 5th and 6th grade students submitting original essays written as a tribute to a special senior citizen. One student from each of the 50 states and the District of Columbia receives $100 and a $50 KFC gift certificate. One grand prize winner receives $5,000 and a new computer. The teacher of the grand prize winning student receives $2,500 and a $50 KFC gift certificate. The first 5 teachers to submit 20 or more essays receive $500 and a $25 KFC gift certificate. Contact KFC Corporation Contributions Program, c/o Corp. Contributions, P.O. Box 32070, Louisville, KY 40232. 502-456-8300; Application address for Colonel's Way Award: KFC Colonel's Way Award, 200 E. Randolph Drive, 63rd Floor, Chicago, IL 60601. 800-874-3273; {http://www.yum.com/community/colway.htm}; {email: alison.franklin@edelman.com}.

Free Cards, Letters and Photos From the White House

Whether it's about more money for your school or your solution to problems with the environment, all you need to do is send a note to the White House. You will receive a response on official White House stationary that will also include a picture of the President. Or you can simply write and ask for an 8x10 of the President and/or First Lady. Just make sure to include the name and address of where the note or pictures should be sent. If the mail is not quite fast enough for you, then check out the White House website. You can e-mail the President, Vice-President, or First Lady. If you can't make the trip to Washington, you can take a virtual tour of the White House, as well as view pictures and biographies of past presidents. There is even a special White House web page for kids! Contact The White House, 1600 Pennsylvania Avenue, NW, Washington, DC 20500; {www. whitehouse.gov}.

Volcano Hotline

Volcanoes can erupt at any time, and are one of the most destructive forces on Earth. You can request several free publications from the U.S. Geological Survey that describe volcanoes and volcanic activity, including: *Volcanoes, Volcanoes of the United States* and *Volcano Information for the General Public*. These publications are also available online at the address below. With a visit to the website, you can download how to make a paper volcano, and you can be connected with the volcano observatories in Alaska, the Cascade Mountains and Hawaii. Contact U.S. Geological, P.O. Box 25286, Denver, CO 80225; 888-ASK-USGS; {http://volcanoes. usgs.gov}; {www.usgs.gov/education. html}.

Money Money Money

You can learn a lot about your money from the Bureau of Engraving and Printing. Some information sheets available include: *Change in $1 From July 1929*, that describes the value of $1, *Engravers and Engraving*, that gives the history of the printed dollar, *Fun Facts About Dollars*, that contains money trivia, and *The Story of Money*. All of these are free and may help when the kids argue for a raise in their

allowance. Contact Bureau of Engraving and Printing, U.S. Department of the Treasury, 1500 Pennsylvania Avenue, NW, Washington, DC 20220; 202-622-2000; {www.treas.gov}.

Free Endangered Species Information

The time that threatened or endangered plants or species have left in this world is limited, but there are steps you can take to help them continue. It is important to teach children about endangered animals, so they can learn how their actions effect wildlife, as well as how to protect these animals from extinction. The U.S. Fish and Wildlife Service has several publications that explain how a plant or animal becomes endangered, and what is being done to protect them. Publications include *Endangered Species* and *Why Save Endangered Species?* Contact Publications Unit, U.S. Fish and Wildlife, National Conservation Training Center, Conservation Library, Rt. 1, Box 166, Shepherdstown, WV 25443; 304-876-7399, Fax: 304-876-7231; {http:// endangered.fws.gov/index.html}.

Earthquake Hotline

The National Earthquake Information Center (NEIC) located approximately 20,000 earthquakes each year, but these are only the most important of the many million earthquakes that are estimated to occur each year. To learn more about epicenters, the Richter scale, and seismology, contact the NEIC, as it is the foremost collector of rapid earthquake information in the world and is responsible for publications and dissemination of earthquake data. You can receive free publications on the severity of earthquakes and safety and survival in an earthquake. Contact the National Earthquake Information Center, U.S. Geological Survey, Box 25046, MS 967, Denver, CO 80225; 303-273-8500; Fax: 303-273-8450; {http://neic.cr.usgs.gov}.

Why Do Leaves Change Color?

The *Why Leaves Change Color* booklet can be used to learn why leaves change yellow, orange and red each fall. It also contains instructions on how to copy leaves with crayons and how to make leaf prints with a stamp pad. Contact Forest Service, U.S. Department of Agriculture, 12th and Independence Avenue, SW, P.O. Box 96090, Washington, DC 20090-6090; 202-205-8333; {www.fs.fed.us}

Free Water Safety Coloring Book

Spending a lot of time on your boat this summer? Make sure you follow all the boating safety rules, so your fun-filled summer is accident free. To help educate your kids on water and boating safety without sounding like you are lecturing, contact the Boating Safety Hotline. They have two coloring books for kids called *Water 'N Kids* and *Boats 'N Kids* that explain the basic concepts of water and boat safety. You can even sign up for very inexpensive boating classes. Contact Boating Safety Hotline, Consumer and Regulatory Affairs Branch, (G-NAB-5), Auxiliary, Boating and Consumer Affairs Division, Office of Navigation

Safety and Waterways Services, U.S. Coast Guard, 2100 2nd Street, SW, Room 1109, Washington, DC 20593; 800-368-5647; {www.uscgboating, org}.

Archeology Information

If archeology is your thing, then check out the National Park Service. They have the *Archeology and Ethnography Program* that has developed fascinating materials about our country's past and can help spur on your interests. They have several publications available including *Participate in Archeology* and *Archeology and Education*, and the website includes links to other archeology resources. Contact Publications, Archeology and Ethnography Program (2275), National Park Service, 1849 C Street, NW, Washington, DC 20240; 202-208-6843; {www.cr.nps.gov}

Help Kids Clean-Up

Let's Reduce and Recycle: Curriculum for Solid Waste Awareness provides lesson plans for grades K-12, and includes activities, skits, bibliographies, and other resources. Other booklets include *A Resource Guide of Solid Waste Educational Materials; School Recycling Programs; Recycle Today!*; and more. Contact RCRA/Superfund Hotline, Office of Solid Waste (5305W), 1200 Pennsylvania Avenue, NW, Washington, DC 20460; 800-424-9346; {www.epa.gov/epaoswer/education/teachers.htm}.

Free Art Videos

You don't need to leave the comfort of your home or school to view great works of art. The National Gallery of Art's Extension Program is an attempt to develop awareness in the visual arts and make its collections accessible to everyone, no matter how far away the Gallery they may live. The Gallery offers free loans of over 150 videos, slide sets, films, teaching packets, and videodiscs, covering a wide variety of topics and time periods. Contact the Department of Education Resources, Education Division, National Gallery of Art, 2000B South Club Drive, Landover, MD 20785; 202-737-4215; {www.nga.gov}.

Learn About Solar Energy

You can learn more about alternative sources of energy through the Energy Efficiency and Renewable Energy Clearinghouse. They have many publications just for kids including: *Learn About Renewable Energy; Solar Heating; Learn About Saving Energy*; and even *Solar Power Science Experiments*. Contact Energy Efficiency and Renewable Energy Clearinghouse, Mail Stop EE-1, Department of Energy, Washington, DC 20585; 202-586-9220; {www.eere .energy.gov/kids/}.

Learn About Bike Safety

The U.S. Consumer Product Safety Commission has several free publications targeting bicycle use. *Sprocket Man* is a comic book that teaches your child how to ride safely and provides important tips on dealing with traffic and pedestrians. *Ten Smart Routes to Bicycle Safety* gives ten rules everyone should follow while riding. *Kids Speak Out On Bike Helmets* provides facts on bike safety and the importance of wearing a helmet. And *Bicycle Safety: Message to Parents, Teachers and Motorists* is a two page fact sheet urging parents and teachers to teach proper bicycle riding skills and habits to children. Contact the U.S. Consumer Product Safety

Commission, Washington, DC 20207; 800-638-2772; 301-504-6816; {www.cpsc.gov}.

Archeology Vacations

"Passport In Time" helps you open a window to the past by allowing you to join activities such as archeological excavation, site mapping, drafting, laboratory and art work, collecting oral histories, restoration, and much more. Projects vary in length and there is no registration fee. Kids are allowed on many of the projects. Contact Passport In Time Clearinghouse, P.O. Box 31315, Tucson, AZ 85751; 800-281-9176; 520-722-2716; {www.passport intime.com}.

Help to Care for Your Kids Pet

A household pet needs special care, and no one knows this better than the Center for Veterinary Medicine. For this reason, they have published several fact sheets that help explain to children how to care for pets properly. So, write today. Your dog (cat or even horse) will thank you. Contact Center for Veterinary Medicine, Food and Drug Administration, 7519 Standish Place, HFV-12, Rockville, MD 20855; 301-827-3800; {www. fda.gov/cvm}.

Cyberspace Safety

If you're concerned for your children's well being on the Information Super Highway, get a free copy of *Parents Guide to the Internet*, or read it on the Internet. The American Academy of

Pediatrics worked with the U.S. Department of Education to develop this brochure, which showcases the Internet as an educational tool and gives tips on Internet safety for children, and highlights web sites for families and parents. Contact the American Academy of Pediatrics, 141 Northwest Point Boulevard, Elk Grove Village, IL 60007-1098; {www. aap.org}; 847-434-4000; 800-USA-LEARN-for free booklet; {www.ed. gov/pubs/parents/internet} - to download booklet.

"Give a Hoot. Don't Pollute"

The *Woodsy Owl Activity Guide* is jam-packed with ideas for classroom activities, list of kid's books, coloring pages, and more! There is a $2 charge for the guide. Contact The Smokey Bear-Woodsy Owl Center of Excellence, 402 SE 11th Street, Grand Rapids, MN 55744; {www.fs. fed.us/spf/woodsy/}.

"Only You Can Prevent Forest Fires"

Smokey the Bear is 60 years old and he is still teaching kids about forest fires. He now has a web site that gives kids all kinds of free information including: coloring pages, activities books, a story maker, and information on camping. Check out the web site for all kinds of information at {www. smokeybear.com}.

Help Your Child Learn

ED Pubs offers hundreds of brochures, pamphlets and other information to help your child learn. Titles include: *Put Reading First: Helping Your Child Learn to Read, Helping Your Child Learn History, Helping Your Child Learn Mathematics* and many more. Most titles are free on line or through the mail. Contact ED Pubs, P.O. Box

1398, Jessup, MD 20794-1398; 877-4-ED-PUBS; {www.edpubs.org}.

Send Your Kids to Outer Space

Space Camp, located in Huntsville, Alabama, offers kids ages 9-18, camp opportunities from weekends to 13 days in length. Full scholarships are available based on financial need, special learning needs or academic achievement for students in fourth through twelfth grades. Scholarships are available only for the specific 6-day programs. Scholarship students may choose from the Space Camp or the Aviation Challenge. Contact the Space Camp Scholarship Office, P.O. Box 070015, Huntsville, AL 35807; 800-63-SPACE; {www.spacecamp. com/scholarships/}.

Free Reading Information

Reading is Fundamental has something for everyone involved with children: parents, teachers, grandparents or even an older brother or sister. RIF programs throughout the country bring books to children at the greatest risk of failure. The web site offers individuals, as well as organizations a wide variety of information on reading. Parents can access activities, reading lists, motivation ideas and tips and tricks for children of all ages. Do your kids love to put on plays? There is a search that will list drama activities for each specific age group. There are many other searches including: art connections, vocabulary, writing, rainy day activities and home-to-school connections. They also offer brochures and handouts. They can be copied free online or you can contact them for multiple copies. Contact Reading Is Fundamental, 1825 Connecticut Avenue, NW, Suite 400, Washington, DC 20009; 877-RIF-READ; 202-673-0020; {www.rif.org}.

Get In Shape A Fun Way

The President's Challenge will help motivate all Americans to get fit and stay active. The Challenge offers a whole series of programs designed to help improve anyone's activity level. The Active Lifestyle Program is for those just getting started with daily fitness. You choose an activity from a long list of activities provided and participate in them 60 minutes a day, 5 days a week for children 18 and younger, for a total of six weeks. Track your activity on your personal activity log online and when you are finished you can order Presidential Active Lifestyle Award. The Presidential Champions Program is for those athletes who already active and want a new challenge. You choose an activity from the list and track your activities on the online log. You earn points for each activity you log. Points are based on the amount of energy each activity burns. You can work for the Bronze, Silver or Gold awards and order them when you have attained your goal. Contact The President's Challenge, 501 N. Morton, Suite 104, Bloomington, IN 47404; 800-258-8146; {www.presidentschallenge.org}.

Make Sure The Kids' Toys Are Safe

Is that toy you just bought safe for your child or has it been recalled? You can check the Consumer Product Safety Commissions *Toy Safety Recall* list. If you have found a toy that you feel isn't safe, you can report the product to the CPSC's hotline or report it online. They also offer a number of publications including: *BB Guns Can Kill, Dangers Associated with Children's Balloons, Strings and Straps on Toy Can Strangle Young Children* and more. Contact U.S. Consumer Product Safety Commission (CPSC), Publication Request, Washington, DC 20207-0001; 800-638-2772; {www.cpsc.gov}.

Get Your Child Ready For Kindergarten

Getting Your Child Ready for School, Parents as Partners Series is just one of a million bibliographic reports on educational-related resources in the ERIC database. You can download many of these articles at no cost. Contact ERIC Project, c/o Computer Sciences Corporation, 4483-A Forbes Boulevard, Lanham, MD 20706; 800-LET-ERIC; {http://eric.gov}.

How to Choose and Locate a Child Care Provider

Choosing child care is a very important decision for parents to make. Local Child Care Resources and Referral (CCR&R) organizations can help you. They can make referrals; provide information on state licensing requirements, availability of child care subsidies and other information. You can find your local CCR&R on the web site below. The Child Care Connector is a search engine to research the child care options in your area. They also publish many brochures including: *Finding Help Paying for Child Care, Choosing Quality Child Care for a Child with Special Needs, Matching Your Infant's or Toddler's Style to the Tight Child Care Setting* and more for no charge online or they will send you one in the mail. Contact Child Care Aware, 1319 F Street, NW, Suite 500, Washington, DC 20004; 800-424-2246; {www.childcareaware.org}.

Take Time Off When You Have A Baby

The Family and Medical Leave Act provides up to 12 weeks of unpaid leave in a 12 month period to take care of a new born baby or the adoption of a new family member. There are some limitations, so you'll need to check with your employer or the U.S. Department of Labor for additional information. Contact U.S. Department of Labor, Frances Perkins Building, 200 Constitution Avenue, NW 20210; 866-4-USWAGE; {www.dol.gov/esa/whd/fmla/}.

Help Collecting Child Support

The Office of Child Support Enforcement is a great resource for parents dealing with child support issues. They offer a number of publications and offer links to every states Child Support Enforcement Office. Contact the Office of Child Support Enforcement, Administration for Children and Families, 370 L'Enfant Promenade, SW, Washington, DC 20201; 202-401-9383; {www.acf.hhs.gov/programs/cse/}.

More Child Support Assistance

The Association for Children for Enforcement and Support is a non-profit organization working to improve child support enforcement. Memberships are available on a sliding scale based on income from$5 to $25 a year. Membership includes: Child Support Collection Guide, child support newsletter, workshops at reduced rates, and additional information. They also have an Absent Parent Locator Service. Contact ACES, P.O. Box 7842, Fredericksburg, VA 22404-7842; 800-738-ACES (2237); {www.childsupport-aces.org/}.

Legal Assistance

Legal Services Corporation offers civil legal assistance to those in need. The web site has a map of LSC Programs throughout the country. Contact Legal Services Corporation, 3333 K Street, NW, 3rd Floor, Washington, DC 20007-3522; 202-295-1500; {www.lsc.gov}.

Computer Repair and Training

Tech Corps is a non-profit organization designed to address the technology needs of the k-12 education group. There are branches in many states where volunteers train teachers and students in computer technology. They also repair and install computers, offer seminars and work with teachers to improve use of computers in the classroom. Contact Tech Corps, P.O. Box 334, Maynard, MA 01754; 978-897-8282; {www.techcorps.org}.

Free Learning Guide To Ellis Island

What would you bring to America? How would it feel to travel in steerage? What do all the symbols on the Statue of Liberty mean? These and other questions are answered in activity sheets distributed by the

National Park Service. In addition, educators can request a two week free loan of "Park In A Pack" which is a kit containing a teacher's guide, several videos, and educational activities dealing with Ellis Island. Contact Statue of Liberty National Monument, Liberty Island, New York, NY 10004; 212-263-3200; {www.nps.gov/stli/prod02.htm}.

Help Save the Planet

Teach your kids about the environment in a fun way. The U.S. Environmental Protection Agency has coloring books, activity sheets and even a Planet Protector Club for kids. The activities help increase your child's awareness of the Earth and recycling. Contact the U.S. Environmental Protection Agency, Office of Solid Waste, 1200 Pennsylvania, NW, Washington, DC 20460; {www.epa.gov/kids}.

What is Water?

The U.S. Geological Survey has developed a Water Resources Outreach Program webpage that provides a wealth of information on the Earth's water, water basics and more. They have also developed a series of posters that provide basic knowledge of water resources and cover topics such as wastewater, wetlands, groundwater, water quality and navigation. Contact U.S. Geological Survey Branch Information Services, Box 25286, Denver, CO

80225; 888-ASK-USGS; {http://water. usgs.gov/outreach/order.html}.

Have Your Kids Do A Family Oral History

The Grand Generation: Interviewing Guide & Questionnaire lists guidelines for collecting folklore and oral history from older tradition-bearers. It includes a general guide to conducting interviews, a list of sample questions, and examples of ways to preserve and present findings. This can be accessed for free at the following web site {http://smithsonianeducation.org/migr ations/seek1/grand1.html}. The Smithsonian Center for Folklore and Cultural Heritage offers the publication, *The Smithsonian Folklore and Oral History Interviewing Guide* with all kinds of suggestions for kids to record their family's oral history. You can view this document at {www.folklife.si.edu/resources/pdf/Int erviewingGuide.pdf}. Contact Smithsonian Institution Center for Folklore and Cultural Heritage, 750 9th Street, NW, Suite 4100, Washington, DC 20560-0953; 202-275-1150.

Create Your Own Family Tree

There is nothing like bringing a family together and showing them they all share the same roots. The Archives maintains ship passenger arrival records dating back to the 1820's, and its staff will even do research for you if you supply some basic information, such as the port of entry, passenger name, and date of arrival. If they find your ancestor, they will send you a notice. The manifests consist of 2-by-3 foot sheets. Listing passengers' age and occupations, and if after 1906 the information will include amount of money, language spoken, even height and weight. If you want to purchase a copy of the page of the manifest, the cost is $1.90 per page with a minimum of $10 for mail order. Contact The National Archives and Records Administration, 8601 Adelphi Road, College Park, MD 20740-6001; 866-272-6272; {www.nara.gov}.

We The People

We all had to memorize the Preamble of the Constitution during our school years. It might be fun to see the whole text of the Constitution, Bill of Rights, and The Declaration of Independence. You could test you kids' knowledge of each of the documents. The documents can be found at the National Archives & Records Administration website. To view the documents, go to their web site at {www.archives.gov/welcome/index.html}. You may also contact them at U.S. National Archives & Records Administration, 8601 Adelphi Road, College Park, MD 20740-6001; 866-272-6272.

Bring a Cast-Iron Umbrella

Acid Rain: A Student's First Sourcebook is a great way to teach kids about the environment and what needs to be done to protect it. Designed for grades 4-8, the sourcebook describes the effects of acid rain, solutions, experiments, and activities. The website also has links to other acid rain resources. Contact Acid Rain Division, Environmental Protection Agency, Ariel Rios Building, 1200 Pennsylvania Avenue, NW, Washington, DC 20460; 202-272-0167; {www.epa.gov/Region4/topics/air/acidrain.html}.

Become A Disaster Action Kid

Herman the FEMA spokescrab, will help your kids become ready for any disaster. Floods, wildfires, hurricanes, tornadoes, earthquakes, winter storms,

even National Security Emergencies are all disasters that can happen that you can prepare for. What can you and your kids do to prepare your family, siblings, and pets before the disaster strikes? Contact the Federal Emergency Management kid's web site for all kinds of informational brochures, fact sheets, posters and more. Contact, FEMA, P.O. Box 2012, Jessup, MD 20794-2012; 800-480-2520; {www. fema.gov/kids/}.

The Next Thomas Edison

If your kid loves to take things apart and create new things, then he/she has the inventor's spirit. The Patent and Trademark Office has developed a great kids web site. They offer links, puzzles, games and information about obtaining patents. The web site also provides information for parents, teachers and coaches. Contact The United States Patent and Trademark Office, Mail Stop USPTO Contact Center, P.O. Box 1450, Alexandria, VA 22313-1450; 800-786-9199; 703-308-4357; {www.uspto.gov/go/kids/}.

Bring The Birds To You

Kids love to look at pictures of birds in books. Why not teach them to go outside and look at the real thing? The U.S. Fish & Wildlife Service has a web site for students and educators to learn all about animals. They can view pictures and videos online not just on birds, but many other kinds of animals. For additional information call 800-344-WILD or check out their web site at {http://educators.fws.gov/}.

Free or Low Cost Rocks

Lots of fourth graders across the country study about rocks and minerals. Contact your state geologist located at your state capital. They have informational sheets, brochures, videos, slides, and activities designed to bring rocks alive to kids. Some states even have field trips for teachers and kids to learn more about the rocks and minerals in their region. Many states, like Ohio, offer free rock samples to give kids that hands-on experience at rock and mineral identification and classification.

Free Information On Outer Space

Want to help your child build a solar system? *Solar System Puzzle Kit* is an activity where kids are asked to assemble an eight-cube paper puzzle, and when solved, they can create a miniature solar system. Information on rockets, the moon, all of the planets, current Space Shuttle information, space exploration and more is available through NASA's incredible educational resources system for educators, parents and students. You can download hundreds of publications, chat with experts, and look at the latest pictures form space. Each state has an Educators Resource Center that can provide you with information as well. Contact NASA, Education Division, Washington, DC 20546; {http:// spacelink.nasa.gov}.

International Studies

What is the leading export from Ireland? How many people live in Ethiopia? The federal government has two websites that can provide enough information for a two page country report, and it doesn't even involve going to the library! Check out {http://lcweb2.loc.gov/frd/cs/cshome.html#about} and {www.state.gov/r/pa/ei/bgn/}.

What To Read

Sometimes choosing a book is difficult, and sometimes kids need a little encouragement to keep reading. The Sylvan Learning Foundation has a website where you can plug in your child's reading level, type of books the child finds interesting, and the computer will do a search for you for free. You will be able to print a list of books, including grade level and subject focus, to take with you to the library. Your kids can take quizzes on books they read, as well as earn points and prizes. To sign up, check out Sylvan Learning Foundation at {www.bookadventure.com}.

Free Help For Parenting Kids

KidsPeace has parenting brochures including: *24 Ways You Can Prevent Child Abuse, 7 Standards for Effective Parenting, 15 Ways to Help Your Kid Through Crisis, What Every Preteen Really Wants You To Know, Grief Packet, Street Drug Information,* and *Join the Fight: Help Kids Eat Right.* To receive your free information, print out the form on the KidsPeace website, or view online. KidsPeace Fulfillment Department, 4125 Independence Drive, Suite #4, Schnecksville, PA 18078; {www.kidspeace.org}.

$5,000 to Help Low and Moderate Income Families Adopt a Child

The Gift of Adoption Fund provides adoption funding, grants, and financial assistance to low and moderate-income families seeking to adopt, and who could not otherwise afford adoption without assistance. Applicants are evaluated based on their income, assets, liabilities, earning potential and other financial resource opportunities. Average grants to individual families range from $2,000 to $5,000. Contact Gift of Adoption Fund, 101 E. Pier St., 1st Fl., Port Washington, WI 53074; 262-268-1386, 877-905-ADOP (2367); Fax: 262-268-1387.

FREE MONEY FOR ELEMENTARY AND HIGH SCHOOL

Private Voucher Clearinghouse

CFA Children First America) serves as a national clearinghouse for privately funded voucher programs that provide everything from support services to new programs on videotapes for K-12 grades. These private tuition grants and tax funded options give low-income families the power to choose the K-12 school that will best accomplish their needs. The website has a list of the U.S. programs. Just click on the area of the program that is located near or in your hometown. The website also gives you a history about school choice legislation, school choice research, and some testimonies on how you can make a difference in the program. Contact the Children First America, P.O. Box 29928, Austin, TX 78755; 512-345-1083; {www.childrenfirstamerica.org}

$1,700 Washington Scholarship Fund, Inc.

The Washington School Fund provides financial assistance for children to attend either private or parochial schools in the Washington, D.C. area for grades K through 12th. The maximum amount received per child is $7,500 for low-income students. Contact the Washington Scholarship

Fund, Inc., 1133 15th Street, NW, Suite 580, Washington, DC 20005; 202-293-5560; Fax: 202-293-7893; {www.washingtonscholarshipfund.org}.

$1,400 For Elementary Students In New York City

The School Choice Scholarships Foundation provides funds to cover the annual tuition costs up to $1,400 maximum per child and it is guaranteed for at least three years. Scholarships are only for elementary school children who are currently enrolled in a New York City's public schools, and meet the income levels requirements. Students are selected by a lottery drawing with priority given to children who attend the lowest performing schools. Contact the Children's Scholarship Fund, 8 West

38th Street, 9th Floor, New York, NY 10018; 215-515-7137; Fax: 212-750-2840; {www.scholarshipfund.org/nyc}.

Dentist Offers Scholarships for Elementary School Children

For several years Dr. Albert Landucci has sponsored awards and scholarships to the less fortunate. Scholarships are based on academic excellence, community service, volunteering, science and mathematics excellence and dental assisting. Scholarships are offered in the San Mateo Elementary School District and all the high schools in San Mateo For more information about the awards, scholarships and to see if your school is in the district, visit Dr. Landucci's website. Contact: Albert O. J. Landucci, D.D.S, 2720 Edison Street, San Mateo, CA 94403-2495; 650-574-4444; 650-574-4441; {www. drlanducci.com}.

Free Private Schools For Kids of Color

A Better Chance's mission is work with minority students from the 6th grade through eleventh to open opportunity doors that otherwise would not be open without a helping hand. There are several programs that include helping students receive financial aid for attending private local schools, boarding schools, or summer programs to help prepare for college. Contact A Better Chance, 240 West 35th Street, 9th Floor, New York, NY 10001-2506; 646-346-1310; Fax: 646-562-7865; {www.abetterchance.org}.

Tuition Assistance for Black Students

The Black Student Fund has provided financial assistance and support services to African American students and their families in the Washington, DC area for over 34 years. All financial assistance is based on a sliding scale. Contact the Black Student Fund, 3636 16th Street, NW, 4th Floor, Washington, DC 20010; 202-387-1414; {www.blackstudent fund.org}; Email: {mail@blackstudent fund.org}.

Money For Future Writers

For those future award-winning writers, Amelia Magazine awards $200 for a high school student's first publication. First publications can be a previously unpublished poem, a nonfiction essay or a short story. Deadline for the contest is May 15. Write or call for further information. Amelia Student Award, Amelia Magazine, 329 East Street, Bakersfield, CA 93304; 805-323-4064.

$2,000 For Children In Arizona

Arizona children in K-12, with incomes up to $29,693 can receive up to $2,000 per child per school year with a minimum three-year commitment to qualified children. Contact the Arizona Scholarship Fund, P.O. Box 2576, Mesa, AZ 85214; 480-497-4564; Fax: 480-497-4737; Email: {Cham Bria@Azscholarships.org}; or Arizona Scholarship Fund, P.O. Box 31354, Tucson, AZ 85751-1354; 502-271-6857; or Arizona Scholarship Fund, P.O. Box 293, Flagstaff, AZ 86002; 928-286-0233; Email: {Sandy@AZ scholarships.org}.

Education Loans Up To $20,000 For Grades K Thru 12

As with college loans, there are many financial institutions that provide loans for families to send their children to private or parochial schools at the elementary and secondary school levels. Listed below are some of the organizations that are providing these types of loans. Be sure to be aware that you can always contact your state banking commissioner by calling your state capitol operator listed in the Appendix.

1) The Education Resources Institute (TERI)
   P.O. Box 312
   Boston, MA 02117
   800-255-TERI
   {www.teri.org}

2) First Marblehead Corporation
   The Prudential Tower
   800 Boylston Street, 34th Floor
   Boston, MA 02199-8157
   617-638-2231
   {http://gateloan.com}

3) FACTS SCHOLAR Loan Program
   P.O. Box 67037
   100 N. 56th Street, Suite 306
   Lincoln, NE 68504
   800-624-7092
   402-466-1063
   Fax: 402-466-1136
   {www.factsmgt.com}

$25,000 for an Audio Essay

The 57-year-old contest is open to 9th through 12th graders. Students should submit a 3-5 minute essay based on a patriotic theme established by VFW. Contact your school counselor or principal to apply, or contact the VFW listed and they will tell you where your local chapter is located. First place national winners receive a $25,000 savings bond. Contact VFW Voice of Democracy Essay Contest, Veterans of Foreign Wars of the United States, VFW Building, 406 West 34th Street, Kansas City, MO 64111; 816-986-

1117; {www.vfw.org}, {info@vfw.org}.

Money For Young Writers

Contestants receive a cash award for writing a short story that promotes brotherhood and is 4,000 words maximum. The money can be used for anything. Contact Aim Magazine Short Story Contest, P.O. Box 1174, Maywood, IL 60153; 708-344-4414; {www.aimmagazine.org}.

$10,000 for Artists

Any high school students that need help with furthering their education can enter the VFW Ladies Auxiliary National Patriotic Creative Art Competition. Students should submit their entry through the VFW Ladies Auxiliary Local Chapter first. Finalists from the local chapters are selected for the grand prize competition. First place grand prize winners receive $10,000, and an all expense paid trip to the VFW Ladies Auxiliary Conference for Community Service in Washington, DC. Second place winners receive $5,000, and 3rd place winners receive $2,500. Contact VFW Ladies Auxiliary National Patriotic Creative Art Competition, Ladies Auxiliary to the VFW National Headquarters, 406 West 34th Street, Kansas City, MO 64111; 816-561-8655; Fax: 816-931-4753; {www.ladiesauxvfw.com}.

$1,500 For Young Science Types

Each year General Learning Communication with Dupont sponsors a science essay contest for children in grades 7-12. First place winners of each division receive $1,500, and an expense paid trip to Space Center Houston with their parents. This trip includes airfare, hotel and an allowance. Four finalists receive a

$500 prize and honorable mentions receive $50. The deadline for the contest is January 23. Write or visit the website to obtain the entry application and mail first class in a 9x12 envelope. Contact Dupont Science Challenge, Science Essay Awards Program, c/o General Learning Communications, 900 Skokie Blvd, Suite 200, Northbrook, IL 60062; 847-205-3000; Fax: 847-564-8197; {www.glcomm.com/dupont}.

$150 For Young Artists

American Automobile Association (AAA) awards prizes up to $150 for children in K to 12th grade and $5,000 for college students in their School Traffic Safety Program. In the K-12 division, children submit posters. In the senior high division, students can submit essays, brochures, and even creative videos. Contact your local AAA office and ask for the School Traffic Safety Division; {www.aaa.com}.

$40,000 Scholarships For Kids From K to 8th Grade

There are 40 programs nationwide and each serves local families. The scholarships averaged $1,100 for children from K through 8th grade to attend private schools. Check the web site for the local offices throughout the country. Contact the Children's Scholarship Fund, 8 West 38th St. 9th Floor, New York, N Y 10018; 212-515-7100; {www.scholarshipfund.org}.

$10,000 For Young Inventors

Craftsman sponsors a program where students either invent or modify a tool independently. Two winners from grades 2-5 and 6-8 will receive a $10,000 savings bond. Ten finalists, five from each grade will receive a

$5,000 savings bond. The teachers of these winners and their schools will receive prizes from Sears. Every contestant will receive a gift and certificate of appreciation. Contact Craftsman/NSTA Young Inventors Awards Program, National Science Teachers Association, 1840 Wilson Boulevard, Arlington, VA 22201; 888-494-4994; {www.nsta.org/programs/craftsman}, {younginventors@nsta.org}.

$1,000 For Writing About Technology

Students in K-12 from the U.S. and Canada can use their imagination and creative writing and illustrating skills to compose a ten page or less essay to indicate what technology would be like 20 years from now. There are four categories for students to participate: grades K-3, grades 4-6, grades 7-9 and grades 10-12. Final first place winners receive a $10,000 savings bond, second place winners receive a $5,000 savings bond, and teachers receive Toshiba prizes. Contact Toshiba/NSTA Explora Vision Awards Program, 1840 Wilson Boulevard, Arlington, VA 22201; 800-EXPLORE9; {www.exploravision.org}, {exploravision@ nsta.org}.

$1,000 a Year for 3 Years In Kentucky

School Choice Scholarships Inc. (SCSI) in Jefferson County, Kentucky awards its kids with 100 new partial-scholarships per year in addition to the 325 scholarships awarded just last year! If your Jefferson County child is in K-6 and your family meets the Federal School Lunch regulations, you can be awarded 50%-60% of all tuition (up to $2000) for THREE YEARS! SCSI is willing to make a three-year commitment to making sure your child can enjoy the freedom of school choice! Contact SCSI, P.O. Box 221546, Louisville, KY 40252-1546; 502-254-7274; {www.schoolchoice ky.com}.

$1,450 For Families In Texas

The Childrens Educational Opportunity Foundation is a private scholarship program that will pay one-half of a child's tuition at any private school or out-of-district public school in Harris County (up to $1450). If your Harris County, TX family meets the Federal School Lunch Program requirements, your child enrolled in 1st to 8th grade may apply. This year, the Foundation hopes to award 550 students with the ability to practice school choice! Contact The Childrens Educational Opportunity Foundation, 109 North Post Oak Lane, Suite 350, Houston, TX 77024; 713-722-8555; Fax: 713- 722-7442; {www.houston ceo.org}.

$1,200 in Arizona

Arizona School Choice Trust (coupled with the Childrens Scholarship Fund) will grant 25%-75% towards your child's choice of educational institution (up to $3000). If you live in Arizona, meet the Federal School Lunch Program guidelines, and your child is in a grade from K-12, you are eligible to apply! The Arizona School Choice Trust has awarded more than 500 four-year awards and through tax-deductible donations adds more

students to the program each year. To ensure your child's success in the program, ASCT requires that while enrolled, your student must maintain a 90% attendance rate. Contact Arizona School Choice Trust, Inc., 1951 W. Camelback Rd., Suite 445, Phoenix, AZ 85015; 602-454-1360; Fax: 602-995-1449; {www.asct.org}.

Over $5 Million More For Texas Children

The Today Foundation of Dallas, Texas joins with the Children's Education Fund and the Children's Scholarship Fund (CSF) to be able to grant Dallas students in grades K-8 with help to attend their schools of choice. The assistance pays half of the tuition (up to $1500) to any Dallas area school parent. Contact Children's Education Fund, P.O. Box 225748, Dallas, TX 75222-5748; 972-298-1811; Fax: 972-296-6369; {www.TodayFoundation.org}, {today@todayfoundation.org}.

Up to $1,800 in Michigan

The Education Freedom Fund provides low-income Michigan families with school choice for their K-8 students by providing tuition assistance through scholarships. Scholarships are need-based to families that qualify for the federal government's free or reduced lunch program. Maximum annual scholarships are $1000 annually. Parents must pay a minimum of $500 tuition. Education Freedom Fund, P.O. Box 230078, Grand Rapids, MI 49523-0078; 800-866-8141; {www.education freedomfund.org}.

Free Classes For Kids With A.D.D.

The nonprofit organization, *Children and Adults with Attention Deficit Disorder (CHADD)*, identifies a number of federal laws that require the government to provide children with this disorder special educational services. It is only recently that these children became eligible for such services, so many eligible children may not be receiving what they deserve.

To learn more about these free educational services, or to find out more and how to treat a child with ADD, contact: CHADD, 8181 Professional Place, Suite 150, Landover, MD 20785; 800-233-4050, 301-306-7070, Fax: 301-306-7090; {www.chadd.org}.

LEGAL SERVICES

Did you know that the government Will Fight For You For Free? Our government offers a great benefit to every consumer that has a problem with any company, organization or professional. There is some government office that regulates them all and if you find that government office, they will investigate your problem and get you justice all for free. And the  greatest thing about using the government is not that they are free, but they are more powerful than any lawyer you can ever dream of hiring, even Johnny Cochran.

For example, if your insurance company does not pay a claim, you can call the company and they will tell you about some bureaucratic rule about why they won't pay you. So what do you do? Don't hire an attorney to fight that insurance company, because the insurance company's attorneys are better than your attorney at fighting claims, and the insurance company has very little to lose if they fight you. The worst they can lose is your business, which they probably lost already. Or they can lose by having to pay what they owe you anyway. So they are willing to fight you all day while you are being charged big lawyer fees.

But if you contact the government office that regulates insurance companies (your state insurance commissioner's office), they will contact your insurance company for you, even if you are wrong. Now the insurance company has an entirely new problem. The insurance commissioner allows the insurance company to do business in the state, so if they really do something wrong in dealing with the commissioner, they can lose ALL OF THEIR BUSINESS, not just your business. Plus, the insurance company knows it costs a lot of money just to communicate back and forth with a government agency and it could be a lot cheaper just to give you what you want. You now have the power, so use it.

1) Help Finding Who Regulates Any Company You Are Having Trouble With

Most organizations and professionals are regulated at the state level including: insurance companies, credit card companies, banks, mail order companies, retail companies, contractors, doctors, and even lawyers. To find what office regulates your problem, contact your state capitol operator located in your state capital by dialing 411 or go on line to www.govengine.com and search for the regulatory bodies in your state. Your state Attorney General's office (or Secretary of State's office) should also be able to assist you.

2) *To find free legal services*

If a government office can't help, there are two places to contact when you need a lawyer, but can't afford one. The Legal Services Corporation provides free legal services to those that meet certain income requirements. If you exceed those limits, they may be able to refer you to some place for more help. They have offices throughout the country. Legal Services Corporation, 3333 K St., NW, 3rd Floor, Washington, DC 20009; 202-295-1500; {www.lsc.gov}. Many lawyers work pro bono depending upon your situation. Contact your state bar association to see if someone there can help. You can contact your state capitol operator by calling 411, or the American Bar Association, 321 N. Clark St., Chicago, IL 60610; 312-988-5000; {www.abanet.org/soc/probono/pip.html}.

3) *Help From Your Elected Officials*

People forget that they can turn to their congressman and senators when they are at a loss for help. Each office has a case manager who can direct you to the appropriate person or office for help in resolving your complaint. You can contact your state representative or senator by contacting your state capitol operator at 411 or online at {www.govengine.gov}. You can contact your representative and senators in Congress by calling U.S. House of Representatives, Washington, DC 20515; 202-224-3121; {www.house.gov} or U.S. Senate, Washington, DC 20510; 202-224-3121; {www.senate.gov}.

Free Lawyers for Millionaires

No matter what your income, you can get the most powerful organization in the world, your government, to fight for you to:

1. Establish paternity;
2. Set up a court order for child support;
3. Track down a missing parent and collect your child support; and even
4. Get the courts to adjust child support orders when circumstances change.

Actually I lied. There are a few states that may charge you up to $25.00. So the maximum you will pay is $25.00. So, why hire an attorney, who may or may not know the law, and will charge you up to $200 an hour, when you can call someone who wrote the law, whose duty is to enforce it for you, and who is free?

Contact your state Child Support Enforcement Office, or contact Office of Child Support Enforcement, U.S. Department of Health and Human Services, 370 L'Enfant Promenade, SW, Washington, DC 20447; 202-401-9383; {www.acf.dhhs.gov/programs/cse/}.

Rid Your Neighborhood of Troublemakers

Some states allow local community groups to get tenants or property owners thrown out of the neighborhood — under civil laws, not criminal laws — if they are involved with drugs or are a nuisance to the community. It's easier to enforce a civil law than a criminal law. Which is probably why O.J. Simpson lost his civil trial, but won his criminal trial.

The Community Law Center in Maryland provides free legal assistance to communities in Maryland to enforce these laws. Their services are free to non-profit community groups who seek to rid their neighborhood of troublemakers.

To find out if your community has similar services, contact your state Attorney General's office. The Community Law Center can be reached at 2500 Maryland Avenue, Baltimore, MD 21218; 410-366-0922; Fax: 410-366-7763; {www.commun itylaw.org}; {clawc@aol.com}.

Free Legal Help with Family, Consumer, Housing Income, Work, Children and Senior Issues

Legal Services Corporation is a collection of over 269 government supported local offices that provide free legal services in their area. Over 5000 attorneys and paralegals are available to individuals and families that are under certain income limits. The maximum income can be up to $30,000 for a family of four, or even more depending on certain financial obligations. Contact your state information operator listed in the Appendix and ask for the Legal Services Office or contact: Legal Services Corporation, 3333 K Street, NW, 3rd Floor, Washington, DC 20009-3522; 202-295-1500; {www. lsc.gov}.

Help for Families Fighting Veterans Benefits

Through low cost publications, training courses and other services, the **National Veterans Legal Services Program** has been helping veterans get their due. Current publications include: *VA Claims*, *Agent Orange*, and *Gulf War Benefits*. Contact: National Veterans Legal Services Program, 2001 S Street, NW, Suite 610, Washington, DC 20009; 202-265-8305; {www.nvlsp.org}.

Free Legal Assistance for Domestic Violence Problems

Seven days a week, 24 hours a day, you can call the hotline and not only get access to sources that will solve your immediate problem, but also get information and sources in your area that can explain your legal options and get you through the legal process. Contact National Domestic Violence Hotline, P.O. Box 161810, Austin, TX 78716; 800-799-SAFE; TTY: 800-787-3224; {ndvh@ndvh.org}; {www. ndvh.org}.

10,000 Lawyers that Work for Free

If your income is less than $32,000 (for a family of 4), it's worth checking out the pro bono legal services that are available in your state. And even if your income is more, it's worth checking because some of these services have flexible requirements. Every year tens of thousands of lawyers volunteer their services to people who need help with almost any kind of problem.

For a listing of pro bono organizations in your state, contact your state bar association listed in your state capitol. The state information operator listed in the Appendix can provide you with a number, or you can contact: American Bar Association 321 N. Clark St., Chicago, IL 60610; 312-988-5000; {www.abanet.org/soc/probono/pip.htm l}.

Free Lawyers Will Fight for Your Rights

We've all heard of the *American Civil Liberties Union (ACLU)*. They have over 300 offices around the country and handle close to 6,000 cases a year. The ACLU has more than 60 staff attorneys who collaborate with at least 2,000 volunteer attorneys in handling cases. They have appeared before the Supreme Court more than any other organization except the U.S. Department of Justice. If you feel that your civil liberties have been violated, they may take your case. Contact the local ACLU office listed in your telephone directory or the main office website can provide you with a local contact: ACLU - American Civil Liberties Union, 125 Broad Street, 18th Floor, New York, NY 10004-2400; {www.aclu.org/}.

Free Legal Help with Sexual Harassment at Work or School

Free assistance to women and girls who are facing sex, or race discrimination, sexual harassment at work or at school, pregnancy, discrimination, or problems with family medical leave and other employment issues related specifically to women. The staff offers information and answers questions, and occasionally can draft "demand" letters, demanding that an employer or other person or organization stop doing something. In some circumstances, they can help you pursue internal grievance or administrative procedures, and in some precedent-setting cases, they will provide legal representation.

Contact Equal Rights Advocates, 1663 Mission Street, Suite 250, San Francisco, CA 94103; 415-621-0672;

Fax: 415-621-6744; Advice and Counseling Line: 800-839-4ERA; {www.equalrights.org}.

Free Legal Help for Breast Cancer Patients

If you are a breast cancer patient living in California, you maybe eligible to receive free legal assistance on issues such as:

♦ Debt collection problems with hospital and doctor bills.

♦ Barriers to access to diagnosis and treatment.

♦ Negotiations with insurance carriers for coverage and payment options.

♦ Housing discrimination.

♦ Employment discrimination.

♦ Temporary guardianships or modification of custody arrangements.

If you don't live in California, ask them if they are aware of similar services in your area. Contact Breast Cancer Legal Project, California Women's Law Center, 3460 Wilshire Blvd., Suite 1102, Los Angeles, CA 90010; 213-637-9900; Fax: 213-637-9909; {www.cwcl.org/}; {cwcl@cwcl.org}.

Free Women's Law Centers

Rich or poor, women in **Maryland** can get free telephone help in filling out the forms to represent themselves in family court matters that are simple and uncontested. The hotline number is *800-845-8550* and it operates Mondays through Fridays 9:30 am to 4:30 pm. Or women can call the hotline for information on family law issues, such as, how to obtain a separation, child custody, child support, and how to escape domestic violence. Contact: The Women's Law Center of Maryland, Inc., 305 West

Chesapeake Ave., Towson, MD 21205; 410-321-8761; {admin@ wlcmd.org}; {www.wlcmd.org}.

Women in the state of **Washington** can call a free legal *Information and Referral Lline* that is staffed with attorneys and paralegals to respond to questions about family law or employment. They also can receive legal rights publications including *Sexual Harassment in Employment and Education*; *Family Law in Washington State: Your Rights and Responsibilities*; and *Options for Unmarried Parents*. You can also attend free legal workshops, or receive help in filling out legal forms, and free legal consultations in domestic violence cases. Contact Northwest Women's Law Center, 3161 Elliott Ave., Suite 101, Seattle WA 98121; 206 682 9552; Fax: 206 682 9556; Legal Information and Referral: 206-621-7691; {NWWLC@nwwlc.org}; {www.nwwlc.org}.

Free Legal Help to Fight Your Union At Work

If you feel your rights have been violated by compulsory unionism, or you simply have a question about your Right to Work, legal experts are available for free to help answer your questions. Contact The National Right to Work Legal Defense Foundation, 8001 Braddock Rd., Springfield, VA 22160; 800-336-3600; {www.nrtw.org}.

Free Legal Help for People with Disabilities

The disability laws not only cover people with disabilities that everyone can see. It's also for children who aren't getting the education they need from the local school, or for the cancer patient who feels discriminated against

at work. A free hotline will help you learn about your rights, help you enforce them, and will even handle some high impact legal cases. Contact Disability Rights Education and Defense Fund, Inc., 2212 Sixth Street, Berkeley, CA 94710; 510-644-2555 V/TTY; Fax: 510-841-8645; {edf@dredf.org}; {www.dredf.org}.

Free Legal Help for Welfare Rights

Over 157 local organizations around the country fight for the rights of low-income people on welfare. These organizations can be a good place to turn to ensure that you are getting the proper benefits, and for knowing your rights in dealing with the bureaucracy.

Contact your local social services agency to locate an office near you or the website for the Welfare Law Center that contains a directory of all the organizations. Contact Welfare Law Center, 275 Seventh Ave., Suite 1205, New York, NY 10001; 212-633-6967; {dirk@ welfarelaw.org}; {www.lincproject.org/}.

Free Legal Help to Fight for Home Schooling Rights

The Home School Legal Defense Association (HSLDA) provides legal help for members on home schooling issues. Families receive legal consultation by letter and phone, and representation for negotiations with local officials, and court proceedings.

HSLDA also takes the offensive, filing actions to protect members against government intrusion and to establish legal precedent. On occasion, HSLDA will handle precedent-setting cases for non-members, as well. Contact: HSLDA, P.O. Box 3000, Purcellville, VA 20134; 540-338-5600; Fax: 540-338-2733; {www.hslda.org}.

Free Consulting in Sex Discrimination Law Suits

If, as a woman, you feel discriminated against in higher education, the Legal Advocacy Fund (LAF) of the American Association of University Women (AAUW) may be able to help by providing financial support for sex discrimination lawsuits. LAF organizes a network of volunteer attorneys and social scientists who consult with women on legal strategy, informational resources, and the strength of current or potential lawsuits. Contact AAUW Legal Advocacy Fund, Dept. LAF.INT., American Association of University of Women, 1111 16th St., NW, Washington, DC 20036; 800-326-AAUW; Fax: 202-872-1425; TDD: 202-785-7777; {info@aauw.org}; {www.aauw.org}.

Free Legal Rights for Women's Issues

Legal Momentum has a hotline that provides free information and referrals on women's issues including reproductive rights, violence against women, economic justice, and gender equity in education. They also provide low-cost legal guides on the following topics:

A Guide to Court Watching in Domestic Violence and Sexual Assault Cases
Divorce and Separation
Domestic Violence and Child Custody
Employment Sexual Harassment & Discrimination (Spanish)
Pregnancy & Parental Leave
Sexual Harassment in Housing
Sexual Harassment in the Schools
Sexual Harassment in the Schools: A Blueprint for Action (Spanish)
Violence Against Women
How to Find a Lawyer (free)

Contact NOW LDEF, 395 Hudson Street, New York, NY 10014; 212-925-6635 (9:30 a.m. to 11:00 p.m. EST); Fax: 212-226-1066; {peo@legalmomentum.org}; {www.legalmomentum.org}.

Legal Assistance for Overseas Teachers

Free legal aid is available for teachers employed in U.S. Department of Defense schools overseas and are members of the *Federal Education Association (FEA)*. The FEA legal staff conducts arbitration and other legal actions to ensure the rights and benefits of teachers. Contact Federal Education Association, 1201 16th St. NW, Washington, DC 20036; 202-822-7850; Fax: 202-822-7867; {FEA_Legal/Pres@odedodea.edu}; {www.feaonline.org}.

Free Legal Help for Pregnant Teens Discriminated in Honors Society

Feminists for Life of America, along with the ACLU, got the a federal court to rule that two high school seniors, whose school denied them National Honor Society membership because they became pregnant and chose to give birth, must be admitted into the society. Contact Feminists for Life of America, 733 15th St. NW, Suite 1100, Washington, DC 20005; 202-737-FFLA; {www.feministforlife.org}.

Free Legal Help with Civil Liberties, Religious Freedom, and Parental Rights

The Rutherford Institute defends people who have been denied civil and human rights without charging them for such services. The issues they cover include civil liberties, religious freedom, parental rights, and sexual harassment. You may remember them from their involvement in the Paula Jones case. Contact The Rutherford Institute, Legal Department, P.O. Box 7482, Charlottesville, VA 22906; 434-978-3888; {www.rutherford.org}.

Free Legal Help for Gays and Those with HIV/AIDS

Lambda carries out legal work on issues such as discrimination in employment, housing, public accommodations, and the military; HIV/AIDS-related discrimination and public policy issues; parenting and relationship issues; equal marriage rights; equal employment and domestic partnership benefits; "sodomy" law challenges; immigration issues; anti-gay initiatives; and free speech and equal protection rights. Contact one of the offices listed below.

National Headquarters Lambda
120 Wall Street, Suite 1500
New York, NY 10005-3904

212-809-8585
Fax: 212-809-0055

Western Regional Office
3325 Wilshire Boulevard
Suite 1300
Los Angeles, CA 90010-1729
213-382-7600
Fax: 213-351-6050

Midwest Regional Office
11 East Adams, Suite 1008
Chicago, IL 60603-6303
312-663-4413
Fax: 312-663-4307

Southern Regional Office
1447 Peachtree Street, NE
Suite 1004
Atlanta, GA 30309-3027
404-897-1880
Fax: 404-897-1884

South Central Regional Office
3500 Oak Lawn Ave., Suite 500
Dallas, TX 75219-6722
214-219-8585
Fax: 214-219-4455

Lambda's website is {www.lambda legal.org}.

Free Help Collecting Child Support

An association of concerned parents helps others learn about their rights and the remedies available for collecting what is due to them. Some services are free, others are for those who join for only $20. They can show you that you don't need to use a professional collection agency, and they will even contact officials on your behalf. Contact Association for Children for Enforcement and Support (ACES), P.O. Box 7842, Fredericksburg, VA 22404-7842; 800-739-2237; {www.childsupport-aces.org}.

Legal Help at a 75% Discount

The only things a paralegal can't do that a lawyer can, is give legal advice and represent you in court. That means they can file uncontested divorce papers, family court petitions, wills and probate, power of attorney, bankruptcy, and more.

There are states where paralegals can represent clients in cases like those involving evictions or government agencies. And if you are seeking a legal opinion from an attorney, you may want to get a paralegal to research the law for you, so that you can make your own decisions.

Remember 50% of all lawyers lose their cases in court. So why pay $200 an hour for a lawyer, when you can get a lot of the same services done for less than $50 an hour. Paralegals are in the yellow pages Contact National Federation of Paralegal Associations, 2517 Eastlake Ave. E, Suite 200, Seattle, WA 98102; 206-652-4120; Fax: 206-652-4122; {www.para legals.org}.

Free Legal Latino Help

The Mexican American Legal Defense and Educational Fund (MALDEF) is a national nonprofit organization whose mission is to protect and promote the civil rights of the more than 29 million Latinos living in the United States in the areas of education, employment,

political access, and more. They take cases to court and provide other legal help for the Latino community.

Contact MALDEF, 634 South Spring St., 11th Floor, Los Angeles, CA 90014; 213-629-2512; Fax: 213-629-0266; {www.maldef.org}.

Free Help with Housing Discrimination

Buying your first home is a very exciting time. But for many, house shopping is more than an eye opening experience. Some people are not shown houses in particular neighborhoods or are denied a home because of their sex, race, or living arrangement. If you feel you have been treated unfairly, contact Office of Fair Housing and Equal Opportunity, U.S. Department of Housing and Urban Development, 451 7th St., SW, Room 5100, Washington, DC 20410; 202-708-4252; 800-669-9777; {www. hud.gov}.

Fight Your Bank, Credit Card Company, etc.

Finding the right bank, savings and loan, or credit union means figuring out your own needs first. How much money can you keep on deposit and how many checks will you write? Examine your future loans and savings needs, as well as look at the convenience of the financial institution, its service charges, fees, and deposit and loan interest rates. You can contact one of the following offices to learn more.

National Banks (banks that have the word "National" in their names or the initials "N.A." after their names)
    Comptroller of the Currency
    U. S. Department of the Treasury
    Customer Assistance Group

1301 McKinney St., Suite 3450
Houston, TX 77010
800-613-6743
www.occ.treas.gov

FDIC-Insured Banks
Office of Consumer Affairs
Federal   Deposit   Insurance
Corporation
550 17th St., NW, Room F-130
Washington, DC 20429-9990
202-736-0000
800-934-3342
www.fdic.gov

Savings and Loans
Office of Thrift Supervision
U.S. Department of Treasury
1700 G St., NW
Washington, DC 20552
202-906-6000
800-842-6929
www.ots.treas.gov

State Banks
Contact your State Government
Banking Commissioner located
in your state capital (look in the
blue pages of your phone book or
contact your state capitol
operator).

Where to Get Help to Stop Sexual Harassment
Call **"9 to 5"** if you experience any of
the following at work:
♦ Suggestive comments about your
   appearance
♦ Unwanted touching or other
   physical contact
♦ Unwanted sexual jokes or
   comments
♦ Sexual advances

Sexual harassment is not only
offensive, it's against the law. It is
illegal even if the harasser is not your
boss, even if he is not threatening that

you will lose your job if you don't go
along. 9to5's **toll free job problem
hotline** and trained job counselors give
information and support to thousands
of working women. If you decide to
pursue a legal remedy, contact your
state discrimination agency or the
federal   Equal   Employment
Opportunity Commission. The federal
agency covers workplaces of 15 or
more. State law covers workplaces
with fewer employees.

Contact: 9to5, National Association of
Working Women, 152 W. Wisconsin,
Suite 408, Milwaukee, WI 30309; 800-
522-0925; {www.9to5.org}.

Discrimination Because You're a Woman, Pregnant, Person of Color, etc.
There's no need to take harassment or
bullying on the job. Here is your
chance to fight back. If you believe
you have been discriminated against
by an employer, labor union, or
employment agency when applying for
a job or while on the job because of
race, color, sex, religion, national
origin, age, or disability, you may file
a charge with the Equal Employment
Opportunity Commission (EEOC).

For more information, contact Equal
Employment Opportunity Commission, 1801 L St., NW, Washington, DC
20507; 202-663-4900; 800-669-4000;
{www.eeoc.gov}.

Fight Lawyers, Accountants, Pharmacists, Doctors, Real Estate Agents and Other Professionals
Lawyer over-charging you? Do you
feel you have been mistreated by your
doctor? These issues and more are
handled by the agency or board that
licenses that particular profession.

These boards will then help you to resolve the problem. To locate the correct board usually located in your state capital, contact your state operator.

Free Help in Writing a Will

Estate planning is not something that people often relish doing, but it is extremely important. It is difficult enough when a loved one dies, but then to have to search through papers trying to find information about insurance, or investments is often too much. When children are involved, estate planning is essential. Who will take care of the children and how can you secure their financial future?

Your local Cooperative Extension Service often offers classes or publications on estate planning. The time to plan ahead is now. Look in the blue pages of your phone book for the nearest Cooperative Extension office, as they are in almost every county across the country.

How an Abuser Can Discover Your Internet Activities

The *American Bar Association's (ABA) Commission on Domestic Violence* has issued a warning concerning possible threats to you if an abuser has access to your email account and thus may be able to read your incoming and outgoing mail. If you believe your account is secure, make sure you choose a password he

or she will not be able to guess. If an abuser sends you threatening or harassing email messages, they may be printed and saved as evidence of this abuse. Additionally, the messages may constitute a federal offense.

Contact your local United States Attorney's Office or American Bar Association Commission on Domestic Violence, 740 15th Street, NW, 9th Floor, Washington, DC 20005-1019; 202-662-1000; Fax: 202-662-1594, {abacdv@abanet.org}; {www.abanet.org}.

Fight Retailers, Mail Order Companies, Auto Dealers, Contractors, etc.

You go to a store to get the best price on the gift for Uncle George, only to learn that the store is out of stock despite the product being advertised in the paper. Did the salesman try to get you to buy a higher priced item? You could be the victim of the old bait and switch scam. Is the paint peeling off of the new toy doll you bought your daughter? Problems dealing with your car dealership or car repair shop? What about the contractor that has yet to finish the job?

There are ways to deal with all these problems and get them resolved to your satisfaction. You just need to pull in the big guns. Attorney General's Offices have Consumer Protection Offices, and many also have separate offices that handle only car complaints. They will take your complaint and try to help you get the satisfaction you deserve. For other problems contact:

Defective Products — contact Consumer Product Safety Commission, Washington, DC

20207-0001; 800-638-2772; {www.cpsc.gov}.

Contractor or Licensed Professional Problems — contact the state Licensing Board for the profession located in your state capitol. You can contact the state operator for assistance in finding the office.

Mail Order Problems — contact the U.S. Postal Service, Public Affairs Branch, 475 L'Enfant Plaza, SW, Room 3140, Washington, DC 202060; 202-268-5400; {www.usps.gov}.

Fraud Issues — contact Federal Trade Commission, Public Reference, 600 Pennsylvania Ave., Washington, DC 20580; 202-382-4357, 877-FTC-HELP; {www.ftc.gov}.

Free Legal Help if Your Child is Suspended from School

"Zero Tolerance" and other school system disciplinary practices can place your child's education in jeopardy if you are not aware of your rights. Your first meeting with the principal on such matters can actually serve as a trial for your child's future. The School House Legal Services of Baltimore, Maryland provides free attorneys and paralegals to represent Maryland families in these matters. Maryland has an income limit for representation that is about $30,000 for a family of four, but information about the process is free.

If you don't live in Maryland, contact your local Legal Services Office or your State Department of Education for more information and help. School House Legal Services can be reached at Maryland Disability Law Center, 1800 N. Charles St., Suite 202,

Baltimore, MD 21201; 410-727-6352; {www.mdlcbalto.org}.

Free Help Fighting an Electric Bill or Stopping a Turn Off

The state utility commissions can help you fight high gas or electric bills. Some will even come out and make sure that your meter is not over charging you. They don't have money to pay for your bills, but they can negotiate payment arrangements with the company for you or suggest non-profit organizations that may have emergency funds to help.

For example, Maryland suggests the Fuel Fund for Central Maryland or the Maryland Energy Assistance program. The office can also force the utility not to cut off your service because of medical emergencies or cold weather. Contact your state utility commission listed in the blue pages of your phone book for further assistance.

Free Legal Help to Fight Car Dealers and Repair Shops

When you can't get satisfaction from the manager or owner, then it is time to bring in the big guns:

♦ Your state attorney general's office is set up to handle automobile complaints. Sometimes all you have to do is send a letter to the attorney general with a copy to the business owner.

♦ Automotive Consumer Action Program (AUTOCAP) is a complaint handling system sponsored by the automobile industry for new or used car purchases from NEW car dealers only. Contact National Automobile Dealers Association, 8400 Westpark Drive, McLean, VA 22102; 703-821-7000; {www.nada.org/}

♦ Better Business Bureau (BBB) Auto Line is a FREE, out-of-court arbitration program, paid for by the business community to handle automobile complaints between consumers and most auto manufacturers. Contact your local Better Business Bureau or BBB Auto Line, Dispute Resolution Division, Council of Better Business Bureaus, Inc., 4200 Wilson Blvd, Suite 800, Arlington, VA 22203-1838; 703-276-0100; {www.bbb.org/complaints.asp}

Emergency Shelter, Housing & Counseling for Violence Victims

If violence is ripping your life apart, you have nowhere to go, and you do not know how to reclaim your life, the YWCA, the nation's leading provider of shelter and services to women and their families can help you! In the United States, more than 650,000 people come to the YWCA each year for services and support to overcome violence. For more information contact your local YWCA.

The YWCA takes a holistic approach to helping women escape, recover from and prevent violence in their lives and the lives of their families. Many local YWCAs offer programs and services including emergency shelter for women and children, transitional housing, support to victims of rape and sexual assault, individual and group counseling, peer support, self-defense training, programs for batterers and legal advocacy.

Contact YWCA U.S.A., 1015 18th Street, NW, Suite 1100, Washington, DC 20036; 202-467-0801; {www.ywca.org}. National Domestic Violence Hotline 800-799-SAFE; hearing impaired 800-787-3224.

Money To Pay Your Legal Bills

Many lawyers around the country offer their services for free to those who cannot cover the costs of legal services. In addition, special Pro Bono projects are underway at the American Bar Association, including the Child Custody Project, Immigration Development Project and the Rural Pro Bono Delivery Initiative.

If you need legal services, you can contact your local bar association to see who is offering to do Pro Bono work or you can contact the American Bar Association, 740 15th St., NW, Washington, DC 20005; 202-662-1000; {www.abanet.org/legalservices/probono/home.html}. A directory of Pro Bono organizations is available on this website.

When All Else Fails

People forget that they can turn to their representative or senators for help resolving a complaint. You vote these people into office, and most of them want to stay there. They know that if they can help you, then you and your family will vote for them in each and every election. Their offices have case managers whose job is to cut the red-tape and push your case through quickly. Look in your phone book for their local office or you can call U.S. House of Representatives, Washington, DC 20515; 202-224-3121; {www.house.gov}; or U.S. Senate, Washington, DC 20510; 202-224-3121; {www.senate.gov}.

Non-Profits

If you have a non-profit organization, or you are thinking of starting a non-profit organization, this is the section for you. It is a collection of programs that are just for non-profit organizations.

<u>Should you become a non-profit organization</u>? The real answer is, "It Depends." You may or may not have to become a non-profit organization. If it is a new venture, I would not worry about the answer to that question until you know for sure where you are going to apply for the money you need. Some sources require you to be a registered non-profit and some do not. There are programs, listed here and elsewhere, that will give you the money to do your good work as an individual, so you don't have to be a non-profit. So why go thru all the time, energy and expense to become a non-profit if you are not positive of where you are going to apply for the money.

Don't waste time. Find out exactly where you are going to apply for the money and if they require you to become a non-profit, then go become one.

Another way around becoming a non-profit is by working with an existing non-profit. For example, you want to start a center training unemployed teenagers to become car mechanics, and you found a program that gives out money for this kind of activity, but only to non-profits. You can contact your local church, community college or any other non-profit and talk with them about an opportunity of doing the project together. Organizations like this can let you use their name, give you a desk and collect maybe 20% of what you get as an overhead activity.

There is always more than one way to accomplish anything. You just have to search for it.

There are over one hundred thousand organizations, both public and private, that give money to individuals or to non-profit groups. This section describes a number of these programs, but certainly not all. To look for more programs that give out money for non-profit organizations contact:

1) *Money From Foundations For Non-Profits*
The following are the major sources of information for finding grants from non-profit organizations. Their databases contain information on most of the non-government grant sources.

The Foundation Center
79 Fifth Avenue
New York, NY 10003
212-620-4230
www.fdncenter.org
They have a database of over 75,000 non-profit organizations that give out grants. This database is accessible on the web for a fee or you can go into one of the Foundation Center libraries around the country and use their database for free. They also publish directories of foundations that give out grant money. You can call their office and they will tell you what libraries in your area have these directories for you to look at for free.

The Foundation Center also gives short courses on topics like "How to Search for Grant Money", or "How to Write a Grant". Don't pay thousands of dollars for courses on these subjects when you can get it from one of the best for a very reasonable price.

Guidestar
4801 Courthouse Street
Suite 220
Williamsburg, VA 23188
757-229-4631
www.guidestar.org
They have a similar database as The Foundation Center, but do not offer training and classes on other aspects of grantsmanship. Their database seems to have much more information in it about any given foundation. The best part is that you can use the database that will only show partial information on the records, but it is good enough for many applications.

2) *Money From The Government For Non-Profits*
Money is available to non-profit organizations from all three levels of government, Federal, State, and local.

Money From The Federal Government

All the major money programs in the Federal government are described in a book called the *Catalog of Federal Domestic Assistance*. This book is available at your local public library or the U.S. Government Printing Office (www.gpo.gov). You can also search the contents of this book for free on the web at {www.cfda.gov}. The government has also recently started a web site devoted to government grants called {www.grants.gov}. In addition they have a web site {http://www.firstgov.gov/Business/Nonprofit.shtml}.

Money From State Governments

There is not likely to be a single source of information at the state level for grants for non-profits from the state government. The best bet seems to be to identify those agencies that may be involved in your area of expertise and to start fishing. For example, if you are interested in training youth, try locating those agencies that are involved with youth like the departments of education, training, and health. If you don't know any likely departments, you can call any department you want and ask them "who deals with youth?" Your state capital operator can help you identify state offices. You can call them in your state capital by calling 411. Or on the web go to {www.govengine.com} and click on your state. Then start looking for web sites for departments that may be relevant. You can also get assistance in forming and registering as a non-profit through your state office of Attorney General or Secretary of State.

Money From City and County Governments

There is not likely a single source for information on non-profits at the local government level. Contact your city and county offices to see if they can provide you with some direction. Your local chamber of commerce can also be of assistance.

3) *Free Help In Starting A Non-Profit*
There are over 1,000 Small Business Development Centers around the country that will help you with any problem you may have in starting or expanding a non-profit organization. They can assist you with becoming a non-profit, finding money (although they themselves do not offer money), management problems, technical issues and more. To find a

Small Business Development Center in your area contact: 1-800-8-ASK-SBA;
{http://www.sba.gov/sbdc/sbdcnear.html}.

4) Money For Arts Or Humanities

The National Endowment for the Arts and the National Endowment for the Humanities are the two main resources for these types of funds offered by the federal government. Money is also handed about by state councils for arts and humanities. You can learn more by checking out the arts site at {www.arts.gov} and the humanities site at {www.neh.fed.us}. Both offer a link to state websites for more information.

So, go start saving the world. There are a lot of problems out there to solve and now you know where to get the money to do it.

$50,000 to Preserve Ecosystems

Grants are awarded with a primary focus on ecological issues. Agriculture, economic globalization, land resources, and international affairs are some of the topics of interest. This foundation is both national and international in giving. Contact Foundation for Deep Ecology, 1062 Fort Cronkhite, Sausalito, CA 94965; Fax: 415-229-9340; {http://www.deepecology.org}; {info@deepecology.org}.

Up to $30,000 to Advocate for Freedom of Choice

Provides grants to grassroots organizations, coalitions and other groups for efforts and projects related to the reproductive and other rights of women. Grants range from $15,000 to $30,000. Grants are given to individual organizations and coalitions implementing grassroots organizing strategies or other collective approaches to improve access to reproductive health services. Contact Ms. Foundation for Women, 120 Wall Street, 33rd Floor, New York, NY 10005; 212-742-2300; Fax: 212-742-1653; {http://www.ms.foundation.org/}; {info@ms.foundation.org}.

$7,500 to Plant and Preserve Trees

Provides grants up to $7,500 to community organizations and volunteer groups to tree-planting, tree preservation and other forestry projects in urban areas in California. Contact California ReLeaf / National Tree Trust, 2311 Tustin Avenue, Newport Beach, CA 92660; 949-642-0127; {http://www.nationaltreetrust.org/relea f/}; {ehoskins@nationaltreetrust.org}.

Money to Sponsor Women-Based Projects

Makes grants to projects designed and implemented by women and girls that reflect the cultural and ethnic diversity of our society and promote the empowerment of women and girls in any and all facets of society. Contact Open Meadows Foundation, P.O. Box 150-607, Van Brunt Station, Brooklyn, NY 11215-607; 718-768-2249; {http://www.openmeadows.org/}; {openmeadows@igc.org}.

Lesbians Get $2,000 for Lesbian-Related Projects

$2,000 grants to fund projects supporting and developed by lesbians age 60 and older. Contact The Edie Windsor Fund for Old Lesbians, Open Meadows Foundation, P.O. Box 150-607, Van Brunt Station, Brooklyn, NY 11215-607; 718-768-2249; {http://www.openmeadows.org/}; {openmeadows@igc.org}.

Up to $233,000 to Foster Awareness for a Better World

Grants ranging from $10,000 up to $233,000 are available for those individuals who want to foster awareness of the power of love and forgiveness in the merging global community through research, education and service programs. The institute does not accept unsolicited proposals, but occasionally offers funding opportunities in the form of fellowships, requests for proposals, and awards that are open for application. Contact John E. Fetzer Institute, Inc., (formerly John E. Fetzer Foundation, Inc., 9292 West KL Ave., Kalamazoo, MI 49009-9398; 269-375-2000; Fax: 269-372-2163; {http://www.fetzer.org}; {info@fetzer.org}

$20,000 Grants Supporting Women's Human Rights

The Global Fund provides general program and operating support grants to women's organizations and individuals focused on advancing the human rights of women and girls. Grants range from $500 to an annual funding of $20,000. The majority of the funding remains devoted to general grants supporting universal issues such as reproductive health and choice, improved access to media and communications, the advancement of women in positions of elected leadership, the rights of sexual minorities, and the prevention of violence against women and children; however, there are grants that support special projects and initiatives. Funding is on an international basis. Contact Global Fund For Women, 1375 Sutter St., Suite 400, San Francisco, CA 94109; 415-202-7640; Fax: 415-202-8604; {www.globalfundforwomen.org}; {gfw@globalfundforwomen.org}.

FREE Computers and Technology Equipment

NCF encourages corporations and individuals to donate surplus and used computers, software, peripherals and related business technology. NCF directs those donations to training and educational organizations. All the organizations are pre-screened and qualified grass-roots partners of NCF. All donated equipment is distributed to these organizations FREE with no charges to the donor or recipients. Contact The Christina Foundation, 500 West Putnam, Greenwich, CT 06830; 203-863-9100; {http://www.cristina.org/}; {ncf@christina.org}.

Up to $5,000 for Activism Efforts

Organizing and Advocacy Grants support organizing and activism work that exists to challenge sexism, racism, homophobia, economic injustice, and other forms of oppression. Support is offered to young women between the ages of 15 and 30 and to projects which serve them in the areas of reproductive health and justice, scholarships and grassroots organizing and advocacy. Projects with a budget over $500,000 are rarely supported. Grants range from $100 to $5,000. Contact Third Wave Foundation, 511 W. 25th Street, Suite 301, New York, NY 10001; 212-675-0700; Fax: 212-255-6653; {http://www.thirdwavefoundation.org/programs/grants.html}; {info@thirdwavefoundation.org}.

$5,000 to Support Women's Rights

There are of two types: 1) Training access, and education grants which are awarded for projects that benefit, target, and are developed by women between the ages of 15 and 30, with an emphasis on low-income women, women of color and lesbian and bisexual women. Projects with budgets exceeding $500,000 are rarely supported. Grants range from $100 to $5,000; and 2) Emergency grants which fund travel, accommodation, and abortion procedures on an on-going and immediate basis. Also, grants are awarded to organizations

that grant money directly and immediately to young women in need of abortions. Contact Third Wave Foundation, 511 W. 25th Street, Suite 301, New York, NY 10001; 212-675-0700; Fax: 212-255-6653; {http://www.thirdwavefoundation.org/programs/grants.html}; {info@thirdwavefoundation.org}.

Up to $5,000 for Activism Efforts

Third Wave Foundation Scholarship Program is available to all full-time or part-time young women and transgender activists age 30 and under who are enrolled in, or have been accepted to, an accredited university, college, vocational/technical school or community college. The primary criteria to qualify for a Third Wave scholarship is vigorous engagement in activist work and financial need. Students applying for grants should also be involved as activists, artists, or cultural workers working on issues such as racism, homophobia, sexism, or other forms of inequality. Scholarships range in amount from $500 and $5,000 each. Contact Third Wave Foundation, 511 W. 25th Street, Suite 301, New York, NY 10001; 212-675-0700; Fax: 212-255-6653; {http://www.thirdwavefoundation.org/programs/grants.html}; {info@thirdwavefoundation.org}.

Over $350,000 for Charitable Causes

Autodesk makes charitable contributions to non-profit organizations involved with arts and culture, education, the environment, health and human services, community development, science and technology, civic affairs, and to disabled people for product donations. Support is given on a national and international basis. Contact Autodesk, Inc. Corporate Giving Program, c/o Community Rels. Department, 111 McInnis Parkway, San Rafael, CA 94903; 415-507-6603; Fax: 415-507-6138; {julie.wilder@ autodesk.com}. Application address for product donations: Gifts In Kind Intl., 333 N. Fairfax St., Alexandria, VA 22314.

$10,000 Grants for Projects Supporting Worldwide Unity

The Eric Berne Fund for the Future awards grants of up to $10,000 to individuals or organizations, both not-for-profit and for-profit, demonstrating an interest in the evaluation of effectiveness of various applications of transactional analysis theory. Priority is given to those applicants who either are current members of the ITAA or have demonstrated a high level of competency in the theory and practice of TA. Contact Eric Berne Fund of the International Transactional Analysis Association, c/o Rosa Krauscz, 436 14th St., Ste. 1301, Oakland, CA 94612-2710; 510-625-7720; Fax: 510-625-7725; {http://www.itaa-net.org}; {itaa@itaa-net.org}.

Grants of $1,500 for Catholic Missions

This Foundation gives primarily to Roman Catholic missionaries selected by the Foundation. Grants range from $50 up to $1,500. Contact Pro Deo

Guild, Inc., P.O. Box 304, Hartsdale, NY 10530-0304; {http://www.para cleteinc.com/pro_deo_guild.htm}.

Financial Assistance for Philanthropy Projects

The Rockefeller Philanthropy Advisors supports organizations and individuals engaged in philanthropy, and administer a donor-advised fund, The Philanthropic Collaborative. Assistance ranges from $5,000 up to $4.0 million. Contact Rockefeller Philanthropy Advisors, Inc. (formerly The Philanthropic Collaborative, Inc.), 437 Madison Ave., 37th Floor, New York, NY 10022; 212-812-4330; Fax: 212-812-4335. West Coast office address: 101 2nd St., 24th Fl., San Francisco, CA 94104; 415-543-0733; Fax: 415-543-0735; {http://www. rockpa.org}; {info@rockpa.org}.

$7,500 for Human Rights and Social Justice

This Foundation offers support to individuals and organizations "for the purpose of enabling them to carry on research, teaching, and education in the areas of civil and human rights and social justice." Grants are available up to $7,500 per individual. Contact Petra Foundation Charitable Trust, c/o Law Firm of Hill & Barlow, One International Pl., 21st Floor, Boston, MA 02110-2600; Application address: c/o Muriel Morisey Spence, Chair., Award Comm., P.O. Box 11579, Washington, DC 20008; 202-364-8964.

Grants up to $20,000 for Community Projects

Grants are currently awarded once a year and are mostly in the $10,000 to $20,000 range. Funding is allocated among three categories: 1) Environment; 2) Social; and 3)

Jewish/. Whatever the specific area of interest, the foundation encourages projects which are concerned with promoting community, social justice, a healthy environment and a sustainable economy, either by developing alternatives to the status quo or by responsibly modifying existing systems, institutions, conditions, and attitudes which block promising innovation. Contact Max and Anna Levinson Foundation, P.O. Box 6309, Santa Fe, NM 87502-6309; 505-995-8802; Fax: 505-995-8982; {http://www.levinsonfoundation.org}; {info@levinson foundation.org}.

Grant Funding for Missionaries

The foundation assists projects of national and international scope which have special importance for the mission of the Catholic Prelature of Opus Dei, including capital expansion projects. Contact Woodlawn Foundation, 524 North Ave., Ste. 203, New Rochelle, NY 10801-3410; 914-632-3778; Fax: 914-632-5502.

Up to $5,000 for Essays on Human Rights

The Elie Wiesel Prize in Ethics offers a first prize of $5,000, second prize of $2,500, third prize of $1,500 and two honorable mentions of $500 each to undergraduates who are or will be registered as full-time juniors or seniors at accredited four-year colleges or universities in the U.S and Canada. All entries must be in the formal or informal voice, ranging from 3,000 to 4,000 words, and may take the form of an analysis that is biographical, historical, literary, philosophical, psychological, sociological or theological. All candidates must be sponsored by a faculty member. The foundation advances the causes of

human rights throughout the world by creating forums for the discussion of urgent ethical and moral issues confronting humankind. Contact The Elie Wiesel Foundation for Humanity, 529 5th Ave., Ste. 1802, New York, NY 10017; 212-490-7777; Fax: 212-490-6006; {http://www.eliewiesel foundation.org}; {info@eliewiesel foundation.org}.

$90,000 to Pursue Your Career Goals

Each year, the Fannie Mae Foundation selects up to six seasoned professionals as Johnson Fellows. These Fellows design and pursue development plans that can include research, travel, study, self-designed internships, and other activities that enhance their skills and knowledge. The program is a unique opportunity for individuals to identify and pursue personal and professional goals in the affordable housing and community development fields. The Johnson fellowship provides each fellow with a $70,000 grant and a stipend of up to $20,000 for travel and education-related expenses. The nonprofit organization with which each fellow is associated may receive a grant of up to $25,000 for transitional costs related to the temporary absence of the employee or volunteer. Contact Fannie Mae Foundation, Policy and Leadership Development, 4000 Wisconsin Ave. N.W., N. Tower, Ste. 1, Washington, DC 20016-2804; 202-274-8066 or 202-274-8057 or 202-274-8000; Fax: 202-274-8100; {http://www.fanniemaefoundation.org}; {llucs@ fanniemaefoundation.org}.

FREE Tuition for Affordable Housing Providers

The Fannie Mae Foundation Fellowship Program is intended to enhance the management and decision-making skills of accomplished leaders experienced in managing housing and community development programs. The State and Local program curriculum focuses on: organizational strategy; political management; policy development; management control and operations; and management of human resources. Fellowship funds cover the cost of the admission deposit, program tuition, and room and board for the session. Applicants must be able to attend the entire three-week session and are responsible for their own transportation and other incidental costs. Contact Fannie Mae Foundation, Policy and Leadership Development, 4000 Wisconsin Ave. N.W., N. Tower, Ste. 1, Washington, DC 20016-2804; 202-274-8066 or 202-274-8057 or 202-274-8000; Fax: 202-274-8100; {http://www.fanniemaefoundation.org}; {llucs@fanniemaefoundation.org}.

$1,500 to Provide Medical Services to Those in Need

The Paul S. McCord, D.O. Memorial Scholarship Fund is awarded annually to one student from the 3rd year class at College of Osteopathic Medicine at Midwestern University (CCOM). The recipient must demonstrate a commitment to providing medical services in an underserved and/or disadvantaged area, provide volunteer services beyond those required by his/her college, demonstrate a high degree of care and concern for the underserved, and show leadership qualities in serving the underserved and the disadvantaged. One $1,500 scholarship will be awarded to a student chosen by CCOM. Contact American Osteopathic Foundation (formerly National Osteopathic Foundation), 142 E. Ontario, Ste. 502, Chicago, IL 60611; 312-202-8232 or 800-621-1773, ext. 8232; Fax: 312-

202-8216; {http://www.aoffoundation.org}; {vheck@aof-foundation.org}.

$70,000 or More for Education, Medicine or Religion

The organization provides educational, medical, and religious support in the U.S. and overseas. Over $70,000 is available for grants to individuals. Contact Voice in the Wilderness, Inc., P.O. Box 210098, Dallas, TX 75211-0098; {www.voice-wilderness.com}.

$25,000 Plus a One-Year Lease on a New Car

Through the Volvo Heroes USA program, Volvo annually awards $5,000 to ten Volvo or Volvo retailer employees for the charity of their choice who go above and beyond the call of duty to act with conscience, care, and character to help others in need in the areas of safety, quality of life, and environment. Special emphasis is directed towards employees working to benefit many people, improve the natural environment, and help underserved communities. The three top winners receive an additional $20,000 for the charity of their choice and the top winner receives a one-year lease on a Volvo automobile. All U.S. citizens or legal residents of the U.S. of any age, including U.S. citizens living abroad, are eligible to submit nominations for the Volvo for life Awards. Contact

Volvo Cars of North America, LLC Corporate Giving Program, 1 Volvo Drive, Rockleigh, NJ 07647-2507; {http://www.volvoforlifeawards.com}; {nominate@volvo4lifeawards.com}; {info@volvoforlifeawards.com}.

$48,000 for Peace and Disarmament

The Ploughshares Fund provides financial support for projects related to preventing the spread of weapons of mass destruction, controlling the sale of conventional weapons, addressing the environmental impact of nuclear weapons production, promoting new approaches to conflict prevention, and building global and regional security. Grant awards to individuals range from a high of $48,000 to a low of $1,500. Contact Ploughshares Fund, Fort Mason Ctr., Bldg. B, Ste. 330, San Francisco, CA 94123; 415-775-2244; Fax: 415-775-4529; {http://www.ploughshares.org}; {email: ploughshares@ploughshares.org}.

Money for All Kinds of Charities

The Philanthropic Ventures Foundation's financial support, including scholarships and grants, covers a wide variety of areas, including the arts, economic development, education, environment, and human services. PVF takes the investment approach to charitable giving, seeking outstanding people and opportunities whose impact in the community will be significant and bringing them to the attention of donors. Applications not accepted. Giving primarily in the San Francisco Bay Area, CA, but extends nationally pursuant to donors' recommendations. Foundation grants to individuals range between $215,000 and $15. Contact Philanthropic Ventures Foundation,

1222 Preservation Park Way, Oakland, CA 94612-1201; 510-645-1890; Fax: 510-645-1892; {http://www.ventures foundation.org/index.html}; {email: info@venturesfoundation.org}.

Funding for Helping People

The Lodestar Foundation seeks to initiate or support innovative nonprofit endeavors that are directed towards the betterment of the human condition, whether physically, educationally, emotionally, or spiritually. Primary consideration will be given to those endeavors that: (1) encourage cooperation, collaboration, best practices and efficiency among nonprofits addressing common or related issues or (2) encourage philanthropy, charity, volunteerism or public service. Contact The Lodestar Foundation, 4455 East Camelback Road, Suite 215A, Phoenix, Arizona 85018; 602-956-2699; Fax: 602-840-1543; {http://www.lodestarfound ation.org/}; {email: lsavage@lodestar foundation.org}.

$250,000 to Improve the World's Food Supply

Grants of up to $250,000 are given to individuals for achievement in improving the world food supply. Giving is both national and international. Contact World Food Prize Foundation, 666 Grand Ave., Ste. 1700, Des Moines, IA 50309; 515-245-3783; Fax: 515-245-3785; {http://www.worldfoodprize.com}; {wfp@worldfoodprize.org}; {jpim@world foodprize.org}. Application Address: World Food Prize Foundation, 1700 Ruan Ctr., 666 Grand Ave., Des Moines, IA 50309.

$12,000 to Do Good for Others

College graduates may be eligible to receive grants ranging from $7,000 up to $12,000 to pursue meaningful projects which can also benefit others. Awards are usually made on a one-year basis and are not renewed. This is a national award program. Contact Ella Lyman Cabot Trust, Inc., c/o Palmer & Dodge, LLP, 111 Huntington Avenue, 19th Floor, Boston, MA 02199. Application Address Ella Lyman Cabot Trust, Inc. c/o Brooks Thompson, 109 Rockland St., Holliston, MA 01746.

$12,000 For Non-Profit To Develop Housing

The PreDevelopment Program provides community-based non-profit funds for "soft costs" of specific projects. Funds are available for housing or economic development projects that target low-income people. Maximum award is $12,000. Funds can be used for costs directly related to the planning of the project, including, but not limited to, architecture drawings, site plans, legal costs, engineering costs, market studies, real estate options, and zoning/permit fees. Contact the Ohio Community Development Finance Fund, 17 South High Street, Suite 900, Columbus, OH 43215; 614-221-1114; {www.financefund.org/pd.html}.

Over $500,000 For Parental Assistance Centers

An average of $513,000 in funding is available to nonprofit organizations to assist them in establishing parental information and resource centers.

These grants will enable centers to assist parents in helping their children to meet State and local standards, develop resource materials and provide information about high-quality family involvement programs; plan, implement, and fund activities for parents that coordinate the education of their children with other programs that serve their children and families. Projects generally include a focus on serving parents of low-income, minority, and limited English proficient children enrolled in elementary and secondary schools. Contact the U.S. Department of Education, Parental Options and Information, 400 Maryland Ave., S.W., Rm. 3E209, FB-6, Washington DC 20202-6100; 202-260-2225; {www.ed.gov/programs/pirc/index.html}.

$500,000 Grants Available To Non-Profits

Through the Challenge Grants program, non-profits can expand their volunteer efforts with up to $1 million in funding. The program has $2.6 million available, and anticipates offering up to four grants this year alone. Contact the Corporation for National and Community Service Headquarters Address, 1201 New York Avenue, NW, Washington, D.C. 20525; 202-606-5000; {http://www.nationalservice.org/news/pr/051304.html}.

$100,000 To Mentor Children of Prisoners

Get up to $5 million through the Family and Youth Services Bureau to make a difference in the lives of children. The Mentoring Children of Prisoners program is looking for organizations that are interested in helping children of incarcerated individuals. Find out how your organization can get involved. Contact Family and Youth Services Bureau, Administration for Children and Families, Department of Health and Human Services, 330 C Street, SW., Washington, DC 20447; 202-205-8102; {www.acf.hhs.gov/programs/fysb/}. For additional information go to {www.nwrel.org/mentoring/children_prisoners.html} and {http://12.46.245.173/pls/portal30/CATALOG.PROGRAM_TEXT_RPT.SHOW?p_arg_names=prog_nbr&p_arg_values=93.616}.

Get $150,000 To Send Donated Supplies Overseas

Get the government to pay for the transporting of donated supplies overseas. Through the Ocean Freight Reimbursement (OFR) Program, Private Voluntary Organizations (PVO) can obtain funding to ship commodities overseas by ocean freight. OFR awards up to $150,000 per year and ships only those commodities and only to those countries approved by USAID. Contact Information Center, U.S. Agency for International Development, Ronald Reagan Building, Washington, D.C. 20523-1000; {www.usaid.gov/our_work/cross-cutting_programs/private_voluntary_cooperation/ofr.html}.

Free Accounting Services For Non-Profits and Small Business

There are a number of organizations around the country that provide free accounting services to help non-profits, small businesses, and even needy individuals get the accounting help they need. They can help with bookkeeping instruction, system analysis, preparation of 990 forms, preparation for audits and free publications. A minimal one-time cost may be required. To find free accounting help in your area, contact Accountants for the Public Interest, University of Baltimore, Thurnel Business Center, Room 155, 1420 North Charles Street, Baltimore, MD 21201; 410-837-6533; Fax: 410-837-6532. You can also contact your state association of Certified Public Accountants, as many may be able to direct you to a volunteer CPA who would be willing to help.

GRANTS FROM THE IRS

The IRS Will Send 3.5 Million Families a Check for Up To $4,300, If They Only Ask*

It's not really a grant, but it looks like a grant, it walks like a grant and it even smells like a grant. They are called tax credits. It's extra money the IRS will give you that's better than a refund because they will give it to you even if you don't pay any taxes. You just have to have some income and the less income you have the bigger the check you get. You can make up to $35,458 and still be eligible.

Free Publications
IRS Publication 596, Earned Income Tax Credit
Call: 1–800–829–3676
Download: http://www.irs.gov/pub/irs-pdf/p596.pdf

This is just one grant from the IRS that millions are missing. The following items will show you more, but don't stop with this book, and don't hire a high priced accountant or lawyer. Use the free tax services listed below or contact your Congressman or Senators' offices to find more free tax services in your area. To locate the offices go to {www. govengine.gov} or {www.congress.org}. You can also contact them at U.S. House of Representatives, Washington, DC 20515; 202-224-3121; {www.house.gov}; Senate, Washington, DC 20510; 202-224-3121; {www. senate.gov}.

1) Free Tax Services
Don't pay professional tax preparers money when you can have an income up to $35,000 or even more as you can get your taxes prepared for free. No matter what your income,

check if the services in your area can help you. The service is called Volunteer Income Tax Assistance (VITA). To find your local VITA program contact your local public library or your Congressman's office at {www.congress.org}. You can also try the IRS hotline at 1-800-TAX-1040; or see {http://www.irs.gov/individuals/article/0,,id=119845,00.html}.

2) *Free Legal Help With Tax Problems*
Families can have incomes up to $50,000, or more even, and get free lawyers to solve their tax problem. There are over 115 Low Income Taxpayer Clinics (LITC) that will help you with legal problems for free. You should check the availability of services in your area no matter what your income is. To find a clinic near you, contact your local public library or your Congressman's office at {www. congress.org}. You can also try the IRS hotline at 1-800-TAX-1040; or see {http://www.irs.gov/pub/irs-utl/pub._ 4134-04.pdf}.

3) *Free Tax Help For Seniors*
With a grant from the IRS, the AARP organizes over 8,000 "Tax Counseling For The Elderly" sites around the country that specialize in providing free tax help for people 60 and over. They may also provide free help for others, so it can't hurt to ask. To find a site near you, call the TCE hotline at 1-800-829-1040 or the AARP Tax Aide hotline at 1-888-227-7669 or visit {http://www.irs.gov/pub/irs-utl/pub._4134-04.pdf} or {http://www.aarp. org/money/taxaide/}. You can also contact your local public library or your Congressman's office at {www.congress.org}.

4) *Government Will Fight The IRS For You*
If you have attempted to deal with an IRS problem unsuccessfully, you should contact your Taxpayer Advocate. They will represent your interests and concerns within the

IRS by protecting your rights and resolving problems that have not been fixed through normal channels. They can clear-up problems that resulted from previous contacts and ensure that your case is given a complete and impartial review. Call 1-877-777-4778 or {www.irs.gov/advocate}.

*Sources
{http://www.acorn.org/fileadmin/ACORN_Reports/National_EITC_Report_-_Final_version_01.pdf }
{http://www.robinhood.org/programs/initiative_details.cfm?initiativeId=5}
{http://en.wikipedia.org/wiki/Earned_Income_Tax_Credit}

More Grants From The IRS

Get a $2,000 Check From Your State

You can claim anywhere from an additional 5% to 50% of what you get from the federal Earned Income Tax Credit from your state government. About 18 states currently offer this credit, as well as a handful of local jurisdictions. Make sure you get this money too. Contact one of the free tax services described above or your state tax office located in your state capital. You can call 411 and ask for this number or go to {www.govengine.com} and click on your state. You can also contact your local public library or your Congressman's office at {www.congress.org}; or see: {http://www.cbpp.org/5-14-04sfp.pdf }.

$1,000 Check For Each Child

The new federal Child Tax Credit gives working people making up to $110,000 a check for up to $1,000 even if they don't pay taxes. Look into it. Use the free tax sources above or call 1-800-TAX-1040. You can also go to: {http://www.irs.gov/newsroom/rticle/0,,id=106182,00.html}.

$2,100 Check For Child Care

This federal Child and Dependent Care Tax Credit is for child care for kids under 13 or for caring for dependents mentally or physically incapable of self-support. You can get a tax credit up to $2,100 depending on your income and the amount you pay for care. Unlike the Child Tax Credit and Earned Income Tax Credit, you get this check only if you are paying taxes. Use the free tax sources above or call 1-800-TAX-1040. Or go to: {http://www.irs.gov/newsroom/article/0,,id=106189,00.html}.

$2,310 Check From Your State For Child Care

Twenty-seven states offer Child and Dependent Care Tax Credit on your state tax returns. About 14 of these states do not require you to pay any taxes in order to get a check. Contact one of the free tax services described above or your state tax office located in your state capital. You can call 411 and ask for this number or go to {www.govengine.com} and click on your state. You can also contact your local public library or your

Congressman's office at {www. congress.org}. Also see: {http:// www.nccp.org/policy_long_descriptio n_15.html} or {http://www.nwlc.org/ pdf/NWLCTaxCreditsOutreachCampa ignToolkit2005.pdf}.

$1,500 Check For Going To College

You can make up to $100,000 and the government will send you a check under the federal Hope Scholarship Tax Credit if you are at least going to college part-time. It's only for the first two years of college and you have to be paying taxes to get the money. Use the free tax sources above, call 1-800-TAX-1040 or go to: {http://www.irs. ov/individuals/article/0,,id=96271,00.h tml}.

$2,000 Check For Taking A Course Or Class

Almost any kind of course that will improve your job skills are eligible under the federal Lifetime Learning Tax Credit. You can make up to $100,000 and still get this credit, but you have to be paying taxes to get the money. Use the free tax sources above, or call 1-800-TAX-1040 or go to http://www.irs.gov/individuals/article/ 0,,id=96273,00.html}.

$5,000 Check To Pay For Health Insurance

The federal Health Coverage Tax Credit is a bit more complicated, but it will pay 65% of health care insurance for people who lost their job because of imports or are receiving certain retirement benefits. Use the free tax sources above, or call 1-800-TAX-1040 or go to {http://www.irs. ov/individuals/article/0,,id=109960,00. html}.

$1,125 Check For Seniors Or Disabled

The Tax Credit for Elderly and Disabled is for citizens who are older than 65 or disabled. Your eligibility is based upon your income. Use the free tax sources above, or call 1-800-TAX-1040 or go to http://www.irs.gov/ pub/irs-pdf/p524.pdf

$10,160 Check For Adoptions

As an adoptive parent you may be able to receive a tax credit up to $10,160. The income limits on this go up to $192,390. Use the free tax sources above, or call 1-800-TAX-1040 or go to {http://www.irs.gov/taxtopics/c607. html}.

$30,000 Check From Your State

In addition to the state tax credit programs mentioned above, every state has other tax credits programs that can send you real money for taking advantage of them. Sample programs include:

- $1,160 for renters or homeowners in Wisconsin http://www.uwex.edu/ces/econ/h omestead.html

☐ $300 for buying new appliances in Oregon
http://www.energy.state.or.us/res/tax/taxcdt.htm

☐ $1,750 for installing solar panels in Hawaii
http://www.hawaii.gov/dbedt/ert/sol_t_hi.html

☐ $2,000 for seniors who pay property taxes in North Dakota
http://www.state.nd.us/taxdpt/property/pubs/senior-credit.pdf

☐ $30,000 to fix-up an old home in North Carolina

http://www.hpo.dcr.state.nc.us/tchome.htm

☐ $250 if you donate to an extracurricular activity at a school in Arizona
http://ww2.chandler.k12.az.us/tax-credit.html

*Contact your state Department of Revenue or Taxes to see what is available in your state. You can call 411 and ask for this number or go to {www.govengine.com} and click on your state. You can also contact your local public library or your Congressman's office at {www.congress.org}.

TEACHERS

What can be more important work in our society than teaching our young? We have included a number of grant items here that we especially reserved for teachers. Although the list is not very big, do not believe that there is very little available for teachers. There is, but the object of this book does not lend it self to providing an extensive section for  teachers. But don't despair, this list of sources before the money program descriptions are places you can turn to search for more programs. Each of these clearinghouses is set up to do free research, either on the web or on the phone, for subjects related to teaching. For example you can contact the Education Resources Information Center and request information on grant programs available for elementary teachers and they will help you with the research. These are free clearinghouses that will do free research on education related topics.

Education Resources Information Center
www.eric.ed.gov
800-LET-ERIC (538-3742)

The Educator's Reference Desk
eduref@eduref.org
http://www.eduref.org/

Center for Applied Linguistics
4646 40th Street, NW
Washington, DC 20016
202-362-0700
http://www.cal.org/resources/update.html

Clearinghouse on Elementary and Early Childhood Education
University of Illinois at Urbana-Champaign
51 Gerty Drive
Champaign, IL 61820
217-333-1386
http://ceep.crc.uiuc.edu/

National Center for ESL Literacy Education
4646 40th Street, NW
Washington, DC 20016
202-362-0700
ncle@cal.org
www.cal.org/ncle

ERIC Clearinghouse on Disabilities and Gifted Education
The Council for Exceptional Children
1110 N. Glebe Road
Arlington, VA 22201
800-328-0272
ericed@cec.sped.org
http://ericec.org

Clearinghouse on Educational Policy and Management
975 High Street, Suite 100
Eugene, OR 97401
541-346-5044
http://eric.uoregon.edu/

1. *Find All Federal Government Money Programs For Teachers….*
They are described in a book called the Catalog of Federal Domestic Assistance. This book is available at your local public library or the U.S. Government Printing Office {www.gpo.gov}. You can also search the contents of this book for free on the web at {www.cfda.gov}.

2. *Find All State Money Programs For Teachers…..*
Every state has money available for schools. Look for your
state office of education. You can find them by dialing 411
and asking for your state capitol operator or by going to the
web at {www.govenegine.com} and clicking on your state.

3. *Find Programs Available Through The Smithsonian*
The Smithsonian offers a wealth of education programs and
resources for teachers and students alike. To learn more
about what they offer, check them out on the web at
{www.si.edu}.

There can't be anything more important in our country than
educating our children. I hope every teacher realizes the
important work they do in our country. Soon we will do an entire
book just for teachers so we can celebrate and encourage their
work.

Teachers Get up to $1,000!

Provides grants to music teachers
through its Teacher Enrichment Grant
program. Grants are awarded in the
amount of $1,000, $750, $500 or $250
and may be used for private study,
college-level course work, or special
projects in performance, pedagogy,
music theory and composition. Contact
Music Teachers National Association
Foundation Fund, Teacher Enrichment
Grant Program, 441 Vine Street, Suite
505, Cincinnati, OH 45202-2811; 513-
421-1420 or 888-512-5278; Fax: 513-
421-2503; {www.mtna.org};
{mtnanet@mtna.org}.

School Teachers Get $250
for Education Activities

The Aerospace Education Foundation
of the Air Force Association (AFA)
offers "Educator Grants" of up to $250
per academic year to elementary,
middle and secondary school teachers

for aerospace education activities.
Funds may be used for anything
aerospace related, from purchasing
textbooks, videotapes, DVDs, model
rockets, radio controlled airplanes to
going on fieldtrips to aviation
museums, military bases or local
airports. Contact Aerospace Education
Foundation, 1501 Lee Highway,
Arlington, VA 22209; 703-247-5839;
Fax: 703-247-5853; {http://www.aef.
org}; {rkay@aef.org}.

$5,000 Grants for Teacher
Education in the Arts

This grantmaker awards one $5,000
grant, one $3,000 grant, and one
$1,000 grant biennially to a grant
recipient with a baccalaureate degree
to promote further study in a selected
field of fine arts. The Foundation also
provides scholarships of $10,000 to
foreign students for study in American
colleges and universities. Foundation

support is primarily for teacher education through scholarships and grants; giving also for the arts. Contact Alpha Delta Kappa Foundation, 1615 W. 92nd Street, Kansas City, MO 64114-3296; 816-363-5525 or 800-247-2311; Fax: 816-363-4010; {http://www.alphadeltakappa.org}; {alphadeltakappa@worldnet.att.net}.

Grants up to $2,000 for Food Service Educators

The Teacher Work-Study Grants offers $2,000 grants to food service/ hospitality educators who are interested in complementing classroom time with hands-on work experience. Through this program, educators work as full-time foodservice employees and gain a better understanding of day-to-day restaurant operations. Applicants must be full-time high school or college educators or administrators of a food service/hospitality program. Contact National Restaurant Association Educational Foundation, (formerly National Institute for the Food Service Industry), 175 W. Jackson Blvd., Ste. 1500, Chicago, IL 60604-2702; 800-765-2122 or 312-715-1010, ext. 733; Fax: 312-715-0807; {http://www. nraef.org}; {info@foodtrain.org}.

FREE Training Software for Teachers and Professors

Through the PTC Design & Technology in Schools Program, PTC makes available licenses for 300 classroom seats of its Pro/DESKTOP software to secondary school teachers.

The Design & Technology in Schools Program introduces students to 3D design technology as early as middle school - so they can become better problem solvers, critical thinkers and collaborators. This is about more than just free software - it's about encouraging technological literacy. Contact PTC Corporate Giving Program, c/o Corp. Contributors, 140 Kendrick Street, Needham, MA 02494; 781-370-5000; Fax: 781-370-5647; {http://www.ptc.com/for/education/index.htm}; {schools@ptc.com}

$1,000 for Social Studies Teachers

The Christa McAuliffe Reach for the Stars Award provides one grant of $1,000 to a teacher of social studies or social studies education to help him/her recognize a unique dream that is otherwise unachievable and that relates to the improvement of social studies education. Applicants must be NCSS members who are teachers or educators currently engaged with K-12 students. Contact National Council for the Social Studies, 8555 16th St., N.W., Ste. 500, Silver Spring, MD 20910; 301-588-1800; Fax: 301-588-2049; {http://www.ncss.org}; {excellence@ncss.org}.

$7,500 to Teach Children History

The CiviConnections Grant awards $7,500 grants to a team of three teachers for implementing a new program that provides teacher teams and students in grades 3-12 with opportunities to link local historical inquiry with community service-learning activities. Contact National Council for the Social Studies, 8555 16th St., N.W., Ste. 500, Silver Spring, MD 20910; 301-588-1800; Fax: 301-588-2049; {http://www.ncss.org}; {excellence@ncss.org}.

$1,500 to Advocate for Academic Freedom

The Defense of Academic Freedom Award is a $1,500 award presented to an individual who has contributed in a significant way to the protection of academic freedom in ways that relate to social studies education. This award is by nomination only. Contact National Council for the Social Studies, 8555 16th St., N.W., Ste. 500, Silver Spring, MD 20910; 301-588-1800; Fax: 301-588-2049; {http://www.ncss.org}; {excellence@ncss.org}.

$20,000 for Social Studies Projects

The Fund for the Advancement of Social Studies Education Demonstration Project Grant offers up to $20,000 in support of an innovative collaborative project to enhance and promote social studies education. The proposal should emphasize a program in which NCSS standards are impacting student learning. Applicants must be NCSS members who are current social studies teachers or social studies teacher educators. Categories include K-5, 6-9, 10-12, and college/university. Contact National Council for the Social Studies, 8555 16th St., N.W., Ste. 500, Silver Spring, MD 20910; 301-588-1800; Fax: 301-588-2049; {http://www.ncss.org}; {excellence@ncss.org}.

$2,500 for Outstanding Teachers!

The Outstanding Social Studies Teacher of the Year Awards provides three outstanding K-12 social studies teachers, who have been NCSS members for at least two years, $2,500, complimentary membership in NCSS, and a commemorative plaque. Winners must make an in-service presentation at the annual conference. The award is by nomination only; self-nominations are accepted. Contact National Council for the Social Studies, 8555 16th St., N.W., Ste. 500, Silver Spring, MD 20910; 301-588-1800; Fax: 301-588-2049; {http://www.ncss.org}; {excellence@ncss.org}.

Good Teacher Award: $10,000 Grant

The State Farm Good Neighbor Teacher Award offers a $10,000 grant to social studies teachers who personify a "good neighbor" philosophy through their interest, involvement, and leadership in the field of education. Innovative teachers of grades K-12 are eligible. Contact National Council for the Social Studies, 8555 16th St., N.W., Ste. 500, Silver Spring, MD 20910; 301-588-1800; Fax: 301-588-2049; {http://www.ncss.org}; {excellence@ncss.org}.

$10,000 to Develop Courses for College Teaching

The Contemplative Practice Fellowships are awarded to regular full-time faculty members at U.S. academic institutions. The stipend may be used for salary support and/or research expenses. The program offers approximately 24 fellowships of up to $10,000 for the development of courses and teaching materials that explore contemplative practice from a variety of disciplinary and interdisciplinary perspectives. Fellowships support the study of contemplation not just as a religious practice but as a method for developing concentration and deeper understanding and for cultivating awareness. Contact American Council of Learned Societies (also known as ACLS), 633 3rd Ave., Ste. 8C, New

York, NY 10017-6795; 212-697-1505; Fax: 212-949-8058; {http://www. acls.org}; {grants@acls.org}.

$32,000 for Psychologists to Take Sabbatical

The James McKeen Cattell Fund Fellowships for psychologists provide funds to supplement the regular sabbatical allowance provided by the recipients' home institutions. The maximum award is limited to the lesser of (1) half the recipient's salary for the academic year, (2) an amount less than half salary that will bring the total of the university allowance plus the award up to the individual's normal academic-year salary, or (3) a ceiling of $32,000. Contact James McKeen Cattell Fund, c/o Duke Univ., Dept. of Psychology, Box 90086, Durham, NC 27708-0086; Fax: 919-660-5726; {http://www.cattell.duke.edu/}; {williams@psych.duke.edu}.

Over $8,000 for Christian University Faculty

This Foundation has over $8,000 in grants available to give to Christian colleges or university faculty. Contact Christian Scholars Foundation, c/o Bernard Draper, 8103 Saguaro Ridge Road, Parker, CO 80138-6713; 303-840-2340.

Up to $10,000 for Christian Scholars

In order to encourage exceptional scholars to complete their Ph.D. work, The Christian Scholarship Foundation, Inc. offers three to five Graduate Fellowship Awards, each ranging from $2,000 to $10,000. The fellowship is available to members of the churches of Christ who are teaching or who plan to teach religion and related subjects in universities, colleges, schools of theology, and Bible chairs. The

applicant must have satisfactorily completed at least one full year of study as a candidate for the Ph.D. or equivalent post-graduate degree prior to the year of application. A person already holding a Ph.D. degree is not thereby excluded from candidacy. Study may be pursued in any field related to the recognized theological disciplines in seminary, college, or university programs of instruction leading toward the Ph.D. or equivalent degree. Contact CSF, Inc., 668 Clifton Road, NE, Atlanta, GA 30307; 404-377-6524; Fax: 404-377-4234; {http://www.csfinc.org/ awards.html}.

Funding over $30,000 for Research or Teaching Students

This Foundation supports two fellowship programs: 1) Fellowship Research Grants that offer support for scholarly research and publication projects in the social sciences and humanities, primarily in economics,

history, philosophy, international affairs, and political science. Support is intended to lead to the advancement of knowledge through teaching, lecturing, and publication. Awarded to individuals who are established professionally and associated with educational or research institutions; and 2) H.B. Earhart Fellowships that offer support for graduate study leading to careers in college or university teaching or research. Students must be nominated by faculty. Applications from non-invited sponsors or directly from students are not accepted. Awards range from $400 to over $30,000. Contact Earhart Foundation, 2200 Green Rd., Ste. H, Ann Arbor, MI 48105; 734-761-8592.

$5,000 for Library Projects

The Carnegie-Whitney Awards have been established to provide grants for the preparation and publication of popular or scholarly reading lists, indexes and other guides to library resources that will be useful to users of all types of libraries. The grants may be used for print and electronic projects of varying lengths. Grants are awarded to individuals, official units of the American Library Association and other groups affiliated with the American Library Association. Grants of up to $5,000 each are awarded annually. Contact American Library Association, 50 E. Huron Street, Chicago, IL 60611-2795; 800-545-2433; Fax: 312-944-0379; {http://www.ala.org}; {ala@ala.org}.

$750 for Librarians to Study Publishing

This grant is known as the WNBA–Ann Heidbreder Eastman Grant. The purpose of the grant is to help provide funds for a librarian to take a course or to participate in an intensive institute devoted to aspects of publishing as a profession, or to provide reimbursement for such study completed within the past year. Librarians holding the MLS or its equivalent master's level credential and having at least two years of post-master's work experience in a library are eligible to apply. Criteria for selecting the winner include the assessment of the likelihood of career benefit to the person taking the course. The size of the grant will be up to $750

annually. Contact American Library Association, 50 E. Huron Street, Chicago, IL 60611-2795; 800-545-2433; Fax: 312-944-0379; {http://www.ala.org}; {ala@ala.org}.

Grants up to $10,000 for Excellent Librarians

Several distinct programs offer support for program development, research activities, grants to individual librarians of merit, seed money, and in-kind support to the various types of libraries, school media centers, and librarians. Grants range from $500 up to $10,000. Contact American Library Association, 50 E. Huron Street, Chicago, IL 60611-2795; 800-545-2433; Fax: 312-944-0379; {http://www.ala.org}; {ala@ala.org}.

$6,000 Grants for Teacher Recognition

The Dolores Kohl Education Foundation conducts workshops and seminars for teachers, pupils, and parents to improve the education of children; awards to teachers for exemplary teaching; some grants for furtherance of education; funding also for a children's museum. Early Childhood Teaching Awards was formed to honor outstanding early childhood educators from the three-county Chicago metropolitan area. The Kohl McCormick Awards is the only teacher recognition program designed to acknowledge the talents and contributions of early childhood educators. There is a $5,000 cash award for the teacher and a $1,000 cash award to his/her school or center. Contact Dolores Kohl Education Foundation, 825 Green Bay Rd., Ste. 130, Wilmette, IL 60091; {http://mccormicktribune.org/education/KMAwards/KMawards.htm}.

$25,000 for Elementary School Teachers

The H. E. Butt Grocery Company makes charitable contributions to non-profit organizations involved with arts and culture, education, food distribution, recreation, economic development, and to food banks. It also awards 30 grants to K-12 teachers whose leadership and dedication inspire a love of learning in students of all backgrounds and abilities, ranging from $1,000 to $25,000. Contact H. E. Butt Grocery Company Contributions Program, 646 S. Main Ave., San Antonio, TX 78204; 210-938-8357 / 800-432-3113; {http://www.heb.com/aboutHEB/HH.jsp}.

$40,000 for University Staff to do Research

The Sabbatical Fellowships program is open to mid-career faculty of universities and 4-year colleges in the United States who have been granted a sabbatical/research leave, but for whom financial support from the parent institution is available for only part of the year. The total of institutional and external support should not exceed the academic year salary for the year in which the fellowship is held. The Society encourages candidates to use the resources of the American Philosophical Society Library, but this is not a requirement. The Sabbatical Fellowship carries a stipend of $30,000 to $40,000. Contact American Philosophical Society, 104 S. 5th Street, Philadelphia, PA 19106-3387; {http://www.amphilsoc.org/grants/sabbatical.htm}; {eroach@amphilsoc.org}.

$8,000 for Math Teachers

The National Council of Teachers of Mathematics provides scholarships and grants between $2,000 and $8,000 to mathematics teachers for training and research in the field of mathematics. Giving activities include $301,768 for 89 grants to individuals ranging from $7,000 to $438. Contact National Council of Teachers of Mathematics, 1906 Association Dr., Reston, VA 20191-1502; 703-620-9840, ext. 2113; Fax: 703-476-2970; {http://www.nctm.org}; {email: infocentral@nctm.org}.

$25,000 for Innovative Teachers

The Walt Disney Company Contributions Program includes the DisneyHand Teacher Awards program, which annually awards forty $10,000 grants to pre-K-12 teachers who demonstrate innovative teaching methods that actively engage students in learning. The schools of each winner receive $5,000 and the top winner receives an additional $15,000. Contact The Walt Disney Company Contributions Program, 500 S. Buena Vista St., Burbank, CA 91521-0893; 877-282-8322; {http://disney.go.com/disneyhand}. Additional application address: DisneyHand Teacher Awards: P.O. Box 10404, Van Nuys, CA 91410-0404.

$1,000 for Teachers and Schools

The Chadwick's of Boston, Inc. Corporate Giving Program makes charitable contributions to K-12 teachers and their schools. Support is given on a national basis. Through the Teacher of the Year Award Program, Chadwick's of Boston annually awards 10 gift certificates worth $300 to K-12 teachers who make a positive impact on their community, school, classroom, or students, and the school of each winner receives $500. Contact

Chadwick's of Boston, Inc. Corporate Giving Program, 35 United Dr., West Bridgewater, MA 02379-1027; application address for Teacher of the Year Award: c/o Chadwick's of Boston Teacher of the Year, c/o Mailboxes Etc., Box 151, Needham, MA 02492; {http://www.chadwicks.com/chadwick s/teacher/teacher.asp}; {email: cobteacher@aol.com}.

$300 for Innovative Teachers

The Curriculum Associates, Inc. Corporate Giving Program awards grants to pre-K-12 educators. Support is given on a national basis. Through the Partners for Growth Matching Grants program, Curriculum Associates annually awards 400 grants of classroom materials worth $300 to pre-K-12 educators who demonstrate an innovative approach to teaching with Curriculum Associates research-based instructional and assessment materials, and matches the grant with an additional $300. Contact Curriculum Associates, Inc. Corporate Giving Program, P.O. Box 2001, North Billerica, MA 01862-9914; 800-225-0248; application address for Partners for Growth: c/o Partners for Growth Prog., 153 Rongeway Rd., North Billerica, MA 01862; 800-225-0248, ext. 265; {http://www.curricassoc. com/grants}; {email: grants@curricu lumassociates.com}.

$750 for Visual Learning Programs

The Inspiration Software Inspired Teacher Scholarships for Visual Learning Program provides grants of $750 to K-12 teachers that champion visual learning in the classroom. Award recipients may use the $750 scholarships for a wide range of professional development activities, including attendance at a conference,

training event or professional education course where visual learning is a key topic. Contact Inspiration Software Inspired Teacher Scholarships for Visual Learning Program, c/o Inspired Teacher Scholarships, 7412 S.W. Beaverton-Hillsdale Hwy., Ste. 102, Portland, Oregon 97225-2167; 503-297-3004 / 800-877-4292; Fax : 503-297-4676; {http://www.inspiration.com/prodev/in dex.cfm?fuseaction=winners}; {email: webmaster@inspiration.com}.

$5,000 for Teachers

The NEA Foundation for the Improvement of Education makes grants to improve public education nationwide. Primary giving interests include: improving professional development for public school teachers, public school education support professionals, and faculty and staff at public higher education institutions; improving arts education; closing the achievement gap; promoting innovation in teaching and learning; and using technology in the curriculum. The foundation provides $2,000 grants to teachers for the development of fine arts program, and $5,000 grants for creative teaching methods. Also provides grants of between $2,000 and $5,000 for professional development programs for public school teachers. Giving activities include $266,626 for 79 grants to individuals ranging from $35,000 to $333. Contact The NEA Foundation for the Improvement of Education, 1201 16th St., N.W., Washington, DC 20036-3207; 202-822-7840; Fax: 202-822-7779; {http://www.nfie.org}.

Fellowships for Future High School Math and Science Teachers

The Knowles Science Teaching Foundation was established to strengthen the quality of science and mathematics teaching, grades 7-12 in United States schools. The foundation provides the Knowles Science Teaching Fellows Program. The teaching fellows are young men and women with a bachelor's or advanced degree in science, engineering or mathematics, and who plan to teach high school science and mathematics. The fellowship supports them for up to five years through a teacher preparation program to eligibility for tenure. Fellows are selected from among students who have earned or are in the process of earning a degree in one of the physical sciences such as physics, chemistry, astronomy, geology and/or engineering. Usually fellows will have earned, or be in the final year of, their undergraduate or graduate degree. Applicants who will be in their first year of teaching are also eligible. The foundation also provides funding for science education research projects. Applicants for these projects may be higher education faculty, doctoral candidates, post-docs, scholars on sabbatical, emeritus professors, teachers and others in science, in education and in related fields. Contact The Knowles Science Teaching Foundation, 20 East Redman Avenue, Haddonfield, NJ 08033; 856-216-8080; Fax: 856-216-9987;

{http://www.kstf.org/programs.htm}; {email: info@kstf.org}.

Funding for Research and Educational Materials about India

The Infinity Foundation seeks to promote a proper understanding of the Indian civilization. The foundation provides grants for projects involving research and/or the development of educational materials that improve the authenticity of portrayal of Indic traditions in the educational system. The foundation particularly wants proposals on the following subjects: the contributions of India to world civilization in math, science, technology, philosophy, religion; India's role in world history; India's influence on literature in the West; Indic contributions to modern psychology; India's influence on the development of European and Asian languages; current social conditions of India; the portrayal of India in American educational materials; and media portrayals about India. An individual grantee must be a scholar, teacher, visionary, or spiritual leader whose work in the topics above would be enhanced by a grant from the foundation. Contact The Infinity Foundation, 66 Witherspoon Street, Suite 400, Princeton, NJ 08542; 609-683-0548; Fax: 609-683-0478; {http://www.infinityfoundation.com}; {email: mail@infinityfoundation. com}.

Grants Up To $18,000 for K-12 Math and Science Teachers

The Toshiba American Foundation offers grants to math and science teachers of students from K-12. These grants are for specific classroom math and science education projects.

Teachers must submit a specific project description with their grant application. Past grants range from approximately $760 to $18,000. Contact Toshiba America Foundation, 1251 Avenue of the Americas, 41st Floor, New York, NY 10020; 212-596-0620; Fax: 212-221-1108; {http://www.toshiba.com/taf/about_us.html}; {email: foundation@tai.toshiba.com}.

Money for Native American and Native Hawaiian Libraries

Over 250 libraries shared $3.5 million dollars to support their core library operations, professional assessment, and the education of their staff. These funds can be used to establish or enhance links among libraries, link libraries electronically with education, social or information services, pay costs for libraries to acquire or share computer systems, and to better serve those who have difficulty using the libraries. In addition there is the Native American Library Services Enhancement Grant which provides up to $150,000 for a one to two year project that enhances existing library services. Contact Institute of Museum and Library Services, Office of Library Services, 1100 Pennsylvania Ave., NW, Room 802, Washington, DC 20506; 202-606-5408; {www.imls.gov}.

Up to $1 Million To Train Librarians

Librarians for the 21st Century is a program that supports efforts to recruit and educate the next generation of librarians and the faculty. It also supports grants for research related to library education and library staffing needs, curriculum development, and continuing education and training. These funds can be used for scholarships and fellowships for Master's and Doctoral programs, recruitment programs to attract promising high school and college students, as well as training and continuing education programs. Contact Institute of Museum and Library Services, Office of Library Services, 1100 Pennsylvania Ave., NW, Room 802, Washington, DC 20506; 202-606-5528; {www.imls.gov}.

School Libraries Can Share $20 Million

That is how much money is available through the Literacy through School Libraries program operated by the U.S. Department of Education. This program is designed to provide students with increased access to up-to-date school library materials, and provide them with a well-equipped technologically advanced school library media center with a trained staff. Money has been used in the past to support a district-wide library revitalization project in elementary schools, development of a full-service library in a rural area, and the implementation of a technology-based reading program. Contact U.S. Department of Education, OESE Academic Improvement and Teacher Quality Programs, 400 Maryland Ave., SW, Room 2W104; Washington, DC 20202; 202-401-3751; {www.ed.gov/programs/lsl/index.html}.

Get A Shelf Of Books FREE

We The People is a program of the National Endowment for the Humanities that explores events and themes in our nation's history. We The People Bookshelf is a set of books given to libraries who sponsor programs, books clubs, plays, etc. that encourage young readers to learn more about our country. Contact National Endowment for the Arts, Office of Public Affairs, 1100 Pennsylvania Ave., NW, Washington, DC 20506; 202-606-8299; {www.wethepeople. gov}.

FREE Art Resources For Your Library

The National Gallery of Art offers a free loan program of videos, slides, DVDs, CD-ROMs and more for libraries to use in art education and humanities programs. If your library would like to promote certain programs, contact Department of Education Resources, National Gallery of Art, 2000B South Club Drive, Landover, MD 20785; {www.nga. gov/education/classroom/loanfinder/}.

Get And Stay Connected

Bill Gates foundation has supported libraries in their attempts to get connected to the internet and to stay technologically advanced. Two programs the foundation offers include:

US Library Program: The foundation has partnered with public libraries to bring access to computers, the Internet, and digital information to low-income and disadvantaged communities.

Staying Connected Challenge Grants: These challenge grants are given to state library agencies so they can assist local libraries with their technology needs, particularly in training staff and keeping their computer systems

running. This is a matching grant program. Staying Connected grants support four activities: hardware upgrades and replacements, internet connectivity upgrades, training support and technical support. A "Toolkit" is available and is designed to help libraries engage local communities in their technology programs. Contact Bill & Melinda Gates Foundation, P.O. Box 23350, Seattle, WA 98102; 206-709-3140; {www.gatesfoundation. org}.

Surplus Books For You

The Library of Congress has surplus books available to non-profit organizations. The books are a mixture of topics with only a small percentage of publications at the primary and secondary school levels. Your library either needs to send or designate someone to choose books from the collection. Shipping the material to your library is your only expense. Contact Anglo-American Acquisitions Division, Library of Congress, 101 Independence Ave., SE, Washington, DC 20540; 202-707-9524; {www.loc. gov/acq/surplus.html}.

Help From The Cell Phone People

The Verizon Foundation is a web based grant organization; you can search for Verizon's support in your community by entering your zip code on their web site.

Verizon Reads: Verizon is committed to helping America raise literacy levels. They offer a variety of literacy programs and grants.

Verizon Works: Verizon encourages nonprofits to use technology as a tool to connect their communities and work force through education and training.

Verizon volunteers: This program encourages Verizon employees to give back to their communities through time and money and provides matching gifts and foundation grants to nonprofit organizations employees support. Libraries can request volunteers through this program. Contact Verizon Foundation; 800-360-7955; Fax: 212-840-6988; {http://foundation.verizon.com}.

Non-profit Guides

Non-profit Guides offers free web-based grant-writing resources for non-profit organizations. The guides are designed to assist established non-profits through the grant-writing process. {www.npguides.org}.

Help Fund Literacy Programs

ProLiteracy Worldwide provides the National Book Scholarship Fund that supplies books and materials to local literacy programs. Priority is given to programs that focus on family literacy. Contact National Book Scholarship Fund, ProLiteracy Worldwide, 1320 Jamesville Avenue, Syracuse, NY 13210; 888-528-2224; 315-422-9121; Fax: 315-422-6369; {www.nbsf.org}.

$350 Literacy and Creativity Money

The Ezra Jack Keats Foundation offers mini-grants of $350 to libraries for programs that encourage literacy and creativity. Programs are not required to be related to the works of Ezra Jack Keats. Contact Ezra Jack Keats Mini-grants, 450-14 Street, Brooklyn, NY 11215-5702; {www.ezra-jack-keats.org}.

Money From The Phone People

AT&T Foundation offers grants to help organizations meet the needs and services of the community members. Specific program areas include education, arts and culture, and civic and community service. In addition, they offer 1/3 of their grant money through their local communities fund. Contact AT&T Foundation at {http://www. att.com/foundation/}.

$5,000 From the Electric Company

Westinghouse has established a Charitable Giving Program with the focus on education and civic and societal needs. Money is awarded to organizations that are located in the areas where Westinghouse has a presence. Contact the Westinghouse Charitable Giving Advisory Board, P.O. Box 355, ECE 575C, Pittsburgh, PA 15230; 412-374-6824; {www. westinghousenuclear.com}.

Free Books For Kids

The First Book program is a national organization focusing on getting books into the hands of children from low-income families. In the past three years, over 20 million new books have been distributed. Books are given to the program through donations from children's book publishers, services donors, and volunteers. To receive books for your program you may contact either a First Book Advisory Board that may be in existence in your community or you can contact the National Book Bank. Contact First Book, 1319 F St., NW, Suite 1000, Washington, DC 20004; 202-393-1222; {www.firstbook.org}.

Protect Your School Library Books

The 3M Corporation has joined with the American Association of School Librarians and offers $1.5 million worth of 3M Detection Systems and Tattle-Tape Security Strips. To learn how to apply to receive the benefits of this program contact American Association of School Librarians, 50 East Huron St., Chicago, IL 60611; 312-280-4382; 800-545-2433; {www.ala.org/ala/aasl/aaslindex.htm}.

$660,000 In Grants For School Library Books

The Laura Bush Foundation awarded that amount of money to fund the purchase of books for school libraries. The funds are to be used to update, extend, and diversify the book collection in a school library. Contact the Laura Bush Foundation for America's Libraries, c/o Community Foundation for the National Capital Region, 1201 15th St., NW, Suite 420, Washington, DC 20005; 202-955-5890; {www.laurabushfoundation.org}.

Books For Rural Libraries

The Libri Foundation helps rural libraries purchase new hard cover children's books which they typically cannot afford. Friends of the Library or other local organizations can contribute up to $350 of which the Libri Foundation will match 2:1, for a total of $1,050 worth of new books.

The local library can choose the book from the Foundation's extensive title list. Contact the Libri Foundation, P.O. Box 10246, Eugene, OR 97440; 541-747-9655; {www.librifoundation.org}.

More Free Books

Children's author Ann M. Martin and friends began Lisa Libraries as a memorial to a friend. Lisa Libraries donates new books to organizations serving children in low-income areas, and helps to start or expand children libraries in places such as day care centers, prison visiting areas, and after school programs. Contact The Lisa Libraries, P.O. Box 430, Boiceville, NY 12412; {www.lisalibraries.org}.

$8,000 in Free Books

The National Book Scholarship Fund provides books and materials to literacy programs. The books are from New Readers Press books. The fund supports family literacy, English as a second language, adult basic education and tutor training. In return for the books, the receiving organization pays the Fund 20% in cash for the worth of their request. Contact Mara Roberts, Program Administration, National Book Scholarship Fund, Pro Literacy Worldwide, 1320 Jamesville Ave., Syracuse, NY 13210; {www.nbsf.org}.

Money To Get Connected

The Schools and Libraries Division of the Universal Service Administrative Company provides access to telecommunications services for all eligible schools and libraries. This program offers discounts on internet access and telecommunications services. To learn if you qualify, contact the Universal Service Administrative Company at 888-203-8100; {www.sl.universalservice.org}.

$10,000 With Your Cup Of Coffee

The Starbucks Foundation has a mission to help the youth in underserved communities through the funding of programs that teach leadership, literacy and respect for diversity. Starbucks Foundation provides grants to programs which focus on literacy and writing for children through the age of 21. Grants are given to organizations in communities in which Starbucks stores are located. Two different programs are available. A $1,000 mini-grant is available to local projects involving the store's employees. A $10,000 Opportunity Grant is available to larger projects that involve Starbucks stores, employees, and customers. Applications for the mini-grants are available from Starbucks stores. Contact Starbucks Foundation, 22401 Utah Ave., South, Seattle, WA 98134; 206-447-7950; {http://www.starbucks. com/aboutus/grantinfo.asp}.

Money And Books From Albertson's

Albertson's stores support the neighborhood by offering more than $78 million in cash and donations to support several different focus areas, including the schools. Last year with a partnership with Coca-Cola Company, Albertson's was able to distribute a half-million books to schools. To learn more about their grant and books programs contact your local Albertson's or Albertson's Inc., 250 E. Parkcenter Blvd., Boise, ID 83706; 877-932-7948; {www.albertsons.com/ abs_inthecommunity/}.

$15 Million from Alcoa

The Alcoa Foundation wants to improve the quality of life in communities where Alcoa is located

worldwide. In order to better serve the community, Alcoa has four Areas of Excellence from which the grants must originate. The Areas include: Conservation and Sustainability, Safe and Health Children and Families, Global Education and Workplace Skills, and Business and Community Partnerships. To learn how to apply for a grant, contact your nearest Alcoa location, or be directed to the correct office by calling Alcoa Foundation, 3029 Alcoa Corporate Center, 201 Isabella Street. Pittsburgh, PA 15212-5858; 412-553-2348; {www.alcoa. com/global/en/community/info_page/F oundation.asp}.

Grants From The Energy People

Alliant Energy offers Community Grants to support programs and initiatives in areas where the energy company is located, in order to improve the lives of their employees and residents of their communities. Grants are awarded in specific areas such as human needs, education, culture and art, civic, and environment. They have a presence in Iowa, Wisconsin, Minnesota and Illinois. To find the exact service areas, please check the website. For more information on the grant program contact Executive Director, Alliant Energy Foundation, P. O. Box 77007, Madison, WI 53707; 608-458-4483;

800-255-4268; {www.alliantenergy.com/stellent/groups/public/documents/pub/comm_cf_index.hcsp}.

Money From Insurance People

The Allstate Foundation offers grants to programs focusing on the areas of safe and vital communities, tolerance, inclusion and diversity, and economic empowerment. Grants to organizations that cross various regions should apply to the National headquarters. Local organizations should send their grant requests to local regional offices found on the website. Contact The Allstate Foundation, 2275 Sanders Rd., Suite F4, Northbrook, IL 60062; 847-402-5502; {www.allstate.com/foundation}.

Electronic Company Offers Grants

The Tyco Electronics Foundation make grants to organizations in communities where Tyco employees live. Because of their electronics focus, Tyco supports grants that encourage science and math, although they do make contributions for community programming with an education component. Contact Mary Rakoczy, The Tyco Electronics Foundation, c/o Tyco Electronics Corp., P.O. Box 3608, MS 140-10, Harrisburg, PA 17105; 717-592-4869; {www.tyco electronics.com/about/foundation/}.

Get Your Money From The Bank

Bank of America Foundation is one of the largest philanthropic organizations of any corporation, offering over $108 million in grants last year. The Foundation has a focus on child development, economic and financial education, and teacher development. Each region that the Bank serves determines their own areas of need,

and these can be found on the website. Your organization must be located in a service area of the Bank. For more information on how to apply for a grant contact Julie Chavez, Bank of America Foundation, 213 S. LaSalle St., Chicago, IL 60604; 888-488-9802; {www.bankofamerica.com/foundation/}.

The Book People Give More Than Books

Barnes and Noble supports local organizations that promote literacy and the arts or education. Organizations that seek support need to be willing to include Barnes and Noble in in-store programming and promotion of project. Proposals should be submitted through the local store, and they will then be forwarded to the district manager. Contact your local store or Mary Ellen Keating, Senior Vice President, Corporate Communications, Barnes & Noble, 122 Fifth Ave., New York, NY 10011; {www.barnes andnobleinc.com/company/codonation/co_donation.html}.

You Can Bank On It

Citigroup Foundation offers grants to organizations in Citigroup areas throughout the world. The areas of focus include financial education, educating the next generation and building communities and entrepreneurs. Literacy development is included in the education component. Contact Charles V. Raymond, President, Citigroup Foundation, 850 Third Ave., 13th Floor, New York, NY 10043; 212-559-9163; {www.citigroup.com/citigroup/citizen/community/index.htm}.

More Than Just Food

Darden Restaurants, which include Red Lobster, Olive Garden, Bahama Breeze, and more wants to improve communities in areas of arts and culture, social services and nutrition, education, and preservation of natural resources. Projects in Atlanta, Cincinnati, Chicago, Dallas, Detroit, Houston, Los Angeles, Miami, Oklahoma City, and the central Florida area are eligible. Contact Foundation Administrator, Darden Restaurant Foundation, P.O. Box 59330; Orlando, FL 32859; 407-245-5213; {www. dardenrestaurants.com}.

More Than A Dollar

The Dollar General Literacy Foundation obviously has a focus area of increasing the literacy of adults and supports organization who have this mission. Organizations must be located within the Dollar General market area. For more information on how to apply for a grant contact The Dollar General Literacy Foundation, P.O. Box 1064, Goodlettsville, TN 37072; {www. dollargeneral.com/community/dglitera cy.aspx}.

$2,000, Papers, Staplers, And More

Office Depot has a program called Caring and Making a Difference that operates in communities where their employees live. Every store makes regular product donations, and the focus of their grant giving is on the health, education, and welfare of children. Nonprofits with those goals in mind can request funds of up to $2,000. Contact Office Depot, 2200 Old Germantown Rd., Delray Beach, FL 33445; attn: Donations; 800-937-3600; {www.community.office depot.com}.

Free Art Books For Rural And Inner City Schools

The Art Resources Transfer Inc. is a non-profit organization that donates

books on art and culture to any library through their Distribution to Underserved Communities Library Program. This program also pays for the shipment of the books to the library. Their goal is to make information on contemporary art and cultural issues available to all. You can view the books available online and fill out a simple request form. Books are available on a first-come, first-served basis. Contact DUC Library Program, Arts Resources Transfer, 526 West 26th St., Room 614, New York, NY 10001; 212-255-2919; {www.duc program.org/index.htm}.

Garth Brooks and Kids

Garth Brooks started the Teammates for Kids Foundation to support non-profits whose focus is on working with children. Grants may be given to help organizations with programs focusing on health and education of children. Contact Teammates for Kids Foundation, 7851 S. Elati St., Suite 200, Littleton, CO 80120; {www. touchmeall.com}.

Money From Coca-Cola

The Coca-Cola Foundation focuses on the educational opportunities for youth to help them become knowledgeable about the world in which they live. Grants are given to colleges, universities, elementary and secondary schools, teacher training, special programs for minority students, and more. They support innovative school programs, and programs to help kids stay in school. Contact The Coca-Cola Foundation, P.O. 1734, Atlanta, GA 30301; 404-676-2568; {www2.coca-cola.com/citizenship/foundation.html}.

Cheap Books

Literacy Empowerment Foundation is a non-profit organization designed to help educational programs by offering low cost books. The Reading Recycling Project runs throughout the year, and offers 100 books free of charge (must pay shipping) new and gently used books to literacy programs. Although the selection is dependent upon availability, the program makes an effort to meet the needs of the program. Classroom libraries can order 100 new books organized for a specific grade for $125. Bruce Larkin, a children's book author, has agreed to donate sets of 25 free books to every kindergarten and first grade classroom in the U.S. Children will be given the book to call their own. Titles will change every month so children can receive 12 different titles during the school year. You must reorder each month. The program also offers a Matching Book Grant which allows libraries to purchase $1,000 worth of books for $500 (can go up to $16,000 value). Contact Literacy Empowerment Foundation, 6323 Salem Park Circle, Mechanicsburg, PA 17050; 717-791-6210; {www. colorcodedbooks.org}.

Money From The Car People
The Ford Motor Company Fund focuses on grants in five areas: education, environment, public policy, health & social programs, civic affairs & community development, and arts & humanities. The Fund wants to help improve the communities and lives where the company operates. Contact Ford Motor Company Fund, One American Road, P.O. Box 1899, Dearborn, MI 48126; 888-313-0102; {www.ford.com}.

Paper and Money
The International Paper Company Foundation helps communities where they operate, especially those in which their employees volunteer. Areas of focused giving include literacy,

education, civic needs, and more. They sponsor teacher workshops and Earth Day activities. A required grant application form is available on the website. Contact Executive Director, International Paper Company Foundation, 400 Atlantic St., Stamford, CT 06921; {www. internationalpaper.com}.

$3,000 From Target
Target awards Arts and Reading Grants to local nonprofit organizations. Contact your local Target store for the $1,000 to $3,000 grants. Grants are made in the area of early education, arts, and family violence prevention. Target gives over $2 million each week back to communities. You can check the web site to locate a store near you. Target also has local teams of volunteers to help out in the community. Target Grant Program; {http://target.com}.

Money From The Cell Phone People
U.S. Cellular focuses on nonprofit organizations that have significant relevance in the following areas: Civic and Community, Education, Health and Human Service, Environment and Arts and Culture. Contributions are available in certain areas of Illinois, Indiana, Iowa, Maine, Minnesota,

Missouri, Nebraska, New Hampshire, North Carolina, Oklahoma, Oregon, Tennessee and Wisconsin. Contact US Cellular, Public Affairs & Communications Department, c/o U.S. Cellular's Connecting With Our Communities Program, 8410 West Bryn Mawr, Suite 700, Chicago, IL 60631; {www.uscc.com/uscellular/SilverStream/Pages/a_charitable.html}

$5.5 Million From Sprint

The Foundation makes grants to nonprofit organizations with major interest in education, arts and culture, community involvement and youth development. Grants are primarily awarded to geographical areas with significant employee presence including Kansas City, Atlanta, Dallas and Sacramento. Contact Sprint Foundation Headquarters, 6200 Sprint Parkway, Overland Park, KS 66251; 800-829-0965; {www.sprint.com/community/sprint_foundation/index.html}.

Money From Cingular

Cingular wants to improve the communities where we work and live. Cingular supports community-based nonprofit organizations in the following areas: educational, cultural, and social issues. Contact Cingular Wireless Headquarters, Glenridge Highlands Two, 5565 Glenridge Connector, Atlanta, GA 30342; 866-CINGULAR; {www.cingular.com/about/community_involvement}.

$150 Million From Walmart

Walmart supports a variety of local programs throughout the United States. Through volunteer commitment and community grants local nonprofits may be eligible for part of the millions of dollars that they provide yearly. Contact your local Walmart or Sam's

Club for information. Contact Walmart Foundation; 800-530-9925; {www.walmartfoundation.org/wmstore/goodworks/scripts/index.jsp}.

Money From Walgreen's

Walgreen's funds are awarded to eligible nonprofit organizations in local Walgreen communities. They provide grants in the health related programs, One-on-One tutorial programs and community and social service agencies. Contact Walgreens Community Relations, Mail Stop #2255, 200 Wilmont Road, Deerfield, IL 60015; 947-914-2500; 847-914-2856 guideline voicemail; {www.walgreens.com/about/community/guidelines.jhtml}.

Up To $10,000 In Railroad Money

The Union Pacific Foundation wants to improve the communities where their employees live. Grants are awarded to nonprofit organizations located within communities serviced by Union Pacific Railroad. You must apply for the grant online. Contact Union Pacific Railroad Foundation, 1400 Douglas Street, Omaha, NE 68179; 402-544-5000; 888-870-8777; {www.up.com/found}.

$22 Million From The Bank

U.S. Bancorp supports many programs including literacy training and mentoring programs, as well as artistic and cultural enrichment. U.S. Bancorp awards grants to nonprofit organizations at a local level. Contact your local branch or check the web site for a location in your area. Contact U.S. Bancorp Charitable Giving; {www.usbank.com/about/community_relations/charit_giving.html}.

Money From Supervalu

The SUPERVALU Foundation provides support to local programs that meet local community's needs. Funding is available for programs within the following guidelines: education, social service, workforce development, hunger relief and fine arts. Contact SUPERVALU Foundation, P.O. Box 990, Minneapolis, MN 55440; {www.supervalu.com/community/comm_main.html}.

Up To $25,000 From Staples

Staples Foundation provides funds to non-profit organizations that support job skills and education for all people especially the disadvantaged youth. Contact Staples Foundation for Learning, 500 Staples Drive, 4 West, Farmington. MA 01702; 508-253-9600; {www.staplesfoundation.org/}.

$2,500 From 7-Eleven

Grants are available from $1,000 to $2,500 to non-profit organizations located in communities where 7-Eleven stores operate. Programs eligible include those that assist adolescents and adults, especially at-risk and economically disadvantaged, with workforce development and literacy as their primary mission. Contact 7-Eleven Community Affairs, P.O. Box 711, Dallas, TX 75221; 214-828-7480; {www.7-eleven.com/about/outreachprograms.asp}.

Travel Overseas

Traditional Fulbright Scholar Program: This traditional program offers U.S. professional and faculty to travel abroad for two months for up to an academic year. The Scholars lecture and conduct research in a wide variety of academic and professional areas. *Fulbright Senior Specialists Program*: This grant program offers short-term Fulbright grants of two to six weeks. Contact Fulbright Program, Office of Academic Exchange Programs, Bureau of Educational and Cultural Affairs, U.S. Department of State, SA-44, 301 4th Street, S.W., Room 234, Washington, DC 20547; 202-619-4360; {http://exchanges.state.gov/education/fulbright/index.htm}.

Money For Author Visits

PEN offers the Readers & Writers program as a grant to sites that cannot afford author visits. Three different authors visit each site over a ten-month period. In addition, the program provides a copy of the author's book for each student. Contact PEN American Center, Readers & Writers Program, 588 Broadway, Suite 303, New York, NY 10012; 212-334-1660, ext 109; {www.pen.org/readers&writers/home.htm}.

Teach Tolerance

Teaching Tolerance provides free multimedia kits to libraries that work with youth. Check the website for the many titles available. Contact Teaching Tolerance, 400 Washington Avenue, Montgomery, AL 36104; 334-956-8376; {www.teachingtolerance.org}.

TRAVEL

Travel and see the world. That is the goal for many people, but how do you do it on the cheap? Look to Uncle Sam to see what he may offer to help you and start packing your bags.

1) Find All Federal Government Money Programs For Travel

They are described in a book call the Catalog of Federal Domestic Assistance. This book is available at your local public library or the U.S. Government Printing Office {www.gpo.gov}. You can also search the contents of this book for free on the web at {www.cfda.gov}.

2) Find Interesting Travel Information

Check online at {www.firstgov.gov} as there is a listing for Travel and Recreation which provides information on a wealth of topics.

3) Find Your State Travel Information

Contact your state tourism board to find great places to see for free or cheap. To locate your state tourism office you can contact your state capitol operator by calling 411 or you can find a link on the website {www.firstgov.gov}.

4) When You Need Help

If you are overseas and in trouble, who do you call? Are there countries you should not visit? What if you lose your passport? How do I get a Visa? All these questions and more are handled by the U.S. Department of State's Office of Citizen Services. They have lists of doctors and lawyers located in various countries that can help you, and more.

Their website has a wealth of information and tips before you even leave this country. For more information contact the Office of Citizens Services, U.S. Department of State, Room 4817 NS, 2201 C St., NW, Washington, DC 20520; 202-647-5225; {http://travel.state.gov}.

5) *Help From The U.S. Department of Education*

U.S. Network for Education Information was created in the fall of 1996 as a national information and referral service to assist American educators, students, and parents with access to reliable information about international education and to provide basic information and referral contacts to resources within U.S. education. The United States Information Service (USIS) administers a worldwide network of overseas Educational Advising Centers (EACs) whose mission is to help persons and organizations in a particular country who are interested in education in the United States. While the main work of these Centers consists in advising local nationals, they can also provide information and assistance to Americans living or working within the areas that they serve. The website has links to study abroad programs, and for teachers interested in teaching overseas. Contact U.S. Network for Education Information, National Library of Education, 400 Maryland Ave., SW, Washington, DC 20202; 800-424-1616; {www.ed.gov/about/offices/list/ous/international/usnei/edlite-index.html}.

Teacher at Sea Program

Teachers from elementary to college can climb aboard a NOAA research and survey ship to work under the tutelage of knowledgeable scientists and crew. Teachers can gain first hand knowledge to help enrich their classrooms. Teachers may choose from one of 15 ships that conduct a variety of scientific research. NOAA-Marine Operations Center, Pacific, 1801 Fairview Avenue, E, Seattle, WA 98102-3767; 206-553-8705; {www.tas.noaa.gov/}.

National Park Service- Volunteers-In-Parks (VIP) Program

The Volunteers-In-Parks volunteers donated 4.5 million hours of their time to national parks in 2003. Volunteers can help in a variety of ways and must contact each park to find out about available opportunities. (http://nps.gov/volunteer/)

International Volunteers-In-Parks Program offers opportunities to individuals from all over the world. Call 202-354-1807 for information on the International Program.

Natural Resource Laureate Program is a new program that hosts science-based professionals in the national parks. The program matches volunteers possessing proven science backgrounds with parks needing specific natural resource expertise. Contact them at 540-788-3274 or {www.nature.nps.gov/partnerships/laureateprogram.htm}.

Take Your Kids On An Archeology Expedition

How about going on a free archeological dig for 2 weeks in Alaska? Or studying marine biology off the coast of Maine? That was what my family and I did for two summers with a U.S. Department of Agriculture program called Passport in Time. Passport in Time helps you open a window to the past by allowing you to join activities such as archaeological excavation, site mapping, drafting, laboratory and art work, collecting oral histories, restoration, and much more. Projects vary in length and there is no registration fee. Kids are allowed on many of the projects. Contact Passport

In Time Clearinghouse, P.O. Box 31315, Tucson, AZ 85751; 800-281-9176; {www.passportintime.com}.

Take Your Craft On The Road Or Even To Other Countries

Many state arts councils support travel, exhibitions and performances throughout the state, region, or even overseas. Illinois has an Access Program which provides funds to bring art to communities normally deprived of performances. They also have money for Touring Art Groups. Most states have funds to help bring art to rural areas or to groups with minimal access. To see what your state has to offer, contact your state Arts Council in your state capitol. If you have trouble locating it, you can call your state operator at 411, or check online at {www.govengine.gov}. Nonprofit arts organizations may be able to access travel funds by applying for a National Endowment for the Arts grants. Contact National Endowment for the Arts, 1100 Pennsylvania Ave., NW, Washington, DC 20506; {http://arts. endow.gov}.

Get Paid To Take Your Work Overseas

Get paid to represent America at a conference in India for 2 weeks, or take your jazz group to tour Japan. These programs are part of the activities at the U.S. Department of State's Office of Citizen Exchanges. The Office manages professional, youth and cultural program exchanges. Grants are awarded to American participants or nonprofit organizations, but individuals are encouraged to have foreign co-sponsors. Cultural exchanges show the creativity and dynamism of American society, and the participants in these programs are enriched through the exposure to other cultures. Contact Office of Citizen Exchanges (ECA/PE/C), Bureau of Educational and Cultural Affairs, U.S. Department of State, SA-44, 301 Fourth Street, S.W., Washington, D.C. 20547; 202-619-5348; {http:// exchanges.state.gov}.

$45,000 To Get A Ph.D. Abroad

Did you know that if you are a doctoral student, you can take your spouse – and even your kids! – overseas with you to do research? The Fulbright-Hays Overseas Doctoral Dissertation provides grants to colleges and universities to fund individual doctoral students to conduct research in other countries in modern foreign languages and area studies for periods of 6 to 12 months. Proposals focusing on Western Europe are not eligible. Financial award includes a basic stipend, air fare for recipient only; dependents allowance for accompanying dependents; allowance for project materials, services, and supplies, tuition payments to foreign institutions, and local travel expenditures; and funds for health insurance. Contact the U.S. Department of Education, OPE, International Education Programs Service, 1990 K Street, N.W., 6th Floor, Washington, DC 20006-8521; 202-502-7632; {www.ed.gov/ programs/iegpsddrap/index.html}. {http://12.46.245.173/pls/portal30/CA TALOG.PROGRAM_TEXT_RPT.SH OW?p_arg_names=prog_nbr&p_arg_v alues=84.022}.

$6,000 For Teachers To Travel

The Fulbright-Hays Faculty Research Abroad Fellowship Program provides grants to colleges and universities to fund faculty to maintain and improve their area studies and language skills by conducting research abroad for periods of 3 to 12 months. Proposals focusing on Western Europe are not eligible. Financial provisions include a stipend in lieu of salary; air fare; allowance for project materials; services and supplies; fees to foreign institutions; and local travel expenditures. Contact the U.S. Department of Education, OPE, International Education Programs Service, 1990 K Street, N.W., Washington, D.C. 20006-8521; 202-502-7633; {www.ed.gov/programs/ iegpsfra/index.html}.

$3,700 For Summer Travel For Teachers

Students aren't the only ones who can get away for the summer. Teachers, and even librarians, are eligible for summer studies that enable them to do a little traveling too. Each year the National Endowment for the Humanities offers teachers opportunities to study humanities topics in a variety of Summer Seminars and Institutes. All teachers selected to participate will be awarded a stipend of $2,800, $3,250, or $3,700 (depending on the length of the seminar) to help cover travel costs, books, research expenses, and living expenses. Full-time teachers in U.S. K-12 schools, as well as librarians and school administrators, may apply. Contact the National Endowment for the Humanities, 1100 Pennsylvania Avenue, NW, Washington, DC 20506; 202-606-8463; {www.neh.gov/pro jects/sischool.html}.

$30,000 To Travel To Italy

You just may be eligible for a fellowship in Italy, Greece, or even Turkey. The National Endowment for the Humanities (NEH) provides fellowships to scholars with a collegial environment and access to resources that might not be available at their home institutions. NEH Fellowship programs may be administered by independent centers for advanced study, libraries, and museums in the U.S., or American overseas research centers or other organizations that have expertise in promoting research on foreign cultures. Contact NEH, 1100 Pennsylvania Avenue, N.W., Washington, DC 20506, 202-606-8400; {www.neh.gov/projects/fpiri.html}.

$7,500 For A Summer At NASA

Did you know you could actually study at NASA? The National Aeronautics and Space Administration is sponsoring the NASA Undergraduate Student Research Program, offering undergraduates research experiences at NASA Centers. The program is accepting applications from undergraduate juniors and seniors enrolled full-time in an accredited U.S. college or university. Eligible fields of study are in engineering, mathematics, computer science, or physical/life sciences. The program will consist of a 10–15 week research experience at a participating

NASA Center under the supervision of a NASA technical mentor. Students will receive a $5,000 (10-week summer session) or $7,500 (15-week fall session) stipend for the research experience plus one round-trip airfare or ground transportation costs to and from the NASA Host Center. Contact the Virginia Space Grant Consortium, Old Dominion University Peninsula Center, 600 Butler Farm Road, Suite 200, Hampton, VA 23666; {www.vsgc.odu.edu/desc.htm}.

$7,000 To Study Overseas

Need money to study overseas? The Benjamin Gilman International Scholarship Program offers scholarships for financially needy U.S. undergraduates to study abroad. Scholarship recipients are chosen by a competitive selection process. The award provides for tuition, room and board, books, local transportation, insurance, and international airfare. Contact the Gilman International Scholarship Program, Institute of International Education, 520 Post Oak Blvd., Suite 740, Houston, TX 77027-9407; 713-621-6300; {www.iie.org/programs/gilman/index.html}.

$9,000 For Art Enthusiasts To Go Overseas

Museum staff can get money to work at a museum overseas. The Cultural Exchange program is an institutional linkage that matches museums in the U.S. with their counterparts abroad. One museum staff member from each institution participates in a one-month exchange visit during which the museums develop and conduct a collaborative project. Partnerships include art museums, botanical gardens, children's museums, science museums, and historic sites. The program covers per diem, international travel expenses, and educational materials for both partners. Contact the Cultural Programs Division Staff, Bureau of Educational and Cultural Affairs, U.S. Department of State, SA-44, 301 4th Street, SW, Suite 568, Washington, D.C. 20547; 202-619-4779; {http://exchanges.state.gov/education/citizens/culture/ipam.htm}.

$25,000 For Performing Artists To Perform Overseas

Get your artwork the exposure it deserves. The Fund for U.S. Artists at International Festivals and Exhibitions awards grants to performing artists and organizations that have been invited to participate in international festivals. The Fund supports the creative and professional development of U.S. artists through the presentation of their work at significant international festivals worldwide. Contact the Cultural Programs Division Staff, Bureau of Educational and Cultural Affairs, U.S. Department of State, SA-44, 301 4th Street, SW, Suite 568, Washington, D.C. 20547; 202-203-7523; {http://exchanges.state.gov/education/citizens/culture/filmfest.htm}.

$24,000 For High School Teachers To Travel Overseas

The Fulbright Teacher and Administrator Exchange Program provides opportunities for teachers to participate in direct exchanges of positions with colleagues from other countries for six weeks, a semester, or a full academic year. U.S. and foreign teachers, from elementary and secondary levels, and 2-year colleges are eligible to apply. The program offers full grants, round trip transportation, and health and accident insurance. Contact the Fulbright Teacher and Administrator Exchange,

600 Maryland Avenue SW, Suite 320, Washington, D.C. 20024; 202-314-3520; {www.fulbrightexchanges.org}.

$2,500 Grant for Federal Employees PLUS a trip to Washington

A $2,500 cash award with an all expense paid trip to Washington DC for the winner and a spouse. Four federal employees will receive the grant for achievements in the following areas: Substance Abuse Prevention and Treatment Award; Fire Prevention and Safety Award; Physical Rehabilitation Award; and Traffic Safety and Accident Prevention Award. Contact: GEICO Philanthropic Foundation, c/o GEICO Corporation, 5260 Western Avenue, Chevy Chase, MD 20815; {www.geico.com/federal/serviceAwards.htm}.

Money to Study Flowers in a Foreign Country!

The Harold F. Wilkins Scholarship administered by the American Floral Endowment provides grants to students to study the floral industry in a foreign country, to pursue a floral industry internship abroad; to attend an International Floricultural Symposium, and/or other related intellectual pursuits. Funding allocations vary depending on the length of the program and anticipated expenses.

Contact: American Floral Endowment, 11 Glen-Ed Professional Park, Glen Carbon, IL 62034; 618-692-0045; Fax: 618-692-4045; {www.htctech.net}; {afe@htctech.net}

Over $20,000 to Travel and Live in Italy!

Independent Research program awards grants of up to $16,500 to travel to and live in Venice and the Veneto. Grants will be awarded for historical research specifically on Venice and the former Venetian empire, and for study of contemporary society and culture in Venice. Grantees eligible for further $4,000 grant to fund publication of research. Contact The Gladys Krieble Delmas Foundation, 521 Fifth Avenue, Suite 1612, New York, NY 10175-1699; 212-687-0011; Fax: 212-687-8877; {www.delmas.org}; {info@delmas.org}.

$5,000 to Pay Travel Costs when Studying Overseas

Offers grants for students to help pay travel costs when traveling to and studying at programs in Central and South America, the Caribbean, Asia, and Africa; must demonstrate academic preparation and financial need. Contact: Council on International Educational Exchange, 7 Custom House Street, 3rd Floor, Portland, ME 04101; 800-40-Study or 207-553-7600; Fax: 207-553-7699; {www.ciee.org}.

$5,000 Grants for Teacher Education in the Arts

This grantmaker awards one $5,000 grant, one $3,000 grant, and one $1,000 grant biennially to a grant recipient with a baccalaureate degree to promote further study in a selected field of fine arts. The Foundation also provides scholarships of $10,000 to foreign students for study in American colleges and universities. Foundation support is primarily for teacher education through scholarships and grants; giving also for the arts. Contact Alpha Delta Kappa Foundation, 1615 W. 92nd Street, Kansas City, MO 64114-3296; 816-363-5525 or 800-247-2311; Fax: 816-363-4010; {www.alphadeltakappa.org}; {alphadeltakappa@worldnet.att.net}.

Live in New Zealand, Get $120 per Week, and MORE!

The Roy W. Dean Editing Grant offers grantees a return ticket to New Zealand and stay in the Wye Cottage in the Wairau Valley outside of Blenheim on the glorious South Island. They will also receive $120.00 NZ per week for the 4 weeks stay for food and gas. They will have a phone card to "call home." Additionally, a computer, CD player, VCR, TV, Fax and a Mitsubishi RUV to run up and down the South Island with are provided. Winners will need a dub of their footage on mini-DV format for this editing. The host will be Paul Davidson, a local filmmaker, who will provide his Non-Linear edit suite and assist as required. Contact: From the Heart Productions, Attn: Roy W. Dean Editing Grant, 1455 Mandalay Beach Road. Oxnard, CA 93035-2845; 866-689-5150; {www.fromtheheartproduc tions.com/g.rant-editing.shtml}; {carole@fromtheheartproductions.com}.

$50,000 Grant to Film in New Zealand

The New Zealand film grant is for all residents of New Zealand. If you are a resident living abroad, you can enter but you must film in New Zealand. This grant is goods and services from heart-felt companies who want to see documentaries made on film that "are unique and make a contribution to society". You will own the rights to this film. From the Heart Productions requests a producer credit and a "thank you credit" on the film to all of the donors, individually. This film grant gives the winner the many benefits. Contact: From the Heart Productions, Attn: Roy W. Dean Film Grant, 1455 Mandalay Beach Road. Oxnard, CA 93035-2845; 866-689-5150; {www. fromtheheartproductions.com/grant-nz.shtml}; {carole@fromtheheartproductions.com}.

Get Money to Research & Write in New Zealand

This Writing/Research Grant for writers of screen plays, short films and documentary films is for important issues that fit certain criteria It must be "unique and make a difference to society". It is for writers who need uninterrupted time to work on projects in a beautiful, remote setting with a good computer, VCR, TV, RUV and a few sheep to tend. Writers will get the following: four to six weeks at the Wye Cottage on the south island of New Zealand, outside of Blenheim in the Wairau Valley; $500.00 NZ free accommodations of three weekday nights in the Queen Charlotte Sounds with Ann Scott-Holt and Branwen Edwards as your hostesses at A Sea View in their own separate accommodations overlooking the water; a Mitsubishi RUV to run around in; one Coach Airline Ticket from your hometown to Blenheim, New Zealand

and return; $120.00 NZ per week for groceries and gas; a TV with cable, BBC news and movies from all over the world; a new computer, scanner and fax program at the Wye Cottage; a $100.00 NZ phone card; $200.00 NZ for "emergency expenses" (car, house, etc.); $300.00 US in software from Screenplay Systems; and a $150.00 NZ Garden Therapy Session at the Organic Leighvander Cottage. There is a $38.00 NZ application fee ($28.00 NZ with proof you are a student). Contact: From the Heart Productions, Attn: Roy W. Dean Writing/Research Grant, 1455 Mandalay Beach Road. Oxnard, CA 93035-2845; 866-689-5150; {www.fromtheheartprodu ctions.com/grant-writing.shtml}; {car ole@fromtheheartproductions.com}.

Library Researchers Get up to $2,500 for Living & Travel Expenses

Library Research Grants support scholars whose research requires use of specific collections housed in the Research Library at the Getty Research Institute. These grants provide partial, short-term support for costs relating to travel and living expenses. Projects must relate to specific items in the library collection. Library Research Grants range from $500 to $2,500, depending on distance traveled and duration of stay, and may only be applied to travel and living expenses. Contact: J. Paul Getty Trust, 1200 Getty Center Drive, Suite 800, Los Angeles, CA 90049-1685; 310-440-7320; Fax: 310-440-7703; {www. getty.edu/grants/research/scholars/libra ry_research.html}.

Money to Live and Work in Asia

The Luce Scholars Program provides stipends and internships for fifteen young Americans to live and work in

Asia each year. Those who already have significant experience in Asia or Asian studies are *not* eligible for the Luce Scholars Program. Candidates must be American citizens who have received at least a bachelor's degree and are no more than 29 years In addition to the basic stipend, a cost of living allowance and a housing allowance may be provided to Scholars living in areas where such costs are high. Contact: The Henry Luce Foundation, Inc., 111 W. 50th Street, Suite 4601, New York, NY 10020; 212-489-7700; Fax: 212-581-9541; {www.hluce.org/4prdesfm.html}; {hlf@hluce.org}.

$3,600 For Researchers to Travel in the U.S.

The Travel Grants Program (TGP) provides short-term travel support to individual scientists, engineers, and managers for travel to the United States to meet with U.S. for-profit companies with the intent of developing collaborative projects and new business opportunities. The CRDF arranges and pays for airfare, lodging expenses, per diem, and medical insurance. Contact: The U.S. Civilian Research and Development Foundation, (also known as CRDF), 1530 Wilson Blvd. 3rd Floor, Arlington, VA 22209; 703-526-9720; Fax: 703-526-9721; {www.crdf.org/Industry/industryfull.html#IndustryOrientation&Travel}; {information@crdf.org}.

$10,000 to Study Turkish Culture

Research Grants in Comparative Studies of Modern Turkey are for graduate students at the dissertation research stage and for post-doctoral scholars in the U.S. who study aspects of the Republic of Turkey (post-1922)

in a comparative context. Applicants must be U.S. citizens or permanent residents in the U.S. and affiliated with a university in the U.S. A significant portion of the project should be devoted comparatively to one or more states or political entities in Europe, Latin America, the Middle East, and Asia in addition to the Turkish Republic. These grants are primarily, but not exclusively, in the field of Political Science. The maximum award is $10,000. Contact: Institute of Turkish Studies, c/o Georgetown University, Intercultural Center, P.O. Box 571033, Washington, DC 20057-1033; 202-687-0295; Fax: 202-687-3780; {www.turkishstudies.org}; {institute_turkishstudies@yahoo.com}

GTI application address: Institute of Turkish Studies, 1524 18th Street, N.W., No. 1, Washington, DC 20036; 202-328-6208.

Travel to Turkey to Study Language, Research and Get $2,000

The Summer Language Study Grants for Graduate Students for summer

travel to Turkey for language study in preparation for graduate research. To be eligible for Summer Language Study Grant applicants must be: graduate students in any field of the social sciences and/or humanities; U.S. citizens or permanent residents; and currently enrolled in a university in the United States. Normally, the recipients

of the Summer Language Study Grants are expected to spend a minimum of two months in Turkey at an established Ottoman or Turkish language training facility. The Summer Research Grants for Graduate Students has the same guidelines and award amounts. Contact: Institute of Turkish Studies, c/o Georgetown University, Intercultural Center, P.O. Box 571033, Washington, DC 20057-1033; 202-687-0295; Fax: 202-687-3780; {www. turkishstudies.org}; {institute_turkishstudies@yahoo.com}
.
GTI application address: Institute of Turkish Studies, 1524 18th Street, N.W., No. 1, Washington, DC 20036; 202-328-6208.

Grants to Help You Teach Turkish Studies

Teaching Aid Grants are intended for the development of instructional materials in the field of Turkish Studies such as language teaching materials, maps, slide kits etc., for academic institutions in the United States. Contact: Institute of Turkish Studies, c/o Georgetown University, Intercultural Center, P.O. Box 571033, Washington, DC 20057-1033; 202-687-0295; Fax: 202-687-3780; {www. turkishstudies.org}; {institute_turkishstudies@yahoo.com}

GTI application address: Institute of Turkish Studies, 1524 18th Street, N.W., No. 1, Washington, DC 20036; 202-328-6208.

FREE Airline Ticket to Turkey for Graduate Work

The Postdoctoral Summer Travel-Research Grants are intended to provide partial support for travel and research to Turkey for those who hold the Ph.D. in a social sciences or humanities discipline. To be eligible, applicants must be U.S. citizens or U.S. permanent residents and currently live/work in the U.S. Maximum award is round-trip airfare to Turkey. Contact: Institute of Turkish Studies, c/o Georgetown University, Intercultural Center, P.O. Box 571033, Washington, DC 20057-1033; 202-687-0295; Fax: 202-687-3780; {www. turkishstudies.org}; {institute_turkishstudies@yahoo.com}

GTI application address: Institute of Turkish Studies, 1524 18th Street, N.W., No. 1, Washington, DC 20036; 202-328-6208.

Help to Publish Written Work on Turkish Studies

Subventions for Publications grants are intended towards the publication costs of journals in the field of Turkish Studies published in the United States; of manuscripts already accepted for publication; and, of texts, documents and translations of works directly related to Turkish Studies. For journals, funding must be requested for the year in which the issue(s) will actually appear in print, and must be used in the year the grant is given. Subventions for books and journals will be disbursed only upon publication of the work and receipt of 25 copies of the work by ITS. The maximum award is 25% of the publication costs. Contact: Institute of Turkish Studies, c/o Georgetown University, Intercultural Center, P.O. Box 571033, Washington, DC 20057-1033; 202-687-0295; Fax: 202-687-3780; {www.turkishstudies.org}; {institute_turkishstudies@yahoo.com}

GTI application address: Institute of Turkish Studies, 1524 18th Street, N.W., No. 1, Washington, DC 20036; 202-328-6208.

$10,000 to Help with Turkish Studies Coursework

To be eligible for a dissertation writing grant, applicants should be: graduate students in any field of the social sciences and/or humanities; U.S. citizens or permanent residents; and currently enrolled in a Ph.D. degree program in the United States. These grants are intended for advanced students who have finished the research stage of their dissertation and they may not be used for dissertation research. Contact: Institute of Turkish Studies, c/o Georgetown University, Intercultural Center, P.O. Box 571033, Washington, DC 20057-1033; 202-687-0295; Fax: 202-687-3780; {www.turkishstudies.org}; {institute_turkishstudies@yahoo.com}

GTI application address: Institute of Turkish Studies, 1524 18th Street, N.W., No. 1, Washington, DC 20036; 202-328-6208.

Grants up to $10,000 to Study Abroad in Turkey!

Grants for Undergraduate Study are for students studying in the United States who wish to participate in study abroad programs in Turkey. These awards will be made to institutions, which will be responsible for their distribution to qualified applicants who are US citizens. Individual applications will not be accepted. The time period for these grants can be either a semester or the whole academic year depending on the length of the study abroad program in Turkey. Contact: Institute of Turkish Studies, c/o Georgetown University, Intercultural Center, P.O. Box 571033, Washington, DC 20057-1033; 202-687-0295; Fax: 202-687-3780; {www.turkishstudies.org}; {institute_turkishstudies@yahoo.com}

GTI application address: Institute of Turkish Studies, 1524 18th Street, N.W., No. 1, Washington, DC 20036; 202-328-6208.

$5,000 for Airport and Air Travel Research

This organization offers up to $5,000 grants for research into airport design, safety, passenger comfort, and all aspects of air travel. Contact: Arnold W. Thompson Charitable Trust, c/o Arnold W. Thompson, 8480 N. Lee Trevino Drive, Tucson, AZ 85742-9709; 520-544-9307.

$40,000 to Research Eastern Europe

Two different fellowships are offered under the East European Studies Fellowships program. Scholars may apply for Post-doctoral Research in East European Studies Fellowships. Applicants are required to hold the Ph.D. as of the application deadline date, or its equivalent, as demonstrated by professional experience and publications. Funds may be used to supplement sabbatical salaries or awards from other sources, provided they would intensify or extend the contemplated research. Also, under the Dissertation Fellowship Program, doctoral candidates may apply for an academic year of support for dissertation research or writing to be undertaken outside of East Europe. The maximum stipend is $15,000 plus expenses. Contact: American Council of Learned Societies (also known as ACLS), 633 3rd Avenue, Suite 8C, New York, NY 10017-6795; 212-697-

1505; Fax: 212-949-8058; {www.acls.org}; {grants@acls.org}.

$3,500 per Month to Research Using Foreign Languages

The Library of Congress Fellowships in International Studies support postdoctoral research in the humanities and social sciences using the foreign language collections at the Library of Congress. Approximately 10 fellowships will be available for four to nine months each, with a stipend of $3,500 per month. Contact: American Council of Learned Societies (also known as ACLS), 633 3rd Avenue, Suite 8C, New York, NY 10017-6795; 212-697-1505; Fax: 212-949-8058; {www.acls.org}; {grants@acls.org}.

Get $62,000 to Travel and Research Social Science Projects

The Charles A. Ryskamp Research Fellowships provide $60,000, plus $2,000 for research and travel to provide time and resources to enable advanced assistant professors in the humanities and related social sciences to conduct their research under optimal conditions. Contact: American Council of Learned Societies (also known as ACLS), 633 3rd Avenue, Suite 8C, New York, NY 10017-6795; 212-697-1505; Fax: 212-949-8058; {www.acls.org}; {grants@acls.org}.

Fellowships to Study in China; Research Assistance for Chinese Scholars

The Chinese Fellowships for Scholarly Development offers fellowships awarded to Chinese scholars in social sciences and humanities with the M.A., Ph.D., or equivalent degree from a Chinese institution to carry out one semester or one year of individual or collaborative research at the invitation of a U.S. host scholar. Candidates must be nominated by the U.S. host. The postdoctoral fellowships provide for a modest living allowance, health insurance, and international airfare. The National Program for Advanced Study and Research in China is offered in graduate study and in research. Contact: American Council of Learned Societies (also known as ACLS), 633 3rd Avenue, Suite 8C, New York, NY 10017-6795; 212-697-1505; Fax: 212-949-8058; {www.acls.org}; {grants@acls.org}.

$3,000 to $5,000 for Caribbean Projects

Research and study grants to graduate students and professional social scientists and projects related to territories of the Caribbean. Other subjects include: race or ethnic relations, gender issues, education in a comparative perspective and problems of aging. The awards seek to encourage outstanding scholarship that will advance their interdisciplinary understanding of the topics specified above. Contact Research Institute for the Study of Man, c/o Lambros Comitas, 162 E. 78th Street, New York, NY 10021-0406; 212-678-4040; {www.rism.org/}.

$17,000 to Study in Belgium

The Foundation will award fellowships for advanced study at one of the Belgian Universities or other academic institutions of higher learning.

Applicants are nominated by the dean of the graduate school or professional school of his/her university. The grant carries a stipend of $17,000 - which includes round-trip travel expenses, lodging, and living expenses in Belgium for a period of six months, as well as tuition or, enrollment fees. In addition, the Foundation will cover health insurance for the Fellow. The candidates should meet the following qualifications: U.S. citizen, preferably less than 30 years of age; speaking and reading knowledge of Dutch, French or German; and have a Masters or equivalent degree, or be working towards a Ph.D. or equivalent degree. Contact Belgian American Educational Foundation, 195 Church Street, New Haven, CT 06510; 203-777-5765; {www.baef.be/content/fellowsh.html}; {emile.boulpaep@yale.edu}.

$1,000 for Medical or Dental Students to go as Missionaries

CMDS offers a program of grants-in-aid, through the James S. Westra Memorial Endowment Fund, that provides selected medical/dental students with clinical experiences of two weeks or more in mission settings in developing countries. The awards cover transportation and project-related expenses up to $1,000. Eligible applicants must be: a CMDS member; a third or fourth year medical/dental student enrolled in a traditional four-year program in an approved US medical or dental school; and able to

demonstrate financial need to enable project participation. Contact The Christian Medical and Dental Society, P. O. Box 5, Briston, TN 37621-0005; 423-844-1000, Fax: 423-844-1005; {www.cmdahome.org/}.

$700 Travel Grants for Medical Students

Global Health Ministries (GHM) may award up to four travel grants annually to assist approved fourth-year medical students to travel to a GHM related hospital or health care center in Tanzania, Madagascar, or Cameroon for an international elective of at least eight weeks duration. Candidates must be active and committed Christians, and a member of a Lutheran church. The maximum award of the grant is $700. Contact Global Health Ministries, 8731 Hickory Street, NE, Minneapolis, MN 55432-2500; 612-586-9590; Fax: 612-586-9591; {www.ghm.org/}; {74023.2466@ compuserve.com}.

Financial Assistance for Medical Students to Travel

The MAP International/Reader's Digest International Fellowship program (MAP-RDIF) encourages lifelong involvement in global health issues by providing selected medical students firsthand exposure in a Christian context to the health, social and cultural characteristics of a developing world community. Third and fourth-year medical students, residents and interns are eligible. Students select a mission agency or hospital that has an outreach among the poor in a rural or urban setting. Students must spend at least eight weeks in the field (six weeks for residents and interns). The fellowship provides 75% of the approved round trip airfare to the destination. In most instances, students pay room and board as well as the remaining 25 percent of travel costs. Contact RDIF Coordinator, MAP International, P.O. Box 215000, Brunswick, GA 31521-5000; 912-280-6633; Fax: 912-265-6170; {www.map.org/main.asp?menu=3&submenu=4}; {rdif@map.org}.

Scholarships to Study Languages in Unstudied Regions

The National Security Education Program (NSEP) - Graduate Fellowships offer scholarships for language study in less commonly studied countries/regions. They may be combined with medical electives. Contact Academy for Educational Development, National Security Education Program Graduate Fellowship Officer, 1875 Connecticut Avenue, NW, Suite 900, Washington, DC 20009-1202; 202-884-8285 or 800-498-9360; Fax: 202-884-8408; {nsep@aed.org}.

$30,000 to Research Cancer in the U.S. or Italy

The Foundation seeks to develop and encourage international cooperation among physicians and researchers in the fight against cancer through research, training, and education. AICF is the U.S. Representative of the European School of Oncology. A major activity is the award of Fellowships to Italian and American scientists so that they might spend a period of research and advanced training in pre-clinical or clinical research centers in the United States or Italy. US fellowships are for one year, but may be renewed for an additional year and carry an annual stipend of $30,000. Italian fellowships are for one year, but may be renewed for an

additional year and carry an annual stipend of $25,000. Contact American-Italian Cancer Foundation, 112 E. 71st Street, 2B, New York, NY 10021; 212-628-9090; Fax: 212-517-6089; {www.aicfonline.org}; {aicf@aicfonline.org}.

Scholarships to Travel and Study Internationally

Graduate scholarships for international study are available in any field and require a one year commitment. The scholarships cover travel expenses and provide a stipend for room and board. The applicant must be able to communicate in the host language. All applications are made and processed through the local Rotary Club. Contact The Rotary Foundation, 1600 Ridge Avenue, Evanston, IL 60201; 312-328-0100 OR Attn: Kristin Petroskey, The Rotary Foundation, 1560 Sherman Avenue, 16th Floor, Evanston, IL 60201; 708-866-3000; {www.rotary.org/foundation/}.

$15,000 to Study Teaching in Alaska

The Masters of Art in Teaching (MAT) Scholarship Program offers five scholarships of up to $5,000 each to Sealaska shareholders and/or descendants who apply and are admitted to the University of Alaska Southeast MAT program and who meet the Foundation's qualification guidelines. Contact Sealaska Heritage Foundation, 1 Sealaska Plz., Suite 201, Juneau, AK 99801-1249; 907-463-4844; Fax: 907-586-9293; {www.sealaskaheritage.org}.

Funding to Study Alaskan Heritage

The Heritage Study Grants ensure the perpetuation of southeast Alaskan native arts and cultural practices with a priority on those arts and practices that are in danger of being lost. The grants help to defray the costs of participating in an instructional pursuit or study related to specific practices or art forms. Contact Sealaska Heritage Foundation, 1 Sealaska Plaza, Suite 201, Juneau, AK 99801-1249; 907-463-4844; Fax: 907-586-9293; {www.sealaskaheritage.org}.

More Money to Study in Alaska

The 7(i) Scholarship Program awards scholarships that are targeted to specific fields of study, such as natural resource management, accounting, engineering, or other fields in which Sealaska Corporation has business operations. The scholarships are intended to help Sealaska shareholders and descendants acquire education skills necessary to support Sealaska Corporation's business operations. Contact Sealaska Heritage Foundation, 1 Sealaska Plaza, Suite 201, Juneau, AK 99801-1249; 907-463-4844; Fax: 907-586-9293; {www.sealaskaheritage.org}.

$20,000 to Research the Environment in Europe

This organization provides scholarships and grants to individuals for the conduct of research to address problems of ecology and the environment, with particular emphasis on the environment of Eastern Europe. Contact The Sendzimir Foundation, Inc., c/o Clark, Schaefer, Hackett & Co., 105 E. 4th Street, Suite 1600, Cincinnati, OH 45202; {www.send zimir.org.pl/}; {office@sendzimir.org.pl}.

Over $3.0 Million for Trips to Israel

The American Israel Education Foundation is an educational foundation affiliated with the American Israel Public Affairs Committee (AIPAC). AIEF sponsors: education programs such as trips to Israel for community leaders and elected officials, seminars on Middle East issues at universities across the country, and other projects that help to educate the general public about U.S.-Israel relations. Contact: American Israel Education Foundation, Inc., 440 1st Street N.W., Suite 600, Washington, DC 20001-2028; {www.aipac.org/}.

Fellowships and Money to Travel to Germany

The Foundation sponsors the Robert Bosch Foundation Fellowship Program that enables young American professionals to participate in an intensive work and study program in Germany. The program provides young American professionals (23-34) with executive level internships in the federal government and private sectors in Germany. Seminars provide an in-depth understanding of issues facing the European Union and Germany today. Candidates are competitively chosen from the fields of business administration, economics, journalism and mass communications, law, political science and public affairs/public policy. Contact CDS International, Inc., 871 United Nations

537

Plaza, 15th Floor, New York, NY 10017; 212-497-3500; Fax: 212-497-3535; {www.cdsintl.org}; {info@cdsintl.org}.

Move to a Foreign Country for Internships & Career Training

CDS International administers international practical training programs that stimulate the exchange of knowledge and technological skills and contribute to the development of a highly-trained and intercultural-competent workforce. The organization provides several programs that allow for foreign travel as well as training. There may be program fees associated with these programs. Contact CDS International, Inc., 871 United Nations Plaza, 15th Floor, New York, NY 10017; 212-497-3500; Fax: 212-497-3535; {www.cdsintl.org}; {info@cdsintl.org}.

$10,000 for Artists to Travel to Europe or Russia

Project grants enable U.S. artists, curators and presenters to implement projects in Central Europe, Russia and Eurasia with grants ranging from $2,000 to $10,000. Cooperative arts projects resulting in the creation of new work or those that establish a mutually beneficial exchange of ideas and expertise among artists, curators and arts organizations are eligible to apply. Applicants must be citizens or permanent residents of the United States. Contact CEC ArtsLink, Inc., 12 West 31st Street, 4th Floor, New York, NY 10001; 212-643-1985; {www.cecip.org/}; {al@cecartslink.org}.

FREE Rent & Utilities for Artists to Go to New Mexico

The Foundation's purpose is to provide a quiet haven where artists may pursue their creative endeavors without pressure to produce while they are in residence. Artists can live in the fully furnished apartments for a period of up to three months rent-free and utility-free. No spouses, children or pets are permitted to reside at the Foundation. Artists are responsible for purchasing and preparing their own meals, paying their own travel expenses and providing their own working material. Contact: The Helene Wurlitzer Foundation of New Mexico, P.O. Box 1891, Taos, NM 87571; 505-758-2413; Fax: 505-758-2559; {hwf@taosnet.com}.

Money for Travel to Chicago to Attend Conference

The Nellie Mae Foundation Graduate Student program provides sponsorship for graduate students to attend AAHE's National Conference. The scholarships cover travel to Chicago, lodging, registration fee, meal expenses, and a one-year AAHE membership. Applicants must attend a New England college or university and be a member of an underserved population. Contact American Association for Higher Education, 1 Dupont Circle, Suite 360, Washington, DC 20036-1110; 202-293-6440; Fax: 202-293-0073; {www.aahe.org}; {info@aahe.org}.

$1,000 Travel Money for Food Writers

The IACP Foundation has a travel grant program for professional food writers whose research requires or will benefit from access to the holdings of specific libraries with significant culinary collections in the U.S. Applicants must demonstrate that they are under contract for a book, magazine or newspaper article. Contact The International Association of Culinary Professionals Foundation,

304 W. Liberty Street, Suite 201, Louisville, KY 40202-3068; 502-587-7953; Fax: 502-589-3602; {www.iacp foundation.com/}.

Funding for Research on India

The American Institute of Indian Studies promotes scholarly studies on India in the U.S. through fellowship support, training, and the maintenance of research facilities. Fellowships are also provided for performing and creative arts. Contact American Institute of Indian Studies, 1130 E. 59th Street, Chicago, IL, 0637-1539; 773-702-8638; {www.indiastudies. org}.

Right-On Write-Offs

There's still time to take advantage of leftover tax laws that favor the well-heeled. The Internal Revenue Service has changed some of the rules regarding business deductions, but there are still ways you can write off parts of your summer vacation as a business expense. Anyone can do it even if you're just an employee. Find out how by calling the IRS at 800-829-3676 and asking for a free copy of Publication 463, Travel, Entertainment, Gift and Car Expenses. You can also check them out online at {www.irs.gov}.

Do Some Research

Going to a country where you've never been before? Background Notes on the Countries of the World is a series of short, factual pamphlets with information on the country's land, people, history, government, political conditions, economy, foreign relations, and U.s. Foreign policy. Each pamphlet also includes a factual profile, brief travel notes, a country map, and a reading list. Contact Public

Affairs Bureau, U.S. Department of State, 2201 C St., NW, Washington, DC 20520; 202-647-2518; {www. state.gov/r/pa/bgn/}.

When You Need Help

Are you overseas and need medical assistance? What about if you are arrested or someone has died in another country? The Department of State has the Office of Citizens Services that can answer all you questions and direct you to places for

further assistance. They have lists of doctors and lawyers located in the various countries that can help you, along with a multitude of other resources to help those in crisis in a foreign land. Contact The Office of Citizens Services, U.S. Department of State, Room 4817 NS, 2201 C St., NW, Washington, DC 20520; 202-647-5225; {http://travel.state.gov/}.

Should I Go There?

Before you pack your bags, everyone should check out the latest news on the country or countries they are planning to visit. Consular Information Sheets are available for every country of the world. They include information as to the location of the U.S. Embassy or Consulate in the country, unusual practices, health conditions, currency, crime, and much more. Travel

Free Money For Everybody

Warnings are issued when the State Department decides based on all relevant information to recommend that Americans avoid travel to a certain country. Contact The Office of Citizens Services, U.S. Department of State, Room 4817 NS, 2201 C St., NW, Washington, DC 20520; 202-647-5225; {http://travel.state.gov/travel_warnings.html}.

Some Nighttime Reading
Know before you go is a good motto to live by when traveling. The Department of State has put together a series of travel publications that provide good tips for travelers to various countries, as well as general information about traveling overseas. These are available for sale at a minimal cost or you can view them for free online. Publications include:
- *U.S. Consuls Help Americans Abroad*
- *Crisis Abroad*
- *Overseas Citizens Services*
- *Travel Warning on Drugs Abroad*
- *Sending Money Overseas to a U.S. Citizen in an Emergency*
- *Your Trip Abroad*
- *A Safe Trip Abroad*
- *Tips for Older Americans*
- *Tips for Students*
- *Tips for Residing Abroad*
- *Tips for Travelers to Canada*
- *Tips for Travelers to the Caribbean*
- *Tips for Travelers to Central and South America*
- *Tips for Travelers to Mexico*
- *Tips for Business Travelers to Nigeria*
- *Nigerian Advance Fee Fraud*
- *Tips for Travelers to Sub-Saharan Africa*
- *Tips for Travelers to the Middle East and North Africa*
- *Tips for Travelers to the Middle*

Contact Superintendent of Documents, P.O. 371954, Pittsburgh, PA 15250; 202-512-1800; {http://travel.state.gov/travel_pubs.html}.

Counterterrorism
Office of Counterterrorism coordinates all U.S. Government efforts to improve counterterrorism cooperation with foreign governments. The U.S. Counterterrorism Policy is: First, make no concessions to terrorists and strike no deals; Second, bring terrorists to justice for their crimes; Third, isolate and apply pressure on states that sponsor terrorism to force them to change their behavior; and Fourth, bolster the counterterrorism capabilities of those countries that work with the U.S. and require assistance. You can also view their annual publication Patterns of Global Terrorism on their website. Contact, Office of the coordinator for Counterterrorism, Office of Public Affairs, Room 2507, Department of State, 2201 C St., NW, Washington, DC 20520; {http://www.state.gov/s/ct/}.

Overseas Security
The Overseas Security Advisory Council (OSAC) was established in 1985 by the U.S. Department of State to foster the exchange of security related information between the U.S. Government and American private sector operating abroad. This has helped the American private sector and colleges and universities protect their investments and their personnel abroad. The OSAC publish a series of publications, including:
- *Security Guidelines for American Families Living Abroad*
- *Security Guidelines for American Enterprises Abroad*
- *Emergency Planning Guidelines for American Businesses Abroad*

- *Security Awareness Overseas*
- *Guidelines for Protecting U.S. Business Information Overseas*
- *Personal Security Guidelines for the American Business Traveler Overseas*
- *Security Guidelines for children Living Abroad*

Contact Overseas Security Advisory council, Bureau of Diplomatic Security, U.S. Department of State, Washington, DC 20522; 202-663-0533; {www.ds-osac.org/default.cfm}.

Be the Face of America to the World!

Get ready for the challenge of a lifetime! Some of the most interesting work in the world is done by U.S. Department of State employees overseas and in Washington, DC. By becoming a Foreign Service Officer, Foreign Service Specialist of Civil Service employee for the U.S, Department of State you can really make a difference. The people of the State Department are at work every day around the world on matters of vital importance. You could be involved in providing background information needed to develop foreign policy, implementing established policies, assisting American citizens in need, and more. Contact Office of Recruitment, Examination and Employment, U.S. Department of State, HR/REE, SA-1, 2401 E St., NW, 5H, Washington, DC 20522; 202-261-8888; {www.state.gov/m/dghr/hr/}.

Want To Teach Overseas?

American-sponsored overseas schools are independent, non-government schools sponsored by Americans or in which American citizens have considerable interest. Although the relationship between our American embassies and the various schools overseas may be close, the schools are private institutions, responsible for hiring their own teachers and staff. Generally, the schools are not joined together under any administrative umbrella; each does its own hiring and establishes its own qualification requirements and application procedures. Although the Department of State does not employ teachers for assignment abroad, they have assembled general information about teaching overseas and a list of organizations that provide teaching opportunities. Contact {www.state.gov/m/a/os/index.cfm?id=1703}.

Student Employment

The U.S. Department of State manages several student employment programs that enable students to get experience in a foreign affairs environment through on-the-job experience. Some students work in Washington, DC and others have the opportunity to work at an embassy overseas. Positions are both paid and unpaid and many are available during spring, summer or fall. Programs include Cooperative Education Program, Fascell Fellowship, Student Internships, the Thomas R. Pickering Foreign Affairs Fellowship, as well as many others. For more information contact Attn: Student Programs, U.S. Department of State, Recruitment Division, SA-1, 2401 E St., NW, 5th Floor, Washington, DC 20522; {www.state.gov/m/dghr/hr/student/}.

High School Students And Teachers Can Visit Russia

The Secondary School Partnership Program objective is to sponsor the exchange of high school students and teachers between the U.S. and the former Soviet Union through grants to private not-for-profit organizations and public institutions. Grants are awarded to fund projects in two program areas: academic year in the U.S., and short-term exchanges of groups of students and teachers between linked schools. The total amount of money available is $15 million. Contact Youth Programs Division, Office of Citizen Exchanges, Bureau of Educational and Cultural Affairs, 301 4th Street, SW, Room 568, Washington, DC 20547; 202-203-7527; Fax: 202-203-7236; {http://exchanges.state.gov/education/citizens/students}.

Spend A Year In Europe On A Mid-Career Break

The Hubert Humphrey Fellowship provides opportunities for accomplished mid-career professionals from designated countries of Africa, Asia, Latin America, the Caribbean, the Middle East, and Eurasia, to come to the United States for a year of study and related practical professional experiences. The program provides a basis for establishing lasting ties between citizens of the United States and their professional counterparts in other countries, fostering an exchange of knowledge and mutual understanding throughout the world. Fellows are placed in groups at selected U.S. universities and design individualized programs of academic coursework and professional development activities. Applicants must have an undergraduate degree, five years of substantial professional experience, demonstrated leadership qualities, and fluency in English. Contact Hubert H. Humphrey Fellowship Program, Humphrey Fellowships and Institutional Linkage Branch (ECA/A/S/U), Institute of International Education, U.S. Department of State, SA-44, 301 4th

Street, SW, Washington, DC 20547; 202-619-5289, 202-326-7701; Fax: 202-326-7702; {http://exchanges.state.gov/education/hhh}, {www.iie.org/template.cfm?&Template=/programs/hhh/default.htm}.

Money For Artists, Filmmakers, Playwrights, And Museum Professionals To Go Overseas

The Culture Program supports projects by U.S. nonprofit organizations for exchanges of professionals in the arts and museum fields. Priority is given to institutionally-based projects involving artists in the creation of their particular art forms and projects which will lead to institutional linkages. Two way exchanges are encouraged and cost sharing is required. This exchange program is designed to introduce American and foreign participants to each other's cultural and artistic life and traditions. It also supports international projects in the United States or overseas involving composers, choreographers, filmmakers, playwrights, theater designers, writers and poets, visual artists, museum professionals, and more. Contact Cultural Programs Division, Bureau of Educational and Cultural Affairs, U.S. Department of State, SA-44, 301 4th St., SW, Suite 568, Washington, DC 20547; 202-203-7523; Fax: 202-203-7525; {http://

exchanges.state.gov/education/citizens
/culture/}.

Money For Students, Teachers, Bankers, Lawyers, And Journalists To Travel Overseas

The Fulbright Scholar Program provides grants to U.S. students, teachers, and scholars to study, teach, lecture, and conduct research overseas, and to foreign nationals to engage in similar activities in the United States to increase mutual understanding and peaceful relations between the people of the United States and the people of other countries. Fields of study and subjects taught include the arts and humanities, social sciences, and physical sciences. In addition to the exchange of students and scholars, the program includes professional exchanges in journalism, law, management, banking, and public administration. Contact Council for International Exchange of Scholars, 3007 Tilden Street, NW, Suite 5L, Washington, DC 20008-3009; 202-686-4000; Fax: 202-362-3442; {www.iie.org/cies}.

Money For English, Law, And Journalism Professionals To Go Abroad

The Professional Exchanges Program sends Americans overseas to aid foreign institutions seeking professional assistance in such academic disciplines as English teaching, law, and journalism. Experts on the United States can consult with academic and professionals at foreign educational or other relevant institutions about special issues, or to conduct seminars/workshops for professional personnel. Contact Office of Citizen Exchanges, Bureau of Educational and Cultural Affairs, U.S.

Department of State, SA-44, 301 4th St., SW, Room 238, Washington, DC 20547; 202-619-5348; Fax: 202-619-4350; {http://exchanges.state.gov/education/citizens/professl}.

Foreign High School Teachers Can Spend Six Weeks In The U.S.

The Fulbright American Studies Institutes — Study Of The United States Program provides grants to foreign secondary and postsecondary school educators for a 4 to 6 week program of academic workshops in U.S. history, culture, and institutions to enhance and update the content of what is taught about the United States abroad. Contact Study of the US Branch, U.S. Department of State, 301 4th St., SW, Room 252, Washington, DC 20547; 202-619-4557; Fax: 202-619-6790; {http://exchanges.state.gov/education/amstudy/fasi.htm}.

Exchange Program For English Teachers

The English Language Specialist Program promotes the study and teaching of English abroad, in host country institutions, and through American educational and binational centers in 41 countries. TEFL/TESL English teaching programs concentrate on training teachers through seminars, exchanges of foreign and American English specialists, and the development and distribution of curricula and materials for teaching the English language and American culture. Contact Office of English Language Programs, U.S. Department of State, Annex #44, 301 4th St., SW, Room 304, Washington, DC 20547; 202-619-5869; Fax: 202-401-1250; {http://exchanges.state.gov/education/engteaching}.

Volunteer In The U.S.

The objective of the Corporation for National and Community Service AMERICORPS program is to supplement efforts of private, nonprofit organizations and federal, state, and local government agencies to eliminate poverty and poverty-related problems by enabling persons from all walks of life and all age groups to perform meaningful and constructive service as volunteers throughout the U.S. AmeriCorps volunteers receive a modest subsistence allowance, an end-of-service stipend, health insurance, and money for college. Contact AmeriCorps State Offices or contact Corporation for National Service, 1201 New York Ave. NW, Washington, DC 20525; 800-942-2677, 202-606-5000; {www. cns.gov}.

$30,000 To Study Farming Internationally

The Scientific Cooperation and Research program enables American scientists to work with foreign researchers to help solve critical problems that are affecting the food

systems, agriculture, fisheries, forestry and the environment in the U.S. and the collaborating country. U.S. researchers from USDA agencies, universities, and private nonprofit agricultural research institutions are eligible. Contact U.S. Department of Agriculture, International Collaborative Research Program, USDA/FAS/ICD/RSED/SCRP, Ag Box 1084, Room 3229 South Building, 14th and Independence Ave., SW, Washington, DC 20250-1084; 202-720-3904; {www.fas.usda.gov/icd/grants/scrp.htm}.

Your Friends In The Ukraine Can Come To The U.S. To Learn Free Enterprise

The Special American Business Internship Training Program awards internships in U.S. firms to business managers and scientific workers from the newly independent states of the former Soviet Union. SABIT provides the intern with a hands-on training program in the business skills necessary to operate in a market economy. A counselor is provided to help with cultural adjustments. Companies provide medical insurance, housing, and any other living expenses beyond those covered by the daily stipend provided by the U.S. A SABIT fact sheet is also available. Contact U.S. Department of Commerce, Special American Business Internship Training Program, 1401 Constitution Ave., NW, FCB-4th Floor-4100 W, Washington, DC 20230; 202-482-0073; {www.mac.doc.gov/sabit/}.

Money For Students And Teachers To Travel Together Overseas

The International Group Projects Abroad program is designed to contribute to the development and improvement of the study of modern foreign languages and area studies in the United States, and provide opportunities for American teachers, advanced students, and faculty to study in foreign countries. Grants allow groups to conduct overseas projects in research, training, and curriculum development. Money can be used for international travel, maintenance allowances, rent of instructional materials in the country of study, and more. Contact International Studies Team, International Education and Grants Programs Service, Office of Postsecondary Education, U.S. Department of Education, 1900 K Street, NW, 6th Floor, Washington, DC 20006-8521; 202-502-7624; Fax: 202-205-7859; {www.ed.gov/programs/iegpsgpa}.

Money For Teachers To Take A Sabbatical Overseas

The Fulbright-Hays Seminars Abroad program is designed to improve understanding and knowledge of people and culture of a different country. There are 7 to 10 seminars that last 4 to 6 weeks held in countries outside of Western Europe. Eligible persons are teachers in social sciences and humanities, administrators, and curriculum specialists of state and local education agencies, college faculty, librarians and museum teachers who are primarily responsible

for teaching undergraduates in the social sciences, humanities, and area studies. Contact Higher Education Programs, U.S. Department of Education, 1990 K Street, NW, 6th Floor, Washington, DC 20006-8521; 202-502-7700; {www.ed.gov/programs/iegpssap}.

Grants To College Teachers Who Want To Create Programs In International Business

The Business and International Education program is designed to promote innovation and improvement in international business education curricula at institutions of higher education and promote linkages between these institutions and the business community. Institutions must enter into an agreement with a business enterprise, trade organization, or association engaged in international economic activity, or a combination or consortium of the named entities. Contact Higher Education Programs, U.S. Department of Education, 1990 K St., NW, 6th Floor, Washington, DC 20006-8500; 202-502-7626; {www. ed.gov/programs/iegpsbie}.

Conduct Cancer Research In a Different Country

The Short-Term Scientist Exchange Program is designed to promote collaborative research between established U.S. and foreign scientists by supporting exchange visits to each country's laboratories. Visits may last from one week to six months time. Candidates must have at least three years postdoctoral experience in cancer research and an invitation from a qualified sponsor. Contact National Cancer Institute, Office of International Affairs, 6130 Executive Boulevard, Suite 100, Bethesda, MD

20892-7301; 301-496-4761; {www.cancer.gov/about_nci/oia}.

Visit The U.S. To Do Health Research

The NIH Visiting Program provides talented scientists throughout the world with the opportunity to participate in the varied research activities of the National Institutes of Health. There are two categories of Visiting Program participants: Visiting Fellows and Visiting Scientists. Each participant works closely with a senior NIH investigator who serves as supervisor or sponsor during the period of award or appointment. The Visiting Fellow award is for obtaining research training experience. Fellows must have a doctoral degree, not more than 3 years of relevant postdoctoral research experience, and cannot be U.S. citizens. Contact International Services Branch, Office of Research Services, National Institutes of Health (NIH), 31 Center Drive, MSC 2028, Bethesda, MD 20892-2028; 301-496-6166; {www.nih.gov/od/ors/dirs/isb/isb.htm}

New U.S. Researchers Can Continue Research In Developing Countries

The International Research Scientist Development Award program provides opportunities for foreign postdoctoral biomedical or behavioral scientists who are in the formative stages of their career to extend their research experience in a laboratory in the United States. Contact International Research Scientists Development Award, Fogarty International Center, Division of International Training and Research, National Institutes of Health, Building 31, Room B2C39, 31 Center Drive, MSC 2220, Bethesda, MD 20892-2220; 301-496-8733; Fax: 301-402-0779; {www.fic.nih.gov/programs/irsda.html}.

Conduct Medical Research With Foreign Scientists

The Fogarty International Research Collaboration Award program provides for collaborative research between U.S. biomedical scientists and investigators in foreign countries. These awards are made for research projects that, for the most part, will be carried out at the foreign research site. Its purpose is to promote discovery and reduce global health disparities. Contact Division of International Research and Training, Fogarty International Center, Building 31, Room B2C39, 31 Center Drive, MSC 2220, Bethesda, MD 20892-2220; 301-496-1653; Fax: 301-402-0779; {www.fic.nih.gov/programs/firca.html}.

Research Internationally

The International Training and Research Program in Emerging Infective Disease program provides the opportunity for research and training needs in emerging and re-emerging infectious diseases in developing countries. ITREID is designed to train laboratory scientists and public health workers in developing countries and the U.S. in research, control and prevention strategies, and their implementation and evaluation related to these diseases. Contact Division of International Training and Research, Fogarty International Center, National Institutes of Health, Building 31, Room B2C39, 31 Center Drive, MSC 2220, Bethesda, MD 20892-2220; 301-496-7614; Fax: 301-402-0779; {www.fic.nih.gov/programs/erid.html}

Money To Study In Japan

The Japan-U.S. Friendship Commission provides grants to institutions and associations to support American studies in Japan, Japanese studies in the United States, exchange programs in the arts, policy-oriented research, and public affairs, and education. The Commission is interested in sponsoring research on Japan-US economic relations and activities in Asia, with priority given to Japanese investment in Asia and its effect on Japan-US economic, trade and political relations. Contact 1201 15th Street, NW, Suite 330, Washington, DC 20005; 202-653-9800; Fax: 202-653-9802; {www.jusfc.gov}.

Go To Japan For 6 Months

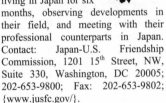

The United States/Japan Creative Artists' Program is designed to allow artists who create original work to pursue their individual artistic goals and interests by living in Japan for six months, observing developments in their field, and meeting with their professional counterparts in Japan. Contact: Japan-U.S. Friendship Commission, 1201 15th Street, NW, Suite 330, Washington, DC 20005; 202-653-9800; Fax: 202-653-9802; {www.jusfc.gov/}.

Money For Artists To Work With the Newly Independent States

Artslink encourages artistic exchange with the newly independent states in Central and Eastern Europe, the former Soviet Union, and Eurasia by offering three categories of support: Artslink Projects, which provides funding to U.S. artists to work on mutually beneficial projects with counterparts abroad; Artslink Residencies, which supports U.S. arts organizations

wishing to host a visiting artist or arts manager for a five-week residency; and Independent Projects, where artists and art managers can work on projects in the U.S. Contact CEC International Partners, 12 West 31st St., Suite 400, New York, NY 10001-4415; 212-643-1985; Fax: 212-643-1996; {http://godai.comset.net/cecip}.

Money For Teachers To Study

Promotion of the Humanities – Fellowships and Stipends Grants program provides support for college and university teachers; individuals employed by schools, museums, libraries, and others to undertake full-time independent study and research in the humanities for two consecutive summer months. Recipients must work full-time on their projects during the two-month period. Contact Fellowships and Stipends, Division of Research, National Endowment for the Humanities, 1100 Pennsylvania Ave., NW, Room 318, Washington, DC 20506; 202-606-8200; {www.neh.gov/grants/guidelines/stipends.html}.

Scientific Collaboration

The International Opportunities for Scientists and Engineers program is designed to advance and benefit U.S. interests by enabling U.S. scientists and engineers to avail themselves of research opportunities in other countries. The Division of International Programs supports efforts to initiate international cooperation involving new foreign collaborators, or new types of activities with established partners. Contact International Programs Division, National Science Foundation, 4201 Wilson Blvd., Room 935, Arlington, VA 22230; 703-292-8710; {www.nsf.gov/sbe/int}

Research In The Tropics

The objective of the Short-Term Fellowships program is to enable selected candidates to work in the tropics and explore research possibilities at the Smithsonian Tropical Research Institute. Fellowships are primarily for graduate students, but awards are made occasionally to undergraduate and postdoctoral candidates. Contact Office of Fellowships, Smithsonian Tropical Research Institution, 955 L'Enfant Plaza, Suite 7302, Washington, DC 20560; 202-633-4010; Fax: 202-786-2557; {www.stri.org/}.

Money To Attend Workshops Overseas

The Citizens Exchanges program awards grants to U.S. nonprofit organizations for projects that link their international exchange interests with counterpart institutions/groups in other countries. Subject areas include environmental protection, trade unionism, education administration and curriculum reform, protection, small business development and management training, and more. The Office of Citizen Exchanges develops a series of Requests for Proposals (RFPs) during the course of the fiscal year. Contact Office of Citizen Exchanges, Bureau of Educational and Cultural Affairs, U.S. Department of State, SA-44, 301 Fourth St., SW, Washington, DC 20547 ; 202-619-5348; Fax: 202-619-4350; {http://exchanges.state.gov/education/ citizens}.

Spend Six Weeks In A Foreign Country Working With Art Colleagues

Participants in the American Cultural Specialists program spend two to six weeks in one country working with foreign colleagues. They may conduct workshops or master classes, direct a play, rehearse a ballet, or advise on arts management. Specialists are provided with economy international travel and a honorarium of $200 per day plus limited allowances for educational and miscellaneous expenses by the Department of State. The U.S. embassy and/or the local co-sponsor provide per diem domestic travel and all local program costs. This is not a grant program from which individuals can request financial assistance for overseas projects, but as a response to a specific request from embassies abroad. Contact Cultural Programs Division, Bureau of Educational and Cultural Affairs, U.S. Department of State, SA-44, 301 4th St., SW, Room 568, Washington, DC 20547; 202-203-7523; Fax: 202-203-7325; {http://exchanges.state.gov/ed ucation/citizens/culture/aculfrs.htm}.

Eight Week Foreign Tours For Jazz Musicians And Bands

The Jazz Ambassador Program is designed to use the wealth of often undiscovered musical talent in the U.S. to enhance the mission of promoting cross-cultural understanding. Jazz Ambassadors travel to four or five countries for a period of four to eight weeks. In addition to public performances, they may conduct workshops and master classes. Nominations of classical musicians in various categories are sought from music schools, conservatories, colleges and universities throughout the U.S. Contact Cultural Programs Division, Bureau of Educational and Cultural Affairs, U.S. Department of State, SA-44, 301 4th St., SW, Room 568, Washington, DC 20547; 202-203-

7523; Fax: 202-619-7525; {http:// exchanges.state.gov/education/citizens /culture/jazzamb.htm}.

Foreign Leaders Can Study In The U.S.

The International Visitor Leadership office arranges programs for foreign leaders and potential leaders designed to develop and foster professional contacts with their colleagues in the United States and provide a broader exposure to American social, cultural, and political institutions. Areas of expertise government, politics, media, education, science, labor relations, the arts, and other fields. Participants are nominated by U.S. embassies. Contact Office of International Visitors, U.S. Department of State, 301 4th St., SW, Room 266, ECA/PE/V/C/P, Washington, DC 20547: 866-283-9090, 202-619-5217; Fax: 202-205-0792; {http://exchanges.state.gov/ education/ivp}.

Do Your Part To Help The World

The Peace Corps' objective is to promote world peace and friendship, to help other countries in meeting their needs for trained manpower, and to help promote understanding between the American people and other peoples served by the Peace Corps. Volunteers serve for a period of 2 years, living among the people with whom they work. Volunteers are expected to become a part of the community and to demonstrate, through their voluntary service, that people can be an important impetus for change. Volunteers receive a stipend and health insurance. Contact: Peace Corps, 1111 20th St., NW, Washington, DC 20526; 800-424-8580; Fax: 202-606-9410; {www.peacecorps.gov}.

Money For Engineering Students To Travel The Country Visiting DOE Laboratories

The Faculty and Student Teams Program objective is to provide college and university science and engineering faculty and students with energy-related training and research experience in areas of energy research at Department of Energy research facilities. Funds can be used to conduct energy research at one of the DOE research facilities. Students can also participate in energy-related workshops and conferences. Successful candidates receive a stipend of $800 per week for each week at the lab, as well as travel and housing expenses. Students must apply to a participating laboratory or university. Contact Science Education Programs, Office of Science Education, U.S. Department of Energy, Washington, DC 20585; 202-586-0987/7174; {www.scied.science.doe.gov/scied/fast /about.html}.

Community College Students Can Intern at Energy Laboratories

The objective of the Community College Institutes program is to give community college students the opportunity to participate in hands-on research at the cutting edge of science at the Department of Energy Laboratories, and to provide training and experience in the operation of sophisticated state-of-the-art equipment and instruments. College students who are majoring in an energy-related field can spend a semester using some of the Federal government's equipment and instruments at many of the Department of Energy's labs. The energy research must be in an area of the laboratory's ongoing research. Students receive a weekly stipend of $400, complimentary housing or a housing allowance, and a round-trip ticket to the lab. Contact Science Education Programs, Office of Science Education, U.S. Department of Energy, Washington, DC 20585; 202-586-7174, 202-586-9770; {www.scied.science.doe.gov/scied/CCI/about.html}.

The Military Could Be Your Ticket Overseas

U.S. Air Force Recruiting Service
550 D St., W, Suite 1
Randolph Air Force Base, TX 78150-4527
800-423-USAF
210-652-5993
www.airforce.com/

Commander
Naval Recruiting Command
4015 Wilson Blvd.
Arlington, VA 22203
800-USA-NAVY
www.navy.com/

Commanding General
Marine Corps Recruiting Command
2 Navy Annex
Washington, DC 20380-1775
800-MARINES
www.usmc.mil/

Army Opportunities
1307 Third Avenue
Fort Knox, KY 40121-2726

800-USA-ARMY
www.goarmy.com/

U.S. Coast Guard Information Center
4200 Wilson Blvd., Suite 450
Arlington, VA 22203
800-GET-USCG
www.uscg.mil
The Army, Navy, Marine Corps, Air Force, and the Coast Guard are responsible for protecting the security of the U.S. There are 2.87 million men and women on active duty, with over 600,000 serving outside the United States. Length of service does vary, as does pay and types of jobs available. You can even earn the chance to go to college. The military has bases all around the country and the world, and your local recruiter can answer all your questions about the opportunities they have to offer.

Thousands Of Government Jobs In Foreign Countries

The Federal government hires personnel to do everything from typing to spying, and there are posts all around the world. Those interested in jobs overseas can contact the Office of Personnel Management to learn current job openings and the skills required. Other government agencies also hire for jobs abroad, and you could contact them directly for information on employment opportunities. Contact Federal Job Information Center, Office of Personnel Management, 1900 E St.,

NW, Washington, DC 20415; 202-606-1800; {http://www.usajobs. opm.gov}; or you may contact the Career America Connection at 912-757-3000. Other agencies that hire for overseas employment include:

Agency For International Development
Information Center
Ronald Reagan Building
Washington, DC 20523
202-712-4810
www.info.usaid.gov

U.S. Customs Service
1300 Pennsylvania Avenue, NW
Washington, DC 20229
202-354-1000
www.customs.treas.gov

Central Intelligence Agency
703-482-0623
Office of Public Affairs
Washington, DC 20505
800-562-7242
Fax: 703-482-1739
www.cia.gov

U.S. Department of Commerce
Human Resources Management Office
U.S. and Foreign Commercial Service
1401 Constitution Ave., NW
Room 5001
Washington, DC 20230
202-482-4883
www.commerce.gov

U.S. Department of Agriculture
Foreign Agricultural Service
Personnel Division
1400 Independence Ave., SW
Washington, DC 20250
703-720-7115
www.fas.usda.gov

Sell Your Goods Overseas

The Trade Information Center is a comprehensive "one-stop-shop" for information on U.S. government programs and activities that support exporting efforts. This hotline is staffed by trade specialists who can provide information on seminars and conferences, overseas buyers and representatives, overseas events, export financing, technical assistance, and export counseling. They offer trade missions to help you find local agents, representatives, distributors, or direct sales. Their Trade Shows promote U.S. products with high export potential. The Agent/ Distributor Service will locate, screen, and assess agents, distributors, representatives, and other foreign partners for your business. Matchmaker Trade Delegations prescreen prospects interested in your product and assist with meetings. If you cannot afford the cost of traveling overseas, the Trade Information Center can refer you to several programs that offer loans to help you start exporting. You can also receive assistance from your own state's Department of Economic Development. Contact: Trade Information Center, U.S. Department of Commerce, Washington, DC 20230; 202-482-4473, 800-USA-TRADE; {www. trade.gov/td/tic}.

Work On Assignment for U.S. Embassies

The English Language Specialists program recruits American academics in the fields of TEF:/TES: and Applied Linguistics to complete assignments needed by overseas American Embassies. These assignments may include curriculum projects, teacher training seminars, textbook development, English for Specific Purposes and program evaluation. If a candidate is not specified by the Embassy, one will be recruited by the

Office of English Language Programs. Eligible Specialists will hold a MA or Ph.D., and have overseas and teacher training experience. Benefits include an honorarium of $200 per day, round-trip airfare, materials allowance, and basic health insurance. Contact Office of English Language Programs, U.S. Department of State, Annex #44, 301 4th Street, SW, Room 304, Washington, DC 20547; 202-619-5869; {http://exchanges.state.gov/edu cation/engteaching/specialists.htm}.

U.S. and Chinese Students Work Together

The U.S.-China Youth Exchange Initiative program is for secondary school students in the US and China so that they may develop an understanding of their counterpart's community life. Students and educators at selected schools work on Internet-based projects. The top seven partnerships are then involved in a 3 or 4-week exchange. Contact Youth Program Division, U.S. Department of State, SA-44, 301 4th Street, SW, Room 568, Washington, DC 20547; 202-203-7527; {http://exchange.state.gov/education/citizens/students/eap.htm}.

Free Cars and Air Fare To Go On Vacation

Not quite as easy as it sounds, but there are companies out there to help people move their cars. Most of the cars need to be driven across the country and in exchange, many car moving companies offer free gas and airline travel home. This is not to say that you can take your family on a minivan vacation across the country. Certain rules and restrictions apply. But I have known many a college kid that has gotten to drive across the U.S. for free. Obviously, you do not get to

pick your make and model, and you need to be flexible as to the departure time and destination, but this is one way to see America. Contact local moving companies to see what they have to offer. There is a website for those interested in having their cars moves at {www.movecars.com}. Air courier services operate the same way, but you are required to have a valid passport. Most air freight services don't do enough business to send a plane overseas each day. As a courier, you carry a package checked as baggage to an overseas destination. There have been no incidences of contraband problems, and customs is familiar with this service. You deliver the package to a company representative in the customs section of the airport, and then you are on our own. In exchange, you get to fly to exotic ports for FREE or cheap. Children are not allowed to accompany couriers. Contact companies listed in the air courier section of your phone book, do a web search using the terms "air courier service," or contact Air Courier Association at 800-211-5119; or online at {www.aircourier.org}.

Discounts on Car Rentals

You never should pay full-price for car rentals and there are deals aplenty if you keep your eyes open. AAA and AARP membership will save you a few bucks, as will many other membership programs. Car rental agencies also often offer discounts to senior citizens. Many times, if you book your flight and rental car at the same time, you can get a discount rate, plus get miles added to your frequent flier program. All you have to do is ask! The free brochure, *Renting a Car: What Everyone Should Know*, outlines some points to consider and questions to ask when you reserve a rental car. You can learn how to choose a rental car company and understand the terms they use for insurance and charges. Contact Public Reference, Federal Trade Commission, Washington, DC 20580; 202-326-2222, 877-FTC-HELP; or online at {www.ftc.gov}.

Travel Tips For Older Americans

What do you do if you lose your passport or have a health emergency? Is it safe to travel to a particular country? What about your medications? *Travel Tips for Older Americans* explains all this and more, and can be viewed for free online at {http://travel.state.gov}.

Spend Your Vacation as a Moose Crossing Guard at Old Faithful

Each year the National Parks use 80,000 volunteers! Contact your nearest park to discover an interesting way to spend your free time or to receive a free brochure, contact National Park Service, U.S. Department of the Interior, 1849 C Street, NW, Washington, DC 20240; 202-208-3100; {www.nps.gov/interior}.

Get Out of the House and Into the Woods

If you prefer saving spotted owls and counting woodchucks to playing bridge with the girls, you can be a volunteer with the Forest Service and be a nature hike leader or help with fascinating research. Contact your nearest national forest. For a list of national forests nearest you, contact U.S. Forest Service, U.S. Department of Agriculture, 1400 Independence Avenue, SW, Washington, DC 20250-0003; 202-205-8333; {www.fs.fed.us}.

Travel The World and Save it Too, For Free

Provide business assistance in Poland. Teach school in Nepal. These are just two examples of how over 500 seniors spent their time with the Peace Corps. As a volunteer, you serve two years, living among the native people and becoming part of the community. The Peace Corps sends volunteers throughout most of the world to share their expertise in education, agriculture, health, economic development, the environment and more. Contact Peace Corps, 1990 K Street, NW, Washington, DC 20526; 800-424-8580; {www.peacecorps.gov}.

Low Rates and Free Nights at Hotels

Almost all major hotel chains offer discounts 10-30% off the cost of rooms. Some require that you belong to AARP or AAA or other organization, so it is best to call ahead and ask. Three hotel chains Ramada, Hilton and, and Red Roof inns offer special deals to guests who frequent their hotels. Ramada's TripRewards Program is free to join and you can redeem your points for hotel stays and other prizes (800-367-8747). Hilton Senior HHotels program charges $55 ($40 annual renewal fee), and seniors receive up to $50 off rooms and discounts at hotel restaurants (800-548-8690). Red Roof offers the Redicard for their guests. The program is free to join and members can receive many benefits including: free nights, member only reservations, free USA

Today paper during stays and more (800-733-7663).

Discounts on Airline Tickets if You Are a Senior

Most airlines offer discounts to seniors amounting to as much as 10%. What happens though is that some of the airlines' special offers may be exempt from the discount. It is best to see what the lowest available rate is and then inquire about the senior discount. In many instances, the airline only requires that one person meet the age requirements for the discount, so your companion can receive the lower rate as well. Contact the specific airline or check with AARP for discounts currently available.

5-15% Off When You Travel

All car rental chains offer senior discounts, but again AARP or AAA membership may be required. The amount of discount varies from location to location, but usually is 10%. You should call ahead to see if a discount is available. Some chains also require reservations 24 hours in advance. For those that prefer to leave the driving to others, two other discount programs include AMTRAK and Greyhound. AMTRAK offer 15% off any fare available to those 62 and older (800-USA-RAIL). Greyhound bus has a 5% discount for people 55 and over (800-229-8425). Greyhound offers the Student Advantage Discount

Card that can save students 15% on walk-up fares and more. The card costs $20 per year.

Free (Or Cheap) Hunting and Fishing Licenses

Practically every state has a special license rate for seniors. States such as Alabama, Alaska, Delaware, Georgia, Kansas and others do not require that people 65 and older carry fishing and hunting licenses. Other states offer seniors, on average, half off the cost of licenses. These rules change so you will need to contact each state to receive specific details and discounts.

50% Off Camping

Almost all states offer discounts to seniors at state parks. Entrance fees are usually waived for seniors, or states like Illinois offer 50% off camping fees. Eighteen states have no residency requirements to receive the discount, so if you are planning a cross country camping trip, contact the state Parks Department to find out about eligibility criteria. For those wanting to camp in the National Forest, the Golden Age Passport is available to those 62 and over. For $10 you receive free lifetime admission to the parks, plus 50% off camping and many other services. The Passport is available at all National Parks, online at {www. nationalparks.org} or by calling 888-GOPARKS.

APPENDIX

Don't know who to call or where to turn for assistance? Never fear; the Appendix is here! This is a state-by-state listing of starting places for any problem, concern, or issue you may have. We have included address, phone number and website wherever possible. Each listing should be able to either answer your question or direct you to an office near you. Happy hunting!

The *Federal Information Center* can connect you with the appropriate federal government agency that handles your topic of interest.

The *State Information Operator* can connect you to the correct state government office that can answer your question.

State Departments on Aging focus on issues and concerns of the senior population. If you are looking for nutrition, transportation, housing, financial assistance, nursing home resources, or anything else having to do with seniors, then contact this office. They will direct you to local services and resources, as well as tell you about programs offered by the state.

Attorney General's Offices have Consumer Protection Offices where you can call to complain or seek assistance for a problem dealing with a business in the state. Many of these offices have special automobile hotlines that handle car complaints.

Banking Commissioners are in charge of state banks. If you feel a state bank has not treated you fairly or you would like to do research on a bank before you hand over your life savings, then call the *Banking Commissioner*.

Child Care and Development Block Grant Agencies give money to states to help families meet their child care needs. Each state sets up their eligibility requirements and programs offered. To find out what your state provides in the way of child care assistance contact this office.

Child Support Enforcement Agencies are the people to contact if your ex has not been paying all of the child support payment. These offices can help track down your ex and get what you are owed — even across state lines.

The *Cooperative Extension Service* has offices located in almost every county across the U.S. and has a wealth of information regarding finances, child care, home economics, gardening, and more. Many operate special horticulture hotlines where you can find information concerning your garden, plants, and grass. They offer free or cheap courses and publications in cooking, sewing, financial planning and more.

Corporation Division Offices are the people that incorporate businesses in their state. If you are starting a business, you need to talk to this office. If you have a concern about a corporation in your state, they can provide you with information about the corporation's status. You can also find out who owes money to whom through the Uniform Commercial Code.

Day Care Licensing Agencies license daycare facilities in the state. Each state has their own rules the agencies must follow. Contact this agency to learn if a child care setting has had any violations or problems, and to inquire about the rules and regulations they must follow.

Economic Development Offices are a good place to start to learn about business assistance and financing programs offered through the state. Many have one-stop business assistance centers that will answer your licensing questions as well.

State Departments of Education are responsible for the elementary and secondary schools in the state. They can provide you with the amount spent per child, student-teacher ratio, test scores, experiences, and more concerning the different school districts.

The *Departments of Higher Education* are responsible for colleges and universities in the state and can tell you about accreditation concerns. This office usually has information regarding state scholarship and loan programs.

The *Health Departments* are in charge of various health programs offered by the state. They can direct you to local community services, and can answer questions regarding health statistics and other health information. If you cannot afford health insurance, this office can direct you to resources your state may have to provide coverage.

State Housing Offices have a variety of programs to help with the construction and purchase of homes. Contact this office to learn more, and to be referred to county and city offices that may have additional programs. If you are having a problem with your housing needs, call this office for assistance. This office can also refer you to rental assistance programs.

Insurance Commissioners enforce the laws and regulations for all kinds of insurance, and they also handle complaints from consumers. If you have a complaint about your insurance company's policies, and the company won't help you, contact the Insurance Commission in the state. This office can also let you know what insurance companies can do business in the state, and most have informative booklets to help you learn how to choose the best insurance coverage for you.

Labor Departments are in charge of the state's work force. They offer special job training programs to help people get the training they need and offer incentives to companies often in the form of training subsidies. Call this department if you are looking for a job to see what kinds of assistance programs your state offers.

Licensing Offices can provide you with information concerning various licensed professionals, and can direct you to the appropriate office for those professions covered by other agencies or boards. If you are having trouble with your beautician, contractor, veterinarian, or other professional, call this office.

One Stop Career Centers are located throughout the U.S. and offer career services to those looking for a job. Services vary from site to site, but most include help with resume writing, job skills training, job hunting assistance, and more.

Security Regulators license and regulate stock brokers and investment advisers in their state, as well as the securities these people offer and sell. This office can provide information on these various professionals, such as their current standing and will accept complaints, although they will usually only investigate to make sure no laws were broken. These offices usually have information for investors for assistance in making sound investment decisions.

Small Business Development Centers are located in over 700 cities across the U.S. and offer free or very low cost consulting services on most aspects of business ownership, including how to write a business plan, sell your idea, get government contracts, and more.

Social Services Offices are the ones in charge of child care programs, welfare, Medicaid, and other programs designed to help individuals and families get back on their feet. If you are struggling to make ends meet, contact this office to be directed to resources and services in your area.

Temporary Assistance to Needy Families (TANF) is the new office that replaced Aid to Families With Dependent Children (AFDC). This program helps people who need funds to pay for basic necessities as they enter job training programs, finish their education, or care for small children. Welfare-To-Work is often part of this program.

Transportation Departments are in charge of highways, road construction, and can direct you to those in charge of transportation systems and programs throughout their state. Many of these departments offer funds to local organizations to help fill some transportation needs in the community.

Unclaimed Property Offices hold money and other valuables that go unclaimed in the state. Unclaimed funds include savings and checking accounts, certificates of deposit, health insurance payments, stock and dividends, and more. If you think you or someone in your family may have missing funds, contact this office and they can do a search for you.

Unemployment Insurance Offices are the ones that distribute unemployment checks. Contact this office if you are eligible for the checks, want to appeal a denial, or need an extension of your benefits.

Utility Commissioners are in charge of the utility companies in the state. Many companies offer discounts and other special services to seniors or those in need. Contact your local utility company or this office to learn what is available.

In almost every state, there are *Women's Commissions* and similar groups that provide direction or assistance to women. Missions and programs vary, but these groups all share the goal of working toward eliminating the inequities that affect women at home and in the workplace. Some commissions are simply advocacy groups, bringing attention to issues that affect women and working to bring about legislative changes that would improve situations that women face. Others provide information and referrals to help women get ahead and some even provide direct services to help women get the training, education, and financial help they need to succeed.

ALABAMA

Federal Information Center
1-800-FED-INFO
www.firstgov.gov
www.pueblo.gsa.gov/call/

State Information Office
334-242-8000
www.state.al.us

Department on Aging
Department of Senior Services
770 Washington Ave.
Suite 470
Montgomery, AL 36130
334-242-5743
877-425-2243
www.adss.state.al.us

Attorney General's Office
Office of the Attorney General
Alabama State House
11 South Union Street, 3rd Floor
Montgomery, AL 36130
334-242-7300
800-392-5658
www.ago.state.al.us

Banking Commissioner
State Banking Department
Center for Commerce
401 Adams Ave. Suite 680
Montgomery, AL 36130
334-242-3452
www.bank.state.al.us

Child Care and Development Block Grant Lead Agency
Department of Human Resources
Family Services Division
50 Ripley St.
Montgomery, AL 36130
334-242-9500
www.dhr.state.al.us/fsd

Child Support Enforcement Agency
Department of Human Resources
Child Support Enforcement
Division
P.O. Box 30400
Montgomery, AL 36130
334-242-9300
800-284-4347 (in AL and GA)

Fax: 334-242-0606
www.dhr.state.al.us/csed

Cooperative Extension Offices
Dr. W. Gaines Smith, Interim
Director
Alabama Cooperative Extension
Service
109-D Duncan Hall
Auburn University
Auburn, AL 36849-5612
334-844-4444
www.aces.edu

Chinelle Henderson,
Administrator
Alabama A&M University
Cooperative Extension Service
P.O. Box 222
Normal, AL 35762
205-851-5710
http://saes.aamu.edu/

Dr. Moore, Director
Cooperative Extension Program
U.S. Department of Agriculture
Tuskegee University
207 N. Main St.
Suite 400
Tuskegee, AL 36083-1731
334-727-8808
www.tusk.edu/academics/cooper
ative_ext//

Day Care Licensing Agency
Alabama Department of Human
Resources
Office of Child Care
50 Ripley St.
Montgomery, AL 36130
334-242-9500
www.dhr.state.al.us/fsd/child_car
e.asp

Economic Development Office
Alabama Development Office
401 Adams Ave., Suite 670
Montgomery, AL 36130-4106
800-248-0033
334-242-0400
Fax: 334-242-0415
www.ado.state.al.us

Alabama Department of Revenue
50 N. Ripley St.
Montgomery, AL 36132-7123
334-242-1170
www.ador.state.al.us/

Department of Education
Alabama Department of
Education
50 N. Ripley
P.O. Box 302101
Montgomery, AL 36104
334-242-9700
www.alsde.edu/

Department of Higher Education
Alabama Commission on Higher
Education
100 N. Union St.
P.O. Box 30200
Montgomery, AL 36130-2000
334-242-1998
Fax: 334-242-0268
www.ache.state.al.us

Health Department
Alabama Dept. of Public Health
RSA Tower
201 Monroe Street
Montgomery, AL 36104
MAILING ADDRESS:
 RSA Tower
 P.O. Box 303017
 Montgomery, AL 36130-3017
334-206-5300
www.adph.org
Email:
webmaster@alapubhealth.org

Housing Office
Alabama Housing Finance
Authority
P.O. Box 230909

Montgomery, AL 36123-0909
334-244-9200
800-325-AHFA
www.ahfa.com

Insurance Commissioner
Insurance Commissioner
201 Monroe St., Suite 1700
Montgomery, AL 36104
334-269-3550
www.aldoi.org

Labor Department
Alabama Department of Labor
RSA Union, 6th Floor
P.O. Box 303500
Montgomery, AL 36130-3500
334-242-3460
www.alalabor.state.al.us

Licensing Office
Alabama Career Information
Network System (ACINS)
401 Adams Ave.
P.O. Box 5690
Montgomery, AL 36103
334-242-5591
www.adeca.state.al.us/soicc/soic
c/WEBSTAR3.0/SOICC/default.ht
ml

One-Stop Career Center
Department of Industrial
Relations
649 Monroe Street
Montgomery, AL 36131
334-242-8990
Fax: 334-242-3960
http://dir.alabama.gov
Email: director@dir.state.al.us

Security Regulators
Alabama Securities Commission
770 Washington Ave., Suite 570
Montgomery, AL 36130-4700
334-242-2984
800-222-1253
http://asc.state.al.us
3450_alabama.htm

Small Business Development
Center
Alabama Small Business
Development Consortium
University of Alabama at
Birmingham
2800 Milan Ct. Suite 124
Birmingham, AL 35211
205-943-6750
Email: sandefur@uab.edu
www.asbdc.org

Social Services Offices
Alabama Department of Human
Resources
Office of Governmental Affairs
and Public Information
Gordon Pearson Building
Suite 2104, 50 N. Ripley St.
Montgomery, AL 36130
334-242-1310
www.dhr.state.al.us

**Temporary Assistance to
Needy Families (TANF)**
Temporary Aid to Needy Families
Joel Sander
Alabama Department of Human
Resources
Family Assistance Division
Gordon Pearson Bldg.
50 Ripley St.
Montgomery, AL 36130
334-242-1310
www.dhr.state.al.us/

Transportation Department
Alabama Department of
Transportation
1409 Coliseum Blvd.
P.O. Box 303050
Montgomery, AL 36130-3050
334-242-6358
www.dot.state.al.us

William Luckerson
Alabama Department of
Transportation
1409 Coliseum Blvd.
Montgomery, AL 36130-3050

334-242-6083
www.dot.state.al.us

Unclaimed Property Office
Unclaimed Property Division
State Treasurer's Office
Room S-106
State Capitol Building
Montgomery, AL 31630
334-242-7500
888-844-8400
www.treasury.state.al.us/

**Unemployment Insurance
Office**
Unemployment Compensation
Division
Alabama Department of Industrial
Relations
649 Monroe St., Room 4676
Montgomery, AL 36131-4200
334-242-8800
http://dir.alabama.gov/uc
Weekly benefit range: $45-190
Duration of benefits: 15-26 weeks

**Utility Commission (Energy
Division)**
Public Service Commission
P.O. Box 304260
RSA Union, Suite 950
100 N. Union St.
Montgomery, AL 36130
334-242-2696
800-392-8050 (AL only)
www.psc.state.al.us

Your Senator
United States Senate
Washington, DC 20510
202-224-3121
www.senate.gov

Your Representative
United States House of
Representatives
Washington, DC 20515
202-224-3121
www.house.gov

ALASKA

Federal Information Center
1-800-FED-INFO
www.firstgov.gov
www.pueblo.gsa.gov/call/

State Information Office
907-465-2111
www.state.ak.us

Department on Aging
Alabama Commission on Aging
Alaska Department of Health and
Human Services
P.O. Box 110693
Juneau, AK 99811-0693
907-465-3250
www.alaskaaging.org

Attorney General's Office
Office of the Attorney General
P.O. Box 110300
Juneau, AK 99811-0300
907-465-2133
www.law.state.ak.us
Email: Attorney_General@law.
state.ak.us

Banking Commissioner
Division of Banking, Securities
and Corporations
P.O. Box 110807
Juneau, AK 99811-0807
907-465-2521
www.dced.state.ak.us/bsc/

**Child Care and Development
Block Grant Lead Agency**
Alaska Department of Health and
Social Services
Division of Public Assistance
619 E. Ship Creek, Suite 230
Anchorage, AK 99501
907-269-4500
Fax: 907-465-5254
www.hss.state.ak.us

**Child Support Enforcement
Agency**
Barbar Miklos
Child Support Enforcement
Division
550 West 7th Ave.
Suite 310

Anchorage, AK 99501-6699
907-269-6900
800-478-3300
Fax: 907-269-6900
www.csed.state.ak.us/

Cooperative Extension Office
Hollis D. Hall, Director
Alaska Cooperative Extension
University of Alaska Fairbanks
P.O. Box 756180
Fairbanks, AK 99775-6180
907-474-7246
www.uaf.edu/coop-ext/

Corporation Division Office
State of Alaska
Division of Banking, Securities
and Corporation
Corporation Section
P.O. Box 110808
Juneau, AK 99811-0808
907-465-2500
www.dced.state.ak.us/bsc/
corps.htm

Day Care Licensing Agency
Department of Health and Social
Services
Office of Day Care Licensing
619 E. Ship Creek
Suite 230
Juneau, AK 99501
907-465-3170
www.hss.state.ak.us

Economic Development Office
Alaska Department of
Commerce, Community and
Economic Development
P.O. Box 110800
Juneau, AL 98111
907-465-5478
www.dced.state.ak.us/cbd/

Department of Education
Alaska Department of Education
Public Information
801 W. 10th St., Suite 200
Juneau, AK 99801-1878
907-465-2800
www.eed.state.ak.us

**Department of Higher
Education**
Alaska Commission on
Postsecondary Education
3030 Vintage Boulevard
Juneau, AK 99801-7100
800-441-2962
907-465-2962
Fax: 407-465-5316
www.state.ak.us/acpe/home.html

Health Department
Alaska Department of Health &
Social Services
350 Main Street, Room 508
Juneau, AK 99801
MAILING ADDRESS:
P.O. Box 110610
Juneau, AK 99811-0610
907-465-3027
Fax: 907-4654101
www.hss.state.ak.us/dph

Housing Office
Alaska Housing Finance
Corporation
4300 Boniface Parkway
Anchorage, AK 99504
MAILING ADDRESS
P.O. Box 101020
Anchorage, AK 99510-1020
907-338-6100
800-478-2432
www.ahfc.state.ak.us

Insurance Commissioner
Director of Insurance
P.O. Box 110805
Juneau, AK 99811-0805
907-465-2515
Fax: 907-465-3422
www.dced.state.ak.us/insurance

Labor Department
Alaska Department of Labor
P.O. Box 21149
Juneau, AK 99802-1149
907-456-2700
www.labor.state.ak.us/

Licensing Office
Division of Occupational
Licensing

Free Money For Everybody

Department of Commerce and
Economic Development
State of Alaska
P.O. Box 110806
Juneau, AK 99811-0806
907-465-2534
www.dced.state.ak.us/occ

One-Stop Career Center
Alaska Job Center Network
Department of Labor
P.O. Box 21149
Juneau, AK 99802-1149
907-456-2700
www.jobs.state.ak.us

Security Regulators
Division of Banking, Securities
and Corporations
P.O. Box 110807
Juneau, AK 99801
907-465-2521
www.commerce.state.ak.us/bsc/h
ome.htm

**Small Business Development
Center**
Alaska Small Business
Development Center
University of Alaska Anchorage
510 L Street, Suite 310
Anchorage, AK 99501-3550
907-271-4022
Fax: 907-271-4545
www.sba.gov/ak/

Social Services Offices
Alaska Department of Health and
Social Services
350 Main Street Room 404

P.O. Box 110601
Juneau, AK 99811-0601
907465-3030
Fax: 907-465-3068
www.hss.state.ak.us

**Temporary Assistance to
Needy Families (TANF)**
Temporary Aid to Needy Families
Jim Nordlund
Alaska Department of Health and
Social Services
P.O. Box 110640
Juneau, AK 99811-0640
907-465-3347
www.hss.state.ak.us/dpa/progra
ms/atap

Transportation Department
Mike Barton
Alaska Department of
Transportation and Public
Facilities
3132 Channel Dr.
Juneau, AK 99801
907-465-3900
www.dot.state.ak.us

Unclaimed Property Office
Department of Revenue
Unclaimed Property Unit
P.O. Box 110405
Juneau, AK 99811-0405
907-465-3726
www.revenue.state.ak.us

**Unemployment Insurance
Office**
Unemployment Insurance
Program Manager

Employment Security Division
P.O. Box 25509
Juneau, AK 99802-5509
907-465-2712
www.labor.state.ak.us
Weekly benefit range: $44-248
Duration of benefits: 16-26 weeks

Utility Commission
Regulatory Commission of Alaska
701 West 8th Ave., Suite 300
Anchorage, AK 99501-3469
907-276-6222
www.state.ak.us/apuc/

Women's Commission
Safe City
Anchorage Women's Commission
Dept. of Health and Human
Services
P.O. Box 196650
Anchorage, AK 99519-6650
907-343-6302
Fax: 907-343-6730
www.muni.org/healthssd/women.
cfm

Your Senator
United States Senate
Washington, DC 20510
202-224-3121
www.senate.gov

Your Representative
United States House of
Representatives
Washington, DC 20515
202-224-3121
www.house.gov

ARIZONA

Federal Information Center
1-800-FED-INFO
www.firstgov.gov
www.pueblo.gsa.gov/call/

State Information Office
602-542-4900
http://az.gov

Department on Aging
Aging and Adult Administration
Arizona Department of Economic
Security
1789 W. Jefferson
Phoenix, AZ 85007
602-542-4446
Fax: 602-542-6575
www.de.state.az.us/aaa/

Attorney General's Office
Office of the Attorney General
Department of Law
1275 West Washington Street
Phoenix, AZ 85007
602-542-5025
www.ag.state.az.us
Email: ag.inquiries@ag.
state.az.us

Banking Commissioner
Superintendent of Banks
2910 N. 44th St., Suite 310
Phoenix, AZ 85018
602-255-4421
www.azbanking.com

**Child Care and Development
Block Grant Lead Agency**
Department of Economic Security
Child Care Administrator
3150 E. Union Hills
Phoenix, AZ 85020
602-569-4719
Fax: 602-569-6149
www.de.state.az.us/

**Child Support Enforcement
Agency**
Nancy Mendoza
Division of Child Support
Enforcement
Department of Economic Security
P.O. Box 40458

Phoenix, AZ 85067-9917
602-252-4045
800-882-4151
www.de.state.az.us/dcse

Cooperative Extension Office
Jim Christenson, Director
Cooperative Extension Office
P.O. Box 210036
University of Arizona
Forbes 301
Tucson, AZ 85721
520-621-7205
http://ag.arizona.edu/extension

Corporation Division Office
Arizona Corporation Commission
Secretary of State
1300 W. Washington
Phoenix, AZ 85007-2929
602-542-3026
www.cc.state.az.us/corp/
index.htm

Day Care Licensing Agency
State Department of Health
Services
Office of Child Care Licensure
150 North 18th Avenue
Phoenix, AZ 85007
602-364-2536
Fax: 602-364-4808
www.hs.state.az.us/als/ childcare/
index.htm

Economic Development Office
Department of Commerce
1700 W. Washington
Suite 600
Phoenix, AZ 85007
602-771-1100
800-528-8421
www.commerce.state.az.us/

Department of Education
Arizona Department of Education
Research and Policy Division
1535 W. Jefferson
Phoenix, AZ 85007
602-542-5393
800-352-4558
www.ade.state.az.us/

**Department of Higher
Education**
Arizona Commission for
Postsecondary Education
2020 North Central, Suite 550
Phoenix, AZ 85004-4503
602-258-2435
Fax: 602-258-2483
www.acpe.asu.edu

Health Department
Arizona Department of Health
Services
Office of Women's and Children's
Health
150 N. 18th Avenue, Suite 320
Phoenix, AZ 85007
602-364-1400
Fax: 602-220-6551
TDD: 602-364-1495
www.azdhs.gov/phs/owch/index.h
tm

Housing Office
Office of Housing Development
3800 N. Central, Suite 1500
Phoenix, AZ 85012
602-280-1365
www.housingaz.com

Insurance Commissioner
Director of Insurance
2910 N. 44th St., Suite 210
Phoenix, AZ 85018
602-912-8444
800-325-2548
www.state.az.us/id/

Labor Department
Industrial Commission of Arizona
800 W. Washington Street
Phoenix, AZ 85007
602-542-4515
Fax: 602-542-8097
www.ica.stateaz.ux/Labor/laborto
p.htm

Licensing Office
Registrar of Contractors
800 W. Washington St., 6th Floor
Phoenix, AZ 85007
602-542-1525
www.rc.state.az.us

One-Stop Career Center
One Stop Career Center
Arizona Department of Economic
Security
P.O. Box 6123
Site Code 901z
Phoenix, AZ 85005
602-542-3957
www.de.state.az.us/oscc/
index.html
Email: onestop@de.state.az.us

Security Regulators
Arizona Corporation Commission
1300 W. Washington St.. 3rd
Floor
Phoenix, AZ 85007
602-542-4242
www.ccsd.cc.state.az.us

**Small Business Development
Center**
Arizona Small Business
Development Center Network
Maricopa County Community
Colleges
**Small Business Development
Center**
2411 West 14th Street
Tempe, AZ 85281
480-731-8720
Fax: 480-731-8729
www.dist.maricopa.edu/sbdc

Social Services Offices
Arizona Department of Economic
Security
Community Services
P.O. Box 6123
Site Code 086z
Phoenix, AZ 85005

602-542-6600
www.de.state.az.us

**Temporary Assistance to
Needy Families (TANF)**
Cash Assistance
Arizona Department of Economic
Security
1789 West Jefferson St.
Phoenix, AZ 85007
602-542-4791
www.azdes.gov/faa/cash.asp

Transportation Department
Arizona Department of
Transportation
206 South 17th Ave.
Suite 340-B
Phoenix, AZ 85007
602-712-7355
www.dot.state.az.us

Unclaimed Property Office
Department of Revenue
Unclaimed Property Unit
P. O. Box 29026
Phoenix, AZ 85038-9026
602-364-0380
800-397-0256
www.revenue.state.az.us/
unclm/index.htm

**Unemployment Insurance
Office**
ESA Administrator
P.O. Box 29225
Phoenix, AZ 85038
602-364-2722
www.de.state.az.us/esal
Weekly benefit range: $60-240
Duration of benefits: 12-26 weeks

Utility Commission
Corporation Commission
1200 W. Washington St.
Phoenix, AZ 85007-2996
602-542-4251
800-222-7000 (AZ only)
www.cc.state.az.us/utility/
index.htm

Women's Commission
Phoenix Women's Commission
Equal Opportunity Department
200 West Washington
Phoenix, AZ 85003
602-261-8242
Fax: 602-256-3389
www.ci.phoenix.az.us/
PHXWOMEN/index.html

Tucson Women's Commission
240 North Court Ave.
Tucson, AZ 85701
520-624-8318
Fax: 520-624-5599
Email: pctwc@mindspring.com
www.geocities.com/pctwc

Your Senator
United States Senate
Washington, DC 20510
202-224-3121
www.senate.gov

Your Representative
United States House of
Representatives
Washington, DC 20515
202-224-3121
www.house.gov

ARKANSAS

Federal Information Center
1-800-FED-INFO
www.firstgov.gov
www.pueblo.gsa.gov/call/

State Information Office
501-682-3000
www.state.ar.us

Department on Aging
Division of Aging and Adult
Services
Box 1437, Slot S-530
Little Rock, AR 72203
501-682-2441
Fax: 501-682-8155
www.state.ar.us/dhs/aging/
index.html

Attorney General's Office
Office of the Attorney General
323 Center Street, Suite 200
Little Rock, AR 72201
501-682-2007
800-482-8982
www.ag.state.ar.us
Email: oag@ag.state.ar.us

Banking Commissioner
Bank Commissioner
400 Hardin Rd., Suite 100
Little Rock, AR 72211
501-324-9019
www.state.ar.us/bank/

**Child Care and Development
Block Grant Lead Agency**
Arkansas Department of Human
Services
Division of Child Care and Early
Childhood Education
P.O. Box 1437, Slot S-140
Little Rock, AR 72203-1437
501-682-4891
Fax: 501-682-2317
www.state.ar.us/childcare

**Child Support Enforcement
Agency**
Dan McDonald
Office of Child Support
Enforcement
Division of Revenue

400 E. Capitol
P.O. Box 8133
Little Rock, AR 72203
501-682-6169
800-264-2445 (in AR)
Fax: 501-682-6002
www.state.ar.us/dfa/childsupport/
index.html

Cooperative Extension Offices
David Foster, Director
Cooperative Extension Service
2301 s. University Ave.
Little Rock, AR 72204
501-671-2000
www.uaex.edu

Corporation Division Office
Secretary of State
Corporations Division
State Capitol, Room 256
Little Rock, AR 72201
501-682-3409
888-233-0325
www.sosweb.state.ar.us

Day Care Licensing Agency
State Department of Human
Services
Child Care Licensing Unit
P.O. Box 1437, Slot 720
Little Rock, AR 72203-1437
501-682-8590
www.state.ar.us/childcare

Economic Development Office
Arkansas Economic Development
Commission
1 Capitol Mall
Little Rock, AR 72201
501-682-1121
800-ARKANSAS
Fax: 501-682-7394
www/1800arkansas.com

Department of Education
Arkansas Department of
Education
Office of Accountability
4 State Capitol Mall, 204-B
Little Rock, AR 72201
501-682-4475
http://arkedu.state.ar.us

**Department of Higher
Education**
Arkansas Department of Higher
Education
114 East Capitol
Little Rock, AR 72201
501-371-2000
Fax: 501-371-2001
www.arkansashighered.com

Health Department
Arkansas Department of Health
4815 West Markham
Little Rock, AR 72205
501-661-2000
800-235-0002
www.healthyarkansas.com/

Housing Office
Arkansas Development Finance
Authority
P.O. Box 8023
423 Main St., Suite 500
Little Rock, AR 72201
501-682-5900
www.state.ar.us/adfa

Insurance Commissioner
Insurance Commissioner
Arkansas Insurance Department
1200 W. 3rd St.
Little Rock, AR 72201
501-371-2600
800-282-9134
www.state.ar.us/insurance/

Labor Department
Arkansas Department Of Labor
10421 West Markham
Little Rock, AR 72205
501-682-4500
Fax: 501-682-4535
www.ark.org/labor

Licensing Office
Boards and Commissions
Governor's Office
State Capitol Building
Little Rock, AR 72201
501-682-3570
www.state.ar.us/governor

One-Stop Career Center
Arkansas Career Development
Network
Arkansas Employment Security
Department
#1 Pershing Circle
Little Rock, AR 72114
501-682-2003
www.state.ar.us/esd/

Security Regulators
Arkansas Securities Department
Heritage West Building
201 East Markham, Suite 300
Little Rock, AR 72201
501-324-9260
www.accessarkansas.org/arsec

**Small Business Development
Center**
Arkansas Small Business
Development Center
University of Arkansas at Little
Rock
2801 S. University
Little Rock, AR 72201
501-324-9043
Fax: 501-324-9049
Email: jmnye@ualr.edu
www.asbdc.ualr.edu

Social Services Offices
Arkansas Department of Human
Services
Donaghey Plaza West
Slot 5201

P.O. Box 1437
Little Rock, AR 72203-1437
501-682-8650
www.state.ar.us/dhs/

**Temporary Assistance to
Needy Families (TANF)**
Temporary Aid to Needy Families
Arkansas Department of Human
Services
TEA Support Center
101 East Capitol
P.O. Box 1437, Slot S-301
Little Rock, AR 72203
501-682-8299
www.state.ar.us/dhs/tea/

Transportation Department
James Gilbert
Arkansas State Highway and
Transportation Department
P.O. Box 2261
Little Rock, AR 72203
501-569-2000
Fax: 501-569-2400
www.ahtd.state.ar.us

Unclaimed Property Office
Auditor of State
Unclaimed Property Division
1400 West 3rd Street
Suite 100
Little Rock, AR 72201-1811
501-682-6000
800-252-4648
www.accessarkansas.org/auditor

**Unemployment Insurance
Office**
Unemployment Insurance
Director
Arkansas Employment Security
Department
One Pershing Circle
Little Rock, AR 72114
501-682-3200
www.accessarkansas.org/esd
Weekly benefit range: $47-264
Duration of benefits: 9-26 weeks

Utility Commission
Public Service Commission
1000 Center St.
P.O. Box 400
Little Rock, AR 72203-0400
501-682-2051
800-482-1164 (AR only)
www.accessarkansas.org/psc

Women's Commission
Closed 96-99

Your Senator
United States Senate
Washington, DC 20510
202-224-3121
www.senate.gov

Your Representative
United States House of
Representatives
Washington, DC 20515
202-224-3121
www.house.gov

CALIFORNIA

Federal Information Center
1-800-FED-INFO
www.firstgov.gov
www.pueblo.gsa.gov/call/

State Information Office
916-322-9900
www.ca.gov

Department on Aging
California Department of Aging
1600 K St.
Sacramento, CA 95814
916-322-3887
Fax: 916-324-4989
www.aging.state.ca.us/

Attorney General's Office
Office of the Attorney General
P.O. Box 944255
Sacramento, CA 94244-2550
916-322-3360
800-952-5225
http://caag.state.ca.us

Banking Commissioner
Department of Financial
Institutions
111 Pine St., Suite 1100
San Francisco, CA 94111-5613
415-263-8500
www.dfi.ca.gov

**Child Care and Development
Block Grant Lead Agency**
Child Development Division
California Dept. of Education
1430 N. Street
Sacramento, CA 95814
916-322-6233
Fax: 916-323-6853
www.cde.ca.gov/sp/cd

**Child Support Enforcement
Agency**
Leslie Frye
California Department of Child
Support Services
P.O. Box 419064
Rancho Cordova, CA 95741-
9064
916-464-5050

866-249-0773 (in CA)
www.childsup.cahwnet.gov

Cooperative Extension Office
Kenneth Farrell, Vice President
University of California
Division of Agriculture and
Natural Resources
300 Lakeside Drive, 6th Floor
Oakland, CA 94612-3560
510-987-0060
www.ucanr.org
(programs are at county level)

Corporation Division Office
Corporations Unit
Secretary of State
1500 11th St.
Sacramento, CA 95814
916-657-5448
www.ss.ca.gov/business/
business.htm

Day Care Licensing Agency
Department of Social Services
Community Care Licensing
Division
744 P St., Mail Station 19-50
Sacramento, CA 95814
916-445-6951
www.dss.cahwnet.gov/
default.htm

Economic Development Office
Business, Transportation and
Housing Agency
980 9th Street, Suite 2450
Sacramento, CA 95814-2719
916-323-5400
http://commerce.ca.gov

Department of Education
California Department of
Education
1430 N. Street
Sacramento, CA 95814
916-319-0818
www.cde.ca.gov/

**Department of Higher
Education**
California Student Aid
Commission

P.O. Box 419026
Rancho Cordova, CA 95741-
9026
888-224-7268
Fax: 916-526-8002
www.csac.ca.gov

Health Department
California Department of Health
Services
P. O. Box 997413
Sacramento, CA 95899-7413
906-445-4171
www.dhs.ca.gov

Housing Offices
California Housing Finance
Agency
1121 L St., 7th Floor
Sacramento, CA 95814
916-322-3991
www.calhfa.ca.gov

California Department of Housing
and Community Development
P.O. Box 952050
Sacramento, CA 94252-2050
916-445-4782
http://housing.hcd.ca.gov

Insurance Commissioner
Commissioner of Insurance
300 S. Spring St., SouthTower
Los Angeles, CA 90013
213-897-8921
800-927-HELP (complaints)
www.insurance.ca.gov/

Labor Department
California Employment
Development Department
800 Capital Mall
Sacramento, CA 95814
800-758-0398
www.edd.cahwnet.gov/

Licensing Office
State of California
Department of Consumer Affairs
400 R Street
Sacramento, CA 95814
916-445-1254
800-952-5210
www.dca.ca.gov

Free Money For Everybody

One-Stop Career Center
One-Stop Office
800 Capitol Mall, MIC 83
Sacramento, CA 95814
800-758-0398
Fax: 916-654-9863
www.sjtcc.cahwnet.gov/
SJTCCWEB/ONE-STOP/
Email: onestop@edd.ca.gov

Security Regulators
Department of Corporations
1515 K Street, Suite 200
Sacramento, CA 95814-4052
916-445-7205
www.corp.ca.gov

Small Business Development Center
California Small Business
Development Center
California Trade and Commerce
Agency
980 9th Street, Suite 2450
Sacramento, CA 95814-2719
916-323-5400
www.commerce.ca.gov

Social Services Offices
California Department of Social
Services
Office of Community Relations
744 P Street
Sacramento, CA 95814
916-445-6951
www.dss.cahwnet.gov

Temporary Assistance to Needy Families (TANF)
Temporary Aid to Needy Families
Eloise Anderson
California Department of Social
Services
744 P Street
Sacramento, CA 95814
916-445-6951
www.dss.cahwnet.gov/cdssweb

Transportation Department
California Department of
Transportation - CALTRANS
P.O. Box 942873
Sacramento, CA 94273-0001
916-654-5266
www.dot.ca.gov
Tory Harris

Unclaimed Property Office
Division of Collections
Bureau of Unclaimed Property
P.O. Box 942850
Sacramento, CA 94250-5873
916-445-2636
www.sco.ca.gov

Unemployment Insurance Office
Unemployment Insurance
Employment Development
Department
800 Capitol Mall, MIC 83
Sacramento, CA 95814
800-300-5616

www.edd.ca.gov/fleclaim.htm
Weekly benefit range: up to $450
Duration of benefits: 12-26 weeks

Utility Commission
Public Utilities Commission
505 Van Ness Ave.
San Francisco, CA 94102-3298
415-703-2782
www.cpuc.ca.gov

Women's Commission
California Commission on the
Status of Women
1303 J St., Suite 400
Sacramento, CA 95814-2900
916-445-3173
Fax: 916-322-9466
Email: csw@sna.com
www.statusofwomen.ca.gov

Your Senator
United States Senate
Washington, DC 20510
202-224-3121
www.senate.gov

Your Representative
United States House of
Representatives
Washington, DC 20515
202-224-3121
www.house.gov

COLORADO

Federal Information Center
1-800-FED-INFO
www.firstgov.gov
www.pueblo.gsa.gov/call/

State Information Office
303-866-5000
www.colorado.gov

Department on Aging
Office of Adult and Veterans
Services
Social Services Department
1575 Sherman St., 10th Floor
Denver, CO 80203
303-866-2800
Fax: 303-866-2696
www.cdhs.state.co.us/

Attorney General's Office
Office of the Attorney General
Department of Law
1525 Sherman Street, 5th Floor
Denver, CO 80203
303-866-4500
Fax: 303-866-5691
www.ago.state.co.us

Banking Commissioner
State Bank Commissioner
Division of Banking
Denver Post Bldg.
1560 Broadway, Suite 1175
Denver, CO 80202
303-894-7575
Fax: 303-894-7570
www.dora.state.co.us/banking

**Child Care and Development
Block Grant Lead Agency**
Office of Child Care Services
Colorado Dept. of Human
Services
1575 Sherman St.
Denver, CO 80203-1714
303-866-5958
Fax: 303-866-4453
www.cdhs.state.co.us/childcare/
home.html

**Child Support Enforcement
Agency**
Pauline Burton

Division of Child Support
Enforcement
Department of Human Services
1575 Sherman St., 5th Floor
Denver, CO 80203
303-866-4300
303-866-4360
www.childsupport.state.co.us/

Cooperative Extension Office
Milan Rewets, Director
Colorado State University
Cooperative Extension
1 Administration Building
Fort Collins, CO 80523-4040
970-491-6281
www.ext.colostate.edu

Corporation Division Office
Corporate Division
Secretary of State
1560 Broadway, Suite 200
Denver, CO 80202
303-894-2200
www.sos.state.co.us/

Day Care Licensing Agency
State Department of Human
Services
Office of Social Services
Child Care Licensing
1575 Sherman St.
Denver, CO 80203-1714
303-866-5958
www.cdhs.state.co.us/childcare/li
censing.htm

Economic Development Office
Office of Economic Development
and International Trade
1625 Broadway, Suite 1700
Denver, CO 80202
303-892-3840
Fax: 303-892-3848
TDD: 800-659-2656
www.state.co.us/gov_dir/oed.html

Department of Education
Colorado Department of
Education
Planning and Evaluation Unit
201 E. Colfax
Denver, CO 80203-1799

303-866-6600
www.cde.state.co.us/

**Department of Higher
Education**
Colorado Commission on Higher
Education
1380 Lawrence St., Suite 1200
Denver, CO 80204
303-866-2723
www.state.co.us/cche_dir/
hecche.html

Health Department
Colorado Department of Public
Health & Environment
4300 Cherry Creek Drive South
Denver, CO 80246-1530
303-692-2000
www.cdphe.state.co.us/

Housing Office
Colorado Housing and Finance
Authority
1981 Blake St.
Denver, CO 80202-1272
303-297-2432
800-877-2432
www.colohfa.org

Insurance Commissioner
Commissioner of Insurance
1560 Broadway, Suite 850
Denver, CO 80202
303-894-7499
800-930-3745
Fax: 303-894-7455
www.dora.state.co.us/insurance/
index.htm

Labor Department
Colorado Department of Labor
and Employment
1515 Arapahoe
Tower 2, Suite 400
Denver, CO 80202
303-318-8000
www.cdle.state.co.us

Licensing Office
Department of Regulatory
Agencies
State Services Building

1560 Broadway, Suite 1550
Denver, CO 80202
303-894-7855
Fax: 303-894-7885
www.dora.state.co.us

One-Stop Career Center
Job Service Centers
Colorado Department of Labor
and Employment
Office of Employment and
Training
1515 Arapahoe Street
Tower 2, Suite 400
Denver, CO 80202-2117
303-318-8000
http://navigator.cdle.state.co.us

Security Regulators
Division of Securities
1580 Lincoln St., Suite 420
Denver, CO 80203
303-894-2320
www.dora.state.co.us/Securities/i
ndex.htm

**Small Business Development
Center**
Colorado Small Business
Development Center
Office of Business Development
1625 Broadway, Suite 1710
Denver, CO 80202
303-892-3794
Fax: 303-892-3848
www.state.co.us/oed/sbdc

Social Services Offices
Colorado Department of Human
Services
1575 Sherman Street
Denver, CO 80203-1714
303-866-5700

Fax: 303-866-4047
www.cdhs.state.co.us

**Temporary Assistance to
Needy Families (TANF)**
Temporary Aid to Needy Families
Sue Tuffin
Colorado Department of Human
Services
1575 Sherman St., Third Floor
Denver, CO 80203-1714
303-866-5981
www.cdhs.state.co.us/oss/
Self_Sufficiency.html

Transportation Department
Colorado Department of
Transportation
4201 East Arkansas Ave.
Denver, CO 80222
303-757-9011
www.dot.state.co.us

Unclaimed Property Office
Unclaimed Property Division
The Great Colorado Payback
1120 Lincoln St., Suite 1004
Denver, CO 80203
303-894-2443
800-825-2111
www.treasurer.state.co.us/
payback/index.htm

**Unemployment Insurance
Office**
Office of Unemployment
Insurance
1515 Arapahoe St.
Tower 2, Suite 400
Denver, CO 80202
303-318-8000
http://unempben.cdle. state.co.us
Weekly benefit range: $25 -272
Duration of benefits: 13-26 weeks

Utility Commission
Public Utilities Commission
1580 Logan St.
Logan Tower, Office Level 2
Denver, CO 80203
303-894-2000
800-888-0170 (CO only)
Fax: 303-894-2065
www.dora.state.co.us/PUC/
index.htm

Women's Commission
Denver Women's Commission
201 West Colfax, Dept 1102
Denver, CO 80204
720-913-8450
Fax: 303-913-8470
www.denvergov.org/
Chaer Robert, Director

Fort Collins City Commission on
the Status of Women
c/o Human Resources
City of Ft. Collins
P.O. Box 580
Fort Collins, CO 80522
970-221-6091
970-224-6050
www.ci.fort-collins.co.us
Laurie Fonken-Joseph, Chair

Your Senator
United States Senate
Washington, DC 20510
202-224-3121
www.senate.gov

Your Representative
United States House of
Representatives
Washington, DC 20515
202-224-3121
www.house.gov

CONNECTICUT

Federal Information Center
1-800-FED-INFO
www.firstgov.gov
www.pueblo.gsa.gov/call/

State Information Office
860-240-0222
www.ct.gov

Department on Aging
Elderly Services
Department of Social
Services
25 Sigourney St.
Hartford, CT 06106-5033
860-424-5277
800-994-9422
www.ctelderlyservices.state
.ct.us

Attorney General's Office
Office of the Attorney
General
55 Elm Street
P.O. Box 120
Hartford, CT 06141-0120
860-808-5318
Fax: 860-808-5387
www.cslib.org/attygenl
Email: attorney.general@
po.state.ct.us

Banking Commissioner
Banking Commissioner
260 Constitution Plaza
Hartford, CT 06103-1800
860-240-8299
800-831-7225 (toll free in
CT)
www.state.ct.us/ dob/

**Child Care and
Development Block Grant
Lead Agency**
Office of Child Care
Connecticut Dept. of Social
Services
25 Sigourney St., 10th Floor
Hartford, CT 06106-5033
800-842-4524
www.dss.state.ct.us/ccare

**Child Support
Enforcement Agency**
Diane Fray
Bureau of Child Support
Enforcement
Department of Social
Services
25 Sigourney St.
Hartford, CT 06106
800-842-1508
www.dss.state.ct.us/csrc/cs
rc.htm

**Cooperative Extension
Office**
Associate Director
Cooperative Extension
System
University of Connecticut
1376 Storrs Road
Storrs, CT 06269-4134
860-486-1987
www.canr.uconn.edu/ces/
index.html

**Corporation Division
Office**
Office of Secretary of State
Commercial Recording
Division
30 Trinity St.
Hartford, CT 06106
860-509-6212
www.sots.state.ct.us

**Day Care Licensing
Agency**
State of Connecticut
Department of Public Health
Child Day Care Licensing
410 Capital Ave.
P.O. Box 340308
Hartford, CT 06134-3038
860-509-8045
800-282-6063
www.dph.state.ct.us

**Economic Development
Office**
Department of Economic
and Community
Development

505 Hudson Street
Hartford, CT 06106
860-270-8000
www.ct.gov/ecd

Department of Education
Connecticut Department of
Education
Public Information Office
165 Capitol Ave.
Hartford, CT 06145
860-713-6548
www.state.ct.us/sde/

**Department of Higher
Education**
Department of Higher
Education
61 Woodland Street
Hartford, CT 06105-2326
860-947-1800
Fax: 860-947-1310
www.ctdhe.org

Health Department
Connecticut Dept. of Public
Health
410 Capitol Avenue
P.O. Box 340308
Hartford, CT 06134-0308
860-509-8000
800-282-6063
TDD: 860-509-7191
www.dph.state.ct.us

Housing Office
Connecticut Housing
Finance Authority
999 West St.
Rocky Hill, CT 06067-4005
860-721-9501
www.chfa.org

Insurance Commissioner
Insurance Commissioner
P.O. Box 816
Hartford, CT 06142-0816
860-297-3800
800-203-3447
Fax: 860-560-7410
www.state.ct.us/cid/

Free Money For Everybody

Labor Department
Connecticut Department of
Labor
200 Folly Brook Blvd.
Wethersfield, CT 06109-
1114
860-263-6000
www.ctdol.state.ct.us

Licensing Office
Occupational Licensing
Division
Department of Consumer
Protection
165 Capitol Ave.
Hartford, CT 06106
860-713-6050
Fax: 860-713-7239
www.dcp.state.ct.us/licensing

One-Stop Career Center
Connecticut Works
Connecticut Department of
Labor
200 Folly Brook Boulevard
Wethersfield, CT 06109
860-263-6000
www.ctdol.state.ct.us/ctwor
ks/ ctworks.htm

Security Regulators
Department of Banking
260 Constitution Plaza
Hartford, CT 06013-1800
860-240-8230
800-831-7225
www.state.ct.us/dob

**Small Business
Development Center**
Connecticut Small Business
Development Center
University of Connecticut
School of Business
Administration

2100 Hillside Rd., Unit 1094
Storrs, CT 06269-1094
860-486-4135
Fax: 860-486-1576
www.sbdc.uconn.edu

Social Services Offices
Connecticut Department of
Social Services
25 Siqourney Street
Hartford, CT 06106
800-842-1508
www.dss.state.ct.us

**Temporary Assistance to
Needy Families (TANF)**
Temporary Aid To Needy
Families
Patricia Wilson-Cooker
Connecticut Dept. of Social
Services
25 Sigourney St.
Hartford, CT 06106
800-842-1508
www.dss.state.ct.us/svcs/ta
nf.htm

**Transportation
Department**
Lynn DiNallo
Connecticut Department of
Transportation
P.O. Box 317546
2800 Berlin Turnpike
Newington, CT 06131-7546
806-594-2000
www.ct.gov/dot

**Unclaimed Property
Office**
Unclaimed Property Unit
Office of State Treasurer
55 Elm ST.
Hartford, CT 06106
860-702-3126

800-618-3404
www.state.ct.us/ott

**Unemployment Insurance
Office**
State Labor Department
200 Folley Brook Blvd.
Wethersfield, CT 06109
860-263-6785
www.ctdol.state.ct.us/
Duration of benefits: 26
weeks

Utility Commission
Department of Public Utility
Control
10 Franklin Square
New Britain, CT 06051
860-827-1553
Fax: 860-827-2613
800-382-4586 (CT only)
www.state.ct.us/dpuc/

Women's Commission
Connecticut Permanent
Commission of the Status of
Women
18-20 Trinity St.
Hartford, CT 06106
860-240-8300
Fax: 860-240-8314
Email: pcsw@po.state.ct.us
www.cga.state.ct.us/pcsw/

Your Senator
United States Senate
Washington, DC 20510
202-224-3121
www.senate.gov

Your Representative
United States House of
Representatives
Washington, DC 20515
202-224-3121
www.house.gov

DELAWARE

Federal Information Center
1-800-FED-INFO
www.firstgov.gov
www.pueblo.gsa.gov/call/

State Information Office
302-739-4000
http://delaware.gov

Department on Aging
Aging Division
Health and Social Services
Department
1901 N. Dupont Hwy.
New Castle, DE 19720
800-223-9074
www.state.de.us/dhss/dsaapd

Attorney General's Office
Office of the Attorney General
Carvel State Office Building
820 North French Street
Wilmington, DE 19801
302-577-8400
www.state.de.us/attgen/index.htm
Email:
Attorney.General@state.DE.US

Banking Commissioner
State Bank Commissioner
555 E. Lockerman St., Suite 210
Dover, DE 19901
302-739-4235
Fax: 302-739-3609
www.state.de.us/ bank/

**Child Care and Development
Block Grant Lead Agency**
Social Services Administrator
Delaware Department of Health
and Social Services
1901 N. DuPont Highway
Lewis Building
New Castle, DE 19720
302-255-9040
Fax: 302-255-4429
www.state.de.us/dhss/main/childr
en.htm

**Child Support Enforcement
Agency**
Charles E. Hayward
Division of Child Support
Enforcement

Department of Health and Social
Services
P. O. Box 904
84A Christiana Road
New Castle, DE 19720
302-577-7171
Fax: 302-326-6239
www.state.de.us/dhss/dcse/
index.html

Cooperative Extension Office
Dr. Starlene Taylor
Assistant Administrator
Delaware State College
Cooperative Extension Service
1200 N. DuPont Highway
Dover, DE 19901
302-274-7100
http://ag.udel.edu/extension/
index.html#

Corporation Division Office
Delaware Department of State
Division of Corporations
Secretary of State
P.O. Box 898
Dover, DE 19903
302-739-3073
www.state.de.us/corp/

Day Care Licensing Agency
Department of Health and Social
Services
Office of Child Care Licensing
DSCYF, 1825 Falkland Rd.
Wilmington, DE 19805
302-892-5800
www.state.de.us/kids/occl.htm

Economic Development Office
Delaware Economic
Development Office
John D. Wilk
99 Kings Highway
P.O. Box 1401
Dover, DE 19901
302-739-4271
Fax: 302-739-2535
www.state.de.us/dedo/ index.htm

Department of Education
Delaware Department of
Education

John G. Townsend Building
P.O. Box 1402
Dover, DE 19903-1402
302-739-4601
Fax: 302-739-4654
www.doe.state.de.us/

**Department of Higher
Education**
Delaware Higher Education
Commission
820 North French Street
Carvel State Office Building
Wilmington, DE 19801
800-292-7935
302-577-3240
Fax: 302-577-6765
www.doe.state.de.us/high-ed

Health Department
Delaware Division of Public
Health
417 Federal Street
Dover, DE 19901
302-744-4700
Fax: 302-739-3008
www.state.de.us/dhss/dph/
index.htm

Housing Office
Delaware State Housing Authority
Division of Housing and
Community Development
18 the Green
Dover, DE 19901
302-739-4263
www2.state.de.us/dsha

Insurance Commissioner
Insurance Commissioner
841 Silver Lake Blvd.
Rodney Bldg.
Dover, DE 19904
302-739-4251
800-282-8611
Fax: 302-739-6278
www.state.de.us/inscom/index.ht
ml

Labor Department
Delaware Department of Labor
4425 North Market Street
Wilmington, DE 19802

302-761-8085
www.delawareworks.com/

Licensing Office
Division of Professional
Regulation
861 Silver Lake Blvd.
Cannon Building, Suite 203
Dover, DE 19904
302-744-4500
800-464-4357
www.professionallicensing.state.d
e.us

One-Stop Career Center
Delaware Career Network
Department of Labor,
Employment and Training
4425 North Market Street
Wilmington, DE 19809-0828
302-761-8102
www.vcnet.net

Security Regulators
Delaware Division of Securities
Carvel State Office Building
820 North French St., 5th Floor
Wilmington, DE 19801
302-577-8424
www.state.de.us/securities

**Small Business Development
Center**
Delaware Small Business
Development Center
University of Delaware
1318 N. Market St.
Wilmington, DE 19801
302-571-1555
Fax: 302-571-5222
www.delawaresbdc.org

Social Services Offices
Delaware Department of Health
and Social Services
Health and Social Service
Campus
1901 North DuPont Highway
Main Building
New Castle, DE 19720
302-255-9040
www.state.de.us/dhss/

**Temporary Assistance to
Needy Families (TANF)**
Temporary Aid to Needy Families
Nina Licht
Delaware Social Services
Lewis Building
1901 North Dupont Highway
New Castle, DE 19720
302-255-9500
800-372-2022
www.state.de.us/dhss/dss/tanf.ht
m/

Transportation Department
Delaware Department of
Transportation
800 S. Bay Rd.
P.O. Box 778
Dover, DE 19903
800-652-5600
302-760-2080
www.state.de.us/deldot/

Unclaimed Property Office
Delaware State Escheater
P.O. Box 8931
Wilmington, DE 19899
302-577-8200
www.state.de.us/revenue/escheat
/escheat.htm

**Unemployment Insurance
Office**
Division of Unemployment
Insurance
4425 N. Market Street
Wilmington, DE 19802
302-761-8446
www.delawareworks.com/division
s/unemployment/ welcome.htm
Weekly benefit range: $20-300
Duration of benefits: 24-26 weeks

Utility Commission
Public Service Commission
861 Silver Lake Blvd.
Suite 100, Cannon Bldg.
Dover, DE 19904
302-739-4247
800-282-8574 (DE only)
www.state.de.us/delpsc/index.ht
ml

Women's Commission
Delaware Commission for
Women
4425 N. Market St., 4th Floor
Wilmington, DE 19802
302-761-8005
Fax: 302-761-6652
www.delawareworks.com/dcw

Your Senator
United States Senate
Washington, DC 20510
202-224-3121
www.senate.gov

Your Representative
United States House of
Representatives
Washington, DC 20515
202-224-3121
www.house.gov

DISTRICT OF COLUMBIA

Federal Information Center
1-800-FED-INFO
www.firstgov.gov
www.pueblo.gsa.gov/call/

District of Columbia Information Office
202-727-1000
www.dc.gov/

Department on Aging
Aging Office
441 4th St., NW, Suite 900S
Washington, DC 20001
202-724-5626
Fax: 202-724-4979
www.dcoa.dc.gov

Attorney General's Office
Office of the Corporation Counsel
1350 Pennsylvania Avenue NW,
Suite 409
Washington, DC 20004
202-727-3400
http://occ.dc.gov/main.shtm

Banking Commissioner
810 1st Street NE, Suite 701
Washington, DC 20002
202-727-8000
http://disb.dc.gov

Child Care and Development Block Grant Lead Agency
Office of Early Childhood Development
Department of Human Services
717 14th Street SE
Suite 700
Washington, DC 20005
202-727-1839
www.dhs.dc.gov

Child Support Enforcement Agency
Bureau of Paternity and Child Support Enforcement
441 4th Street
Suite 550N
Washington, DC 20001
202-442-9900
www.csed.dc.gov

Cooperative Extension Office
Reginald Taylor, Acting Director
Cooperative Extension Service
University of the District of Columbia
4200 Connecticut Ave., NW
Washington, DC 20008
202-274-5000
www.universityofdc.orgl

Corporation Division Office
Corporations Division
Consumer and Regulatory Affairs
941 N. Capitol St., NE
Washington, DC 20002
202-442-4400
Fax: 202-442-9445
www.dcra.dc.gov

Day Care Licensing Agency
Child and Residential Care Facilities Division
825 North Capitol St. NE
2nd Floor
Washington, DC 20002
202-442-5888
www.dchealth.dc.gov

Economic Development Office
Office of Economic Development
1350 Pennsylvania Ave., NW
Suite 317
Washington, DC 20004
202-727-6365
www.dcbiz.dc.gov

Department of Education
Public Schools
825 North Capitol Street, NE
Washington, DC 20002
202-724-4222
www.K12.dc.us

Department of Higher Education
State Education Office
441 4th Street NW
Suite 350 North
Washington, DC 20001
202-727-6436
http://seo.dc.gov

Health Department
District of Columbia Department of Health
825 N. Capitol St., NE
Washington, DC 20002
202-442-5999
Fax: 202-442-4788
www.dchealth.dc.gov/index.asp

Housing Offices
DC Housing Finance Agency
815 Florida Ave., NW
Washington, DC 20001
202-777-1600
Fax: 202-986-6705
www.dchfa.org

District of Columbia Department of Housing and Community Development
801 N. Capitol St., NE
Suite 8000
Washington, DC 20002
202-442-7200
http://dhcd.dc.gov

Insurance Commissioner
Commissioner of Insurance
801 First St., NE, Suite 701
Washington, DC 20001
202-727-8000
www.disr.dc.gov

Labor Department
Department of Employment Services
609 H Street, NE
Washington, DC 20002
202-724-7000
www.does.dc.gov

Licensing Office
Department of Consumer and Regulatory Affairs
941 N. Capitol St., NE
Washington, DC 20002
202-442-4400
Fax: 202-442-9445
www.dcra.dc.gov

One-Stop Career Center
DOES One-Stop Career Center

Free Money For Everybody

Department of Employment
Services
609 H Street, NE
Washington, DC 20002
202-724-7000
www.does.dc.gov

Security Regulators
Securities Bureau of the District
of Columbia
810 First Street, NE, Suite 701
Washington, DC 20002
202-727-8000
www.disr.dc.gov

**Small Business Development
Center**
Small Business Development
Center
1110 Vermont Ave., NW
9th Floor
Washington, DC 20005
202-606-4000
www.sba.gov/dc

Social Services Offices
Department of Human Services
64 New York, NE, 6th Floor
Washington, DC 20002
202-671-4200

Fax: 202-279-6014
www.dhs.dc.gov

**Temporary Assistance to
Needy Families (TANF)**
Welfare Reform
Washington DC Department of
Human Services
64 New York Ave. NE, 6th Floor
Washington, DC 20002
202-671-4200
www.dhs.dc.gov

Transportation Department
Radamese Cabrera
Washington DC Department of
Public Works
2000 14th St., 6th Floor
Washington, DC 20009
202-673-6813
Fax: 202-671-0642
www.ddot.dc.gov

Unclaimed Property Office
Office of Chief Financial officer
Unclaimed Property Unit
1350 Pennsylvania Ave., NW
Room 203
Washington, DC 20004
202-442-8181
www.cfo.dc.gov

**Unemployment Insurance
Office**
Office of Unemployment
Compensation
Department of Employment
Services
609 H. Street, NE
Washington, DC 20002
202-724-7000
Fax: 202-724-5683
www.does.dc.gov

Utility Commission
Public Service Commission
1333 H St., NW
Suite 200 West Tower
Washington, DC 20005
202-626-5110
www.dcpsc.org

Your Senator
United States Senate
Washington, DC 20510
202-224-3121
www.senate.gov

Your Representative
United States House of
Representatives
Washington, DC 20515
202-224-3121
www.house.gov

FLORIDA

Federal Information Center
1-800-FED-INFO
www.firstgov.gov
www.pueblo.gsa.gov/call/

State Information Office
850-488-1234
www.myflorida.com

Department on Aging
Department of Elder Affairs
4040 Esplanade Way, Suite 315
Tallahassee, FL 32399-7000
850-414-2000
Elder Helpline:
800-96-ELDER (in FL)
www.state.fl.us/doea/

Attorney General's Office
Office of the Attorney General
The Capitol
Tallahassee, FL 32399-1050
850-487-1963
866-966-7226
Fax: 850-410-1630
http://myfloridalegal.com

Banking Commissioner
State Comptroller
Florida Department of Financial
Services
200 E. Gaines St.
Tallahassee, FL 32399-0300
850-410-9111
800-848-3792 (toll free in FL)
www.dbf.state.fl.us

**Child Care and Development
Block Grant Lead Agency**
Chief, Child Care Services
Florida Department of Children
and Families
1317 Winewood Blvd.
Building 1, Room 202
Tallahassee, FL 32399-0700
850-487-1111
Fax: 850-487-1111
www.state.fl.us/cf_web/

**Child Support Enforcement
Agency**
Patricia Piller
Child Support Enforcement
Program

Department of Revenue
P.O. Box 8030
Tallahassee, FL 32314
800-622-5437
Fax: 850-488-4401
http://sun6.dms.state.fl.us/
dor/childsupport/

Cooperative Extension Offices
Christine Taylor-Stephens, Dean
Florida Cooperative Extension
Service
P.O. Box 110210
University of Florida
Gainesville, FL 32611-0210
352-392-1761
www.ifas.ufl.edu/www/extension/
ces.htm

Corporation Division Office
Division of Corporations
Secretary of State
409 Gaines St.
Tallahassee, FL 32399
800-755-5111
www.dos.state.fl.us/doc/
index.html

Day Care Licensing Agency
Florida Department of Children
and Families
1317 Winewood Blvd.
Building 8, Room 202
Tallahassee, FL 32399-0700
850-487-1111
www.state.fl.us/cf_web/

Economic Development Office
Florida Economic Development
Council
P.O. Box 3186
Tallahassee, FL 32315-3186
850-201-FEDC
Fax: 850-201-3330
www.fedc.net

Enterprise Florida
390 N. Orange Ave.
Suite 1300
Orlando, FL 32801
407-316-4600
Fax 407-316-4599
www.floridabusiness.com

Department of Education
Florida Department of Education
Turlington Building, Suite 1514
325 W. Gaines St.
Tallahassee, FL 32399
850-245-0505
www.fldoe.org

**Department of Higher
Education**
Florida Department of Education
Turlington Buidling, Suiete 1514
325 West Gaines Street
Tallahassee, FL 32399
850-245-0505
www.fldoe.org

Health Department
Florida Department of Health
4052 Bald Cypress Way
Tallahassee, FL 32399-1701
850-245-4443
www.doh.state.fl.us
Email: dhs@doh.state.fl.us

Housing Office
Florida Housing Finance
Corporation
227 N. Bronough St.
Suite 5000
Tallahassee, FL 32301-1329
850-488-4197
www.floridahousing.org

Insurance Commissioner
Insurance Commissioner
200 E. Gaines St.
Tallahassee, FL 32399-0300
850-413-3100
800-342-2762
www.fldfs.com

Licensing Office
Florida Department of Business
and Professional Regulation
1940 N. Monroe St.
Tallahassee, FL 32399-1027
850-487-1395
www.state.fl.us/dbpr

One-Stop Career Center
Agency for Workforce Innovation
107 East Madison Street

Free Money For Everybody

Carldwell Building
Tallahasse, FL 32399-4120
850-245-7105
Fax: 850-921-3223
www.floridajobs.org

Security Regulators
Division of Securities
200 East Gaines St.
Tallahassee, FL 32399
850-410-9805
800-848-3792
www.dbf.state.fl.us/index.html

Small Business Development Center
Florida Small Business
Development Center
University of West Florida
401 E. Chase Street
Suite 100
Pensacola, FL 32502
850-473-7830
Email: fsbdc@uwf.edu
www.sbdc.uwf.edu

Social Services Offices
Florida Department of Children
and Families
1317 Winewood Boulevard
Building 1, Room 202
Tallahassee, FL 32399-0770
850-487-1111
www.state.fl.us/cf_web/

Temporary Assistance to Needy Families (TANF)
Temporary Aid to Needy Families
Florida Department of Children
and Families
1317 Winewood Blvd.
Tallahassee, FL 32399-0770
850-487-1111
www.state.fl.us/cf_web

Transportation Department
Department of Transportation
605 Suwannee St.
Tallahassee, FL 32399-0450
850-414-4100
www.dot.state.fl.us

Unclaimed Property Office
Department of Banking and
Finance
Abandoned Property Division
209 East Gaines St.
Tallahassee, FL 32399-0358
850-410-9253
http://up.dbf.state.fl.us/

Unemployment Insurance Office
Division of Unemployment
Compensation
Agency for Workforce Innovation
107 East Madison Street
Caldwell Building

Tallahassee, FL 32399-4120
850-245-7105

Utility Commission
Public Service Commission
2540 Shumard-Oak Blvd.
Tallahassee, FL 32399-0850
850-413-6100
800-342-3552 (FL only)
www.psc.state.fl.us

Women's Commission
Florida Commission on the Status
of Women
Office of the Attorney General
The Capitol PL-01
Tallahassee, FL 32399-1050
850-414-3300
Fax: 850-921-4131
www.fcsw.net

Your Senator
United States Senate
Washington, DC 20510
202-224-3121
www.senate.gov

Your Representative
United States House of
Representatives
Washington, DC 20515
202-224-3121
www.house.gov

GEORGIA

Federal Information Center
1-800-FED-INFO
www.firstgov.gov
www.pueblo.gsa.gov/call/

State Information Office
404-656-2000
www.georgia.gov

Department on Aging
Division of Aging Services
Georgia Department of Human
Resources
2 Peachtree St., NW, Suite 9-385
Atlanta, GA 30303-3142
404-657-5258
Fax: 404-657-5285
www2.state.ga.us/
departments/dhr/aging.html

Attorney General's Office
Office of the Attorney General
40 Capitol Square, SW
Atlanta, GA 30334
404-656-3300
http://ganet.org/ago

Banking Commissioner
Commissioner of Banking and
Finance
2990 Brandywine Rd., Suite 200
Atlanta, GA 30341-5565
707-986-1633
www.ganet.org/dbf/dbf.html

**Child Care and Development
Block Grant Lead Agency**
Family Support Unit
Division of Family and Children
Services
Georgia Dept. of Human
Resources
Two Peachtree St., NW
Suite 29-213
Atlanta, GA 30303
404-651-6316
http://dfcs.dhr.georgia.gov

**Child Support Enforcement
Agency**
Robert Riddle
Child Support Enforcement
Department of Human Resources

2 Peachtree St.
Atlanta, GA 30303
404-463-8800
800-227-7993 (in GA)
Fax: 404-657-3326
www.cse.dhr.state.ga.us

Cooperative Extension Offices
Bob Isaac, Interim Director
Cooperative Extension Service
University of Georgia
1111 Conner Hall
Athens, GA 30602-7504
706-542-3824
http://extension.caes.uga.edu

Cooperative Extension Service
Fort Valley State College
Fort Valley, GA 31030
478-825-6296
www.aginfo.fvsu.edu/ces/overvie
w.htm

Corporation Division Office
Corporations Division
Secretary of State
315 West Tower
#2 M.L. King Dr.
Atlanta, GA 30334-1530
404-656-2817
Fax: 404-657-2248
www.sos.state.ga.us/corporations/

Day Care Licensing Agency
Department of Human Resources
Child Care Licensing Unit
2 Peachtree St., NW, 32nd Floor
Atlanta, GA 30303-3142
404-657-5562
http://dhr.georgia.gov

Economic Development Office
Office of Economic Development
60 Executive Park South, NE
Suite 250
Atlanta, GA 30329-2231
404-679-4940
Fax: 800-736-1155
www.dca.state.ga.us

Department of Education
Georgia Department of Education
2054 Jesse Hill Jr. Dr.

Twin Towers East, Suite 1654
Atlanta, GA 30334
404-656-2800
800-311-3627 (in GA)
www.doe.k12.ga.us/

**Department of Higher
Education**
Student Finance Commission
2082 East Exchange Place
Tucker, GA 30084
800-505-GSFC
770-724-9000
Fax: 770-724-9089
www.gsfc.org

Health Department
Georgia Division of Public Health
Two Peachtree Street, NW
Atlanta, GA 30303-3186
404-657-2700
www.ph.dhr.state.ga.us/
Email: gdphinfo@ dhr.state.ga.us

Housing Office
Georgia Residential Finance
Authority
60 Executive Park South
Suite 250
Atlanta, GA 30329
404-679-4940
www.dca.state.ga.us

Insurance Commissioner
Insurance Commissioner
West Tower, Suite 704
2 Martin Luther King, Jr. Dr.
Atlanta, GA 30334
404-656-2070
800-656-2298
www.gainsurance.org

Labor Department
Georgia Department of Labor
148 International Boulevard
Atlanta, GA 30303-1751
404-232-7300
www.dol.state.ga.us

Licensing Office
Examining Board Division
Secretary of State
237 Coliseum Dr.

Macon, GA 31217
478-207-1300
www.sos.state.ga.us/plb

One-Stop Career Center
Department of Labor
Employment Services
148 International Boulevard, NE
Atlanta, GA 30303-1751
404-232-3540
www.state.ga.us/index/gaemp.
html

Security Regulators
Securities and Business
Regulation Division
802 West Tower
Suite 802
2 Martin Luther King Jr. Dr., SE
Atlanta, GA 30334
404-656-3920
Fax: 404-657-8410
www.sos.state.ga.us/Securities/
default.htm

Small Business Development Center
Georgia Small Business
Development Center
University of Georgia
Chicopee Complex
1180 East Broad Street
Athens, GA 30602-5412
706-542-6776
Fax: 706-542-6776
Email:SBDCDIR@ sbdc.uga.edu
www.sbdc.uga.edu

Social Services Offices
Georgia Department of Human
Resources
2 Peachtree St., NW
Atlanta, GA 30303-3142
404-656-4937
www.state.ga.us/Departments/
DHR

Temporary Assistance to Needy Families (TANF)
Temporary Aid to Needy Families
Tommy Olmstead
Georgia Department of Human
Resources
2 Peachtree St., NW
Suite 29-213
Atlanta, GA 30303
404-651-6316
www2.state.ga.us/
departments/dhr/tanf.html

Transportation Department
Georgia Dept. of Transportation
No. 2 Capitol Square, S. W.
Atlanta, GA 30334
404-656-5267
www.dot.state.ga.us

Unclaimed Property Office
Department of Revenue
Property Tax Division
Unclaimed Property
4245 International Parkway
Hapeville, GA 30354-3903
404-968-0490
www2.state.ga.us/departments/
dor/ptd/ucp/index.html

Unemployment Insurance Office
Assistance Commissioner
Unemployment Insurance
Georgia Department of Labor
148 International Blvd., NE
Suite 718
Atlanta, GA 30303
404-232-3990
www.dol.state.ga.us/ui/
Weekly benefit range: $39-274
Duration of benefits: 8-26 weeks

Utility Commission
Public Service Commission
244 Washington Street, SW
Atlanta, GA 30334
404-656-4501
800-282-5813 (GA only)
www.psc.state.ga.us

Women's Commission
GA State Commission of Women
148 International Blvd., NE
Atlanta, GA 30303
404-657-9260
Fax: 404-657-2963

Your Senator
United States Senate
Washington, DC 20510
202-224-3121
www.senate.gov

Your Representative
United States House of
Representatives
Washington, DC 20515
202-224-3121
www.house.gov

HAWAII

Federal Information Center
1-800-FED-INFO
www.firstgov.gov
www.pueblo.gsa.gov/call/

State Information Office
808-548-6222
www.state.hi.us

Department on Aging
Aging Office
250 S. Hotel St., Room 406
Honolulu, HI 96813-2831
808-586-0100
www2.state.hi.us/eoa

Attorney General's Office
Dept. of the Attorney General
425 Queen Street
Honolulu, HI 96813
808-586-1500
Fax: 808-586-1239
www.state.hi.us/ag

Banking Commissioner
Commissioner of Financial
Institutions
P.O. Box 2054
Honolulu, HI 96805
808-586-2820
www.state.hi.us/dcca/dfi

*Child Care and Development
Block Grant Lead Agency*
Hawaii Department of Human
Services
Benefits, Employment and
Support Services Division
Child Care Program Office
1390 Miller St., Room 209
Honolulu, HI 96813
808-586-4996
Fax: 808-586-4890
www.state.hi.us/dhs

*Child Support Enforcement
Agency*
Mike Meaney
Child Support Enforcement
Agency
Department of Attorney General
601 Kamokila Blvd., Suite 251
Kapolei, HI 96707

808-692-8265
888-317-9081
Fax: 808-587-3716
www.state.hi.us/csea/csea.htm

Cooperative Extension Office
Dr. Po'Yung Lai, Assistant
Director
Cooperative Extension Service
3050 Maile Way
Honolulu, HI 96822
808-956-8139
www.ctahr.hawaii.edu/

Corporation Division Office
Business Registration Division
Department of Commerce and
Consumer Affairs
335 Merchant Street
P.O. Box 40
Honolulu, HI 96813
808-586-2744
www.businessregistrations.com

Day Care Licensing Agency
Department of Human Services
Employment/Child Care Program
Office
1390 Miller St., Room 209
Honolulu, HI 96813
808-586-4996
www.hawaii.gov/dhs

Economic Development Office
Department of Business and
Economic Development and
Tourism
P.O. Box 2359
Honolulu, HI 96804
No. 1 Capitol District Bldg.
250 S. Hotel Street
Honolulu, HI 96813
808-586-2423
Fax: 808-587-2790
www2.hawaii.gov/DBEDT

Department of Education
Hawaii Department of Education
Information Branch
P.O. Box 2360
Honolulu, HI 96804
808-586-3230

Fax: 808-586-3234
www.doe.k12.hi.us

*Department of Higher
Education*
Hawaii State Postsecondary
Education Commission
2444 Dole Street, Room 209
Honolulu, HI 96822
808-956-8213
www.hawaii.edu/offices/bor

Health Department
Hawaii Department of Health
1250 Punchbowl Street
Honolulu, HI 96813
808-586-4400
Fax: 808-586-4444
www.state.hi.us/health/

Housing Office
Housing and Community
Development
677 Queen Street, Suite 300
Honolulu, HI 96813
808-586-4882
www.hcdch.state.hi.us

Insurance Commissioner
Insurance Commissioner
Department of Commerce and
Consumer Affairs
335 Merchant Street, Room 213
Honolulu, HI 96813
808-586-4882
www.state.hi.us/dcca/ins

Labor Department
Hawaii Department of Labor and
Industrial Relations
830 Punchbowl Street
Honolulu, HI 96813
808-586-8842
http://dlir.state.hi.us/

Licensing Office
Office of the Director
Department of Commerce and
Consumer Affairs
P.O. Box 3469
Honolulu, HI 96801
808-586-3000
www.hawaii.gov/dcca/

Free Money For Everybody

One-Stop Career Center
Workforce Development
Department of Labor
Workforce Development Division
830 Punchbowl Street, #112
Honolulu, HI 96813
808-586-8842
Fax: 808-586-9099
http://dlir.state.hi.us/

Security Regulators
Hawaii Corporate & Securities
Commission
P.O. Box 40
Honolulu, HI 96810
808-586-2744
www.state.hi.us/dcca/
breg-seu/compliance.html

**Small Business Development
Center**
Hawaii Small Business
Development Center Network
University of Hawaii at Hilo
308 Kamehameha Ave.,
Suite 201
Hilo, HI 96720
808-974-7515
Fax: 808-974-7683
Email: darrylm@interpac.net
www.hawaii-sbdc.org

Social Services Offices
Hawaii Department of Human
Services
P.O. Box 339
Honolulu, HW 96809

808-586-4996
www.state.hi.us/dhs

**Temporary Assistance to
Needy Families (TANF)**
Temporary Aid to Needy Families
Kathleen Stanley
Hawaii Department of Human
Services
P.O. Box 339
Honolulu, HI 96809
808-586-4996
www.state.hi.us/dhs/

Transportation Department
Brian Minaai
Hawaii Department of
Transportation
Aliiaimoku Bldg.
869 Punchbowl St.
Honolulu, HI 96813
808-587-2150
www.hawaii.gov/dot/

Unclaimed Property Office
Unclaimed Property Section
P.O. Box 150
Honolulu, HI 96810
808-586-1589
www.ehawaii.gov/bf/ucp

**Unemployment Insurance
Office**
Administrator
Unemployment Insurance
Division
Department of Labor and
Industrial Relations

830 Punchbowl Street, Room 325
Honolulu, HI 96813
808-586-9077
http://dlir.state.hi.us
Weekly benefit range: $5-395
Duration of benefits: 26 weeks

Utility Commission
Public Utilities Commission
465 South King Street
Room 103
Honolulu, HI 96813
808-586-2020
www.state.hi.us/budget/puc/
puc.htm

Women's Commission
Hawaii State Commission on the
Status of Women
235 S. Beretaniast, # 401
Honolulu, HI 96813
808-586-5757
Fax: 808-586-5756
www.state.hi.us/hscsw

Your Senator
United States Senate
Washington, DC 20510
202-224-3121
www.senate.gov

Your Representative
United States House of
Representatives
Washington, DC 20515
202-224-3121
www.house.gov

IDAHO

Federal Information Center
1-800-FED-INFO
www.firstgov.gov
www.pueblo.gsa.gov/call/

State Information Office
208-334-2411
www.state.id.us

Department on Aging
Aging Office
P.O. Box 83720
Boise, ID 83720-0007
208-334-3833
www.idahoaging.com/abouticoa/index.htm

Attorney General's Office
Office of the Attorney General
Statehouse
700 West Jefferson Street
P.O. Box 83720
Boise, ID 83720-0100
208-334-2400
Fax: 208-334-2530
www2.state.id.us/ag/

Banking Commissioner
Department of Finance
P.O. Box 83720
700 W. State St.
Boise, ID 83720-0031
208-332-8000
http://finance.state.id.us/industry/bank.section.asp

Child Care and Development Block Grant Lead Agency
Department of Health and Welfare Policy
450 W. State Street
Boise, ID 83720-0036
208-334-5500
www.healthandwelfare.idaho.gov

Child Support Enforcement Agency
Bureau of Child Support Services
Department of Health and Welfare
450 W. State Street
Boise, ID 83720-0036
208-334-5500

800-356-9868
www.healthandwelfare.idaho.gov

Cooperative Extension Office
Cooperative Extension System
College of Agriculture
University of Idaho
Twin Falls R & E Center
P. O. Box 1827
315 Falls Avenue
Twin Falls, ID 83303-1827
208-736-3603
www.uidaho.edu/ag/extension/

Corporation Division Office
Corporate Division
Secretary of State
Room 203, Statehouse
Boise, ID 83720-0080
208-334-2300
www.idsos.state.id.us/

Day Care Licensing Agency
Department of Health and Welfare
Bureau of Family and Children's Services
450 W. State St., 10th Floor
Boise, ID 83720-0036
208-334-5500
www.healthandwelfare.idaho.gov

Economic Development Office
Idaho Commerce and Labor
700 West State Street
P.O. Box 83720
Boise, ID 83720-0093
208-334-2470
Fax: 208-334-2631
http://cl.idaho.gov

Department of Education
Idaho Department of Education
P.O. Box 83720
Boise, ID 83720-0027
208-332-6800
www.sde.state.id.us/dept/

Department of Higher Education
Office of the State Board of Education
P.O. Box 83720

Boise, ID 83720-0037
208-334-2270
www.idahoboardofed.org

Health Department
Idaho Department of Health & Welfare
450 W. State St., 10th Floor
P.O. Box 83720
Boise, ID 83720-0036
208-334-5500
www.healthandwelfare.idaho.gov

Housing Office
Idaho Housing Agency
565 W. Myrtle
P.O. Box 7899
Boise, ID 83707-1899
208-331-4882
www.ihfa.org

Insurance Commissioner
Director of Insurance
P.O. Box 83720
Boise, ID 83720-0043
208-334-4250
www.doi.state.id.us/

Labor Department
Idaho Commerce and Labor
317 Main Street
Boise, ID 83735
208-332-3570
http://cl.idaho.gov

Licensing Office
State of Idaho
Department of Self-Governing Agencies
Bureau of Occupational Licenses
Owyhee Plaza
1109 Main, #220
Boise, ID 83720-5642
208-334-3233
www.ibol.idaho.gov

One-Stop Career Center
Idaho Works
Idaho Commerce and Labor
317 Main Street
Boise, ID 83735
208-332-3570

Fax: 208-334-6300
www.idahoworks.state.id.us

Security Regulators
Idaho Securities Bureau
P.O. Box 83720
Boise, ID 83720
208-332-8000
www.finance.state.id.us/home.asp

Small Business Development Center
Idaho Small Business
Development Center
Boise State University
College of Business
1910 University Drive
Boise, ID 83725-1655
208-426-1640
800-225-3815
www.idahosbdc.org

Social Services Offices
Idaho Department of Health and
Welfare
450 West State Street
Boise, ID 83720-0036
208-334-5500
www.healthandwelfare.idaho.gov

Temporary Assistance to Needy Families (TANF)
Temporary Aid to Needy Families

Social Services Block Grant
Idaho Department of Health and
Welfare
450 W. State Street
Boise, ID 83720
208-334-5500
www.healthandwelfare.idaho.gov

Transportation Department
Idaho Department of
Transportation
P.O. Box 7129
Boise, ID 83707
208-334-8848
www.itd.idaho.gov

Unclaimed Property Office
Unclaimed Property Division
P.O. Box 36
Boise, ID 83722
208-334-7627
http://tax.idaho.gov/unclaimed.htm

Unemployment Insurance Office
Administrator
Unemployment Insurance
Division
Department of Employment
317 Main St.
Boise, ID 83735
208-334-3570

http://cl.idaho.gov
Weekly benefit range: $51-320
Duration of benefits: 10-26 weeks

Utility Commission
Public Utilities Commission
P.O. Box 83720
Boise, ID 83720-0074
208-334-0300
www.puc.state.id.us

Women's Commission
Idaho Commission on the
Women's Program
P.O. Box 83720
Boise, ID 83720-0111
208-334-2110
800-643-7798
www.state.id.us/women

Your Senator
United States Senate
Washington, DC 20510
202-224-3121
www.senate.gov

Your Representative
United States House of
Representatives
Washington, DC 20515
202-224-3121
www.house.gov

ILLINOIS

Federal Information Center
1-800-FED-INFO
www.firstgov.gov
www.pueblo.gsa.gov/call/

State Information Office
217-782-2000
www.illinois.gov

Department on Aging
Aging Department
421 E. Capitol Ave. #100
Springfield, IL 62701-1789
217-785-3356
www.state.il.us/aging/

Attorney General's Office
Office of the Attorney General
100 West Randolph Street
Chicago, IL 60601
312-814-3000
TTY: 312-814-3374
www.ag.state.il.us

Banking Commissioner
Commissioner of Banks and
Trust Companies
500 E. Monroe St.
Springfield, IL 62701
217-782-3000
www.obre.state.il.us/default2.htm

**Child Care and Development
Block Grant Lead Agency**
Office of Child Care and Family
Services
Illinois Dept. of Human Services
100 South Grand Avenue, East
Springfield, IL 62762
217-557-1601
www.dhs.state.il.us

**Child Support Enforcement
Agency**
Jackie Garner
Child Support Enforcement
Division
Illinois Department of Public Aid
509 South 6th St., 6th Floor
Springfield, IL 62701
800-447-4278
www.ilchildsupport.com

Cooperative Extension Office
Dennis Campion, Director
University of Illinois
Cooperative Extension Service
214 Mumford Hall
1301 W. Gregory Drive
Urbana, IL 61801
217-333-5900
www.extension.uiuc.edu/
welcome.html

Corporation Division Office
Department of Business Services
501 s 2nd Street, Room 328
Springfield, IL 62756
217-782-6961
www.sos.state.il.us/

Day Care Licensing Agency
Department of Children and
Family Services
406 E. Monroe St.
Springfield, IL 62701-1498
217-785-2509
www.state.il.us/dcfs/index.shtml

Economic Development Office
Department of Commerce and
Economic Opportunity
620 E. Adams
Springfield, IL, 62701
100 West Randolph St.
Suite 3-400
Chicago, IL 60601
217-782-7500
www.commerce.state.il.us

Department of Education
Illinois State Board of Education
100 N. First St.
Springfield, IL 62777-0001
217-782-8535
866-262-6663
www.isbe.state.il.us/

**Department of Higher
Education**
Illinois Student Assistance
Commission
1755 Lake Cook Drive
Deerfield, IL 60015-5209
847-948-8550 ext.3503

800-899-4722
www.collegezone.com

Health Department
Illinois Department of Public
Health
535 West Jefferson Street
Springfield, IL 62761
217-782-4977
www.idph.state.il.us

Housing Office
Illinois Housing Development
Authority
401 N. Michigan Ave., Suite 900
Chicago, IL 60611
312-836-5200
www.ihda.org

Insurance Commissioner
Director of Insurance
320 W. Washington St., 4th Floor
Springfield, IL 62767-0001
217-782-4515
800-548-9034
www.idfpr.com

Labor Department
Illinois Department of Labor
State of Illinois Building
160 North LaSalle, SuiteC-1300
Chicago, IL 60601
312-793-2800
www.state.il.us/agency/idol

Licensing Office
State of Illinois
Department of Professional
Regulations
320 W. Washington, Third Floor
Springfield, IL 62786
217-785-0800
www.idfpr.com

One-Stop Career Center
Illinois Employment and Training
Center (IETC) Network
Dept. of Employment Security
Employment Services
850 East Madison Street
Springfield, IL 62702-5603
217-785-5069
www.ides.state.il.us/

Security Regulators
Illinois Securities Department
Lincoln Tower, Suite 200
520 South Second St.
Springfield, IL 62701
217-782-2256
800-628-7937
www.sos.state.il.us/

Small Business Development Center
Illinois Small Business
Development Center
Department of Commerce &
Economic Opportunity
620 East Adams Street, 3rd Floor
Springfield, IL 62701
217-782-7500
www.illinoisbiz.biz

Social Services Offices
Illinois Department of Human
Services
Office of Communications
100 S. Grand Ave., E
Springfield, IL 62762
800-843-6154
www.dhs.state.il.us

Temporary Assistance to Needy Families (TANF)
Temporary Aid to Needy Families
Amina Everett

Illinois Department of Human
Services
Harris Bldg.
100 South Grand Ave.
Springfield, IL 62762
217-782-1210
www.dhs.state.il.us

Transportation Department
Kirk Brown
Illinois Department of
Transportation
2300 S. Dirksen Pkwy.
Springfield, IL 62764
217-782-7820
www.dot.state.il.us

Unclaimed Property Office
Unclaimed Property Division
Office of State Treasurer
P.O. Box 19495
Springfield, IL 62794-9495
217-785-6992
www.cashdash.net

Unemployment Insurance Office
Unemployment Insurance
Manager
Illinois Department of
Employment Security
850 East Madison Street
Chicago, IL 62702

312-793-1900
www.ides.state.il.us

Utility Commission
Commerce Commission
527 E. Capitol Ave.
Springfield, IL 62701
217-782-7295
www.icc.state.il.us

Women's Commission
Governor's Commission on the
Status of Women
100 W. Randolph, Suite 16-100
Chicago, IL 60601
312-814-5743
Ellen Solomon, Executive
Director
www.state.il.us/commission/wom
en/commis.htm

Your Senator
United States Senate
Washington, DC 20510
202-224-3121
www.senate.gov

Your Representative
United States House of
Representatives
Washington, DC 20515
202-224-3121
www.house.gov

INDIANA

Federal Information Center
1-800-FED-INFO
www.firstgov.gov
www.pueblo.gsa.gov/call/

State Information Office
317-232-1000
www.state.in.us

Department on Aging
Aging and Rehabilitative Services
Division
Family and Social Services
Administration
402 W. Washington St.
Room W454
Indianapolis, IN 46207
317-232-4454
www.in.gov/fssa/elderly

Attorney General's Office
Office of the Attorney General
Indiana Government Center
South, 5th Floor
402 West Washington Street
Indianapolis, IN 46204
317-232-6201
www.in.gov/attorneygeneral

Banking Commissioner
Department of Financial
Institutions
30 S. Meridian St., Suite 300
Indianapolis, IN 46204
317-232-3955
800-382-4880 (toll free in IN)
www.in.gov/dfi

**Child Care and Development
Block Grant Lead Agency**
Indiana Family and Social
Services Administration
Division of Family and Children
402 W. Washington St.
Room W392
P.O. Box 7083
Indianapolis, IN 46204-7083
317-233-4704
www.in.gov/fssa/families

**Child Support Enforcement
Agency**
Joe Mamlin

Child Support Bureau
402 W. Washington St.
Room W392
Indianapolis, IN 46204
317-232-4885
www.in.gov/fssa

Cooperative Extension Office
Dr. Wadsworth, Director
1140 AGAD
CES Administration
Purdue University
West Lafayette, IN 47907-1140
317-494-8489
888-398-4636
www.ces.purdue.edu

Corporation Division Office
Office of Corporation
Secretary of State
Room E018
302 West Washington St.
Indianapolis, IN 46204
317-232-6576
www.state.in.us/sos/

Day Care Licensing Agency
Indiana Family and Social
Services Administration
Division of Family and Children
Child Care Licensing Unit
402 W. Washington St., Room
386
Indianapolis, IN 46204
317-232-4469 for centers
317-232-4521 for family care
www.in.gov/fssa

Economic Development Office
Indiana Department of
Commerce
One North Capitol, Suite 700
Indianapolis, IN 46204
317-232-8800
Fax: 317-232-4146
www.state.in.us/doc/index.html

Department of Education
Indiana Department of Education
Education Information Systems
Room 229, State House
Indianapolis, IN 46204-2798
317-232-6610

www.doe.state.in.us/

**Department of Higher
Education**
State Student Assistance
Commission of Indiana
150 West Market St., Suite 500
Indianapolis, IN 46204
317-232-2350
Fax: 317-232-3260
www.in.gov/ssaci

Health Department
Indiana State Department of
Health
2 North Meridian Street
Indianapolis, IN 46204
317-233-1325
www.state.in.us/isdh

Housing Office
Indiana Housing Finance
Authority
115 W. Washington St.
Suite 1350, South Tower
Indianapolis, IN 46204
317-232-7777
800-872-0371
www.in.gov/ihfa

Insurance Commissioner
Commissioner of Insurance
311 W. Washington St., Suite 300
Indianapolis, IN 46204-2787
317-232-2385
www.in.gov/idoi/

Labor Department
Indiana Department of Labor
Indiana Government Center-
South
402 W. Washington St.
Room W 195
Indianapolis, IN 46204
317-232-2655
www.in.gov/labor

Licensing Office
Indiana Professional Licensing
Agency
Indiana Government Center S.
302 W. Washington St.
Room E-034

Indianapolis, IN 46204
317-232-2980
www.in.gov/pla

One-Stop Career Center
Workforce Development
Indiana Department of Workforce
Development
Indiana Government Center
10 North Senate Avenue
Indianapolis, IN 46204
317-232-4259
Fax: 317-233-4793
www.dwd.state.in.us
Email: workone@dwd-
is.state.in.us

Security Regulators
Securities Division
302 W. Washington St.
Room E-111
Indianapolis, IN 46204
317-232-6681
www.state.in.us/sos

Small Business Development Center
Small Business Development
Center
One North Capitol, Suite 900
Indianapolis, IN 46204
317-234-2082
Email: sbdc@isbdcorp.org
www.isbdc.org

Social Services Offices
Indiana Family and Social
Services Administration
402 West Washington Street

P.O. Box 7083
Indianapolis, IN 46204
317-233-4454
www.state.in.us/fssa/index.html

Temporary Assistance to Needy Families (TANF)
Temporary Aid to Needy Families
James Hmurovich
Indiana Division of Family and
Children
402 West Washington St.
Room W392
Indianapolis, IN 46204
317-232-4705
www.state.in.us/fssa/families

Transportation Department
Brian Jones
Indiana Department of
Transportation
100 N. Senate Ave.
Room IGCN755
Indianapolis, IN 46204
317-232-5533
www.in.gov/dot/

Unclaimed Property Office
Attorney General's Office
Unclaimed Property Division
302 West Washington St.
5th Floor
Indianapolis, IN 46204
317-232-6201
www.state.in.us/attorneygeneral/
ucp/index.htm

Unemployment Insurance Office
Dept. of Workforce Development

Indiana Government Center
South
10 N. Senate Ave., Room 302
Indianapolis, IN 46204
317-233-4838
Weekly benefit range: $50-312
Duration of benefits: 8-26 weeks

Utility Commission
Utility Regulatory Commission
302 W. Washington St.
Suite E306
Indianapolis, IN 46204
317-232-2700
www.in.gov/iurc/

Women's Commission
Indiana State Commission for
Women
10 N. Senate Ave.
Room SE204
Indianapolis, IN 46204
317-232-6720
Fax: 317-232-7485
Email: icw@state.in.us
www.state.in.us/icw

Your Senator
United States Senate
Washington, DC 20510
202-224-3121
www.senate.gov

Your Representative
United States House of
Representatives
Washington, DC 20515
202-224-3121
www.house.gov

IOWA

Federal Information Center
1-800-FED-INFO
www.firstgov.gov
www.pueblo.gsa.gov/call/

State Information Office
515-281-5011
www.iowa.gov

Department on Aging
Elder Affairs Department
Clemens Building
200 W. 10th St., Third Floor
Des Moines, IA 50309-3609
515-242-3333
www.state.ia.us/elderaffairs/

Attorney General's Office
Office of the Attorney General
1305 East Walnut Street
Des Moines, IA 50319
515-281-5164
515-281-5926 (consumer
advocate)
Fax: 515-281-4209
www.state.ia.us/government/ag/
index.html

Banking Commissioner
Superintendent of Banking
200 E. Grand, Suite 300
Des Moines, IA 50309-1827
515-281-4014
www.idob.state.ia.us/

**Child Care and Development
Block Grant Lead Agency**
Federal Day Care Program
Manager
Iowa Dept. of Human Services
Hoover State Office Bldg., 5th Flr.
Des Moines, IA 50319-0114
800-972-2017
www.dhs.state.ia.us/

**Child Support Enforcement
Agency**
Bureau of Collections
Department of Human Services
P.O. Box 9125
Des Moines, IA 50306
515-281-5647

800-229-9223
http://childsupport.dhs.state.ia.us

Cooperative Extension Office
Dr. Nolan R. Hartwig
Interim Director
Cooperative Extension Service
315 Beardshear Hall
Iowa State University
Ames, IA 50011
515-294-9434
www.extension.iastate.edu

Corporation Division Office
Corporate Division
Secretary of State
Lucas Building
321 E. 12th St.
Des Moines, IA 50319
515-281-5204
www.sos.state.ia.us

Day Care Licensing Agency
Department of Human Services
Child Care Licensing Department
Hoover State Office Bldg.
5th Floor
Des Moines, IA 50319
515-281-3582
www.dhs.state.ia.us/

Economic Development Office
Department of Economic
Development
200 East Grand Ave.
Des Moines, IA 50309-1827
515-242-4700
Fax: 515-242-4809
TTY: 800-735-2942
www.state.ia.us/ided

Department of Education
Iowa Department of Education
Grimes State Office Bldg.
Des Moines, IA 50319-0146
515-281-5294
www.state.ia.us/educate/

**Department of Higher
Education**
Iowa College Student Aid
Commission
200 Tenth Street, 4th Floor

Des Moines, IA 50309-2036
515-242-3344
www.iowacollegeaid.org

Health Department
Iowa Department of Public Health
Lucas Building
321 East 12th Street
DesMoines, IA 50319
515-281-7689
www.idph.state.ia.us

Housing Office
Iowa Finance Authority
100 E. Grand Ave., Suite 250
Des Moines, IA 50309
515-242-4990
800-432-7230
www.ifahome.com

Insurance Commissioner
Insurance Commissioner
330 Maple St.
Des Moines, IA 50319-0065
515-281-5705
877-955-1212
www.iid.state.ia.us/

Labor Department
Iowa Workforce Development
1000 East Grand Avenue
DesMoines, IA 50319-0209
515-281-5387
www.iowaworkforce.org

Licensing Office
Bureau of Professional Licensing
Iowa Department of Health
Lucas State Office Building
321 E. 12th St.
Des Moines, IA 50319-0075
515-281-7689
www.idph.state.ia.us/licensure

One-Stop Career Center
Workforce Development
Department of Workforce
Development
1000 East Grand Avenue
Des Moines, IA 50319-0209
515-281-5387
800-JOB-IOWA
www.iowaworkforce.org

Security Regulators
Securities Division
330 Maple St.
Des Moines, IA 50319-0065
515-281-5705
www.iid.state.ia.us/

Small Business Development Center
Iowa Small Business
Development Center
Iowa State University
College of Business
Administration
2501 N. Loop Drive
Building 1, Suite 615
Ames, IA 50010-8283
515-296-6714
Fax: 515-292-0020
Email: rmanning@iastate.edu
www.iabusnet.org/sbdc/index.html

Social Services Offices
Iowa Dept. of Human Services
Hoover Street Office Building
DesMoine, IA 50319
515-281-4847
www.dhs.state.ia.us

Temporary Assistance to Needy Families (TANF)
Temporary Aid to Needy Families
Chuck Palmer

Iowa Department of Human
Services
Hoover State Office
Building E
Des Moines, IA 50319
515-281-5452
www.dhs.state.ia.us/

Transportation Department
Mark Wandro
Iowa Department of
Transportation
800 Lincoln Way
Ames, IA 50010
515-239-1101
www.dot.state.ia.us/

Unclaimed Property Office
Treasurer
Unclaimed Property Division
State Capitol Bldg.
Des Moines, IA 50319
515-281-5368
www.treasurer.state.ia.us

Unemployment Insurance Office
Bureau Chief of Job Insurance
Dept. of Employment Services
1000 E. Grand Ave.
Des Moines, IA 50319-0209
515-281-4748
www.iowaworkforce.org/ui
Duration of benefits: 11-26 weeks

Utility Commission
Iowa Utilities Board
350 Maple St.
Des Moines, IA 50319-0069
515-281-5979
www.state.ia.us/
government/com/util/util.htm

Women's Commission
Iowa Commission on the Status
of Women
321 E. 12th
Lucas State Office Building
Des Moines, IA 50319
515-281-4461
Fax: 515-242-6119
www.state.ia.us/dhr/sw
Charlotte Nelson, Exec. Director
Kathryn Burt, Chair

Your Senator
United States Senate
Washington, DC 20510
202-224-3121
www.senate.gov

Your Representative
United States House of
Representatives
Washington, DC 20515
202-224-3121
www.house.gov

KANSAS

Federal Information Center
1-800-FED-INFO
www.firstgov.gov
www.pueblo.gsa.gov/call/

State Information Office
785-296-0111
800-4KANSAS
www.state.ks.us

Department on Aging
Kansas Department on Aging
New England Building
503 S. Kansas Ave.
Topeka, KS 66603-3404
800-432-3535
785-296-4986
Fax: 785-296-0256
www.agingkansas.org/kdoa

Attorney General's Office
Office of the Attorney General
120 SW 10th Avenue, 2nd Floor
Topeka, KS 66612-1597
785-296-2215
800-432-2310
Fax: 785-296-6296
www.ink.org/public/ksag

Banking Commissioner
State Bank Commissioner
700 Jackson St.
Suite 300
Topeka, KS 66603-3714
785-296-2266
Fax: 785-296-0168
www.osbckansas.org

Child Care and Development Block Grant Lead Agency
Coordinator of Child Care Services
Kansas Department of Social and Rehabilitation Services
915 SW Harrison, Room 681W
Topeka, KS 66612
785-296-3959
Fax: 785-296-2173
www.srskansas.org

Child Support Enforcement Agency
John Badger

Child Support Enforcement Program
Department of Social and Rehabilitation Services
P.O. Box 497
Topeka, KS 66601-0497
785-296-3237
Fax: 785-296-5206
www.srskansas.org/ cse/cse.htm

Cooperative Extension Office
Mark Johnson, Interim Director
Cooperative Extension Service
Kansas State University
119 Umberger Hall
Manhattan, KS 66506
785-532-3519
www.oznet.ksu.edu

Corporation Division Office
Corporate Division
Secretary of State
Memorial Hall, 1st Floor
120 SW 10th Avenue
Topeka, KS 66612
785-296-4564
www.kssos.org

Day Care Licensing Agency
Kansas Department of Health and Environment
Child Care Licensing and Registration
1000 SW Jackson, Suite 200
Topeka, KS 66612-1274
785-296-1270
Fax: 785-296-0803
www.kdhe.state.ks.us/kidsnet

Business Development Division
Department of Commerce and Housing
1000 SW Jackson St., Suite 100
Topeka, KS 66612-1357
785-296-3481
Fax 785-296-5055
TTY 785-296-3487
http://kdoch.state.ks.us/public

Department of Education
Kansas State Department of Education

120 SE 10th Ave.
Topeka, KS 66612-1182
785-296-3201
Fax: 785-296-7933
www.ksbe.state.ks.us/

Department of Higher Education
Kansas Board of Regents
1000 SW Jackson St., Suite 520
Topeka, KS 66612-1368
785-296-3421
Fax: 785-296-0983
www.kansasregents.org

Health Department
Kansas Division of Health & Environment
1000 SW Jackson St.
Suite 300
Topeka, KS 66612-1365
785-296-1500
Fax: 785-368-6368
www.kdhe.state.ks.us

Housing Development Division
Kansas Housing Resources Corp.
1000 SW Jackson St., Suite 100
Topeka, KS 66612-1354
785-296-5865
Fax: 785-296-8985
www.kshousingcorp.org

Insurance Commissioner
Commissioner of Insurance
420 SW 9th St.
Topeka, KS 66612-1678
785-296-3071
800-432-2484
www.ksinsurance.org

Labor Department
Kansas Department of Labor
401 SW Topeka Boulevard
Topeka, KS 66603-3182
785-296-5000
Fax: 785-296-5286
www.dol.ks.gov

Licensing Office
Access Kansas
534 S. Kansas Ave.

Free Money For Everybody

Suite 1210
Topeka, KS 66603-3434
800-4KANSAS
785-296-5059
www.accesskansas.org

One-Stop Career Center
Kansas Job Service Career
Centers
Department of Human Resources
Division of Employment and
Training
401 SW Topeka Boulevard
Topeka, KS 66603-3182
785-296-5000
http://entkdhr.state.ks.us

Security Regulators
Kansas Securities Commission
618 S. Kansas Ave., 2nd Floor
Topeka, KS 66603
785-296-3307
800-232-9580
Fax: 785-296-6872
www.ink.org/public/ksecom

**Small Business Development
Center**
Fort Hays State University
Kansas Small Business
Development Center
214 SW 6th Street, Suite 301
Topeka, KS 66603-3179
785-296-6514
Fax: 785-291-3261
www.fhsu.edu/ksbdc

Social Services Offices
Kansas Department of Social and
Rehabilitation Services
915 Harrison Street, SW
Topeka, KS 66612
785-296-3959
Fax: 785-296-2173
www.srskansas.org

**Temporary Assistance to
Needy Families (TANF)**
Temporary Aid to Needy Families
Rochelle Chronister
Kansas Department of Social and
Rehabilitation Services
915 Harrison St.
Topeka, KS 66612
785-296-3959
www.srskansas.org

Transportation Department
James Van Sickel
Kansas Department of
Transportation
915 Harrison, Room 754
Docking State Office Bldg.
Topeka, KS 66612-1568
785-296-3566
www.ksdot.org

Unclaimed Property Office
Unclaimed Property Division
900 Jackson, Suite 201
Topeka, KS 66612-1235
785-296-3171
www.treasurer.state.ks.us

**Unemployment Insurance
Office**
Director
Division of Employment Security
Department of Human Resources
401 Topeka Ave.
Topeka, KS 66603-3182
785-296-5000
www.hr.state.ks.us/ui/html/
enui.htm

Utility Commission
Kansas Corporation Commission
1500 SW Arrowhead Rd.
Topeka, KS 66604-4027
785-271-3100
800-662-0027 (KS only)
Fax: 785-271-3354
www.kcc.state.ks.us

Your Senator
United States Senate
Washington, DC 20510
202-224-3121
www.senate.gov

Your Representative
United States House of
Representatives
Washington, DC 20515
202-224-3121
www.house.gov

KENTUCKY

Federal Information Center
1-800-FED-INFO
www.firstgov.gov
www.pueblo.gsa.gov/call/

State Information Office
502-564-3130
www.kentucky.gov

Department on Aging
Aging Services Division
Cabinet for Families and Children
275 E. Main St. 5C-D
Frankfort, KY 40621
502-564-6930
Fax: 502-564-4595
http://chs.state.ky.us/aging

Attorney General's Office
Office of the Attorney General
700 Capital Center Dr., Suite 118
Frankfort, KY 40601-3499
502-696-5300
502-696-5389 (consumer protection)
http://ag.ky.gov

Banking Commissioner
Commissioner
Department of Financial Institutions
1025 Capital Center Dr.
Suite 200
Frankfort, KY 40601
502-573-3390
800-223-2579
Fax: 502-573-8787
www.dfi.state.ky.us/

Child Care and Development Block Grant Lead Agency
Department for Social Services
Cabinet for Families and Children
275 E. Main St., 6W
Frankfort, KY 40621
502-564-7130
Fax: 502-564-3866
http://cfc.state.ky.us

Child Support Enforcement Agency
Child Suport Enforcement Commission

700 Capitol Avenue, Suite 126A
Frankfort, KY 40601
502-696-5675
http://ag.ky.gov/childsupport

Cooperative Extension Offices
Cooperative Extension Service
S-107 Ag. Science Bldg., North
University of Kentucky
Lexington, KY 40546-0091
606-257-4302
www.ca.uky.edu

Dr. Harold Benson, Director
Kentucky State University
Cooperative Extension Program
400 E. Main Street
Frankfort, KY 40601
502-227-6310
www.kysu.edu/landgrant/CEP/cep.htm

Corporation Division Office
Corporate Division
Secretary of State
700 Capitol Ave. Suite 152
Frankfort, KY 40601
502-564-3490
Fax: 502-564-5687
www.sos.state.ky.us/

Day Care Licensing Agency
Cabinet for Health Services
Office of Inspector General
Division of Licensed Child Care
275 E. Main St., 5E-A
Frankfort, KY 40621
502-564-2800
Fax: 502-564-6546
http://chs.state.ky.us/oig/childcare

Economic Development Office
Kentucky Cabinet for Economic Development
2300 Capital Plaza Tower
500 Mero Street
Frankfort, KY 40601
502-564-7670
www.thinkkentucky.com

Department of Education
Kentucky Department of Education

500 Mero Street
Frankfort, KY 40601
502-564-4770
www.kde.state.ky.us/

Department of Higher Education
Kentucky Higher Education Assistance Authority
P.O. Box 798
Frankfort, KY 40601-0798
800-928-8926, ext. 3963
502-564-7990
www.kheaa.com

Health Department
Kentucky Cabinet for Health Services
275 East Main Street
Frankfort, KY 40621
502-564-3970
Fax: 502-564-2556
http://chs.state.ky.us

Housing Office
Kentucky Housing Corporation
1231 Louisville Rd.
Frankfort, KY 40601-6191
502-564-7630
800-633-8896
www.kyhousing.org

Insurance Commissioner
Insurance Commissioner
215 W. Main St.
P.O. Box 517
Frankfort, KY 40602
502-564-3630
800-595-6053
www.doi.state.ky.us/

Labor Department
Kentucky Cabinet for Workforce Development
500 Mero Street
Frankfort, KY 40601
502-564-6606
Fax: 502-564-7967
www.kycwd.org

Licensing Office
Division of Occupations and Professions

P.O. Box 1360
Frankfort, KY 40601
502-564-3296
Fax: 502-564-4818
www.state.ky.us/agencies/finance
/ occupations

One-Stop Career Center
One-Stop Career Centers System
Capitol Plaza Tower
500 Mero Street
Frankfort, KY 40601
502-564-6606
Fax: 502-564-7967
www.kycwd.org

Security Regulators
Kentucky Department of Financial
Institutions
1025 Capital Center Dr.
Suite 200
Frankfort, KY 40601
502-573-3390
800-223-2579
Fax: 502-573-8787
www.dfi.state.ky.us

Small Business Development Center
Kentucky Small Business
Development Center
University of Kentucky
Center for Entrepreneurship
225 College of Business and
Economics
Lexington, KY 40056-0034
859-257-7744
888-475-SBDC
www.ksbdc.org

Social Services Offices
Kentucky Cabinet for Families
and Children

275 East Main Street
Frankfort, KY 40621
502-564-6180
Fax: 502-564-3866
http://cfc.state.ky.us/

Temporary Assistance to Needy Families (TANF)
Temporary Aid to Needy Families
Dietra Paris
Dept. of Community Based
Services
275 East Main St.
Third Floor, West
Frankfort, KY 40621
502-564-7050
Fax: 502-564-6907
http://cfc.state.ky.us

Transportation Department
Kentucky Transportation Cabinet
200 Mero Street
Frankfort, KY 40622
502-564-4890
Fax: 502-564-4809
www.kytc.state.ky.us

Unclaimed Property Office
Unclaimed Property Branch
Kentucky State Treasury
Department
Suite 183, Capitol Annex
Frankfort, KY 40601
502-564-4722
800-465-4722
www.kytreasury.com

Unemployment Insurance Office
Director, Division for
Unemployment Insurance
Dept. of Employment Services
275 E. Main St., 2nd Floor

Frankfort, KY 40621
502-564-2900
www.des.state.ky.us/agencies/
wforce/des/ui/ui.htm
Weekly benefit range: $39-341
Duration of benefits: 15-26 weeks

Utility Commission
Public Service Commission
211 Sower Boulevard
P.O. Box 615
Frankfort, KY 40602-0615
502-564-3940
800-772-4636
Fax: 502-564-3460
www.psc.state.ky.us/

Women's Commission
Kentucky Commission on Women
500 Mero Street
CPT 2nd Floor
Frankfort, KY 40601
502-564-6643
Fax: 502-564-2315
Email: kcw@mail.state.ky.us
http://women.state.ky.us
Betsy Nowland-Curry, Executive
Director

Your Senator
United States Senate
Washington, DC 20510
202-224-3121
www.senate.gov

Your Representative
United States House of
Representatives
Washington, DC 20515
202-224-3121
www.house.gov

LOUISIANA

Federal Information Center
1-800-FED-INFO
www.firstgov.gov
www.pueblo.gsa.gov/call/

State Information Office
225-342-6600
www.louisiana.gov

Department on Aging
Elderly Affairs
412 N. 4th St.
Baton Rouge, LA 70802
225-342-7100
Fax: 225-342-7133
www.gov.state.la.us/depts/
elderly.htm

Attorney General's Office
Office of the Attorney General
P.O. Box 94095
Baton Rouge, LA 70804-9095
225-342-7876
800-351-4889 (consumer hotline)
Fax: 225-342-3790
www.ag.state.la.us

Banking Commissioner
Commissioner of Financial
Institutions
8660 United Plaza Blvd.
2nd Floor
P.O. Box 94095
Baton Rouge, LA 70804-9095
504-925-4660
Fax: 225-925-4548
www.ofi.state.la.us

**Child Care and Development
Block Grant Lead Agency**
Child Care Assistance Program
Louisiana Dept. of Social
Services
Office of Family Support
P.O. Box 94065
Baton Rouge, LA 70804
225-342-3950
Fax: 225-219-9399
www.dss.state.la.us

**Child Support Enforcement
Agency**
Lisa Woodruff-White

Support Enforcement Services
Office of Family Support
P.O. Box 94065
Baton Rouge, LA 70804-9065
225-342-3950
800-256-4650
Fax: 225-219-9399

Cooperative Extension Offices
Dr. Jack Bagent, Director
Cooperative Extension Service
Louisiana State University
P.O. Box 25100
Baton Rouge, LA 70894-5100
225-388-4141
www.lsuagcenter.com/nav/extens
ion/extensio.asp

Dr. Leadrey Williams,
Administrator
Cooperative Extension Program
Southern University and A&M
College
P.O. Box 10010
Baton Rouge, LA 70813
225-771-2242
www.subr.edu

Corporation Division Office
Commercial Division
Secretary of State
P.O. Box 94125
Baton Rouge, LA 70804-9125
225-925-4704
www.sec.state.la.us/

Day Care Licensing Agency
Department of Social Services
Child Care Licensing Division
P.O. Box 3078
Baton Rouge, LA 70821
225-922-0015
Fax: 225-922-0014
www.dss.state.la.us/

Economic Development Office
Department of Economic
Development
P.O. Box 94185
Baton Rouge, LA 70804-9185
225-342-3000
www.lded.state.la.us

Department of Education
Louisiana Department of
Education
P.O. Box 94064
Baton Rouge, LA 70804-9064
225-342-3625
877-453-2721
www.doe.state.la.us/

**Department of Higher
Education**
Office of Student Financial
Assistance
P.O. Box 91202
Baton Rouge, LA 70821-9202
225-922-1011
Fax: 225-922-0790
800-259-LOAN
www.osfa.state.la.us

Health Department
Louisiana Department of Health
and Hospitals
1201 Capitol Access Road
P.O. Box 629
Baton Rouge, LA 70821-0629
225-342-9500
Fax: 225-342-5568
www.dhh.state.la.us
Email: Webmaster@
dhhmail.dhh.state.la.us

Housing Office
Louisiana Housing Finance
Agency
2415 Quail Dr.
Baton Rouge, LA 70808
225-763-8700
888-454-2001
Fax: 225-763-8710
www.lhfa.state.la.us

Insurance Commissioner
Commissioner of Insurance
P.O. Box 94214
Baton Rouge, LA 70804-9214
225-342-5900
800-259-5300
www.ldi.state.la.us/

Labor Department
Louisiana Department of Labor
1001 North 23rd

P.O. Box 94094
Baton Rouge, LA 70804-9094
225-342-3111
www.ldol.state.la.us

Licensing Office
First Stop Shop
Secretary of State
P.O. Box 94125
Baton Rouge, LA 70804-9125
225-922-2675
800-259-0001
www.sec.state.la.us

One-Stop Career Center
Louisiana Works
Louisiana Occupational
Information System (L.O.I.S.)
P.O. Box 94125
Baton Rouge, LA 70804-9125
225-922-2675
800-259-0001
www.ldol.state.la.us

Security Regulators
Office of Financial Institutions
P.O. Box 94095
Baton Rouge, LA 70804-9095
225-925-4660
Fax: 225-925-4548
www.ofi.state.la.us

Small Business Development Center
Louisiana State University
One University Place
Shreveport, LA 71115
318-797-5144
www.lsus.edu/sbdc

Social Services Offices
Louisiana Department of Human
Services
P.O. Box 3776
Baton Rouge, LA 70821
225-342-0286
www.dss.state.la.us

Temporary Assistance to Needy Families (TANF)
Temporary Aid to Needy Families
Louisiana Dept. of Social
Services
P.O. Box 3776
Baton Rouge, LA 70821
225-342-0286
www.dss.state.la.us/

Transportation Department
Carol Cranshaw, Public
Transportation Administrator
Louisiana Department of
Transportation and Development
P.O. Box 94245
Baton Rouge, LA 70804-9245
225-379-1200
www.dotd.state.la.us

Unclaimed Property Office
Louisiana Department of
Treasury
Unclaimed Property Section
P.O. Box 91010
Baton Rouge, LA 70821
225-219-9400
888-925-4127 (in state)
www.treasury.state.la.us

Unemployment Insurance Office
Director, Unemployment
Insurance

Louisiana Department of Labor
P.O. Box 94094
Baton Rouge, LA 70804-9094
225-342-3111
Fax: 225-342-5208
www.ldol.state.la.us/

Utility Commission
Public Service Commission
P.O. Box 91154
Baton Rouge, LA 70821-9154
225-342-4404
800-256-2397
Fax: 225-342-2831
www.lpsc.org

Women's Commission
Governor's Office of Women's
Services
1885 Woodale Blvd.
P.O. Box 94095
Baton Rouge, LA 70804-9095
504-922-0960
Fax: 504-922-0959
www.ows.state.la.us/

Your Senator
United States Senate
Washington, DC 20510
202-224-3121
www.senate.gov

Your Representative
United States House of
Representatives
Washington, DC 20515
202-224-3121
www.house.gov

MAINE

Federal Information Center
1-800-FED-INFO
www.firstgov.gov
www.pueblo.gsa.gov/call/

State Information Office
207-624-7700
www.state.me.us

Department on Aging
Elder and Adult Services
Human Services Department
11 State House Station
442 Civic Center Drive
Augusta, ME 04333
207-287-9200
800-262-2232
www.state.me.us/dhs/beas/

Attorney General's Office
Office of the Attorney General
6 State House Station
Augusta, ME 04333
207-626-8800
TTY: 207-626-8865
www.state.me.us/ag/homepage.
htm

Banking Commissioner
Bureau of Financial Institutions
#36 State House Station
Augusta, ME 04333-0036
207-624-8570
800-965-5235
Fax: 207-624-8590
www.state.me.us/
pfr/bkg/bkg_index.htm

**Child Care and Development
Block Grant Lead Agency**
Office of Child Care and Head
Start
Maine Dept. of Human Services
221 State St.
Augusta, ME 04333-0011
207-287-5060
Fax: 207-287-5031
www.state.me.us/dhs/

**Child Support Enforcement
Agency**
Stephen Hussey
Division of Support Enforcement
and Recovery

Bureau of Income Maintenance
Department of Human Services
State House Station 11
Whitten Rd.
Augusta, ME 04333
207-287-3110
Fax: 207-287-2334
www.state.me.us/dhs/bfi/dser

Cooperative Extension Office
Vaughn Holyoke, Director
Cooperative Extension Service
University of Maine
5741 Libby Hall
Room 102
Orono, ME 04469-5741
207-581-2811
www.umext.maine.edu

Corporation Division Office
Information and Report Section
Bureau of Corporations
Secretary of State
State House Station 101
Augusta, ME 04333-0101
207-624-7752
Fax: 207-287-5874
www.state.me.us/sos/cec/corp

Day Care Licensing Agency
Bureau of Child and Family
Services
221 State St., Station 11
Augusta, ME 04333
207-287-5060
Fax: 207-287-5031
TTY: 207-287-5048
www.state.me.us/dhs/

Economic Development Office
Office of Business Development
Department of Economic and
Community Development
59 State House Station
Augusta, ME 04333
207-624-9804
Fax: 207-287-5701
www.econdevmaine.com

Department of Education
Maine Department of Education
Educational Bldg.
Station No. 23

Augusta, ME 04333
207-624-6620
Fax: 207-624-6601
www.state.me.us/education/
homepage.htm

**Department of Higher
Education**
Finance Authority of Maine
(FAME)
Maine Education Assistance
Division
5 Community Drive
P.O. Box 949
Augusta, ME 04332-0949
207-623-0095
800-228-3734
TDD: 207-626-2717
www.famemaine.com

Health Department
Maine Dept. of Human Services
221 State Street
Augusta, ME 04333
207-287-3707
www.state.me.us/dhs/

Housing Office
Maine State Housing Authority
353 Water St.
Augusta, ME 04330-4633
207-626-4600
800-452-4668
Fax: 207-626-4678
TTY: 800-452-4603
www.mainehousing. org

Insurance Commissioner
Superintendent of Insurance
34 State House Station
Augusta, ME 04333-0034
207-624-8475
800-300-5000 (in state)
Fax: 207-624-8599
www.state.me.us/pfr/ins/
ins_index.htm

Labor Department
Maine Department of Labor
P.O. Box 259
Augusta, ME 04332-0259
207-624-6400
Fax: 207-287-8394
www.state.me.us/labor/

Licensing Office
Department of Professional and
Financial Regulation
State House Station 35
August, ME 04333
207-624-8500
Fax: 207-624-8690
TTY: 207-624-8563
www.state.me.us/pfr/
pfrhome.htm

One-Stop Career Center
Maine Career Centers
Department of Labor
Bureau of Employment Services
55 State House Station
Augusta, ME 04333-0055
207-624-6390
888-457-8883
TTY: 888-313-9400
www.mainecareercenter.com

Security Regulators
Maine Securities Division
121 State House Station
Augusta, ME 04333
207-624-8551
Fax: 207-624-8590
www.state.me.us/pfr/sec/
sec_index.htm

**Small Business Development
Center**
Small Business Development
Center
University of Southern Maine
MAILING ADDRESS:
   96 Falmouth Street
   P.O. Box 3000
   Portland, ME 04104-9300
207-780-4420
800-679-SBDC
Fax: 207-780-4810

TTY: 207-780-5646
www.mainesbdc.org

Social Services Offices
Maine Dept. of Human Services
221 State Street
Augusta, ME 04333
207-287-3707
www.state.me.us/dhs/

**Temporary Assistance to
Needy Families (TANF)**
Temporary Aid to Needy Families
Maine Dept. of Human Services
Bureau of Family Independence
11 Statehouse Station
Augusta, ME 04333
207-287-5089
Fax: 207-287-5096
TTY: 207-287-6948
www.state.me.us/dhs/bfi

Transportation Department
Office of Passenger
Transportation
16 Statehouse Station
Augusta, ME 043333
207-624-3000
www.state.me.us/mdot/
homepage.htm

Unclaimed Property Office
Treasury Department
Abandoned Property Division
39 State House Station
Augusta, ME 043333
207-624-7477
www.state.me.us/treasurer/
property.htm

**Unemployment Insurance
Office**
Director, Unemployment
Compensation Division

Maine Department of Labor
P.O. Box 309
Augusta, ME 04332
207-287-2316
www.state.me.us/labor/
unemployment
Weekly benefit range: $47-272
Duration of benefits: 21-26 weeks

Utility Commission
Public Utilities Commission
18 State House Station
242 State Street
Augusta, ME 04333-0018
207-287-3831
Fax: 207-287-1039
TTY: 800-437-1220
www.state.me.us/mpuc

Women's Commission
Maryland Commission for
Women
45 Calvert Street
Annapolis, MD 21401
410-260-6047
877-868-2196
Fax: 410-974-2307
TTY: 800-925-4434
www.dhr.state.md.us/mcw

Your Senator
United States Senate
Washington, DC 20510
202-224-3121
www.senate.gov

Your Representative
United States House of
Representatives
Washington, DC 20515
202-224-3121
www.house.gov

MARYLAND

Federal Information Center
1-800-FED-INFO
www.firstgov.gov
www.pueblo.gsa.gov/call/

State Information Office
800-811-8336
www.maryland.gov

Department on Aging
Aging Office
301 W. Preston St.
Suite 1004
Baltimore, MD 21201-2374
410-767-1100
800-AGE-DIAL
Fax: 410-333-7943
www.mdoa.state.md.us

Attorney General's Office
Office of the Attorney General
200 St. Paul Place
Baltimore, MD 21202
410-576-6300
888-743-0023
TDD: 410-576-6372
www.oag.state.md.us

Banking Commissioner
Commissioner of Financial
Regulation
500 North Calvert St., Room 402
Baltimore, MD 21202
410-230-6100
Email: finreg@dllr.state.md.us
www.dllr.state.md.us/finance

**Child Care and Development
Block Grant Lead Agency**
Child Care Administration
Maryland Department of Human
Resources
311 W. Saratoga St., 1st Floor
Baltimore, MD 21201
410-767-7128
Fax: 410-333-8699
www.dhr.state.md.us/cca

**Child Support Enforcement
Agency**
Clifford Layman
Child Support Enforcement
Administration

311 West Saratoga St.
Baltimore, MD 21201
410-962-1110
800-332-6347 (in MD)
TTY: 800-925-4434
www.dhr.state.md.us/csea/index.
htm

Cooperative Extension Offices
Dr. Thomas Fretz
Regional Directors Office
Cooperative Extension Service
1296 Symons Hall
University of Maryland
College Park, MD 20742-5551
301-405-2072
www.agnr.umd.edu/MCE/index.cfm

Cooperative Extension Service
UMES
2122 Henson Ctr.
Princess Anne, MD 21853
410-651-6206
http://umesde.umes.edu/ 1890-
mce/

Corporation Division Office
Corporate Charter Division
Dept. of Assessments and
Taxation
301 W. Preston St.
Baltimore, MD 21201
410-767-1184
888-246-5941
www.dat.state.md.us/

Day Care Licensing Agency
Department of Human Resources
Child Care Administration
Licensing Division
311 W. Saratoga St.
Baltimore, MD 21201
410-767-7128
www.dhr.state.md.us/

Economic Development Office
Department of Business and
Economic Development
217 East Redwood St.
Baltimore, MD 21202
800-CHOOSEMD
Fax: 410-767-6300
www.dbed.state.md.us/

Department of Education
Maryland Department of
Education
Office of Planning
Results and Information
Management
200 W. Baltimore St.
Baltimore, MD 21201
410-767-0600
www.msde.state.md.us/

**Department of Higher
Education**
Maryland Higher Education
Commission
839 Bestgate Rd., Suite 400
Annapolis, MD 21401-1781
410-260-4500
800-974-0203
Fax: 410-260-3200
www.mhec.state.md.us

Health Department
Maryland Department of Health &
Mental Hygiene
State Office Building Complex
201 West Preston Street
Baltimore, MD 21201-2399
410-767-6860
877-463-3464 (in state)
TDD: 800-735-2258
www.dhmh.state.md.us/index.html

Housing Office
Department of Housing and
Community Development
100 Community Place
Crownsville, MD 21032-2023
410-514-7000
800-756-0119(in state)
www.dhcd.state.md.us

Insurance Commissioner
Insurance Commissioner
525 St. Paul Place
Baltimore, MD 21202-2272
410-468-2000
800-492-6116
TTY: 800-735-2258
www.mdinsurance.state.md.us

Labor Department
Maryland Department of Labor,
Licensing and Regulation

1100 North Eutaw Street
Baltimore, MD 21201
410-767-2357
www.dllr.state.md.us

Licensing Office
Division of Occupational and
Professional Licensing
Department of Labor, Licensing
and Regulation
500 N. Calvert St., 3rd Floor
Baltimore, MD 21202
410-230-6220
www.dllr.state.md.us/license/
occprof/index.html

One-Stop Career Center
CareerNet
Department of Labor, Licensing
and Regulation
Employment Services
500 North Calvert Street
Baltimore, MD 21202-2272
410-230-6220
www.careernet.state.md.us/

Security Regulators
Maryland Division of Securities
200 St. Paul Place, 20th Floor
Baltimore, MD 21202
410-576-6360
www.oag.state.md.us/Securities

**Small Business Development
Center**
Maryland Small Business
Development Center
7100 Baltimore Ave., Suite 402
College Park, MD 20740
301-403-0501
www.mdsbdc.umd.edu

Social Services Offices
Maryland Department of Human
Resources

Saratoga State Center
311 West Saratoga Street
Baltimore, MD 21201
410-767-7214
800-332-6347
TTY: 800-925-4434
www.dhr.state.md.us/

**Temporary Assistance to
Needy Families (TANF)**
Temporary Aid to Needy Families
Maryland Department of Human
Resources
311 W. Saratoga St.
Baltimore, MD 21201
410-767-7214
www.dhr.state.md.us/fia/
p_assist.htm

Transportation Department
Maryland Mass Transit
Administration
6 St. Paul St.
Baltimore, MD 21201-1614
410-539-5000
800-RIDE-MTA
www.mtamaryland.com

Unclaimed Property Office
Unclaimed Property Section
301 West Preston St.
Baltimore, MD 21201
410-767-1700
800-782-7383
http://in1.comp.state.md.us/
unclaim/default.asp

**Unemployment Insurance
Office**
Executive Director
Office of Unemployment
Insurance
Department of Labor, Licensing,
and Regulation

1100 N. Eutaw St., Room 414
Baltimore, MD 21201
410-949-0022
www.dllr.state.md.us/employment
/ unemployment.html
Weekly benefit range: $25-310
Duration of benefits: 26 weeks

Utility Commission
Public Service Commission
6 St. Paul St., 16th Floor
Baltimore, MD 21202
410-767-8000
800-492-0474 (MD only)
www.psc.state.md. us/psc/

Women's Commission
Maryland Commission for
Women
45 Calvert Street
Baltimore, MD 21401
410-260-6047
877-868-2196
Fax: 410-974-2307
TTY: 800-925-4434
Email: mcw@dhr.state.md.us
www.dhr.state.md.us/mcw/
index.htm

Your Senator
United States Senate
Washington, DC 20510
202-224-3121
www.senate.gov

Your Representative
United States House of
Representatives
Washington, DC 20515
202-224-3121
www.house.gov

MASSACHUSETTS

Federal Information Center
1-800-FED-INFO
www.firstgov.gov
www.pueblo.gsa.gov/call/

State Information Office
617-722-2000
www.mass.gov

Department on Aging
Elder Affairs Department
1 Ashburton Place
5th Floor, Room 506
Boston, MA 02108
617-727-7750
800-243-4636
TTY: 800-872-0166
www.state.ma.us/elder

Attorney General's Office
Office of the Attorney General
One Ashburton Place
Boston, MA 02108-1698
617-727-2200
617-727-8400 (consumer hotline)
www.ago.state.ma.us

Banking Commissioner
Commissioner of Banks
One South Station
Boston, MA 02110
617-956-1500
Fax: 617-956-1599
TDD: 617-956-1577
www.state.ma.us/ dob/

Child Care and Development Block Grant Lead Agency
Office of Child Care Services
600 Washington Street, 6th Floor
Suite 6100
Boston, MA 02111
617-988-6600
Fax: 617-988-2451
www.qualitychildcare.org

Child Support Enforcement Agency
Jerry Fay
Child Support Enforcement
Division
Department of Revenue
Boston, MA 02204

617-626-3894
800-332-2733
TDD: 800-255-5587
www.cse.state.ma.us/

Cooperative Extension Office
Dr. John Gerber, Associate
Director
40 Campus Center Way
University of Massachusetts
Amherst, MA 01003-9244
413-545-4800
www.umassextension.org

Corporation Division Office
Corporate Division
Secretary of State
1 Ashburton Place, 17th Floor
Boston, MA 02108
617-727-9640
Fax: 617-742-4528
www.state.ma.us/sec/cor/coridx.h
tm

Day Care Licensing Agency
Department of Health
Office of Child Care Services
Day Care Licensing Division
600 Washington Street, 6th Floor
Suite 6100
Boston, MA 02111
617-988-6600
Fax: 617-988-2451
www.qualitychildcare.org

Economic Development Office
Massachusetts Office of Business
Development
10 Park Plaza, Suite 4510
Boston, MA 02116
617-973-8600
800-5-CAPITAL
Fax: 617-727-8797
www.state.ma.us/mobd

Department of Education
Massachusetts Department of
Education
Information and Outreach
350 Main St.
Malden, MA 02148-0523
781-388-3000
www.doe.mass.edu

Department of Higher Education
Board of Higher Education
Office of Student Financial
Assistance
454 Broadway, Suite 200
Revere, MA 02151
617-727-9420
Fax: 617-727-0667
www.osfa.mass.edu

Health Department
Massachusetts Department of
Public Health
250 Washington Street
Boston, MA 02108-4619
617-624-6000
www.state.ma.us/dph/
dphhome.htm

Housing Offices
Massachusetts Housing Finance
Agency
1 Beacon St.
Boston, MA 02108-3110
617-854-1000
Fax: 617-854-1029
TDD: 617-854-1025
www.mhfa.com/

Massachusetts Department of
Housing and Community
Development
100 Cambridge Street, Suite 300
Boston, MA 02114
617-573-1100
www.mass.gov/dhcd

Insurance Commissioner
Division of Insurance
One South Station, 5th Floor
Boston, MA 02210-2208
617-521-7794
Consumer Hotline: 617-521-7794
Fax: 617-521-7575
www.state.ma.us/doi

Labor Department
Massachusetts Department of
Labor and Workforce
Development
One Ashburton Place
Room 2112

Boston, MA 02108
617-727-6573
Fax: 617-727-1090
www.mass.gov/dlwd

Licensing Office
Division of Professional Licensure
239 Causeway St.
Boston, MA 02114
617-727-3074
Fax: 617-727-2197
TTY: 617-727-2099
www.state.ma.us/dpl

One-Stop Career Center
Massachusetts One-Stop Career
Center Network
Division of Career Services
19 Staniford Street
Boston, MA 02114
617-626-5300
www.detma.org/jobseeker/
centers/careercenters.htm

Security Regulators
Massachusetts Securities
Division
One Ashburton Place, 17th Floor
Boston, MA 02108
617-727-3548
800-269-5428 (in state)
Fax: 617-248-0177
www.state.ma.us/sec/sct/
sctidx.htm

**Small Business Development
Center**
Massachusetts Small Business
Development Center
University of Massachusetts
Amherst
227 Isenberg School of
Management

Amherst, MA 01003-9310
413-545-6301
http://msbdc.som.umass.edu

Social Services Offices
Massachusetts Health and
Human Services
1 Ashburton Place, 11th Floor
Boston, MA 02108
617-573-1600
www.masscares.org

**Temporary Assistance to
Needy Families (TANF)**
Temporary Aid to Needy Families
Claire McIntire
Massachusetts Department of
Transitional Assistance
600 Washington St.
Boston, MA 02111
617-348-8500
800-249-2007
www.state.ma.us/dta

Transportation Department
Kevin J. Sullivan
Massachusetts Executive Office
of Transportation and
Construction
10 Park Plaza
Boston, MA 02116
617-973-7000
Fax: 617-523-6454
www.eotc.org

Unclaimed Property Office
Abandoned Property Division
1 Ashburton Place, 12th Floor
Boston, MA 02108-1608
617-367-0400
800-647-2300
www.state.ma.us/treasury

**Unemployment Insurance
Office**
Unemployment Insurance
Director
Department of Employment and
Training
19 Staniford St., 2nd Floor
Boston, MA 02114
617-626-6560
www.detma.org/claimant/

Utility Commission
Department of
Telecommunications and Energy
One South Station
Boston, MA 02110
617-305-3500
www.mass.gov/dte

Women's Commission
Massachusetts Governor's
Advisory Committee on Women's
Issues
Statehouse Governor's Office
Room 111
Boston, MA 02133
617-727-3600
Fax: 617-727-9725
Joanne Thompson, Chair
www.state.ma.us/womenissues

Your Senator
United States Senate
Washington, DC 20510
202-224-3121
www.senate.gov

Your Representative
United States House of
Representatives
Washington, DC 20515
202-224-3121
www.house.gov

MICHIGAN

Federal Information Center
1-800-FED-INFO
www.firstgov.gov
www.pueblo.gsa.gov/call/

State Information Office
517-373-1837
www.michigan.gov

Department on Aging
Michigan Office of Services to the
Aging
P.O. Box 30676
Lansing, MI 48909-8176
517-373-8230
www.miseniors.net

Attorney General's Office
Office of the Attorney General
G. Mennen Williams Bldg., 7th Fl.
525 West Ottawa Street
P.O. Box 30212
Lansing, MI 48909
517-373-1110
517-373-1140 (consumer
protection)
Fax: 517-373-3042
www.ag.state.mi.us
Email: miag@michigan.gov

Banking Commissioner
Commissioner of Financial
Institutions Bureau
P.O. Box 30220
Lansing, MI 48909
517-373-0220
877-999-6442
Fax: 517-335-4978
www.michigan.gov/cis

**Child Care and Development
Block Grant Lead Agency**
Family Independence Agency
P.O. Box 30037
Lansing, MI 48909
517-373-2035
Fax: 517-335-6101
www.michigan.gov/fia

**Child Support Enforcement
Agency**
Family Independence Agency
P.O. Box 30037

Lansing, MI 48909
517-373-2035
Fax: 517-373-4980
www.michigan.gov/fia

Cooperative Extension Office
Arlen Leholm, Director
Michigan State University
Extension
Room 108, Agriculture Hall
Michigan State University
East Lansing, MI 48824-1039
517-355-2308
www.msue.msu.edu/home

Corporation Division Office
Corporation Division
Corporation and Securities
Bureau
Michigan Department of
Commerce
P.O. Box 30053
6546 Mercantile
Lansing, MI 48909
517-241-6470
www.cis.state.mi.us/corp

Day Care Licensing Agency
Division of Child Day Care
Licensing 7109 W. Saginaw, 2nd
Floor
Lansing, MI 48909
517-241-2488
866-685-0006
www.michigan.gov/fia

**Economic Development
Corporation**
Michigan Economic Development
300 North Washington Square
Lansing MI 48913
517-373-9808
http://medc.michigan.org

Department of Education
Michigan Department of
Education
Information Center Data Services
P.O. Box 30008
Lansing, MI 48909
517-373-3324
www.michigan.gov/mde

**Department of Higher
Education**
Michigan Department of Treasury
Higher Education Assistance
Authority
P.O. Box 30466
Lansing, MI 48909-7966
877-323-2287
517-373-3394
www.michigan.gov/mistudentaid

Health Department
Michigan Department of
Community Health
Lewis Cass Building, Sixth Floor
320 South Walnut Street
Lansing, MI 48913
517-373-3740
www.michigan.gov/mdch
Email: arias@michigan.gov

Housing Office
Michigan State Housing
Development Authority
735 E. Michigan Ave.
P.O. Box 30044
Lansing, MI 48912
517-373-8370
Fax: 517-335-4797
TTY: 800-382-4568
www.mshda.org

Insurance Commissioner
Office of Financial and insurance
Services
P.O. Box 30220
Lansing, MI 48909
517-373-0220
877-999-6442
Fax: 517-335-4978
www.michigan.gov/cis

Labor Department
Michigan Jobs Commission
300 North Washington Square
Lansing, MI 48913
800-946-6829
http://jobs.michigan.org

Licensing Office
Michigan Department of
Consumer and Industry Services
P.O. Box 30018

Lansing, MI 48909
517-241-9288
Fax: 517-241-9280
www.michigan.gov/cis

One-Stop Career Center
Michigan Works!
2500 Kerry Street
Suite 210
Lansing, MI 48912
517-371-1100
www.michiganworks.org

Security Regulators
Michigan Corporation &
Securities Bureau
P.O. Box 30220
Lansing, MI 48909
517-373-0220
877-999-6442
Fax: 517-335-4978
www.michigan.gov/cis

Small Business Development Center
Michigan Small Business
Development Center
Grand Valley State University
510 W. Fulton St.
Grand Rapids, MI 49504
616-336-7480
Fax: 616-336-7485
www.mi-sbdc.org

Social Services Offices
Michigan Family Independence
Agency
P.O. Box 30037
Lansing, MI 48909

General Info: 517-373-2035
www.michigan.gov/fia

Temporary Assistance to Needy Families (TANF)
Temporary Aid to Needy Families
Michigan Family Independence
Agency
P.O. Box 30037
Lansing, MI 48909
General Info: 517-373-2035
www.michigan.gov/fia

Transportation Department
Gus Lluberes
Michigan Department of
Transportation
425 West Ottawa St.
P.O. Box 30050
Lansing, MI 48909
517-373-2090
www.mdot.state.mi.us/

Unclaimed Property Office
Department of Treasury
Unclaimed Property Division
P.O. Box 30756
Lansing, MI 48909
517-636-5320
Fax: 517-636-5324
www.michigan.gov/treasury

Unemployment Insurance Office
Unemployment Agency
Consumer and Industry Services
Cadillac Place
3024 W. Grand Blvd.
Detroit, MI 48202

313-456-2180
800-638-3995
www.cis.state.mi.us/ua/
homepage.htm
www.michigan.gov/uia

Utility Commission
Public Service Commission
6545 Mercantile Way, Suite 7
P.O. Box 30221
Lansing, MI 48909
517-241-6180
800-292-9555 (MI only)
Fax: 517-241-6181
www.michigan.gov/mpsc

Women's Commission
Michigan Women's Commission
110 W. Michigan Avenue
Suite 800
Lansing, MI 48933
517-373-2884
Fax: 517-355-1649
www.michigan.gov/mdcr

Your Senator
United States Senate
Washington, DC 20510
202-224-3121
www.senate.gov

Your Representative
United States House of
Representatives
Washington, DC 20515
202-224-3121
www.house.gov

MINNESOTA

Federal Information Center
1-800-FED-INFO
www.firstgov.gov
www.pueblo.gsa.gov/call/

State Information Office
651-296-2881
www.state.mn.us

Department on Aging
Minnesota Board on Aging
Department of Human Services
444 LaFayette Rd. North
St. Paul, MN 55155-3843
651-296-2770
800-882-6262
www.mnaging.org

Attorney General's Office
Office of the Attorney General
1400 NCL Tower
445 Minnesota Street
St. Paul, MN 55101
651-296-3353
800-657-3787
www.ag.state.mn.us

Banking Commissioner
Department of Commerce
Division of Financial
Examinations
85 7th Place East, Suite 500
St. Paul, MN 55101-2198
651-296-2135
www.commerce.state.mn.us/

**Child Care and Development
Block Grant Lead Agency**
Child Care Program Administrator
Minnesota Department of Human
Services
444 Lafayette Road North
St. Paul, MN 55155
651-296-3800
www.dhs.state.mn.us

**Child Support Enforcement
Agency**
Child Support Enforcement
Division
Department of Human Services
444 Lafayette Rd., 4th Floor
St. Paul, MN 55155

651-296-2542
www.dhs.state.mn.us/ecs/
program/csed.htm

Cooperative Extension Office
Minnesota Extension Service
University of Minnesota
240 Coffey Hall
1420 Eckles Avenue
St. Paul, MN 55108-6068
612-624-1222
www.extension.umn.edu

Corporation Division Office
Business Services Division
Secretary of State
180 State Office Building
St. Paul, MN 55155
651-296-2803
877-551-6SOS (6767)
www.sos.state.mn.us/business/
index.html

Day Care Licensing Agency
Department of Human Services
Licensing Division
444 Lafayette Rd. North
St. Paul, MN 55155
651-296-3971
www.dhs.state.mn.us/

Economic Development Office
Department of Employment and
Economic Development
500 Metro Square Bldg.
121 7th Place East
St. Paul, MN 55101-2146
651-297-1291
800-657-3858
www.deed.state.mn.us

Department of Education
Minnesota Department of
Children, Families & Learning
1500 Highway 36 West
Roseville, MN 55113-4266
651-582-8200
http://children.state.mn.us/

**Department of Higher
Education**
Minnesota Higher Education
Programs

1450 Energy Park Dr.
Suite 350
St. Paul, MN 55108-5227
651-642-0533
800-657-3866
www.mheso.state.mn.us

Health Department
Minnesota Department of Health
717 Delaware Street Southeast
P.O. Box 64975
St. Paul, MN 55164-0975
651-215-5800
www.health.state.mn.us

Housing Office
Minnesota Housing Finance
Agency
400 Sibley St., Suite 300
St. Paul, MN 55101
651-296-7608
800-657-3769
www.mhfa.state.mn.us

Insurance Commissioner
Commissioner of Commerce
85 7th Place East, Suite 500
St. Paul, MN 55101-2362
651-296-4026
800-657-3602
800-657-3978 (license status)
www.commerce.state.mn.us/

Labor Department
Minnesota Economic Security
390 North Robert Street
St.Paul, MN 55101
651-296-3711
800-GET-JOBS
www.deed.state.mn.us

Licensing Office
Department of Commerce
85 7th Place East, Suite 500
St. Paul, MN 55101
651-296-6319
800-657-3978
www.commerce.state.mn.us

One-Stop Career Center
Minn WorkForce Center
Department of Employment and
Economic Development

Free Money For Everybody

390 North Robert Street
St. Paul, MN 55101
888-GET-JOBS
www.deed.state.mn.us

Security Regulators
Department of Commerce
85 7th Place East, Suite 500
St. Paul, MN 55101
651-296-4973
www.commerce.state.mn.us/

Small Business Development Center
Minnesota Small Business
Development Center
Minnesota Department of
Employment and Economic
Development
500 Metro Square Bldg.
121 7th Place East
St. Paul, MN 55101-2146
651-297-1291
Fax: 651-296-1290
www.mnsbdc.com

Social Services Offices
Minnesota Dept. of Human
Services
444 Lafayette Road North
St.Paul, MN 555155
651-297-3933
www.dhs.state.mn.us

Temporary Assistance to Needy Families (TANF)
Temporary Aid to Needy Families
David Doth

Minnesota Department of Human
Services
444 Lafayette Rd. North
St. Paul, MN 55155
651-297-3933
www.dhs.state.mn.us/

Transportation Department
Elwyn Tinkenberg
Minnesota Department of
Transportation
Transportation Bldg.
395 John Ireland Blvd.
St. Paul, MN 55155
800-657-3774
651-296-3000
www.dot.state.mn.us

Unclaimed Property Office
Minnesota Commerce
Department
Unclaimed Property Division
85 7th Place East, Suite 600
St. Paul, MN 55101
651-296-2568
800-925-5668
www.commerce.state.mn.us/
pages/UnclaimedMain.htm

Unemployment Insurance Office
Minnesota Department of
Employment and Economic
Development
390 N. Robert St. 2nd Floor
St. Paul, MN 55101-1812
651-296-3644
888-438-5627 (888-GET-JOBS)

www.uimn.org/ui
Weekly benefit range: $38-493
Duration of benefits: up to 26
weeks

Utility Commission
Public Utilities Commission
121 7th Place East, Suite 350
St. Paul, MN 55101-2147
612-296-0406
800-657-3782 (MN only)
www.puc.state.mn.us

Women's Commission
Minnesota Commission on the
Economic Status of Women
G-22 State Capitol
St. Paul, MN 55155
651-296-8590
800-657-3949
Email: lcesw@commissions.
leg.state.mn.us
www.commissions.leg.state.
mn.us/lcesw

Your Senator
United States Senate
Washington, DC 20510
202-224-3121
www.senate.gov

Your Representative
United States House of
Representatives
Washington, DC 20515
202-224-3121
www.house.gov

MISSISSIPPI

Federal Information Center
1-800-FED-INFO
www.firstgov.gov
www.pueblo.gsa.gov/call/

State Information Office
601-359-1000
www.state.ms.us

Department on Aging
Aging and Adult Services Division
Human Services Department
750 North State Street
Jackson, MS 39205
601-359-4929
800-948-3090
www.mdhs.state.ms.us/aas.html

Attorney General's Office
Office of the Attorney General
P.O. Box 220
Jackson, MS 39205
601-359-3680
www.ago.state.ms.us

Banking Commissioner
Commissioner of Banking and
Consumer Finance
501 N. West St.
901 Woolfolk Bldg., Suite A
P.O. Box 23729
Jackson, MS 39225-3729
601-359-1031
800-844-2499
www.dbcf.state.ms.us/

**Child Care and Development
Block Grant Lead Agency**
Office for Children and Youth
Mississippi Dept. of Human
Services
750 N. State St.
Jackson, MS 39205
601-359-4544
800-877-7882 (in state)
Fax: 601-359-4422
www.mdhs.state.ms.us/ocy.html

**Child Support Enforcement
Agency**
Alsee McDaniel
Division of Child Support
Enforcement

Department of Human Services
750 N. State St.
Jackson, MS 39205
800-948-4010 (in MS)
www.mdhs.state.ms.us/cse.html

Cooperative Extension Offices
Ronald A. Brown, Director
Cooperative Extension Service
Mississippi State University
P.O. Box 9601
Mississippi State, MS 39762-
9601
662-325-3036
http://msucares.com

LeRoy Davis, Dean
Cooperative Extension Service
1000 ASU Dr., #690
Lorman, MS 39096-7500
601-877-6137
www.alcorn.edu/academic/
academ/ags.htm

Corporation Division Office
Office of Corporations
Secretary of State
700 North Street
P.O. Box 136
Jackson, MS 39205
800-256-3494
601-359-1633
www.sos.state.ms.us/busserv/
corp/corporations.asp

Day Care Licensing Agency
Mississippi State Dept. of Health
Child Care Facilities Licensure
Branch
570 E. Woodrow Wilson Dr.
Jackson, MS 39216
601-576-7613
www.msdh.state.ms.us/

Economic Development Office
Mississippi Development
Authority
P.O. Box 849
Jackson, MS 39205-0849
601-359-3449
Fax: 601-359-2832
www.mississippi.org

Department of Education
Mississippi Dept. of Education
Central High School
359 N. West St.
P.O. Box 771
Jackson, MS 39205
601-359-3513
www.mde.k12.ms.us

**Department of Higher
Education**
Mississippi Institution of Higher
Learning
3825 Ridgewood Road
Jackson, MS 39211
601-432-6493
800-327-2980
www.ihl.state.ms.us

Health Department
Mississippi State Dept of Health
570 E. Woodrow Wilson Dr.
P.O. Box 1700
Jackson, MS 39215-1700
601-576-7400
www.msdh.state.ms.us/

Housing Office
Mississippi Home Corporation
P.O. Box 23369
Jackson, MS 39225-3369
601-718-INFO
601-718-4642
www.mshomecorp.com

Insurance Commissioner
Commissioner of Insurance
1001 Woolfolk State Office Bldg.
501 N. West St.
P.O. Box 79
Jackson, MS 39205
601-359-3569
800-562-2957
www.doi.state.ms.us

Labor Department
Mississippi Employment Security
Commission
1520 W. Capitol St.
MESC P.O. Box 1699
Jackson, MS 31295-1699
601-354-8711
http://mdes.ms.gov

Licensing Office
Secretary of State
P.O. Box 136
Jackson, MS 39205-0136
601-359-1350
www.sos.state.ms.us

One-Stop Career Center
Employment Security
Commission
1520 W. Capitol St.
P.O. Box 1699
Jackson, MS 39215-1699
601-354-8711
http://mdes.ms.gov

Security Regulators
Securities Division
700 North Street
P.O. Box 136
Jackson, MS 39205
601-359-2663
800-804-6364
www.sos.state.ms.us/

Small Business Development Center
Mississippi Small Business
Development Center
University of Mississippi
B19 Jeanette Philips Dr.
P.O. Box 1848
University, MS 38677-1848
662-915-5001
800-725-7232 (in state)
Fax: 662-915-5650
Email: msbdc@olemiss.edu
www.olemiss.edu/depts/mssbdc

Social Services Offices
Mississippi Department of Human
Services
750 North State Street
Jackson, MS 39202
601-359-4500
800-345-6347 (in state)
www.mdhs.state.ms.us

Temporary Assistance to Needy Families (TANF)
Temporary Aid To Needy
Families
Division of Economic Assistance
Department of Human Services
750 State St.
Jackson, MS 39202
601-359-4810
800-948-4060
Email: leden@mdhs.state.ms.us
www.mdhs.state.ms.us/
ea_tanf.html

Transportation Department
Dick Hall
Mississippi Dept. of
Transportation
401 N. West St.
P.O. Box 1850
Jackson, MS 39215-1850
601-359-7001
www.gomdot.com

Unclaimed Property Office
Unclaimed Property Division
P.O. Box 138
Jackson, MS 39205-0138
601-359-3600
www.treasury.state.ms.us/

Unemployment Insurance Office
Director, Unemployment
Insurance Division
Employment Security
Commission
1520 W. Capitol St.
P.O. Box 1699
Jackson, MS 39215-1699
601-961-7755
http://mdes.ms.gov

Utility Commission
Public Service Commission and
Public Utilities Staff
501 N. West Street
201-A Woolfolk State Office Bldg.
Jackson, MS 39201
601-961-5400
www.psc.state.ms.us/mpsc/
psc-home.htm

Women's Commission
Inactive

Your Senator
United States Senate
Washington, DC 20510
202-224-3121
www.senate.gov

Your Representative
United States House of
Representatives
Washington, DC 20515
202-224-3121
www.house.gov

MISSOURI

Federal Information Center
1-800-FED-INFO
www.firstgov.gov
www.pueblo.gsa.gov/call/

State Information Office
573-751-2000
www.state.mo.us

Department on Aging
Department of Health and Senior
Services
P.O. Box 570
Jefferson City, MO 65102
573-751-6400
www.dhss.mo.gov

Attorney General's Office
Office of the Attorney General
Supreme Court Bldg.
207 West High Street
P.O. Box 899
Jefferson City, MO 65102
573-751-3321
800-392-8222 (consumer
protection hotline)
Fax: 573-751-0774
Email: attgenmail@moago.org
www.ago.state.mo.us

Banking Commissioner
Commissioner of Finance
Harry S. Truman Office Bldg.
Room 630
P.O. Box 716
Jefferson City, MO 65102
573-751-3242
800-722-3321
www.ded.mo.gov

**Child Care and Development
Block Grant Lead Agency**
Family Support Division
Missouri Department of Social
Services
P.O. Box 2320
Jefferson City, MO 65102-2320
573-751-3221
800-735-2466
www.dss.state.mo.us/dfs/
index.htm

**Child Support Enforcement
Agency**
Division of Child Support
Enforcement
Department of Social Services
221 West High Street
P.O. Box 1527
Jefferson City, MO 65102-1527
573-751-4815
800-859-7999
www.dss.state.mo.us/cse/
index.htm

Cooperative Extension Offices
Ronald J. Turner, Interim Director
Cooperative Extension Service
University of Missouri
108 Whitten Hall
Columbia, MO 65211
573-882-7754
http://extension.missouri.edu

Dyremple Marsh, Director
Cooperative Extension Service
Lincoln University
110A Allen Hall
P.O. Box 29
Jefferson City, MO 65102-0029
573-681-5547
www.lincolnu.edu

Corporation Division Office
Business Services Department
Corporate Division
Secretary of State
James C. Kirkpatrick State
Information Center
P.O. Box 778
Jefferson City, MO 65102-0778
573-751-4153
www.sos.state.mo.us/business/co
rporations

Day Care Licensing Agency
State Department of Health and
Senior Services
Bureau of Child Care, Safey and
Licensure
P.O. Box 570
Jefferson City, MO 65102
573-751-6400
www.dhss.state.mo.us

Economic Development Office
Department of Economic
Development
P.O. Box 1157
Jefferson City, MO 65102
573-751-4962
www.ded.mo.gov

Department of Education
Missouri Department of
Elementary and Secondary
Education
P.O. Box 480
Jefferson City, MO 65102-0480
573-751-4212
www.dese.state.mo.us

**Department of Higher
Education**
Missouri Department of Higher
Education
P.O. Box 1438
3515 Amazonas Drive
Jefferson City, MO 65109-5717
573-751-2361
800-473-6757
Fax: 573-751-6635
www.mocbhe.gov

Health Department
Missouri Department of Health
920 Wildwood
P.O. Box 570
Jefferson, MO 65102-0570
573-751-6400
Fax: 573-751-6041
www.dhss.state.mo.us

Housing Office
Missouri Housing Development
Commission
3435 Broadway
Kansas City, MO 64111
816-759-6600
www.mhdc.com

Insurance Commissioner
Director of Insurance
301 W. High St.
P.O. Box 690
Jefferson City, MO 65102-0690
573-751-4126

800-726-7390 (consumer hotline)
www.insurance.state.mo.us/

Labor Department
Missouri Department of Labor
and Industrial Relations
3315 West Truman Boulevard,
Room 213
P.O. Box 504
Jefferson, MO 65102-0504
573-751-4091
www.dolir.state.mo.us

Licensing Office
Division of Professional
Registration
Department of Economic
Development
3605 Missouri Blvd.
Jefferson City, MO 65102
573-751-0293
Email: profreg@mail.state.mo.us
www.ecodev.state.mo.us/pr

One-Stop Career Center
Greathires.org
Department of Economic
Development
P.O. Box 1157
Jefferson City, MO 65102
888-728-JOBS
www.greathires.org

Security Regulators
Securities Division
Missouri State Information Center
600 W. Main Street, 2nd Floor
Jefferson City, MO 65101
573-751-4136
800-721-7996 (investor hotline)
www.sos.state.mo.us/securities

Small Business Development Center
Missouri Small Business
Development Center
University of Missouri-System
1205 University Avenue

Suite 300
Columbia, MO 65211
573-882-0344
Fax: 573-884-4297
www.missouribusiness.net/sbdc

Social Services Offices
Missouri Department of Social
Services
221 West High Street
P.O. Box 1527
Jefferson City, MO 65102-1527
573-751-4815
800-735-2466
Email: askdss@mail.state.mo.us
www.dss.state.mo.us

Temporary Assistance to Needy Families (TANF)
Temporary Assistance
Missouri Department of Social
Services
Division of Family Services
P.O. Box 1527
Jefferson City, MO 65102-1527
573-751-4815
800-735-2466
www.dss.state.mo.us/dfs/
tempa.htm

Transportation Department
Missouri Department of
Transportation
105 W. Capitol Ave.
Jefferson City, MO 65102
573-751-2551
888-ASK-MODOT
Email: comments@mail.modot.
state.mo.us
www.modot.state.mo.us

Unclaimed Property Office
Unclaimed Property Division
P.O. Box 1004
Jefferson City, MO 65102
573-751-2411
www.treasurer.missouri.gov/ucp/
ucp1.asp

Unemployment Insurance Office
Director
Unemployment Insurance
Division of Employment Security
421 E. Dunklin St.
P.O Box 59
Jefferson City, MO 65102-0059
573-751-3215
www.dolir.state.mo.us/es/

Utility Commission
Public Service Commission
Governor Office Bldg.
200 Madison St.
P.O. Box 360
Jefferson City, MO 65102-0360
573-751-3234
800-392-4211 (MO only)
www.psc.state.mo.us

Women's Commission
Missouri Women's Council
Department of Economic
Development
P.O. Box 1684
Jefferson City, MO 65102
573-751-0810
877-426-9284 (in state)
Fax: 573-751-5005
Email:
wcouncil@mail.state.mo.us
www.womenscouncil.org

Your Senator
United States Senate
Washington, DC 20510
202-224-3121
www.senate.gov

Your Representative
United States House of
Representatives
Washington, DC 20515
202-224-3121
www.house.gov

MONTANA

Federal Information Center
1-800-FED-INFO
www.firstgov.gov
www.pueblo.gsa.gov/call/

State Information Office
406-444-2511
www.state.mt.us

Department on Aging
Senior and Long Term Care
Division
Department of Public Health and
Human Services
111 North Sanders, Room 210
Helena, MT 59604
406-444-4077
800-332-2272 (aging hotline)
www.dphhs.state.mt.us/sltc/index
.htm

Attorney General's Office
Office of the Attorney General
P.O. Box 201401
Helena, MT 59620-1401
406-444-2026
Fax: 406-444-3549
www.doj.state.mt.us/

Banking Commissioner
Commissioner of Banking and
Financial Institutions
301 South Park, Suite 316
Helena, MT 59601
MAILING ADDRESS:
    P.O. Box 200546
    Helena, MT 59620-0546
406-841-2920
Fax: 406-841-2930
www.discoveringmontana.com/
doa/banking

**Child Care and Development
Block Grant Lead Agency**
Human and Community Services
Division
Montana Dept. of Public Health
and Human Services
1400 Broadway, Rm. C-118
Helena, MT 59601
MAILING ADDRESS:
    P.O. Box 8005
    Helena, MT 59604-8005

406-444-5900
Fax: 406-444-5956
www.dphhs.state.mt.us

**Child Support Enforcement
Agency**
Mary Ann Wellbank
Child Support Enforcement
Division
Department of Social and
Rehabilitation Services
3075 N. Montana Ave.
Helena, MT 59601
MAILING ADDRESS:
    P.O. Box 202943
    Helena, MT 59620-2943
406-444-9855
800-346-5437 (in MT)
Fax: 406-444-1370
www.dphhs.state.mt.us

Cooperative Extension Office
Vice Provost for Outreach and
Director of Extension
110 B Culbertson Hall
P.O. Box 172230
Montana State University
Bozeman, MT 59717-2230
406-994-1752
http://extn.msu.montana.edu

Corporation Division Office
Business Bureau
Secretary of State
Room 260, Capitol
P.O. Box 202801
Helena, MT 59620-2801
406-444-3665
Email: sos@state.mt.us
http://sos.state.mt.us/css/
BSB/BSB.asp

Day Care Licensing Agency
Department of Health and Human
Services
Quality Assurance Division
Licensure Bureau
P.O. Box 202953
Helena, MT 59620-2953
406-444-2012
Email: mdalton@state.mt.us/ccrd
www.dphhs.state.mt.us

Economic Development Office
Department of Commerce
Economic Development Division
301 South Park Avenue
PO Box 200501
Helena, MT 59620-0501
406-841-2700
Fax: 406-841-2701
http://commerce.state.mt.us/

Department of Education
Montana Office of Public
Instruction
P.O. Box 202501
Helena, MT 59620-2501
406-444-3095
888-231-9393
www.opi.state.mt.us

**Department of Higher
Education**
Office of the Commissioner of
Higher Education
2500 Broadway St.
P.O. Box 203101
Helena, MT 59620-3101
406-444-6570
Fax: 404-444-1469
www.montana.edu/wwwoche

Health Department
Montana Department of Public
Health & Safety Division
Cogswell Building
1400 Broadway
P.O. Box 202951
Helena, MT 59620
406-444-4540
Fax: 406-444-1861
www.dphhs.state.mt.us

Housing Office
Department of Commerce
Housing Division
301 South Park Avenue
Helena, MT 59601
MAILING ADDRESS:
    P.O. Box 200501
    Helena, MT 59620-0501
406-841-2700
Fax: 406-841-2701
http://commerce.state.mt.us/Hous
ing/Hous_Prog_BHB.html

Insurance Commissioner
Commissioner of Insurance and
Securities
State Auditor's Office
840 Helena Ave.
Helena, MT 59601
406-444-2840
800-332-6148
www.discoveringmontana.com/sa
o/default.htm

Labor Department
Montana Department of Labor
and Industry
P.O. Box 1728
Helena, MT 59624-1728
406-444-9091
Email: dwest@state.mt.us
http://dli.state.mt.us/

Licensing Office
Business Standards Division
Licensing, Business Regulation
Department of Commerce
301 S. Park, 4th Floor
Helena, MT 59602
P.O. Box 200513
Helena, MT 59620-0513
406-841-2300
www.discoveringmontana.com/dli
/bsd/license/bus_index.htm

One-Stop Career Center
Job Service Workforce Centers
Department of Labor and Industry
Workforce Services Division
P.O. Box 1728
Helena, MT 59624
406-444-4571
http://jsd.dli.state.mt.us

Security Regulators
Montana State Auditor's Office
Securities Department
840 Helena Ave.
Helena, MT 59601
406-444-2040
800-332-6148
www.discoveringmontana.com/
sao/securities/secintro.htm

**Small Business Development
Center**
Montana Small Business
Development Center
Montana Dept. of Commerce
301 South Park
Helena, MT 59601
MAILING ADDRESS:
  P.O. Box 200505
  Helena, MT 59620-0505
406-841-2707
Fax: 406-841-2731
http://commerce.state.mt.us/
BRD/BRD_SBDC.html

Social Services Offices
Montana Department of Public
Health and Human Services
111 North Sanders
Helena, MT 59620
MAILING ADDRESS:
  P.O. Box 4210
  Helena, MT 59604-4210
406-444-5622
Fax: 406-444-1970
www.dphhs.state.mt.us
Email: dphhstech@state.mt.us

**Temporary Assistance to
Needy Families (TANF)**
Temporary Aid to Needy Families
Montana Department of Public
Health and Human Services
1400 Broadway, Rm. C-118
P.O. Box 8005
Helena, MT 59604-8005
406-444-5900
Fax: 406-444-5956
www.dphhs.state.mt.us

Transportation Department
Janis Winston
Montana Dept. of Transportation
2701 Prospect Ave.
P.O. Box 201001
Helena, MT 59620-1001
406-444-6200
www.mdt.state.mt.us

Unclaimed Property Office
Unclaimed Property
Department of Revenue
P.O. Box 5805
Helena, MT 59604-5805
406-444-6900
Fax: 406-444-0722
www.state.mt.us/revenue/css/2for
individuals/08unclaimedproperty.
asp

**Unemployment Insurance
Office**
Administrator
Unemployment Insurance
Division
P.O. Box 8020
Helena, MT 59604-8020
406-444-2545
http://uid.dli.state.mt.us

Utility Commission
Public Service Commission
1701 Prospect Ave.
P.O. Box 202601
Helena, MT 59620-2601
406-444-6199
www.psc.state.mt.us

Women's Commission
Interdepartmental Coordinating
Committee for Women (ICCW)
P.O. Box 1728
Helena, MT 59624
406-444-2055
www.mdt.state.mt.us/iccw

Your Senator
United States Senate
Washington, DC 20510
202-224-3121
www.senate.gov

Your Representative
United States House of
Representatives
Washington, DC 20515
202-224-3121
www.house.gov

NEBRASKA

Federal Information Center
1-800-FED-INFO
www.firstgov.gov
www.pueblo.gsa.gov/call/

State Information Office
402-471-2311
www.state.ne.us

Department on Aging
Aging and Disability Services
P.O. Box 95044
Lincoln, NE 68509-5044
402-471-4623
800-942-7830
www.hhs.state.ne.
us/ags/agsindex.htm

Attorney General's Office
Office of the Attorney General
State Capitol, Room 2115
Lincoln, NE 68509402-471-2682
800-727-6432 (consumer
protection)
www.ago.state.ne.us

Banking Commissioner
Director of Banking and Finance
P.O. Box 95006
1200 N. Street
The Atrium, Suite 311
Lincoln, NE 68509-5006
402-471-2171
www.ndbf.org

**Child Care and Development
Block Grant Lead Agency**
Child Care and Development
Fund
Nebraska Department of Health
and Human Services
P.O. Box 95044
Lincoln, NE 68509-5044
402-471-2306
www.hhs.state.ne.us/
chs/chc/chcindex.htm

**Child Support Enforcement
Agency**
Child Support Enforcement Office
Department of Health and Human
Services
P.O. Box 94728

Lincoln, NE 68509-4728
402-441-8715
877-631-9973
www.hhs.state.ne.us/cse/cseinde
x.htm

Cooperative Extension Office
Randall Cantrell, Director
University of Nebraska-Lincoln
S.E. Research and Extension
Center
Room 211, Agriculture Hall
Lincoln, NE 68583-0714
402-472-2966
http://extension.unl.edu/

Corporation Division Office
Corporations Division
Secretary of State
State Capitol
P.O. Box 94608
Room 1301
Lincoln, NE 68509-4608
402-471-4079
Fax: 402-471-3666
www.sos.state.ne.us/htm/corpme
nu.htm

Day Care Licensing Agency
Nebraska Health and Human
Services System
Department of Services
P.O. Box 95044
Lincoln, NE 68509-5044
402-471-2306
www.hhs.state.ne.us/
chs/chc/chcindex.htm

Economic Development Office
Department of Economic
Development
P.O. Box 94666
301 Centennial Mall South
Lincoln, NE 68509-4666
402-471-3111
800-426-6505 (in NE)
Fax: 402-471-3778
TDD: 800-833-7352
www.neded.org

Department of Education
Nebraska Department of
Education

301 Centennial Mall South
Lincoln, NE 68509
402-471-2295
www.nde.state.ne.us/

**Department of Higher
Education**
Nebraska Coordinating
Commission for Postsecondary
Education
P.O. Box 95005
Lincoln, NE 68509-5005
402-471-2847
Fax: 402-471-2886
www.ccpe.state.ne.us/
PublicDoc/CCPE/Default.asp

Health Department
Nebraska Health & Human
Services System
Department of Services
P.O. Box 95044
Lincoln, NE 68509-5044
402-471-2306
www.hhs.state.ne.us/index.htm

Housing Office
Nebraska Investment Finance
Authority
200 Commerce Court
1230 O St.
Lincoln, NE 68508-1402
402-434-3900
800-204-NIFA (6432)
www.nifa.org

Insurance Commissioner
Director of Insurance
941 O St., Suite 400
Lincoln, NE 68508-3639
402-471-2201
TDD: 800-833-7352
www.nol.org/home/ndoi/

Labor Department
Nebraska Workforce
Development
550 South 16th Street
P.O. Box 94600
Lincoln, NE 68509-4600
402-471-9000
Fax: 402-471-2600
www.dol.state.ne.us

Free Money For Everybody

Licensing Office
Regulation and Licensure
Credentialing Division
Nebraska Department of Health
and Human Services
301 Centennial Mall South
P.O. Box 94986
Third Floor
Lincoln, NE 68509-9486
402-471-2115
Fax: 402-471-3577
www.hhs.state.ne.us/crl/
crlindex.htm
Email: marie.mcclatchey@hhss.
state.ne.us

One-Stop Career Center
Nebraska Office of Workforce
Services
Department of Labor
550 South 16th Street
Lincoln, NE 68509
402-471-2600
Fax: 402-471-9867
www.dol.state.ne.us

Security Regulators
Nebraska Securities Bureau
Department of Banking & Finance
1200 "N" Street
The Atrium, Suite 311
P.O. Box 95006
Lincoln, NE 68509-5006
402-471-3445
www.ndbf.org/sec.htm

**Small Business Development
Center**
Nebraska Business Development
Center
College of Business
Administration
Roskens Hall, Room 415
University of Nebraska at Omaha
Omaha, NE 68182-0248

402-554-2521
http://nbdc.unomaha.edu

Social Services Offices
Nebraska Health and Human
Services System
Department of Services
P.O. Box 95044
Lincoln, NE 68509-5044
402-471-2306
www.hhs.state.ne.us

**Temporary Assistance to
Needy Families (TANF)**
Temporary Aid to Needy Families
Dan Cillessen
Nebraska Department of Health
and Human Services
P.O. Box 95044
Lincoln, NE 68509-5044
402-471-2306
www.hhs.state.ne.us/ fia/adc.htm

Transportation Department
Jerry Wray
Nebraska Department of Roads
1500 Highway 2
Lincoln, NE 68502
MAILING ADDRESS:
    P.O. Box 94759
    Lincoln, NE 68509
402-471-4759
www.dor.state.ne.us

Unclaimed Property Office
Unclaimed Property Division
P.O. Box 94788
Lincoln, NE 68509-4788
402-471-2455
www.nebraska.treasurer.org

**Unemployment Insurance
Office**
Unemployment Insurance
Director

Nebraska Department of Labor
P.O. Box 94600
550 S. 16th St.
Lincoln, NE 68509
402-471-2600
www.dol.state.ne.us/
Weekly benefit range: $30-280
Duration of benefits: 20-26 weeks

Utility Commission
Public Service Commission
300 The Atrium
1200 N St.
Lincoln, NE 68508
402-471-3101
800-526-0017
www.nol.org/home/NPSC

Women's Commission
Nebraska Commission on the
Status of Women
301 Centennial Mall South
Box 94985
Lincoln, NE 65809-4985
402-471-2039
Fax: 402-471-5655
Email: ncswmail@mail.
state.ne.us
www.women.state.ne.us

Your Senator
United States Senate
Washington, DC 20510
202-224-3121
www.senate.gov

Your Representative
United States House of
Representatives
Washington, DC 20515
202-224-3121
www.house.gov

NEVADA

Federal Information Center
1-800-FED-INFO
www.firstgov.gov
www.pueblo.gsa.gov/call/

State Information Office
775-687-5000
www.nv.gov

Department on Aging
Aging Services Division
Human Resources Dept.
3416 Goni Road
Bldg. G, Suite 132
Carson City, NV 89706
775-687-4210
http://aging.state.nv.us

Attorney General's Office
Office of the Attorney General
100 North Carson Street
Carson City, NV 89701-4717
775-684-1100
Fax: 775-684-1108
http://ag.state.nv.us
Email: aginfo@ag.state.nv.us

Banking Commissioner
Commissioner of Financial
Institutions
406 E. Second St., Suite 3
Carson City, NV 89701-4758
775-684-1830
Fax: 775-684-1845
http://fid.state.nv.us

*Child Care and Development
Block Grant Lead Agency*
CCDBG Coordinator
Nevada Department of Human
Resources
Welfare Division
1470 E. College Pkwy.
Carson City, NV 89706
775-684-0500
http://welfare.state.nv.us

*Child Support Enforcement
Agency*
Nancy Kathryn Ford
Child Support Enforcement
Program
Nevada State Welfare Division

1470 E. College Pkwy.
Carson City, NV 89706-7924
775-684-0500
http://welfare.state.nv.us/child.ht
m

Cooperative Extension Office
Janet Usinger, Director
Nevada Cooperative Extension
2345 Redrock, Suite 330
Las Vegas, NV 89146-3157
702-251-7531
www.unce.unr.edu

Corporation Division Office
Corporations Division
Secretary of State
202 N. Carson Street
Las Vegas, NV 89701-4201
775-684-5725
http://sos.state.nv.us

Day Care Licensing Agency
Division of Child and Family
Services
Bureau of Services for Child Care
711 E. 5th Street
Carson City, NV 89701
775-684-4400
Fax: 775-684-4464
http://dcfs.state.nv.us/page23.html

Economic Development Office
State of Nevada Commission on
Economic Development
108 E. Proctor St.
Carson City, NV 89701
775-687-4325
800-336-1600
Fax: 775-687-4450
www.expand2nevada.com/

555 E. Washington Avenue
Suite 5400
Las Vegas, NV 89101
702-486-2700
Fax: 702-486-2701

Department of Education
Nevada Department of Education
700 E. Fifth St.
Carson City, NV 89701-5096
775-687-9200

Fax: 775-687-9101
www.nde.state.nv.us

*Department of Higher
Education*
University and Community
College System of Nevada
System Administration North
2601 Enterprise Rd.
Reno, NV 89512
775-784-4905
Fax: 775-784-1127
www.nevada.edu

University and Community
College System of Nevada
System Administration South
5550 West Flamingo Rd.
Suite C-1
Las Vegas, NV 89103
702-889-8426
Fax: 702-889-8492
www.nevada.edu

Health Department
Nevada State Health Division
505 East King Street
Room 201
Carson City, NV 89710-4797
775-684-4200
http://health2k.state.nv.us

Housing Offices
Department of Business &
Industry
Housing Division
1802 N. Carson St.
Suite 154
Carson City, NV 89701
775-687-4258
800-227-4960
Fax: 775-687-4040
Email: nhd@govmail.state.nv.us
http://nvhousing.state.nv.us

Insurance Commissioner
Commissioner of Insurance
788 Fairview Drive
Suite 300
Carson City, NV 89701
775-687-4270
Fax: 775-687-3937
http://doi.state.nv.us

Labor Department
Nevada Department of
Employment, Training and
Rehabilitation
500 East Third Street
Carson City, NV 89713
775-684-3849
Email: detradmn@nvdetr.org
www.detr.state.nv.us

Licensing Office
Consumer Affairs Division
Department of Business and
Industry
1850 E. Sahara Ave., Suite 101
Las Vegas, NV 89104
702-486-7355
800-326-5202
Fax: 702-486-7371
www.fyiconsumer.org

One-Stop Career Center
Nevada Department of
Employment, Training and
Rehabilitation
Job Connect
500 East Third Street
Carson City, NV 89713-0021
775-684-0400
www.nevadajobconnect.com

Security Regulators
Securities Division
Secretary of State
555 E. Washington St.
Suite 5200
Las Vegas, NV 89101
702-486-2440
Fax: 702-486-2452
Email:
nvsec@govmail.state.nv.us
http://sos.state.nv.us/securities/in
dex.htm

**Small Business Development
Center**
Nevada Small Business
Development Center

University of Nevada, Reno
College of Business
Administration
Business Building, Room 411
Reno, NV 89557-0100
775-784-1717
Fax: 775-784-4337
Email: nsbdc@unr.nevada.edu
www.nsbdc.org

Social Services Offices
Nevada Department of Human
Resources
505 East King Street, Room 600
Carson City, NV 89701-3708
775-684-4000
www.hr.state.nv.us

**Temporary Assistance to
Needy Families (TANF)**
Temporary Aid to Needy Families
Welfare Division
1470 E. College Pkwy.
Carson City, NV 89701
775-684-0500
www.welfare.state.nv.us/elig_pay
/ tanf_home.htm

Transportation Department
Tom Stephens, P.E.
Nevada Department of
Transportation
1263 South Stewart St.
Carson City, NV 89712
775-888-7000
Fax: 775-888-7115
www.nevadadot.com
Email: info@dot.state.nv.us

Unclaimed Property Office
Unclaimed Property Division
55 E. Washington Ave.
Suite 4200
Las Vegas, NV 89101
702-486-4140
800-521-0019
Fax: 702-486-4177
http://nevadatreasurer.gov

**Unemployment Insurance
Office**
Unemployment Insurance
Employment Security Department
500 E. Third St.
Carson City, NV 89713
775-684-3849
www.detr.state.nv.us/uiben/
uiben_uiben.htm
Email: detrui@nvdetr.org
Northern Nevada: 775-684-0350
Southern Nevada: 702-486-0350
Rural Nevada: 888-890-8211

Utility Commission
Public Service Commission
1150 E. William St.
Carson City, NV 89701
771-687-6001
800-992-0900
Fax: 775-687-6110
www.puc.state.nv.us

Women's Commission
Nevada Women's Fund
770 Smithridge Dr.
Suite 300
Reno, NV 89502
775-786-2335
Fax: 775-786-8152
www.nevadawomensfund.org
Email:
info@nevadawomensfund.org

Your Senator
United States Senate
Washington, DC 20510
202-224-3121
www.senate.gov

Your Representative
United States House of
Representatives
Washington, DC 20515
202-224-3121
www.house.gov

NEW HAMPSHIRE

Federal Information Center
1-800-FED-INFO
www.firstgov.gov
www.pueblo.gsa.gov/call/

State Information Office
603-271-1110
www.state.nh.us

Department on Aging
Elderly and Adult Services
Division
129 Pleasant St.
Concord, NH 03301-3857
603-271-4680
800-351-1888
www.dhhs.state.nh.us/
DHHS/DEAS

Attorney General's Office
Office of the Attorney General
33 Capitol Street
Concord, NH 03301
603-271-3658
TDD: 800-735-2964
Fax: 603-271-2110
http://doj.nh.gov

Banking Commissioner
Bank Commissioner
64B Old Suncook Rd.
Concord, NH 03301
603-271-3561
Fax: 603-271-1090
www.nh.gov/banking

Child Care and Development Block Grant Lead Agency
Child Development Bureau
Division for Children, Youth and Families
New Hampshire Department of Health and Human Services
129 Pleasant St.
Concord, NH 03301-3857
603-271-4451
800-852-3345
Fax: 603-271-7982
www.dhhs.state.nh.us/DHHS/CDB

Child Support Enforcement Agency
Division of Child Support
Services

Department of Health and Human
Services
129 Pleasant St.
Concord, NH 03301-3857
603-271-4745
800-852-3345, ext 4745 (in NH)
Fax: 603-271-4787
www.dhhs.state.nh.us/DHHS/DC
SS

Cooperative Extension Office
Peter J. Horne, Dean and
Director
UNH Cooperative Extension
59 College Road, Taylor Hall
Durham, NH 03824-3587
603-862-4582
http://ceinfo.unh.edu/

Corporation Division Office
Corporate Division
Secretary of State
107 N. Main Street
Concord, NH 03301-4989
603-271-3244
www.state.nh.us/sos/corporate/in
dex.htm

Day Care Licensing Agency
State Department of Health and
Human Service
Program Support
Office, Child Care Licensing Unit
129 Pleasant St.
Health and Human Services Bldg.
Concord, NH 03301-3857
603-271-4814
www.dhhs.state.nh.us/DHHS/LRS

Economic Development Office
State of New Hampshire
Department of Resources and
Economic Development
172 Pembroke Road
Concord, NH 03302-1856
603-271-2591
Fax: 603-271-6784
www.nheconomy.com
Email: info@nheconomy.com

Department of Education
New Hampshire Dept. of
Education

101 Pleasant St.
Concord, NH 03301-3860
603-271-3494
Fax: 603-271-1953
www.ed.state.nh.us

Department of Higher Education
New Hampshire Postsecondary
Education Commission
3 Barrell Court, Suite 300
Concord, NH 03301-8543
603-271-2555
TDD: 800-735-2964
Fax: 603-271-2696
www.nh.gov/ postsecondary

Health Department
New Hampshire Department of
Health & Human Services
Office of Community and Public
Health
20 Hazen Drive
Concord, NH 03301
603-271-4501
Fax: 603-271-4827
www.dhhs.state.nh.us/DHHA/OC
PH

Housing Office
Housing Finance Authority
32 Constitution Dr.
Bedford, NH
MAILING ADDRESS:
   P.O. Box 5087
   Manchester, NH 03108
603-472-8623
800-640-7239
TDD: 603-472-2089
www.nhhfa.org

Insurance Commissioner
Insurance Commissioner
21 South Fruit Street
Suite 14
Concord, NH 03301-
603-271-2261
800-852-3416
www.nh.gov/insurance

Labor Department
New Hampshire Department of
Labor

95 Pleasant Street
Concord, NH 03301
603-271-3176
www.labor.state.nh.us

Licensing Office
New Hampshire Joint Board of
Licensure and Certification
57 Regional Dr.
Concord, NH 03301
603-271-2219
Fax: 603-271-6990
Email: llavertu@nhsa.state.nh.us
www.state.nh.us/jtboard/
home.htm

One-Stop Career Center
New Hampshire Works
Dept. of Employment Security
32 South Main Street
Concord, NH 03301
603-224-3311
800-852-3400
www.nhes.state.nh.us
Email: webmaster@nhes.state.
nh.us

Security Regulators
Bureau of Securities Regulation
State House, Room 204
Concord, NH 03301-4989
603-271-1463
Fax: 603-271-7933
www.sos.nh.gov/securities

**Small Business Development
Center**
New Hampshire Small Business
Development Center
University of New Hampshire
The Whittemore School of
Business
108 McConnell Hall
Durham, NH 03824
603-862-2200

Fax: 603-862-4876
http://.nhsbdc.org

Social Services Offices
New Hampshire Department of
Health and Human Services
129 Pleasant St.
Concord, NH 03301-3857
603-271-4331
800-852-3345, ext. 4331 (in NH)
www.dhhs.state.nh.us/

**Temporary Assistance to
Needy Families (TANF)**
Temporary Aid to Needy Families
Division of Family Services
New Hampshire Department of
Health and Human Services
129 Pleasant St.
Concord, NH 03301-3857
603-271-4238
800-852-3345, ext. 4238 (in NH)
www.dhhs.state.nh.us/
DHHS/DFA

Transportation Department
New Hampshire Department of
Transportation
John O. Morton Bldg.
7 Hazen Dr.
P.O. Box 483
Concord, NH 03302-0483
603-271-3434
Fax: 603-271-3914
www.nh.gov/dot

Unclaimed Property Office
Abandoned Property Division
Treasury Department
25 Capitol St., Room 121
Concord, NH 03301
603-271-2621
800-791-0920
www.state.nh.us/treasury/
divisions/AP/APindex.htm

**Unemployment Insurance
Office**
Unemployment Compensation
Bureau
Department of Employment
Security
32 South Main St.
Concord, NH 03301
603-224-3311
www.nhes.state.nh.us

Utility Commission
Public Utilities Commission
21 S. Fruit Street
Suite 10
Concord, NH 03301-2429
603-271-2431
800-852-3793 (NH only)
Fax: 603-271-3878
TDD: 800-735-2964
Email: puc@puc.state.nh.us
www.puc.state.nh.us/

Women's Commission
New Hampshire Commission on
the Status of Women
25 Capitol Street
State House Annex, Room 414
Concord, NH 03301
603-271-2660
Fax: 603-271-4032
Email:
cmswweb@admin.state.nh.us
www.state.nh.us/csw

Your Senator
United States Senate
Washington, DC 20510
202-224-3121
www.senate.gov

Your Representative
United States House of
Representatives
Washington, DC 20515
202-224-3121
www.house.gov

NEW JERSEY

Federal Information Center
1-800-FED-INFO
www.firstgov.gov
www.pueblo.gsa.gov/call/

State Information Office
609-292-2121
www.state.nj.us

Department on Aging
Division of Senior Affairs
Dept. of Health and Senior
Services
P.O. Box 360
Trenton, NJ 08625-0360
609-292-7874
800-792-8820 (hotline)
www.state.nj.us/health/senior/

Attorney General's Office
Office of the Attorney General
Hughes Justice Complex
25 Market Street
P.O. Box 080
Trenton, NH 08625-0080
609-292-4925
Fax: 609-292-3508
www.state.nj.us/lps

Banking Commissioner
Commissioner of Banking and
Insurance
20 W. State St.
P.O. Box 040
Trenton, NJ 08625
609-292-5360
www.state.nj.us/dobi/index.html

Child Care and Development
Block Grant Lead Agency
Division of Family Development
New Jersey Department of
Human Services
Quakerbridge Plaza, Bldg. 6
P.O. Box 716
Trenton, NJ 08625-0716
609-588-2400
www.state.nj.us/humanservices/d
fd

Child Support Enforcement
Agency
Child Support

Division of Family Development
Department of Human Services
Quakerbridge Plaza
Building 6
P.O. Box 716
Trenton, NJ 08625-0716
609-588-2400
877-NJKIDS1
www.njchildsupport.org

Cooperative Extension Office
Zane Helsel, Director
Rutgers Cooperative Extension
88 Lipman Drive
New Brunswick, NJ 08901-8525
732-932-9306
www.rce.rutgers.edu

Corporation Division Office
Commercial Recording Division
Secretary of State
225 W. State St.
P.O. Box 308
West Trenton, NJ 08625
609-292-9292
www.state.nj.us/treasury/revenue
/ dcr/dcrpg1.html

Day Care Licensing Agency
Division of Youth and Family
Services
Bureau of Licensing
P.O. Box 717
Trenton, NJ 08625-0717
609-292-1018
800-331-3937
www.state.nj.us/humanservices/
dyfs/licensing.html

Economic Development Office
New Jersey Economic
Development Authority
P.O. Box 990
Trenton, NJ 08625-0990
609-292-1800
www.njeda.com
Email: njeda@njeda.com

Department of Education
New Jersey Department of
Education
Office of Public Information
100 River View Executive Dr.

P.O. Box 500
Trenton, NJ 08625-0500
609-292-4469
www.state.nj.us/education/

Department of Higher
Education
New Jersey Commission of
Higher Education
20 West State St.
P.O. Box 542
Trenton, NJ 08625-0542
609-292-4310
Fax: 609-292-7225
www.state.nj.us/highereducation
Email: nj_che@che.state.nj.us

Health Department
New Jersey Department of Health
& Senior Services
P.O. Box 360
John Fitch Plaza
Trenton, NJ 08625-0360
609-292-7874
www.state.nj.us/health/

Housing Office
New Jersey Housing and
Mortgage Finance Agency
637 S. Clinton Ave.
P.O. Box 18550
Trenton, NJ 08650-2085
609-278-7400
800-NJ-HOUSE
www.state.nj.us/dca/hmfa/
index.html

Insurance Commissioner
Commissioner
Department of Banking and
Insurance
20 W. State St.
P.O. Box 325
Trenton, NJ 08625-0325
609-292-5360
www.state.nj.us/dobi

Labor Department
New Jersey Department of Labor
John Fitch Plaza
P.O. Box 110
Trenton, NJ 08625
609-292-2323

Email: cmycoff@dol.state.nj.us
www.state.nj.us/labor

Licensing Office
Division of Consumer Affairs
P.O. Box 45027
Newark, NJ 07101
973-504-6200
800-242-5846 (complaints)
Fax: 973-648-3538
www.state.nj.us/lps/ca/
nonmed.htm
Email: askconsumeraffairs@
ps.state.nj.us

One-Stop Career Center
Workforce New Jersey
Division of Employment and
Training
P.O. Box 940
Trenton, NJ 08625
609-292-5834
www.wnjpin.state.nj.us

Security Regulators
Bureau of Securities
P.O. Box 47029
153 Halsey St.
Newark, NJ 07101
973-504-3600
www.state.nj.us/lps/ca/bos.htm

Small Business Development Center
New Jersey Small Business
Development Center
Rutgers Graduate School of
Management
49 Bleeker Street
Newark, NJ 07102-1913
973-353-1927
www.njsbdc.com

Social Services Offices
New Jersey Department of
Human Services
P.O. Box 700
Trenton, NJ 08625-0700
609-292-3717
www.state.nj.us/humanservices/

Temporary Assistance to Needy Families (TANF)
Temporary Aid to Needy Families
New Jersey Department of
Human Services
Quakerbridge Plaza, Bldg. 6
P.O. Box 716
Trenton, NJ 08625-0716
609-292-3717
www.state.nj.us/humanservices/
DFD/wfnjws.html

Transportation Department
Jeffrey Warsh
New Jersey Transit Corporation
1 Penn Plaza East
Newark, NJ 07105
973-491-7900
800-772-2222 (in NJ)
www.njtransit.com

Unclaimed Property Office
Department of the Treasury
Unclaimed Property Section
P.O. Box 240
Trenton, NJ 08695-0240
609-984-8234
Email: taxation@tax.state.nj.us
www.state.nj.us/treasury/
taxation/

Unemployment Insurance Office
Director, Division of
Unemployment Insurance

New Jersey Department of Labor
John Fitch Plaza
P.O. Box 058
Trenton, NJ 08625-0058
609-292-7162
www.state.nj.us/labor/ui/uiindex.h
tml
Weekly benefit range: $60-475
Duration of benefits: up to 26
weeks

Utility Commission
Board of Public Utilities
Two Gateway Center
Newark, NJ 07102
973-648-2026
800-624-0241 (NJ only)
www.bpu.state.nj.us

Women's Commission
New Jersey Department of
Community Affairs
Division of Women
101 South Broad St.
P.O. Box 801
Trenton, NJ 08625-0801
609-292-8840
Fax: 609-633-6821
www.state.nj.us/dca/dow
Linda B. Bowker

Your Senator
United States Senate
Washington, DC 20510
202-224-3121
www.senate.gov

Your Representative
United States House of
Representatives
Washington, DC 20515
202-224-3121
www.house.gov

NEW MEXICO

Federal Information Center
1-800-FED-INFO
www.firstgov.gov
www.pueblo.gsa.gov/call/

State Information Office
505-827-9632
800-825-6639
www.state.nm.us

Department on Aging
State Agency on Aging
2550 Cerrillos Road
Santa Fe, NM 87505
505-476-4799
800-432-2080 (in NM)
www.nmaging.state.nm.us
Email: nmaoa@state.nm.us

Attorney General's Office
Office of the Attorney General
407 Galisteo Street
Bataan Memorial Bldg.
Room 260
Santa FE, NM 87501
P.O. Drawer 1508
Santa Fe, NM 87504-1508
505-827-6000
800-678-1508 (in NM)
Fax: 505-827-5826
www.ago.state.nm.us

Banking Commissioner
Financial Institutions Division
Regulation and Licensing
Department
2550 Cerrilos Road
Santa Fe, NM 87505
505-476-4885
Fax: 505-476-4670
www.rld.state.nm.us/fid/index.htm

Child Care and Development Block Grant Lead Agency
Bureau Chief
Child Care Services Bureau
Department of Children, Youth and Families
P.O. Drawer 5160
1120 Paseo de Peralta
Santa Fe, NM 87502-5160
505-827-8400

Fax: 505-827-8480
www.cyfd.org

Child Support Enforcement Agency
J. Barry Bitzer
Child Support Division
Department of Human Services
P.O. Box 25110
Santa Fe, NM 87504
505-476-7040
800-288-7207 (in NM)
800-585-7631 (in NM)
www.state.nm.us/hsd/csed.html

Cooperative Extension Office
Dr. Jerry Schickenanz
New Mexico State University
Box 3AE Martin Hall, Rm. 309
Las Cruces, NM 88003
505-646-3016
http://cahe.nmsu.edu/ces/

Corporation Division Office
New Mexico Public Regulation Commission
Corporations Bureau
1120 Paseo De Peralta
P.O. Drawer 1269
Santa Fe, NM 87504-1269
505-827-4508
800-947-4722 (NM only)
www.nmprc.state.nm.us/
corporations/corpshome.htm

Day Care Licensing Agency
Children, Youth and Families
Department
Prevention and Intervention
Division
Child Care Licensing Bureau
P.O. Drawer 5160
Santa Fe, NM 87502-5160
505-827-8400
800-827-8480
www.cfd.org

Economic Development Office
Economic Development
Department
Joseph M. Montoya Bldg.
1100 S. St. Francis Drive

Santa Fe, NM 87503
505-827-0300
800-374-3061
Fax: 505-827-0407
www.edd.state.nm.us

Department of Education
New Mexico Department of Education
Education Bldg.
Public Outreach Office
300 Don Gaspar Ave.
Santa Fe, NM 87501-2786
505-827-5800
http://sde.state.nm.us/

Department of Higher Education
New Mexico Commission On Higher Education
1068 Cerrillos Road
Santa Fe, NM 87505
505-476-6500
Fax: 505-476-6511
www.nmche.org

Health Department
New Mexico Department of Health
1190 St. Francis Drive
P.O. Box 26110
Sante Fe, NM 87502-6110
505-827-2613
Fax: 505-827-2530
www.health.state.nm.us

Housing Offices
Mortgage Finance Authority
344 4th Street, SW
Albuquerque, NM 87102
505-843-6880
800-444-6880
www.nmmfa.org

Insurance Commissioner
Superintendent of Insurance
P.O. Drawer 1269
Santa Fe, NM 87504-1269
505-827-4601
800-947-4722 (in NM)
www.nmprc.state.nm.us/insuranc
e/inshm.htm

Labor Department
New Mexico Department of Labor
401 Broadway NE
Albuquerque, NM 87102
505-841-8409
www.dol.state.nm.us

Licensing Office
Regulation and Licensing
Department
2550 Cerrillos Road
Santa Fe, NM 87505
505-476-4800
www.rld.state.nm.us

One-Stop Career Center
New Mexico Works
Department of Labor
401 Broadway, NE
Albuquerque, NM 87102
505-841-8409
www.dol.state.nm.us/

Security Regulators
New Mexico Securities Division
Regulation and Licensing
Department
2550 Cerrillos Drive
Santa Fe, NM 87505
505-476-4580
800-704-5533 (in NM)
www.rld.state.nm.us/sec

**Small Business Development
Center**
New Mexico Small Business
Development Center
Santa Fe Community College
6401 Richards Avenue
Santa Fe, NM 87508
505-428-1362
800-281-7232
www.nmsbdc.org

Social Services Offices
New Mexico Human Services
Department
P.O. Box 2348
Santa Fe, NM 87504
888-473-3676
www.state.nm.us/hsd/home.htm

**Temporary Assistance to
Needy Families (TANF)**
Temporary Aid to Needy Families
New Mexico Department of
Human Services
P.O. Box 2348
Santa Fe, NM 87504
505-827-7250
888-473-3676
www.state.nm.us/hsd/isd.html

Transportation Department
Peter Rahn
New Mexico Highway and
Transportation Department
P.O. Box 1149
1120 Cerrillos Rd.
Santa Fe, NM 87504-1149
505-827-5100
www.nmshtd.state.nm.us

Unclaimed Property Office
Dept. of Revenue & Taxation
Special Tax Programs and
Services
P.O. Box 25123
Santa Fe, NM 87504-5123
505-827-0769
www.state.nm.us/tax/

**Unemployment Insurance
Office**
Chief, Unemployment Insurance
Bureau

New Mexico Department of Labor
401 Broadway Blvd., NE
P.O. Box 1928
Albuquerque, NM 87103
505-841-4000
www.dol.state.nm.us/dol_UIclaim
s.html
Weekly benefit range: $57-277
Duration of benefits: 19-26 weeks

Utility Commission
Public Utility Commission
224 E. Palace Ave.
Santa Fe, NM 87501-2013
505-827-6940
www.nmprc.state.nm.us/utilitydiv
home.htm

Women's Commission
New Mexico Commission on the
Status of Women
4001 Indian School Rd., NE
Suite 300
Albuquerque, NM 87110
505-841-8920
800-432-9168
www.state.nm.us/womenscommi
ssion

Your Senator
United States Senate
Washington, DC 20510
202-224-3121
www.senate.gov

Your Representative
United States House of
Representatives
Washington, DC 20515
202-224-3121
www.house.gov

NEW YORK

Federal Information Center
1-800-FED-INFO
www.firstgov.gov
www.pueblo.gsa.gov/call/

State Information Office
518-474-2121
www.state.ny.us

Department on Aging
Office for the Aging
2 Empire State Plaza
Albany, NY 12223-1251
518-474-5731
800-342-9871 (NY only)
http://aging.state.ny.us/nysofa/

Attorney General's Office
Office of the Attorney General
The Capitol
Albany, NY 12224-0341
518-474-7330
800-771-7755
www.oag.state.ny.us

Banking Commissioner
Superintendent of Banks
New York State Banking
Department
One State Street
New York, NY 10004-1417
212-709-3501
877-BANK-NYS
www.banking.state. ny.us/

**Child Care and Development
Block Grant Lead Agency**
Office of Children and Family
Services
Child Day Care Services
52 Washington St.
Rensselaer, NY 12144-2735
518-474-9324
www.ocfs.state.ny.us/main/ becs/

**Child Support Enforcement
Agency**
Robert Doar
Office of Child Support
Enforcement
Office of Temporary and
Disability Services
40 N. Pearl St.

Albany, NY 12243
518-474-9081
800-343-8859 (in NY)
http://newyorkchildsupport.com

Cooperative Extension Office
Cornell Cooperative Extension
365 Roberts Hall
Ithaca, NY 14853-5905
607-255-2237
www.cce.cornell.edu/

Corporation Division Office
New York State
Department of State
Division of Corporations, State
Records, and UCC
41 State St.
Albany, NY 12231-0001
518-473-2492
Fax: 518-474-1418
Email: corporations@dos.state.
ny.us
www.dos.state.ny.us/corp/
corpwww.html

Day Care Licensing Agency
State Department of Family
Assistance
Bureau of Early Childhood
Services
Office of Children and Family
Services
Child Day Care Services
52 Washington St.
Rensselaer, NY 12144-2735
518-474-9454
www.ocfs.state.ny.us/main/
becs/default.htm

Economic Development Office
Empire State Development
30 S. Pearl St.
Albany, NY 12245
and
633 Third Ave.
New York, NY 10017-6706
800-STATE-NY (782-8369)
www.empire.state.ny.us

Department of Education
New York Department of
Education

Education Building
89 Washington Ave.
Albany, NY 12234
518-474-3852
www.nysed.gov/

**Department of Higher
Education**
New York Higher Education
Services Corporation
Grants and Scholarship
Information
99 Washington Avenue
Albany, NY 12255
518-473-1574
888-NYSHESC
Email: webmail@hesc.com
www.hesc.com

Health Department
New York Department of Health
Corning Tower Building
Empire State Plaza
Albany, NY 12237
518-474-2011
www.health.state.ny.us
Email: nyhealth@health.state.
ny.us

Housing Offices
State of New York
Division of Housing and
Community Renewal
Hampton Plaza
38-40 State St.
Albany, NY 12207
518-402-3728
www.dhcr.state.ny.us

New York Housing Finance
Agency
641 Lexington Avenue
New York, NY 10022
212-688-4000
www.nyhomes.org

State of New York
Division of Housing and
Community Renewal
25 Beaver St.
New York, NY 10004
212-480-6700
866-ASK-DHCR (3427)

Email:
DHCRInfo@dhcr.state.ny.us
www.dhcr.state.ny.us

Insurance Commissioner
Superintendent of Insurance
25 Beaver St.
New York, NY 10004
212-480-6400
800-342-3736 (in NY)
www.ins.state.ny.us

Labor Department
New York Department of Labor
State Office Bldg. Campus
Room 500
Albany, NY 12240-0003
518-457-9000
www.labor.state.ny.us

Licensing Office
New York State Education Dept.
Office of the Professions
State Education Building, 2nd
Floor
89 Washington Ave.
Albany, NY 12234
518-474-3817
800-442-8106
Email: op4info@mail.nysed.gov
www.op.nysed.gov

One-Stop Career Center
Workforce Development and
Training
Department of Labor
Workforce Development
Building 12, State Campus
Albany, NY 12240
518-457-0380
Email: onestop@labor.state.ny.us
www.wdsny.org

Security Regulators
New York Bureau of Investor
Protection and Securities
120 Broadway, 23rd Floor
New York, NY 10271
212-416-8000
www.oag.state.ny.us

**Small Business Development
Center**
New York Small Business
Development Centers
State University of New York
(SUNY)
41 State St.
Albany, NY 12246
518-443-5398
800-732-SBDC (in NY)
Fax: 518-465-4992
Email: kingjl@nysbdc.org
www.smallbiz.suny.edu/

Social Services Offices
New York State Department of
Family Assistance
52 Washington St.
Rensselaer, NY 12144-2735
518-473-8437
www.dfa.state.ny.us

**Temporary Assistance to
Needy Families (TANF)**
Temporary Aid to Needy Families
John Johnson
Office of Temporary and
Disability Assistance
40 North Pearl St.
Albany, NY 12243
518-474-9222
800-342-3009
www.otda.state.ny.us

Transportation Department
Joseph H. Boardman
New York Department of
Transportation
5-504 Harriman State Office
Campus
1220 Washington Ave.
Albany, NY 12232
518-457-4422
www.dot.state.ny.us

Unclaimed Property Office
Office of Unclaimed Funds
Office of State Comptroller
110 State St.
Albany, NY 12236

518-270-2200
800-221-9311 (in NY)
www.osc.state.ny.us

**Unemployment Insurance
Office**
Director
Unemployment Insurance
Division
New York State Dept. of Labor
State Office Building Campus,
Room 500
Albany, NY 12240-0003
518-457-9000
888-209-8124 (to file a claim)
www.labor.state.ny.us/
working_ny/unemployment_
insurance/unemployment_
insurance.html

Utility Commission
Public Service Commission
Empire State Plaza
Agency Bldg. 3
Albany, NY 12223-1350
518-474-3280
800-342-3377 (NY only)
www.dps.state.ny.us

Women's Commission
New York State Division for
Women
633 Third Ave., 38th Floor
New York, NY 10017
212-681-4547
Fax: 212-681-7626
www.state.ny.us/women

Your Senator
United States Senate
Washington, DC 20510
202-224-3121
www.senate.gov

Your Representative
United States House of
Representatives
Washington, DC 20515
202-224-3121
www.house.gov

NORTH CAROLINA

Federal Information Center
1-800-FED-INFO
www.firstgov.gov
www.pueblo.gsa.gov/call/

State Information Office
919-733-1110
www.ncgov.com

Department on Aging
Aging Division
Human Resources Dept.
693 Palmer Dr.
MAILING ADDRESS:
2101 Mail Service Center
Raleigh, NC 27699-2101
919-733-3983
Fax: 919-733-0443
www.dhhs.state.nc.us/aging

Attorney General's Office
Office of the Attorney General
Department of Justice
9001 Mail Service Center
Raleigh, NC 27699-9001
919-716-6400
877-NO-SCAM (consumer
protection)
www.ncdoj.com

Banking Commissioner
Commissioner of Banks
316 Edenton St.
Raleigh, NC 27603
MAILING ADDRESS:
4309 Mail Service Center
Raleigh, NC 27699-4309
919-733-3016
Fax: 919-733-6918
www.banking.state. nc.us/

**Child Care and Development
Block Grant Lead Agency**
Department of Health and Human
Services
Division of Child Development
2201 Mail Service Center
Raleigh, NC 27699-2201
919-662-4499
800-859-0829 (in NC)
Fax: 919-661-4845
http://ncchildcare.dhhs.state.nc.u
s

**Child Support Enforcement
Agency**
Child Support Enforcement
Section
Division of Social Services
P.O. Box 20800
Raleigh, NC 27619-0800
252-789-5225
800-992-9457 (in NC)
www.dhhs.state.nc.us/dss/ cse/

Cooperative Extension Offices
Dr. Jon F. Ort, Director
Cooperative Extension Service
North Carolina State University
Box 7602
Raleigh, NC 27695-7602
919-515-2811
www.ces.ncsu.edu/

Cooperative Extension Program
North Carolina A&T State
University
P.O. Box 21928
Greensboro, NC 27420-1928
336-334-7956
www.ag.ncat.edu/extension/
index.htm

Corporation Division Office
Division of Corporation
Secretary of State
P.O. Box 29622
Raleigh, NC 27626-0622
919-807-2225
Fax: 919-807-2039
www.secretary.state.nc.us/
corporations

Day Care Licensing Agency
Department of Family Assistance
Division of Child Development
Child Care Licensing
319 Chapanoke Rd., Suite 120
Raleigh, NC 27603
MAILING ADDRESS:
2201 Mail Service Center
Raleigh, NC 27699-2201
919-662-4499
800-859-0829
http://ncchildcare.dhhs.state.nc.u
s

Economic Development Office
Department of Commerce
Commerce Finance Center
301 N. Wilmington St.
Raleigh, NC 27001
MAILING ADDRESS:
4301 Mail Service Center
Raleigh, NC 27699-4301
919-733-4151
Fax: 919-715-9265
www.commerce.state.nc.us/

Department of Education
North Carolina Department of
Public Instruction
301 N. Wilmington St.
Raleigh, NC 27601-2825
919-807-3300
www.dpi.state.nc.us/

**Department of Higher
Education**
North Carolina State Education
Assistance Authority
P.O. Box 14103
Research Triangle Park, NC
27709
919-549-8614
Fax: 919-549-8481
Email: information@ncseaa.edu
www.ncseaa.edu

Health Department
North Carolina State Center for
Health Statistics
Cotton Classing Building
222 North Dawson Street
Raleigh, NC 27603-1392
MAILING ADDRESS:
1908 Mail Service Center
Raleigh, NC 27699-1908
919-733-4728
Fax: 919-733-8485
www.schs.state.nc.us/SCHS

Housing Office
North Carolina Housing Finance
Agency
3508 Bush St.
Raleigh, NC 27609-7509
919-877-5700
800-393-0988

Email: webmaster@nchfa.com
www.nchfa.com

Insurance Commissioner
Commissioner of Insurance
1201 Mail Service Center
Raleigh, NC 27699-1201
919-733-2032
800-JIM-LONG
Email: consumer@ncdoi.net
www.ncdoi.com/

Labor Department
North Carolina Dept. of Labor
1101 Mail Service Center
Raleigh, NC 27699-1101
919-733-7166
800-LABOR-NC
www.dol.state.nc.us/

Licensing Office
Department of the Secretary of
State
4344 Mail Service Center
Raleigh, NC 27699-4344
919715-2864
800-228-8443 (in NC)
www.nccommerce.com/servicent
er/blio

One-Stop Career Center
Joblink Career Centers
Commission on Workforce
Development
NC Department of Commerce
301 N. Wilmington St.
4327 Mail Service Center
Raleigh, NC 27699-4327
919-715-3300
Fax: 919-715-3974
www.joblink.state.nc.us

Security Regulators
North Carolina Securities Division
300 N. Salisbury St., Room 302
Raleigh, NC 27603
MAILING ADDRESS:
   P.O. Box 29622
   Raleigh, NC 27626-0622
919-733-3924

800-688-4507 (complaints)
www.secretary.state.nc.us/sec

**Small Business Development
Center**
North Carolina Small Business
and Technology Development
Center
University of North Carolina
5 West Hargett St., Suite 600
Raleigh, NC 27601-1348
919-715-7272
800-2580-UNC
Fax: 919-715-7777
www.sbtdc.org

Social Services Offices
North Carolina Department of
Health and Human Services
Albemarle Bldg.
325 N. Salisbury St.
Raleigh, NC 27603
MAILING ADDRESS:
   2401 Mail Service Center
   Raleigh, NC 27601
919-733-3055
www.dhhs.state.nc.us/dss

**Temporary Assistance to
Needy Families (TANF)**
Temporary Aid to Needy Families
Work First
Division of Social Services
325 North Salisbury St.
Raleigh, NC 27603
MAILING ADDRESS:
   2401 Mail Service Center
   Raleigh, NC 27699-2401
919-733-3055
www.dhhs.state.nc.us/dss/workfir
st/index.htm

Transportation Department
Lynda Tippett
North Carolina Department of
Transportation
1500 Mail Service Center
Raleigh, NC 27699-1500
919-733-2520
www.ncdot.org

Unclaimed Property Office
Escheat & Unclaimed Property
325 North Salisbury St.
Raleigh, NC 27603-1385
919-508-5176
www.treasurer.state.nc.us

**Unemployment Insurance
Office**
Unemployment Insurance
Division
Employment Security
Commission of North Carolina
700 Wade Ave.
Raleigh, NC 27605
919-715-8502
www.ncesc.com

Utility Commission
Utilities Commission
430 N. Salisbury St.
Dobbs Bldg.
4325 Mail Service Center
Raleigh, NC 27603-5918
919-733-7328
www.ncuc.commerce.state.nc.us

Women's Commission
North Carolina Council for
Women
1320 Mail Service Center
Raleigh, NC 27699-1320
919-733-2455
Fax: 919-733-2464
www.doa.state.nc.us/doa/
cfw/cfw.htm

Your Senator
United States Senate
Washington, DC 20510
202-224-3121
www.senate.gov

Your Representative
United States House of
Representatives
Washington, DC 20515
202-224-3121
www.house.gov

NORTH DAKOTA

Federal Information Center
1-800-FED-INFO
www.firstgov.gov
www.pueblo.gsa.gov/call/

State Information Office
701-328-2000
http://discovernd.com

Department on Aging
Aging Services Division
Human Services Dept.
600 E. Boulevard Avenue
Dept. 325
Bismarck, ND 58505-0250
701-328-4601
800-451-8693 (senior info)
Email: dhsaging@state.nd.us
http://lnotes.state.nd.us/dhs/
dhsweb.nsf/ServicePages/
AgingServices

Attorney General's Office
Office of the Attorney General
State Capitol Building
600 East Boulevard Ave.
Department 125
Bismarck, ND 58505-0040
701-328-2210
800-472-2600
www.ag.state.nd.us

Banking Commissioner
Commissioner of Banking and
Financial Institutions
2000 Schafer St., Suite G
Bismarck, ND 58501-1204
701-328-9933
TDD: 800-366-6888
www.state.nd.us/dfi

Child Care and Development
Block Grant Lead Agency
Early Childhood Services
Children and Family Services
North Dakota Department of
Human Services
600 E. Boulevard Ave.
Bismarck, ND 58505-0250
701-328-2316
800-245-3736
Fax: 701-328-3538

www.state.nd.us/humanservices/
services/childfamily

Child Support Enforcement
Agency
Child Support Enforcement
Division
Department of Human Services
1600 E. Century Avenue, Suite 7
P.O. Box 7190
Bismarck, ND 58507-7190
701-328-3582
Fax: 701-328-6575
TDD: 800-366-6888
www.state.nd.us/humanservices/
childsupport

Cooperative Extension Office
Dr. Sharon Anderson, Director
Cooperative Extension Service
North Dakota State University
Morrill Hall, Room 311, Box 5437
Fargo, ND 58105
701-231-8944
www.ext.nodak.edu/

Corporation Division Office
Business Info/Registration
Division
Secretary of State
Capitol Building
600 E. Boulevard Ave.
Bismarck, ND 58505
701-328-4284
800-352-0867, ext. 4284
www.state.nd.us/sec/Business/
businessinforegmnu.htm

Day Care Licensing Agency
Department of Human Services
Children and Family Services
Early Childhood Services
600 E. Boulevard
Bismarck, ND 58505-0250
701-328-4809
www.ndchildcare.org/splash

Economic Development Office
Department of Economic
Development and Finance
1600 E. Century Ave., Suite 2
P.O. Box 2057
Bismarck, ND 58502-2057

701-328-5300
Fax: 701-328-5320
TTY: 800-366-6888
www.growingnd.com

Department of Education
Department of Public Instruction
600 E. Boulevard Ave.
Department 201
Floors 9, 10, and 11
Bismarck, ND 58505-0440
701-328-2260
Fax: 701-328-2461
www.dpi.state.nd.us/

Department of Higher
Education
University Systems
10th Floor, State Capitol
600 East Boulevard Ave.
Department 215
Bismarck, ND 58505-0230
701-328-2960
Fax: 701-328-2961
www.ndus.edu

Health Department
North Dakota Department of
Health
600 East Boulevard Avenue
Bismarck, ND 58505-0200
701-328-2372
Fax: 701-328-4727
www.health.state.nd.us
Email: tdwelle@state.nd.us

Housing Office
Housing Finance Agency
P.O. Box 1535
Bismarck, ND 58502-1535
701-328-8080
800-292-8621
Fax: 701-328-8090
TTY: 800-366-6888
www.ndhfa.org

Insurance Commissioner
Commissioner of Insurance
Capitol Bldg., 5th Floor
600 E. Boulevard Ave.
Bismarck, ND 58505-0320
701-328-2440

800-247-0560 (in ND)
www.state.nd.us/ndins

Labor Department
600 E. Boulevard Ave.
Department 406
Bismarck, ND 58505-0340
701-328-2660
800-582-8032 (in ND)
Email: labor@state.nd.us
www.state.nd.us/labor

Licensing Office
Licensing Section
Office of the Attorney General
600 East Boulevard
Department 125
Bismarck, ND 58505-0040
701-328-2329
www.ag.state.nd.us/

One-Stop Career Center
Job Service North Dakota
P.O. Box 5507
Bismarck, ND 58506-5507
800-732-9787
701-328-2868
TTY: 800-366-6888
Fax: 701-328-1025
www.jobsnd.com
Email: jsndweb@state.nd.us

Security Regulators
North Dakota Securities
Commissioner's Office
State Capitol Building, 5th Floor
600 East Boulevard Ave.
Bismarck, ND 58505-0510
701-328-2910
800-297-5124 (in ND)
www.state.nd.us/securities

Small Business Development Center
North Dakota Small Business
Development Center
University of North Dakota

118 Gamble Hall, Box 7308
Grand Forks, ND 58202-7308
701-777-3700
800-445-7232 (SBDC)
Fax: 701-777-3225
Email: ndsbdc@sage.und.
nodak.edu
www.ndsbdc.org

Social Services Offices
Department of Human Services
State Capitol, Judicial Wing
600 E. Boulevard Ave.
Department 325
Bismarck, ND 58505-0250
701-328-2310
800-472-2622
Fax: 701-328-2359
TTY: 701-328-2359
www.state.nd.us/humanservices

Temporary Assistance to Needy Families (TANF)
Temporary Aid to Needy Families
Public Assistance Division
Department of Human Services
600 East Boulevard Ave.
Department 325
Bismarck, ND 58505-0250
701-328-2332
800-755-2716
www.state.nd.us/humanservices

Transportation Department
David A. Sprynczynatyk
North Dakota Department of
Transportation
608 East Boulevard Ave.
Bismarck, ND 58505-0700
701-328-2500
Email: dot@state.nd.us
www.state.nd.us/dot

Unclaimed Property Office
Unclaimed Property Division
State Land Department
P.O. Box 5523

Bismarck, ND 58506-5523
701-328-2800
Email: lfisher@state.nd.us
www.land.state.nd.us

Unemployment Insurance Office
Director, Job Insurance Division
Job Service North Dakota
P.O. Box 5507
Bismarck, ND 58506-5507
701-328-2868
888-263-3453
www.state.nd.us/jsnd/

Utility Commission
Public Service Commission
600 E. Boulevard, Dept. 408
Bismarck, ND 58505-0480
701-328-2400
Fax: 701-328-2410
TTY: 800-366-6888
www.psc.state.nd.us/

Women's Commission
North Dakota Governor's
Commission on the Status of
Women
P.O. Box 1913
Bismarck, ND 58502
701-328-2219
Fax: 701-328-2205
www.governor.state.nd.us/boards

Your Senator
United States Senate
Washington, DC 20510
202-224-3121
www.senate.gov

Your Representative
United States House of
Representatives
Washington, DC 20515
202-224-3121
www.house.gov

OHIO

Federal Information Center
1-800-FED-INFO
www.firstgov.gov
www.pueblo.gsa.gov/call/

State Information Office
614-466-2000
http://ohio.gov

Department on Aging
Department of Aging
50 W. Broad St., 9th Floor
Columbus, OH 43215-3363
614-466-5500
Fax: 614-466-5741
Email: ODAMAIL@age.state.
oh.us
www.goldenbuckeye.com

Attorney General's Office
Office of the Attorney General
Montgomery State Office Tower
30 East Broad Street, 17th Floor
Columbus, OH 43215-3428
614-466-4320
800-282-0515 (OH)
(consumer protection)
www.ag.state.oh.us

Banking Commissioner
Superintendent of Financial
Institutions
77 S. High St., 21st Floor
Columbus, OH 43215-6120
614-728-8400
Email:
webdfi@dfi.com.state.oh.us
www.com.state.oh.us/ODOC/dfi

**Child Care and Development
Block Grant Lead Agency**
Department of Job and Family
Services
Office for Children and Families
30 E. Broad St., 32nd Floor
Columbus, OH 43215-3414
614-466-6282
Fax: 614-466-2815
http://jfs.ohio.gov

**Child Support Enforcement
Agency**
Office of Child Support

Department of Jobs and Family
Services
30 East Broad St., 32nd Floor
Columbus, OH 43215-3414
614-752-6561
800-686-1556 (in OH)
Fax: 614-752-9760
http://jfs.ohio.gov.ocs

Cooperative Extension Office
Keith Smith, Director
OSU Extension
2120 Fiffe Road
Agriculture Administration
Building
Columbus, OH 43210
614-292-4067
www.ag.ohio-state.edu/

Corporation Division Office
J. Kenneth Blackwell
Ohio Secretary of State
180 E. Broad Street, 16th Floor
Columbus, OH 43215
614-466-3910
877-SOS-FILE
www.state.oh.us/sos/business_se
rvices_information.htm
Email: busserv@sos.state.oh.us

Day Care Licensing Agency
Department of Jobs and Family
Services
Child Care Licensing Section
255 E. Main St., 3rd Floor
Columbus, OH 43215
614-466-3822
Fax: 614-728-1043
http://jfs.ohio.gov

Economic Development Office
Ohio Department of Development
77 S. High St.
P.O. Box 1001
Columbus, OH 43216-1001
614-466-2317
800-848-1300
Fax: 614-466-3379
www.odod.state.oh.us

Department of Education
Ohio Department of Education
25 S. Front St.

Columbus, OH 43215-4183
614-995-1545
877-644-6338
Email:
contact.center@ods.state.oh.us
www.ode.state.oh.us

**Department of Higher
Education**
Ohio Board of Regents
State Grants and Scholarship
Department
30 East Broad St., 36th Floor
Columbus, OH 43215-3414
888-833-1133
614-466-6000
Fax: 614-466-5866
Email:
regents@regents.state.oh.us
www.regents.state.oh.us

Health Department
Ohio Department of Health
246 North High Street
P.O. Box 118
Columbus, OH 43216-0118
614-466-3543
www.odh.state.oh.us

Housing Office
Ohio Housing Finance Agency
57 E. Main St.
Columbus, OH 43215-5135
614-466-7970
TDD: 614-466-1940
www.odod.state.oh.us/ohfa

Insurance Commissioner
Director of Insurance
2100 Stella Court
Columbus, OH 43215-1067
614-644-2658
800-686-1526 (consumer)
800-686-1527 (fraud)
800-686-1578 (senior health)
www.ohioinsurance.gov

Labor Department
Workforce Development
Department of Jobs and Family
Services
145 South Front Street
Columbus, OH 43215

614-466-3817
www.ohioworkforce.org

Licensing Office
State of Ohio
Dept. of Administrative Services
State Information Office
30 East Broad St., 40th Floor
Columbus, OH 43215
614-466-6511

One-Stop Career Center
One-Stop Systems
One-Stop Employment and
Training System
Bureau of Employment Services
145 Front Street, 6th Floor
Columbus, OH 43215
614-466-3817
Fax: 614-728-5938
www.ohioworkforce.org

Security Regulators
Department of Commerce
Ohio Division of Securities
77 South High St., 22nd Floor
Columbus, OH 43215
614-644-7381
800-788-1194
(Investor Protection Hotline)
www.securities.state.oh.us

**Small Business Development
Center**
Ohio Small Business
Development Center
Department of Development
77 South High Street, 28th Floor
Columbus, OH 43216-1001
614-466-2711
800-848-1300
Fax: 614-466-0829
www.odod.state.oh.us/edd/osb/sb
dc

Social Services Offices
Ohio Department of Jobs and
Family Services
30 East Broad Street, 32nd Floor
Columbus, OH 43215
614-466-6282
http://ifs.ohio.gov

**Temporary Assistance to
Needy Families (TANF)**
Ohio Works First
Ohip Department of Jobs and
Family Services
30 E. Broad Street, 32nd Floor
Columbus, OH 43215
614-466-6282
http://jfs.ohio.gov

Transportation Department
Gordon Proctor
Ohio Department of
Transportation
1980 W. Broad St.
Columbus, OH 43223
614-466-7170
www.dot.state.oh.us

Lynn Rathke
Ohio Department of
Transportation
1980 W. Broad St.
Columbus, OH 43215
614-644-7362
www.dot.state.oh.us

Unclaimed Property Office
Division of Unclaimed Funds
77 South High St., 20th Floor
Columbus, OH 43215-6108
614-466-4433
Email: unfd.claims@com.state.
oh.us

www.com.state.oh.us/ODOC/
unfd/default.htm

**Unemployment Insurance
Office**
Director
Unemployment Insurance
Ohio Bureau of Employment
Services
Office of Unemployment
Compensation
P.O. Box 182404
Columbus, OH 43218-2404
614-995-7066
http://jfs.ohiogov/ouc
Weekly benefit range: $66-414
Duration of benefits: 20-26 weeks

Utility Commission
Public Utilities Commission
180 E. Broad St.
Columbus, OH 43215-3793
614-466-3016
800-686-7826 (OH only)
TTD/TTY: 800-686-1570
www.puc.state.oh.us/

Women's Commission
Closed June 15, 2001

Your Senator
United States Senate
Washington, DC 20510
202-224-3121
www.senate.gov

Your Representative
United States House of
Representatives
Washington, DC 20515
202-224-3121
www.house.gov

OKLAHOMA

Federal Information Center
1-800-FED-INFO
www.firstgov.gov
www.pueblo.gsa.gov/call/

State Information Office
405-521-2011
www.state.ok.us

Department on Aging
Aging Services Division
Human Services Dept.
2401 NW 23rd, Suite 40
Oklahoma City, OK 73107-2422
405-521-2327
800-211-2116 (senior info)
www.okdhs.org/aging

Attorney General's Office
Office of the Attorney General
2300 N. Lincoln Blvd. , Suite 112
Oklahoma City, OK 73105
405-521-3921
www.oag.state.ok.us/

Banking Commissioner
Bank Commissioner
4545 N. Lincoln Blvd.
Suite 164
Oklahoma City, OK 73105-3427
405-521-2782
Fax: 405-522-2993
www.state.ok.us/ ~osbd/

**Child Care and Development
Block Grant Lead Agency**
Administrator of CCDF
Office of Child Care
Oklahoma Department of Human
Services
Sequoyah Memorial Office Bldg.
2400 N. Lincoln Blvd.
P.O. Box 25325
Oklahoma City, OK 73125
405-521-3561
800-347-2276
Fax: 405-521-0391
www.okdhs.org/childcare

**Child Support Enforcement
Agency**
Child Support Enforcement
Division

Department of Human Services
P.O. Box 53552
Oklahoma City, OK 73152
405-522-2273
800-522-2922 (in OK) (kids line)
www.okdhs.org/childsupport

Cooperative Extension Offices
Dr. C.B. Browning, Director
Oklahoma Cooperative Extension
Service
Oklahoma State University
139 Agriculture Hall
Stillwater, OK 74078
405-744-5398
www1.dasnr.okstate.edu/oces

Corporation Division Office
Secretary of State
Business Filing Department
101 State Capitol Building
2300 N. Lincoln Blvd., Room 101
Oklahoma City, OK 73105-4897
405-521-3912
Fax: 405-521-3771
www.sos.state.ok.us/

Day Care Licensing Agency
Department of Human Services
Division of Child Care
Sequoyah Memorial Office Bldg.
2400 N. Lincoln Blvd.
P.O. Box 25352
Oklahoma City, OK 73125
405-521-3561
800-347-2276
www.okdhs.org/childcare

Economic Development Office
Department of Commerce
900 North Stiles
P.O. Box 26980
Oklahoma City, OK 73126-0980
405-815-6552
800-879-6552.
www.locateok.com
www.odoc.state.ok.us/index.html

Department of Education
Oklahoma State Department of
Education
2500 N. Lincoln Blvd.
Oklahoma City, OK 73105-4599

405-521-3301
www.sde.state.ok.us/

**Department of Higher
Education**
Oklahoma State Regents for
Higher Education
655 Research Pkwy., Suite 200
Oklahoma City, OK 73104
405-225-9100
Fax: 405-225-9230
www.okhighered.org

Health Department
Oklahoma State Department of
Health
1000 NE 10th Street
Oklahoma City, OK 73117
405-271-5600
www.health.state.ok.us

Housing Office
Oklahoma Housing Finance
Agency
100 NW 63rd Street, Suite 200
P.O. Box 26720
Oklahoma City, OK 73126-0720
405-848-1144
800-256-1489
TDD: 405-848-7471
www.ohfa.org

Insurance Commissioner
Insurance Commissioner
2401 NW 23rd, Suite 28
P.O. Box 53408
Oklahoma City, OK 73152-3408
405-521-2828
800-522-0071
www.oid.state.ok.us

Labor Department
Oklahoma Department of Labor
4001 North Lincoln Boulevard
Oklahoma City, OK 73105
405-528-1500
888-269-5353
Fax: 405-528-5751
www.oklaosf.state.ok.us/~okdol

Licensing Office
Oklahoma Business Licensing
System

P.O. Box 26980
Oklahoma City, OK 73126-0980
800-879-6552
http://busdev3.odoc5.odoc.state.o
k.us

One-Stop Career Center
Oklahoma Workforce Centers
Employment Security
Commission
P.O. Box 52003
Oklahoma City, OK 73152-2003
405-557-5469
www.oesc.state.ok.us

Security Regulators
Oklahoma Dept. of Securities
First National Center
120 North Robinson, Suite 860
Oklahoma City, OK 73102
405-280-7700
Fax: 405-280-7742
www.securities.state.ok.us

**Small Business Development
Center**
Oklahoma Small Business
Development Center
Southeastern Oklahoma State
University
Durant, OK 74701
580-924-0277
800-522-6154
Fax: 580-920-7471
www.osbdc.org

Social Services Offices
Oklahoma Department of Human
Services
2401 North Lincoln Boulevard
P.O. Box 25352
Oklahoma City, OK 73125
405-521-6602
www.okdhs.org

**Temporary Assistance to
Needy Families (TANF)**
Temporary Aid to Needy Families
Peggy Butcher
Oklahoma Department of Human
Service
Family Support Services Division
P.O. Box 25352
Oklahoma City, OK 73125
405-521-3076
Fax: 405-521-4158
www.okdhs.org/fssd/ProgramInfo
rmation.htm#Temporary

Transportation Department
Gary Ridley
Oklahoma Dept. of
Transportation
Transportation Bldg.
200 NE 21st St.
Oklahoma City, OK 73015-3204
405-521-2631
www.okladot.state.ok.us

Unclaimed Property Office
Oklahoma State Treasurer
Unclaimed Property Section
4565 Lincoln Blvd., Suite 106
Oklahoma City, OK 73105-3413
405-521-4273
www.unclaimed.state.ok.us

**Unemployment Insurance
Office**
Unemployment Insurance
Director
Employment Security
Commission
P.O. Box 52003
2401 N. Lincoln Blvd.
Oklahoma City, OK 73152-2003
405-557-7190
www.oesc.state.ok.us/ui/
default.htm

Weekly benefit range: $16-275
Duration of benefits: 20-26 weeks

Utility Commission
Corporation Commission
P.O. Box 52000
Oklahoma City, OK 73152-2000
405-521-2211
www.occ.state.ok.us

Women's Commission
Oklahoma Governor's
Commission on the Status of
Women
2101 North Lincoln Blvd.
Oklahoma City, OK 73105-4897
405-522-6897
www.opm.state.ok.us/ocsw

Lawton Mayor's Commission on
the Status of Women
102 SW 5th St.
Lawton, OK 73501
405-581-3260

Tulsa Mayor's Commission on the
Status of Women
c/o Department of Human Rights
200 Civic Center
Tulsa, OK 74103
918-582-0558
918-592-7818

Your Senator
United States Senate
Washington, DC 20510
202-224-3121
www.senate.gov

Your Representative
United States House of
Representatives
Washington, DC 20515
202-224-3121
www.house.gov

OREGON

Federal Information Center
1-800-FED-INFO
www.firstgov.gov
www.pueblo.gsa.gov/call/

State Information Office
503-378-6500
www.oregon.gov

Department on Aging
Seniors and People with
Disabilities
500 Summer St., NE, E02
Salem, OR 97301-1073
503-945-5811
800-282-8096
www.dhs.state.or.us/seniors

Attorney General's Office
Office of the Attorney General
Department of Justice
1162 Court Street, NE
Salem, OR 97301-4096
503-378-4400
877-877-9392 (OR consumer
hotline)
www.doj.state.or.us
Email: doj.info@state.or.us

Banking Commissioner
Administrator
Division of Finance and
Corporate Securities
350 Winter St., NE, Room 410
Salem, OR 97301-3881
503-378-4140
Fax: 503-947-7862
Email: dcbs.dfcsmail@state.or.us
www.cbs.state.or.us/dfcs/

**Child Care and Development
Block Grant Lead Agency**
Child Care Division
Department of Employment
875 Union St., NE
Salem, OR 97311
503-947-1400
800-556-6616
Fax: 503-947-1428
http://findit.emp.state.or.us/
childcare/ccdf.cfm

**Child Support Enforcement
Agency**
P.O. Box 14506
Salem, OR 97309
503-373-7300
800-850-0228 (OR only)
www.dcs.state.or.us

Cooperative Extension Office
Dr. Lyla Houghlum, Director
Oregon State Extension
Service Administration
Oregon State University
Ballard Extension Hall #101
Corvallis, OR 97331-3606
541-737-2713
http://extension.oregonstate.edu

Corporation Division Office
Corporation Division
Secretary of State
Public Service Bldg.
255 Capitol St., NE, Suite 151
Salem, OR 97310-1327
503-986-2200
www.sos.state.or.us/corporation

Day Care Licensing Agency
Employment Department
Child Care Division
875 Union Street, NE
Salem, OR 97311
503-947-1400
800-556-6616
www.emp.state.or.us

Economic Development Office
Economic and Community
Development Department
775 Summer St., Suite 200
Salem, OR 97301-1280
503-986-0123
www.econ.state.or.us/

Department of Education
Oregon Department of Education
255 Capitol St., NE
Salem, OR 97310-0203
503-378-3569
Fax: 503-378-5156
www.ode.state.or.us/

**Department of Higher
Education**
Oregon Student Assistance
Commission
1500 Valley River Drive
Suite 100
Eugene, OR 97401
800-452-8807
541-687-7400
www.osac.state.or.us

Health Department
Oregon Health Division
800 NE Oregon Street
Portland, OR 97232
503-731-4000
800-422-6012
www.ohd.hr.state.or.us
Email: ohd.info@state.or.us

Housing Office
Oregon Housing and Community
Services Department
P.O. Box 14508
Salem, OR 97309-0409
503-986-2000
TTY: 503-986-2100
Email: info@hcs.state.or.us
www.hcs.state.or.us/

Insurance Commissioner
Department of Consumer and
Business
Insurance Commissioner
P.O. Box 14480
Salem, OR 97309-0405
503-947-7980
Fax: 503-378-4351
Email: dcbs.insmail@state.or.us
www.cbs.state.or.us/external/
ins/index.html

Labor Department
Oregon Employment Department
875 Union Street NE
Salem, OR 97311
503-947-1670
www.emp.state.or.us/

Licensing Office
Department of Consumer and
Business Services

P.O. Box 14480
Salem, OR 97309-0405
503-986-2200
http://lic.oregon.gov/cfmx/lic

One-Stop Career Center
Oregon Career Network
Oregon Employment Department
875 Union Street, NE
Salem, OR 97311
503-947-1470
www.emp.state.or.us
Email: info@emp.state.or.us

Security Regulators
Division of Finance and
Corporate Securities
Department of Consumer &
Business Services
350 Winter St., NE, Room 410
Salem, OR 97301-3881
503-378-4140
Fax: 503-947-7862
Email: dcbs.dfcsmail@state.or.us
www.cbs.state.or.us/external/
dfcs/

**Small Business Development
Center**
Oregon Business Development
Center
Lane Community College
1445 Willamette St., Suite 1
Eugene, OR 97401-4087
541-687-0611
Fax: 541-686-0096
Email: contact@lanebdc.com
www.lanebdc.com

Social Services Offices
Oregon Department of Human
Services

500 Summer Street, NE, E15
Salem, OR 97301-1097
503-945-5944
TTY: 503-947-5330
Fax: 503-378-2897
Email: dhr.info@state.or.us
www.dhs.state.or.us

**Temporary Assistance to
Needy Families (TANF)**
Temporary Aid to Needy Families
Sandie Hoback
Oregon Department of Human
Resources
500 Summer St., NE E-46
Salem, OR 97301-1067
503-945-5651
800-359-9517
www.dhs.state.or.us/assistance

Transportation Department
Oregon Department of
Transportation
355 Capitol St., NE
Salem, OR 97301-3871
503-986-3450
888-275-6368
www.oregon.gov/ODOT

Unclaimed Property Office
Unclaimed Property Unit
775 Summer St., NE
Salem, OR 97301
503-378-3805
Email: claims@dsl.state.or.us
http://statelands.dsl.state.or.us/
upintro.htm

**Unemployment Insurance
Office**
Programs and Methods
Employment Department

875 Union St., NE
Salem, OR 97311
503-947-1707
800-237-3710
http://findit.emp.state.or.us/
uiinfo.cfm
Weekly benefit range: $98-419
Duration of benefits: 4-26 weeks

Utility Commission
Public Utility Commission
550 Capital St., NE, Suite 215
Salem, OR 97301-2551
503-378-6611
800-522-2404 (OR only)
www.puc.state.or.us

Women's Commission
Oregon Commission for Women
P.O. Box 751-CW
Portland, OR 97207
503-725-5889
Fax: 503-725-8152
Email: ocfw@pdx.edu
Roslyn Farrington, Executive
Director

Your Senator
United States Senate
Washington, DC 20510
202-224-3121
www.senate.gov

Your Representative
United States House of
Representatives
Washington, DC 20515
202-224-3121
www.house.gov

PENNSYLVANIA

Federal Information Center
1-800-FED-INFO
www.firstgov.gov
www.pueblo.gsa.gov/call/

State Information Office
717-787-2121
www.state.pa.us

Department on Aging
Department of Aging
555 Walnut St., 5th Floor
Harrisburg, PA 17101-1919
717-783-1550
Fax: 717-783-6842
Email: aging@state.pa.us
www.aging.state.pa.us/aging/site/
default.asp

Attorney General's Office
Office of the Attorney General
16th Floor, Strawberry Square
Harrisburg, PA 17120
717-787-3391
www.attorneygeneral.gov
Email: info@attorneygeneral.gov

Banking Commissioner
Secretary of Banking
333 Market St., 16th Floor
Harrisburg, PA 17101-2290
717-787-2665
800-PA-BANKS (toll free in PA)
www.banking.state.pa.us/

*Child Care and Development
Block Grant Lead Agency*
CCDBG Administrator
Office of Children, Youth and
Families
Pennsylvania Department of
Public Welfare
Health and Welfare Building
Room 131
P.O. Box 2675
Harrisburg, PA 17105-2675
717-783-3856
877-4-PA-KIDS
www.dpw.state.pa.us/

*Child Support Enforcement
Agency*
Office of Income Maintenance

Department of Public Welfare
Health and Welfare Building
Room 432
P.O. Box 2675
Harrisburg, PA 17105-2675
717-787-1894
800-932-0211
www.dpw.state.pa.us/

Cooperative Extension Office
Dr. Ted Alter, Director
Pennsylvania State University
Room 217, A.G. Administration
University Park, PA 16802
814-863-3438
www.extension.psu.edu

Corporation Division Office
Corporation Bureau
Department of State
206 N. Office Building
Harrisburg, PA 17120
717-787-1057
www.dos.state.pa.us/corps/

Day Care Licensing Agency
Child Care Works
Office of Children, Youth and
Families
Health and Welfare Building
Room 131
P.O. Box 2675
Harrisburg, PA 17105-2675
717-783-3856
877-4-PA-KIDS
www.dpw.state.pa.us/

Economic Development Office
Department of Community and
Economic Development
4th Floor, Commonwealth
Keystone Bldg. North Street
Harrisburg, PA 17120-0225
800-379-7448
Email: ra-DCEDCS@state.pa.us
www.inventpa.com

Governor's Action Team
100 Pine Street, 9th Floor
Harrisburg, PA 17101
717-233-1375
888-4TEAMPA
www.teampa.com

Department of Education
Pennsylvania Dept. of Education
333 Market St.
Harrisburg, PA 17126-0333
717-783-6788
www.pde.psu.edu

*Department of Higher
Education*
Office of Postsecondary and
Higher Education
333 Market St.
Harrisburg, PA 17126-0333
717-783-6788
www.pdehighered.state.pa.us/hig
her/site/default.asp?g=O

Pennsylvania Higher Education
Assistance Agency
1200 North 7th Street
Harrisburg, PA 17102
717-720-2850
800-692-7392
TTY: 800-654-5988
Fax: 717-720-3907
www.pheaa.org

Health Department
Pennsylvania Dept. of Health
P.O. Box 90
Health & Welfare Building
Harrisburg, PA 17108
877-PA-HEALTH
www.dsf.health.state.pa.us
Email:
webmaster@heath.state.pa.us

Housing Office
Pennsylvania Housing Finance
Agency
2101 North Front St.
P.O. Box 8029
Harrisburg, PA 17105-8029
717-780-3800
TDD: 717-780-1869
www.phfa.org

Insurance Commissioner
Insurance Commissioner
1326 Strawberry Square
Harrisburg, PA 17120
717-787-6174
877-881-6388 (hotline)

TTY/TDD: 717-783-3898
www.ins.state.pa.us

Labor Department
Pennsylvania Department of
Labor and Industry
Room 1700, 7th and Forster Sts.
Harrisburg, PA 17120
717-787-5279
www.dli.state.pa.us/

Licensing Office
Bureau of Professional and
Occupational Affairs
P.O. Box 2649
Harrisburg, PA 17105-2649
717-787-8503
800-822-2113 (PA only)
(complaints)
www.dos.state.pa.us/

One-Stop Career Center
Team Pennsylvania CareerLink
Department of Labor and Industry
Room 1720, Seventh & Foster St.
Harrisburg, PA 17120
717-787-5279
www.pacareerlink.state.pa.us

Security Regulators
Pennsylvania Securities
Commission
Eastgate Office Building
2nd Floor
1010 N. 7th St.
Harrisburg, PA 17102-1410
717-787-8061
800-600-0007 (in PA)
www.psc.state.pa.us

**Small Business Development
Center**
Pennsylvania Small Business
Development Center
Vance Hall, 4th Floor
3733 Spruce Street
Philadelphia, PA 19104-6374

215-898-1219
Fax: 215-573-2135
www.pasbdc.org

Social Services Offices
Pennsylvania Department of
Public Welfare
333 Health and Welfare Building
Harrisburg, PA 17105
717-787-4592
www.dpw.state.pa.us/

**Temporary Assistance to
Needy Families (TANF)**
Temporary Aid to Needy Families
Pennsylvania Department of
Public Welfare
Health and Welfare Building
Room 432
P.O. Box 2675
Harrisburg, PA 17105
717-787-1894
800-692-7462
TDD: 800-451-5886
www.dpw.state.pa.us

Transportation Department
Pennsylvania Department of
Transportation
Keystone Bldg., 400 North St.
Harrisburg, PA 17120
717-787-2838
www.dot.state.pa.us

Unclaimed Property Office
Pennsylvania State Treasury
Office of Unclaimed Property
P.O. Box 1837
Harrisburg, PA 17105-1837
800-222-2046
www.treasury.state.pa.us/
unclaimed.html

**Unemployment Insurance
Office**
Bureau of U.C. Benefits and
Allowances

Department of Labor and Industry
Labor and Industry Building
6th Floor
Seventh and Forster Sts.
Harrisburg, PA 17121
717-783-3140
888-313-7284
Email: 4C-news@dli.state.pa.us
www.dli.state.pa.us
Weekly benefit range: $33-461
Duration of benefits: 16-26 weeks

Utility Commission
Public Utility Commission
Commonwealth Keystone Bldg.
400 North St.
Harrisburg, PA 17120
MAILING ADDRESS:
    P.O. Box 3265
    Harrisburg, PA 17105
717-783-1740
800-782-1110 (complaints-PA
only)
http://puc.paonline.com/

Women's Commission
Pennsylvania Commission for
Women
Finance Building, Room 504
Harrisburg, PA 17120
888-615-7477
717-787-8128
Fax: 717-772-0653
www.pcw.state.pa.us

Your Senator
United States Senate
Washington, DC 20510
202-224-3121
www.senate.gov

Your Representative
United States House of
Representatives
Washington, DC 20515
202-224-3121
www.house.gov

RHODE ISLAND

Federal Information Center
1-800-FED-INFO
www.firstgov.gov
www.pueblo.gsa.gov/call/

State Information Office
401-222-2000
www.state.ri.us

Department on Aging
Department of Elderly Affairs
Benjamin Rush
Building #55
5 Howard Avenue
Cranston, RI 02920
401-462-3000
www.dea.state.ri.us

Attorney General's Office
Office of the Attorney General
150 South Main Street
Providence, RI 02903
401-274-4400
www.riag.state.ri.us

Banking Commissioner
Director and Superintendent of
Banking
Department of Business
Regulation
233 Richmond St.
Providence, RI 02903
401-222-2246
Fax: 401-222-6098
www.dbr.state.ri.us

**Child Care and Development
Block Grant Lead Agency**
Rhode Island Department of
Human Services
Individual and Family Support
Services
Louis Pasteur Bldg.
600 New London Ave.
Cranston, RI 02920
401-462-5300
www.dhs.state.ri.us/dhs/
dserfch.htm

**Child Support Enforcement
Agency**
Child Support Enforcement
101 Friendship Street

Providence, RI 02903-3716
401-528-3548
www.dcyf.ri.gov

Cooperative Extension Office
Cooperative Extension Education
Center
University of Rhode Island
9 East Alumni Avenue
12 Woodward Hall
Kingston, RI 02881-0804
401-874-2900
www.uri.edu/ce/index1.html

Corporation Division Office
Corporations Division
Secretary of State
100 North Main St., 1st Floor
Providence, RI 02903-1335
401-222-3040
Fax: 401-222-1309
Email: corporations@sec.state.
ri.us
www2.corps.state.ri.us/corporatio
ns

Day Care Licensing Agency
Department of Children, Youth
and Families
101 Friendship Street
Providence, RI 02903-3716
401-528-3624
www.dcyf.state.ri.us

Economic Development Office
Economic Development
Corporation
One West Exchange St.
Providence, RI 02903
401-222-2601
www.riedc.com

Department of Education
Rhode Island Department of
Education
255 Westminster St.
Providence, RI 02903
401-222-4600
www.ridoe.net

**Department of Higher
Education**
Rhode Island Office of Higher
Education

301 Promenade St.
Providence, RI 02908
401-222-6560
Fax: 401-222-6111
www.ribghe.org

Health Department
Rhode Island Department of
Health
3 Capitol Hill
Providence, RI 02908
401-222-2231
Fax: 401-222-6548
TTY: 711
www.health.state.ri.us/
Email: library@doh.state.ri.us

Housing Office
Rhode Island Housing and
Mortgage Finance Corporation
44 Washington St.
Providence, RI 02903-1721
401-751-5566
TDD: 401-427-9799
www.rihousing.com

Insurance Commissioner
Insurance Commissioner
Department of Business
Regulation
233 Richmond St., Suite 233
Providence, RI 02903
401-222-2246
Fax: 401-222-6098
www.dbr.state.ri.us

Labor Department
Rhode Island Department of
Labor and Training
Pastore Government Center
1511 Pontiac Ave.
Cranston, RI 02920
401-462-8000
www.dlt.state.ri.us

Licensing Office
Department of Labor and Training
Professional Regulation Division
1511 Pontiac Ave. Bldg. 70
Cranston, RI 02920
401-462-8000
www.dlt.state.ri.us/

Free Money For Everybody

One-Stop Career Center
NetWorkri
Department of Labor and Training
1511 Pontiac Ave.
Cranston, RI 02920
401-462-8000
Email: brutherford@networkri.org
www.networkri.org

Security Regulators
Department of Business
Regulation
Division of Securities Regulation
233 Richmond St.
Providence, RI 02903
401-222-2246
www.dbr.state.ri.us

Small Business Development Center
Bryant College
Small Business Development
Center
1150 Douglas Pike
Smithfield, RI 02197-1284
401-232-6111
Fax: 401-232-6933
www.RISBDC.org

Social Services Offices
Rhode Island Department of
Human Services
600 New London Avenue
Cranston, RI 02920
401-462-5300
www.dhs.state.ri.us

Temporary Assistance to Needy Families (TANF)
Family Independence Program
Louis Pasture Bldg.
600 New London Ave.
Cranston, RI 02920
401-462-5300
800-DHS-3322
www.dhs.state.ri.us/

Transportation Department
Robert Letourneau
Rhode Island Department of
Transportation
Two Capitol Hill
Providence, RI 02903
401-222-1362
www.dot.state.ri.us

Unclaimed Property Office
Unclaimed Property Division
P.O. Box 1435
Providence, RI 02901
401-222-6505
TDD: 401-222-3399
Email: ups@treasury.state.ri.us
www.treasury.ri.gov/money/st.ht
m

Unemployment Insurance Office
Assistant Director
Unemployment Insurance
Department of Employment and
Training
1511 Pontiac Ave.

Cranston, RI 02920
401-243-9100
www.dlt.state.ri.us

Utility Commission
Public Utilities Commission
89 Jefferson Blvd.
Warwick, RI 02888
Providence, RI 02903
401-941-4500
www.ripuc.org

Women's Commission
Rhode Island Advisory
Commission on Women
One Capitol Hill
Providence, RI 02098
401-222-6105
Fax: 401-222-5638
Email: ricw@doa.state.ri.us
www.ricw.state.ri.us

Your Senator
United States Senate
Washington, DC 20510
202-224-3121
www.senate.gov

Your Representative
United States House of
Representatives
Washington, DC 20515
202-224-3121
www.house.gov

SOUTH CAROLINA

Federal Information Center
1-800-FED-INFO
www.firstgov.gov
www.pueblo.gsa.gov/call/

State Information Office
803-896-0000
www.myscgov.com

Department on Aging
Bureau of Senior Services
South Carolina Department of
Health and Human Services
P.O. Box 8206
Columbia, SC 29202-8206
803-898-2850
www.dhhs.state.sc.us/

Attorney General's Office
Office of the Attorney General
Rembert Dennis Building
1000 Assembly Street, Room 519
P.O. Box 11549
Columbia, SC 29211
803-734-3970
www.scattorneygeneral.com
Email:
info@scattorneygeneral.org

Banking Commissioner
Commissioner of Banking
309 Calhoun St.
Columbia, SC 29201
803-734-2001

**Child Care and Development
Block Grant Lead Agency**
Advocates for Better Care
South Carolina Health and
Human Services
Bureau of Community Services
P.O. Box 8206
Columbia, SC 29202-8206
803-898-2570
www.dhhs.state.sc.us/

**Child Support Enforcement
Agency**
Child Support Enforcement
Division
Department of Social Services
P.O. Box 1469
Columbia, SC 29202-1469
803-898-9210
800-768-5858 (in SC)

www.state.sc.us/dss/csed/
index.html

Cooperative Extension Offices
Carroll Culvertson, Director
Clemson University
Cooperative Extension Service
103 Barre Hall
Clemson University
Clemson, SC 29634-0101
864-656-3382
http://virtual.clemson.edu/groups/
extension/

Corporation Division Office
Division of Corporations
Secretary of State
P.O. Box 11350
Columbia, SC 29211
803-734-2158
www.scsos.com/

Day Care Licensing Agency
Department of Social Services
Division of Child Day Care
Licensing and Regulation
P.O. Box 1520
Columbia, SC 29202-1520
803-253-4049
Fax: 803-252-1364
www.state.sc.us/dss/cdclrs/
index.html

Economic Development Office
Department of Commerce
1201 Main Street, Suite 1600
Columbia, SC 29201-3200
803-737-0400
Fax: 803-737-0418
www.callsouthcarolina.com

Department of Education
South Carolina Department of
Education
1429 Senate St.
Columbia, SC 29201
803-734-8500
www.myscschools.com

**Department of Higher
Education**
South Carolina Commission on
Higher Education
Tuition Grants Commission
101 Business Park Blvd.

Suite 2100
Columbia, SC 29203-9498
803-896-1120
Fax: 803-896-1126
Email: info@sctuitiongrants.org
www.sctuitiongrants.com

Commission on Higher Education
1333 Main St., Suite 200
Columbia, SC 29201
803-737-2660
Fax: 803-737-2297
www.che400.state.sc.us

Health Department
South Carolina Department of
Health & Environmental Control
2600 Bull Street
Columbia, SC 29201
803-898-3432
www.scdhec.net

Housing Office
South Carolina State Housing
Financing and Development
Authority
919 Bluff Rd.
Columbia, SC 29201
803-734-2000
www.sha.state.sc.us

Insurance Commissioner
Chief Insurance Commissioner
300 Arbor Lark Dr., Suite 1200
Columbia, SC 29223
MAILING ADDRESS:
  P.O. Box 100105
  Columbia, SC 29202-3105
803-737-6160
800-768-3467
Email: cnsmmail@doi.state.sc.us
www.doi.state.sc.us

Labor Department
South Carolina Department of
Labor, Licensing and Regulation
Public Information Office
110 Centerview Drive
P.O. Box 11329
Columbia, SC 29211-1329
803-896-4300
Email: contactllr@mail.llr.
state.sc.us
www.llr.state.sc.us

Free Money For Everybody

Licensing Office
South Carolina Department of
Labor, Licensing, and Regulation
110 Centerview Dr.
P.O. Box 11329
Columbia, SC 29211
803-896-4300
www.llr.state.sc.us/

One-Stop Career Center
1 Stop Partnership
Employment Security
Commission
P.O. Box 995
1550 Gadsden Street
Columbia, SC 29202
803-737-2258
Fax: 803-737-0140
www.sces.org/
Email: jobs@sces.org

Security Regulators
Office of the SC Attorney General
Securities Division
P.O. Box 11549
Columbia, SC 29211-1549
803-734-9916
www.scsecurities.org/index.html

Small Business Development Center
South Carolina Small Business
Development Center
University of South Carolina
Moore School of Business
Columbia, SC 29208
803-777-5118
Fax: 803-777-4403
www.uscbiz.net

Social Services Offices
South Carolina Department of
Social Services
1535 Confederate Ave.
P.O. Box 1520
Columbia, SC 29202-1520
803-898-7601
800-311-7220
www.state.sc.us/dss

Temporary Assistance to Needy Families (TANF)
Temporary Aid to Needy Families
South Carolina Department of
Social Services
P.O. Box 1520
Room 605
Columbia, SC 29202
803-898-7601
800-768-5700
www.state.sc.us/dss/

Transportation Department
Elizabeth S. Marby
South Carolina Department of
Transportation
P.O. Box 191
955 Park St.
Columbia, SC 29202-0191
803-737-2314
www.dot.state.sc.us

Unclaimed Property Office
State Treasurer's Office
Unclaimed Property Division
P.O. Box 11778
Columbia, SC 29211
803-734-2101
www.state.sc.us/treas/

Unemployment Insurance Office
Deputy Executive Director
Unemployment Compensation
Employment Security
Commission
P.O. Box 995
Columbia, SC 29202
803-737-3071
www.sces.org/ui/index.htm
Weekly benefit range: $20-292
Duration of benefits: 15-26 weeks

Utility Commission
Public Service Commission
101 Executive Center Dr.
Columbia, SC 29210
803-896-5100
800-922-1531 (SC only)
www.psc.state.sc.us

Women's Commission
Governor's Office Commission on
Women
1205 Pendleton St., Room 366
Columbia, SC 29201
803-734-1609
Fax: 803-734-0241
www.govoepp.state.sc.us/

Your Senator
United States Senate
Washington, DC 20510
202-224-3121
www.senate.gov

Your Representative
United States House of
Representatives
Washington, DC 20515
202-224-3121
www.house.gov

SOUTH DAKOTA

Federal Information Center
1-800-FED-INFO
www.firstgov.gov
www.pueblo.gsa.gov/call/

State Information Office
605-773-3011
www.state.sd.us

Department on Aging
Adult Services on Aging Office.
Social Services Department
700 Governors Dr.
Pierre, SD 57501
605-773-3656
www.state.sd.us/social/ASA/inde
x.htm

Attorney General's Office
Office of the Attorney General
500 East Capitol Avenue
Pierre, SD 57501-5070
605-773-3215
800-300-1986 (SD consumer
hotline)
Fax: 605-773-4106
www.state.sd.us/attorney/index.ht
ml
Email:
consumerhelp@state.sd.us

Banking Commissioner
Director of Banking and Finance
State Capitol Bldg.
217 1/2 West Missouri
Pierre, SD 57501-4590
605-773-3421
Fax: 605-773-5367
Email:
tammi.watkins@state.sd.us
www.state.sd.us/drr2/reg/bank/ba
nkinfo.htm

**Child Care and Development
Block Grant Lead Agency**
Child Care Services
South Dakota Department of
Social Services
700 Governors Dr.
Pierre, SD 57501-2291
605-773-4766
800-227-3020

www.state.sd.us/social/ccs/ccsho
me.htm

**Child Support Enforcement
Agency**
Terry Walter
Office of Child Support
Enforcement
Department of Social Services
700 Governors Dr.
Pierre, SD 57501
605-773-3641
Fax: 605-773-7295
www.state.sd.us/social/CSE/inde
x.htm

Cooperative Extension Office
Mylo Hellickson, Director
SDSU
Box 2207D
AG Hall 154
Brookings, SD 57007
605-688-4792
http://sdces.sdstate.edu

Corporation Division Office
Corporate Division
Secretary of State
Capitol Bldg.
500 East Capitol Ave., Suite 204
Pierre, SD 57501-5070
605-773-4845
www.state.sd.us/sos/corporations
/corpcover.htm

Day Care Licensing Agency
Department of Social Services
Child Care Services
Child Care Licensing Division
700 Governors Dr.
Pierre, SD 57501-2291
605-773-4766
800-227-3020
Email: ccs@state.sd.us
www.state.sd.us/state/social/

Economic Development Office
Governor's Office of Economic
Development
711 East Wells Ave.
Pierre, SD 57501-3369
605-773-5032
800-872-6190

Fax: 605-773-3256
Email: goedinfo@state.sd.us
www.sdgreatprofits.com

Department of Education
South Dakota Department of
Education and Cultural Affairs
Office of Finance Management
Kneip Bldg.
700 Governors Dr.
Pierre, SD 57501-2291
605-773-3248
605-773-6139
www.state.sd.us/deca/

**Department of Higher
Education**
South Dakota Board of Regents
306 E. Capitol Ave., Suite 200
Pierre, SD 57051-2545
605-773-3455
Email: info@ris.sdbor.edu
www.ris.sdbor.edu

Health Department
South Dakota Department of
Health
Health Building
600 East Capitol
Pierre, SD 57501-2563
605-773-3361
800-738-2301 (in SD)
Fax: 605-773-5683
www.state.sd.us/doh
Email: doh.info@state.sd.us

Housing Office
South Dakota Housing
Development Authority
221 S. Central Ave.
P.O. Box 1237
Pierre, SD 57501-1237
605-773-3181
www.sdhda.org

Insurance Commissioner
Director of Insurance
Insurance Bldg.
118 W. Capitol St.
Pierre, SD 57501
605-773-3563
www.state.sd.us/insurance/

Labor Department
South Dakota Dept. of Labor
700 Governors Drive
Pierre, SD 57501-2291
605-773-3101
Fax: 605-773-4211
www.state.sd.us/dol/dol.htm

Licensing Office
Department of Commerce and
Regulation
Professional and Occupational
Licensing
118 E. Capitol Ave.
Pierre, SD 57501-2000
605-773-3178
Fax: 605-773-3018
www.state.sd.us/dcr/boards/
boardhom.htm

One-Stop Career Center
Job Service of South Dakota
SD Department of Labor
Kneip Building
700 Governors Drive
Pierre, SD 57501-2291
605-773-3101
Fax: 605-773-4211
www.state.sd.us/dol/sdjob/
js-home.htm
Email: infor@dol-pr.state.sd.us

Security Regulators
Department of Commerce and
Regulation
Division of Securities
118 W. Capitol Ave.
Pierre, SD 57501
605-773-4823
Fax: 605-773-5953
Email: secur@crpr1.state.sd.us
www.state.sd.us/dcr/securities/

**Small Business Development
Center**
South Dakota Small Development
Center
University of South Dakota
School of Business
414 East Clark Street/
Vermillion, SD 57069-2390
605-677-5287
Fax: 605-677-5427
Email: stracy@charlie.usd.edu
Email: wdruin@usd.edu
www.usd.edu/brbinfo/sbdc

Social Services Offices
South Dakota Department of
Social Services
700 Governors Drive
Pierre, SD 57501-2291
605-773-3165
www.state.sd.us/social

**Temporary Assistance to
Needy Families (TANF)**
TANF Work Program
South Dakota Department of
Social Services
700 Governors Dr.
Pierre, SD 57501
605-773-4678
Email: tanf@state.sd.us
www.state.sd.us/social/
tanf/index.htm

Transportation Department
South Dakota Department of
Transportation
Becker-Hansen Bldg.
700 E. Broadway Ave.
Pierre, SD 57501
605-773-3265
www.sddot.com

Unclaimed Property Office
Unclaimed Property Division
500 East Capitol Ave.
Pierre, SD 57501-5070
605-773-3378
Email: unclaimed.property@
state.sd.us
www.sdtreasurer.com/unclaimed.
asp

**Unemployment Insurance
Office**
Director, Unemployment
Insurance Division
Department of Labor
700 Governors Drive
Pierre, SD 57501
605-773-3101
Fax: 605-773-4211
www.state.sd.us/dol/dol.asp

Utility Commission
Public Utilities Commission
Capitol Bldg., 1st Floor
500 E. Capitol Ave.
Pierre, SD 57501-5070
605-773-3201
800-332-1782
www.state.sd.us/puc

Women's Commission
Abolished

Your Senator
United States Senate
Washington, DC 20510
202-224-3121
www.senate.gov

Your Representative
United States House of
Representatives
Washington, DC 20515
202-224-3121
www.house.gov

TENNESSEE

Federal Information Center
1-800-FED-INFO
www.firstgov.gov
www.pueblo.gsa.gov/call/

State Information Office
615-741-3011
www.state.tn.us

Department on Aging
Aging Commission
500 Deaderick St., 9th Floor
Nashville, TN 37243-0860
615-741-2056
www.state.tn.us/comaging

Attorney General's Office
Office of the Attorney General &
Recorder
425 5th Avenue
Nashville, TN 37243
P.O. Box 20207
Nashville, TN 37202-0207
615-741-3491
www.attorneygeneral.state.tn.us

Banking Commissioner
Commissioner of Financial
Institutions
511 Union Street, Suite 400
Nashville, TN 37219
615-741-2236
www.state.tn.us/financialinst/

**Child Care and Development
Block Grant Lead Agency**
Child Care Services
Tennessee Department of
Human Services
Citizens Plaza - 14th Floor
400 Deaderick St.
Nashville, TN 37248
615-313-4700
www.state.tn.us/humanserv/

**Child Support Enforcement
Agency**
Child Support Services
Department of Human Services
Citizens Plaza Bldg., 12th Floor
400 Deaderick St.
Nashville, TN 37248
615-253-4394

800-838-6911
www.state.tn.us/humanserv/
child_support.htm

Cooperative Extension Offices
Agricultural Extension Service
University of Tennessee
2621 Morgan Circle
121 Morgan Hall
Knoxville, TN 37996
865-974-7114
www.utextension.utk.edu

Cherry Lane Zon Schmittou,
Extension Leader
Davidson County Agricultural
Service
Tennessee State University
3500 John A. Merritt Blvd.
Nashville, TN 37209-1561
615-963-1351
www.tnstate.edu/cep/

Corporation Division Office
Office of Secretary of State
Business Services Division
312 8th Ave. North
6th Floor, Snodgrass Tower
Nashville, TN 37243
615-741-2286
www.state.tn.us/sos/soshmpg.htm

Day Care Licensing Agency
Department of Human Services
Day Care Licensing Division
400 Deaderick St.
Nashville, TN 37248-0001
615-313-4700
www.state.tn.us/humanserv/

Economic Development Office
Department of Economic and
Community Development
312 Eighth Avenue North
Eleventh Floor
Nashville, TN 37243-0405
615-741-1888
Fax: 615-741-7306
www.state.tn.us/ecd

Department of Education
Tennessee Dept. of Education

Office of Accountability
Andrew Johnson Tower
6th Floor
Nashville, TN 37243-0375
615-741-2731
www.state.tn.us/education

**Department of Higher
Education**
Tennessee Student Assistance
Corporation
404 James Robertson Pkwy.
Suite 1900
Nashville, TN 37243
615-741-3605
Fax: 615-741-6230
www.state.tn.us/thec/

Health Department
Tennessee Department of Health
Cordell Hull Building, 3rd Floor
Nashville, TN 37247-0101
615-741-3111
www.state.tn.us/health

Housing Office
Tennessee Housing
Development Agency
404 James Robertson Pkwy.
Suite 1114
Nashville, TN 37243-0900
615-741-2400
www.state.tn.us/thda

Insurance Commissioner
Commissioner of Insurance
500 James Robertson Parkway,
Davy Crockett Tower
Nashville, TN 37243-0565
615-741-2241
www.state.tn.us/commerce

Labor Department
Tennessee Department of Labor
Andrew Johnson Tower, 8th Floor
Nashville, TN 37243-0655
615-741-6642
www.state.tn.us/labor-wfd/

Licensing Office
Division of Regulatory Boards
Department of Commerce and
Insurance

500 James Robertson Parkway
Nashville, TN 37243-0565
615-741-2241
www.state.tn.us/commerce

One-Stop Career Center
Tennessee Career Center
Office of Workforce Development
Andrew Johnson Bldg., 8th Floor
Nashville, TN 37243-0655
615-741-6652
www.state.tn.us/labor-wfd/

Security Regulators
Tennessee Securities Division
Davy Crockett Tower
500 James Robertson Pkwy.
Nashville, TN 37243-0565
615-741-2241
www.state.tn.us/commerce/
securities

Small Business Development Center
Tennessee Small Business
Development Center
MTSU
P.O. Box 98
Murfreesboro, TN 37132
615-849-9999
877-898-3900
www.tsbdc.org

Social Services Offices
Tennessee Department of
Human Services
Citizens Plaza Building

400 Deaderick Street
Nashville, TN 37248-0001
615-313-4700
www.state.tn.us/humanserv

Temporary Assistance to Needy Families (TANF)
Temporary Aid to Needy Families
Wanda Moore
Tennessee Department of
Human Services
400 Deaderick St., 15th Floor
Nashville, TN 37248-0001
615-313-4700
www.state.tn.us/humanserv/
famfir.htm

Transportation Department
Tennessee Department of
Transportation
JK Polk Bldg., Suite 700
Nashville, TN 37243-0349
615-741-2848
www.tdot.state.tn.us

Unclaimed Property Office
Unclaimed Property Division
Tennessee State Capitol
Nashville, TN 37243
615-741-6499
www.treasury.state.tn.us

Unemployment Insurance Office
Deputy Commissioner
Tennessee Department of
Employment Security

Andrew Johnson Tower, 8th Floor
Nashville, TN 37243-0655
615-253-4809
www.state.tn.us/labor_wfd/ui/ui/htm

Utility Commission
Tennessee Regulatory Authority
460 James Robertson Parkway
Nashville, TN 37243-0505
615-741-2904
800-342-8359 (TN only)
www.state.tn.us/tra/

Women's Commission
Tennesse Economic Council on
Women
Snodgrass Tower, Third Floor
312 Eighth Avenue North
Nashville, TN 37243
615-253-4264
www.state.tn.us/sos/ecw

Your Senator
United States Senate
Washington, DC 20510
202-224-3121
www.senate.gov

Your Representative
United States House of
Representatives
Washington, DC 20515
202-224-3121
www.house.gov

TEXAS

Federal Information Center
1-800-FED-INFO
www.firstgov.gov
www.pueblo.gsa.gov/call/

State Information Office
512-463-4630
www.state.tx.us

Department on Aging
Aging Department
701 W. 51st Street
Austin, TX 78751
512-438-3011
www.dads.state.tx.us

Attorney General's Office
Office of the Attorney General
P.O. Box 12548
Austin, TX 78711-2548
512-463-2100
800-621-0508 (consumer protection)
www.oag.state.tx.us
Email: cac@oag.state.tx.us

Banking Commissioner
Banking Commissioner
2601 N. Lamar Blvd.
Austin, TX 78705-4294
512-475-1300
877-276-5554
www.banking.state.tx.us

Child Care and Development Block Grant Lead Agency
Texas Workforce Commission
Child Care Services
Work and Family Clearinghouse
101 E. 15th St., Suite 440-T
Austin, TX 78778-0001
512-936-3137
Fax: 512-936-3255
www.twc.state.tx.us/

Child Support Enforcement Agency
David Vela
Child Support Division
Office of the Attorney General
P.O. Box 12017
Austin, TX 78711-2017
512-479-6478

800-252-8014
www.oag.state.tx.us/child/

Cooperative Extension Offices
Texas Agricultural Extension Service
Texas A&M University
Administration Bldg., Room 112
College Station, TX 77843-7101
979-845-7800
http://tce.tamu.edu

Cooperative Extension Program
P.O. Box 3059
Prairie View, TX 77446-3059
936-857-2023
http://pvcep.pvamu.edu

Corporation Division Office
Corporation Section
Statue Filing Division
Secretary of State
P.O. Box 13697
Austin, TX 78711
512-463-5555
www.sos.state.tx.us/

Day Care Licensing Agency
Department of Protective and Regulatory Services
Child Care Licensing
P.O. Box 149030
Austin, TX 78714-9030
512-438-4800
800-252-5400
www.tdprs.state.tx.us/

Economic Development Office
Department of Economic Development
P.O. Box 12728
Austin, TX 78711-2728
512-936-0100
www.tded.state.tx.us

Department of Education
Texas Education Agency
Division of Public Information
1701 N. Congress
Austin, TX 78701
512-463-9734
www.tea.state.tx.us/

Department of Higher Education
Texas Higher Education Coordinating Board
Box 12788, Capitol Station
Austin, TX 78711
512-427-6101
www.thecb.state.tx.us/

Health Department
Texas Department of Health
1100 West 49th Street
Austin, TX 78756-3199
512-458-7111
888-963-7111
www.tdh.texas.gov/

Housing Office
Texas Housing Agency
507 Sabine
Austin, TX 78701
P.O. Box 13941
Austin, TX 78711-3941
512-475-3800
www.tdhca.state.tx.us

Insurance Commissioner
Director
Claims and Compliance Division
State Board of Insurance
P.O. Box 149104
Austin, TX 78714-9104
512-463-6169
800-252-3439
www.tdi.state.tx.us

Labor Department
Texas Workforce Commission
101 East 15th Street
Austin, TX 78778
512-936-3137
www.twc.state.tx.us

Licensing Office
Department of Licensing and Regulation
P.O. Box 12157
Austin, TX 78711
512-463-6599
800-803-9202
www.license.state.tx.us

Free Money For Everybody

One-Stop Career Center
Texas Workforce Information
System (TWIST)
Texas Workforce Commission
101 East 15th Street
Austin, TX 78778
512-463-2654
www.twc.state.tx.us

Security Regulators
State Securities Board
P.O. Box 13167
Austin, TX 78711-3167
512-305-8300
www.ssb.state.tx.us

**Small Business Development
Center**
North Texas Small Business
Development Center
Dallas County Community
College
1402 Corinth Street
Dallas, TX 75215
214-860-5831
Fax: 214-860-5813
www.ntsbdc.org

Social Services Offices
Texas Health and Human
Services Commission
4900 N. Lamar Blvd., 4th Floor
Austin, TX 78751-2316
MAILING ADDRESS:
    P.O. Box 13247
    Austin, TX 78711
512-424-6500
www.hhsc.state.tx.us

**Temporary Assistance to
Needy Families (TANF)**
Temporary Aid to Needy Families
Texas Health and Human
Services
P.O. Box 13247
Austin, TX 78711-3247
512-424-6500
www.hhsc.state.texas.us

Transportation Department
Texas Department of
Transportation
125 East 11th St.
Austin, TX 78701-2483
512-416-2000
www.dot.state.tx.us

Unclaimed Property Office
Comptroller of Public Accounts
Unclaimed Property Section
P.O. Box 12019
Austin, TX 78711-2019
512-463-3120
800-654-FIND
www.window.state.tx.us/up

**Unemployment Insurance
Office**
Director
Unemployment Insurance
Texas Workforce Commission
15th and Congress, Room 668
Austin, TX 78778
512-463-7234
www.twc.state.tx.us/ui/bnfts/
claimantinfo.html

Weekly benefit range: $47-287
Duration of benefits: 9-26 weeks

Utility Commission
Public Utility Commission
1701 N. Congress Ave.
Austin, TX 78701
MAILING ADDRESS:
    P.O. Box 13326
    Austin, TX 78711-3326
512-936-7000
888-782-8477
www.puc.state.tx.us

Women's Commission
Texas Governor's Commission
for Women
P.O. Box 12428
Austin, TX 78711
512-463-2000
800-843-5789
Fax: 512-463-1849
www.governor.state.tx.us/women/

Your Senator
United States Senate
Washington, DC 20510
202-224-3121
www.senate.gov

Your Representative
United States House of
Representatives
Washington, DC 20515
202-224-3121
www.house.gov

UTAH

Federal Information Center
1-800-FED-INFO
www.firstgov.gov
www.pueblo.gsa.gov/call/

State Information Office
801-538-3000
www.utah.gov

Department on Aging
Aging and Adult Services Division
Human Services Dept.
120 North, 200 West
Room 325
Salt Lake City, UT 84103
801-538-3910
www.hsdaas.state.ut.us

Attorney General's Office
Office of the Attorney General
P.O. Box 142320
Salt Lake City, UT 84114-2320
801-538-9600
800-244-4636
www.attygen.state.ut.us
Email: uag@utah.gov

Banking Commissioner
Commissioner of Financial
Institutions
P.O. Box 146800
Salt Lake City, UT 84114-6800
801-538-8830
www.dfi.state.ut.us

**Child Care and Development
Block Grant Lead Agency**
Utah Dept. of Workforce Services
Policy and Program Unit
140 East 3rd South
Salt Lake City, UT 84111
801-526-4340
800-622-7390
Fax: 801-526-4349
http://occ.dws.state.ut.us/occ

**Child Support Enforcement
Agency**
Bureau of Child Support Services
Department of Human Services
P.O. Box 45011
Salt Lake City, UT 84145-0011
801-536-8500/8509

800-662-8525
www.ors.state.ut.us/

Cooperative Extension Office
Dr. Robert Gilliland
Vice President for Extension and
Continuing Education
U.M.S. 4900
Utah State University
Logan, UT 84322-4900
435-797-1000
http://extension.usu.edu/cooperati
ve

Corporation Division Office
Corporations and UCC
Division of Business Regulations
P.O. Box 146705
160 East 300 South St., 1st Floor
Salt Lake City, UT 84145
801-530-4849
www.commerce.utah.gov

Day Care Licensing Agency
Child Care Licensing
288 N. 1460 West
P.O. Box 142003
Salt Lake City, UT 84114-2003
801-538-9299
www.health.ut.gov/licensing

Economic Development Office
Business and Economic
Development Division
324 South State St.
Suite 500
Salt Lake City, UT 84111
801-538-8700
www.utah.org/dbed/welcome.htm

Department of Education
Utah Board of Education
Department of Finance
250 E. 500 South
P.O. Box 144200
Salt Lake City, UT 84114-4200
801-538-7500
www.usoe.k12.ut.us/

**Department of Higher
Education**
Utah System of Higher Education
60 South 400 West

Salt Lake City, UT 84101-1284
801-321-7101
www.utahsbr.edu

Health Department
Utah Department of Health
P.O. Box 141010
Salt Lake City, UT 84114-1010
801-538-6101
www.health.state.ut.us
Email: pwightma@doh.state.ut.us

Housing Office
Utah Housing Corporation
554 South, 300 East
Salt Lake City, UT 84111
801-521-6950
800-284-6950 (in UT)
www.utahhousingcorp.org

Insurance Commissioner
Commissioner of Insurance
3110 State Office Bldg.
Salt Lake City, UT 84114-6901
801-538-3800
800-439-3805
www.insurance.state.ut.us

Labor Department
Utah Department of Workforce
Services
P.O. Box 45249
Salt Lake City, UT 84145-0249
801-526-9675
http://jobs.utah.gov

Licensing Office
Division of Occupational and
Professional Licensing
Department of Commerce
P.O. Box 146741
Salt Lake City, UT 84114-6741
801-530-6628
866-275-3675
www.commerce.state.ut.us/opl

One-Stop Career Center
Career Centers
Department of Workforce
Services
P.O. Box 45249
Salt Lake City, UT 84145-0249
801-526-9675

Fax: 801-526-9211
http://jobs.utah.gov

Security Regulators
Securities Division
P.O. Box 146760
Salt Lake City, UT 84114-6760
801-530-6600
www.commerce.state.ut.us/

Small Business Development Center
Small Business Development Ctr.
Salt Lake Community College
1623 South State Street
Salt Lake City, UT 84115
801-957-3480
Fax: 801-957-3489
Email: FinnerMi@slcc.edu
www.slcc.edu/sbdc

Social Services Offices
Utah Dept. of Human Services
120 North 200 West
Salt Lake City, UT 84103
801-538-4100
www.dhs.state.ut.us

Temporary Assistance to Needy Families (TANF)
Temporary Aid to Needy Families
Robin Arnold Williams
Utah Dept. of Human Services

120 North 200 West, Suite 225
Salt Lake City, UT 84103
801-538-4100
www.dhs.state.ut.us

Transportation Department
Glenda Seelos
Utah Department of
Transportation
Mail Stop 141200
4501 South 2700 West
Salt Lake City, UT 84114-1200
801-965-4000
www.dot.state.ut.us

Unclaimed Property Office
State Treasurer's Office
Unclaimed Property Division
E315 Capitol Complex
P.O. Box 142315
Salt Lake City. UT 84114-2315
801-538-1042
www.treasurer.state.ut.us

Unemployment Insurance Office
Director Unemployment
Insurance
Workforce Services
140 East 300 South
P.O. Box 45249
Salt Lake City, UT 84145-0249
801-526-9675

http://ui.dws.state.ut.us
Weekly benefit range: $20-377
Duration of benefits: 10-26 weeks

Utility Commission
Public Service Commission
160 East, 300 South
Salt Lake City, UT 84111
801-530-6716
www.psc.state.ut.us

Women's Commission
Utah Governor's Commission for
Women and Families
140 East, 300 South
Salt Lake City, UT 84111
801-526-9281
Fax: 801-526-9238
www.governor.state.ut.us/women/

Your Senator
United States Senate
Washington, DC 20510
202-224-3121
www.senate.gov

Your Representative
United States House of
Representatives
Washington, DC 20515
202-224-3121
www.house.gov

VERMONT

Federal Information Center
1-800-FED-INFO
www.firstgov.gov
www.pueblo.gsa.gov/call/

State Information Office
802-828-1110
http://vermont.gov

Department on Aging
Vermont Department of Aging
and Independent Living
103 S. Main St.
Waterbury, VT 05671
802-241-2400
www.dad.state.vt.us/

Attorney General's Office
Office of the Attorney General
109 State Street
Montpelier, VT 05609-1001
802-828-3171
TTY: 802-828-3665
Fax: 802-828-2154
www.state.vt.us/atg
Email: consumer@uvm.edu

Banking Commissioner
Commissioner of Banking and
Insurance Securities
89 Main St., Drawer 20
Montpelier, VT 05620-3101
802-828-3301
www.bishca.state.vt.us

**Child Care and Development
Block Grant Lead Agency**
Child Care Services Division
Vermont Department of Social
and Rehabilitation Services
103 S. Main St., 2nd Floor
Waterbury, VT 05671
802-241-3110
Fax: 802-241-1220
www.state.vt.us/srs/childcare

**Child Support Enforcement
Agency**
Jeffery Cohen
Office of Child Support
103 South Main St.
Waterbury, VT 05671-1901
800-786-3214

Fax: 802-244-1483
www.ocs.state.vt.us

Cooperative Extension Office
Dr. Larry Forchier, Dean
Division of Agriculture, Natural
Resources, and Extension
University of Vermont
601 Main Street
Burlington, VT 05405
802-656-8679
www.uvm.edu/extension

Corporation Division Office
Corporate Division
Secretary of State
81 River Street
Montpelier, VT 05609-1104
802-828-2386
www.sec.state.vt.us

Day Care Licensing Agency
Department of Social and
Rehabilitation Services
Child Care Licensing Unit
103 S. Main St.
Montpelier, VT 05761-2901
802-241-2131
www.state.vt.us/srs/

Economic Development Office
Dept. of Economic Development
National Life Building, Drawer 20
Montpelier, VT 05620-0501
802-828-3080
Fax: 802-828-3258
www.thinkvermont.com

Department of Education
Vermont Department of
Education
School Finance Department
State Office Bldg.
120 State St.
Montpelier, VT 05620-2501
802-828-3135
www.state.vt.us/educ/

**Department of Higher
Education**
Vermont Student Assistance
Corporation
P.O. Box 2000

Winooski, VT 05404
888-253-4819
802-654-3798
www.vsac.org

Health Department
Vermont Department of Health
108 Cherry Street
Burlington, VT 05402-0070
802-863-7200
800-464-4343
Fax: 802-865-7754
www.healthyvemonters.info

Housing Offices
Vermont Housing Finance
Agency
One Burlington Sq.
164 St. Paul St.
Burlington, VT 05401-4364
802-864-5743
www.vhfa.org

Vermont State Housing Authority
1 Prospect St.
Montpelier, VT 05602
802-828-3295
800-820-5119
www.vsha.org

Insurance Commissioner
Commissioner of Banking and
Insurance
89 Main St., Drawer 20
Montpelier, VT 05620-3101
802-828-3301
www.bishca.state.vt.us/

Labor Department
Vermont Department of
Employment and Training
5 Green Mountain Drive
P.O. Box 488
Montpelier, VT 05601-0488
802-828-4000
www.det.state.vt.us

Licensing Office
Office of Professional Regulation
Secretary of State
26 Terrace Street
Drawer 09
Montpelier, VT 05609-1101

802-828-2363
http://vtprofessionals.org

One-Stop Career Center
One-Stop Career Resource
Department of Employment and
Training
Division of Jobs and Training
5 Green Mountain Drive
P.O. Box 488
Montpelier, VT 05601-0488
802-828-4000
Fax: 802-828-4022
www.det.state.vt.us

Security Regulators
Department of Banking,
Insurance, Securities & Health
Care Administration
Securities Division
89 Main St., Drawer 20
Montpelier, VT 05620-3101
802-828-3420
www.bishca.state.vt.us

Small Business Development Center
Vermont Small Business
Devlopment Center
P.O. Box 188
Randolph, VT 05061-0188
802-728-9101
800-464-SBDC
Fax: 802-728-3026
www.vtsbdc.org
Email: dkelpins@vtsbdc.org

Social Services Offices
Vermont Agency of Human
Services

103 South Main Street
Waterbury, VT 05671-0201
802-241-2220
www.ahs.state.vt.us

Temporary Assistance to Needy Families (TANF)
Temporary Aid to Needy Families
Jane Kitchel
Vermont Dept. of Social Welfare
103 South Main St.
Waterbury, VT 05671-0201
802-241-2889
www.dsw.state.vt.us/
wrp/tanf_stp.htm

Transportation Department
William Peabody
Vermont Agency of
Transportation
133 State St.
Montpelier, VT 05633
802-828-2828
www.aot.state.vt.us

Unclaimed Property Office
Abandoned Property Division
State Treasurer's Office
133 State St.
Montpelier, VT 05633
802-828-2301
www.tre.state.vt.us

Unemployment Insurance Office
Unemployment Insurance
Dept. of Employment and
Training
5 Green Mountain Dr.
P.O. Box 488

Montpelier, VT 05601-0488
802-828-4242
www.det.state.vt.us/

Utility Commission
Public Service Board
112 State St.
Chittenden Bank Bldg.
4th Floor, Drawer 20
Montpelier, VT 05620-2701
802-828-2358
www.state.vt.us/psb

Women's Commission
Vermont Governor's Commission
on the Status of Women
126 State St.
Montpelier, VT 05633-6801
802-828-2851
800-881-1561
Fax: 802-828-2930
www.women.state.vt.us

Your Senator
United States Senate
Washington, DC 20510
202-224-3121
www.senate.gov

Your Representative
United States House of
Representatives
Washington, DC 20515
202-224-3121
www.house.gov

VIRGINIA

Federal Information Center
1-800-FED-INFO
www.firstgov.gov
www.pueblo.gsa.gov/call/

State Information Office
804-786-0000
www.virginia.gov

Department on Aging
Aging Department
1600 Forest Ave., Suite 100
Richmond, VA 23229
804-662-9333
800-552-3402
www.aging.state.va.us/

Attorney General's Office
Office of the Attorney General
900 East Main Street
Richmond, VA 23219
804-786-2071
www.oag.state.va.us
Email: mail@oag.state.va.us

Banking Commissioner
Bureau of Financial Institutions
1300 E. Main St., Suite 800
P.O. Box 640
Richmond, VA 23218-0640
804-371-9657
www.state.va.us/scc/division/
banking/index.htm

Child Care and Development Block Grant Lead Agency
Virginia Department of Social
Services
Child Day Care
7 N. Eighth Street
Richmond, VA 23219
804-726-7000
www.dss.state.va.us/

Child Support Enforcement Agency
Asst. Commissioner for Child
Support Enforcement
Department of Social Services
7 North Eighth Street
Richmond, VA 23219
804-726-7000
800-257-9986 (in VA)

www.dss.state.va.us/family/dcse.
html

Cooperative Extension Offices
Virginia Cooperative Extension
Virginia Tech
Blacksburg, VA 24061-0402
540-231-5299
www.ext.vt.edu/

Corporation Division Office
Clerk of Commission
State Corporation Commission
Secretary of State
P.O. Box 1197
Richmond, VA 23218
804-371-9967
800-552-7945
www.state.va.us/scc/index.html

Day Care Licensing Agency
Department of Social Services
Child Care Licensing Division
7 North EighthStreet
Richmond, VA 23219-1849
804-726-7000
www.dss.state.va.us/

Economic Development Office
Economic Development
Partnership
901 East Byrd Street
P.O. Box 798
Richmond, VA 23218-0798
804-371-8100
Fax: 804-371-8112
www.yesvirginia.org/

Department of Education
Virginia Department of Education
Management Information Office
101 N. 14th St., 22nd Floor
Richmond, VA 23219
MAILING ADDRESS:
P.O. Box 2120
Richmond, VA 23218
804-225-2540
800-292-3820
www.pen.k12.va.us/

Department of Higher Education
Virginia State Council of Higher
Education

Office of Financial Aid
James Monroe Building
101 North 14th Street, 9th Floor
Richmond, VA 23219
804-225-2600
Fax: 804-225-2604
www.schev.edu/

Health Department
Virginia Department of Health
P.O. Box 2448
Richmond, VA 23218-2448
804-864-7001
www.vdh.state.va.us/

Housing Office
Virginia Housing Development
Authority
601 S. Belvedere St.
Richmond, VA 23220
804-782-1986
800-968-7837
www.vhda.com

Insurance Commissioner
Commissioner of Insurance
1300 E. Main St.
P.O. Box 1157
Richmond, VA 23218
804-371-9741
800-552-7945 (VA only)
www.state.va.us/scc/division/
boi/index.htm

Labor Department
Virginia Department of Labor and
Industry
13 South Thirteenth Street
Richmond, VA 23219-4104
804-371-2327
www.dli.state.va.us

Licensing Office
Virginia Dept. of Professional and
Occupational Regulation
3600 W. Broad St.
Richmond, VA 23230
804-367-8500
www.state.va.us/dpor/

One-Stop Career Center
Workforce Development System
Employment Commission

P.O. Box 1358
Richmond, VA 23218-1358
804-786-1485
800-828-1140
www.vec.state.va.us/

Security Regulators
Virginia Division of Securities
P.O. Box 1197
Richmond, VA 23218
804-371-9051
800-552-7945
www.state.va.us/scc/division/srf/index.htm

Small Business Development Center
Virginia Small Business
Development Center
4031 University Drive
Suite 200
Fairfax, VA 22030
703-277-7700
www.virginiasbdc.org

Social Services Offices
Virginia Dept. of Social Services
7 North Eighth Street
Richmond, VA 23219
804-726-7000
www.dss.state.va.us

Temporary Assistance to Needy Families (TANF)
Temporary Aid to Needy Families
Department of Social Services
7 North Eighth Street
Richmond, VA 23219
804-726-7000
www.dss.state.va.us/benefit/tanf.html

Transportation Department
Virginia Department of
Transportation

1221 E. Broad Street
Richmond, VA 23219
804-786-2801
http://virginiadot.org

Virginia Department of Rail and
Public Transportation
1313 East Main Street
Suite 300
Richmond, VA 23218-0590
804-786-4440
www.drpt.state.va.us

Unclaimed Property Office
Division of Unclaimed Property
Department of Treasury
P.O. Box 2478
Richmond, VA 23218-2478
804-225-2142
800-468-1088
www.trs.state.va.us/

Unemployment Insurance Office
Field Operations
Virginia Employment Commission
703 E. Main St.
Richmond, VA 23219
804-786-3466
www.vec.state.va.us
Weekly benefit range: $55-326
Duration of benefits: 12-26 weeks

Utility Commission
State Corporation Commission
P.O. Box 1197
Richmond, VA 23218-1197
804-371-9420
800-552-7945 (VA only)
www.state.va.us/scc/division/puc/index.htm

Women's Commission
Alexandria Council on the Status
of Women

421 King Street, Suite 400
Alexandria, VA 22314
703-838-5030
Fax: 703-838-4976
http://ci.alexandria.va.us/alexandria/oow

Arlington Commission on the
Status of Women
2100 Clarendon Blvd., Suite 414
Arlington, VA 22201
703-228-3314
TTY: 703-228-4611
www.arlingtonva.us

Fairfax City Commission for
Women
10455 Armstrong St.
Fairfax, VA 22030
703-385-7894
Fax: 703-385-7811
www.ci.fairfax.va.us/host/women/cfw.html

Fairfax County Commission for
Women
12000 Government Center Pkwy.
Suite 318
Fairfax, VA 22035
703-324-5720
Fax: 703-324-3959
TTY: 703-324-5706

Your Senator
United States Senate
Washington, DC 20510
202-224-3121
www.senate.gov

Your Representative
United States House of
Representatives
Washington, DC 20515
202-224-3121
www.house.gov

WASHINGTON

Federal Information Center
1-800-FED-INFO
www.firstgov.gov
www.pueblo.gsa.gov/call/

State Information Office
360-753-5000
http://access.wa.gov

Department on Aging
Aging and Adult Services
P.O. Box 45050
Olympia, WA 98504-5600
800-422-3263
www.aasa.dshs.wa.gov

Attorney General's Office
Office of the Attorney General
P.O. Box 40100
1125 Washington Street, SE
Olympia, WA 98504-0100
360-753-6200
800-551-4636
www.wa.gov/ago

Banking Commissioner
Department of Financial
Institutions
Division of Banking
P.O. Box 41200
Olympia, WA 98504-1200
360-902-8700
800-372-8303
www.dfi.wa.gov/banks

**Child Care and Development
Block Grant Lead Agency**
Division of Child Care and Early
Learning
Washington Department of Social
and Health Services
P.O. Box 45480
Olympia, WA 98504-5480
360-413-3209
Fax: 360-413-3482
www1.dshs.wa.gov

**Child Support Enforcement
Agency**
Meg Sollenberger
Division of Child Support, DSHS
P.O. Box 11520
Tacoma, WA 98411-5520

360-586-3162
360-586-3274
800-442-KIDS
www1.dshs.wa.gov

Cooperative Extension Office
Dr. Harry Burcalow, Director
Cooperative Extension
411 Hulbert
Washington State University
Pullman, WA 99164-6230
509-335-2837
http://ext.wsu.edu

Corporation Division Office
Corporate Division
Secretary of State
P.O. Box 40234
Olympia, WA 98504-0234
360-753-7115
www.secstate.wa.gov

Day Care Licensing Agency
Office of Child Care Policy
Child Care Licensing Division
P.O. Box 45480
Olympia, WA 98504
360-902-8038
www1.wa.gov/dshs

Economic Development Office
Department of Community,
Trade, and Economic
Development
128 10th Ave., SW
P.O. Box 42525
Olympia, WA 98504-2525
360-725-4000
www.cted.wa.gov

Department of Education
Washington State Board of
Education
P.O. Box 47206
Olympia, WA 98504
360-725-6025
www.sbe.wa.gov

**Department of Higher
Education**
Higher Education Coordinating
Board
917 Lakeridge Way

P.O. Box 43430
Olympia, WA 98504-3430
360-753-7800
www.hecb.wa.gov

Health Department
Washington State Department of
Health
P.O. Box 47890
Olympia, WA 98504-7890
360-236-4030
800-525-0127
www.doh.wa.gov/

Housing Office
Washington State Housing
Finance Commission
1000 Second Ave., Suite 2700
Seattle, WA 98104-1046
206-464-7139
800-767-4663
www.wshfc.org

Insurance Commissioner
Insurance Commissioner
Insurance Bldg. AQ21
P.O. Box 40255
Olympia, WA 98504-0255
360-725-7200
800-562-6900
www.insurance.wa.gov

Labor Department
Washington Workforce Training
and Education Coordinating
Board
128-10th Avenue SW
P.O. Box 43105
Olympia, WA 98504-3105
360-753-5662
www.wtb.wa.gov

Licensing Office
Department of Licensing
P.O. Box 9020
Olympia, WA 98507-9020
360-902-3600
www.wa.gov/dol/

One-Stop Career Center
Washington One-Stop Career
Center System
Employment Security Department

212 Maple Park
P.O. Box 9046
Olympia, WA 98507-9046
360-902-9302
877-348-0502
www.wa.gov/esd/1stop

Security Regulators
Department of Financial
Institutions
Securities Division
P.O. Box 9033
Olympia, WA 98507-9033
360-902-8760
800-372-8303
www.dfi.wa.gov/sd

Small Business Development Center
Washington State Small Business
Development Center
Washington State University
College of Business and
Economics
501 Johnson Tower
MAILING ADDRESS:
P.O. Box 644851
Pullman, WA 99164-4851
509-335-1576
Fax: 509-335-0949
Email: riesenbe@wsu.edu
www.wssbdc.org

Social Services Offices
Washington Department of Social
and Health Services
DSHS Constituent Services
P.O. Box 45130

Olympia, WA 98504-5130
360-902-7892
www1.dshs.wa.gov

Temporary Assistance to Needy Families (TANF)
Temporary Aid to Needy Families
Roxane Lowe
Department of Social and Health
Services
P.O. Box 45100
Olympia, WA 98504
360-725-4668
www1.dshs.wa.gov

Transportation Department
Barbara Savary
Washington State Department of
Transportation
P.O. Box 47300
Olympia, WA 98504-7300
306-705-7000
www.wsdot.wa.gov/

Unclaimed Property Office
Unclaimed Property Section
Department of Revenue
P.O. Box 47477
Olympia, WA 98504-7477
360-705-6706
http://dor.wa.gov/

Unemployment Insurance Office
Assistant Commissioner
Employment Security Department
P.O. Box 9046
Olympia, WA 98507

360-902-9303
http://fortress.wa.gov/esd/portal/u
nemployment
Weekly benefit range: $82-384
Duration of benefits: 10-30 weeks

Utility Commission
Utilities and Transportation
Commission
1300 S. Evergreen Park Dr. SW
Olympia, WA 98504-7250
360-664-1160
800-562-6150 (WA only)
www.wutc.wa.gov/

Women's Commission
Seattle Women's Commission
c/o Seattle Office for Civil Rights
700 Third Ave, Suite 250
Seattle WA 98104-1849
206-684-4537
Fax: 206-684-0332
www.cityofseattle.net/womensco
mmission

Your Senator
United States Senate
Washington, DC 20510
202-224-3121
www.senate.gov

Your Representative
United States House of
Representatives
Washington, DC 20515
202-224-3121
www.house.gov

WEST VIRGINIA

Federal Information Center
1-800-FED-INFO
www.firstgov.gov
www.pueblo.gsa.gov/call/

State Information Office
304-558-3456
www.wv.gov

Department on Aging
Bureau of Senior Services
1900 Kanawha Blvd.
State Capitol
Holly Grove, Building #10
Charleston, WV 25305-0160
304-558-3317
www.state.wv.us/seniorservices

Attorney General's Office
Office of the Attorney General
1900 Kanawha Blvd., Room 26E
Charleston, WV 25305-9925
304-558-2021
800-368-8808
www.wvs.state.wv.us/wvag

Banking Commissioner
Commissioner of Banking
State Capitol Complex
1900 Kanawha Blvd. East
Bldg. 3, Room 311
Charleston, WV 25305-0240
304-558-2294
www.wvdob.org

**Child Care and Development
Block Grant Lead Agency**
Day Care and Licensing
Division of Early Care and
Education
350 Capitol Street
Room B-18
Charleston, WV 25301
304-558-1885
Fax: 304-558-2059
www.wvdhhr.org/

**Child Support Enforcement
Agency**
Child Support Enforcement
Division
Department of Health and Human
Resources

350 Capitol Street, Room 147
Charleston, WV 25301-3703
304-558-3780
Fax: 304-558-4092
www.wrdhhr.org/bcse

Cooperative Extension Office
Robert Maxwell, Interim Director
Cooperative Extension
507 Knapt Hall
P.O. Box 6031
West Virginia University
Morgantown, WV 26506-6031
304-293-4221
www.wvu.edu/~exten

Corporation Division Office
Corporate Division
Secretary of State
Room 139 West, State Capitol
Charleston, WV 25305
304-558-6000
866-SOS-VOTE
www.wvsos.com

Day Care Licensing Agency
Department of Health and Human
Resources
Day Care Licensing
350 Capitol Street
Room B-18
Charleston, WV 25301
34-558-1885
www.wvdhhr.org/oss/

Economic Development Office
West Virginia Development Office
1900 Kanawha Blvd., East
Charleston, WV 25305-0311
304-558-2234
800-982-3386
Fax: 304-558-0449
www.wvdo.org

Department of Education
West Virginia Dept. of Education
Dept. of Statistical Information
Bldg. 6, Room 351
1900 Kanawha Blvd. E.
Charleston, WV 25305-0330
304-558-3660
http://wvde.state.wv.us/

**Department of Higher
Education**
State College and University
Systems Central Office
1018 Kanawha Boulevard East,
Suite 700
Charleston, WV 25301-2800
304-558-2101
www.hepc.wvnet.edu

Health Department
West Virginia Bureau for Public
Health
350 Capitol Street, Room 702
Charelston, WV 25301-2971
304-558-2971
Fax: 304-558-1035
www.wvdhhr.org/bph/index.htm

Housing Office
West Virginia Housing
Development Fund
814 Virginia St., East
Charleston, WV 25301
304-345-6475
www.wvhdf.com/

Insurance Commissioner
Insurance Commissioner
1124 Smith Street
Charleston, WV 25301
304-558-3354
888-879-9842
www.state.wv.us/insurance/

Labor Department
West Virginia Bureau of
Employment Programs
112 California Avenue
Charleston, WV 25305-0112
304-558-7800
800-252-5627
www.state.wv.us/bep

Licensing Office
Secretary of State
State Capitol
Charleston, WV 25305
304-558-6000
www.wvsos.com

One-Stop Career Center
Job Service

Bureau of Employment Programs
Jobs/Job Training
112 California Avenue
Charleston, WV 25305-0112
304-558-1138
Fax: 304-558-1136
www.state.wv.us/bep/jobs/

Security Regulators
West Virginia Securities Division
State Capitol, Building 1
Room W-100
Charleston, WV 25305
304-558-2257
www.wvauditor.com

Small Business Development Center
West Virginia Small Business
Development Center
West Virginia Development Office
1900 Kanawha Boulevard
Charleston, WV 25305-0311
304-558-2960
Fax: 304-558-0127
Email: palmeh@mail.wvnet.edu
www.sbdcwv.org

Social Services Offices
West Virginia Department of
Health and Human Resources
State Capital Complex
Building 3, Room 218
Charleston, WV 25305
304-558-0684
www.wvdhhr.org

Temporary Assistance to Needy Families (TANF)
Temporary Aid to Needy Families
West Virginia Department of
Health and Human Resources
350 Capitol Street
Room 730
Charleston, WV 25301
304-558-4069
www.wvdhhr.org/bcf/tanf.asp

Transportation Department
Toni Boyd
West Virginia Department of
Transportation
1900 Kanawha Boulevard
East Building 5, Room 803
Charleston, WV 25305
304-558-3505
www.wvdot.com

Unclaimed Property Office
One Players Club Drive
Charleston, WV 25305
304-558-2937
800-642-8687
www.wvtreasury.com

Unemployment Insurance Office
Director, Unemployment
Compensation Division
Bureau of Employment Programs
112 California Ave. Room 508
Charleston, WV 25305
304-558-2624

www.state.wv.us/bep/uc/
default.htm

Utility Commission
Public Service Commission
201 Brooks St.
Charleston, WV 25301
304-340-0300
800-344-5113 (WV only)
www.psc.state.wv.us

Women's Commission
West Virginia Women's
Commission
Building 6, Room 850
Capitol Complex
Charleston, WV 25305
304-558-0070
Fax: 304-558-5167
www.wvdhhr.org/women/index.asp

Your Senator
United States Senate
Washington, DC 20510
202-224-3121
www.senate.gov

Your Representative
United States House of
Representatives
Washington, DC 20515
202-224-3121
www.house.gov

WISCONSIN

Federal Information Center
1-800-FED-INFO
www.firstgov.gov
www.pueblo.gsa.gov/call/

State Information Office
608-266-2211
www.wisconsin.gov

Department on Aging
Division of Disability and Elderly
Services
P.O. Box 7851
Madison, WI 53707-7851
608-266-0554
www.dhfs.state.wi.us

Attorney General's Office
Office of the Attorney General
Department of Justice
State Capitol, Suite 114 East
P.O. Box 7857
Madison, WI 53707-7857
608-266-1221
www.doj.state.wi.us

Banking Commissioner
Commissioner of Banking
345 W. Washington Ave., 4th
Floor
Madison, WI 53703
608-261-7578
www.wdfi.org/

**Child Care and Development
Block Grant Lead Agency**
Wisconsin Department of
Workforce Development
Office of Child Care
P.O. Box 7946
Madison, WI 53707-7935
608-266-0327
Fax: 608-261-6376
www.dwd.state.wi.us/dws/progra
ms/childcare

**Child Support Enforcement
Agency**
Bureau of Child Support
Division of Economic Support
P.O. Box 7946
Madison, WI 53707-7946
608-266-9909

Fax: 608-627-2824
www.dwd.state.wi.us/bcs/

Cooperative Extension Office
Dr. Aeyse Somersan, Director
432 North Lake Street, Room 601
Madison, WI 53706
608-262-3980
www.uwex.edu/ces

Corporation Division Office
Corporate Division
P.O. Box 7846
Madison, WI 53707-7846
608-266-7577
www.wdfi.org

Day Care Licensing Agency
Department of Health and Social
Services
Child Care Licensing Division
P.O. Box 8916
Madison, WI 53708-8916
608-266-9314
www.dhfs.state.wi.us/rl_dcfs

Economic Development Office
Department of Commerce
201 W. Washington Avenue
Madison, WI 53703
608-266-1018
www.commerce.state.wi.us

Department of Education
Wisconsin Department of Public
Instruction
Center for Education Statistics
125 S. Webster
P.O. Box 7841
Madison, WI 53707-7841
608-266-3390
800-441-4563
www.dpi.state.wi.us/

**Department of Higher
Education**
State of Wisconsin Higher
Educational Aids Board
P.O. Box 7885
Madison, WI 53707-7885
608-267-2206
Fax: 608-267-2808
http://heab.state.wi.us

Health Department
Wisconsin Department of Health
& Family Services
1 West Wilson Street
Madison, WI 53702-0007
608-266-1865
TTY: 608-267-7371
www.dhfs.state.wi.us

Housing Office
Wisconsin Housing and
Economic Development Authority
P.O. Box 1728
Madison, WI 53701-1728
608-266-7884
800-334-6873
www.wheda.com

Insurance Commissioner
Commissioner of Insurance
P.O. Box 7873
Madison, WI 53707-7873
608-266-3585
800-236-8517
http://oci.wi.gov/oci_home.htm

Labor Department
Wisconsin Department of
Workforce Development
P.O. Box 7946
Madison, WI 53707-7946
608-266-1093
www.dwd.state.wi.us

Licensing Office
Department of Regulation and
Licensing
P.O. Box 8935
Madison, WI 53708-8935
608-266-2112
http://drl.wi.gov

One-Stop Career Center
Partnership for Full Employment
(PFE)
Department of Workforce
Development
201 East Washington Avenue
P.O. Box 7946
Madison, WI 53707-7946
608-266-3131
Fax: 608-261-1784
www.dwd.state.wi.us/dwd

Security Regulators
Division of Securities
P.O. Box 1768
Madison, WI 53701-1768
608-266-1064
www.wdfi.org

Small Business Development Center
Wisconsin Small Business
Development Center
University of Wisconsin
Center of Innovation
278 Jarvis Hall
UW-Stout
Menomonie, WI 54715-0790
715-232-1457
www.wisconsinsbdc.org

Social Services Offices
Wisconsin Department of Health
and Family Services
1 West Wilson Street
Madison, WI 53702
608-266-1683
www.dhfs.state.wi.us

Temporary Assistance to Needy Families (TANF)
Temporary Aid to Needy Families
Work Force Development

P.O. Box 7946
Madison, WI 53707
608-266-3131
www.dwd.state.wi.us/dws/tanf

Transportation Department
Wisconsin Bureau of Transit and
Local Roads
P.O. Box 7910
Madison, WI 53707-7910
608-262-7988
www.dot.state.wi.us

Unclaimed Property Office
Unclaimed Property Division
State Treasurer's Office
P.O. Box 2114
Madison, WI 53701-2114
608-267-7977
www.ost.state.wi.us/

Unemployment Insurance Office
Administrator
Division of Unemployment
Insurance
201 E. Washington Ave.
Room 371
P.O. Box 7905
Madison, WI 53707-7905
608-266-3100

800-494-4944
www.dwd.state.wi.us/ui/

Utility Commission
Public Service Commission
610 North Whitney Way
Madison, WI 53707
608-266-2001
800-225-7729
www.psc.state.wi.us

Women's Commission
Wisconsin Women's Council
101 East Wilson, 8th Floor
Madison, WI 53702
608-266-2219
Fax: 608-267-0626
http://womenscouncil.wi.gov

Your Senator
United States Senate
Washington, DC 20510
202-224-3121
www.senate.gov

Your Representative
United States House of
Representatives
Washington, DC 20515
202-224-3121
www.house.gov

WYOMING

Federal Information Center
1-800-FED-INFO
www.firstgov.gov
www.pueblo.gsa.gov/call/

State Information Office
307-777-7011
http://wyoming.gov

Department on Aging
Division on Aging
Department of Health
6101 Yellowstone Rd, Room 259B
Cheyenne, WY 82002
307-777-7986
800-442-2766
http://wdhfs.state.wy.us/aging

Attorney General's Office
Office of the Attorney General
123 Capitol Building
200 West 24th Street
Cheyenne, WY 82002
307-777-7841
800-438-5799 (consumer complaints)
TDD: 307-777-5351
http://attorneygeneral.state.wy.us

Banking Commissioner
Banking Commissioner
Division of Banking
Department of Audit
Herschler Bldg., 3rd Floor E.
Cheyenne, WY 82002
307-777-7797
http://audit.state.wy.us/ banking/

Child Care and Development Block Grant Lead Agency
CCDBG Administrator
Wyoming Department of Family Services
Hathaway Building
2300 Capitol Ave.
Cheyenne, WY 82002-0490
307-777-6595
http://dfsweb.state.wy.us/

Child Support Enforcement Agency
James Mohler

Child Support Enforcement Program
Department of Family Services
Hathaway Building
2300 Capital Ave.
Cheyenne, WY 82002-0490
307-777-6948
Fax: 307-777-3693
http://dfsweb.state.wy.us/ csehome/cs.htm

Cooperative Extension Office
Darryl Kautzman, Director
CES
University of Wyoming
Box 3354
Laramie, WY 82071-3354
307-766-5124
www.uwyo.edu/ces/ceshome.htm

Corporation Division Office
Corporate Division
Secretary of State
State of Wyoming
Capitol Building, Room 110
Cheyenne, WY 82002-0020
307-777-7311
http://soswy.state.wy.us

Day Care Licensing Agency
Department of Family Services
Office of Child Care Licensing
Hathaway Building, Room 323
2300 Capitol Ave.
Cheyenne, WY 82002-0490
307-777-6285
http://dfsweb.state.wy.us/

Economic Development Office
Wyoming Business Council
214 W. 15th St.
Cheyenne, WY 82002-0204
307-777-2800
800-262-3425
Fax: 307-777-2838
www.wyomingbusiness.org

Department of Education
Wyoming Department of Education
Statistical Department
Hathaway Bldg., 2nd Floor
2300 Capitol Ave.

Cheyenne, WY 82002-0050
307-777-7673
www.k12.wy.us/

Department of Higher Education
Wyoming Department of Higher Education
Hathaway Building
2300 Capitol Avenue
Cheyenne, WY 82002
307-777-6213

Health Department
Wyoming Department of Health
2300 Capitol Avenue
MAILING ADDRESS:
117 Hathaway Building
Cheyenne, WY 82002
307-777-7657
Fax: 307-777-7439
TTY: 307-777-5648
http://wdhfs.state.wy.us/wdh/
Email: wdh@missc.state.wy.us

Housing Office
Wyoming Community Development Authority
155 North Beach
Casper, WY 82602
307-265-0603
www.wyomingcda.com

Insurance Commissioner
Commissioner of Insurance
Herschler Bldg. 3 East
122 W. 25th St.
Cheyenne, WY 82002
307-777-7401
800-438-5768
http://insurance.state.wy.us

Labor Department
Wyoming Dept. of Employment
122 West 25th Street
Cheyenne, WY 82002
307-777-7672
http://wydoe.state.wy.us/

Licensing Office
Governor's Office
State Capitol
Cheyenne, WY 82002

307-777-7434
www.state.wy.us/governor/
governor_home.html

One-Stop Career Center
Employment Resource Centers
Department of Employment
Employment Resource Division
100 West Midwest
Casper, WY 82602
307-235-3254
http://wydoe.state.wy.us/erd

Security Regulators
Securities Division
Secretary of State
24th Street & State Capitol Ave.
Cheyenne, WY 82002
307-777-7370
http://soswy.state.wy.us

Small Business Development Center
Wyoming Small Business
Development Center
University of Wyoming
P.O. Box 3922
Laramie, WY 82071-3922
307-766-3505
800-348-5194
Fax: 307-766-3406
Email: DDW@uwyo.edu
www.uwyo.edu/sbdc

Social Services Offices
Wyoming Department of Family
Services
Hathaway Building

Cheyenne, WY 82002-0490
307-777-3679
dfsweb.state.wy.us

Temporary Assistance to Needy Families (TANF)
Temporary Aid to Needy Families
Marianne Lee
Department of Family Services
2300 Capitol Ave.
Hathaway Building, 3rd Floor
Cheyenne, WY 82002
307-777-7531
http://dfsweb.state.wy.us/

Transportation Department
John Black
State Highway Department
P.O. Box 1708
Cheyenne, WY 82003
307-777-4375
http://wydotweb.state.wy.us

Unclaimed Property Office
Unclaimed Property Division
State Treasurer's Office
1st Floor West, Herschler Bldg.
122 West 25th St.
Cheyenne, WY 82008
307-777-5590
http://treasurer.state.wy.us

Unemployment Insurance Office
Administrator, Division of
Unemployment Insurance
Department of Employment
P.O. Box 2760

Casper, WY 82602
307-235-3254
http://wydoe.state.wy.us/
Weekly benefit range: $18-250
Duration of benefits: 12-26 weeks

Utility Commission
Public Service Commission
2515 Warren Ave.
Hansen Bldg., Suite 300
Cheyenne, WY 82002
307-777-7427
http://psc.state.wy.us

Women's Commission
Wyoming State Government
Commission for Women
c/o Department of Employment
Herschler Building
122 West 25th St.
Cheyenne, WY 82002
307-777-7671
http://wydoe.state.wy.us
Amy McClure, Chair

Your Senator
United States Senate
Washington, DC 20510
202-224-3121
www.senate.gov

Your Representative
United States House of
Representatives
Washington, DC 20515
202-224-3121
www.house.gov

Index

A

Abbott Laboratories
  financial assistance for employees,
  404
Abortions, 134
Accounting
  free services, 64
Acid rain, 464
Activism
  grants for projects, 454
  money for non-profit organizations,
  491
Actors
  financial assistance, 293
  health care programs, 293
  money for shoes, 274
  scholarship programs, 293
Adoption, 122, 423, 465
  tax credits, 501
Advocacy groups
  medical, 126, 127
African Americans
  college money programs, 330
  education grants, 327
Agency For International
  Development, 551
Aggression
  money for research, 336
Aging benefits checkup, 410
Agriculture graduates
  student loan forgiveness, 384
Agriculture, U.S. Department of
  Foreign Agricultural Service, 551
  SBIR grants, 92
AIDS
  financial assistance for victims, 407
  housing programs for persons with,
  201
  money for actors, 294
  money for artists, 282
  money for writers, 294
Air courier services, 421
Air Force, U.S., 550
Air travel
  research, 533
  bereavement fares, 420
Airfare reduced, 420

Airline discounts, 426
Airlines
  business assistance, 75
  commuter, 65
Airports
  business grants, 74
  financial assistance, 91
Alabama
  discount drug programs, 138
Alaska
  community development programs,
  207
  discount drug programs, 139
  student loan forgiveness, 383
Alaskan Natives
  college money programs, 322
Alcohol
  substance abuse treatment, 121, 124
Alcoholism
  treatment programs, 134
Alliant Energy
  community grants, 517
Allstate
  community grants, 518
All-Volunteer Force Educational
  Assistance, 368
American art
  money programs for doctoral
  dissertations, 283
American Bar Association, 482
American Cancer Society, 124, 131
American Civil Liberties Union, 476
American Lung Association, 122
American Red Cross, 415
  assistance for veterans, 415
American University
  student loan forgiveness, 382
AmeriCorps, 369, 544
  loan forgiveness, 375
Angel Tree, 416
Anthropological research
  scholarships, 350
Apartment buildings, 202
  grants, 221
  mortgages, 195
Apprenticeship programs, 440, 442
Aquariums
  financial assistance, 85

Botanical gardens
   financial assistance, 85
Breakfast programs, 126
Breast cancer, 125
   legal assistance, 476
Brooklyn Law School
   student loan forgiveness, 381
Bureau of Health Professions, 360
Bureau of Indian Affairs, 366
Bus companies
   business grants, 75
Business
   certified loans, 108
   city money programs, 60
   county money programs, 60
   development assistance, 87
   development loans, 66
   disabled persons, 309
   employee purchase programs, 63
   federal money programs, 59
   financial assistance, 67, 72, 76, 86,
      87, 91, 106, 107, 108, 273, 274
   free accounting services, 64
   incubators, 72, 108
   mentoring services, 87
   money from non-profit
      organizations, 60
   money to help disabled persons, 84
   SBIR grants, 92
   starting, 61
   state money programs, 60
   technical assistance, 92
   technology transfer programs, 93
   training programs overseas, 544
Business education, 351
Business schools
   funding, 351
Businesses, starting
   child care centers, 409

C

California
   disability insurance, 309
   discount drug programs, 140
California State University
   student loan forgiveness, 380

Camping
   discounts, 426
   for children of prisoners, 416
   Salvation Army, 415
Cancer
   research overseas, 536
Cancer patients, 128
Cancer services, 131
   legal assistance, 476
Canine Companions for Independence,
   312
Canine Working Companions, 313
Career One-Stop, 447
Caregivers, 314
   financial benefits, 133
Cars
   complaints about, 483, 484
   free lease, 494
   free publications, 417
   how to buy, 418
   moving, 420, 421
   recalls, 419
   rental discounts, 422, 552
   repair, 417, 418
   tax deductions, 421
Caribbean
   study grants, 534
Catalog of Federal Domestic
   Assistance, 59, 487
Catholic Charities, 396
Catholic missions, 492
Center for International Education, 355
Central Intelligence Agency, 551
Cervical cancer, 125
Challenge grants, 496
Child care, 436, 451, 452
   block grants, 408
   business assistance, 65, 66
   corporate, 422, 423
   for Americorps and VISTA workers,
      422
   for teens with disabilities, 422
   how to choose a provider, 461
   money programs, 450
   subsidies, 408, 409, 422
   tax credits, 500
   Temporary Assistance for Needy
      Families, 422
   through nonprofit groups, 408

Eurasian and East European Research
and Training Program, 365
Europe
art project grants, 538
Export assistance, 64
Exports
agricultural products, 90
business assistance, 82
dairy products, 90
financial assistance, 71
Eyeglasses
discounts, 401

F

Faculty Loan Repayment Program,
360
Fair Housing Act
education, 209
Fair Housing and Equal Opportunity,
482
Fair housing programs, 210
Families
money to help, 453
Family and Medical Leave Act, 462
Family planning
government programs, 133
Farm labor
housing programs, 214
job training, 448
Farmers
conservation assistance, 90
financial assistance, 69, 70, 71
loans, 71
Federal Education Association, 478
Federal Employee Education
Assistance Program, 371
Federal Family Education Loans, 355
Federal government employees
student loan forgiveness, 384
Federal money programs, 393
Federal Perkins Loan Program, 356
Federal Supplemental Education
Opportunity Grants, 354
Federal Trade Commission, 101, 102,
423
Federal Transit Administration, 421

Fellowship programs, 332, 334, 335,
337
arts, 369
child welfare, 439
Etruscan studies, 349
math teachers, 512
medical students, 339
physical therapy, 338
religion teachers, 508
research Eastern Europe, 533
research foreign language
collections, 534
research in India, 539
research social sciences, 534
science teachers, 512
study in China, 534
study in Germany, 537
study overseas, 542
Film editors
study in New Zealand, 529
Films
money programs, 273, 274, 277,
279, 280, 297
money programs for high school
students, 287
money programs for women, 280
Financial aid websites, 370
Financial assistance
grades K-12, 466
rural housing, 215, 216
Fire safety, 460
First-time homebuyers programs, 167,
169
Fisheries
business assistance, 79
Fishermen
financial assistance, 73
Flight training, 440
Flood insurance, 212
Floral industry
study overseas, 528
Florida
discount drug programs, 142
Flu shots, 122
Food and Agricultural Science
National Needs Graduate
Fellowship Grants, 366
Food and Nutrition Service, 413, 414

Muslim students
  college money programs, 344, 345

N

National Administration on Aging, 413
National Adoption Foundation, 122, 423
National Aeronautics and Space Administration
  SBIR grants, 93
  technology transfer programs, 94
  undergraduate research, 527
National Association of Housing and Redevelopment Officials, 167
National Association of Working Women, 481
National Endowment for the Humanities, 364
National Health Service Corps Loan Repayment, 364
National Highway Traffic Safety Administration, 420
National Immunization Information Hotline, 123
National Institute for Literacy, 321
National Institutes of Health, 118
National Library Service, 427
National Oceanic and Atmospheric Administration
  mortgage subsidies, 193
National Park Service
  volunteers, 524, 553
National Rehabilitation Association, 304
National SAFEKIDS Campaign, 420
National Science Foundation, 368
  SBIR grants, 93
  technology transfer programs, 94
National Senior Service Corps, 428
Native Americans
  business assistance, 74
  college money programs, 322
  economic development assistance, 82
  farm assistance, 82
  financial assistance for artists, 282
  food distribution programs, 413

grant programs, 340
grants for housing, 222
grants for libraries, 513
home repair programs, 223
housing programs, 222, 223
job training, 448
money programs for artists, 280
mortgage assistance, 223
student aid, 361
Natural resources
  environmental quality programs, 219
Nature
  why leaves change color, 458
Nature centers
  financial assistance, 85
Navy, U.S., 550
Nebraska
  discount drug programs, 151
Nevada
  discount drug programs, 152
New Hampshire
  discount drug programs, 152
New Jersey
  disability insurance, 310
  discount drug programs, 153
New Mexico
  discount drug programs, 154
New York
  disability insurance, 310
  discount drug programs, 154
New York University School of Law
  student loan forgiveness, 383
Non-profit organizations, 485, 491
  disabled housing projects, 198
  fair housing programs, 210
  federal money programs, 487
  foreclosed properties, 212
  free staffing, 429
  government assistance, 497
  grants to help the Hispanic community, 205
  grants, 219, 220, 221, 490, 492
  help to start, 488
  help with child care, 408
  housing programs, 193
  loans to build cooperative housing, 189
  loans to buy land, 220

community development, 493
Direct Loan Program, 354
Federal Family Education Loans, 355
Federal Student Aid Information Center, 354, 356
for Alaskan Natives, 361
for American Indians, 361, 365, 366
for community development majors, 366
for criminal justice majors, 367
for food and agricultural sciences, 366
for graduate studies, 355, 357, 358
for humanities studies, 364
for international studies, 354, 355, 365
for low income, first generation college students, 358
for merchant marines, 367
for minorities, 369
for Native Hawaiians, 362
for nurse anesthetists, 365
for nursing students, 359, 363, 365
for occupational health and safety training, 363
for persons providing rehabilitation services, 357
for public health degrees, 363
for social, behavioral, and economic science majors, 368
for speech interpreters for the deaf, 357
for undergraduates, 354, 356
for veterans children, 368
for veterans, 367
health profession loans, 359, 361, 362, 364
health profession scholarships, 360, 363
housing field, 493
Jacob K. Javits Fellowships, 357
loan forgiveness, 372
low-interest loans, 356
medical students, 494
National Security Agency grants, 361
nursing loan repayment money, 362
Pell Grants, 356

Robert C. Byrd Honors Scholarships, 357
Student Financial Assistance Programs, 356
temporary employment, 358
work study programs, 438
Students
employment, 541
Study help, 356
Substance abuse treatment, 124
Salvation Army, 134
Summer Food Service Program, 414
Supervalu Foundation
community grants, 522
Supplemental Security Income, 306, 400
Supportive housing
elderly, 197
Surplus books
libraries, 514
Surplus money, 402
Survivors and Dependents Educational Assistance, 368
Sweat equity, 216

T

Target
grants, 520
Tax credits, 498
Taxes
adoption credits, 501
car deductions, 421
child care credit, 500
child tax credit, 500
credits for disabled, 501
credits for seniors, 501
Earned Income Tax Credit, 414, 500
education credits, 501
free help for seniors, 499
free help with problems, 499
free services, 498
health coverage tax credit, 501
property, 181
state credits, 501
Taxpayer Advocate, 402, 499
Teachers
education grants, 437

Y